An Anxious Pursuit

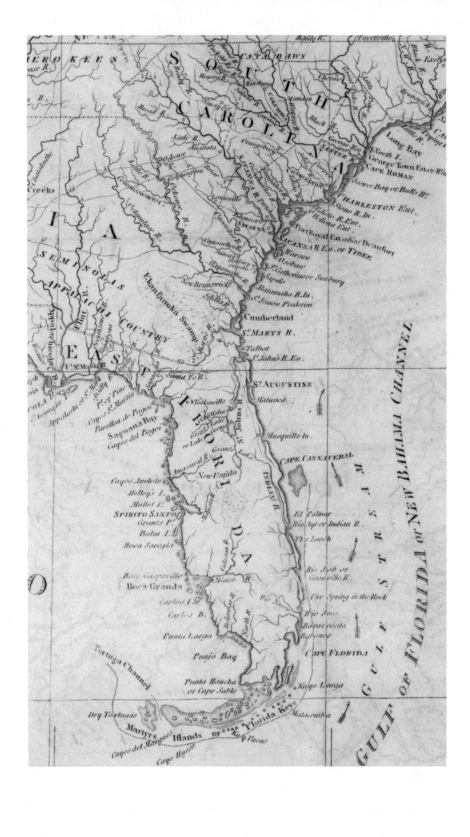

An Anxious Pursuit

AGRICULTURAL INNOVATION

AND MODERNITY IN THE LOWER

SOUTH, 1730–1815

Joyce E. Chaplin

 PUBLISHED FOR THE INSTITUTE OF EARLY

AMERICAN HISTORY AND CULTURE, WILLIAMSBURG,

VIRGINIA, BY THE UNIVERSITY OF NORTH CAROLINA

PRESS, CHAPEL HILL & LONDON

The

Institute of

Early American

History and

Culture is

sponsored

jointly by the

College of

William and

Mary and the

Colonial

Williamsburg

Foundation.

© 1993 The University of North Carolina Press

Manufactured in the United States of America

Library of Congress Cataloging-in-Publication Data

Chaplin, Joyce E.

An anxious pursuit : agricultural innovation and modernity in the lower South, 1730–1815 / Joyce E. Chaplin.

    p.   cm.

Includes bibliographical references and index.

ISBN 0-8078-2084-9 (cloth : alk. paper)

ISBN 0-8078-4613-9 (pbk. : alk. paper)

1. Southern States—History—Colonial period, ca. 1600–1775.   2. Southern States—History—1775–1865.   3. Agriculture—Southern States—History.   4. Slavery—Southern States—History.   5. Plantation life—Southern States—History.   I. Institute of Early American History and Culture (Williamsburg, Va.)   II. Title.

F212.C47   1993

975'.02—dc20

92-21432

CIP

FRONTISPIECE:

Map 1. The Lower South. *From Jedidiah Morse,* The American Gazetteer (*Boston, 1797*)

Plates 6 and 7 were drawn by John Perrine. Details of plantation maps have been artistically highlighted.

This volume received indirect support from an unrestricted book publication grant awarded to the Institute by the L. J. Skaggs and Mary C. Skaggs Foundation of Oakland, California.

00   99   98   97   96   6   5   4   3   2

For my father and the memory of my mother

꧁

Preface

This book began as a study of historical continuity, but it ended up emphasizing change as well as persistence—in other words, it turned out truly to be a history. It is a history of a region of early America that has been little examined. Compared to other portions of English-speaking North America, only frontier areas have drawn less scholarly attention than the Lower South. The antebellum history of the region has tended to overshadow its earlier development—something that misled me as I started my research. Influenced by historical and anthropological writing on modes of production and on work culture, I had originally intended to examine how the colonial Lower South's method of production heralded the static plantation economy that would dominate in the antebellum period. But I soon detected factors that did not seem prototypically southern. Many projects elicit from their researchers a moment of epiphany. Mine came when I was sitting over yet another planter's library inventory, which contained, yet again, all the latest (circa 1800) in improving literature. An argument that this was a static society seemed not to explain the actual society at hand.

In addition to being a study of a place, this book is a study of an era, of the first phase of modernity in the West. It is in the conjunction of place and time—in the fate of modernity in a provincial area—that I seek to elucidate how Western progress both was and was not congruent with the motivations of those who lived in a seemingly backward-looking slave society and plantation economy. My intention is not only to illuminate the Lower South in an era of modern history but also to examine modern notions of progress according to how they upheld socioeconomic forms that seemed, then and now, less than modern. I have therefore tried to direct my analysis, equally, both at the Lower South and at late-Enlightenment ideas of progress that still inform our thinking but that may impede as well as promote societal betterment. I wanted my study to achieve balance: by placing the slaveholding culture of the Lower South within contemporary ideas of progress, I did not intend to provide a defense of that culture; by criticizing modern progress because of its accessibility to slaveholders, I did not mean to dismiss out of hand the ideal of improvement in human society, in which I believe. My study is critical and skeptical but not, I hope, cynical.

I have been fortunate, throughout my work on this project, to receive assistance and encouragement from many sources. The book began as a doctoral thesis written for Jack P. Greene, and I am grateful to Jack for countless pieces of advice, for his willingness to share his own work and insights, and for his continued interest in and support of the project. William W. Freehling and Philip D. Morgan read and gave excellent advice on the dissertation; Jack Pole and Owen Hannaway suggested ways to sharpen its analysis. Peter A. Coclanis and Robert M. Weir responded to a revised version of the text. Portions of the work were read and improved by David L. Carlton, Lacy K. Ford, Jr., Donald L. Winters, Paul G. E. Clemens, Eugene D. Genovese, John Harley Warner, Arleen M. Tuchman, Matthew Ramsey, Russell R. Menard, Daniel C. Littlefield, James H. Williams, Jack Temple Kirby, and David Armitage. Thad Tate has given encouragement ever since I described the dissertation to him. Conversations with Brad Thompson and Mart Stewart were also helpful. Robert Tracy McKenzie and Richard A. Pride helped with the statistics. John Perrine did the drawings for Plates 6 and 7. I received financial support from the History Department of the Johns Hopkins University, the Fulbright Council, the Vanderbilt University Research Council, the Economic History Association, and the National Endowment for the Humanities. The Institute for Southern Culture at the University of South Carolina and the John Carter Brown Library at Brown University also provided support for my research. I owe a debt to Tim Breen for starting me, when I was an undergraduate, in my researches on the Lower South, agriculture, and culture. I was very fortunate in having a superb editor for, at times, a difficult manuscript. Fredrika Teute—who read many a version of this text—was patient and tireless in her assistance. Gil Kelly, who copyedited the manuscript, pointed out even my worst missteps with remarkable good humor.

Research for this book depended on the help of curators and librarians from the Savannah River to the Spey Valley. I am delighted to have the opportunity of thanking the Georgia Historical Society; the Georgia Department of Archives and History; the libraries of the University of Georgia; the South Carolina Historical Society; the South Caroliniana Library; the South Carolina Department of Archives and History; the Charleston Library Society; the College of Charleston; the Southern Historical Collection (University of North Carolina at Chapel Hill); the William R. Perkins Library of Duke University;

Mr. Thomas Pinckney of Richmond, Virginia, and the Library of Congress; Yale University Library; the John Carter Brown Library; the British Library; the Royal Society for the Encouragement of Arts, Manufactures and Commerce (London); the Linnean Society of London; Guildhall Library and the Worshipful Society of Apothecaries; the National Register of Archives–Scotland; the Scottish Record Office; the National Library of Scotland; Sir John Clerk of Penicuik; and Mr. Oliver Russell of Ballindalloch Castle. I received help, as well, from the special collections division of the Jean and Alexander Heard Library at Vanderbilt University and from the History Library at the University of Leeds, England. Portions of chapters 2 and 4 appeared in the *Journal of Social History* (1990); portions of chapters 6 and 8 in the *Journal of Southern History* (1991); and parts of chapters 6 and 7 in the *William and Mary Quarterly*, 3d Ser. (1992). I thank the editors and publishers concerned for permission to reprint this material. Any errors or awkwardness that remains in my work reveals my failure to profit from the advice of the individuals and assistance of the agencies listed above.

For more years than I care to count, I have promised relatives and friends that this project was reaching completion—I am thankful that they kept believing my claims even when I didn't. I would like to express my gratitude to Clint Chaplin, Lee Ann Sunderman, Gayle Hales Ward, Arleen Tuchman, Phyllis Frus, David Carlton, and David Armitage for helping me to concentrate on my work or for diverting me from it, as needed. I am, above all, grateful to my parents, to whom this book is dedicated.

Contents

Illustrations and Tables

Abbreviations

AH	*Agricultural History*
AHR	*American Historical Review*
Ballindalloch	Estate Office, Ballindalloch Castle, Banffshire, Scotland
BL	British Library, British Museum, London
Duke	William R. Perkins Library, Duke University, Durham, N.C.
FHQ	*Florida Historical Quarterly*
GDAH	Georgia Department of Archives and History, Atlanta
GHQ	*Georgia Historical Quarterly*
GHS	Georgia Historical Society, Savannah
Jour. Econ. Hist.	*Journal of Economic History*
Jour. So. Hist.	*Journal of Southern History*
Jour. Soc. Hist.	*Journal of Social History*
LC	Manuscripts Division, Library of Congress, Washington, D.C.
LP	Laurens Papers Project, University of South Carolina, Columbia
LSL	Linnean Society of London
NLS	National Library of Scotland, Edinburgh
RSA	American Correspondence of the Royal Society of Arts, London (microfilm)
SCHM	*South Carolina Historical Magazine / South Carolina Historical and Genealogical Magazine*
SCHS	South Carolina Historical Society, Charleston
SCL	South Caroliniana Library, University of South Carolina, Columbia
SHC	Southern Historical Collection, University of North Carolina, Chapel Hill
SRO	Scottish Record Office, Edinburgh
UGA	Manuscripts, University of Georgia Libraries, Athens
WMQ	*William and Mary Quarterly*

An Anxious
Pursuit

Chapter 1

Perspectives on the Development of a Plantation Region

In 1768, Frederick George Mulcaster, a young Scottish planter in East Florida, described to a correspondent the most important attributes of the new British settlement at an early stage in its English-speaking history. "There is a certain some thing in the Air of St. Augustine or some curs'd power," Mulcaster claimed, "which actually turns the Brain." To justify his hyperbole, he recounted a recent dream. "I stood in a Hall and beneath me was Indigo Rice Cotton etc, in great abundance [and] at my Command my slaves . . . instantly gathered the Crop and put it on Board Vessells" that set sail for England. To Mulcaster's surprise the cargo of New World exotica had turned—Behold!— into "Corn Wine and Oyl" by the time it was unloaded. This startling turn of events awakened the new settler, who hastened out to his plantation to judge whether it was in an actual or an ethereal condition. Mulcaster's dream presented (albeit unconsciously) three crucial images of the early Lower South, the region stretching from Florida north through Georgia and South Carolina: the dizzying plenty of its agriculture and the mutability of its crops but also the dependence of these two happy phenomena on the labor of black slaves. The self-transforming crops enhance the significance of slavery. The American staples become, as they cross the Atlantic, classical and biblical symbols of plenty—the "corn" grown by Ruth and Boaz, the wine that stupefied Cyclops, the oil of Hesiod's bucolic estates. (The reverie omitted only the figs of ancient tradition.) And thus Mulcaster's dream underscored how the Lower South resembled venerated societies of the past that had also relied on slavery. The Briton noted the feature of his adopted region that did not change, whatever crops the place produced, but he concealed this increasingly unwelcome fact behind a screen of biblical and classical allusion. Mulcaster's initial vision of himself standing in a great "Hall" filled with his retainers further evidenced New World planters' desire to resemble genteel landowners in the Old World, perhaps those from a lost age of paternal relations between lord and retainer.[1]

"I'll tease you no more," Mulcaster assured his correspondent, lest the distant friend "perhaps catch the infection" that continued to entice British subjects to settle and plant in the Lower South. But he went on to extol the exotic and lucrative character of commercial agriculture there by adding that he had "Plants from all Parts" of the world on his estate, which had increased in value, he mentioned, by 30 percent since he had begun cultivation on it just a few years earlier.[2] Notwithstanding Mulcaster's calculatedly promotional tone, his statements reveal how the whites engaged in commercial agriculture in the early Lower South believed themselves to be participants within a dynamic and lucrative economy. He also called attention to the growing doubts they had about the stability of their endeavor, an uncertainty, as they entered the modern era, over their increasingly archaic method of getting wealth.

Displaying a different form of concern, South Carolinian Henry Laurens looked, not back to the ancients, but forward to the invisible hand when he contemplated how modern his fellows already were. Observing the post-Revolutionary scramble to repair property and restore agricultural production, Laurens asserted that "each one [was] anxious in the pursuit of his own" but "at the same time without seeming to know or mean it, contributing to the public Weal."[3] Mulcaster and Laurens marked out the two boundaries between which denizens of the Lower South charted their course: the promise of plenty brought by plantation slavery, despite its attached archaisms; and the lure of efficient modernity, complete with a sense of anxiety about self and society. The two men were right to use examples of agriculture to make their points, because agriculture was the characteristic activity of the region. White proper-

---

1. F. George Mulcaster to ———, Nov. 6, 1768, Manigault Family Papers, box 1, folder 4, SCL.

2. *Ibid.*

3. Henry Laurens to Edward Bridgen, Sept. 23, 1784, LP.

tyholders' desire to innovate within this activity best shows their anxious pursuit of a modern future for themselves and their descendants, one, in fact, that their children or grandchildren may not have welcomed.

This study is a cultural history of the early Lower South that uses changes in agriculture to trace the extent to which white inhabitants redefined themselves as a modern people. It unites intellectual history with social and economic history—the history of people thinking with the history of people's behavior. The work examines the years from 1730, when South Carolina's plans to implant slaveless townships in the interior betrayed an early concern among free residents over the path the slaveholding colony was taking, to 1815 and the end of the Napoleonic Wars, which would mark expansion of a European market for cotton and the rapid emergence of an industrial order slaveholders would find less enticing. Before 1815, the modern era that whites in the Lower South were entering was one that defined a secular vision of humanity. Contemporary secular theories examined human society in scientific, or empirical, terms that constituted a set of predictions about future development of society. Sometimes these predictions cheerfully declared that human society was improving its material basis and its ability to respond systematically to crises. But the modern era also defined an ambivalent stance toward societal dynamism, a self-criticizing impulse that accompanied definitions of progress.[4] If the Lower South seemed idiosyncratic—it was a provincial and plantation region considering progress toward modernity—its idiosyncrasies reflected the modern age's own unusual combination of optimism and pessimism over economic change. To say that whites in the Lower South were modern is, not to praise them, but to comment on the ambivalence of modernity in the face of dilemmas like slavery, which inspired both desire for and revulsion against dramatic societal change.

Agricultural innovation in the Lower South is the best measure of the overall

4. This is not necessarily the modernity that celebrated only efficiency and rationalism (see Richard D. Brown, "Modernization and the Modern Personality in Early America, 1600–1865: A Sketch of a Synthesis," *Journal of Interdisciplinary History*, II, no. 3 [Winter 1972], 201–228). This narrower definition would neglect, for example, the romantic temperament (see Michael O'Brien, *Rethinking the South: Essays in Intellectual History* [Baltimore, 1988], 38–56) and skepticism (Henry F. May, *The Enlightenment in America* [New York, 1976], pt. 2), which were also modern. Cf. Paul Johnson, *Birth of the Modern: World Society, 1815–1830* (New York, 1991), which emphasizes characteristics of modernity as they flourished after 1815, not as they began earlier.

dynamism of the place. This activity reflects how white residents accepted modern theory about economic improvement and then manipulated information and resources to make the region yield more wealth—but also how residents were uneasy over social change, something they felt themselves to be effecting as they increased or improved control over material resources. Their accomplishments were impressive—meaning both striking and appalling. Innovation was a kind of economic domination over labor, soil, water, germ plasm, and ideas by those people who were the dominant group in one region of North America. But as important as their tangible achievements is how whites defined economic success to arrive at a distinctive view of themselves and their region. This study therefore explains the actions and behaviors that sustained a high level of economic success in the Lower South and thereby contributes to a historical understanding of the cultural meaning of this success.[5]

The period under scrutiny, the years between 1730 and 1815, constituted the region's golden era—for its white population. The sun still shone on plantation agriculture, and political crises like Nullification lay in the unforeseeable future. At this time, the population and economy in Georgia, South Carolina, and British East Florida expanded rapidly and steadily. Initial colonization had begun along the coastline (see Map 2), where the British established or appropriated ports first at Charleston (1670), then Savannah (1733), then St. Augustine (1763). By the early 1700s, South Carolina's white population was moving into the middle coastal plain and, by midcentury, crossed the fall line into the piedmont; a similar pattern of inward expansion occurred in post-Revolutionary Georgia. The region's population changed as its economy shifted from frontier exchange among Indians, Europeans, and Africans to settled cultivation controlled by whites but often performed by slaves. Along the way, the Indian population declined or moved westward, a significant and growing percentage of the people who replaced Indians were black, and the whites who displaced Indians and brought in slaves tended to prosper by growing, processing, and exporting an array of agricultural commodities. This

---

5. This study connects agriculture (a set of economic behaviors) to the meaning of agriculture (a set of ideas). The period under study was not yet one in which southern agriculture had taken on a rhetorical life of its own. Cf. Drew Gilpin Faust, "The Rhetoric and Ritual of Agriculture in Antebellum South Carolina," *Jour. So. Hist.*, XLV (1979), 541–568.

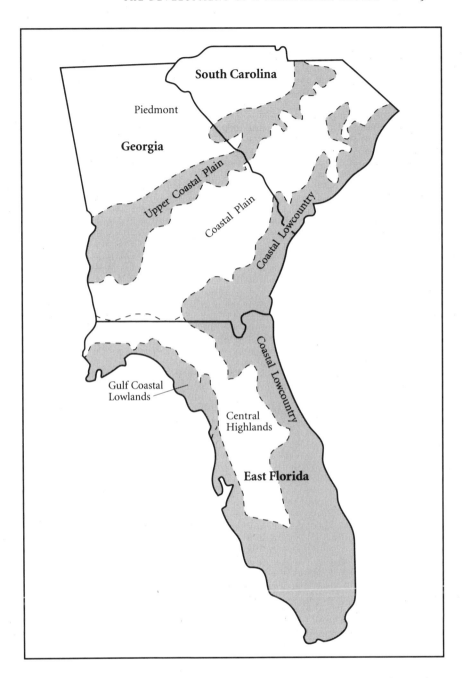

Map 2. Land-use Areas in the Lower South. *After Lewis Cecil Gray,* A History of Agriculture in the Southern United States to 1860 *(Washington, D.C., 1933), I, xxi*

was a place where climate and soil were eminently suited to commercial production of crops; Frederick George Mulcaster's image of an "infection" in the "Air," playing on early modern notions of the physical attributes of particular places, asserted whites' sense of the semitropical luxuriance of the region. The Lower South therefore gained its wealth from subtropical crops, the most important of which were (as Mulcaster conveniently noted) rice, indigo, and cotton.

Plantation agriculture and black slavery were pronounced features of the early Lower South, more so than in any other region on the continent. Both characteristics cohered during South Carolina's initial colonization from the 1670s to 1710s. Indeed, Carolina settlers (many of whom were from the West Indies and had Caribbean expectations for agriculture) had not even bothered to wait until they had a staple crop requiring chattel slavery; they simply brought in substantial numbers of African slaves and expected a suitable crop to materialize. By the 1720s, about fifty years after British colonization, blacks formed a majority in South Carolina's population, a unique phenomenon on the continent.[6] So strongly embedded was slavery, both within the economy and in the mind-set of white settlers, that the 1730 plan to settle the Carolina frontier with free white workers clustered in townships staggered and fell during settlers' race for profits. Reliance on slavery and plantations next became characteristic of Georgia in the 1740s, although that colony's founders had initially envisaged a colony without slaves. Within twenty years of initial settlement, slaves and commercial cultivation of rice were increasing in tandem in Georgia; the number of slaves rose from five hundred in 1751 to fifteen thousand in 1773. In the meantime, Georgia had the distinction of being the only British colony whose white residents had made a sustained and public argument that black slavery was a necessary and even beneficial element of

6. Richard S. Dunn, "The English Sugar Islands and the Founding of South Carolina," *SCHM*, LXXII (1971), 81–93; Converse D. Clowse, *Economic Beginnings in Colonial South Carolina: 1670–1730* (Columbia, S.C., 1971), chaps. 5, 6; Peter H. Wood, *Black Majority: Negroes in Colonial South Carolina from 1670 through the Stono Rebellion* (New York, 1975), chap. 5; Clarence L. Ver Steeg, *Origins of a Southern Mosaic: Studies of Early Carolina and Georgia* (Athens, Ga., 1975), 117, 129, 177. On concentrations of slaves in plantation areas, see Philip D. Morgan, ed., "A Profile of a Mid-Eighteenth Century South Carolina Parish: The Tax Return of Saint James', Goose Creek," *SCHM*, LXXXI (1980), 53.

colonization—a conspicuous fall from grace for the onetime utopia on the Savannah.[7]

The newest third of the Lower South, Florida, was also its shortest-lived component. The British occupied East Florida for only twenty years, between 1763 and 1783, bracketed by phases of Spanish settlement. But British settlers in this most southerly portion of the Lower South made a significant endorsement of the view that slaves and plantation agriculture were essential ingredients of economic success. This was the case, in part, because whites from Georgia and South Carolina took an interest in Florida's colonization, regarding the new province as a pool of opportunity on whose surface they saw reflected their region's successes and into which they could plunge in search of more success. Some of these investors caught a sort of land fever as they rushed to acquire tracts along the St. Johns River, on which they raised indigo for the English market. As in South Carolina townships and early Georgia, experimental settlements in Florida that eschewed slavery in favor of bonded white laborers soon earned reputations as risible failures—critics pointed out that white workers were treated as harshly as imported Africans yet failed to produce the profits of plantations worked by them. The short-lived province replicated both the larger region's persistent attempts to diversify its economy and its attachment to plantation slavery, its conviction that slavery laid a path to a modern, commercial economy.[8]

7. On South Carolina townships, see Robert L. Meriwether, *The Expansion of South Carolina, 1729–1765* (Kingsport, Tenn., 1940), 19–22 (the plan), 38–39 (its failure). On Georgia: Kenneth Coleman, "The Southern Frontier: Georgia's Founding and the Expansion of South Carolina," *GHQ*, LVI (1972), 163–174; David R. Chesnutt, "South Carolina's Penetration of Georgia in the 1760's: Henry Laurens as a Case Study," *SCHM*, LXXIII (1972), 194–208; Chesnutt, "South Carolina's Expansion into Colonial Georgia, 1720–1765" (Ph.D. diss., University of Georgia, 1973); Betty Wood, "Thomas Stephens and the Introduction of Black Slavery in Georgia," *GHQ*, LVIII (1974), 24–40; Wood, *Slavery in Colonial Georgia, 1730–1775* (Athens, Ga., 1984); Ralph Gray and Betty Wood, "The Transition from Indentured to Involuntary Servitude in Colonial Georgia," *Explorations in Economic History*, XIII (1976), 353–370; Milton Ready, "The Georgia Trustees and the Malcontents: The Politics of Philanthropy," *GHQ*, LX (1976), 264–281. The figures are from Wood, *Slavery in Colonial Georgia*, 88–90, 104.

8. E. P. Panagopoulos, *New Smyrna: An Eighteenth-Century Greek Odyssey* (Gainesville, Fla., 1966); Daniel L. Schafer, "Plantation Development in British East Florida: A Case Study of the Earl of Egmont," *FHQ*, LXIII (1984), 172–183; Bernard Bailyn,

By every available measure, the general region had considerable wealth. Economic growth was especially apparent just before the Revolution; in South Carolina the annual value of rice exports from 1770 to 1773 was about 30 percent above the annual average from 1761 to 1766. At this time, the Lower South was the richest region in North America. By 1774, the Upper and Lower South together held one-half of the total private wealth in colonial America, not including the value of slaves—a stunning testament to the material success of staple agriculture in the area between the Potomac and St. Marys rivers. But even the prosperity of the older Chesapeake region seemed trifling compared to that of the new Lower South. By one historian's estimate for 1774, the nine persons with greatest inventoried wealth in British North America were South Carolinians. Overseas commerce created and maintained their wealth. Pre-Revolutionary values of exports per capita (of white population) reveal that South Carolina and Georgia had the highest among the thirteen continental colonies.[9]

Because of the region's reputation for riches, on the eve of the Revolution its population grew more vigorously than anywhere else in British America. Economic gains were never evenly distributed, but the mere prospect of available land and lucrative cash crops promised a success that invited many Europeans and white Americans to emigrate to the Lower South. Contemporary estimates of the profitability of plantations were often what lured migrants. Such calculations ranged from 8 percent to (by the end of the century) an astounding 37.5 percent (see Table 1), and whites still reckoned returns above 10 percent into the first decade of the nineteenth century. By this time, the greatest economic expansion was in the West, as Indian cession and aggressive white migration propelled new settlement inland. Especially after the American Revolution, whites (bringing with them more black slaves) poured into up-country areas and produced a variety of crops, of which indigo, cotton, grain, and tobacco were most successful. These settlers pulled commercial agricul-

Voyagers to the West: A Passage in the Peopling of America on the Eve of the Revolution (New York, 1986), chap. 12; Charles Loch Mowat, *East Florida as a British Province, 1763–1784* (Gainesville, Fla., 1964), chaps. 4, 5.

9. Lewis Cecil Gray, *A History of Agriculture in the Southern United States to 1860*, 2 vols. (Washington, D.C., 1933), I, 289; Alice Hanson Jones, *Wealth of a Nation to Be: The American Colonies on the Eve of the Revolution* (New York, 1980), 50–53, 171; James F. Shepherd and Gary M. Walton, "Trade, Distribution, and Economic Growth in Colonial America," *Jour. Econ. Hist.*, XXXII (1972), 133.

TABLE 1. *Estimated Return on Investment in Planting, 1768–1810*

Year	Profit	Place	Crop
1768	26.7%	Georgia	rice
1771	8.0–12.0	Florida	rice, indigo
1772	23.5	Georgia	rice
1775	16.5	South Carolina	cattle, wheat, lumber
1796	37.5	Georgia	rice or cotton
1810	12.5	Georgia	cotton

Sources: (1768) Philip M. Hamer *et al.,* eds., *The Papers of Henry Laurens* (Columbia, S.C., 1968–), V, 668; (1771) John Farquharson to Sir Archibald Grant, May 11, 1771, Misc. Muniments, GD.1, sect. 32, bundle 38, item 12, SRO; (1772) Louis De Vorsey, Jr., ed., *De Brahm's Report of the General Survey in the Southern District of North America* (Columbia, S.C., 1971), 162–163; (1775) Harry J. Carman, ed., *American Husbandry* (1775) (New York, 1939), 292–294—the profit was after two years of investment; (1796) Nathaniel Pendleton, "Short Account of the Sea Coast of Georgia in Respect to Agriculture, Ship-Building, Navigation, and the Timber Trade," ed. Theodore Thayer, *GHQ,* XLI (1957), 80; (1810) Thomas Fitch to Daniel Mulford, Feb. 16, 1811, Daniel Mulford Papers, II, GHS.

ture after them, establishing the rudiments of a plantation economy in the interior. The transformation was rapid in the midlands of South Carolina, slower in its upcountry and in the interior of Georgia. Exported crops and imported slaves were the vehicles, nevertheless, that carried wealth to the interior. Indeed, during the period from 1790 to 1826, the greatest wealth increases in South Carolina occurred in the upcountry rather than along the coast.[10] All white inhabitants suffered from the Revolution's combined effects of commercial disruption and property damage, but the coastline never recovered its once-fabled riches and became an area of lessened opportunity compared to the upcountry. The size of an average decedent's estate thus shrank along the coast but steadily increased in the upcountry after a severe

10. On increases in slaveholding, see Rachel N. Klein, *Unification of a Slave State: The Rise of the Planter Class in the South Carolina Backcountry, 1760–1808* (Chapel Hill, N.C., 1990), 23, 25, 151–153. On post-Revolutionary patterns of growth, see Marjorie Stratford Mendenhall, "A History of Agriculture in South Carolina, 1790 to 1860: An Economic and Social Study" (Ph.D. diss., University of North Carolina–Chapel Hill, 1940), 9–11.

decline in the early 1790s, signifying how a still-considerable level of regional prosperity had shifted westward in the years after the Revolution.[11]

Although scholars have noted these shifts, there has been little examination of the mechanisms behind them, but economic historians have noted that innovative behavior must surely have been at work.[12] Whites' strategies for maintaining their success truly were innovations, unlike two historical examples of efforts to achieve more limited agricultural advance: European improvement of temperate-climate agriculture in the seventeenth and eighteenth centuries, and efforts to improve crop yield and to diversify the economy in the antebellum South. Planters in the Lower South did, like their British counterparts, call themselves improvers, and some of their efforts did simply make better what they already had. Much innovation, however, reflected not only improvement of existing cultivation but introduction of new crops, development of new mechanisms, and significant adaptation of old methods for growing new staples as well as continual experimentation that led up to these developments.

This examination therefore contributes to shifts in analysis of plantation regions in early America. Through innovation, white residents of the Lower South created, by the measures of economic output and accumulation of wealth, a successful economy, one in which slavery and commercial agriculture continued to yield impressive profits. Most scholarly attention to economic change of this sort has focused on regions above the Lower South and, especially, on the Revolutionary era with its parallel shifts in politics and political economy. The Chesapeake's transition from tobacco monoculture to grain and mixed farming, the mid-Atlantic region's rise to commercial prominence, and the northern states' slow shift to industrialization have all been explored.[13]

11. Marc Egnal, "The Economic Development of the Thirteen Colonies, 1720–1775," *WMQ*, 3d Ser., XXXII (1975), 197. On levels of wealth, see Tables 6, 11, below.

12. See John J. McCusker and Russell R. Menard, *The Economy of British America, 1607–1789* (Chapel Hill, N.C., 1985), 168, 178, 183–184.

13. See Paul G. E. Clemens, *The Atlantic Economy and Colonial Maryland's Eastern Shore: From Tobacco to Grain* (Ithaca, N.Y., 1980); Thomas M. Doerflinger, *A Vigorous Spirit of Enterprise: Merchants and Economic Development in Revolutionary Philadelphia* (Chapel Hill, N.C., 1986); Jonathan Prude, *The Coming of Industrial Order: Town and Factory Life in Rural Massachusetts, 1810–1860* (Cambridge, 1983); Diane Lindstrom, *Economic Development in the Philadelphia Region, 1810–1850* (New York, 1978); Robert F. Dalzell, Jr., *Enterprising Elite: The Boston Associates and the World They*

But scholars, beginning with those of the West Indies, have also emphasized the high level of development in plantation societies—their considerable amounts of wealth, their vigorous contribution to the world of Atlantic trade, their ability to adapt slave labor to fulfill urban and skilled economic functions (including semi–wage labor and work with machinery), their creation of creole cultures that drew on the cosmopolitan culture of the mother country, and their efforts at reform and to adopt Enlightenment thought. Many historians who have examined the North American continent for patterns of economic success have, therefore, shifted their focus from North to South, detecting there the wealth and societal development that (albeit at more modest levels) characterized the West Indies but eluded most white settlers in regions above the Potomac River.[14] The Lower South's contemporary adjustments reveal, accordingly, how it was typical and not yet exceptional: it was

---

Made (Cambridge, Mass., 1987); James A. Henretta, "The War for Independence and American Economic Development," in Ronald Hoffman *et al.*, eds., *The Economy of Early America: The Revolutionary Period, 1763–1790* (Charlottesville, Va., 1988), 45–87. Much of Henretta's essay focuses on the North and mid-Atlantic regions. For comparison, see Russell R. Menard's essay "Slavery, Economic Growth, and Revolutionary Ideology in the South Carolina Lowcountry," 244–274, in the same volume, which emphasizes how economic growth rather than development characterized the Lower South.

14. See Richard B. Sheridan, *Sugar and Slavery: An Economic History of the British West Indies, 1623–1775* (Baltimore, 1973); Sheridan, "Samuel Martin, Innovating Sugar Planter of Antigua, 1750–1776," *AH*, XXXIV (1960), 126–139; Edward Brathwaite, *The Development of Creole Society in Jamaica, 1770–1820* (Oxford, 1971). There have been parallel developments in the study of Latin America, particularly in Brazil. See J. H. Galloway, "Agricultural Reform and the Enlightenment in Late Colonial Brazil," *AH*, LIII (1979), 763–779; Stuart B. Schwartz, *Sugar Plantations in the Formation of Brazilian Society: Bahia, 1550–1835* (Cambridge, 1985), esp. 131, 252–257, 313–337, 428–433.

On the North-South shift, see the synthetic study by Jack P. Greene, *Pursuits of Happiness: The Social Development of Early Modern British Colonies and the Formation of American Culture* (Chapel Hill, N.C., 1988), esp. 1–5, 28–54. On the Lower South, see Richard Waterhouse, "The Responsible Gentry of Colonial South Carolina: A Study in Local Government, 1670–1770," in Bruce C. Daniels, ed., *Town and County: Essays on the Structure of Local Government in the American Colonies* (Middletown, Conn., 1978), 160–185; and "The Development of Elite Culture in the Colonial American South: A Study of Charles Town, 1670–1776," *Australian Journal of Politics and History*, XXVIII (1982), 391–404.

part of a general adaptation to maturing colonial economies, to a new independence from Britain, and to the contested creation of a national identity—including debate over the place of slavery in the new Republic. Compared to its neighbors, the Lower South seemed unusual only in the greater amount of wealth it could invest in new ventures or reinvest in going concerns and in the fact that most wealth continued to result from staple agriculture, and much of it from slave labor.

These discoveries stand to counter a long-held view of plantation regions as disasters in the waiting. Critics of New World plantation economies have contended that white settlers merely erected a golden palace on quicksand. The early profitability of the system dissuaded residents from investing their gains in economic ventures that would have supported more sustained patterns of development. A preference for slavery over free labor was one significant archaism that would tell against planters. At least as damning was the distorted growth common to plantation regions, whose profits continued to perpetuate monoculture rather than fanned out into railroads, public schools, factories—anything that might create a sturdily diversified economy. Planters seemed to lack the entrepreneurial, risk-taking characteristics that would have allowed them to join northerly creoles in moving all portions of the new nation into the modern, industrial age. They instead relied on enslaved labor and a bountiful nature for their way of life, little considering the enduring consequences of their decisions. In the United States, this socioeconomic preference would combine with a politics of proslavery to bring the slaveholding South to its eventual decline and defeat, a husk that once was temporarily animated by an outmoded political economy.[15]

As a long-term view, this analysis is valid; but because it marks the early history of commercial agriculture with its later failures, it is teleological and applies anachronistic standards to the past. Present-day theories of economic development assume that industrialism is the inevitable goal of modern soci-

---

15. See Fred Bateman and Thomas Weiss, *A Deplorable Scarcity: The Failure of Industrialization in the Slave Economy* (Chapel Hill, N.C., 1981); Gavin Wright, *The Political Economy of the Cotton South: Households, Markets, and Wealth in the Nineteenth Century* (New York, 1978); Peter A. Coclanis, "Bitter Harvest: The South Carolina Low Country in Historical Perspective," *Jour. Econ. Hist.*, XLV (1985), 251–259; Coclanis, *The Shadow of a Dream: Economic Life and Death in the South Carolina Low Country, 1670–1920* (New York, 1989); Doerflinger, *Vigorous Spirit of Enterprise*, 356–364. Doerflinger notes that merchants in Baltimore were able to pull Maryland out of the declining South before it was too late.

eties—the natural outcome of capital investment, the perfect arena for com-
moditized labor. Entrepreneurship seeking to create new markets for new
goods now seems to have been the behavior that catalyzed this shift. But at the
start of the modern era, from the mid-1700s into the first two decades of the
1800s, New World planters were only just beginning to witness the trend
toward industrialism. In the meantime, though contemporary observers knew
plantations had their drawbacks, New World commercial agriculture was
nonetheless widely recognized as one of the most dynamic economic ventures
in the world. This view had credence because commerce, not industry, was the
towering achievement of the early modern era; New World agriculture, as well
as manufactures, contributed to the commercial wealth of nations and the
expansion of the Atlantic world. Observers did not even always view commercialization as progress. Commercial activities were too recently abstracted as
unique social behaviors (the market had only lately become a concept rather
than a place) and were not yet highly rationalized—the market was an arena
for deceptive and speculative actions along with socially beneficial ones, and
economic change seemed as hazardous as it was promising.[16] The economic
path from commerce to manufacturing that the early South failed to follow
was, therefore, not yet clearly signposted and was widely suspect as a route that
might lead away from societal harmony and political virtue.

The unsteady development of capitalism and its implications for the American South have long been recognized by certain scholars of slavery. (Marxists
especially have been equipped with a critical view of the operations that led
from commerce to industry.) Indeed, some of the most intriguing studies of
the New World in the modern era have examined the crucial transition, from
the 1760s to the 1820s, when slavery and plantation agriculture were hoisted
out of theories of economic expansion and social progress that had considered
them positively, then dropped into newer and much less approving frameworks. Condemnation of plantation economies evolved during the decades
when capitalism spat out the slavery it might once have used to accumulate its

16. On the inappropriateness of 20th-century development economics for early
America (which lacked Third World characteristics of scarce resources and abundant
population), see McCusker and Menard, *Economy of British America*, 17–18. On the rise
of commerce and debate over commercial development, see J.G.A. Pocock, "To Market, to Market: Economic Thought in Early Modern England," *Jour. Interdisc. Hist.*, X
(1979–1980), 303–309; and Ronald Hamowy, "Progress and Commerce in Anglo-
American Thought: The Social Philosophy of Adam Ferguson," *Interpretation: A
Journal of Political Philosophy*, XIV (1986), 61–87.

initial wealth, when revolution challenged systems of human bondage, when slavery became a problem for reformers in industrializing regions, and when slaveholders adopted a defense of the archaisms of their way of life (redolent of praise for the classical, biblical, and feudal ages) against a money-grubbing and impersonal capitalist order.[17]

Views of plantations and slavery have thus fallen into, to borrow briefly from Hayden White's tropological schema, the narrative modes belonging to comedy, tragedy, and satire. The view of the early South as a comedy (as a narrative in which the dominant characters manage to harmonize the disparate elements of the world around them) portrays planters as active and intelligent exploiters of their region's comparative advantage over northern and colder areas in producing exotic agricultural products. The tragic view of plantation regions emphasizes the eventual decline of these areas and the intimations its residents had (or ought to have had) of their impending doom. The satiric view reverses the reader's expectation of a tidy and predictable denouement, focusing instead on the paradoxical and contradictory elements in the development of New World regions that depended on plantations and slavery during the era when the market began to redefine social relations.[18]

17. See Eric Williams, *Capitalism and Slavery* (Chapel Hill, N.C., 1944); David Brion Davis, *The Problem of Slavery in the Age of Revolution, 1770–1823* (Ithaca, N.Y., 1975); Davis, *Slavery and Human Progress* (Oxford, 1984); Thomas L. Haskell, "Capitalism and the Origins of the Humanitarian Sensibility," *AHR,* XC (1985), 339–361, 547–566; Eugene D. Genovese, *The World the Slaveholders Made: Two Essays in Interpretation* (New York, 1971); Elizabeth Fox-Genovese and Eugene D. Genovese, "The Slave Economies in Political Perspective," *JAH,* LXVI (1979–1980), 7–23; Fox-Genovese and Genovese, *Fruits of Merchant Capital: Slavery and Bourgeois Property in the Rise and Expansion of Capitalism* (New York, 1983). For an assessment of the debate over capitalism and slavery, see forum in *AHR:* David Brion Davis, "Reflections on Abolitionism and Ideological Hegemony," John Ashworth, "The Relationship between Capitalism and Humanitarianism," and Thomas L. Haskell, "Convention and Hegemonic Interest in the Debate over Antislavery: A Reply to Davis and Ashworth," *AHR,* XCII (1987), 797–878. See also O'Brien, *Rethinking the South,* 35–37; Robert William Fogel, *Without Consent or Contract: The Rise and Fall of American Slavery* (New York, 1989), 388–417.

18. On modes of emplotment, see Hayden White, *Metahistory: The Historical Imagination in Nineteenth-Century Europe* (Baltimore, 1973), 7–11. Narratives that fit White's fourth trope, romance, a drama of transcendence over worldly obstacles, have had little to say about economic affairs. They generally take up biographical themes or examine

This last, ironic view of economic development underpins the present study. Such an interpretation is not the only way of viewing the fortunes of the region. A long-term view would be better served by the tragic mode; and a short-term view of the area's economic beginnings, from the perspective of white settlers and ignoring the human cost of slavery, might ill-advisedly take up a comic vision. But examination of the Lower South's innovation in its method of subsistence demonstrates how whites constructed an economy that, though it later and notoriously deviated from patterns of modern development, nonetheless used materials from the modern age to fabricate a place that later seemed antimodern—truly a paradoxical situation. Whites embraced, for example, developments offered by science and by new social-scientific views of humanity in their quest to make a stronger economy. They resembled many other groups in the modern era who used science not simply to enlighten individuals and to improve society but also to apologize for forms of exploitation and social control—especially when these justifications were done in racist terms.[19]

Propertyholding whites also took up an ironic view of historical development; the tone of this present analysis thus amplifies an interpretation people in the past had of themselves. Shaped in the Enlightenment, a view of history as a risky exchange of traditional values for modern mores deeply influenced Americans in the late eighteenth and early nineteenth centuries. The tension this view embodied, between past and future, began with the consciousness of historicism that emerged during the Renaissance. It continued as many major figures of the Enlightenment delivered trenchant criticisms of commercial development and questioned whether humans had benefited from the rapid pace of change in the era of the American, French, and Industrial revolutions. In *The History of Rasselas, Prince of Abissinia* (1759), Samuel Johnson character-

---

southern blacks' struggle to establish independence and dignity for themselves. On biography as romance, see, for example, C. Vann Woodward, *Tom Watson: Agrarian Rebel* (New York, 1963); and Eli N. Evans, *Judah P. Benjamin: The Jewish Confederate* (New York, 1988). On blacks' struggle for freedom, see Eric Foner, *Nothing but Freedom: Emancipation and Its Legacy* (Baton Rouge, La., 1983); and Leon F. Litwack, *Been in the Storm So Long: The Aftermath of Slavery* (New York, 1979).

19. See Robert Proctor, *Racial Hygiene: Medicine under the Nazis* (Cambridge, Mass., 1988), esp. 2–3, 10–13; and Chapter 4 (on medical theory and racism), below. I am indebted to Owen Hannaway for bringing the parallel between Nazi doctors and improving planters to my attention.

ized the modern position as one between fears of "evils recollected" and "evils anticipated." Informed by this tension, whites in the Lower South regarded economic development with skepticism.[20] Their ambivalent attitude helps explain why Mulcaster and Laurens referred both to the ancients and to the moderns to make sense of the Lower South. This skeptical view of economic development would be exemplified in whites' reception of the Scottish historical theory that underpinned political economy, one that postulated an advance from the bracing impoverishment of savagery to the luxurious and commercial glories of modernity.

The present study therefore connects intellectual and social history, relating discussions of economic theory to changes in the Lower South's economic base. This approach is informed by debate over the methodology of the new social history, especially as played out in analysis of the capitalist transformation of early America. Social historians in America have stumbled over the difficulty of relating theory to the behavior of historical actors. They have relied on theoretical frameworks (often inherited from the Enlightenment thought known to whites in the Lower South) filled with dichotomous categories that probably distort the experience and expectations of early Americans. Social history too often has relied on paired and opposing concepts like traditional/modern or communal/individual; scholars who look for the origins of capitalism in America have also used the categories preindustrial/industrial or subsistence/market. These categories can give order and meaning to historical information, but researchers have not always made clear whether these divisions actually existed in the past or are instead misleading artifacts of theories imposed on the past.[21]

20. On the ironic or skeptical mode of the Enlightenment, see May, *Enlightenment in America,* pt. 2; and White, *Metahistory,* 38–39. I disagree with May's view that pessimism emanated from Paris—for the colonies, Edinburgh was probably more influential in this regard—and I cannot follow White's contention that this was a "rationalist" view of history (see Chapter 2, below). On early modern thought and its tension between traditional and modern, see Michael Zuckerman, "The Fabrication of Identity in Early America," *WMQ,* 3d Ser., XXXIV (1977), 183–214. The quotation from Johnson occurs at the end of chap. 2 in *Rasselas.*

21. On social history in general, see Joyce Appleby, "Value and Society," in Jack P. Greene and J. R. Pole, eds., *Colonial British America: Essays in the New History of the Early Modern Era* (Baltimore, 1984), 290–316. On the specific debate over the transition to capitalism, see the excellent summary in Allan Kulikoff, "The Transition to Capital-

The categories continue to reflect the uncertainty, arising early in the modern era, whether social transformation erased an earlier social harmony and spiritual meaning to create a more chaotic and less satisfying world, or instead engendered democracy and material plenty where exploitative social relations and conditions of want and suffering had existed. Recognizing that this ambivalence was an issue for early Americans themselves, some scholars examine the economic motives and beliefs of Americans, a newer elaboration on an established tradition of investigating the nature of American identity and a return to an emphasis on ideas and to a revitalized intellectual history.[22] Contemporary economic motivation reflected, historians have discovered, a strategic positioning in relation to the market as populations went through shifting phases of commercial and domestic activities according to individual, household, or community needs. At the start of the modern era—even into the early nineteenth-century—noncommercial and commercial activities functioned not only as stages in a unilinear theory but also as cycles shaped by the needs and doubts of actual historical actors, *some* of which may have shot off into linear trajectories toward the market and factory. This is a more promising line of analysis and can be joined to examination of economic ideas to give a fuller picture of economic life in early America.[23]

---

ism in Rural America," *WMQ*, 3d Ser., XLVI (1989), 120–144. This work is not a cultural history in the sense recently defined by David Hackett Fischer in *Albion's Seed: Four British Folkways in America* (New York, 1989), vii–xi, 3–11—as a history of folkways that united high and low cultures, short-term and long-term cultural trends. Since Fischer's book does not take into account the Lower South, it is to be assumed that his methodology would make little sense of the region anyway.

22. See, especially, Jack P. Greene, "Search for Identity: An Interpretation of the Meaning of Selected Patterns of Social Response in Eighteenth-Century America," *Jour. Soc. Hist.*, III (1969–1970), 189–220; J. E. Crowley, *This Sheba, Self: The Conceptualization of Economic Life in Eighteenth-Century America* (Baltimore, 1974); Zuckerman, "Fabrication of Identity," *WMQ*, 3d Ser., XXXIV (1977), 183–214. Modified elements of the Protestant identity or ethic—characteristic of New England—are nonetheless also apparent in the Lower South. See Philip Greven, *The Protestant Temperament: Patterns of Child-Rearing, Religious Experience, and the Self in Early America* (New York, 1977), 225–226, 249–250.

23. On some work that stresses both commercial and domestic activities, see Kulikoff, "Transition to Capitalism," *WMQ*, 3d Ser., XLVI (1989), 137–140, which also stresses gender roles as bridges between domestic and commercial economies; Daniel

This study is an analysis of a North American region that probably had the most striking contrast in economic forms: slavery used for agricultural production in its most commercialized incarnation. Both archaism and modernity were present and interconnected. The insights of late-twentieth-century scholarship—the need to look at motives for economic behaviors, the stress on lack of absolute barriers between commercial and noncommercial activities, and the emphasis on contemporary ideas of economic development—are of great use in looking at this idiosyncratic portion of the New World. Such examination helps explain what it was whites thought they were doing when they innovated yet continued their reliance on slavery and agriculture; it recognizes that their rationalization may seem dismayingly eclectic from the perspective of the late twentieth century.

This work falls into two sections, the first establishing a historical context for understanding economic behavior, the second the behaviors themselves. The first examines contemporary analyses of the Lower South, emphasizing two kinds of tension: between criticism of the region's material base and recognition of its considerable prosperity and success (for whites), and between whites' own desire to alter their economy and their emerging defensiveness over their distance from more modern economic forms. It begins with an analysis of the contemporary economic theories that gave whites an ambivalent vision of social development and their place within the modern age. It then assesses the critical view of outsiders and white residents' own self-criticism. This section concludes with a chapter examining the most important types of innovation within commercial agriculture; it emphasizes how whites themselves disagreed over the proper form of social change—especially when it involved slavery—and how slave rebelliousness and desire for independence was an important variable in whites' plans and projects. Promotion of agricultural schemes designed to lessen dependence on slavery and opposition to these schemes were both strong tendencies within Lower South visions of improvement. Too, debate over government schemes that gave advantages to some free citizens but not others engendered parallel controversy.

The second section examines actual innovations, first in the lowcountry, then in the newer western upcountry. In the lowcountry's maturing plantation

---

Vickers, "Competency and Competition: Economic Culture in Early America," *WMQ,* 3d Ser., XLVII (1990), 3–29; Carolyn Merchant, *Ecological Revolutions: Nature, Gender, and Science in New England* (Chapel Hill, N.C., 1989), 149–197.

economy, agricultural experiments depended on a system of power and patronage revolving around the efforts of wealthy planters, and they saw fruition
only when a crisis jeopardized existing agricultural activities. In the interior,
innovation represented settlers' attempts to create a commercial economy
through halting steps to introduce and market agricultural staples and through
creative adaptation of old agricultural techniques to service the new crop of
cotton. The final product was a region that would have been familiar to
antebellum southerners: the coastline had a wealthy and closed elite of rice
planters; the interior, an expanding plantation economy based on cotton and
slavery. But while this looked like the South that would later be defiantly
antinorthern and antimodern, neither of these characteristics had helped
create the region. Instead, a steady influx of northern settlers and a selection
among essential components of the modern era (rather than an outright
rejection of modernity) brought the Lower South into its early nineteenth-
century form. Only a final economic crisis engendered by the War of 1812
uncovered a disinclination to follow the path to the factory, notwithstanding
free residents' continuing admiration for industry outside the Lower South
itself.

Whites' selectivity was informed by the doubt of their age, an uncertainty
whether rapid change (let alone revolution) was beneficial. Most dominant
groups in the West felt a similar tension between stability and transformation—only the idealistic or disaffected broke from this pattern and pointed up
the hesitancy of their cohort. Again, the emphasis is on how whites in the
Lower South were remarkably typical of their time. They believed that they
varied from the rest of the Western world, not in kind, but in degree, insisting
that local peculiarities could be overcome or could be used (like plantation
wealth) to acquire sophisticated features of a more advanced society. To a large
extent, any quarrel Lower South whites had over modernity was, not with the
outside world, but with each other. To a remarkable degree, slavery proved the
divisive issue. This was not due to any moral objection to human bondage:
whites argued over who should have new slaves and why other forms of labor
might be encouraged but rarely suggested extirpating slavery where it already
existed.

Although an indication of growing doubts over slavery, this doubt was not
yet an invasive, external criticism that prompted whites in the South to
consider anathema any troubling public discussion of slavery's drawbacks.
They were instead willing to argue about slavery even as they fought to
maintain it. Even more striking was whites' acknowledgment of slaves' desire

for independent socioeconomic activity, something usually feared only in new or otherwise unstable settlements. A product of Enlightenment views of human nature, whites' newfound ability to see slaves as individuals with minds of their own also enabled them cruelly to manipulate their human needs and desires. Here were the stirrings of modern racism, a theory of humanity that depended on modern science and social science. This last point makes clear how whites in the Lower South are not to be congratulated on their cleverness at adapting their socioeconomic system to a more modern age—blame would be more appropriate. But blame is also due flawed and self-congratulatory notions of progress for providing as many loopholes for slaveholders' peculiar customs as they did incentives for achieving a more consistent notion of modern improvement. Assessments of the American South that rely on crudely triumphal notions of modernity risk narcissism and construct a highly selective moral analysis. Better to criticize slaveholders within the intellectual context of their era than to remove them from it in order to protect the very ideals *they* found so appealing. Understanding the appeal of the modern from the perspective of all its witnesses—however benighted they might seem now—will deepen historical knowledge of their worldview and of ours.

Part I

Considering Modernity

"In your New World, which is some ages behind hand,

an Ingenious Man may find Infinite Satisfaction

from the Good he may do."

—To Alexander Garden, 1756

Chapter 2

The Fate of Progress in the Early Lower South

Arguments for the gradual improvement of human society abounded in the eighteenth century and set the stage for much of the modern era's social thought. Though some scholars have modified the old view that residents of southern North America were always reluctant to entertain these modern ideas, many still stress how southerners gradually came to suspect that theories of progress were inimical to their interests. Historians have argued that the South's material basis—plantations and slavery—made white southerners choke on modern prescriptions for social advance. Slaveholders grew critical of contentions that slavery was, ipso facto, inefficient and reprehensible and questioned whether industrial capitalism was a positive development in Western culture, the latter query curiously similar to radical critiques of capitalism that emerged from very different quarters later in the nineteenth century. Scholarship has also stressed that, as the Western world increasingly associated progress with free labor, slaveholders chose to turn their backs on that world and chart their own course.[1]

This parting of ways may have taken place during the antebellum era, when

1. Michael O'Brien and David Moltke-Hansen, eds., *Intellectual Life in Antebellum Charleston* (Knoxville, Tenn., 1986), 3–44; epigraph in —— to Alexander Garden, June 30, 1756, Dr. Templeton's transactions, RSA, XI, reel 1. On slaveholders' critique of capitalism, see Eugene D. Genovese, *The World the Slaveholders Made: Two Essays in Interpretation* (New York, 1971), 169–194. On how slaveholders (and slavery) gradually were defined as antiprogressive, see David Brion Davis, *Slavery and Human Progress* (Oxford, 1984).

industrial capital truly began to dominate economy and society and slave-holders could not but see the writing on the wall. But they arrived at this realization quite late, long contemplating contemporary social theory with little sense that they might need to exclude themselves from it. Free residents of slaveholding regions could consider themselves modern and improving, in part because theories of progress did not yet stigmatize slavery and other throwbacks to earlier eras as the only or even worst problems of the age. Social theorists criticized rapid economic change as well as stubborn archaisms like slavery. A tension fundamental to the modern age—between the fixed past and the changes of future times, Samuel Johnson's recollection and anticipation— was at the center of this ambivalent assessment of historical development. Either past or future could be romanticized or vilified in shifting, complementary patterns that, as yet, provided no set blueprint for socioeconomic improvement. A nostalgic view that mourned the loss of a past with greater social cohesion would denounce the impersonal motion of modern society, but another interpretation that praised modernity might decry the barbarities of earlier ages and fear impending stagnation.[2] Optimism over the ascent of a modern order came up against questions over the more dubious achievements or outright failures of the moderns. The debate never ended decisively before 1815. If readers in the Lower South felt doubtful over their place in the world whenever they closed a book of social theory, the doubt was as much within their reading material as over themselves.

Much of the social thought that expressed ambivalence over the modern age focused on the question of economic change. In the English-speaking world, theorists who praised economic development for its own sake emerged in the early 1600s, starting off a debate between champions of a new economic order and critics who harked back to earlier ages. The argument assessed, though it did not always distinguish between, two kinds of change: development, or qualitative alteration in economic production; and growth, or quantitative

2. For a general overview of these 18th-century interpretations of the past, see Peter Gay, *The Enlightenment: An Interpretation*, I, *The Rise of Modern Paganism* (New York, 1966), 32–38, II, *The Science of Freedom* (New York, 1969), 3–6, 100–125; J. E. Crowley, *This Sheba, Self: The Conceptualization of Economic Life in Eighteenth-Century America* (Baltimore, 1974), 10–11; and David Spadafora, *The Idea of Progress in Eighteenth-Century Britain* (New Haven, Conn., 1990). See also Philip Abrams, "The Sense of the Past and the Origins of Sociology," *Past and Present*, no. 55 (May 1972), 18–32, though Abrams focuses on the mid-19th century.

increases in production. Observers wondered whether either transformation benefited humanity: development might disrupt social relations even as it brought prosperity; growth could bring degeneracy to classes most likely to gain wealth. Denizens of the modern world, including those in the Lower South, considered several smaller yet still critical questions within the larger issue of economic change. Debate raged, for instance, whether the state ought to play any role in economic development, or whether government-funded ventures instead represented corrupt misuse of power to tax and otherwise intervene in the affairs of free propertyholders. Theorists wondered, too, about the effects of a new economic order on individual humans: did people gain better qualities by living in more complex socioeconomic structures, or did they lose primary virtues? These lines of inquiry contributed to the nascent social sciences, defining an ethnography of peoples at varied levels of economic development and a psychology of people within the highest, commercial level.

By the mid-eighteenth century, the Scottish historical school (precursor of political economy) formed the most influential interpretation of economic development. The school's conjectural history was the first modern theory that linked cultural progress to material production, rather than made simple contrasts between past and present that might not refer to discrete forms of economic activity. Whites in the Lower South were interested in Scottish history because they wanted to determine their own place within its comparative sociological framework. They inserted themselves, with great care, somewhere between the two value-laden extremes of nomadic savagism and commercial civility set out by this theory, the first stage epitomized, for them, by Indians who lingered in relative economic underdevelopment, the last by Europeans who embodied the most highly polished and commercial form of human society.

Their concern over modern theory revealed whites' continuing anxiety over their progress, their uncertainty whether they moved in a circle (advancing only to degenerate) or as an arrow—forward to a better existence. The question remained open until the early 1800s, when whites began to adopt the studied devotion to archaism and societal staticism that characterized their antebellum descendants. Yet even this new uneasiness did not represent a break with contemporary theory so much as recognition of its uneasy regard of progress. After all, the question of which economic form most benefited humanity concerned not only free residents of slaveholding societies but nearly everybody else in the modern age.

℘ℴ *The Idea of Material Progress*

In the early modern era, social theory shifted away from a long-standing assumption that human society was an organic entity, one composed of hierarchical ranks whose members strove for the same (though unequally divided) material goals. This premodern belief had discouraged improvement in material production for its own sake, regarding the harmony and well-being of society as a much higher aim. To be sure, Christians were admonished to work hard, and everyone considered wealth a badge of merit. Christians, too, as Adam's heirs, believed the physical earth their domain, and domination of nature part of God's assignment to them in their carnal state. But the economy that resulted from human exploitation of natural resources was supposed to be part of a moral society; members of society were to be protected from material hardship that resulted, not from natural causes like drought and famine (products of God's providence), but from human sins like greed and pride. No economic behavior could be separated from prevailing moral concerns, and thus individual pursuit of gain was deemed a dubious, if not injurious, activity. Similar ideas about individual discipline and communal gain had earlier appeared in classical republican theory, which, after its revival in the Renaissance, often ran parallel to Christian ideas of a moral economy. In England, however, analysts used the economic crises of the 1620s as starting points for a new argument. Observing how recent economic affairs had taken on a life of their own, these theorists speculated that the economy was a human and secular realm that could be manipulated with other than moral imperatives. They postulated that human action, separated from irrelevant concerns, might create better material circumstances that would then benefit the whole society. This early praise for individual striving after economic advance blazed a trail for modern theorists, from John Locke to Adam Smith, who explicated the ability and right of humans to work for their own good.[3]

Though proponents of the new economic freedom swallowed large doses of criticism, religious and secular, because they abandoned the widely accepted belief in an organically connected social order, their views informed political thought in later years when economic change was manifest. Historians of Britain have labeled the late seventeenth and the eighteenth centuries an Age of

3. Joyce Appleby, *Economic Thought and Ideology in Seventeenth Century England* (Princeton, N.J., 1978); and "Ideology and Theory: The Tension between Political and Economic Liberalism in Seventeenth-Century England," *AHR*, LXXXI (1976), 499–515.

Improvement. This tag, too credulous to be wholly accurate, nonetheless points to the significance of the years from the agricultural reforms of the late 1600s to the acceleration in industrial production at the end of the 1700s. Improvers who increased crop yields and invested in early factories were most likely to see good in their deeds. Others feared that the new wealth could be more a source of degeneracy and corrupt power than a signal of progress.[4]

In the early 1700s, Britons optimistic about the merits of prosperity crafted a literature of improvement. Daniel Defoe was the outstanding contributor. Defoe's *Essay upon Projects* (1697) defined the "projecting spirit" or "humour" that animated men who assumed society benefited from practical experiments and who believed themselves able to experiment in this manner. *Projects* might entail either improvements in existing economic behaviors or innovations that replaced the old with the new; in contemporary parlance, improvement, or *projecting*, referred to both. Although projects included down-to-earth tasks like inventing new tools and machinery or planting better crops, other improvements fed a newfound fascination with intangible properties: stocks, banks, and credit systems. The growth of finance and commerce offered new ways for the government to intervene in economic ventures. Praise of all these projects filled political rhetoric, particularly that of Whiggish defenders of expanded financial powers for the government in the age of Walpole. Bernard Mandeville proposed improvement of a more vexing sort in his *Fable of the Bees; or, Private Vices, Publick Benefits* (1714), his notorious, rhyming explanation of how a private vice like avarice served the public good: greed shook humans out of their natural preference for leisure, thereby increasing industry and prosperity for all.[5]

Mercantilism was the keystone of the new economic thought. Mercantilists, taking up Mandeville's assumption that humans naturally desired wealth and leisure, sought ways to harness human nature to work for the public good. This was not a revival of the old moral tradition, but a nationalistic assessment of economic needs based on a gap mercantilists perceived between England's actual and potential wealth. To fulfill the nation's potential, citizens needed to be shaped into better economic actors. They needed incentives to work, rewards for performing specific tasks, and deterrents against laziness or stub-

---

4. Isaac Kramnick, *Bolingbroke and His Circle: The Politics of Nostalgia in the Age of Walpole* (Cambridge, Mass., 1968), 39–55, 63–83.

5. *Ibid.*, 188–205; J.G.A. Pocock, *The Machiavellian Moment: Florentine Political Thought and the Atlantic Republican Tradition* (Princeton, N.J., 1975), 423–461.

bornly unproductive habits. Properly disciplined, individual interest contributed to the common good, an assumption that liberal economists like Adam Smith later attacked by contending that individual interests, left unregulated, constructed a better welfare for all. Mercantilism elaborated its theory in imperial terms by specifying how a nation could plan and invest its way to wealth through trade. Commerce was the key—not even actual production of raw or manufactured goods was more important. The proof of this was Holland, a place poorly equipped to produce anything but made stunningly wealthy through trade. An optimal balance of trade would minimize payments to other nations for any goods, especially payment in scarce specie. To maintain this balance, England needed to manipulate colonial production of essential or expensive goods, making colonists (even more than subjects in Britain) objects of economic policy and America the arena for many a project.[6]

Projecting remained, however, a questionable pursuit. It seemed an activity that ominously strengthened the state or enriched the elite, a spur to corruption or selfishness. Disaffected Whigs and Tory critics (moving in and out of the circle around Henry St. John, Viscount Bolingbroke) crafted a dissenting literature to dampen the projecting spirit. Their diatribes flourished after the Bank Crisis of 1710 and the South Sea Bubble of 1720, two episodes that revealed the frailty of credit-dependent projects and the avarice of their architects. Jonathan Swift was the best-known skeptic. Swift praised improvement detached from political gain or self-interest, as when a character in *Gulliver's Travels* (1726) said, "Whoever could make two ears of corn or two blades of grass to grow upon a spot of ground where only one grew before, would deserve better of mankind . . . than the whole race of politicians put together" (pt. 2, chap. 7). Yet Swift parodied the dizzy and selfish spirit of projecting, as in two caustic pieces on the Bank of Ireland that he anthologized, *The Wonderfull Wonder of Wonders* (1720) and *The Wonder of All the Wonders, That Ever the World Wondered At* (1721); in the character of a scientist said by Lemuel Gulliver to pursue "a project for extracting sunbeams out of cucumbers"; and most savagely in his *Modest Proposal* (1729) to butcher the children of the poor for meat—a suggestion that satirized the assumption that private vices served the public good by observing how cannibalism might alleviate hunger and overpopulation. Less flamboyant but as insistent were protests

6. On mercantilism and its impact in the colonies, see Crowley, *This Sheba, Self,* 34–49; and Cathy D. Matson and Peter S. Onuf, *A Union of Interests: Political and Economic Thought in Revolutionary America* (Lawrence, Kans., 1990), 15–20.

against centralized and corrupting financial power that came from adherents of republican theory.[7]

Political debate over a changing economy continued through the eighteenth century. Nostalgic interpretations of the British past (begun by James Harrington, taking definitive form with Bolingbroke, and continued in working-class demands for a renewed moral economy) questioned rapid socioeconomic change. In the meantime, the spirit of improvement became associated more with the emerging school of political economy than with any specific political party. By midcentury, agricultural and commercial achievements formed a base of capital for the industrial expansion that emerged before the turn of the century. British observers began to define the socioeconomic characteristics of this process, usually defending them as signs of progress. Banking, credit, and commerce were evidence of their society's increased cultural civility as well as emblems of its economic prosperity. Commerce, especially, seemed the agent of progress. Elaborating on mercantilists' praise of trade, publicists like Joseph Addison and Richard Steele made commerce even appear a civilizing activity, a polisher of individuals and savior of societies in danger of sinking into barbarous poverty.[8]

Hopes of economic growth took a drubbing before midcentury, however, when recession and war brought gloom even to inveterate optimists. Victory in the Seven Years' War and economic upturn renewed cheer; at this time, clergymen like Joseph Priestley and Richard Price joined secular proponents of progress in arguing for an almost unlimited perfectibility in human society. A Christian view of history saw secular progress going hand in hand with improvement of spiritual understanding and diffusion of the faith. By the second half of the century, secular theorists began realizing a long-held goal: to reduce societal phenomena to scientific terms just as Bacon and Newton had subjected the physical world to a science of inquiry. This represented a new form of reflection on the subject of human endeavor. Economists in the 1600s had started this scrutiny by presenting economic activity as a distinct, secular phenomenon conducive to human happiness; Britons next entered into a variety of projects that expanded and diversified the economy; last, a new and more exacting breed of economists analyzed the complex society that had

7. Kramnick, *Bolingbroke and His Circle*, 206–217. On colonial response to projects, see Matson and Onuf, *Union of Interests*, 12–14.

8. Edward A. Bloom and Lillian D. Bloom, *Joseph Addison's Sociable Animal: In the Market Place, on the Hustings, in the Pulpit* (Providence, R.I., 1971).

resulted. The final group brought the frame of analysis full circle by positing that humans could actually improve the physical world (making the earth more fruitful and the climate more temperate), altering the material universe that had originally interested the early physical scientists who had inspired early social scientists.[9]

The Scots pioneered the scientific method of social analysis, fashioning a theory of material progress that defined distinct stages of society, then examining in detail the final, commercial stage. Earlier observers had set out broad contrasts between past and present, primitive and civil, but the Scottish school merged historical and sociological levels of analysis systematically, placing specific societal characteristics into chronological sequence. The resulting theory, a descendant of English musings on the relative benefits of economic advance, was also cousin to French thought on the same subject (especially that of Montesquieu and Turgot) and parent to the emerging field of political economy. Adam Smith briefly reviewed modern society's rise above three earlier stages before getting down to the task of examining the commercial stage in his *Inquiry into the Nature and Causes of the Wealth of Nations* (1776). The Scottish historical school provided assumptions for German historians like Herder and continued in Marx's theory of material development. Its antecedents (which included theorists of epistemology) and descendants cannot all be traced here (nor would such tracings have been relevant to the first audience for Scottish history, which tended even to overlook French authors in favor of British ones). These readers were therefore most familiar with the theory as it appeared in works by Henry Home, Lord Kames; David Hume; Adam Ferguson; John Millar; William Robertson; Edward Gibbon (who used conjectural history in his widely read *Decline and Fall of the Roman Empire*); and Adam Smith.[10]

9. On cycles of pessimism and optimism, see Spadafora, *Idea of Progress*, 213–214, on religious progress, 85–132, and on environmental improvement, 233–234. Pocock, *Machiavellian Moment*, 462–505; and "To Market, To Market: Economic Thought in Early Modern England," *Journal of Interdisciplinary History*, X (1979–1980), 303–309.

10. On contrasts between past and present, see, for example, William G. Batz, "The Historical Anthropology of John Locke," *Journal of the History of Ideas*, XXXV (1974), 663–670; and Ronald L. Meek, *Social Science and the Ignoble Savage* (Cambridge, 1976).

On Gibbon's debt to the Scots, see J.G.A. Pocock, "Gibbon's *Decline and Fall* and the World View of the Late Enlightenment," in Pocock, *Virtue, Commerce, and History: Essays on Political Thought and History, Chiefly in the Eighteenth Century* (Cambridge,

This group of scholars posited they could scientifically analyze any human trait, any social institution. Starting, like Montesquieu, with the premise that human nature was (like gravity) a constant, the Scots analyzed humans' universal characteristics. Humanity's most significant feature was sociability, an innate sympathy for others and a desire to be socially bonded to them. This associational quality meshed with human intelligence, or reason, which created verbal abilities needed for social interactions. Despite their belief in an essential humanity that cut across time and culture, the Scots conceded that individual variation emerged within society according to the varied natural abilities and inclinations of individuals. While innately gregarious and sympa-

---

1985), 143–156; and "Gibbon and the Shepherds: The Stages of Society in the *Decline and Fall,*" *History of European Ideas,* II (1981), 193–202.

For general overviews of early Scottish sociology, see Anand C. Chitnis, *The Scottish Enlightenment: A Social History* (London, 1976), chap. 5; Istvan Hont and Michael Ignatieff, eds., *Wealth and Virtue: The Shaping of Political Economy in the Scottish Enlightenment* (Cambridge, 1983); Meek, *Social Science and the Ignoble Savage;* Gladys Bryson, *Man and Society: The Scottish Inquiry of the Eighteenth Century* (New York, 1968). On connections between Scottish and French theory, see Meek, *Social Science and the Ignoble Savage,* chaps. 3, 5; Meek, *Smith, Marx, and After: Ten Essays in the Development of Economic Thought* (London, 1977), 18–32; John Alan Baum, *Montesquieu and Social Theory* (Oxford, 1979), esp. 97–119; Melvin Richter, *The Political Theory of Montesquieu* (Cambridge, 1977), 3, 51–53. Despite their debt to Montesquieu, the Scottish school (like English theory) was independent of parallel French thought—see Spadafora, *Idea of Progress,* 346–347, 381–385. On Scottish sociological thought's descent from liberal English thought and its relation to political economy, see Pocock, "Virtues, Rights, and Manners: A Model for Historians of Political Thought," in Pocock, *Virtue, Commerce, and History,* 37–50; and John Dunn, "From Applied Theology to Social Analysis: The Break between John Locke and the Scottish Enlightenment," in Hont and Ignatieff, eds., *Wealth and Virtue,* 119–135. On the Scottish school's fortunes in Germany, see Roy Pascal, "Herder and the Scottish Historical School," *English Goethe Society Publications,* XIV (1938–1939), 23–42; Ronald L. Meek, *Economics and Ideology and Other Essays: Studies in the Development of Economic Thought* (London, 1967), 34–50; Meek, *Smith, Marx, and After,* 1–17; Alexander Gillies, *A Hebridean in Goethe's Weimar: The Reverend James Macdonald and the Cultural Relations between Scotland and Germany* (Oxford, 1969). But see the dissenting opinion of Andrew Skinner, "A Scottish Contribution to Marxist Sociology?" in Ian Bradley and Michael Howard, eds., *Classical and Marxian Political Economy: Essays in Honor of Ronald L. Meek* (New York, 1982), 79–114.

thetic toward each other, people were unequal in complementary ways and formed societies in which they each had specialized social roles.[11]

Once a universal human psychology was shown to be the foundation of human society, scholars could go on to study the finer detail within this larger, ubiquitous pattern. In his *Theory of Moral Sentiments* (1759), Adam Smith (following Francis Hutcheson) expanded the sensationalist philosophy of John Locke to establish a calculus of human passions. Smith stressed two senti-ments: *sympathy* (sign of humanity's innate sociable nature), which bound individuals into society; and *emulation,* which motivated humans constantly to improve self and society by imitating others. Smith showed the connection between these two impulses by insisting that "emulation" made people "pur-sue riches" so they might "be taken notice of with sympathy." By stressing human qualities they assumed were universal, the Scots moved away from economic theory's earlier emphasis on how political authorities needed to shape individual behavior. The deepest and most beneficial social mecha-nisms, the Scots countered, were subrational and followed a pattern individ-uals could not escape anyway. Ferguson claimed that true improvements resulted from "human action" but not "human design"; Smith stated that self-conscious "projectors disturb nature in the course of her operations in human affairs," an assertion indicative of his wider questioning of policies like mer-cantilism that officiously damaged the economy. The laws of human nature, rather than positive human law, effected the best changes.[12]

11. On these points, see William Robertson, *The History of America* (London, 1777), II, 277–279; Adam Ferguson, *An Essay on the History of Civil Society* (Edinburgh, 1767), 15, 24; David Hume, "Of the Origin of Government," in Hume, *Essays Moral, Political, and Literary,* rev. ed., ed. Eugene F. Miller (Indianapolis, Ind., 1987), 37. The Scots recognized that they were elaborating on Montesquieu's statement of human similar-ity—Ferguson admitted to this in *Civil Society,* 24. See Charles Secondat, Baron de Montesquieu, *The Spirit of Laws,* ed. David Wallace Carrithers (Berkeley, Calif., 1977), pt. 1, book 1, chap. 2.

12. See Philip Mercer, *Sympathy and Ethics: A Study of the Relationship between Sympathy and Morality, with Special Reference to Hume's Treatise* (Oxford, 1972), chaps. 2–4 (on Hume); John B. Stewart, *The Moral and Political Philosophy of David Hume* (New York, 1963), 57–68; Kenneth MacLean, "Imagination and Sympathy: Sterne and Adam Smith," *Jour. Hist. Ideas,* X (1949), 399–410; and Robert Boyden Lamb, "Adam Smith's System: Sympathy Not Self-Interest," *Jour. Hist. Ideas,* XXXV (1974), 671–682. For a full examination of the question of human passions and modern political

The Scots next traced how humans had unconsciously elaborated their societies in a predictable pattern through four stages, each of greater complexity: hunting, pasturage, farming, and commerce. The four-stage theory (called "conjectural" or "philosophic" history because the true conditions of historically remote societies could only be guessed at) presupposed dynamic progression from one stage to another and assumed that such change increased human sociability and improved civilization. Ferguson claimed, for example, that humanity tended to "advance" from "rudeness to civilization" in an unfailing progression. Material circumstances grounded each social stage. This was not, however, materialism in its reductionist sense. The Scots conceded that environment, laws, religion, and the like affected human culture as well but insisted that, as economics encouraged different human activities, so the resulting culture would take on a different form. As Robertson stated: "In every inquiry concerning the operations of men when united together in society, the first object of attention should be their mode of subsistence. Accordingly as that varies, their laws and policy must be different."[13]

Commercial peoples were the final products of the natural development of human society. The Scots focused on one feature, voluntarism, to distinguish modern and commercial societies from ancient ones. Whereas master-slave (or lord-tenant) relationships created artificial restraints on human behavior that inhibited further development, a free society unshackled sympathy and emulation, allowing people to be swept forward by their liberated natural potentials. Humans who freely constructed their political system made superior citizens, those who freely offered their work did so with greater productivity and efficiency, and those who freely chose among commodities better supported a modern market economy. A labor system based on slavery could be a temporary method of production whenever free labor happened to be scarce and expensive, but then required demolition. The ancient world had not followed this path, and served as negative example: its agricultural production had stagnated, its commerce had languished, and its politics had de-

---

thought, see Albert O. Hirschman, *The Passions and the Interests: Political Arguments for Capitalism before Its Triumph* (Princeton, N.J., 1977). The first quotation is from Adam Smith, *The Theory of Moral Sentiments*, ed. D. D. Raphael and A. L. Macfie (Oxford, 1976), 50; the second and third from Meek, *Smith, Marx, and After*, 19, 26.

13. Ferguson, *Civil Society*, 1; Robertson, *History of America*, I, 324.

pended on primitive conceptions of civic virtue that enhanced an elite's ability to control events at the expense of the people.[14]

While this denunciation of the ancients and this faith that a modern, commercial society would free humanity have often placed the Scots (especially Smith) in the liberal ranks, the principles of the Scottish school also provided a conservative vision of humanity. With its premise that humans were instinctively sociable and naturally tended to elaborate social networks, conjectural history warned against rapid alteration of social structure. Revolution threatened the spontaneously created order to which all humans unconsciously contributed. (No accident, then, that this antirationalist argument appeared in the work of Edmund Burke.) Rapid improvement and rapid retrogression were equally appalling prospects. The deliberated handiwork of humanity was always problematic; conscious improvement was as much a threat to modern progress as it might be a process within it. This was the reason Smith denounced "projectors" who meant well but moved too fast.[15]

A cautious approach to meliorism was related to an ambivalent view of the past. Though the Scottish school condemned atavistic institutions like slavery, it did not reject precommercial ages out of hand. By the end of the eighteenth century, Europeans were busy sentimentalizing certain qualities of precommercial societies—a reassertion of the old desire for an organically connected society that seemed a casualty of an overly modern age. Nostalgia underpinned Ferguson's concern, for instance, that the division of labor snapped the "bands" that held together precommercial societies. In modern societies, he lamented, no one's personality was "animated with the spirit of society itself." Europeans' fondness for the premodern counterbalanced their praise of modernity, but not to the extent of summarily rejecting the present. Not even so-called primitivists like Rousseau preferred primitive society, but merely used it to emphasize virtues modern society needed to protect or restore. Unwillingness to categorize modernity as an unqualified success,

14. Istvan Hont and Michael Ignatieff, "Needs and Justice in the *Wealth of Nations:* An Introductory Essay," 1–10, 42–44, and Nicholas Phillipson, "Adam Smith as Civic Moralist," 185–189, 199, in Hont and Ignatieff, eds., *Wealth and Virtue.* On the ancient world, see, esp., Hume, "Of the Populousness of Ancient Nations," in his *Essays Moral, Political, and Literary,* ed. Miller, 377–464.

15. Ronald Hamowy, *The Scottish Enlightenment and the Theory of Spontaneous Order* (Carbondale, Ill., 1987), 3–4, 34–36. For a more critical view of the Enlightenment idea of human nature, see Alasdair MacIntyre, *After Virtue: A Study in Moral Theory* (Notre Dame, Ind., 1981), 49–59.

however, opened the way to a complicated, romantic vision of human beings as eager perpetrators of progress who nevertheless kept weeping over the lost ways of the past.[16]

Socioeconomic change thus provoked ambivalent feelings. Progress might, for example, be a deceptive stage within degeneration—societies could fall back even after they had moved forward. Some theorists even suspected that progress brought about its own downfall. Greater wealth and the division of labor were both mixed blessings, prosperity because it eroded human virtue, and the division of labor because it turned each citizen into a fragmented version of the human personality unable to sustain social and political duties. Did society move, theorists wondered anew, like an arrow's flight, or in a circle? Those who feared circular development dusted off Polybian and Machiavellian images of cyclic growth and corruption, but set them out in social rather than political terms; the stability of a socioeconomic system, rather than the virtue of a republic, was the central concern.[17] This skeptical view of progress expressed in a more complex way doubts over economic advance that had pursued theorists of development, from critiques of seventeenth-century liberal thought to the debate over projecting.

Members of the Scottish school themselves disagreed whether the nature of material progress was cyclic. They were not as boundlessly optimistic as English contemporaries who waxed enthusiastic over the absolute perfectibility of human society. Because the Scots fixed boundaries on improvement, sticking to historical evidence rather than utopian design, they scrupulously defined the possibility of failure. Ferguson was the gloomiest of the lot, concerned that commercialized people, with their newly fragmented person-

16. Ferguson, "Part Fifth: Of the Decline of Nations," *Civil Society,* quotation from 334. On Europeans' admiration of primitivism, see P. J. Marshall and Glyndwr Williams, *The Great Map of Mankind: Perceptions of New Worlds in the Age of Enlightenment* (Cambridge, Mass., 1982), 193–222, 258–298; J. B. Bury, *The Idea of Progress: An Inquiry into Its Origin and Growth* (London, 1920), 177–182. See Gay, *Enlightenment,* II, 96, on Rousseau and the limits of European primitivism.

17. On the Scottish controversy over the possibility of societal retrogression, see Istvan Hont, "The 'Rich Country–Poor Country' Debate in Scottish Classical Political Economy," in Hont and Ignatieff, eds., *Wealth and Virtue,* 271–315. On Machiavellian themes of growth and corruption, see Pocock, *Machiavellian Moment,* 462–505; Drew R. McCoy, *The Elusive Republic: Political Economy in Jeffersonian America* (Chapel Hill, N.C., 1980), 13–47. On the Enlightenment's lingering fear of cyclic ascent and decline, see Gay, *Enlightenment,* I, 34–36, II, 100–101.

alities, were bound to lapse into personal apathy and societal anarchy. Hume was slightly more optimistic, denying Andrew Fletcher's stern condemnation of wealth and luxury and defending the power of commercial riches to make politics, arts, and manners flourish. Hume did admit, however, that in any given society the arts and sciences tended to reach a certain zenith and thereafter decline. Smith, unsurprisingly, was more cheerful, arguing that division of labor and free international trade gave commercial societies a permanent advantage over poorer countries; once a commercial nation made its ascent, its citizens would perversely have to strive for error in order to enter a Polybian cycle of decline. But even the champion of commercial splendor allowed pessimism to creep into his writings. Smith conceded that "it is in the progressive stage" of a society, not after "it has acquired its full complement of riches," that the population achieved the highest standard of living. He also believed, like Ferguson, that the division of labor could dehumanize the people and recommended that the state take an interest in educating all its citizens to prevent this outcome.[18]

Smith was not, of course, making a statement about the absolute merits of modernity; his was a more balanced and less partisan view. It was, instead, his contention that a modern economy had a *relative* advantage over precommercial economic relations: the detectable gap between the material conditions of the poor and rich in a commercial nation was still preferable to the want they all would suffer in a more primitive social form. This approach did not settle doubts, however, about the continuing vitality of modern, expanding economies—Thomas Malthus would later ask whether prosperity itself might not

18. On the Scots' view of finite improvement, see Spadafora, *Idea of Progress*, 254–255. I disagree with Spadafora's contention (275–284) that the Scots were not pessimists and did not consider how corruption might be a result of progress itself. On Ferguson's prevailing doubt, see Hirschman, *Passions and Interests*, 119–122. See John Robertson, "The Scottish Enlightenment at the Limits of the Civic Tradition," in Hont and Ignatieff, eds., *Wealth and Virtue*, 137–178, for Hume's responses to Fletcher's doleful Machiavellianism. An example of Hume's pessimism can be found in his *Essays Moral, Political, and Literary*, ed. Miller, 135.

On Smith, see Hont and Ignatieff, "Needs and Justice in the *Wealth of Nations*," 1–44, and Hont, "The 'Rich Country–Poor Country' Debate," 271–315, in Hont and Ignatieff, eds., *Wealth and Virtue* (on his optimism); Gay, *Enlightenment*, II, 360–364 (pessimism). The quotation is from *An Inquiry into the Nature and Causes of the Wealth of Nations*, ed. R. H. Campbell and A. S. Skinner, 2 vols. (Oxford, 1976), I, 99.

prove an eventual curse by breeding more population than any nation could support.

Uncertainty over social progress thus left a troubling legacy for the modern age. Economic theorists, especially the Scots, claimed to describe a pattern of social progress that was universal. Yet while asserting that all societies went through the same stages, theorists warned of the perils that could befall them in every stage: from the incivility of barbarism and slavery to the luxury and corruption of commercial society. In the late eighteenth and early nineteenth centuries, most westerners had to worry about their checkered progress toward the final stage of commercial civility; slaveholding societies had to worry about this prospect *and* about their resemblance to earlier and regressive societal stages. If modern economic theory—especially conjectural history and early political economy—was remarkably thorough in pointing out all advantages and disadvantages of economic development, American slaveholders were remarkably suited to read themselves into each promise and threat of modernity.

🍂 Local Discussion

British economic debates gave free inhabitants of the Lower South a method of interpreting themselves, one that congratulated them for their achievements but also revealed unsolved problems. Ideas about improvement and societal progress had powerful appeal to all early Americans, who saw themselves in a constant and vivid process of social development no longer familiar to most Europeans. Americans recognized themselves as recent products of European colonization, and, even into the nineteenth century, they realized their creole society was still in flux. Creoles feared that their underdeveloped economy and provincial status indicated a lingering backwardness and dependence on European markets and culture.

The export-led economy of the Lower South was indeed that of a colony. By the 1720s, commercial agriculture and black slavery were in place in the Carolina lowcountry; the colony produced raw materials for overseas consumers and was gaining a reputation for considerable prosperity. Its economic form, market-oriented agricultural estates and slaves, was slowly moving into new areas toward the West and South. The economy lost its earlier, frontier diversity, and the accretion of an ever larger black population (one that, along the coast, already outnumbered whites) seemed an unstoppable process. Both features were potential weaknesses. Monoculture created an unbalanced economy; slavery brought in an alien and rebellious population, one likely to turn against whites if there was armed conflict with Indians or with the Spanish who still held (until 1763) St. Augustine.

To address these problems, whites in the region used the range of economic arguments and options (from the traditional economy, through mercantilism, to free trade) that had emerged early in the modern era. Various improvers supported projects that moved the society either backward or forward on the hypothetical spectrum between the moral tradition and an industrial economy. (Motives behind the two kinds of projects were, however, not always distinct.)[19] The two extremes roughly bounded the period from 1730 to 1815. Earlier promoters revived moral economies that were linked to mercantilist expectations of economic diversification in the 1730s, when the plantation economy was disturbed by imperial warfare and threat of slave insurrection. A later generation of investors established factories during the commercial upsets of the Napoleonic Wars that ended in 1815; this phase culminated a series of nationalistic pleas for economic self-sufficiency that began during the pre-Revolutionary nonimportation movement.

Earlier, the moral tradition was often imposed on areas outside the plantation perimeter. Economically diversified settlements free of slavery were set in place along the frontier as buffers against western warfare with Indians and as containment of the threat of slave insurrection. Governor Robert Johnson drew up the first such scheme in South Carolina in 1729, a plan for eleven western townships supported in 1730 by Britain's Board of Trade. The towns were to be subsidized by revenue from the slave trade and to be settled by poorer whites instead of planters and slaves; with diversified farm-and-market economies, townships would resist the advance of plantation agriculture. The Trustees for Establishing the Colony of Georgia in America copied Johnson's design when they planned their own colony later in the 1730s. The trust restricted land sales and prohibited slavery to prevent plantations from creeping down from Carolina. The people who settled in townships and Trustee Georgia fulfilled several expectations drawn from mercantilism and the moral

19. The moral tradition, for instance, also emerged during the Revolution and the War of 1812 in republican calls for independence from European economies. See Matson and Onuf, *Union of Interests*, 21–26, on neomercantilist and republican definitions of public sacrifice during the Revolution.

tradition. They produced commodities Britons would otherwise have to buy from foreigners and were (supposedly) better able to resist military threat. Without slaves and plantation-sized tracts, settlers worked more for a common benefit than for individual gain and could not display the laziness and luxury common to people freed from labor.[20] Other mercantilist variations on this alternative to plantation agriculture appeared in British East Florida, where, again, white settlers were supposed to produce goods needed by the empire and where new communities promised to fulfill a mercantilist goal of full employment for British subjects who could emigrate to new colonies to find work. In Georgia and Florida, more than in South Carolina's townships, promoters stated a complex goal: creation of cohesive societies that contrasted with the economic pell-mell characteristic of the larger region and of the Old World itself.[21] Nostalgia, military security, and imperial wealth all came in the same package.

This complicated bundle also included significant doubts over the wisdom of continuing to use slavery. In part an unease over the economic consequences of slavery, this position also reflected fear of slaves' discontent. Slave resistance to white authority had deep roots in the lowcountry. The region stood out among the other areas of early America because of its culturally distinct and more Africanized black population, the members of which were sometimes willing to take up arms to defy white power. Slaves' ability to win freedom, or at least some demonstrable measure of autonomy for their community or themselves, is nevertheless debatable. They could not completely remove themselves from white authority, like maroons in places like Jamaica or Surinam; they did not maintain the communal independence enjoyed by serfs or peasants, who used collective action and internal leadership to distance themselves from the power of landlords; nor could they wring important concessions from masters as slaves on sugar plantations occasionally did. Lower South slaves had, instead, to make the most of the few moments when

20. Robert L. Meriwether, *The Expansion of South Carolina, 1729–1765* (Kingsport, Tenn., 1940), 19–22; David Leroy Coon, "The Development of Market Agriculture in South Carolina, 1670–1785" (Ph.D. diss., University of Illinois, Urbana/Champaign, 1972), 270–299; Kenneth Coleman, *Colonial Georgia: A History* (New York, 1976), 11–12; Lewis Cecil Gray, *A History of Agriculture in the Southern United States to 1860* (Washington, D.C., 1933), I, 186–187; Harold E. Davis, *The Fledgling Province: Social and Cultural Life in Colonial Georgia, 1733–1776* (Chapel Hill, N.C., 1976), 8–13.

21. Bernard Bailyn, *Voyagers to the West: A Passage in the Peopling of North America on the Eve of the Revolution* (New York, 1986), 430–474, 545–572.

they could directly challenge whites. Such an opportunity occurred during the War of Jenkins's Ear when a group of slaves cut and ran for Spanish Florida in the 1739 Stono Rebellion, killing about twenty whites along the way. The Revolution provided a second important chance to defy whites openly.[22]

If these rebellions did not add up into the triumphs won by peasants and slaves elsewhere, Lower South slaves were powerful enough to make one important point clear to their masters: even if their role was legally to act as the property of others, they might always modify if not defy this societal assumption, thus making life unpredictable if not dangerous for whites. Warily assessing the hazard of slave rebellion, colonial officials and lowcountry slaveholders found the old ideal of a tight-knit organic community, united in a common good and against common threats, of considerable value. They insisted that, if newer areas restricted themselves to free and white populations, the Lower South would better be able to promote safety as well as production of mercantile commodities.

Experiments with the moral tradition had plenty of critics, the best known of whom were the Georgia Malcontents. In the 1730s and 1740s, these propertyholders complained against trustee restrictions on land sales and slavery that prevented them from controlling what should be their freehold. The Malcontents drew mostly on the English tradition of law that gave subjects the right to manipulate their property free from interference by the state. Malcontents also used liberal assumptions that individuals, acting independently, were the best

---

22. On slave culture and resistance in the region, see Peter H. Wood, *Black Majority: Negroes in Colonial South Carolina from 1670 through the Stono Rebellion* (New York, 1975), 285–326; Jane Landers, "Gracia Real de Santa Teresa de Mose: A Free Black Town in Spanish Colonial Florida," *AHR*, XCV (1990), 9–30. On community strength among other groups held in bondage, see James C. Scott, *Weapons of the Weak: Everyday Forms of Peasant Resistance* (New Haven, Conn., 1985); Stuart B. Schwartz, *Sugar Plantations in the Formation of Brazilian Society: Bahia, 1550–1835* (Cambridge, 1985), esp. 154–159 and chap. 14; Michael Craton, *Testing the Chains: Resistance to Slavery in the British West Indies* (Ithaca, N.Y., 1982); Richard Price, *First Time: The Historical Vision of an Afro-American People* (Baltimore, 1983); David Barry Gaspar, *Bondmen and Rebels: A Study of Master-Slave Relations in Antigua, with Implications for Colonial British America* (Baltimore, 1985); Peter Kolchin, *Unfree Labor: American Slavery and Russian Serfdom* (Cambridge, Mass., 1987), chaps. 5, 6. For pessimistic assessments of the ability of North American slaves to achieve real autonomy, see Jean Butenhoff Lee, "The Problem of Slave Community in the Eighteenth-Century Chesapeake," *WMQ*, 3d Ser., XLIII (1986), 333–361; and Kolchin, *Unfree Labor*, esp. 233–239.

support of a prosperous and improving economy. This was a more direct attack on mercantilists' insistence that individual interest would undermine the commonwealth unless disciplined by political authorities. Georgia settlers also argued for their right to own slaves, which British subjects had elsewhere. This was a regional twist on liberal economic thought, one that reiterated the region's idiosyncrasies: planners like the trustees who harked back to earlier economic forms nevertheless had no place for slavery within their nostalgic view of society; Malcontents who argued for slave labor drew more extensively on modern defenses of individuals' economic rights. The South Carolina Regulators would, a few decades later, similarly argue for their right to hold and improve property.

Schemes to hedge in or to alter the Lower South's economic form bore little fruit; plantations instead moved into new territory, dominating the region on the eve of the Revolution and supplying the continuing context for reform. Political troubles with Britain brought a new phase of debate over the economy. Republican outcry against luxury helped organize boycotts of British goods and encourage domestic production of necessary articles. After the Revolution, citizens wanted to improve their ability to compete with European economies. During the Confederation, neomercantilist demands for commercial prosperity within each state continued the trend toward the Republic's economic independence. A newly nationalized vision of the economy emerged in discussion of the federal Constitution even as Americans remained convinced that a centralized government might increase economic meddling and erode individual incentive to work toward prosperity. For the most part, however, Americans in the Jeffersonian period were optimists, looking forward to commercial growth brought about by independent American propertyholders who sold their produce abroad. Commercial disruptions of the Napoleonic Wars underscored Americans' desire for independence from Europe; patriots, as during the Revolution, called for a self-sufficient domestic economy that produced its own manufactured goods and urged improvement of established economic activities, the better to entice Old World merchants and consumers.[23] In this context, investors in the Lower South (as elsewhere in the Republic) tentatively supported domestic production of many goods and industrial production of textiles, a brief and inconclusive phase of import substitution. Though this episode shows how slaveholders and others in the

23. Joyce Appleby, *Capitalism and a New Social Order: The Republican Vision of the 1790s* (New York, 1984), chap. 4.

region were unafraid to trek into modern territory marked out by the factory, they beat a hasty retreat once peace in 1815 reopened European markets for plantation products.

However willing whites were to alter their economy, even in ways that contrast with the region's later anti-industrial stance, they were still reluctant to change significantly the region's material base. In all phases of debate over the local economy, no one directly attacked the prevailing pattern: commercial agriculture and slavery. Promoters of various schemes disagreed only whether the existing plantation region (with boundaries that shifted over the years) should be surrounded with another economic form or dotted with more diverse economic activities. Most argument over the future of the region focused on its commercial fortunes—how its contribution to the modern era's expanding field of trade might continue or increase progress without disrupting what was already in place. Whites' discussion of this central question did not result in a consistent or intellectually rigorous position. Their ideas about economic progress were, at best, products of well-read amateurs and part-time intellectuals, the latter being historians rather than economists. The result was an eclectic set of attitudes, most of them responses to specific problems and circumstances. Too inconsistent and particular to be any important contribution to modern theory (unlike contemporary American innovation in political thought and later contributions to economics), debate in the Lower South was nevertheless intriguing.[24] The rest of this chapter sketches the general parameters of their debates with each other; detailed discussion of arguments over the moral tradition, government intervention, and qualitative changes like manufacturing will appear later in the specific contexts that stimulated them. The larger question—Was the region progressing?—is the present focus of this chapter.

24. The economic analysis of Virginian John Taylor of Caroline, formed during the early Republic, was still cast mostly in political terms, specifically in response to debates over the government's role in economic development. Taylor's economic writings, nevertheless, were more rigorous and systematic than those of his contemporaries in the Lower South. Serious study of economics did not take place until the antebellum period; in the South, political economy would first flourish with the work of Jacob N. Cardozo and Thomas Cooper in the 1820s, then develop with the analyses of Thomas R. Dew in the 1830s. See Paul K. Conkin, *Prophets of Prosperity: America's First Political Economists* (Bloomington, Ind., 1980), chap. 3 (John Taylor), chap. 6 (Cardozo and Cooper); Allen Kaufman, *Capitalism, Slavery, and Republican Values: Antebellum Political Economists, 1819–1848* (Austin, Tex., 1982), chaps. 5, 6 (Dew).

The answer always turned on trade. Few questioned mercantilism's insistence that commerce was key to wealth. Indeed, planters, like colonists elsewhere, took this teaching so seriously that they tended to refer to their provinces' commercial standing as if they belonged to independent nations rather than to dependencies of a European nation. James Habersham reported in 1772 how Georgia was "making a rapid progress in her Commerce, Wealth and Population," as if the place should be judged as an economic actor in its own right. In the same year, Habersham used similar language to tell James Wright of the encouraging "Prospect of our soon becoming a rich, commercial People." Economic expectations based on overseas trade continued well after the Revolution, when the submerged nationalism of mercantilist belief made more sense. The *Southern Patriot, and Commercial Advertiser* of Charleston lamented in 1815 how America had yet to realize the capabilities of more advanced societies because it lacked "the great accumulation of riches that takes place in a commercial era." Arguments for free trade, which grew in strength late in the colonial period, emerged again during the Napoleonic Wars, when Americans felt themselves controlled by the whims of European rulers. In 1808, the *Carolina Weekly Messenger* complained how war had "rent asunder" trade, the "link that associated the great society of man" and "converted the labour and industry of man to the greatest advantages."[25]

Local whites also absorbed mercantilism's uneasiness over the fruits of trade, temptations that might encourage lassitude and vicious consumerism among citizens. Here, criticisms of what was labeled "luxury" probably joined with republicanism's premodern suspicion of material splendor. South Carolina Governor James Glen believed that luxury retarded "our Increase both in People and Wealth." Public sacrifice was the order of the day. The patriotic side of this uneasiness was evident in the Revolutionary era. The *South-Carolina Gazette; And Country Journal* set out a doleful portrait of commercial societies in 1773, warning that the degenerative effects of luxury would weaken Ameri-

---

25. *The Letters of Hon. James Habersham, 1756–1775* (GHS, *Collections*, VI [Savannah, 1904]), 162, 167; *Southern Patriot and Commercial Advertiser* (Savannah), Nov. 16, 1815; *Carolina Weekly Messenger* (Charleston), Apr. 26, 1808. On mercantilism in the Lower South, see C. Robert Haywood, "Mercantilism and South Carolina Agriculture, 1700–1763," *SCHM*, LX (1959), 15–27; Haywood, "The Influence of Mercantilism on Social Attitudes in the South, 1700–1763," *Jour. Hist. Ideas*, XX (1959), 577–586; Crowley, *This Sheba, Self*, 86–91. On free-trade theory, see Matson and Onuf, *Union of Interests*, 21–26, 68–70.

can virtue, for which "we ought to labour with emulation." This exhortation was meant, probably, to bolster patriots' resolve against British imports.[26]

Labor could be used to more advantage, in any case, if citizens sought to invigorate their economy. In the Lower South, as in England, projecting rhetoric urged improvements. South Carolinian Edward Rutledge, paraphrasing in a letter to cotton gin entrepreneur Phineas Miller, considered that "if, as Deen Swift said, a Man who could make two blades of Grass grow, where but one grew before, had more merit than all the Ministers of State from the Days of Adam," then any "man who can enrich a poor Country, by giving it a new Staple [crop], or who can give a four fold value to an old one, is at least on a footing with all the Ministers of State since the Deluge." In 1809, David Ramsay contemplated how rice culture in "Carolina has been in a state of constant progressive improvement" since the colony's beginnings in the seventeenth century. Ramsay also emphasized how individuals could, by improving their state, promote the common good. "Every carolinian who plants a field—builds a house—fills a pond—or drains a bog," he stated, "deserves well of his country." Somewhat later, an enthusiastic Agricultural Society of South Carolina lauded a "public spirit" responsible for improvements that would "benefit" not just the new nation but the "whole human race."[27]

In assessing their prospects for improvement, whites in the Lower South often used the historical framework of the Scottish school. Scholars have noted the Scottish influence in the colonies, though this has fostered debate whether the Scottish tradition really influenced early Americans as much as, say, concepts of Christian or civic virtue.[28] By focusing on the Scottish school, this

26. [James Glen], *A Description of South Carolina* (London, 1791), 43–44, facs. rpt., in Chapman J. Milling, ed., *Colonial South Carolina: Two Contemporary Descriptions* (Columbia, S.C., 1951), 51–52; *South-Carolina Gazette; And Country Journal* (Charleston), Nov. 2, 1773.

27. Edward Rutledge to Phineas Miller, Sept. 26, 1794, Edward Rutledge Papers, SCL; David Ramsay, *History of South-Carolina, from Its First Settlement in 1670 to the Year 1808* . . . (Charleston, S.C., 1809), II, 75, 206; Agricultural Society of South Carolina, *Papers Published by Order of the Agricultural Society of South Carolina* (Columbia, S.C., 1818), 3, 7.

28. Garry Wills, *Inventing America: Jefferson's Declaration of Independence* (New York, 1978), pt. 3; Douglas Sloan, *The Scottish Enlightenment and the American College Ideal* (New York, 1971); Andrew Hook, *Scotland and America: A Study in Cultural Relations, 1750–1835* (Glasgow, 1975); William R. Brock, *Scotus Americanus: A Survey of the Links between Scotland and America in the Eighteenth Century* (Edinburgh, 1982);

present analysis of the Lower South lays no claims to its primacy in the region; in volumes of books read, hours of political debate articulated, other theories were probably more evident, and much interest in other printed materials (from religious tracts to novels) was also manifest. But Scottish theory is useful as a qualitative measure, as the best index of whites' acceptance of the most advanced theory about modern society and its economic underpinnings. It shows, above all, how slaveholders were willing to engage with elements of the new political economy that would trouble their antebellum children.

Free residents of the Lower South, even slaveholding planters, did prove surprisingly receptive to modern theory and read through the corpus of socioeconomic thought. Newspapers were the most important medium through which they learned of available books, and newspaper advertisements give a sense of their taste in secular nonfiction. For example, the *South-Carolina and American General Gazette* announced in 1771 the publication of an edition of William Robertson's *History of Charles V* and advertised Hume's *History of England* for sale. A decade later, the same newspaper advertised an edition of Smith's *Wealth of Nations* and a collection of Robertson's histories. Charleston's *Royal Gazette* in 1781 contained a news column from England that discussed the undertakings of Robertson, Gibbon, and Smith. In 1812, Milledgeville's *Georgia Journal* mentioned the reprinting of Robertson's historical works for interested readers.[29]

Private papers also testify to whites' interest in the Scottish school. In 1781, for example, Georgian James Jackson looked at books in a London Cheapside shop; he bought Robertson's *History of America* and Gibbon's *Decline and Fall.* The *Augusta Chronicle* of February 22, 1794, advertised items from Angus Dallas's estate, including a copy of Smith's *Wealth of Nations* and Robertson's *History of America.* Donald McIver's 1810 estate inventory in Richmond County, Georgia, included Smith's *Wealth of Nations,* Robertson's *Charles V,*

Ronald Hamowy, "Progress and Commerce in Anglo-American Thought: The Social Philosophy of Adam Ferguson," *Interpretation: A Journal of Political Philosophy,* XIV (1986), 61–87.

29. *South-Carolina and American General Gazette* (Charleston), July 22, 1771, Jan. 27, 1781; *Royal Gazette* (Charleston), May 12, 1781; *Georgia Journal* (Milledgeville), June 3, 1812. On the role colonial newspapers played in the Lower South's book trade with Britain, see David Moltke-Hansen, "The Empire of Scotsman Robert Wells, Loyalist South Carolina Printer-Publisher" (master's thesis, University of South Carolina–Columbia, 1984).

and a collection of Hume's essays. In 1789, South Carolinian John Ball ordered works by Ferguson and Robertson from his bookseller. Six years later, fellow Carolinian Rawlins Lowndes (1721–1800) ordered Robertson's *History of America* along with some other works. In 1813, Langdon Cheves I ordered books from a New York dealer, including Smith's *Wealth of Nations*, Robertson's *Works*, and Ferguson's and Gibbon's histories of Rome. Two years later, Cheves bought Malthus's work on human population. The Reverend Alexander Findlay's South Carolina estate appraisal included, among other books, a copy of Hume's *History of England*. A partial (yet impressive) list of South Carolinian Ralph Izard's library, probably drawn up in the early 1800s, contains Robertson's *History of Charles V,* Smith's *Wealth of Nations,* and Gibbon's *Decline and Fall.* Another voluminous book list, from about the same time and belonging to a member of South Carolina's Bevard family, includes Hume's *History of England* and his *Essays;* Robertson's *America, Scotland,* and *Charles V;* Ferguson's *Civil Society;* and Gibbon's *Decline and Fall.*[30]

Scottish theory was also available to citizens who borrowed rather than bought their books. The 1812 shelf list for the Savannah Library Society contained Ferguson's *Civil Society;* John Millar's *Origin of the Distinction of Ranks;* Robertson's *America, Scotland,* and *Charles V;* Hume's *History of England;* Smith's *Wealth of Nations;* and Gibbon's *Decline and Fall.* It was Gibbon, above all, whom Americans read as avidly as they might have a novelist, in an age when history was a form of literature that entertained as well as instructed. Siblings Mary Hering Middleton and Oliver Hering discussed Gibbon, nearly chapter by chapter, in a barrage of letters from summer of 1791 through early winter of 1792. While Henry Laurens languished in the Tower of London (the British had nabbed him en route to Holland in 1780, accusing him of high treason), he diverted himself by reading Gibbon and writing a pointed essay comparing contemporary Britain with imperial Rome in its declining condition.[31]

30. Bill from William Nicholl, bookseller, June 7, 1781, James Jackson Papers, section A, Duke; inventory of Donald McIver, July 31, 1810, microfilm for Richmond County, drawer 48, reel 51, p. 467, GDAH; receipts, Ball Family Papers, series 11-515-42, SCHS; receipts dated Oct. 6, 1813, Oct. 12, 1815, Rawlins Lowndes Papers, microfilm, SHC; Langdon Cheves I Papers, series 12-56-15, SCHS; Findlay estate appraisal, Jan. 24, 1784, pp. 30–35, Hezekiah Maham Papers, SCL; typed list of Ralph Izard's books donated to the College of Charleston, Ralph Izard Papers, SCL; manuscript volume with booklist (beginning ca. 1794), Bevard Papers, SHC.

31. "Rules for the Government of the Savannah Library Society," 1812, shelf list appended, Telfair Family Papers, folder 183, item 519, GHS. See the letters from Oliver

Like Laurens, local historians of the Lower South drew inspiration from the Scottish school. The Reverend Alexander Hewatt and physician David Ramsay, for instance, wrote histories using elements of conjectural history. Hewatt, a Scotsman who studied at the University of Edinburgh, emigrated to South Carolina in 1763 and took up duties as pastor of Charleston's First Presbyterian Church. In the 1770s he wrote a history of his adopted province, the very title of which—*An Historical Account of the Rise and Progress of the Colonies of South Carolina and Georgia*—revealed the nature of his analysis. Ramsay, a Pennsylvanian who settled in Charleston, was the preeminent North American historian of his day, praised as the Tacitus of the Western Hemisphere by patriotic contemporaries. His professional descendants regard him, with somewhat more accuracy, as the creator of United States history. Ramsay wrote an astonishing range of works on medical, political, and historical topics; his whiggish histories include the first *History of the American Revolution* (1789) and *The History of South-Carolina* (1809). In the latter work, Ramsay intended a social-scientific study modeled on the efforts of Sir John Sinclair, who did the first statistical survey (of Scotland) in modern history and introduced the word *statistics* to a large reading public. Ramsay acknowledged his debt in an 1809 letter; he had "followed S[i]r John SinClair's Statistical Account of Scotland in a great measure" and had "grafted statistics on history" in accordance with the new, scientific method of analyzing the past and measuring a progress toward modernity.[32]

Hering to Mary Hering Middleton, Aug. 29, Nov. 18, 1791, folder 5, Feb. 11, 1792, folder 6, Hering-Middleton Papers, series 24-63, SCHS. (In later years, the brother and sister moved on to Buffon and Wollstonecraft.) On Laurens, see "A Narrative of the Capture of Henry Laurens, of His Confinement in the Tower of London, etc., 1780, 1781, 1782," SCHS, *Collections,* I (1857), 43. Laurens was accused of spying on behalf of the Continental Congress; the formal charge of treason underscored Britain's refusal to recognize American independence.

32. Elmer D. Johnson, "Alexander Hewat: South Carolina's First Historian," *Jour. So. Hist.,* XX (1954), 50–62. Sinclair had drawn up his *Statistical Account of Scotland* while a lay member of the General Assembly of the Church of Scotland, using parish ministers to gather information in the 1790s. Published in 21 volumes between 1791 and 1799, Sinclair's *Account* was a pioneering effort in the history of the social sciences. See Chitnis, *Scottish Enlightenment,* 15–16.

On Ramsay: Ramsay to Dr. Lettsom, Oct. 29, 1809, David Ramsay Papers, SCL. Ramsay had sent out a "circular letter" to chosen informants in the various South Carolina districts for data on the agriculture, demography, salubrity, and natural

In making such analyses, free residents of the Lower South often began with the premise of innate human sociability. Christopher Gadsden remarked, "So kind and careful is the Author of our beings, in linking us one with another." Timothy Ford, in line with the antirationalism of the Scots, denied the Lockean notion that human society was an artificial construction, the product of a deliberated covenant among men who had lived in a state of nature. Ford maintained, instead, that "a state of nature never in fact existed" and argued: "Man was no sooner born, than he was associated under some common tie, which bound the human race together. . . . Nature implanted the ties." Ford also asserted, as had the Scots, that "inequality of condition is one of nature's laws"; unequal ability interacted with sociability to determine rank within society.[33]

Whites also assumed that humans, naturally able to define ever more complex social connections, created societies that progressed through stages. They insisted on this graduated development, dwelling especially on its first, hunter-gatherer stage because, probably, they had before them an arresting example of people in this stage: native Americans. Accounts of Indian primitivism were nothing new—they had typified the whole history of colonization. Whites in the Lower South brought the process up to date by using the four-stage theory to explain the material base of "savagery" (a word not yet entirely an epithet, but still a social-scientific term that described as well as abused).[34] George Milligen-Johnston, in his *Short Description of South Carolina* (1770), stated that Indians "enjoyed great Liberty, which must be the Case of all People who depend on Hunting, and not on the Cultivation of the Earth For Subsis-

---

history of each county or district. He published a copy of his letter in the preface to his *History of South-Carolina*, and much of the material he received is in that work's appendix. Some of his informants' letters are in the Charleston Library Society and are on microfiche 51-132 of the South Carolina Historical Society. On Ramsay himself, see Arthur H. Shaffer, "David Ramsay and the Limits of Revolutionary Nationalism," in O'Brien and Moltke-Hansen, eds., *Antebellum Charleston*, 47–84; Joseph Ioor Waring, *A History of Medicine in South Carolina, 1670–1825* ([Columbia, S.C.], 1964), 279–299.

33. Gadsden cited in Robert M. Weir, ed., *The Letters of Freeman, etc.: Essays on the Nonimportation Movement in South Carolina, Collected by William Henry Drayton* (Columbia, S.C., 1977), 82; Timothy Ford [Americanus, pseud.], *The Constitutionalist . . .* (Charleston, S.C., 1794), 4, 33.

34. See Roy Harvey Pearce, *Savagism and Civilization: A Study of the Indian and the American Mind* (Baltimore, 1967), chaps. 3, 4.

tence." Milligen-Johnston then explained the modern significance of money, which could, among litigants, calculate a justice unknown to the moneyless Indians, who instead used vengeance as justice. Alexander Hewatt contended that Indians were "instructive" because they "serve to throw light on several earlier periods of history" beyond which white Americans had progressed; they provided a contrast between savage and civil stages of society within the Lower South itself. Emphasizing the material basis of societal progression, Hewatt described how Indians, as seminomadic hunters, were "unacquainted with the advantages of pasturage and agriculture" and thus required "a greater extent of hunting lands . . . for their subsistence."[35]

David Ramsay echoed Hewatt by asserting that it was "well known that population every where keeps pace with the means of subsistence." Thus, South Carolina's dispersed Indians could not thrive, as a hunting and fishing people, once they lost their extensive lands to a more concentrated and sedentary white population; their numbers had declined precipitously since the beginning of English settlement. Ramsay further explained that Indians, as hunters, were "savages, unrestrained by social order" and lacked those elaborate cultural structures (especially laws defining property) that allowed greater social cohesion. What Milligen-Johnston called "liberty," Ramsay dismissed as lack of order. Ramsay hoped that contact with whites might change Indians, "that by treating indians with gentleness and humanity, they would by degrees lose their savage spirit and become civilized."[36]

Concurring that Indians revealed how societies progressed through stages, Governor James Wright of Georgia stated, "The Cherokees I think are half a Century before the Creeks, they are much more civilized and I believe better disposed yet still they are Savages." In his *Oration on the Cession of Louisiana to the United States* (1804), Ramsay claimed that a new economic base would bring about this change: whites could "transform savage warriors to peaceful farmers" in the southern Indian nations newly appropriated by the Republic.

---

35. [George Milligen (-Johnston)], *A Short Description of the Province of South-Carolina* . . . (London, 1770), 74–75, facs. rpt. in Milling, ed., *Colonial S.C.*, 185; [Alexander Hewatt], *An Historical Account of the Rise and Progress of the Colonies of South Carolina and Georgia* (London, 1779), I, 57, 65, 70.

36. Ramsay, *History of S.-C.*, I, 192–193, 194. Ramsay lifted this last phrase about civilizing Indians from Hewatt's *Historical Account*, II, 271. See Johnson, "Alexander Hewat," *Jour. So. Hist.*, XX (1954), 50–62, on how Ramsay's critics accused him of plagiarizing Hewatt.

Thomas Fitch believed that, influenced by United States agents, members of the Creek nation had "advance[d] from the Hunting [stage] to the Shepherds and to the agricultural and manufacturing life, and are becoming Commercial." "I have no doubt," Fitch concluded, "but in ten years or so the savage race will be incorporated into our social system"—a remarkably swift progress through all four of the Scottish stages.[37]

As their statements indicate, whites had little patience with the idea that savagery was noble. They seemed, rather, to regard Indians as markers by which they could congratulate themselves on their cultural advance, however much they might lag behind Europe. The cause of whites' antipathy was obvious. The Lower South had, among the original regions of the United States, the most powerful Indian presence; it was difficult for whites to bestow patronizing and romanticized sentiments on native groups still able to repel their advance. Even when presented with Revolutionary opportunities to characterize themselves as a simple, virtuous, American people (in contrast to Britain's luxury and vice), planters donned native garb with distaste—certainly compared to the eager but ersatz Mohawks of the Boston Tea Party, the fur-hatted Benjamin Franklin, the heroized Virginia Hunting-Shirts. A statement that (with typical caution) identified creoles with aborigines occurred during debate over nonimportation in Charleston in John Mackenzie's "Second Letter to the People." Mackenzie exhorted the reluctant citizenry to realize the exigency of the situation: "It will be more to your honour, to go, for a time, if necessary, even like the Indian, clouted, blanketted, and with bare feet." The hesitant parenthesis, "for a time, if necessary," points up how Indian masquerade was a very last resort.[38]

Reluctance to court any kind of primitive poverty evidenced whites' continued sense of flux and fear of potential failure. Alexander Hewatt admitted that South Carolina lagged behind Europe in its commerce and manufactures. He proposed, as well, that Carolinians judged personal distinction by attributes like beauty, wealth, strength, and agility, because in "the progress of society they have not advanced beyond that period in which men are distinguished more by their external than internal accomplishments." But Hewatt

---

37. "Letters from Sir James Wright," GHS, *Colls.*, III (Savannah, 1873), 170; David Ramsay, *An Oration on the Cession of Louisiana to the United States* (Charleston, S.C., 1804), 13; Thomas Fitch to Daniel Mulford, July 12, 1810, Daniel Mulford Papers, I, GHS. By manufacturing, Fitch meant crafts, not industrialization.

38. Weir, ed., *Letters of Freeman*, 25.

was confident of residents' capacity to pull themselves above this simple state. He asserted, for instance, that planters had shown a good deal of economic acumen, enough that some invested in Georgia land at midcentury when a "spirit of emulation broke out among them for securing tracts of the richest ground" in the new colony. Ramsay also had tentative praise for his fellows' achievements. He believed that "colonists of modern times have many advantages over those of antiquity, for they carry with them the civilization, arts, and refinements" of commercial society. South Carolina colonists also had made admirable progress from "rude woodsmen to polished citizens."[39]

But whites continued to fear societal degeneration. They worried that their society, faltering between rudeness and civility, might slip back into the savagery they observed in nearby Indian societies. An advertisement for Charleston's Library Society raised the alarm: "As the gross Ignorance of the naked *Indian* must raise our Pity . . . it is our Duty as Men, our Interest as Members of a Community, to take every Step, pursue every Method in our Power, to prevent our Descendants from sinking into a similar Situation." Convinced of the danger of incipient barbarism, the society assigned itself the crucial role of "handing down the European Arts and Manners of the latest Times" to the colonial population. The Agricultural Society of South Carolina likewise believed that "the civilized state" was superior to "the savage" but warned that, unless citizens were vigilant, "we should soon loose our claim to civilization, and sink into a state of savage barbarism, nothing better than that of the wild Indian." This was a painful prospect. When a new royal governor, Lord Charles Montagu, arrived in South Carolina in 1766, he offered plans to "polish the native Roughness of the Indians," but William Drayton felt Montagu secretly believed it was the creole whites who needed a good polishing. Stung by the insult, Drayton hoped "that as he polishes us, we shall smoothe him."[40]

Polish required a commercial economy, possibly even one that minimized use of slave labor. Proper attention to this goal would prevent social retrogression. South Carolinian Edmund Caiger lamented how poor colonists who did not grow salable crops and lived by raiding other settlers' herds of livestock were "Like Tartars" (whom European theorists used as a pristine example of

39. [Hewatt], *Historical Account*, I, 134, 293, 304; Ramsay, *History of S.-C.*, I, vii, II, 352 (first quotation).

40. [Milligen (-Johnston)], *Short Description*, 39, in Milling, ed., *Colonial S.C.*, 149; Agr. Soc. S.C., *Papers*, 8, 13; William Drayton to James Grant, July 16, 1766, MacPherson-Grant Papers, bundle 482, Ballindalloch.

nomadic barbarism). South Carolina's Lieutenant Governor William Bull also denounced frontier settlers "who choose to live by the wandering indolence of hunting." David Ramsay, while emphasizing that religion helped "in softening the manners of dispersed colonists, who from the want of school-masters and clergymen were in danger of degenerating into savages," also worried that frontiersmen were too prone to "a melancholy retrogradation in useful habits and pursuits." Whites well knew that, however much they improved their habits, slavery still made their economy and society appear backward. Alexander Hewatt criticized his adopted region by contrasting slavery and free labor. Hewatt's analysis pointed to free-labor advocates' key emphasis on voluntarism, a factor essential not only for economic liberty but for all the political rights that slaves lacked. Even the "servitude which still remains in Britain among the labourers in the coal mines, etc. is very different from that to which the natives of Africa are subjected in the western world." The British "labourers voluntarily enter on such servitude." "They acquire wages as their reward," Hewatt continued, "and both their persons and properties are under the protection of the laws of the realm." By not granting these liberties to blacks, Lower South whites admitted to the backwardness of their homeland, which relied on tyranny and force where civil societies used law and free competition.[41]

But if whites squirmed when reminded of their anachronisms—their barbaric frontiersmen and exploited slaves—they also dreaded what might lie ahead if they brought their society into conformity with Britain's; they felt threatened by (and therefore included in) the process of commercialization. Hewatt, despite his praise of free labor, worried how commercial and manufacturing nations were luxurious and "oppressed" their lower classes. Ramsay likewise lamented that entry into a modern economy would swap advantages for drawbacks: one clear sign of his state's economic backwardness was the high wages paid to free workers, who were, accordingly, free from much exploitation. But in "improved countries where commerce and manufacture have long been established, and luxury prevails," the lower classes are "oppressed and miserable." As Ramsay's double-edged assessment of "improved"

---

41. Edmund Caiger to Samuel Moore, Sept. 15, 1766, RSA, reel 2; Bull quoted in Rachel N. Klein, "Ordering the Backcountry: The South Carolina Regulation," *WMQ*, 3d Ser., XXXVIII (1981), 668; Ramsay, *History of S.-C.*, II, 6, 252; [Hewatt], *Historical Account*, II, 92, 94. On fear of frontier barbarism, see Matson and Onuf, *Union of Interests*, 63–66.

nations indicated, he only hesitantly recommended advance into a more developed economy. The example of the Old World usually offered little reassurance. Deciding that a developed economy did not support any cultural refinements, William James Ball declared of London in 1805, "It certainly is the largest commercial City, but how any one except the Man of Business can prefer living here to any where else astonishes me exceedingly." In Georgia, the *Monitor* delivered a more vehement denunciation of Birmingham in 1810. Focusing on the poor conditions in working-class districts, the newspaper declared that the "devil has certainly fixed upon this spot for his own nursery garden and *HOT HOUSE*."[42]

Cautious at every turn, whites hankered after advantages characteristic of industrializing economies but had enough distance from them to see their disadvantages, hence their growing reluctance to move further away from the plantation model. If an external critic of slavery objected that slavery, the region's real obstacle to socioeconomic progress, remained in place—as more critics were doing—whites would have to agree on a defense, without the internecine bickering that had emerged with the Georgia Malcontents. Unease over slavery, combined with lingering fears over underdevelopment, made whites concentrate on creating a more coherent explanation of themselves than their earlier, more omnivorous debates and experiments had yielded.

✌ Slavery, Sentiment, and Stasis

Modern economic theory encouraged conservatism along with reform. As well as innovating within their economy, therefore, whites in the Lower South hammered out a defense of it, one foreshadowing later antebellum discourse. They formulated two interpretations of themselves still recognizably dependent on modern theory but also adapted to local problems. The first interpretation defended slavery as a social system that obeyed the human passions essential to societal cohesion. Here, planters adopted the emphasis on human sentiments apparent in modern thought, but used the concept of a uniform and malleable humanity to advance their own ends. This alteration of sentiment emerged just before the American Revolution, increasing as external

42. [Hewatt], *Historical Account,* II, 134; Ramsay, *History of S.-C.,* I, 116; William James Ball to Isaac Ball, Oct. 2, 1805, Ball Family Papers, box 2, folder 23, SCL; *Monitor* (Washington, Ga.), Sept. 1, 1810.

criticism of slavery gave planters reason to reassess the institution. Their second analysis modified conjectural history by denying that human societies moved through the four stages in an inevitable manner. Whites seemed to find comfort in the possibility of societal stasis: they remained at a stage behind what seemed an impersonal, luxurious, and immoral commercial society, yet were in no danger of moving back to the equally repellent rudeness of Indian society. They selected a golden mean along the continuum of Scottish history's four stages, one, they claimed, that still had a tender concern for the human passions of its members. This second shift occurred later, mostly after the Revolution, when a perceived need to take up new land from Indians (especially in Georgia) fostered an attitude much more critical of primitive societies.

Defense of slavery was the more important development. Scholars have tended to trace this transition to the period during and after the Revolution.[43] But the shift began earlier, resulting more from local conditions than from the grander Revolutionary milieu that would only amplify what had already been stated. Planters began midway through the eighteenth century to reconsider the ways they thought about and treated slaves. During the second half of the eighteenth century and first two decades of the nineteenth they made the discovery (chillingly—it truly surprised them) that blacks were fellow humans deserving of humane treatment. As well as a reaction to new and external criticism, planters' attitudinal shift resulted from slaves' successful creation of a creole culture during the mid-eighteenth century. Creole slaves, unlike Africans, were able to impress upon Eurocentric whites their essentially human nature. Creolization of the black population was possible because the plantation economy had stabilized. Planters were earlier more interested in producing wealth than in the well-being of their slaves. During the 1720s boom in rice, white Carolinians rapidly imported African slaves, thereby embedding a powerful, discontented population in the region. White apprehensions over security peaked with the Stono Rebellion of 1739. As plantation workers, therefore, blacks were treated harshly, and as potential or actual rebels they were subject to strict regulation. Because of worsening conditions, rates of natural increase for blacks declined in the first half of the century. At this time, whites tended to think of blacks, especially Africans, as subhuman and sav-

43. David Brion Davis, *The Problem of Slavery in the Age of Revolution, 1770–1823* (Ithaca, N.Y., 1975); Willie Lee Rose, "The Domestication of Domestic Slavery," in Rose, *Slavery and Freedom*, ed. William W. Freehling (New York, 1982), 18–36; Eugene D. Genovese, *Roll, Jordan, Roll: The World the Slaves Made* (New York, 1974), 49–70.

age; labor management, accordingly, relied on overt coercion and physical punishment.[44]

After midcentury, when staple-crop planting was firmly established and prices for rice stabilized, planters discovered that a reproducing slave force served their interests better. By the early 1750s, slaves lived longer than had an earlier generation, and they raised children. In these assimilated and creole slaves, whites recognized people like themselves, persons who spoke English, went to Christian churches, dressed and behaved much like Euro-Americans, and lived amid a growing network of family ties through which they displayed sentiments like those among white family members. James Habersham, living among his domestic slaves in Savannah, expressed astonishment that he developed sympathy for them after years of taking little notice of them. He reported to Willet Taylor in 1764, "Oronoko's wife dyed last Night, and the poor fellow is inconsolable, and as she was a favourite of my dear deceased wife and nursed two of my Daughters, I must own the Sight of her has affected me more than all the other negroes I have ever lost." Habersham's candid and troubling statement reveals a rapid switch in emotional stances: from a long-standing disregard for the deaths of many humans he had held in bondage to a sudden, personal concern for one individual. Many planters began to see that blacks' sentiment for their kin revealed their essential humanity, something wrenchingly apparent in the anguished Oronoko. Henry Laurens denounced forced separation of slave families through sale because it ignored blacks' fellow

44. On the period before the 1720s, when South Carolina passed through a frontier stage of development (in which there was a rough equality between most blacks and whites and a surprisingly high level of racial cooperation), see Wood, *Black Majority*, 95–130; on worsening conditions after the spread of rice cultivation, 218–238, 277–284; on increasing racial tensions and the Stono Rebellion, 308–326.

On creolization, see Daniel C. Littlefield, "Plantations, Paternalism, and Profitability: Factors Affecting African Demography in the Old British Empire," *Jour. So. Hist.*, XLVII (1981), 172–173, 176; Ira Berlin, "Time, Space, and the Evolution of Afro-American Society on British Mainland North America," *AHR*, LXXXV (1980), 61. Cf. Michael Craton, "Hobbesian or Panglossian? The Two Extremes of Slave Conditions in the British Caribbean, 1783–1834," *WMQ*, 3d Ser., XXXV (1978), 324–356. On whites' view of blacks as savages, see Winthrop D. Jordan, *White over Black: American Attitudes toward the Negro, 1550–1812* (Chapel Hill, N.C., 1969), 28–32, 230–234. On physical punishment, see Daniel E. Meaders, "South Carolina Fugitives as Viewed through Local Colonial Newspapers with Emphasis on Runaway Notices, 1732–1801," *Journal of Negro History*, LX (1975), 296–297.

feeling and sympathy. This cruelty was inappropriate abuse of those "who tho Slaves are still human Creatures." Blacks' familial bonds—their expression of human sociability—continued to affect James Habersham. In 1772, a slave boy who lived in Habersham's household died of rabies, and the child's final agony impressed his "Humanity." "I never can forget," he wrote, the "Cries and Intreaties of the Mother begging her Child to be put to Death."[45]

This is all very touching, but the sympathy Laurens and Habersham felt posed no radical challenge to human slavery: their sentiments relied on a conceptualization of humanity that assumed social relations were based on inequality. Planters were, after all, taking up the conservative, Scottish stress on innate sociability. Human propensity for social interconnection blindly led people into more complex stages of culture with more specialized (and un-equal) roles for its members. This antirationalist interpretation made no attack on social inequality, but defended it in the name of social cohesion, warning against willful attempts to alter the social order—a message agreeable to slaveholders in an era when slavery was suspect.[46]

The principle of humanity could thus increase the amount and quality of discipline over slaves. Rather than resorting to haphazard methods of physical abuse, slaveholders manipulated slaves' sympathies for each other in order to make them more tractable. Georgia resident William Simpson, after selling a slave who "disobliged me," coolly noted how "the fellow writes to his wife frequently, and appears by his letters to be in great distress for want of her." Simpson believed the slave was "now sufficiently punished" and considered buying him back and reuniting him with his spouse. Humanity toward slaves implied a *system* of control over them, not lessened control, an emphasis stated

45. Habersham to Willet Taylor, Apr. 2, 1764, to William Knox, Feb. 11, 1772, *Letters of Habersham* (GHS, *Colls.*, VI [1904]), 23, 163–164; Philip M. Hamer *et al.*, eds., *The Papers of Henry Laurens* (Columbia, S.C., 1968–), IV, 596. On the creolization of blacks in South Carolina (there is little work on this phenomenon in Georgia), see Philip D. Morgan, "Black Society in the Lowcountry, 1760–1810," in Ira Berlin and Ronald Hoffman, eds., *Slavery and Freedom in the Age of the American Revolution* (Charlottes-ville, Va., 1983), 85–91; Berlin, "Time, Space, and the Evolution of Afro-American Society on British Mainland North America," *AHR*, LXXXV (1980), 54–67; Michael P. Johnson, "Runaway Slaves and the Slave Communities in South Carolina, 1799 to 1830," *WMQ*, 3d Ser., XXXVIII (1981), 418–441; John C. Inscoe, "Carolina Slave Names: An Index to Acculturation," *Jour. So. Hist.*, XLIX (1983), 544.

46. See Chaplin, "Slavery and the Principle of Humanity," *Jour. Soc. Hist.*, XXIV (1990–1991), 301–302.

in a petition from white residents of Orangeburg District, South Carolina. They complained of the permissiveness of men who let their slaves grow and sell cotton, thus facilitating other slaves' ability (the signatories claimed) to vend stolen cotton passed off as their own product. This policy was the result of "a false or a mistaken humanity" on the part of some whites.[47]

The creative adaptations slaves made to their enslavement played, unfortunately, into whites' idea that their society was improving. Having native-born slaves was better, slaveholders conceded, than taking new workers from Africa—which even planters began to see as an unjust use of power. As blacks struggled to maintain family relations, to craft a syncretic Christianity, and to gain better conditions for living and working, whites merely concluded that these efforts improved and creolized a society under their own control. It seemed as if slaves actively, if not voluntarily, adapted to the region. They and whites, slaveholders assumed, created more complex and more interconnecting social ties—as if they all belonged to the same creole family. John Moultrie summarized this position when he wrote how he was glad his overseer was "humane to my Negroes," who as they had "been so long in my family I have a respectful attachment for them as my fellow Creatures."[48]

If whites assumed that there were social connections between slaves and themselves, and that these were valuable societal accretions, they next insisted that the ties should not be cut or even loosened. For that reason Henry Laurens rejected his son's proposal to free slaves who fought against the British in the War of Independence. Here, Revolutionary criticism of slavery was stifled by the more self-interested meliorism that was several decades older. In his father, John Laurens probably had his most sympathetic critic. (Henry stated, "I will undertake to say there is not [another] Man in America of your opinion.") But the older man believed the situation more complicated than his son realized. John was suggesting a revolutionary change for all *society*, not merely for the individual men who might enlist with white Americans. Slaves who considered joining the Continental army would have to make a decision not only for themselves but for "their Wives and Children"; and John was willing to recruit

---

47. William Simpson to James Grant, June 15, 1767, MacPherson-Grant Papers, bundle 243, Ballindalloch; Petitions to the General Assembly, 1816, no. 56, SCDAH. See also Isaac Shelby to Thomas Hart, Apr. 15, 1809, Isaac Shelby Papers, GHS.

48. Chaplin, "Slavery and the Principle of Humanity," *Jour. Soc. Hist.*, XXIV (1990–1991), 305–307; John Moultrie to Isaac Ball, Aug. 17, 1815, Ball Family Papers, box 3, folder 31, SCL.

the men without freeing their families. Henry showed how this contradicted his son's assumption that he offered personal liberty to slaves: If each person deserved liberty, how could the actions of some black men and of John himself affect the fortunes of others? "What right have you to exchange and Barter 'Women and Children' . . . ?" Convinced that a dramatic change in slavery would snap all the sinews of society, with disastrous consequences for all, Laurens answered that his son's scheme, and the slaves themselves, would be objects of abuse from "rooted habits and prejudices, than which there is not in the history of Man recited a more arduos [sic] engagement."[49]

More disturbing was the father's claim that slaves were content with their lot. The dubious basis of this assertion was the sentiment and custom with which whites surrounded slavery. "Have you considered," he asked John, "that your kind intentions towards your Negroes would be deemed by them the highest cruelty?" Slaves would "interpret your humanity to be an Exchange of Slavery[,] a State and circumstances not only tolerable but comfortable from habit, for an intolerable" state where they risked loss of their families, garden plots ("little Plantations"), life, and limb. But a planter who postulated, as Henry Laurens did, that slaves were "strongly attached to me," was often surprised. Though slaves were indeed embedded in their own web of social relations, this was not enough to prevent them from risking its loss in pursuit of freedom. They fulfilled John Laurens's passionate faith that, as human creatures, their "Self-Love" would "induce ardent wishes for a change" in their condition.[50] When a planter like Henry Laurens fulminated about laws of human affection that supposedly overcame love of self, he overlooked the network of positive law that maintained slaves' subordination. Slaves who chose to run away to British forces during the Revolution were entirely willing to lose kin and home once forces that had oppressed them were suspended in the chaos of battle. But whites kept insisting that the invisible, gradually constructed net of social relations that held people together also held them down—should hold them down, lest revolution lead to regression and rude chaos. This opinion would counter ideas about individual liberty that gained strength in the decades between the Revolution and the emergence of radical abolitionism.

49. Quotations are from Hamer *et al.*, eds., *Papers of Laurens*, XII, 368 (second), 412 (first and third); and Henry to John Laurens, Sept. 21, 1779 (fourth), LP.

50. Quotations are from Hamer *et al.*, eds., *Papers of Laurens*, XI, 223 (second), XII, 368 (first), 391 (third).

Rather than propose any real solution to the problem of slavery, whites in the Lower South instead wanted to improve the institution, to polish its rough edges and make it resemble systems of labor in other parts of the world. Some of this talk about humanizing slavery was pitched at an external audience that might not realize how some improvements were easy to make. (Lowcountry planters who already had plenty of workers, for instance, professed horror over the Atlantic slave trade, irritating would-be slaveholders in the upcountry.) When David Ramsay published his history of South Carolina in 1809, he knew northerners would read it and garnished his text with portraits of kindly slaveholders. Ramsay claimed that Gabriel Manigault, for example, was "well known to his friends and neighbors" to have treated his slaves "with great humanity." Other planters had in mind a developmental scheme to make slaves resemble other, less offensively exploited workers. Henry Laurens described improvements he made on his plantation as "the pleasure of my life more particularly as they contribute to bring my poor Blacks to a level with the happiest Peasants to be found in Europe." John Lloyd of South Carolina also compared his slaves with European peasants (as well as West Indian slaves) and concluded that they enjoyed better material conditions, had more incentive to produce goods on their own time, and lived in more stable families. Here then is an early formulation of the antebellum "mudsill" theory that every society, ancient or modern, has its oppressed groups—slave regions were no exception. An editorial in the *Georgia Gazette* asserted, "In all societies subordination and servitude are in some degree necessary." At the federal Constitutional Convention, delegate Charles Pinckney even more boldly stated that "the blacks are the labourers, the peasants of the Southern States," a warning to would-be abolitionists to keep their hands off the South lest they destroy a society that erred only as much as any other.[51]

This was not yet the aggressively antimodern stance of the antebellum era, but one that still took up modern assumptions of psychology and comparative economics. The era's musing over slavery was flexible enough, for instance, to support local critics of slavery who wondered aloud or in print about ways to reform the institution. Georgia planter William Baldwin conceded that racial slavery was "subversive of every idea of moral as well as political justice," but

51. Ramsay, *History of S.-C.*, II, 502; Henry Laurens to Edward Bridgen, Feb. 13, 1786, LP; John Lloyd to E. H. Champion, June 14, 1796, John Lloyd Letterbook, SCL; *Georgia Gazette*, Sept. 24, 1789; Max Farrand, ed., *The Records of the Federal Convention of 1787*, rev. ed. (New Haven, Conn., 1937), II, 371.

disagreed with Lord Kames's idea of freedom as a positive condition admitting of no gradation and believed that slaves were still better off than the poor in Europe.[52] Baldwin's vacillation indicated the plasticity allowed in this era, a flexible tendency to see how the Lower South's mode of subsistence, though flawed, was merely one way of exploiting labor to produce commercial wealth. Local whites conceded their sins while pointing out those of others.

They made a more straightforward assault on the idea of progress by questioning whether advance from one socioeconomic stage to the next was a universal or even beneficial phenomenon. A belief that "savagery" could be a fixed rather than fleeting condition grounded this change of thought, an assumption that characterized many southerners by the early nineteenth century.[53] Georgian Benjamin Lincoln provided, in the 1790s, a series of essays on Indians that represented this modification. Lincoln took up some elements of philosophic history—assuming, for instance, that societies did fall into categories, depending on their mode of subsistence. But he denied that these societal types were succeeding stages of development. Biblical history, Lincoln argued, bore this out with examples of how the four stages had appeared at the same time: Abel and Cain were, variously but contemporaneously, shepherd and farmer; Esau was a roving hunter even as his brother Jacob herded sheep and dwelled in tents. Lincoln then combined Scripture with John Locke to praise farmers above all other productive agents. He cited the "duty of man to cultivate the earth" as a "part of the original plan of the creator" and "the express declaration of holy writ," and he recited Locke's argument that labor alone gave humans a right to property. Land belonged to those who cultivated it, and their efforts created most of the wealth worth talking about. In contrast, Indian hunters only skimmed over the earth in their desultory wandering. Scottish historians recognized this condition but posited that it could change. Lincoln was skeptical. He asserted that Indian contact with whites had had disastrous effects; Indian "misfortunes" arose because they became "connected with the Europeans in a commercial line, while they retained . . . savage ideas,

52. William Baldwin to Thomas Forman, May 6, 1813, Forman-Bryan-Screven Papers, folder 2, GHS.

53. See Pearce, *Savagism and Civilization,* 135–168. Cf. Gary B. Nash, "The Image of the Indian in the Southern Colonial Mind," *WMQ,* 3d Ser., XXIX (1972), 197–230, on how some late-18th-century observers (usually distant from Indians) began to romanticize native Americans.

customs and modes of life." Though Lincoln felt whites should continue to give Indians the civil benefits of agriculture, Christianity, and education, he believed Indians could never truly be civilized, but must "retire and dwindle before the combined effects of civilization and the arts of agriculture."[54]

Georgia settler Daniel Mulford gloated in verse over the prospect that white farmers would displace native hunters. Mulford wrote a paean to Milledgeville (published in the *Milledgeville Argus* in 1808), a rabid denunciation of native American life. His poem took up the classical form of georgic, didactic agricultural poetry, but digressed into a contrast between civil and savage methods of using the landscape:

> Long had the savage stroll'd, o'er plain and hill,
>   And left them rude, wild, unproductive still,—
> 'Tis Industry [and] Enterprise afford
>   This truly rich, but not unjust, reward.
>
> .   .   .   .
>
> So soon the murd'rous scalping-knife and bow
>   Have yielded to the axe, the plough and hoe.

Jonas Fauche completed this triumphal line of thought later in the nineteenth century by denying earlier fears that whites might reenter the savage condition of their Anglo-Saxon forebears, thereafter resembling American Indians. Fauche, who had lived along Georgia's frontier in the 1780s and 1790s, stated, "We, the whites, have advanced, and were we even willing it would be impossible for us to retrograde and return to the hunting state of society."[55]

For similar reasons, Charlestonian William Johnson rejected the graduated progression from gathering to cultivating in his *Nugae Georgicae* (1815). Johnson, like Benjamin Lincoln, claimed that God had revealed agriculture to humanity at one providential moment. Human society did not undergo secular progress; people relied on a "divine source" for their improvement. Johnson left the commercial stage of society out of his essay, concentrating

54. Benjamin Lincoln Papers, UGA, 143–197: quotation on Indian "misfortunes" from 183; remaining quotations from 146–148; biblical history on 149–150; Lockean argument on 160–162.

55. Entry for Dec. 1808, Daniel Mulford Papers, I, GHS; Lilla Mills Hawes, ed., "The Frontiers of Georgia in the Late Eighteenth Century: Jonas Fauche to Joseph Vallance Bevan," *GHQ*, XLVII (1963), 89.

instead on the agricultural nature of South Carolina and on the preeminent role of "the Carolina Farmer"—not a merchant or even a commercially oriented planter—as the most important member of the society. He chided the "sullen" planter who thought only of "the acquisition of wealth" and left his estate and slaves to the direction of hirelings, neglecting his human capacity to experience "those sympathies which connect man to man": another assertion that slavery was an organic social system, not a perversion of natural freedom.[56]

The Agricultural Society of South Carolina, in 1818, also followed this reasoning. Members of the society argued that raising food was the basis for "truly great, happy, and independent" nations. They described how humans moved from hunting to "a pastoral and wandering life" and then to "a different system" in which they "derive their support from the soil which they occupy." This third condition was the final one, the key to "the civilized state" and beyond which it was not necessary to progress. Some cultures would also adopt nonagricultural pursuits that supported the efforts of rural cultivators; commerce and manufactures both serviced agriculture. Farmers could exploit the inventions of these other economies without direct involvement in them. The Agricultural Society believed "innovations" were necessary to keep productivity at a high level in South Carolina, "now that the virgin soil is nearly exhausted"—the paper mentioned, for instance, the benefits of railways and the steam engine. But the authors praised the fruits of modern production only because they improved agriculture, not because they might accelerate progress toward a more commercial or industrial form of production. They formed a defense of a rural life that paralleled rather than intersected an emerging industrial economy, though this was not yet an outright attack on such an economy.[57]

In certain ways, planters' vision of bucolic bliss was similar to physiocracy. In this French theory, farmers and agricultural production (not merchants and trade) were the basis of national wealth and individual virtue. Several American beliefs that grew out of physiocratic assumptions, such as denial of Indian claims to land that they did not cultivate and the right of settlers to take

56. William Johnson, *Nugae Georgicae: An Essay, Delivered to the Literary and Philosophical Society of Charleston, South Carolina, October 14, 1815* (Charleston, S.C., 1815), 3, 5, 6–8.

57. Agr. Soc. S.C., *Papers*, 5, 6, 8, 9, 12–13.

up unused land, appeared in other parts of the nation. But if physiocratic thought was known in the Lower South, whites there more openly acknowledged Christian Scripture as an authority for tilling the earth.[58] Repeated assertions of divine revelation—which had taught humans to farm and which had established, once and for all, a civil form of society—supported faith in agriculture. A similar emphasis on God's primary position in history had been present in the English improving literature, though not among the Scots. It is likely that rhetorics of religious and secular improvement were becoming interdependent in the Lower South, particularly in inland areas more affected by early nineteenth-century revivals. In this melding of religion and social theory, development of an idealized societal stasis paralleled efforts to improve slavery. A "humane" form of slavery fulfilled evangelical demands for reform of the institution that had begun during the revivals of the 1740s and continued past the Revolution. A regional tendency to temper modern, secular theory with Christian belief thus took shape.[59]

Modern definitions of human psychology and historical sociology made their way erratically and unevenly through the Lower South. Emphasis on slaves' humanity and on the sentiments linking slaves to each other (and purportedly to their masters) took strongest hold in the lowcountry; the focus on agrarianism and Indians' essentially retrograde nature was stronger in the western hinterland. This variation reflected differing stages of development in the region. Lowcountry planters had large numbers of creole slaves, people they began to recognize as individual actors and with whom they negotiated whenever they wanted to alter prevailing patterns of agricultural production. In the upcountry, on the other hand, whites were sometimes more in contact with Indians than with black slaves. Finding themselves in competition for land with the former group, whites developed a passionate dislike of peripa-

58. Chester E. Eisinger, "The Influence of Natural Rights and Physiocratic Doctrines on American Agrarian Thought during the Revolutionary Period," *AH*, XXI (1947), 13–23. George Logan's *Letters Addressed to the Yeomanry of the United States* (Philadelphia, 1791) closely resembled Benjamin Lincoln's tract on land use (see Eisinger's discussion of Logan, 15–17).

59. See Spadafora, *Idea of Progress*, 248–251, 378–380; Leland J. Bellot, "Evangelicals and the Defense of Slavery in Britain's Old Colonial Empire," *Jour. So. Hist.*, XXXVII (1971), 19–40; Alan Gallay, "The Origins of Slaveholders' Paternalism: George Whitefield, the Bryan Family, and the Great Awakening in the South," *Jour. So. Hist.*, LIII (1987), 369–394.

tetic savagery and insisted that settled agriculture represented an optimal condition and paramount measure of civilization.

Further variations in economic thought emerged during national debate in the early Republic. The Walpolean controversy over financial innovation and its relation to the power of the state reappeared in controversy over Alexander Hamilton's proposals for a national economy (and later echoed in the political rhetoric of Andrew Jackson and John C. Calhoun). Tension between politicians who favored more government control over revenue and increased spending on internal improvements, and politicians who viewed these possibilities as corruption of republican principles of government continued also in state arenas, including the Lower South. Until the early 1800s, Federalism was strong in the Lower South, the preference of coastal planters who controlled state politics. But in western areas, which tended toward Jeffersonian republicanism, whites were wary of modern instruments of finance that stimulated a commercial economy. They preferred a simpler economic basis, often through open defiance of coastal planters who had a Federalist faith in the benefits of commercial development and were projectors in the model cast by Defoe.[60]

Ambivalence over the price of social change continued among all Americans, not just those in plantation regions. This worrying peaked at the turn of the century, as shock over the consequences (intended or unintended) of the American, French, and Haitian revolutions reverberated throughout the English-speaking world. Lower South whites at this time—the time when slavery was newly attacked—were more than ever trapped between the ideal of societal progress and the fear that their society depended on a form of labor that impeded its own progress or its acceptance in the world. But their unease over their economic development still reflected tension within the most advanced theory of economic development of their time. Though their statements increasingly resembled antebellum attacks on industrial society, whites' worry over their place in the world was not yet an antimodern mode of

60. See John M. Murrin, "The Great Inversion, or Court versus Country: A Comparison of the Revolution Settlements in England (1688–1721) and America (1776–1816)," in J.G.A. Pocock, ed., *Three British Revolutions: 1641, 1688, 1776* (Princeton, N.J., 1980), 368–453; McCoy, *Elusive Republic*, esp. 136–165; Mark D. Kaplanoff, "Charles Pinckney and the American Republican Tradition," in O'Brien and Moltke-Hansen, eds., *Antebellum Charleston*, 85–122; Lacy K. Ford, "Republican Ideology in a Slave Society: The Political Economy of John C. Calhoun," *Jour. So. Hist.*, LIV (1988), 405–424.

thought, but a modern skepticism over the nature and disputed promise of economic development.

Whites' ability to insert themselves into a modern schema of development does not mean they truly were progressive—this is not the real significance of their actions. Instead, their all-too-easy appropriation of modern ideas shows the selectivity of modern theories of progress. The moderns' nostalgia for social cohesion, especially, hindered radical critique of certain forms of exploitation.[61] Of all modern social theories, political economy had the most troubled inheritance from the ancient, organic ideal. Affective bonds, optimally the product of free choices, constructed a natural harmony—a premise meant to rebut fears of Hobbesian atomization in a postmedieval world, but one that made modern folk dread the loss of any sentimental ties, even those fashioned through exploitation. In the face of such ambivalence, whites in the Lower South were unusual neither in rejecting nor in swallowing whole the promises of their age. They, like most in the Scottish school, stood poised between Defoe's bland optimism over economic change and Swift's persistent doubt.

Whites were only too aware of their tenuous position as keen observers of a modern world but peripheral inhabitants of it. At their relatively backward stage, they could either leap forward or languish. As an observer at London's Royal Society of Arts put it, the unusual elements of their "New World, which is some ages behind hand" could stimulate them to perform "Experiments" not possible in Europe. This kind of statement, a compliment that also managed to be an insult, would gall whites in the Lower South, who felt both the advantages and disadvantages of their distance from the modern world they so much admired and who smarted from the patronizing opinions of those who dwelt nearer the heart of that world. External criticism would combine with whites' own sense of their provinciality to provide incentive for innovations meant to bring the region closer to a more modern form.

61. On the limits of moral theory in the modern era, especially the effects of skepticism on ideas of human morality, see MacIntyre, *After Virtue*, 49–59.

Chapter 3

Being Exotic

Residents of the Lower South realized that, by the early eighteenth century, their society had entered an uncertain stage of development. Their region had acquired attributes of a Western and even cosmopolitan society like that in the mother country, yet still it had a recognizably provincial culture, one not entirely made over in the image of the Old World. External opinion reinforced natives' unease. To Europeans, even to creoles in northern areas of America, the Lower South seemed exotic and beyond the pale—lurid and larger than life. Nature was at the bottom of it all: much of the perception of exoticism had to do with the region's physical environment, its warm climate and lush terrain. The Lower South's uncultivated products (both flora and fauna) were alien to Western eyes, and the products of colonial cultivation (like plantation monoculture and slavery) were nearly as unfamiliar. Though planters knew that their region's environment gave them the edge over temperate Europe in producing rarities like rice, indigo, and, later, cotton, they feared that this strength was lost on an audience of outsiders, which persisted in seeing southern areas of North America in the stigmatizing terms of exoticism. As northerner Eli Whitney put it when he moved to Georgia in 1792, he had entered "a new natural world" and had left "the moral world" entirely.[1]

As whites in the Lower South sought to make sense of their place in the world, they were constantly reminded of what outsiders concluded about them. Residents worried, especially, that their exotic environment, though conferring upon them particular advantages, also posed problems. The warm climate and fertile soil, albeit sources of agricultural wealth, bred malaria and yellow fever and encouraged dissipation among whites and exploitation of

1. Whitney to Josiah Stebbins, Nov. 1, 1792, Eli Whitney Papers, Yale University.

slaves; the same conditions that brought riches brought hazards. These assumptions have survived the centuries. Historians too have largely concurred that southern regions of North America sequestered white inhabitants who were ruined by an ill-favored climate and too much wealth: they were lazy, perversely attached to every archaism inherent in slave-based labor, uninterested in improving themselves and their society, and more concerned with leisure-class pastimes than with productive activities.[2]

Lower South whites, seeking to counteract such negative imagery in their own time, often took to scientific pursuits. Science was a good choice because it demarcated what was natural from what was artificial. If residents of the Lower South could analyze the alien environment around them, they would gain control over it; they would prove themselves products of human cultivation—masters of nature, not slaves to the dangerous forces huddled in their natural environs. By the seventeenth century, science was a specialized pursuit requiring intelligence and some training, but still accessible to educated classes anywhere, in Europe or the colonies. Of all forms of intellectual endeavor, science was the most modern, and it most distinguished Western culture from Asia, Africa, and pre-Columbian America. If colonists and creoles wanted a way to demonstrate their similarity to cosmopolitan societies in Europe—for them, the center of political and cultural authority—science seemed the most promising avenue. But while science represented a method of societal redefinition, it was nonetheless a tricky alternative. The international scientific com-

2. For examples of this interpretation, see W. J. Cash, *The Mind of the South* (New York, 1941), which emphasizes the leisure, hedonism, and romanticism of southern culture, 3–55; William R. Taylor, in *Cavalier and Yankee: The Old South and American National Character* (New York, 1957), which historicizes the process by which southerners acquired a stereotypical character and emphasizes the importance of external, northern opinion in the creation of this stereotype—see especially 95–141; David Bertelson, *The Lazy South* (New York, 1967); Eugene D. Genovese, *The Political Economy of Slavery: Studies in the Economy and Society of the Slave South* (New York, 1967), esp. 3–19, 130–141; C. Vann Woodward, "The Southern Ethic in a Puritan World," *WMQ*, 3d Ser., XXV (1968), 343–349, 357–360. Bertram Wyatt Brown has reemphasized the extent to which slavery, racism, and whites' concern over social status created an archaic form of society in the South in his *Southern Honor: Ethics and Behavior in the Old South* (New York, 1982). See also A. Cash Koeniger, "Climate and Southern Distinctiveness," *Jour. So. Hist.*, LIV (1988), 21–44; and Edmund S. Morgan, *American Slavery, American Freedom: The Ordeal of Colonial Virginia* (New York, 1976), 44–70, on cultures of idleness in 17th-century Virginia.

munity (stretching from Linnaeus's Uppsala to Britain's Calcutta) resisted Americans' attempts to enter its charmed circle, and scientific accounts of the Lower South continued to label the region as backward and brutally provincial: exotic in the worst sense of the word. The modern physical sciences and social sciences would, therefore, continue to remind residents of their awkward stage of development between savagery and civility.

❦ Species of Eternity

Whites in the Lower South had the best chance of making a name for their region among scientists by promoting it as a source of information about the natural world. Intellectual interest in sublunary nature (plants, animals, and geological formations) increased during the 1700s, expanding modern science beyond the mechanics that had earlier created the field. At the time, most naturalists were biologists. They classified the natural world (notably in the Linnaean system) then later asked questions about how the classes might change, queries that paved the way to the Darwinian revolution. But because of the concern to classify all natural phenomena, each corner of the globe came under scrutiny. Naturalists raced to discover and name new species, often using latinized versions of their own names or of their patrons'. Naming a plant or animal for a person could confer a species of eternity—fame as everlasting as anyone cared to reckon. Equally, a region with a well-publicized variety of unusual species could gain fame, a factor that made colonial outposts compete for primacy in claiming similar specimens.

Much of the scramble to claim and name took place within patron-client relations between Europe and America. European natural historians either sent protégés to the New World to collect specimens or acquired willing American assistants who packed off samples of their homeland. Organizations such as the Royal Society in London, the Royal Botanic Gardens at Kew, the Royal Academy in Paris, and the Botanic Garden of Madrid—as well as luminaries connected with these and similar institutions—wanted information from and clients in North America to speed the flow of information across the Atlantic. This exchange rapidly increased. Before 1600, only a half-dozen American botanical species were known in Europe; by the 1730s, about three hundred species were known; by the American Revolution, this number had probably doubled, as collectors crammed more specimens into their gardens, museums, and treatises. The rarer a plant, the more prized; and areas like the Lower South, with flora adaptable yet unfamiliar to European gardens, were raked over for samples. (When John Rutledge visited Luigi Castiglioni in Italy, he said of the aristocrat's garden of American plants that most were "from Carolina.")[3]

Under the guidance of patrons, a continual stream of naturalists traipsed through the Lower South, gathering specimens and jotting down notes. Supported by Carolina's proprietors, John Lawson wrote his *New Voyage to Carolina* in 1709, not only describing the land and its natural products but also providing vivid descriptions of its aboriginal inhabitants and the uses they made of the environment. A later generation exhibited similar interest in the new colony of Georgia. London's Worshipful Society of Apothecaries, for instance, paid for "sending persons to Georgia to collect Plants" in the early 1730s. Mark Catesby wrote his two-volume *Natural History of Carolina, Florida, and the Bahama Islands* (1730–1748) with the assistance of Sir Hans Sloane of the Royal Society. Quaker naturalists John Bartram and son William traveled in and wrote about Carolina, Georgia, and Florida in the era of the American Revolution; in 1791 the younger Bartram published an account widely read in Europe not only by scientists but also by those who shaped an early romantic sensibility about nature's wilds. Describing a swamp near Lake George, Florida, William's tone was wondering: "Neither nature nor art could any where present a more striking contrast." The chiaroscuro he perceived depended on "the glittering water pond [which] played on the sight, through the dark grove, like a brilliant diamond, on the bosom of the illumined savanna, bordered with various flowery shrubs and plants; and as we advanced into the plain, the sight was agreeably relieved by a distant view of the forests."

3. On botanical specimens, see Joseph Kastner, *A Species of Eternity* (New York, 1978), 49; 1788 Journal, John Rutledge, Jr., Papers, Duke.

For a general overview of these transatlantic connections, see Brooke Hindle, *The Pursuit of Science in Revolutionary America, 1735–1789* (Chapel Hill, N.C., 1956), chap. 2. On the Lower South, see David Leroy Coon, "The Development of Market Agriculture in South Carolina, 1670–1785" (Ph.D. diss., University of Illinois, Urbana/Champaign, 1972); Coon, "Eliza Lucas Pinckney and the Reintroduction of Indigo Culture in South Carolina," *Jour. So. Hist.*, XLII (1976), 61–76; Sarah P. Stetson, "The Traffic in Seeds and Plants from England's Colonies in North America," *AH*, XXIII (1949), 45–56. See William Tatham's "Botanical Observations," UGA, for a description of North American flora he wrote for the Botanic Garden of Madrid.

The effect was sublime. Thus did an era influenced by a rationalist desire to describe natural phenomena close with a more sentimental view of nature.[4]

In addition to playing host to naturalists, some residents of the Lower South were themselves scientists. South Carolinian Dr. Alexander Garden, a transplanted Scotsman, had the strongest connections with Europe's scientific elite. He corresponded with the great Linnaeus (Carl von Linne) himself as well as John Ellis of London's Royal Society and other leading figures in Edinburgh, London, and the colonies. More than anyone else in the Lower South, Garden gained a species of eternity: Linnaeus named the gardenia for him as reward for his careful description of local plants and patient packing of specimens. (In one 1756 shipment to the Royal Society, Garden prepared no fewer than ninety small trees.) Garden won recognition, as well, for his own contributions to the world of science; he described some new species and cleared up misunderstanding about American specimens—correcting Ellis and even Linnaeus in their confusions. Others with lesser talents also formed connections with the scientific circle. Charleston physicians were particularly active in natural history; Dr. John Lining made elaborate meteorological observations correlated with measurements of his own excretions. Some contributions traveled strange routes. When Swedish natural historian Daniel Charles Solander saw a drawing John Laurens had made of a soft-shelled turtle, he passed it among admiring members of the Royal Society. Solander then asked John's father, Henry, whether his son would act as sketch artist for Captain James Cook's first expedition to the South Seas, from 1768 to 1771. (Laurens declined.)[5]

4. On John Lawson, see his *New Voyage to Carolina*, ed. Hugh Talmage Lefler (Chapel Hill, N.C., 1967). On Georgia as a source of pharmaceuticals, see Rough Court Minute Book, 1727–33, Society of Apothecaries, IX, Guildhall Library MS.8201/9, London. On Sloane's patronage of Catesby, see the introduction to *Catesby's Birds of Colonial America*, ed. Alan Feduccia (Chapel Hill, N.C., 1985); Richard Beale Davis, *Intellectual Life in the Colonial South, 1585–1763* (Knoxville, Tenn., 1978), II, 845–849; and Hindle, *Pursuit of Science*, 16, and also chaps. 10, 16. On the Bartrams, see Gordon DeWolf, introduction to William Bartram's *Travels through North and South Carolina, Georgia, East and West Florida . . .* (London, 1792; facs. ed., Charlottesville, Va., 1980), 97–99 (quotation); and John C. Greene, *American Science in the Age of Jefferson* (Ames, Iowa, 1984), chap. 5.

5. Hindle, *Pursuit of Science*, 51–54; Kastner, *Species of Eternity*, 68–78; Raymond Phineas Stearns, *Science in the British Colonies of America* (Urbana, Ill., 1970), 593–619. Edmund Berkeley and Dorothy Smith Berkeley, *Dr. Alexander Garden of Charles Town* (Chapel Hill, N.C., 1969), shipment recounted on 72, Garden's scientific activities

Despite their accomplishments, natural historians in the Lower South were never confident that they were valued by outsiders other than as sources of raw data. They might be trusted to pack up boxes of specimens but not to interpret them. The European prejudice against American science was not against the Lower South alone, but part of a disdain for the Americas that culminated in the comte de Buffon's claim that New World flora and fauna were stunted and degenerate compared to European specimens. Garden himself felt snubbed by Europeans. He complained of the Royal Society's tendency to "stumble" over any opinions or information "promulgated by one in America tho supported by the Clearest reasoning and Demonstration." (This was a complaint from a man described in Europe as "the phoenix and unique Carolinian"!)[6] The region's cultural life seemed to parallel its economy: just as the Lower South gained wealth by providing exotic commodities to European consumers, so it gained its intellectual reputation by sending exotic specimens to European luminaries. It remained provincial in every sense. Even worse, residents of the Lower South feared that they were themselves exotics—objects to be ogled and categorized like so many magnolias and parakeets. They were material for the new social-scientific impulse to examine the civil as well as natural world. Exoticism was, for this reason, a double disadvantage.

❦ Travelers' Accounts—Science and Fiction

The image of the American South as an underdeveloped place—one filled with persons enervated by a warm climate, ruined by extremes of wealth and poverty, corrupted or exploited by slavery—took shape in the early mod-

---

discussed esp. on 175–198, 325–333. On medicine, see G. Edmund Gifford, Jr., "The Charleston Physician-Naturalists," *Bulletin of the History of Medicine*, XLIX (1975), 556–574. Lining published his results in the Royal Society's *Philosophical Transactions* (London, 1744), LXII. On Laurens, see Philip M. Hamer *et al.*, eds., *The Papers of Henry Laurens* (Columbia, S.C., 1968–), VIII, 86–87, 87n.

6. First quotation from a letter of 1758 cited in Berkeley and Berkeley, *Garden of Charles Town*, 252, second from a 1766 account of Garden's discovery of a new amphibian, 194. On prejudice against American science and against America as suitable object of serious scientific inquiry, see Hindle, *Pursuit of Science*, 255, 307–308, 322; Antonello Gerbi, *The Dispute of the New World: The History of a Polemic, 1750–1900*, trans. Jeremy Moyle (Pittsburgh, Pa., 1973), 3–79 (on American responses, see 240–267).

ern era, largely the product of travelers who wrote accounts of the region. Travelers' narratives, from John Smith to Frederick Law Olmsted to V. S. Naipaul, create a static image of the region as a place without societal dynamism. Though they hold some truths, such accounts are not unbiased descriptions, but meant to be bold and entertaining statements about the human condition.[7] Between the 1500s and 1800s, travel literature evolved as nonfiction prose that nonetheless resembled contemporary forms of fiction (especially the early novel) in its concern to create engaging descriptions of human society even as it incorporated elements of the early social sciences known to Lower South whites through their reading of history and economic theory. A traveler's account was a mixture of entertainment and analysis, fiction and science. Descriptions of the region, for example, reveal how observers exaggerated the unfamiliarity of the Lower South to make more compelling narratives.

The impetus to make travel narratives into scientific writings composed in descriptive language was a reaction against earlier accounts that were quite the opposite. In the Middle Ages, Europeans had regarded travel as an unworthy activity; unless part of a pilgrimage or crusade, a voyager's peregrination was tainted with the sin of *curiositas,* an amalgam of pride, vanity, and aimless secularity. Only during the fourteenth century did Christians begin to see voyaging as a positive pursuit. Between the fourteenth and seventeenth centuries, nonetheless, travel beyond one's native land was rare, a pastime of nobles, an unenviable necessity for merchants, soldiers, and emigrants. Accounts of voyages tended, therefore, to stress the fantastic (miraculous occurrences, monstrous creatures, diabolical peoples, the mythical kingdom of Prester John), except in practical guides for pilgrims. Both the fantastic and prosaic appeared, for example, in the *Travels of Marco Polo* (1271–1295). Ac-

7. On historians' use of travel narratives in defining the southern colonies, see Carl Bridenbaugh, *Myths and Realities: Societies of the Colonial South* (New York, 1963), quotations from travelers Charles Woodmason (76), Timothy Ford (73), Johann David Schoepf (76), and Josiah Quincy (76); Peter H. Wood, *Black Majority: Negroes in Colonial South Carolina from 1670 through the Stono Rebellion* (New York, 1975), 64–88; Rhys Isaac, *The Transformation of Virginia, 1740–1790* (Chapel Hill, N.C., 1982), see chap. 4 for extensive citations from New Jerseyman Philip Vickers Fithian and from other external observers, used to establish the domestic character of Virginians. Grady McWhiney, *Cracker Culture: Celtic Ways in the Old South* (Tuscaloosa, Ala., 1988), defends the use of travelers' accounts in examining the South, see his introduction; ditto for David Hackett Fischer, *Albion's Seed: Four British Folkways in America* (New York, 1989).

curacy in describing different places and cultures was not yet a preeminent goal of writers. A fictive and fantastic account like *The Travels of Sir John Mandeville* (circa 1356) was taken as a worthy description of actual travels; Christopher Columbus, Thomas More, and Walter Ralegh read *The Travels* as if it were geographically sound, and Mandeville was often held to be true when Polo was not.[8]

In the seventeenth and eighteenth centuries, traveling became more common, and travel narratives lost much of their fantastic quality. By the end of the seventeenth century, services (like coaches and hotels) that made touring easier multiplied. As European nations expanded over the globe, westerners found it congenial to visit locations once hostile to them. A system of packet boats between Britain and its North American colonies in 1755, for example, speeded British travelers to the New World. The middle and upper classes took trips to spas, toured exotic locales, and visited friends and kin in far-flung places as part of a widening range of leisure activities. Travel, or "the Tour," became a standard part of the education of men in the middle and upper classes.[9] Travel accounts therefore proliferated. Individuals kept diaries of their

8. Christian K. Zacher, *Curiosity and Pilgrimage: The Literature of Discovery in Fourteenth-Century England* (Baltimore, 1976), esp. 154 (on Mandeville); Mary B. Campbell, *The Witness and the Other World: Exotic European Travel Writing, 400–1600* (Ithaca, N.Y., 1988), chap. 2 (on fantastic), chaps. 4–6; Donald R. Howard, *Writers and Pilgrims: Medieval Pilgrimage Narrations and Their Posterity* (Berkeley, Calif., 1980), 29–32, 54–59 (Mandeville); Percy G. Adams, *Travel Literature and the Evolution of the Novel* (Lexington, Ky., 1983), 73 (on belief in Mandeville's account).

On medieval travel literature, see Howard, *Writers and Pilgrims*, 19–28, 93–95. On later writing, see P. J. Marshall and Glyndwr Williams, *The Great Map of Mankind: Perceptions of New Worlds in the Age of Enlightenment* (Cambridge, Mass., 1982); Adams, *Travel Literature*, 39–40. On the fantastic or grotesque elements of travel writing, see Campbell, *Witness and the Other World*, 47–86.

9. On the grand tour, genteel travel, and the increasing popularity of spas and resorts in England, see G. E. Mingay, *English Landed Society in the Eighteenth Century* (London, 1963), 139–141, 153–156; and Mingay, *The Gentry: The Rise and Fall of a Ruling Class* (New York, 1976), 144–146, 162, 176; Neil McKendrick, John Brewer, and J. H. Plumb, *The Birth of a Consumer Society: The Commercialization of Eighteenth-Century England* (Reading, 1973), 283–284. Charles L. Batten, Jr., has discussed the economic and technological advances that led to more traveling in the 18th century in his *Pleasurable Instruction: Form and Convention in Eighteenth-Century Travel Literature* (Berkeley, Calif., 1978), 2. On imperial packet boat service, see Jack P. Greene, "An Uneasy Con-

journeys in which they commented on the manners and customs of foreign people; other travelers, or authors drawing on travelers' accounts, published gazetteers that described the world known to westerners. All travel narratives reflected, and probably increased, interest in the variety of human societies. These accounts—"an enlargement of the Grand Tour by proxy"—became part of a recognizable if difficult-to-classify literary genre. Narrators sought to avoid the fantastic elements that had appeared in earlier accounts but still tended to color their discourse, believing that a skillful fiction was a delicate art rather than an outright deceit.[10]

Travel accounts multiplied just when the novel was increasing in popularity; and, as the two genres grew up together, authors had a cheerful disregard of the distinction between fiction and nonfiction that emerged later. Someone like Daniel Defoe, for example, concocted travels for a fictional Moll Flanders, turned the real voyager Alexander Selkirk into the literary character Robinson Crusoe, passed off a fake *New Voyage round the World* as true, and inscribed an account of his own tour through Britain. Some accounts that claimed to be truthful were fabricated—their authors scanned gazetteers and penned stories without leaving their armchairs or embellished narratives of tours they had taken with descriptions of sights they never saw. More than a few narratives were hoaxes, as with George Psalmanazar's notorious *Historical and Geographical Description of Formosa,* foisted on the unwary British public in 1704. By the eighteenth century, many readers were so hardened that they suspected even truthful accounts of deception; when James Bruce published an account of Abyssinia's actual (though unusual) dietary customs in 1790, everyone assumed he was lying.[11]

To make travel narratives more credible, some writers began to emphasize

---

nection: An Analysis of the Preconditions of the American Revolution," in Stephen G. Kurtz and James H. Hutson, eds., *Essays on the American Revolution* (Chapel Hill, N.C., 1973), 41. On the rise of travel for pleasure, see also Peter Clark, "Migration in England during the Late Seventeenth and Early Eighteenth Centuries," *Past and Present,* no. 83 (May 1979), 81; and Jeremy Black, *The British and the Grand Tour* (London, 1985), 38–67, 134–141.

10. Percy G. Adams, *Travelers and Travel Liars, 1660–1800* (Berkeley, Calif., 1962), 88; Marshall and Williams, *Great Map of Mankind,* 7–9, 45–63 (quotation, 60); Batten, *Pleasurable Instruction,* 1, 5–7, 25–28.

11. Adams, *Travelers and Travel Liars,* 105–107 (on Defoe), 93–97 (Psalmanazar), and 45–63 (Bruce); Adams, *Travel Literature,* 81–102; Batten, *Pleasurable Instruction,* 47–69.

that certain factual material needed to be included in accounts of voyages, making each tourist an amateur historian, geographer, and ethnographer. Indeed, scholars have pointed to travel narratives as the earliest form of anthropology, derived from Herodotus and then systematized in the modern era. Travel literature thus borrowed from and lent to the novel and the emerging social sciences—it kept features meant to entertain readers (being dull was never a virtue) but adopted a verisimilitude that could give it authority. Travel had long been a metaphor for acquisition of wisdom about the self and the world; a scientific apparatus would now help it explicitly to fulfill this goal. Instead of describing the fantastic, the unbelievable, travelers were now supposed to explain the exotic, the believable though unfamiliar aspects of an enlarging mental world.[12]

Three elements—use of categories, a concern to define national character, and a belief that climate was a major influence on culture—dominated this new approach. Travelers were supposed to order their observations within a grid of social-scientific categories that chopped the foreign into manageable pieces; here, social observers paralleled naturalists' efforts systematically to categorize all objects in the world. Bernhard Varen, in his *Geographia generalis* (1650), listed ten classes of phenomena, both material and social, that travelers were to use when composing their thoughts. Scientist Robert Boyle gave similar instructions in the *Philosophical Transactions* of the Royal Society in 1666. Varen and Boyle also asked travelers to pay attention to the distinguishing characteristics of foreign people, especially their morals, manners, and customs. By the eighteenth century, this was an accepted goal of the social sciences; John Coakley Lettsom's *Naturalist's and Traveller's Companion* (1772) included "Learning, Antiquities, religious Rites, polite Arts, etc." and "Commerce, Manufacture, Arts, Trade, etc." as two important categories.[13]

The concept of national character grew out of an older debate, begun by the ancient Greeks, over the qualities citizens acquired under different forms of

12. On journey as metaphor, see Howard, *Writers and Pilgrims*, 6–7, 106; Ronald Paulson, "Life as Journey and as Theater: Two Eighteenth-Century Narrative Structures," *New Literary History*, VIII (1976–1977), 43–58. On the influence of the social sciences, see Batten, *Pleasurable Instruction*, 84–101; Adams, *Travel Literature*, 78. Cf. J. M. Coetzee, *White Writing: On the Culture of Letters in South Africa* (New Haven, Conn., 1988), 14–15, 34.

13. On Varen and Boyle, see Marshall and Williams, *Great Map of Mankind*, 45; on Tucker and Lettsom, see Batten, *Pleasurable Instruction*, 146 n. 17.

government. Montesquieu's *L'esprit des lois* (1748) was the most influential articulation of the modern concept of national character. Montesquieu asserted that any given people exhibited a distinctive spirit—or taste, temper, genius, or character—and had laws, manners, and customs adapted to this national spirit. He elucidated the different spirits or characters that existed in various societies, the "vivacity" of the ancient Athenians contrasted with the "gravity" of the Spartans. Others followed Montesquieu's lead in defining temperaments for different peoples. Edmund Burke, in his *Speech on Conciliation with the Colonies* (1775), analyzed Britain's efforts to regain control over its recalcitrant colonists. Burke concluded that Americans' peculiar spirit of liberty was so important to their very existence as a people that Britain should neither change their character nor persecute them for it.[14]

Writers who theorized about national character explored a network of variables (similar to travelers' grid of societal categories) that shaped a people's shared characteristics. Climate was often the independent variable of choice: the more extreme the climate, the stronger its effects on human culture. Montesquieu was here again an important figure. Hypothesizing that "the character of the mind, and the passions of the heart are extremely different in different climates," he analyzed how specific environments created certain cultural patterns. In extremely hot zones, Montesquieu asserted, "indolence constitutes the utmost happiness," and the atmosphere was more conducive to slavery than a cold one would be. All the same, Montesquieu conceded that cultural factors—"the religion, the laws, the maxims of government . . . precedents, morals and customs"—also contributed to a people's temperament, along with climate. Adam Ferguson and David Hume concurred that hot areas tended more to lassitude, hence poverty and incivility, than did cold ones. Hume nonetheless allowed that moral, political, and economic factors

---

14. J.G.A. Pocock, *The Machiavellian Moment: Florentine Political Thought and the Atlantic Republican Tradition* (Princeton, N.J., 1975), 49–80 (on ancient idea of national character); Charles Secondat, Baron de Montesquieu, *The Spirit of Laws*, ed. David Wallace Carrithers (Berkeley, Calif., 1977), pt. 3, book 19, chaps. 4–5 (spirit of nation), chap. 7 (Athenians and Spartans); Edmund Burke, *The Speech . . . on . . . Conciliation with the Colonies . . .* (London, 1775), 24, 33–34, 37, 38–51. On the significance of Montesquieu's social analysis, see Peter Gay, *The Enlightenment: An Interpretation*, II, *The Science of Freedom* (New York, 1969), 326–331; in his essay "Of National Characters," David Hume expounded on how certain sociopolitical forms created various types of human characteristics—see *Essays Moral, Political, and Literary*, rev. ed., ed. Eugene F. Miller (Indianapolis, Ind., 1987), 197–214.

could outweigh climatic influences in most societies, reiterating Montesquieu's balance between material and cultural factors.[15]

Overall, the complex of ideas about social-scientific categories, national character, and climate prescribed a static image of a given society. These were not criteria that encouraged descriptions of change over time, but gave fixed portraits. This was in accordance with the form of the genre: the observer moved (he or she was a traveler, after all) rather than what was observed. Journeys still had significance as pilgrimages, searches, ventures; they were metaphors for self-discovery and transformation and paid less attention to the change that could occur in the world beyond the self. Though travel literature of the modern era made the world a smaller and more recognizable place, it did so by reducing different countries and peoples to stereotypical images: the wilds of America, the mystic East; the barbarous Turk, the noble savage.

As in other travel narratives, description of character and social customs appeared in accounts of the Lower South throughout the period under study.[16] Luigi Castiglioni, an Italian aristocrat, noted in the mid-1780s that Georgians modeled their "customs and manners" on those of South Carolinians. Johann David Schoepf, a German natural historian, was interested in the "manners of the inhabitants of Charleston" when he visited them in the 1790s.[17] In his

15. Montesquieu, *Spirit of Laws,* ed. Carrithers, pt. 3, book 14, first quotation from chap. 1, second from chap. 2; Adam Ferguson, *An Essay on the History of Civil Society* (Edinburgh, 1767), 174–175; Hume, *Essays Moral, Political, and Literary,* ed. Miller, 198–214, 267. See Marshall and Williams, *Great Map of Mankind,* 129–138, on how the idea of climate shaped 18th-century descriptions of human cultures, and 138–139 for Hume's emphasis on "moral" factors.

16. Alexis de Tocqueville, somewhat later, employed the concept of national character, in *Democracy in America,* ed. Phillips Bradley (New York, 1945), I, 27–28.

17. Luigi Castiglioni, *Viaggio: Travels in the United States of North America, 1785–87,* ed. and trans. Antonio Pace (Syracuse, N.Y., 1983), 127; Johann David Schoepf, *Travels in the Confederation, 1783–1784,* ed. and trans. Alfred J. Morrison (1911; rpt., New York, 1968), II, 167. The English sailor and novelist John Davis, visiting South Carolina in the same decade as Schoepf, expressed a desire to obtain "the true estimate of manners" in that state. See his *Travels of Four Years and a Half in the United States of America . . . [1798–1802]* (London, 1803), 63. Englishman John Melish composed a list of a dozen questions to ask himself during his tour of the Southwest, the sixth of which had to do with the "manners and customs" of the people—see Melish, *Travels through the United States of America, in the Years 1806 and 1807, and 1809, 1810, and 1811* (London, 1818), 291–292.

popular *American Gazetteer* (first published in 1789), Jedidiah Morse sought to explain "the manners of the people" in South Carolina; and Dr. Daniel Turner, a Rhode Island doctor who moved to south Georgia, wrote in 1805 his opinions of the "morals and manners" of Georgians. Describing local customs was a step toward explaining the general character of local people. Timothy Ford, a New Jersey lawyer, referred to "the genius of the planting interest" in South Carolina during the 1780s and set up a contrast between "the active spirit" of a martial people, whom the South Carolinians were not, and "the effeminate spirit of luxury and dissipation," which did characterize them. Emphasizing the static nature of the resulting image, John Melish explained in the early 1800s that a traveler's account, "when judiciously compiled, presents a *living picture* of the state of the country through which he passes."[18]

Travelers in the Lower South also followed convention in emphasizing how climate affected culture. A diary-keeping visitor to Charleston, Savannah, or St. Augustine invariably described the weather, and the author of a gazetteer usually analyzed the physical attributes of the region before writing about its people. Travelers singled out the heat, humidity, and prevalence of diseases (especially malaria and yellow fever) as important cultural influences, believing that these factors created inescapable sickliness, enervation, and mortality. The anonymous author of *American Husbandry,* analyzing South Carolina in the 1770s, wrote that "the maritime part of the country is in one of the most unhealthy climates in the world." To add insult to injury, he claimed that "this immoderate and excessive heat of climate is in a country the major part of which is spread with stagnated waters" and that "from the mud of these stinking sinks and sewers the heat exhales such putrid effluvia as must necessarily poison the air" for any who inhaled it. Though they realized that a semitropical environment contributed to the agricultural productivity—and therefore the commercial wealth—of this region, visitors harbored suspicions of vegetal and economic growth that was too rapid, because the same condi-

---

18. Jedidiah Morse, *The American Gazetteer* (Boston, 1797), I, s.v. "South Carolina"; Richard K. Murdoch, ed., "Letters and Papers of Dr. Daniel Turner: A Rhode Islander in South Georgia," *GHQ,* LIII (1969), 487; Joseph W. Barnwell, ed., "Diary of Timothy Ford, 1785–1786," *SCHM,* XIII (1912), 201; Melish, *Travels,* iii. Francisco de Miranda, Spanish nobleman and South American revolutionary, similarly wanted to determine what the characteristics of South Carolinians "generally" were. See John S. Ezell, ed., Judson P. Wood, trans., *The New Democracy in America: Travels of Francisco de Miranda in the United States, 1783–84* (Norman, Okla., 1963), 23–24.

tions also facilitated rapid decay and death. Luigi Castiglioni claimed that, though Georgia's climate was "excellent for vegetation," it was "very unhealthy" for the people who dwelt there.[19]

Going beyond even this negative assessment, Johann David Schoepf axiomatically stated in the 1780s that Carolina was "in the spring a paradise, in the summer a hell, and in the autumn a hospital." He concluded, "Carolina would be for many a toper a loved country; it is the doctrine here that during the warm months one should think and work little, and drink much." Francisco de Miranda found Charleston in the summer of 1783 to be scarcely bearable, as its "heat and diabolic multitude of mosquitoes exceed all exaggeration." Its residents were "so accustomed" to the ravages of malaria "that if, in greeting them, one asks, 'How are you?' they answer, their teeth chattering with the cold of the ague, 'Pretty well, only the fever!'" J. B. Dunlop claimed that Savannah, surrounded as it was by marshes and flooded rice fields, was "in Summer much more unhealthy than Charleston." He also thought that so many men in Liberty County, Georgia, had died that widowed women owned nearly all the land there.[20]

Travelers singled out black slavery, in addition to the heat and disease, as an important influence on whites' character. Some observers believed climate created a propensity to employ slaves. On the eve of the Revolution, Bernard Romans claimed that physical conditions in East Florida made African slavery an unavoidable choice for planters. Jedidiah Morse wrote of the fever-ridden South Carolina coast, "No white man, to speak generally, ever thinks of settling a farm, and improving it for himself, without negroes." Some travelers were not certain, on the other hand, that they could draw a clear line from climate to slavery, from nature to culture. Schoepf cautioned that heat did not always explain indolence: "Has not every science flourished at one time or another in other parts of the world where there has been exposure to quite as burning a

19. Harry J. Carman, ed., *American Husbandry* (1775) (New York, 1939), 264; Castiglioni, *Viaggio*, ed. Pace, 131. On contemporary perceptions of climate, see Karen Ordahl Kupperman, "Fear of Hot Climates in the Anglo-American Colonial Experience," *WMQ*, 3d Ser., XLI (1984), 213–240; Richard S. Dunn, *Sugar and Slaves: The Rise of the Planter Class in the English West Indies, 1624–1713* (Chapel Hill, N.C., 1972), chaps. 8–9.

20. Schoepf, *Travels*, ed. Morrison, II, 172, 218; Ezell, ed., Wood, trans., *Travels of Miranda*, 25, 33; Raymond A. Mohl, ed., "A Scotsman [J. B. Dunlop] Visits Georgia in 1811," *GHQ*, LV (1971), 261.

sun?" Timothy Ford disagreed, concluding that the "dronish ease and torpid inactivity" of creoles resulted "from the climate" rather than "from the multiplicity of servants and [their] attendance," which was a custom that reinforced but did not cause a culture of lassitude.[21]

Observers maintained that, whatever its causes, black slavery made native whites haughty and lazy. Whites used slaves as symbols of wealth and of the leisure wealth brought. Ford reported that when he and some companions saw a man on horseback near Charleston, "one of the company" decided the man " 'cannot be a gentleman for he is riding without servants.' " Luckily for the distant stranger, two servants joined him, and Ford's companions decided that he was indeed of their class. Along similar lines, John Davis wrote that a Charlestonian "who is without horses and slaves incurs always contempt" from those in the slaveholding ranks. Travelers believed, however, that slavery constituted only one aspect of whites' total wealth that created an atmosphere of luxury and inertia. Observers again stressed that the heat and damp created incredible agricultural fertility, conducive to easily won riches for whites. Jedidiah Morse explained that the least healthy areas of Georgia were nevertheless the most fertile and "an unfailing source of wealth." Impressed with the abundance of South Carolina's crops, the author of *American Husbandry* wrote, "No husbandry in Europe can equal this of Carolina; we have no agriculture in England . . . that will pay any thing like this." Similarly amazed, the author of a London-published *American Gazetteer* (1762) claimed that Charleston, filled with "rich people," was one of "the richest [cities] in America." Ford warned that "the facility with which money may be made . . . has also a very considerable influence upon manners and customs" and in fact contributed to the degeneracy of the people. Schoepf chimed in that "luxury in Carolina has made the greatest advance, and their manner of life, dress, equipages, furniture, everything denotes a higher degree of taste and love of show" than in the northern states of America. Travelers thus saw laziness, wealth, and luxury as mutually reinforcing components of the character of whites.[22]

21. Bernard Romans, *A Concise Natural History of East and West Florida* (1775; facs. ed., Gainesville, Fla., 1962), 104–107; Morse, *Gazetteer*, I, s.v. "South Carolina"; Schoepf, *Travels*, ed. Morrison, II, 215; Barnwell, ed., "Diary of Ford," *SCHM*, XIII (1912), 143.

22. Barnwell, ed., "Diary of Ford," *SCHM*, XIII (1912), 189; Davis, *Travels*, 117; Morse, *Gazetteer*, I, s.v. "Georgia"; Carman, ed., *American Husbandry*, 301; *The American Gazetteer* (London, 1762), I, s.v. "Charleston"; Schoepf, *Travels*, ed. Morrison, II, 168.

Luxury was the most glaring fault within their degraded character, a comment that drew on neoclassical and Christian denunciations of material splendor. Visitor after visitor emphasized that, because whites gained so much wealth with so little effort, they were free to display their status through preening conspicuous consumption rather than take pains to maintain their income by attention to productive activities. Bostonian Josiah Quincy, visiting Charleston in 1773, found that "State, magnificence and ostentation, the natural attendants of riches, are conspicuous among this people." Captain Michael Gaffney complained of Charleston in 1791 that one "cannot go afoot without being run over by some kind of fop or other" who was "out to take the air" on horseback or in "a chaise." Daniel Mulford, who moved from Connecticut to Georgia in the early 1800s, offered his brother a scathing summary of white Savannahians: the *Ruling Characteristic* in that city was "to get money and display it in a fashionable hospitality." "*Amusements for Gentlemen,*" he claimed, were to "get money—dance—gamble—run horses" while Savannah's ladies could only "spend money—play piano—contemplate their own beauty."[23]

The most striking form of wasteful, ostentatious consumption was gambling, in which money denoted status according to a gambler's willingness to gain or lose material assets by chance: the activity showcased a person's ability to throw away wealth. John Lambert remarked on Georgia planters' passion for gaming, and Josiah Quincy thought that "cards, dice, the bottle and horses engross[ed] prodigious portions of time and attention" in colonial Carolina. Such was whites' penchant for gambling that they even placed bets on annual harvests and slave workers. One South Carolinian observed of the 1771 rice crop, "Bets are laid that there will not be 100,000 Barrels made." Charles William Janson wrote in 1807 that slaves "even become the stake of the [South Carolina] gamester who, with unconcern attaches their fate to the cast of a die, or the turn of a card."[24]

23. Mark Antony DeWolfe Howe, ed., "Journal of Josiah Quincy, Junior, 1773," Massachusetts Historical Society, *Proceedings*, XLIX (1915–1916), 455; Michael Gaffney Journal, 1797, SCL; Daniel Mulford to Levi Mulford, Jan. 28, 1809, Daniel Mulford Papers, I, GHS.

24. John Lambert, *Travels through Lower Canada and the United States of North America, in the Years 1806, 1807, and 1808* (London, 1810), III, 35; Howe, ed., "Journals of Quincy," Mass. Hist. Soc., *Procs.*, XLIX (1915–1916), 455; Manigault to Benjamin Stead, Sept. 6, 1771, Peter Manigault Letterbook, series 11-493, SCHS; Charles William Janson, *The Stranger in America* . . . (London, 1807), 360. Cf. T. H. Breen, "Horses and

Travelers claimed that whites maintained such an indifference to business that they never improved their methods of planting, a particularly stinging accusation for this agricultural society. The author of *American Husbandry*, even as he marveled at South Carolinians' wealth, scorned their mode of subsistence. "All our American colonists are very bad farmers," the anonymous critic wrote, but Carolinians seemed particularly ignorant. They cultivated corn carelessly (using hoes, not plows), sowed no pasture, used little clover, and built few fences. Theirs was a "miserable husbandry" by British standards. Timothy Ford, in his blistering appraisal of South Carolinians, claimed they had not improved much by the early nineteenth century. "There are many who call themselves planters who know little about the process and art of planting. . . . They owe their wealth neither to art, genius, invention, or industry—but it seems to be showered upon them in the copious productions of a fertile soil and a prolific climate." He concluded that "with regard to manners and customs" South Carolinians had "reached their climact[e]ric," but with "regard to some kinds of improvement they would seem to be in an early period of Society."[25]

Descriptions of the lazy Lower South tended to focus on the coastline (as the above quotations indicate), though a variant of this image appeared in writings on inland areas. Coastal residents greeted more external observers than did people inland, because their region contained port cities easily accessible to visitors. Travelers paid less attention to the upcountry area, which had a more temperate climate, fewer black slaves, and less wealth. Outsiders who did discuss upcountry areas often contrasted them—in terms of climate and relative wealth—to coastal regions rather than considered them as distinct and equally important zones. The author of *American Husbandry* believed that, unlike the lowcountry, upland regions had a climate "which in health and agreeableness yields to none in the world." Jedidiah Morse explained how in the Lower South's midlands, "negroes are not so numerous. The master attends personally to his own business."[26]

Gentlemen: The Cultural Significance of Gambling among the Gentry of Virginia," *WMQ*, 3d Ser., XXIV (1977), 239–257; and Clifford Geertz, "Deep Play: Notes on the Balinese Cockfight," in Geertz, *The Interpretation of Cultures: Selected Essays* (New York, 1973), 412–453.

25. Carman, ed., *American Husbandry*, 315–318, 320, 324; Barnwell, ed., "Diary of Ford," *SCHM*, XIII (1912), 143.

26. Carman, ed., *American Husbandry*, 265; Morse, *Gazetteer*, I, s.v. "South Carolina."

Visitors sometimes concluded, however, that upcountry whites were as shiftless as their lowcountry counterparts, though the theme of poor white aimlessness was not yet as elaborate as in the antebellum era. Here, a cool climate and relative poverty replaced lowcountry features of heat and wealth as explanations for laziness; having neither a climate nor a source of labor suited to plantation riches, upcountry residents languished in a state far below the commercial splendors of modernity. J. B. Dunlop claimed that Georgia's impoverished "Crackers" had little else to do but drink, fight, and sue each other over their meager properties. When in court, "they shew their character in a conspicuous manner which is something similar to the idea generally entertained of nations in the first stages of Barbarity." Castiglioni complained that, near Augusta, whites would "occupy themselves with little else but card games and horse races," and in South Carolina "the people of the more internal and mountainous regions . . . are composed of the most vile rabble." J. F. D. Smyth maintained that, on a scale of universal human development, the leather-clad and savage frontiersmen resembled native Americans. But these criticisms of the upcountry were neither as frequent nor as emphatic as the sustained denunciations most visitors gave of the torrid and slave-filled coastline, which continued to give the region, as a whole, its unflattering character. Indeed, Smyth extended the lowcountry's pernicious environment to Camden in western South Carolina, where the whites seemed to him as feeble and sallow as their enervated coastal cousins.[27]

Narratives of travels in the Lower South thus supplied data for the eighteenth century's sociological complex of ideas about climate and human culture; the literature helped give the region a lasting reputation for lassitude. Within these accounts are statements that would develop into romantic notions of differences between northern and southern peoples and into the regional particularism that would underpin nineteenth-century sentiment about place and personal identity.[28] But such observations failed, even within their own social-scientific pretensions, to distinguish among all the wildly different societies that could be fitted into stock images of warm regions. Cultures ranging from India to Persia to Georgia shared stereotypic features of

27. Mohl, ed., "A Scotsman Visits Georgia," *GHQ*, LV (1971), 263–265; Castiglioni, *Viaggio*, ed. Pace, 144, 165; J.F.D. Smyth, *A Tour in the United States of America . . .* (London, 1784), I, 179–180, 205–206.

28. Michael O'Brien, *Rethinking the South: Essays in Intellectual History* (Baltimore, 1968), 50, 67–70, 90–110.

semitropical luxuriance, sensual indolence, and enslavement—nothing in this caricature specified what might be distinctive about any given people in any region that happened to be warm and outside western Europe.

Prefabricated images of distant places easily reverted to the fiction that early champions of travel literature as scientific source had wished to avoid. Caricatures of sultry New World locations appeared, for instance, in Aphra Behn's *Oroonoko* (1688), Abbé Prévost's *Manon Lescaut* (1731), and Voltaire's *Candide* (1759); indeed, the authors of these works relied on travel narratives to recreate, variously, the local colors of Surinam, Louisiana, and Peru. Some travelers recognized that they were subjective observers who mixed *dulce* and *utile* to make more pleasing narratives. Naturalist John Bartram lamented: "Travellers . . . are very deficient in relating the true methods of agriculture, which the inhabitants practise in their respective countries. They think, if they relate their observations of . . . the extravagant diversions of the people, their government, and superstition,—then, they think they have done much; although it is little more than what many of the former travellers have done long before them."[29]

The similarity between fictional and nonfictional narratives was evidenced by the exaggerated language of those who wrote about the Lower South. References that compared the lowcountry's swamps to "stinking sinks and sewers," its summer to "hell," and its mosquitoes to a "diabolic multitude" show some touches of hyperbole. Travelers made other unlikely claims, as when Daniel Turner asserted that he had "not heard a Sermon" for nearly a year while he was in Georgia and explained how he disdained to court any local female because "I conceive the education, morals and manners of this country renders the heart incapable of entertaining . . . pure affection and sensibility." Elkanah Watson, writing how rich South Carolina planters lived "in almost Asiatic luxury," made a similarly strained statement.[30]

Travelers themselves knew that, if they wanted to describe the Lower South, they had more to do than simply rough out its exotic features, but had at least to fill in the sketch. Slaves, for instance, required particular explanation.

29. William Darlington, ed., *Memorials of John Bartram and Humphry Marshall* . . . (Philadelphia, 1849), 374. On caricatures in fiction, see Batten, *Pleasurable Instruction*, 109–110; and Adams, *Travel Literature*, 103–147.

30. Murdoch, ed., "Dr. Daniel Turner," *GHQ*, LIII, 487, 497; Elkanah Watson, *Men and Times of the Revolution* . . . , ed. Winslow C. Watson (New York, 1856), 56.

Though careful to point out how the region's whites were uninterested in work and enamored of luxury, observers also conceded that not all residents displayed these characteristics. Not only did blacks seem to live and work outside the stereotype, but they actively defied its constraints through their industry. Planter absenteeism, travelers noted, necessitated black industriousness. Because of the heat and disease near rice swamps, visitors explained, whites fled the mephitic atmosphere of their plantations. Referring to Georgia's coastal residents, Jedidiah Morse claimed, "Before the sickly season approaches, the rich planters, with their families, remove to the sea-islands or some elevated, healthy situation," leaving plantation affairs under the direction of subalterns. Luigi Castiglioni thought that "most" South Carolina planters "were raised in England" and as adults lived "for the most part in Charleston, visiting their lands two or three times a year." Because planters absented themselves from their properties, travelers reported, slaves took up the work of estate management. Visitors recounted how planters hired white overseers, but also observed that black "drivers" managed much of the day-to-day direction of agricultural activities. Johann Martin Bolzius explained that pre-Revolutionary South Carolina and Georgia planters would "install the most loyal Negroes as Negro drivers (*Treiber*) and beaters (*Schläger*)." Johann David Schoepf claimed in the 1780s that the "head-men" who directed the tricky process of making indigo were "commonly negroes" on whom whites depended for a successful crop.[31]

Even more remarkable to travelers, all slaves tended to work with a minimum of supervision by anyone, black or white. Here, outsiders detected a truly distinctive feature of the Lower South. Many commented on the lowcountry "task system"—so called because workers completed specific tasks in the field rather than labored for set periods of time—that predominated in the coastal areas of Georgia, South Carolina, and East Florida. Planters could leave daily decisions about apportionment of time and labor to their slaves so long as the initial assignment of tasks was properly done. William De Brahm asserted that the "tasking of a Negroe and providing Employ" for her or him was "one of a Planters principal Studies." Planters did not seem to care how slaves did their tasks or how, within certain broad limits, they spent their free time. When

31. Morse, *Gazetteer*, I, s.v. "Georgia"; Castiglioni, *Viaggio*, ed. Pace, 164; Klaus G. Loewald *et al.*, eds. and trans., "Johann Martin Bolzius Answers a Questionnaire on Carolina and Georgia," *WMQ*, 3d Ser., XIV (1957), 234; Schoepf, *Travels*, ed. Morrison, II, 159.

evangelist George Whitefield preached in Georgia in 1740, for example, he claimed that "several of the negroes did their work in less time than usual, [so] that they might come to hear me."[32]

Observers concluded that, in addition to attending sermons, slaves worked on their own initiative. Blacks seemed not only competent workers for whites but eager and self-disciplined laborers for themselves and shrewd participants in local markets. Dr. Turner said that in Georgia a "field negro frequently completes his task of a days work by 12 oclock A. M. and his master feels no right to call on him after" the task was done. The slave could then spend "the remainder of the day at work in his own corn field." Johann Martin Bolzius noticed that Carolina slaves would plant "their tobacco on Sundays, and thus buy something for themselves, their wives, and children." They had to "plant their own food and . . . earn their few clothes by [doing] Sunday work" for neighboring whites. Josiah Quincy also called attention to this latter practice when he wrote that South Carolina "slaves who don't frolic on the Sabbath, do all kinds of work for themselves on hire." Whites sometimes arranged to hire out some of their skilled slaves by the year or month, a situation in which they did not supervise their own workers for long periods. Impressed by the range of skills slaves acquired—they were carpenters, smiths, coopers, carters, seam- stresses, house servants, plowmen, or machine operators—Bolzius decided that "since the Negroes learn all kinds of common and useful crafts, the poor [white] craftsmen cannot succeed." Schoepf calculated that a hired-out slave made 15 to 20 percent annual profit for the master or mistress. "Thus many idlers place their capital in negroes," he wrote, "and, in the strict sense, are by them supported, living careless on the bitter sweat of the hired."[33]

To round out their characterization of the hardworking slave, travelers described how blacks participated in local markets and took up a commercial identity of their own. Slaves traded their crops and services for other goods or even for cash—much to the astonishment of visitors. Bolzius, for instance,

32. Louis De Vorsey, Jr., ed., *De Brahm's Report of the General Survey in the Southern District of North America* (Columbia, S.C., 1971), 94; William V. Davis, ed., *George Whitefield's Journals (1737–1741)* . . . (Gainesville, Fla., 1969), 444.

33. Murdoch, ed., "Dr. Daniel Turner," *GHQ*, LIV (1970), 102; Loewald *et al.*, eds. and trans., "Bolzius Questionnaire," *WMQ*, 3d Ser., XIV (1957), 236, 242; Howe, ed., "Journal of Quincy," Mass. Hist. Soc., *Procs.*, XLIX (1915–1916), 455; Schoepf, *Travels*, ed. Morrison, II, 201–202. John Lambert observed that, in Charleston, "many persons obtain a handsome living by letting out their slaves, for 6 to 10 dollars per month" (*Travels*, II, 403).

tried to buy corn for his horse from the white overseer on a Georgia plantation and was surprised when the man declined. "He had no authority over it and directed me to the Negroes. One of them gave me some, but I had to give him a half crown of local paper currency for it." When itinerant preacher Joseph Pilmore was stranded on the banks of South Carolina's Santee River in 1773, he hired a few slaves who had "finished their task" to ferry him across the river.[34]

Travelers conceded, to be sure, that not all slaves were energetic farmers and ferrymen and often argued that blacks' busy schedule was due not only to their self-discipline but also to their masters' coercion.[35] But travelers' narratives of the early Lower South do not contain the sustained—and racist—denunciation of lazy slaves that would appear in later nineteenth-century accounts, most notably in Frederick Law Olmsted's. On the other hand, foreign whites, like natives, were using blacks for their own purposes. Where planters saw assimilated slaves meekly working their way into a subordinate role within their society, travelers saw steadfast workers proving how a desire for independent activity (within the margins of coerced labor) overcame disincentives of climate and oppression. A native white's sentimentalized mudsill was a visitor's phalanx of Poor Richards. Both views resembled each other because they avoided simply saying how slavery was unjust to slaves, no matter how affective their human nature nor how admirable their work habits. The theme of slaves' resilience and autonomy would remain a contested one throughout the Lower South's history, and one not easily summarized by any contemporary white, whether native or visitor.

Travelers' praise for slaves' attention to work nonetheless raised questions about their own image of the Lower South. They described a society in which the controlling white class might have stepped out of the humid and languorous atmosphere of a Kipling story, but one in which the subordinate black class was more at home in a brisk tale by Horatio Alger. Yet travelers maintained that only the former group defined the region's national character, whereas the efforts of a large portion of the population did little to change this collective ethos. This selective attention to the characteristics of a human

---

34. George Fenwick Jones, ed. and trans., "John Martin Boltzius' Trip to Charleston, October 1742," *SCHM*, LXXXII (1981), 104; Frederick E. Maser and Howard T. Maag, eds., *The Journal of Joseph Pilmore, Methodist Itinerant: For the Years August 1, 1769, to January 2, 1774* (Philadelphia, 1969), 188. Like native whites, travelers tended to emphasize male slaves' activities over those of female workers.

35. See, for example, Schoepf, *Travels*, ed. Morrison, II, 221.

population was consistent with the concept of national character and again reveals the biases of eighteenth- and nineteenth-century observers. Fascination with a people's collective spirit had always been imbued with concern over their political abilities, their laws and government. The characteristics of slaves were unimportant: slaves were not citizens, they had no political rights and needed no political abilities. Since they had a subordinate role in society, slaves could not give it definition. This assumption informed Josiah Quincy's division of South Carolina's inhabitants into "opulent and lordly planters, poor and spiritless peasants and vile slaves."[36] Slavery was important only for its effects on the white population, not for its effects on blacks; it was significant because it reinforced whites' wealth and lassitude, but its ability to energize blacks was only a secondary phenomenon.

Travelers qualified their narratives twice over: blacks did not fit into the stereotyped image of the Lower South, nor did all whites. Visitors introduced to their tales white residents who, by overcoming the debilitating effects of climate and disregarding the luxurious ethos of their compatriots, mustered more effort. When George Whitefield first visited Georgia in 1738, for example, he commented on Swiss settlers' accomplishments and exclaimed, "Surely they speak not truth, who say that the Georgia people have been idle; for I never saw more laborious people than are in these villages." Whitefield had similar praise for Saltzburger immigrants in the town of Ebenezer, Georgia. Nor did exceptions exist only among poor immigrants, but also among the richest planters. In the 1740s, Edward Kimber wrote of Noble Jones's Wormsloe Plantation in Georgia that it was "one of the most agreeable spots I ever saw, and the improvements of that ingenious man are very extraordinary." In 1745, James Pemberton visited Charleston and reported that a "Cap. Horton took us out about a mile" to Jekyll Island "to see a field of Barley which is an uncommon thing in this colony but he having a particular Inclin[ation] to Farming hath made many good Improvem[en]ts on this Island and has one of the Largest barns I have ever seen." Josiah Quincy, who liked few South Carolinians, nonetheless overflowed with praise for Joseph Allston, whose "plantation, negroes, gardens, etc., are in the best order of any I have seen!" Engineer Gerard De Brahm observed before the Revolution that South Carolina's rice mill dams "testify of the great Skill, Industry and Improvement of this Province."[37]

36. Howe, ed., "Journal of Quincy," Mass. Hist. Soc., *Procs.*, XLIX (1915–1916), 454.

37. Davis, ed., *Whitefield's Journals*, 150, 153; Edward Kimber, *Itinerant Observations in America [1744]*, Keith Read Collection, box 15, UGA; entry for Oct. 3, 1745, Pember-

Even Timothy Ford, despite his spirited invectives against the luxurious character of whites, praised certain South Carolinians who were neither sensual nor idle. "One may here and there be found," Ford conceded, "who rising above the prejudices and shaking off the supine carelessness of the country ventures into the use of machinery and the contrivances of art" on his plantation. Such men, he further related, "are generally very successful and find their account in such undertakings." The grudgingly admiring Ford was particularly impressed with South Carolinian Henry Laurens and his Mepkin plantation: "He is a rare instance of method, whereby his plantation raises itself above those of this country in which everything is [usually] done immethodically by the round about means of force and Labour" of slaves. Daniel Turner also gave backhand praise to Georgians. Though he railed against the residents living near St. Marys River and regretted settling among them, Turner did admit in an 1805 letter to his parents that "the place affords a small circle of well informed and tolerably agreeable people." Four years later, Alexander Wilson made a similar assessment. The abundance of slaves "have ruined the energy and activity of the people" in South Carolina, he confided to a correspondent in Philadelphia. "In Charleston, however, I met with some excellent exceptions, among the first ranks of Society there."[38]

Just as their denunciations of the Lower South often went over the top, travelers also exaggerated in their praise. Alexander Cluny's *American Traveler* (1769) was a rare work which had nothing *but* praise for the region. Cluny dismissed discussion of "the Persons, Manners, Customs, etc." of the colonists and focused on the area's "aptitude by Climate and Situation for agriculture and Commerce." He claimed that "of all the British Colonies in *America*," South Carolina "has been cultivated with most Attention, Spirit, and Expence; and the Success has been answerable. The Country is well peopled; and bears a Face of Improvement and Civilization, scarce inferior to any Part of *Europe*." Cluny concluded that South Carolina's "aboriginal Products are cultivated with proper care; and the Products of other countries introduced, and carried nearer to the perfection of their nature" than "Exoticks in any Country we know." Finally, Edmund Burke claimed that it was the energetic and talented

ton Diary, SCL; Howe, ed., "Journal of Quincy," Mass. Hist. Soc., *Procs.*, XLIX (1915–1916), 452; De Vorsey, ed., *De Brahm's Report*, 79.

38. Barnwell, ed., "Diary of Ford," *SCHM*, XIII (1912), 189; Murdoch, ed., "Dr. Daniel Turner," *GHQ*, LIII (1969), 476; Alexander Wilson to Samuel Bradford, Mar. 5, 1809, Alexander Wilson Papers, SCL.

minority of whites—detected by Turner, Wilson, and Ford—who led their more enervated cohort in the agricultural innovations Cluny saw. Burke wrote of the introduction of indigo into South Carolina's plantation economy, "No sooner had a few shewn a spirited and successful example than all went into it so heartily" that the crop became a general success. In his 1791 poem, *Carolina; or, The Planter,* George Ogilvie gave another sympathetic if unlikely account of the lowcountry. In his georgic, Ogilvie classicized the Lower South, making its rice swamps and plantation houses seem to be Mediterranean groves and Roman villas. His verses made the region appear benign because it appeared to be nothing like itself. Flattering allusion to the antique past may have reinforced some planters' nostalgic vision of themselves but did not explain their own society—which was significantly different from the pagan and martial ancient world.[39]

Despite these occasional words of praise, the prevailing barrage of criticism explained why whites in the Lower South worried so much about finding an adequate explanation for themselves, their society, their economy. Most outsiders either condemned them out of hand or damned them with faint or unconvincing praise. Little pleased travelers, who used images of both impoverished savagery and vicious wealth to criticize the region: underdeveloped areas of the Lower South were barbaric; the commercial riches of the settled coast brought the perils of luxury. Not all this invective should be disregarded; people made wealthy through slavery deserved criticism. But travelers' attacks on slavery were faltering—they usually disliked the institution because it degenerated whites, not because it exploited blacks. Such a position displayed the era's continued waffling over the question of which economic form most benefited humanity. In the end, contemporary external accounts were inadequate descriptions of the region though effective goads to resident whites.

Individuals who were not typical of the mores and behavior of the majority of whites in the Lower South played a role that external observers barely

39. [Alexander Cluny], *The American Traveler . . .* (London, 1769), 9, 93; Edmund Burke, *An Account of the European Settlements in America* (London, 1775), II, 261; section from Ogilvie, *Carolina; or, The Planter* (London, 1791), in Berkeley and Berkeley, *Garden of Charles Town,* 354–357. When Abigail Capers moved from Charleston to rural South Carolina in 1791, she complained to a friend that "Carolina is too often represented as the Seat of Gaiety and extravagance," arguing that "few Travellers are well acquainted" with the true nature of the hardworking countryside (Abigail Capers to Elizabeth Russel, Mar. 25, 1791, Mrs. Edith M. Dabbs letter, SHC).

identified, let alone analyzed. The point is not so much whether most whites fitted the stereotype—many probably did. But a volatile group actively shaped exotic climate, slavery, and plantation wealth to their own purposes, rather than were passively shaped by them. This shift in emphasis does not laud their actions, but, indeed, may blame them all the more for what they accomplished. Whites were not, for instance, helplessly driven to use slaves because of their climate—many of them willfully expanded and defended the institution with or without environmental arguments. More interesting than external observers' stereotypical belief that residents of the Lower South were victims of climate and wealth was residents' own fear that they might degenerate into such a condition if they did not preach and practice a way of life that encouraged individual and social development. External criticism spurred them on. South Carolinian David Ramsay ruefully recounted, for example, that outsiders' ideas of pre-Revolutionary South Carolina consisted of little more "than that it produced rice and indigo, and contained a large proportion of slaves, and a handful of free men, and that most of the latter were strangers to vigorous health—all self-indulgent, and none accustomed to active exertions either of mind or body."[40] Ramsay and others were determined to prove otherwise.

40. David Ramsay, *History of South-Carolina, from Its First Settlement in 1670 to the Year 1808* . . . (Charleston, S.C., 1809), II, 512.

Chapter 4

The Local Work Ethic

The energetic whites whom travelers exempted from their critical assessments agreed with yet protested against travelers' stereotypes. Whites resented any stereotypic summation of their society, but their unease manifested itself in two ways: as indignation against the stereotypers and as fear that their society might actually fit the caricature if they and others did not actively work to prevent it. External criticism reinforced their persistent fear that they needed constantly to criticize themselves to prevent their society from sinking into sloth or barbarity. South Carolinian Henry Laurens resentfully replied to two English friends who had poked fun at his homeland, "I beg you will not abuse my Country as you have done, true as all you say may be, I can't bear to hear it from anybody but myself."[1] Life behind the lush curtain of exoticism was unacceptable if residents allowed themselves to become objects of abuse, woeful examples of how either advance or retrogression along the primitivism-refinement yardstick could prove humanity's undoing.

Like Laurens, other whites turned their fears over the character of their society into a determination to reform themselves. But they wanted both to retain the unusual material advantages of their society and to bring it up to an optimal, modernized form; achievement of this golden mean required a tricky meliorist role for themselves, again revealing an uneasiness over the attributes of the region. Whites tried to control climate, wealth, and slavery in their plantation society rather than allow these factors to manipulate them and thereby transform them into the stereotypic figures that populated travelers' narratives. The key to controlling self and society lay in an ethos of directed and productive activity, one that established whites' identity through steadfast

---

1. Henry Laurens to Bridgen and Waller, July 14, 1787, LP.

avoidance of lassitude. Not unique to the Lower South, such an outlook was present as well in other southern or even frontier areas that sought to give inhabitants a sense of purpose amid tempting opportunities to avoid effort. In this way too, the Lower South resembled modernizing areas of the West. Propertyholders in Europe and America wanted, especially during the era of industrialization, to create a work ethic (mostly for the working classes) and a broader ethos of self-improvement and intellectual endeavor for themselves, members of classes that reaped the profits of growing economies. Admiration for technology and efficiency was, along with other bourgeois values, prevalent in the Lower South. The region was, therefore, surprisingly typical compared to other parts of the modern West, though it gave some regional twists to what was otherwise common among Euro-Americans. For instance, just as whites used social-scientific definitions of humanity to justify their use of black slavery, so they took up current medical theory to make the same point.

An ethos especially strong among the native planter elite, the local work ethic also affected poorer and recently arrived whites who employed it to establish their own place within the Lower South. Because it regulated the behavior of propertyholders more than it did actual workers, this ethic did not rely on rigorously defined standards of productivity and efficiency—common among other work ethics. Instead, it encouraged efforts to maintain a life of activity directed at self- and social improvement, one that taught an individual how to adjust to the semitropical climate, the prospect of wealth, and the leisure allowed by ownership of slaves without becoming an enervated pawn of these forces. The ethic taught, not avoidance of the peculiarities of the region, but responsible adjustment to them. It emphasized this possibility by showing how visiting outsiders could become honorary natives, an assumption that rejected the static line travelers drew between insiders and outsiders, between Lower South and larger world.

ᛒ Fevers and Strangers

Attitudes about disease were at the heart of whites' ethos of activity and responsibility. In their response to the dangers of malaria and yellow fever, residents interpreted their physical environment quite differently than did external observers, who emphasized natives' lassitude and debility. Indeed, residents maintained that their peculiar climate endowed them with social and physical strengths that differentiated them in a positive way from outsiders who were not adapted to their region. Whites relied on creative interpretations of acquired immunity to malaria and yellow fever for this view of their region.[2] They stressed the significance of becoming "seasoned" to the society, defining a process of assimilation that required exertion and intelligence on the part of those who successfully undertook it, rather than a climate-induced lapse in these faculties that could prove fatal. Theirs was an amalgamation of fear and bravado, a cultural interpretation of the significance of disease that revealed key assumptions about a creole society. Visible, too, are signs of a sentimentalized attachment to place, part of the nostalgic repertoire of modern thought.[3]

Like external observers, residents of the Lower South believed that yellow fever (epidemic fever) and malaria (intermittent or remittent fever) were endemic to their environment. They generally agreed that fevers were infectious (communicated from the environment to a person) rather than contagious (communicated from person to person), hence they did not usually

2. Although scholars have discussed how Lower South blacks were adapted to mosquito-borne ailments (Peter Wood, *Black Majority: Negroes in Colonial South Carolina from 1670 through the Stono Rebellion* [New York, 1975], chap. 3) and although nearly every history of the early settlements of southern colonies—from Virginia to Barbados—has emphasized the "seasoning" process that European settlers endured, few have studied acclimatized, creole populations in English-speaking America. One exception is Jo Ann Carrigan, "Privilege, Prejudice, and the Strangers' Disease in Nineteenth-Century New Orleans," *Jour. So. Hist.,* XXXVI (1970), 568–578; and "Yellow Fever: Scourge of the South," in Todd L. Savitt and James Harvey Young, eds., *Disease and Distinctiveness in the American South* (Knoxville, Tenn., 1988), 55–78, though these works emphasize New Orleans and the 19th century.

3. On the process of seasoning, see John Duffy, "Eighteenth-Century Carolina Health Conditions," *Jour. So. Hist.,* XVIII (1952), 289–309; H. Roy Merrens and George D. Terry, "Dying in Paradise: Malaria, Mortality, and the Perceptual Environment in Colonial South Carolina," *Jour. So. Hist.,* L (1984), 544–550; Gerald L. Cates, "'The Seasoning': Disease and Death among the First Colonists of Georgia," *GHQ,* LXIV (1980), 146–158; John Duffy, "The Impact of Malaria on the South," in Savitt and Young, eds., *Disease and Distinctiveness,* 29–38. On disease and culture, see Susan Sontag, *Illness as Metaphor* (New York, 1978); James O. Breeden, "Disease as a Factor in Southern Distinctiveness," in Savitt and Young, eds., *Disease and Distinctiveness,* 1–21. On the medical profession and the constant preoccupation with health in South Carolina, see Diane Meredith Sydenham, "Practitioner and Patient: The Practice of Medicine in Eighteenth-Century South Carolina" (Ph.D. diss., Johns Hopkins University, 1979).

quarantine ships in hopes of containing fevers as they did for a malady like smallpox.[4] In this respect, they were in the mainstream of an early modern revival of Hippocratic notions about how diseases were specific to particular physical environments and about how the human body or constitution adapted to these specific environments. In the case of fevers, so-called miasmatic environments were particularly suspect, because the invisible vapors from them carried infection to humans. The countryside harbored miasma that gave people malaria, and urban environments nurtured yellow fever. In other parts of the world, a standard preventive for location-specific maladies was avoidance of infectious environments, but whites in the Lower South thought this an unnecessary reaction. They believed that routine medication could prevent most debilitating incidents of malaria and that acquired immunity to yellow fever could prevent most fatal bouts of the disease.[5]

Whites maintained that they could become resistant to malaria, which was to a certain degree true. Malaria affects human victims in recurrent cycles of infection. New infections arise when the mosquito population is abundant enough to transfer at least one of three types of malaria parasites to nearby humans. Unless one has inherited resistance to the disease, one will either die or produce enough antibodies to fight the malarial plasmodium. Individuals suffer from alternate episodes of fever and chills during this stage; even if a person survives the first bout, the parasite can reinvade blood cells and liver several times until immunity builds. *Plasmodium falciparum* tends to cause death in all but a few victims; *Pl. vivax* and *Pl. malariae* are milder, and the latter can continue to plague an infected human for up to thirty years. Two cycles of infection thus occur: between the insect and human populations at large, and within each invaded host.[6] Though observers in the Lower South

4. See Joseph Ioor Waring, *A History of Medicine in South Carolina, 1670–1825* ([Columbia, S.C.], 1964), 55–57, 71n, 130, 214. See also Charles Cotesworth Pinckney's statement about yellow fever ("There is nothing contagious in the disorder") in Pinckney to "Mr. De Villers," Sept. 29, 1817, Pinckney Family Papers, series 38-11-4, SCHS.

5. On environmental views of disease, see Gilbert Chinard, "Eighteenth Century Theories on America as a Human Habitat," American Philosophical Society, *Proceedings,* XCI (1947), 27–57; James C. Riley, *The Eighteenth-Century Campaign to Avoid Disease* (New York, 1987), chaps. 1, 5. For an application of this view to malaria in the Lower South, see Nathaniel H. Rhodes, "Observations on the General Doctrine of Fevers," 1800, SCL.

6. For discussions of malaria, see Macfarlane Burnet, *Natural History of Infectious Disease,* 3d ed. (Cambridge, 1962), 342–345; Todd L. Savitt, *Medicine and Slavery: The*

were unaware that mosquitoes acted as vectors between miasmal swamps and people (they used mosquito netting for comfort, not health) and did not understand the internal cycle of infection within each patient, they nonetheless gave an interesting and coherent explanation of the disease. They saw that infected individuals who did not die continued to suffer from the malady, but that each bout had reduced virulence. It seemed that survivors became seasoned against intermittent fevers though never immune to them. Whites needed, then, to prevent initial attacks from becoming fatal ones and to minimize the effects of each intermittent attack.

Toward this end, whites used cinchona bark. Variously called jesuit's, peruvian, or fever bark, cinchona contained (as doctors in the late nineteenth century would discover) quinine, an antifebrile agent that also acted as a prophylaxis against malaria—indeed, whites tended to use it against all fevers. During the warm months, whites routinely chewed bark or dosed themselves with extract of bark in liquids like rum, fruit juice, or milk or mashed up with onion or garlic to mask quinine's bitter taste. They often used an emetic like ipecac before taking bark to make it work faster. Ann Manigault recorded in July 1755 that her son had a fever that "abated by taking bark." In the fall of 1780, Charles Cotesworth Pinckney did some plantation business in the country and confessed to his mother, "I was last Sunday again attacked with the Fever, and shall be obliged to you to send me three ounces of Bark in half ounce papers that I may again follow Dr. [Alexander] Garden's prescription." Pinckney later resolved to take bark regularly until a severe frost ended the sickly season. Whites emphasized that they had only themselves to blame if they failed to take medicine, thus leaving themselves prey to illness and debility. David Ramsay cautioned all South Carolinians that "the daily use of jesuit's bark, from July till October, is advisable." Alice Izard wrote her daughter that one family member contracted a fever "from want of attention in taking preventive medicines." Henry Laurens resignedly explained to an English friend that during the summer he was necessarily employed with "the alternate Exercise of Fever and Barke," and in 1812, Peter Horry related that he

---

Diseases and Health Care of Blacks in Antebellum Virginia (Urbana, Ill., 1978), 18–20; Richard B. Sheridan, *Doctors and Slaves: A Medical and Demographic History of Slavery in the British West Indies, 1680–1834* (Cambridge, 1985), 9–10. Cf. Darrett B. Rutman and Anita H. Rutman, "Of Agues and Fevers: Malaria in the Early Chesapeake," *WMQ*, 3d Ser., XXXIII (1976), 31–60.

downed a dose of bark before he went to bed at night. In 1814, Mary McDonald admonished her husband that, in cases of malaria, "a good bolus of Bark 2 or 3 times a day is a good preservative and preventative."[7]

Although whites believed that malaria was controllable or even avoidable, and therefore no insurmountable impediment to plantation management or general activity, they conceded that they sometimes needed to be cautious in exposing themselves to disease. *Too* much time spent in the country, they thought, was an open invitation to illness, foolhardy for members of a class that used overseers and slaves to operate plantations. Edward Rutledge reproached himself in 1790, admitting, "Anxious to attend to my Cotton, I ventured too frequently into the Country which brought on a severe fever." In 1778, Eliza Lucas Pinckney warned her son-in-law that "people in general think it wrong" that he was "staying in the Country." His neighbors had "apprehensions of sickness," and should he fall ill, he "would be blamed" for his carelessness.[8] These statements indicated a class difference in reactions to malaria. Overseers and poorer whites, clearly, could not flee the countryside as easily as members of the planter elite. Some precautions were luxuries beyond

7. Mabel L. Webber, ed., "Extracts from the Journal of Mrs. Ann Manigault, 1754–1781," *SCHM*, XX (1919), 60; C. C. Pinckney to Eliza Lucas Pinckney, Sept. 6, 14, 1780, Pinckney Family Papers, box 4, series 1, LC; David Ramsay, *A Dissertation on the Means of Preserving Health in Charleston and the Adjacent Low Country* (Charleston, S.C., 1790), 25; Alice Izard to Mrs. Manigault, Oct. 5, 1814, Ralph Izard Papers, box 3, folder 26, SCL; Philip M. Hamer *et al.*, eds., *The Papers of Henry Laurens* (Columbia, S.C., 1968–), VII, 333; A. S. Salley, ed., "Journal of General Peter Horry," *SCHM*, XXXIX (1938), 125; Mary to Charles McDonald, Sept. 30, 1814, McDonald-Lawrence Papers, folder 10, Isabel P. Lawrence Collection, GHS.

On contemporary understanding of the properties of the cinchona bark, see Rhodes, "Observations on the General Doctrine of Fevers," SCL. For samples of fever recipes, see Charles to Henrietta Drayton, Oct. 3, 1795, Drayton Collection, box 1-A, folder 3, Middleton Place Manuscripts, SCL; Alexander Keith's Commonplace Book, p. 1, SCL; Harriott Horry's Recipe Book, 1770, Pinckney Family Papers, series 38-19, SCHS; Charles Cotesworth Pinckney to Eliza Lucas Pinckney, Nov. 28, 30, Dec. 1, 1780, Pinckney Family Papers, series 1, box 4, LC.

8. Edward Rutledge to Phineas Miller, Aug. 24, 1790, Edward Rutledge Papers, section A, Duke; Eliza Lucas Pinckney to Daniel Horry, Mar. 9, 1768, Pinckney Family Papers, microfiche 38-2-1, SCHS. On absenteeism, see also Carl Bridenbaugh, "Charlestonians at Newport, 1767–1775," *SCHM*, XLI (1940), 43–47.

the reach of many residents, and, while the elite removed themselves from the worst dangers, the poor stayed behind to face them armed only with their acquired resistance and a good bolus of bark.

Though residents may have thought total avoidance of the fever-laden countryside unnecessary, they did take pains to remove pregnant women—who were especially susceptible to malaria and prone to miscarry while fevered—from country plantations during the summer. Richard Hutson warned Isaac Hayne that his pregnant sister was very "liable to the Fever" and should repair to the city until winter. Thomas Pinckney likewise worried to his sister, Harriott Horry, in May 1778: "I am uneasy at the thought of your remaining in the Fever and Ague Swamps of Santee in your Situation, after the End of this month." Whites constructed, therefore, a balance of activity and caution, in which the healthy did not need to fear reasonable exposure to sickly swamps so long as they routinely dosed themselves, whereas the weak needed to avoid them altogether.[9] Their response to malaria showed how they regarded it as an occasionally fatal and always irritating feature of local life, but not a crushing difficulty.

Yellow fever was more difficult. Reaction to this disease, more than to malaria, showed distinct characteristics of this region: though many parts of America harbored malaria and had similar responses to it, only cities suffered from yellow fever, and only cities in the Deep South had to brace themselves against almost annual assaults of the malady. Yellow fever seemed to inflict more deaths than malaria and therefore seemed a more serious problem in areas it visited. Yet survivors of yellow fever could become immune to any future episode of the disease, as was not the case with malarial parasites, which lingered on in their hosts. (Unless they die, victims of the yellow fever virus acquire antibodies that render them resistant to future attacks.)[10] Whites

9. On the effect of malaria on pregnant women, see Rutman and Rutman, "Of Agues and Fevers," *WMQ*, 3d Ser., XXXIII (1976), 52. Richard Hutson to Isaac Hayne, May 27, 1776, Richard Hutson Letters, Charles Woodward Hutson Collection, SHC; Thomas Pinckney to Harriott Horry, May 28, 1778, Pinckney Family Papers, series 1, box 6, folder 1, LC.

10. Burnet, *Infectious Disease*, 112–113, 352–353, 354. The higher mortality of yellow fever was widely assumed among early Americans, who failed to perceive that malaria had a higher rate of fatalities than yellow fever. The latter disease killed large numbers outright, but malaria killed even more by generally weakening many people and leaving them prey to other infections, which were then blamed as the cause of death, rather than the initial malarial infection. Nevertheless, the dramatic and epidemic

concluded that acclimatization to yellow fever, especially during childhood, protected a person from the ravages of disease and was a badge indicating regional identity; anyone who was residentially loyal gained an unusual physical ability that protected against a fatal disease. Residents set up a parallel between acclimatization and acculturation: only cultural outsiders fell easy victim to yellow fever—the visiting strangers who ridiculed locals were very likely to contract yellow fever in the city (and malaria in the country) while acclimatized residents escaped the worst consequences of these maladies. John Lloyd explained of an "epidemic" fever in Charleston in 1796 that it had "proved very fatal to new-comers." Henry William DeSaussure wrote Ezekiel Pickens in August 1804 that in Charleston "some few cases of yellow fever afflict and destroy Strangers—But no Epidemic prevails among our citizens." A year later, DeSaussure wrote Pickens that, while the yellow fever again attacked strangers, it passed "by the settled or acclimatized residents."[11]

Childhood was the phase of life in which individuals became acclimatized with least risk of death. (Children under the age of fourteen survive yellow fever, and many other diseases, much more frequently than adults.) Whites recognized that children went through this phase of adaptation and that youngsters were more liable to get, and survive, yellow fever. One woman recorded that in fall of 1799 the malady affected numbers of "young Country people who were not accustomed to the Town," though she seemed to believe most of them would recover. Her reference to custom, a gradual accretion of characteristics over a long period, was well chosen. Whites did not necessarily believe that resistance to yellow fever resulted from one critical bout with the disease, as was the case with something like smallpox. Immunity related to a single illness was hard to detect because people (especially children) could have yellow fever without displaying dramatic symptoms and because other dis-

---

nature of yellow fever convinced contemporary observers that it was the worse malady. See John Duffy, *Epidemics in Colonial America* (Baton Rouge, La., 1953), 214, 237–238. One characteristic assessment of the relative dangers of the fevers appears in Thomas Pinckney's advice to his sister, Harriott Pinckney Horry: "If you did not come to Town by a certain time you had better continue in the Country all the Autumn"—better to risk malaria, in other words, than yellow fever (Pinckney to Horry, Aug. 31, 1789, Pinckney Family Papers, series 1, box 8, folder 1, LC).

11. John Lloyd to Jane Champion, Sept. 28, 1796, John Lloyd Letterbook, SCL; H. W. DeSaussure to Ezekiel Pickens, Aug. 22, 1804, Oct. 27, 1805, Henry William DeSaussure Papers, SCL.

eases like malaria and dengue fever could be confused with it. An observer would not always know when a child got the critical fever, but might assume that an adult who had grown up in the lowcountry was immune. Whites concluded that only prolonged exposure to the locality delivered resistance to yellow fever and that all of a person's youth might be needed to guarantee this. Gradual adaptation to their region—to its notorious heat, humidity, miasma— slowly modified a person's constitution and made it resistant to local fever. Alice Izard wrote in 1801 "that the disorder attacks the young, and vigorous," yet "seldom commits any ravages on any subject past 40." Agreeing that advanced age signified ability to withstand yellow fever, Mary Izard assured a friend that she did not fear to go to Charleston during the summer, because she was "too old for the yellow fever." Long-settled residents thus conceived of themselves as physically stronger than either their children or their visitors, as uniquely adapted to their region.[12]

Whites nonetheless believed that only continued residence in the region maintained the beneficial alteration in the fibers of their constitutions— mobility weakened health. When he visited Italy in 1788, John Rutledge, Jr., observed that because migrants rather than residents worked in Italian rice fields, "they do not become (as we term it in C[arolina]) season'd." French naturalist François André Michaux discovered that "persons who leave Charleston" were "much more susceptible of catching [yellow fever] than those who staid at home." Physician David Ramsay cautioned native-born absentees, as well as strangers, to journey to South Carolina in November so they would have "at least half a year to be assimilated to the climate." Frederick Rutledge reasserted the connection between social identity and acquired immunity when he warned his absent brother not to return in September, "as the yellow fever (which rages in Charleston) may treat you as a stranger if you go there too early."[13]

12. Jane Ball to John Ball, Jr., Aug. 28, 1799, Ball Family Papers, series 516-11, SCHS; Alice Izard to Mrs. Gabriel Manigault, Aug. 31, 1801, Manigault Family Papers, box 3, folder 30, SCL; Mary Izard to "Mrs. Gen'l Pinckney," June 29, n.y., Robert Francis Withers Allston Collection, series 12-21-17, SCHS. On youth and yellow fever, see Burnet, *Infectious Disease,* 354.

13. 1788 Journal, John Rutledge, Jr., Papers, cabinet 24, Duke; François André Michaux, *Travels to the West of the Alleghany Mountains . . . in the Year 1802,* in Reuben Gold Thwaites, ed., *Early Western Travels, 1748–1846,* III (Cleveland, Ohio, 1904), 118– 119; Ramsay, *Dissertation,* 30; Frederick to John Rutledge, Sept. 22, 1804, John Rutledge Papers, folder 18, SHC.

The problem of peregrination was critical for children: if they lost early contact with their native region, the results might be disastrous. Thomas Legare iterated this concern when he wrote Jedidiah Morse that his nephew feared spending too much time in study at Yale College. Legare's nephew's "greatest dread seems to be his staying so long as to make his return hazardous as respects an Indemic bilious fever." Seth Lothrop recounted a cautionary tale in which two young and unassimilated South Carolinians died of yellow fever when a hurricane devastated Sullivan's Island and forced vacationing absentees to return to Charleston during the early autumn. Both Elizabeth and James Courtney immediately caught yellow fever, and James died because—Lothrop wrote ominously—"neither of them has ever resided in the City during the Summer months." Echoing the fear that an absentee juvenile risked a stranger's death, Henry William DeSaussure lamented that the Colhoun family's children were at school in Newport, Rhode Island. Their absence was "alienating ... [them] so compleatly from the climate and the habits of their country" that it would be difficult for them to return. Young whites had the duty of remaining in contact with their home despite its endemic dangers, as John Ball, Sr., made clear to his son attending Harvard. When yellow fever swept through Boston in 1798, Ball warned his heir to get out of town: "As you are only a student [there] for 4 years, you are not bound by any tie to risk your life, as might be the case were you here among your relations."[14]

Ball was not so much concerned that his son never die of yellow fever as he was that his child not die in a strange environment—better to risk assimilation at home (with the possibility of continued activity in one's native land) than needlessly die from an alien form of the malady. Ball made explicit his synthesis of ideas about disease, duty, and cultural identity by warning his distant son that, even if preserved from an epidemic, he was "in danger of imbibing principles in the Eastern States that will be against the interest of the Southern States, tending to the ruin of your own family and fortune."[15] If John,

14. Thomas Legare to Jedidiah Morse, Aug. 24, 1811, Thomas Legare Papers, section A, Duke; Seth Lothrop to Sylvanus Keith, Sept. 23, 1804, Sylvanus and Cary Keith Papers, folder 1, cabinet 78, Duke; DeSaussure to Ezekiel Pickens, Dec. 1, 1805, DeSaussure Papers, SCL; John Ball, Sr., to John Ball, Jr., Aug. 27, 1798, Ball Family Papers, series 516-10, SCHS.

15. John Ball, Sr., to John Ball, Jr., Sept. 24, 1799, Ball Family Papers, series 516-10, SCHS. Some parents had to decide whether to let a particularly sickly child keep away from the Lower South. George Jones sent his son Noble Jones away to school in the North, explaining to him: "You had previously suffered so many and such severe

Jr., returned from Harvard with his physical constitution and mode of thought altered—especially, as the senior Ball implied, on the subject of slavery—he risked physical and social death within his own society. This was what Henry Laurens had feared for his firebrand son, John, who proposed to extirpate slavery and therefore courted ostracism and disgrace. The dire need firmly to fix humans to the region helps explain why parents believed acclimatization took up much of childhood and youth; like acculturation, it could be achieved only by gradual and prolonged exposure to the local environment and culture.

The idea that they could become seasoned against endemic fevers gave whites in the Lower South an exclusive definition of themselves. It provided those who lived in the swampy lowcountry, particularly, a sense of unique identity. (Throughout the United States, a comparable reaction to yellow fever probably occurred only in New Orleans.) The whole coastline was prone to malaria, as were areas along rivers. In addition, cities near waterways (including Georgetown and Augusta, but especially Charleston and Savannah) harbored yellow fever. Only the upcountry region of South Carolina escaped serious threat, meaning that, for the moment, its residents were strangers to the lowcountry. Dr. John Lining of South Carolina explained that yellow fever afflicted "country people when they came to town." François André Michaux also observed that, like "foreigners," the "natives of Upper Carolina" could easily succumb to yellow fever. But by the end of the eighteenth century, residents saw that malaria had infiltrated the previously healthy upcountry; safety from fevers receded as population expanded. To make matters worse, yellow fever also traveled inward. The *Aëdes aegypti* mosquito, yellow fever's vector, is semidomesticated, in that it prefers to lay eggs in a source of water with an artificial bottom (like a gourd or barrel) rather than a natural one. It devotedly trailed after white invaders, spreading the span of infection over a larger region.[16]

Upcountry settlers and (by the 1800s) their progeny began to notice that

---

attacks of disease, as to render it almost certain that I must part with you forever, unless I pursued this Course." George to Noble W. Jones, June 25, 1807, Jones Family Papers, folder 4, GHS.

16. John Lining, "A Description of the *American* Yellow Fever . . . ," Dec. 14, 1753, *Essays and Observations Physical and Literary*, II (Edinburgh, 1756), 407; Michaux, *Travels*, in Thwaites, ed., *Travels*, III, 118–119; Waring, *Medicine in S.C.*, 147, 285; Duffy, "Impact of Malaria," in Savitt and Young, eds., *Disease and Distinctiveness*, 39. On *Aëdes aegypti*, see William H. McNeill, *Plagues and Peoples* (New York, 1976), 213.

they had cultivated maladies along with crops—in 1800, when John Bedingfield sent the latest cotton prices to Thomas Carr in inland Georgia, he also posted a packet of cinchona bark. As early as 1794, Camden merchants stocked bark in both powder and liquid form. In 1798, John Chesnut expressed concern over the sickliness of the areas around Columbia, Camden, and Kershaw. Two upcountry residents of South Carolina complained that "the upper country has grown more sickly since it became more cleared" and populated—an unforeseen consequence of displacing an aboriginal population that had seen little reason to clear its land and increase its numbers. New diseases included "not only bilious fevers in their various grades from the mild intermittent to a grade nearly approximating to yellow fever, but also other various forms of disease," possibly infections resulting from a denser human population in the upcountry. Observers hoped that this was temporary, claiming that in "the oldest and most highly cultivated settlements" longevity was enhanced. But this was little consolation to settlers putting down stakes along the frontier, who had a period of greater risk ahead of them. (Spread of disease also challenged the Enlightenment belief that human cultivation improved nature.)[17]

Yet any white with a hardy constitution (especially if young) might successfully run the risk of assimilation and become an honorary native. In this regard, residents not only acknowledged the distinction between native and stranger but suggested a process for its obliteration. David Ramsay, who so confidently bestowed medical advice on natives, was himself a relocated and acclimatized Pennsylvanian. Newcomers understood that they would get fevers until they were seasoned. Scotsman James Steuart, who settled in Charleston, reassured his father in 1751 that, although he "had Severall fitts of intermitting fevers" on his arrival, "the Bark always cures" them. Not everyone was so lucky; another Scot, named William Murray, lamented how "there is Something in the Climate of Carolina which don't Suit my Constitution" and suffered without cure. Reuben King, a New Englander who pioneered in lower Georgia, underwent heroic bouts with various fevers. King's encounter with disease revealed an interesting pattern of community support among whites in

17. Bedingfield to Carr, Feb. 15, 1800, Carr Collection, box 3, folder 26, UGA; entry for Aug. 7, 1794, Camden Account Book, microfilm R474, SCL; John Chesnut to Mrs. Sarah Taylor, Sept. 20, 1798, Williams-Chesnut-Manning Papers, box 1, SCL; Reports of "Mr. Anthony Park and Dr. Davis," in David Ramsay, *History of South-Carolina, from Its First Settlement in 1670 to the Year 1808* . . . (Charleston, S.C., 1809), II, appendix, 600 (quotation).

this frontier, cotton-growing region. Once when King was very ill in 1805, a Major Hopkins took him into his home, where Mrs. Hopkins nursed him. In July of the same year, King went to take care of the neighboring Stuarts, laying out the man who had just died and staying to nurse the widow. King finally acquired some resistance and learned to mix effective doses of bark; he then got on with his tasks of building a community and making money.[18]

The arduous process by which a migrant became a successful resident could partly explain how it was that some immigrants were the most ardent defenders of their region. David Ramsay became a fixture of lowcountry society, a reliable Fourth of July orator, local booster, historian of South Carolina, and hagiographer of its leading citizens. Timothy Ford, so free with stinging criticisms of South Carolina when he had first moved from New Jersey in 1785 (he clearly relished the role of external observer), later married into the local elite and entered politics. In 1794, Ford defended the interests of the lowcountry against upcountry arrivistes by, rather incredibly, complaining that the latter were "strangers to *our* interests, *our* customs and *our* concerns."[19] Ford had made a strange personal journey, within less than a decade, but one that revealed how whites visualized themselves within a process of adaptation that turned hardy and willing outsiders into settled and successful insiders.

Whites even believed that, such was their creole harmony with their climate, they had replaced Indians as the region's proper natives. By the eighteenth century, Indian susceptibility to diseases carried by whites had resulted in catastrophic demographic decline. To whites, this tendency increased the likelihood that Indian nations would "retire and dwindle" before white expansion and commercialization of the land. (Such was Indians' own fear of contact with the disease culture of colonization that, when Cherokee prisoners

18. James to John Steuart, Aug. 15, 1751, Steuart of Dalguise Muniments, bundle 2/8, item 65, GD.38, SRO; William to John Murray, June 25, 1765, Murray of Murraythwaite Muniments, bundle 288, item 17, GD.219, SRO; Virginia Steele Wood and Ralph Van Wood, eds., "The Reuben King Journal, 1800–1806," *GHQ*, L (1966), 300–301, 304 (on how King settled into Georgia), LI (1967), 104, 108 (on support among settlers).

19. On Ford's background, see Joseph W. Barnwell, ed., "Diary of Timothy Ford, 1785–1786," *SCHM*, XIII (1912), 132–147, 181–204. The first quotation (my emphasis) is from the pseudonymous Americanus, *The Constitutionalist* . . . (Charleston, S.C., 1794), 25, in which Ford was replying to Appius [Robert Goodloe Harper], *An Address to the People of South-Carolina* . . . (Charleston, S.C., 1794).

returned from white captivity, they were stripped, washed, and quarantined for eight days.)[20] The two-edged ideal that coastal denizens had of themselves, as actual natives and as adapted natives, would come under fire when new, inland settlers—the pesky "strangers" Ford derided—demanded recognition as equals. Newcomers' desire to be considered members of the club followed coastal residents' logic about how whites had taken over Indian claims to the region, but questioned their hostility toward newly arrived and seemingly strange whites.

This loyalty to the region, its fierceness, also helps peel back a layer of strained cheerfulness that masked fear. Mary Izard's brave statement about yellow fever—"*I* am not at all afraid of the Town"—suggested that others were. And for good reason. In the early years of colonization, the death rate in the South Carolina lowcountry had exceeded that of the mother country; in later years it would still be higher than in the less-fevered upcountry.[21] The debilitating summer months that brought fevers were mostly to blame. During the first half of the eighteenth century, 77 percent of residents of Christ Church Parish who died before the age of twenty did so from August through November. David Ramsay reported that Charleston averaged five to eight funerals a day in the blighted August of 1799 and that the summer's mortality list numbered 362 persons (239 of whom were reputedly mere "strangers") from a population slightly over 16,000. Although there was a remedy for malaria, there was none for yellow fever, despite hopeful experiments with quinine and mercury. Doctors offered little or no comfort during epidemics. One doctor lamented how yellow fever "appalls the heart of the boldest physician," and another despairingly confessed, "I wish no person would send for me . . . for let me do as I will[,] puke, purge or bleed still they all die."[22]

20. The quotation is from Benjamin Lincoln Papers, pp. 147–148, UGA. On the Cherokee, see Thomas Griffiths Diary, p. 22, SHC.

21. Quotation from Mary Izard to "Mrs. Gen'l Pinckney," June 29, n.y., Robert Francis Withers Allston Collection, series 12-21-17, SCHS. On the high death rate, see Peter A. Coclanis, *The Shadow of a Dream: Economic Life and Death in the South Carolina Low Country, 1670–1920* (New York, 1989), 42–43, 166–174; and Mark D. Kaplanoff, "Making the South Solid: Politics and the Structure of Society in South Carolina, 1790–1815" (Ph.D. diss., University of Cambridge, 1979), 29–31.

22. Merrens and Terry, "Dying in Paradise," *Jour. So. Hist.*, L (1984), 542; Ramsay cited in Waring, *Medicine in S.C.*, 113, 115; Frederick Dalcho, "An Oration Delivered

To a certain extent, whites' stubborn optimism over their prospects for survival was realistic, reflecting a rough understanding of the advantages of acquired resistance and recognizing a dramatic drop in the mortality rate during the second half of the eighteenth century as the truly abysmal conditions of an earlier period of settlement settled down.[23] They were right: the population was becoming seasoned. But they were also whistling in the graveyard, trying to buck themselves up by emphasizing the few bright features of the local disease culture over the prevailing illness and death. In a sense, residents crafted a shared identity not only because of their acquired immunity but because of their common apprehension, their shared mixture of hope and denial. But actual death rate is not so much at issue here as is cultural interpretation of the threat of death and debility. External observers claimed that the physical environment of the Lower South sucked the vitality out of survivors. The survivors themselves, however, refused to believe they had to knuckle under and kept issuing reminders of the activities necessary for continued survival.

One sign of this nervous energy was a continual effort to reduce the virulence of endemic disease. Whites, though convinced fevers were a permanent part of local life, believed that the effects of disease could be softened if the region and its people were in the best possible condition: land needed improvement, people needed temperance and hygiene. In this regard, residents followed larger trends in United States medicine that emphasized both regional variation *and* a nationalistic impulse to improve the citizens' health through individual and civic discipline—a sort of federal medical theory that celebrated both the state and the larger Republic. Dr. Benjamin Rush, professor of medicine at the University of Pennsylvania from 1789 to 1813, was the main proponent of this theory and trained several noted physicians in the Lower South. One of his students, David Ramsay, championed local improvement; he wanted to see bogs and ponds drained, Charleston streets cleaned,

---

before the Medical Society of South Carolina . . . ," *Philadelphia Medical Museum,* III (1807), 131; Alexander Baron to Benjamin Rush, Oct. 11, 1794, Rush Manuscripts, Library Company of Philadelphia (Dalcho and Baron cited in Waring, *Medicine in S.C.,* 130n, 178).

23. On improved rates of survival, see George D. Terry, " 'Champaign Country': A Social History of an Eighteenth-Century Lowcountry Parish in South Carolina, St. Johns Berkeley County" (Ph.D. diss., University of South Carolina–Columbia, 1981), 95–99.

and citizens in a clean and sober condition. He recommended a stringent "medical police of cities" and claimed that "industry and temperance" had already improved the health of post-Revolutionary South Carolinians. Similarly, Dr. J. E. White constructed a "medical topography" of the area around Savannah for the better understanding of its faults and of the "intimate union" between place and person.[24]

Whites assumed, therefore, that they were deeply connected to their environment, but not slaves of it; the region altered them, but they were themselves busy altering it, hoping thereby to reach some sort of equilibrium between their human constitutions and the natural constitution of the area. Whites' efforts to improve the medical topography accompanied reforms in other parts of their society. Furthermore, their fascination with the natural world around them and their celebration of all its characteristics (even the dangerous ones) paralleled the region's fame for natural history. Since the early eighteenth century, the Lower South's flora and fauna had attracted attention from naturalists throughout the world, and some residents had become prominent natural historians in their own right. Local doctors had always been active in studies of nature, and their analysis of endemic disease inserted a morbid typology into a regional natural history that could include fevers along with alligators, palmettos, and Cherokee herbal remedies.[25] In any case, the

24. Ramsay, *A Review of the Improvements, Progress, and State of Medicine in the Eighteenth Century* (Charleston, S.C., [1801]), 33, 46–47; Ramsay to Benjamin Rush, Aug. 6, 1786, Library Company, Philadelphia (cited in Waring, *Medicine in S.C.*, 287); J[oshua] E[lder] White, "Topography of Savannah and Its Vicinity: A Report to the Georgia Medical Society, May 3, 1806," *GHQ*, I (1917), 237, 239. See also Ramsay's claims that the "intemperate" were susceptible to yellow fever in his *Sketch of the Soil, Climate, Weather, and Diseases of South-Carolina* (Charleston, S.C., 1796); and in Waring, *Medicine in S.C.*, 293. On Rush's influence, see John Harley Warner, "The Idea of Southern Medical Distinctiveness: Medical Knowledge and Practice in the Old South," in Ronald L. Numbers and Todd L. Savitt, eds., *Science and Medicine in the Old South* (Baton Rouge, La., 1989), 190–194. On Ramsay's education, see Arthur H. Shaffer, *To Be an American: David Ramsay and the Making of the American Consciousness* (Columbia, S.C., 1991), chap. 3.

25. On natural history in the region, see G. Edmund Gifford, Jr., "The Charleston Physician-Naturalists," *Bulletin of the History of Medicine*, XLIX (1975), 556–574; Ronald L. Numbers and Janet S. Numbers, "Science in the Old South: A Reappraisal," *Jour. So. Hist.*, XLVIII (1982), 163–184; Joseph Ewan, "The Growth of Learned and Scientific Societies in the Southeastern United States to 1860," in Alexandra Oleson and San-

threat of disease had an effect on local whites opposite to that which travelers expected: it increased opportunities for civic improvement, individual exertion, and intellectual speculation. Instead of making them feel weak, fevers made white survivors feel as if they had triumphed over physical danger.

❧ Duties and Improvements

The better to defend against climate-induced torpor, whites formulated an ethic of industriousness. They felt that activity in and control over the natural environment not only made it healthier but fulfilled a human duty to exploit resources for individual and societal betterment, an assumption founded on centuries of Western ideology about domination of nature—usually a nature anthropomorphized in female terms. David Ramsay lectured a Fourth of July audience in 1778 that Americans should "improve the rough face of Nature" so that, eventually, "gay fields adorned with the yellow robes of ripening harvest, will smile in the remotest depth of our western frontiers, where impassable forests now frown over the uncultivated earth." John Drayton warned of the necessity of constantly maintaining control over nature. "Withold the hand of cultivation," he wrote, "and nature immediately causes weeds and plants to spring up again; and, in course of time, covers them with her dark retreats." Nature's "dark" and "frowning" countenance was thus a constant admonition to people to keep imposing a human order over the world through unflagging activity.[26]

---

born C. Brown, eds., *The Pursuit of Knowledge in the Early American Republic: American Scientific and Learned Societies from Colonial Times to the Civil War* (Baltimore, 1976), 208–218; Raymond Phineas Stearns, *Science in the British Colonies of America* (Urbana, Ill., 1970), 293–336, 593–619; Brooke Hindle, *The Pursuit of Science in Revolutionary America, 1735–1789* (Chapel Hill, N.C., 1956), 37–38, 51–54; John C. Greene, *American Science in the Age of Jefferson* (Ames, Iowa, 1984), 107–115; Richard Beale Davis, *Intellectual Life in the Colonial South, 1585–1763* (Knoxville, Tenn., 1978), II, 859–865, 886–887; James H. Cassedy, "Medical Men and the Ecology of the Old South," in Numbers and Savitt, eds., *Science and Medicine*, 166–178. See also the biographical entries for Stephen Elliott, Alexander Garden, David Ramsay, and John Lewis Edward Whitridge Shecut in Waring, *Medicine in S.C.* I am indebted to John Harley Warner for pointing out the connection between disease and natural history.

26. David Ramsay, "An Oration on the Advantages of American Independence" (1778), ed. Robert L. Brunhouse, American Philosophical Society, *Transactions*, N.S.,

Fearing that a deleterious climate and a culture of wealth would prevent future generations from perceiving their duty, whites were careful to ensure that their children did not learn bad habits of lassitude and self-indulgence. This concern was common to modernizing societies in America and Europe; residents of the Lower South simply adopted, with some modification, a language of middle-class duty. Georgian Seaborn Jones, guardian of his nephew William Hart (whose father had died), told the boy to pay close attention to his lessons, fearing he was "unconquerably addicted to *idleness, play* and *obstinacy.*" Striving to impress a work ethic on young William, Jones told him he had "lost much precious time, and what makes it still worse, it can by no exertions be regained." When the boy's mother died two years later, Jones gave William dire warnings that he now more than ever needed to improve himself, as Jones, his only supporting adult, might "be deprived of the means or inclination of taking care of you." He advised William to double his "diligence to finish" school and be ready to "enter into some kind of business" to support himself rather than expect to live on the industry and charity of others.[27]

Although other whites may not have been as remorseless about teaching children a work ethic, they nonetheless believed a proper education and habits of diligence were necessary for all children. In 1810, Thomas Couper wrote his sister Ann that their mother approved Ann's plan to spend the summer studying in Charleston, "which she well knows must arise from your desire of improvement." Henry Laurens expressed concern that his children learn practical skills along with their more cerebral education. He wrote his daughter Martha: "I have recollected your request for a pair of globes. . . . When you are measuring the surface of this world, remember you are to act a part on it, and think of a plumb pudding and other domestic duties." This balance between domestic skills and book learning was often emphasized to women who would become planters' wives and plantation mistresses. Laurens made this plan explicit when he reminded Martha that she needed to "learn to cut out and make up . . . a Piece of white or blue Woolen for her Negroes." Thomas Pinckney emphasized the other half of the balance to his sister Harriott. "Your

LV, pt. 4 (1965), 184, 188; John Drayton, *A View of South-Carolina, as Respects Her Natural and Civil Concerns* (Charleston, S.C., 1802), 149. On control of nature, see Carolyn Merchant, *The Death of Nature: Women, Ecology, and the Scientific Revolution* (San Francisco, Calif., 1980), esp. chap. 7.

27. Seaborn Jones to William Hart, Dec. 1, 1804, Nov. 29, 1806, Seaborn Jones Papers, folder 1, GHS.

Negro Cloaths must I think be done ere now," he observed late in 1777, "and you [must] set about some valueable researches into History, the Belles Lettres, Law, Phisic," and on into a comically epic list of studies. (Thomas also used his letters to quiz Harriott on her algebra.) Parents wanted their sons, too, prepared for plantation duties. John Ball, Sr., told his son John to acquire at college "some knowledge of Anatomy" as well as "Physic and Surgery" so that he could "afford some assistance to his negroes" when he inherited the family estate.[28]

Adults needed to keep practicing their youthful habits of industry and practicality in order to become productive members of a planting society. Their acquired skill allowed them to use the fruits of their fertile region to societal advantage. David Ramsay argued that "opportunities of enjoying and communicating happiness within the power of humane, good, and liberal planters are great." "Books, leisure to read, and every facility for philosophical experiments or agricultural projects," Ramsay declared, were, for planters, "all within their grasp." Pleading for attentiveness and innovation in planting, Lewis Du Pre hoped, "We may, in time, enjoy the same advantage which is enjoyed in all other agricultural countries, of having a regular and general system, by which agriculture, our most important interest, may be regulated."[29] These blandishments, though similar to statements made throughout the modern world, had a peculiarly regional object: lucrative plantation agriculture.

Energetic whites openly criticized stereotypical members of the planter class who needed prodding into a more energetic life. William Moultrie reproached a male Charlestonian because he led "the life of a lady, [and had] . . . nothing to do but dress . . . for God sake! come away and be in the country where you will have an opportunity of improving yourself in surveying, leveling, and measuring ground and learn something of the planting business." Along similar lines, but adopting a synthesis of Christian and secular demands that humans prove their use through labor, James Habersham complained that an "Idle man is the lumber of Creation and if it could be, I would almost say ought to be expelled

28. Thomas to Ann Couper, June 21, 1810, folder 1, Fraser-Couper Papers, GHS; Hamer *et al.,* eds., *Papers of Laurens,* IX, 457–458, VIII, 91; Thomas to Harriott Pinckney, Oct. 10, June 6 (for the concern with algebra), 1777, Pinckney Family Papers, series 1, box 6, folder 1, LC; John Ball, Sr., to John, Jr., Oct. 21, 1801, Ball Family Papers, series 516-13, SCHS.

29. Ramsay, *History of S.-C.,* II, 223; Lewis Du Pre, *Observations on the Culture of Cotton* (Georgetown, S.C., 1799), copy in the SCL.

[from] Society," rather than suffered to remain. Likewise annoyed with his brother-in-law's trifling life, Georgian Thomas Carr told him to cease "runing or riding through the woods after dogs" and to develop a modicum of "industry and perseverance." Alexander Garden did not bother to single out any particular culprit. He launched a general attack on "the gentlemen planters" of South Carolina, "who are absolutely above every occupation but eating, drinking, lolling, smoking and sleeping, which five modes of action constitute the essence of their life and existence."[30]

Whites would, conversely, mete out praise for individuals who undertook more vigorous modes of existence. Industriousness meshed with bourgeois notions of a stable and affective domestic life for women and men alike. Pleased to see all his kin busy, Thomas Pinckney gave his sister a glowing description of their family in 1778. "I imagine my Mother is very busy planting at Belomont," Pinckney wrote, "Sally taken up with her Brats at Gooseneck, Mr. Horry up to his knees in the [rice] Swamps, raising a fortune for the exporter, Mr. Daniel noting with all the little dirty Boys in Charlestown and your Ladyship knitting stockings or perhaps looking after your Poultry, salting your Bacon or making Soup and Candles." Pinckney deemed these all "sweet employments, and a lovely Group you form." This was all improbably homely, given the Pinckney family's wealth, but it was a revelatory insistence on how they *thought* they had a humble and useful life—even if some members of the family were raising a fortune out in the swamp. Deploring how Charleston's social whirl took men away from home and work, David Ramsay denounced the wastefulness of the Free and Easy Club's ostentatious dinners. The club's funds would be better laid out, Ramsay chided, on "establishments calculated to improve the condition of man indefinitely with the flow of ages."[31]

Shunning as they did frivolity and dedicating themselves to improving activities, energetic whites had a strong abhorrence of gambling. Ramsay boasted that his father-in-law, Henry Laurens, consented to play cards for money only if the company he kept insisted on it. "He so far conformed to

30. Undated letter fragment, William Moultrie Papers, box 3, folder 38, SCL; *The Letters of Hon. James Habersham* (GHS, *Collections*, VI [1904]), 69; Thomas Carr to John P. Bacon, 1799, Carr Collection, box 3, folder 25, UGA; Garden to John Ellis, Nov. 19, 1764, in Sir James Edward Smith, ed., *A Selection of the Correspondence of Linnaeus . . .* (London, 1821), I, 520.

31. Thomas Pinckney to Harriott Horry, May 28, 1778, Pinckney Family Papers, series 1, box 6, folder 1, LC; Ramsay, *History of S.-C.*, II, 554.

their humor as to play for money on a very moderate scale," Ramsay explained, "and in case of loss he promptly paid, but uniformly refused to receive what he won, esteeming it wrong to take any man's money without giving an equivalent." John Ball warned his son, away at college in 1800, to "take care never to gamble in any way whatever." Thomas Cumming wrote his sister Ann from South Carolina's Sweet Springs resort in the summer of 1803, "None of the gambling gentry have yet shewed themselves and we hope they will not soon." In September of the same year, Samuel Du Bose, Jr., visited another South Carolina resort and complained to his brother: "The gentlemen as heretofore play at cards every afternoon. I give the preference to the company of the ladies."[32]

Whites who criticized how the gambling gentry wasted their time and money did so because they believed their advantages should be used for social improvement: the wealth and leisure of plantation society should be used to better it. James Habersham declared in 1770, for instance, "I revere and esteem Men who act out of the narrow Sphere of Self, and communicate their Knowledge for usefull Improvements for the Public good." Four years later, Henry Laurens exclaimed, with his characteristic brew of didacticism and sentiment, "Oh! that my Sons may endeavour to be truly useful in their Generation, and dare to be Singular or among the unfashionable few, who are Still the Cement of Society and the Witnesses of Truth and Virtue." In 1815, following Habersham's and Laurens's mode of argument, William Johnson praised "the independent, enlightened agriculturalist" in his *Nugae Georgicae*. The *Monitor*, of Washington, Georgia, for the same year discussed Thomas Spalding's production of ninety-five hogsheads of sugar on Sapelo Island in a similarly approving tone. Its editorial stated, "The talents, industry and calculation of Mr. Spalding have awakened new schemes of wealth and independence for the planters of Georgia and South Carolina." But it pointed beyond Spalding's shining achievement toward the dimmer, outer circle of "other planters more cautious, [who] have waited for the issue of the experiment" of sugar planting before bestirring themselves to try it on their own estates.[33]

32. Ramsay, *History of S.-C.*, II, 484; John Ball, Sr., to John, Jr., Aug. 14, 1800, Ball Family Papers, series 516-12; SCHS; Thomas to Ann Cumming, July 8, 1803, Hammond, Bryan, Cumming Papers, box 1, folder 4, SCL; Sawyer Du Bose, Jr., to William Du Bose, Sept. 14, 1803, Samuel Du Bose, Jr., Letters, SHC.

33. *Letters of Habersham* (GHS, *Colls.*, VI [1904]), 92; Hamer *et al.*, eds., *Papers of Laurens*, IX, 226; William Johnson, *Nugae Georgicae: An Essay, Delivered to the Literary*

Some whites even complained outright that they had to act as guides for rich but lazy planters who never used their money and prestige to improve their society. Henry Laurens grumbled to an English friend in 1787: "You ask if any of my Neighbours tread in my Steps of Land improvements, I don't know, I hear them applaud those steps but in the End they call upon me for supplies of provisions. [T]he misfortune is they don't live upon their plantations, or are very lazy." Josiah Smith also predicted that plantations run by absentees would never "produce so much profit as those constantly under the Inspection of Proprietors who reside on the Spot, and at [the] same time are able Planters." When Jacob Read settled a South Carolina plantation and built a rice mill of an unusual design, he emphasized (with a touch of megalomania) that the mill was successful, but "by *my own* perseverance and Judgment; *against that of all the Machine Builders Planters,* and all others."[34]

Though whites who defined themselves as energetic lambasted "all others" for their lassitude, they also found that they had to struggle with themselves to keep up their self-imposed standards. Adolescent Eliza Lucas set herself a rigorous schedule of daily duties on her family's South Carolina plantation that would have won even Benjamin Franklin's approval as a model of ostentatious industry. She rose at 5:00 A.M. and planned out intervals for studying, supervising slaves, performing household tasks, and providing schooling to her sister and some slave children. This regimen kept Lucas out of mischief while rusticating with her family at Garden Hill, but she had to fight against Charleston's leisure-class temptations whenever she went downriver to the city. She regretted "that giddy gayety and want of reflection which I contracted when in town; and I was forced to consult Mr. Lock[e] over and over to see wherein personal Identity consisted and if I was the very same self" as she was when hard at work in the country. Alexander Garden—the Phoenix Carolinian—complained to an English friend that the Lower South's climate could break even his "virtuous resolutions" to remain active and industrious: "The first hot, sulky Enervating day, oversets and dissipates all my fortitude—I fall back into sloth and Idleness and really of a new Clothe myself with true American Nonchalance in point of Study." Worse than the necessity of con-

---

and Philosophical Society of Charleston, South Carolina, October 14, 1815 (Charleston, S.C., 1815), 5; *Monitor* (Washington, Ga.), May 5, 1815.

34. Henry Laurens to Edward Bridgen, Jan. 8, 1787, LP; Josiah Smith to George Austin, Jan. 31, 1774, Josiah Smith Letterbook, SHC; Jacob Read to Charles Ludlow, Dec. 19, 1809, Read Family Papers, box 1, folder 19, SCL.

stantly pummeling oneself into disciplined activity was the fear of being unable to sustain *any* activity, degenerating into what James Habersham had termed "the lumber of creation." Rawlins Lowndes admitted to his wife that during the War of 1812, when slaves could at least improve land if not produce staples for European trade, some "spirited Planters" would "clear and ditch and dam," but regretted that he was "not a spirited Planter." George Izard wistfully wrote his kinsman Henry: "With your Rope, your Hemp, your Rice, Cotton and Merinos you now appear to be completely employed. I envy you the Satisfaction of being so agreeably as well as usefully occupied for yourself and the Public."[35]

Izard revealed not only his own jealousy but the tendency of other whites to improve the productivity of their estates. They often investigated such strategies while traveling abroad, where they evidenced a fascination with industrial production. Most people outside the working classes found industrial machinery and the orderliness of factory labor discipline to be both exciting and promising. This was especially easy before the increase in industrialization after 1815 and the concomitant growth of the working classes, the increase in filthy and forbidding industrial landscapes, and the occurrence of proletarian revolts such as Peterloo.[36] Whites in the Lower South who toured abroad were surprisingly typical tourists: wealthy, curious, sympathetic to modernity, con-

---

35. Elise Pinckney, ed., *The Letterbook of Eliza Lucas Pinckney* (Chapel Hill, N.C., 1972), outline of daily schedule for 1742, 33–34, quotation from 19; Alexander Garden to John Ellis, June 20, 1771, Ellis Manuscripts, I, LSL (Garden recorded that it was 91 degrees when he wrote to Ellis); Rawlins Lowndes to "Mrs. Lowndes," Mar. 15, 1812, Rawlins Lowndes Papers, SHC; George to Henry Izard, May 16, 1809, Ralph Izard Papers, box 3, folder 23, SCL.

36. See S. D. Chapman, *The Cotton Industry in the Industrial Revolution* (London, 1972), 18, 25, 29–34, 60–61, for the effects of increased mechanization, use of steam power, increased capitalization, and growth of larger factories from the 1820s onward. John F. Kasson, Brooke Hindle, and Joyce Appleby have discussed how whites in Jeffersonian America—including the supposedly anticapitalist Jefferson himself—were hopeful about how industry, technology, and capitalism could benefit America. See Kasson, *Civilizing the Machine: Technology and Republican Values in America, 1776–1900* (New York, 1976), chap. 1; Hindle, *Emulation and Invention* (New York, 1981), chap. 1; and Appleby, *Capitalism and a New Social Order: The Republican Vision of the 1790s* (New York, 1984). E. P. Thompson reminds us, however, that members of the working classes were always much more critical of industrialism than were the upper classes, in *The Making of the English Working Class* (London, 1963).

vinced that the industrial order would benefit the poor and underemployed as well as the rich. They were not yet critics of industrial capitalism but admired heavily capitalized machinery and feats of engineering with an enthusiasm that might have dismayed their secessionist grandchildren. Confident that industrial mass production and mechanization represented advances in the world's productive capacity, whites eagerly toured European factories to observe the machinery and labor organization therein. When Henry Laurens visited Britain in 1771, for instance, he reported his plans to "go and see a great many honest fellows working at great Looms and great Forges, at Manchester, Birmingham, et ca." James Heyward was most impressed with the new engines and mechanisms that drove factory machinery. In 1793, Heyward wrote Thomas Pinckney, "I have had the opportunity of seeing a Steam Engine, which being the first, could not but strike the Imagination, as the Powers it moved with far exceeded what I had supposed."[37]

Admiration for the industrial order did not diminish over time; instead, whites' fascination intensified as industrialization itself expanded, particularly after American Independence encouraged manufacturing at home. When Mary Stead Pinckney visited Europe in 1797, she mapped out a busy schedule of tours to factories, including the Angoulême porcelain factory, the Sèvres factory, a "plate glass manufactory" in France, and a wire and spangle factory in Amsterdam. William Ball recorded of his visit to Scotland in 1806, "The sights which gave me the greatest satisfaction were a manufactory of printing cotton stuffs in all its various branches, and the aqueduct bridge near Glasgow." One Augusta woman who toured Pennsylvania went to no fewer than two paper mills and two cloth factories—she mentioned how especially "pleased" she was "with the little Boys tending the carding and spinning maschine" in a woolen factory. When Joseph Dulles toured Britain from 1808 to 1810, he went to a "Manufactory of Oyl Cloth and Paper," a stocking and jean factory, and several Manchester factories as well as museums, libraries, and lectures—he scarcely drew a leisured breath. Such was his conviction that disciplined work was commendable that, when Dulles went to London's Newgate Prison, he was disappointed to find the prisoners "all in idleness."[38]

37. Hamer *et al.*, eds., *Papers of Laurens*, VIII, 18; Heyward to Thomas Pinckney, May 5, 1793, Pinckney Family Papers, series 3, box 4, folder for May 1793, LC.

38. Charles F. McCombs, ed., *The Letter-book of Mary Stead Pinckney, November 14th, 1796, to August 29th, 1797* (New York, 1946), 57–58, 62–64; William to Isaac Ball, Nov. 24, 1806, Ball Family Papers, box 3, folder 25, SCL; entries for Aug. 12, 16, 26, 1815

In their desire to see children and prisoners put to work, whites from the Lower South revealed the tendency among propertied groups in the modern age to see productive and social value in factory organization. In addition, whites' interest in European industrial inventions stemmed from their conviction that such gadgetry could prove useful on home ground. Henry Laurens inspected a wind-driven water pump at a saltworks in Lymington in 1774. Twelve years and a War of Independence later, he inquired of his old factors in England whether they could get him the cloth sails and iron ware for these contraptions so he could build three and use them to pump water into a rice-mill reservoir. In 1790, Edward Rutledge solicited Phineas Miller's technical expertise in obtaining information on a mill to press oil out of cotton seed, and in 1793 Thomas Pinckney received a model of a water-powered threshing machine from Englishman Charles Goodwin.[39]

Planters were sometimes pleasantly surprised that the machines they saw while abroad were *already* in use in the Lower South. Elias Ball wrote to his cousin in 1787 that he had viewed carding and spinning machinery at Liverpool and Manchester. Ball claimed it was "the most wonderfull thing to me that Ever I saw," involving up to ten thousand cotton spindles at a time and "this dun with a wheal turn[e]d by water Just Such as you had to your Limrick [plantation] pounding Mill" for rice in South Carolina. Reuben King recorded in his diary in July 1805 that he went "with my brothers up St Marys River about 12 miles to [a] Steam sawmill," a sight with which he was "much pleased." Whites even planned entertainments to celebrate the completion of mechanisms at home. Robert Mackay reported to his wife in 1810 that he had been away from Savannah because "We had last Saturday a famous party at Colerain [rice mill], to witness the whole machinery in motion at once." Mackay's party included a barbecue and dance for the company. Georgian Edward Harden wrote his fiancee that he had been to see a Mr. Main's new mill begin to beat rice for the first time and "dined in a large party of fine ladies and

(quotation from last date), unidentified journal, Charles Colcock Jones, Jr., Collection, box 2, folder 13a, UGA; entries for Aug. 14, 18 (quotation), Nov. 27, Joseph Dulles Journal, SCL.

39. Henry Laurens to Bridgen and Waller, Jan. 7, 1786, LP; Edward Rutledge to Phineas Miller, Aug. 24, 1790, Edward Rutledge Papers, section A, Duke; Charles Goodwin to Thomas Pinckney, May 24, 1793, Pinckney Family Papers, series 3, box 4, folder for May 1793, LC.

gentlemen" to commemorate the event.[40] Planters' sense of a human duty to improve self and society and a need to control nature thus became specified, from the 1780s onward, in industrial terms.

𝔓𝔞 Work and Slavery: A Problem

Parties held in rice mills nevertheless underscored how whites were, despite all their celebrations of their own diligence, very interested in the leisure that property and increased production would bring them. The idea of a society controlled by privileged whites who bustled about only as much as they wished was most harshly exemplified in the existence of black slavery. Slavery gave the lie to the local work ethic: if whites were so energetic, why did another portion of the population do much of the actual work? To provide an answer that satisfied themselves, whites fell back on the idea of climate as a dubious explanation of racially differentiated aptitudes for hard labor, though they arrived at this supposition only after much questioning and public debate.

The most famous debate over work and slavery took place in Georgia. That colony's trustees had forbidden imports of black slaves in the 1730s, envisioning a colony of pious, hardworking, and militarily prepared whites who would create a mercantilistic and imperial bulwark between South Carolina and Spanish Florida. As well as prohibiting trade in slaves, the trust restricted the market for land (to prevent speculation) and regulated the agricultural economy by encouraging silk cultivation above all other activities. After a decade of implementing their plan, the trustees found themselves, by the 1740s, locked in battle with the Malcontents—propertyholders who wished to aggrandize their investments through slavery and rice planting in emulation of South Carolina's successful economy across the Savannah River. Rejecting any part of the Georgia Plan that inhibited individual investment and profit making, the indefatigable Malcontents petitioned Parliament, worked their way around the

---

40. Elias Ball (of Bristol) to Elias Ball (of Charleston), Sept. 11, 1781, Ball Family Papers, box 1, folder 4, SCL; Wood and Wood, eds., "Reuben King Journal," *GHQ*, LI (1967), 90; Robert to Eliza Mackay, June 23, 1810, Mackay-Stiles Papers, microfilm M470, reel 1, SHC; Edward Harden to Mary Ann Randolph, June 18, 1810, Edward Harden Papers, box 1, folder 3, cabinet 38, Duke.

trust's restrictions on property ownership, and finally wore down the trustees, who relinquished control of the colony one year before their parliamentary charter was to expire.[41]

The hub of this controversy was the familiar and self-interested debate over slavery's ill effects, not on blacks, but on whites. An older, organic model of society was the basis for trustees' expectations. The Georgia Plan assumed that labor was best performed for the good of society as a whole, not for the good of the individual. Unless each person worked, the collective good would suffer. If some people could hire or enslave others to labor for them, the result would be accumulation of personal wealth, social inequality, and loss of the social cohesion necessary to settle a frontier and combat imperial enemies. Prohibition of black slavery would raise the overall value of work, both in actual wages or rewards of land and in social value and honor. The Malcontents countered that this plan would slide Georgia down toward primitive underdevelopment and poverty. They also stressed that the plan was not even a basis for the social harmony the trustees sought, questioning whether regulations on an individual's ability to use labor and capital could create a utopia of truly contented humans. Restrictions of markets for slaves, land, and plantation staples were artificial controls that impeded socioeconomic success and incited protest.[42]

This local dispute drew on centuries of debate over the value of work and resounded with pleas for Christian fellowship, the ennobling effect of humble circumstances, and mercantilistic contribution to the empire. These values were arrayed against the idea that only the independence of the propertied individual and the relatively unfettered development of the economy would bring about greater national or imperial wealth. Either side of the argument could have been used to support free white labor; but the Malcontents' view, in practice, tended to emphasize the necessity of whites' freedom to hold blacks in slavery. In this way, they inserted their colony into the plantation economy

41. On the demise of the trustees' plans for a nonslave society, see David M. Potter, Jr., "The Rise of the Plantation System in Georgia," *GHQ*, XVI (1932), 114–135; Milton Ready, "The Georgia Concept: An Eighteenth Century Experiment in Colonization," *GHQ*, LV (1971), 157–172; Ready, "The Georgia Trustees and the Malcontents: The Politics of Philanthropy," *GHQ*, LX (1976); Betty Wood, *Slavery in Colonial Georgia, 1730–1775* (Athens, Ga., 1984), chaps. 2, 3.

42. Crowley, *This Sheba, Self: The Conceptualization of Economic Life in Eighteenth-Century America* (Baltimore, 1974), 16–49.

first established by South Carolina. Malcontents' ideas helped form the dominant ideology of slaveholding for a region that was now expanding.

Above all, Malcontents pleaded for black slavery by referring to the fevered and swampy environment as a fundamental constraint on white labor. Malcontent leader Patrick Tailfer claimed that the "constitutions" of the "Negroes" were "much stronger than white people, and the heat no way disagreeable nor hurtful to them; but in us it created inflammatory fevers of various kinds." Another critic of the trustees maintained that Georgia's rich swampland could never be tilled "by white people. Because the Work is too laborious, the heat very intent, and the Whites can't work in the wett at that Season of the year as Negroes do to weed the Rice." This became a standard justification for slavery in the early Lower South. South Carolinian John Drayton, drawing upon several decades of speculation on race and work in 1802, concluded that rice swamp was "unsuitable to the constitutions of white persons; whilst that of a negro, is perfectly adapted to its cultivation." Planters from the Lower South even threw this neo-Hippocratic speculation into national debates over the place of slavery in the new Republic. Charles Pinckney, delegate to his state's convention on the federal Constitution, daringly declared "that whilst there remained one acre of swamp-land in South Carolina, he should raise his voice against restricting the importation of negroes."[43]

White insistence on black resistance to fevers had a basis in fact. People from western Africa are indeed adapted to malaria and yellow fever. In the case of the first disease, West Africans have several forms of resistance, the most important being the sickle-cell trait. Humans with this trait have deformed blood cells, uninviting to malarial plasmodia but also conducive to anemia. (The sickle-cell trait is genetic but not racial; populations from malarial regions in southern Europe also carry the trait and are susceptible to sickle-cell anemia.) For yellow fever, most African resistance was acquired rather than genetic. Because such a high proportion of the West African population had acquired immunity, however, most children gained antibodies against yellow

---

43. Clarence L. Ver Steeg, ed., *A True and Historical Narrative of the Colony of Georgia by Pat. Tailfer and Others, with Comments by the Earl of Egmont* (Athens, Ga., 1960), 50; South Carolinian Samuel Eveleigh, quoted in Wood, *Black Majority*, 84; John Drayton, *A View of South-Carolina, as Respects Her Natural and Civil Concerns* (Charleston, S.C., 1802), 147; Jonathan Elliot, ed., *Debates in the Several State Conventions on the Adoption of the Federal Constitution . . .* , 2d ed. (Philadelphia, 1876), IV, 273.

fever in utero, which made them appear resistant from birth. But resistance against one form of fever did not guarantee resistance against all. In America, African populations encountered less familiar forms of disease. They were much more resistant to all fevers than Europeans or creole whites, but whites overstated African immunity, partly because of their lack of understanding of the biology of fevers, but mostly because they wanted to believe that Africans were adapted to laboring in semitropical environments.[44]

There was still a gap in their self-interested reasoning. Whites had claimed, after all, that they, too, were adapted to their environment. Had they accepted one logical conclusion, they might have thought that they were becoming, in effect, like Africans—their progeny would eventually resemble their slaves. They might have been unable to assert that they were forever incapable of working in their swampy milieu if they admitted that they were adapting to it. To avoid any such unwelcome conclusions, whites had to draw even further the contrast between their own immunity and that of blacks and did so by stressing the difference between acquired and innate immunities. They held as a general principle the belief that blacks were never as susceptible to yellow fever and malaria as they were, and believed that slaves' stronger resistance was innate, born within them as a racial characteristic. Their speculation was an ugly foreshadowing of the scientific racism of the later nineteenth century. The latent racism appeared in Dr. John Lining's 1753 description of whites' and blacks' immunity. For whites, Lining stated that it was "a great happiness that our constitutions undergo such *alterations* in . . . yellow fever, as for ever afterwards secure us from a second attack." For blacks, he explained: "There is something very singular *in* the constitutions of the negroes, which renders them not liable to this fever." Lining, like many whites, ignored evidence of how blacks did suffer from fevers. If a black succumbed to yellow fever, for instance, whites tended to believe she or he was mulatto; Lining observed that

44. On African and African-American resistance to fevers, see Wood, *Black Majority,* 88–91; Philip D. Curtin, "Epidemiology and the Slave Trade," *Political Science Quarterly,* LXXXIII (1968), 198–199; Kenneth F. Kiple and Virginia H. Kiple, "Black Yellow Fever Immunities, Innate and Acquired, as Revealed in the American South," *Social Science History,* I (1977), 420–422; Todd L. Savitt, "Black Health on the Plantation: Masters, Slaves, and Physicians," in Numbers and Savitt, eds., *Science and Medicine,* 329–331; Joyce E. Chaplin, "Acquired Resistance to Fevers as Cultural Metaphor in Coastal South Carolina and Georgia, 1760–1815," *Bulletin of the History of Medicine* (Summer 1993).

blacks whose ancestry was either part white or part Indian did fall prey to the disease, but did not discuss whether those with only African ancestors could as well. Only later, in the mid-1800s, did doctors begin to admit that all blacks could get yellow fever.[45]

White children acquired immunity through acculturation, which reflected their social identity; black children gained immunity through inheritance, which reflected their racial identity. (Indians seemed unable to acquire immunity; they were doomed in another way.) The logic of creole reasoning about race and disease culminated in the modern era's first scientific description of race as an inherited characteristic that resulted from natural selection. Native Charlestonian and physician William Wells postulated this in 1813 after examining a white woman who had black patches on her skin. To explain why skin color varied—even in patterns as surprising as this woman's—Wells concluded, in contrast to contemporary climatological explanations of skin color, that racial attributes resulted from selective adaptation to disease in specific regions. He presented this thesis to the Royal Society of London, and published it in 1818, several decades before Charles Darwin's own speculations on natural selection. (Darwin himself believed race was a product of sexual selection.)[46]

This was the logical conclusion of regional speculation about the environment, disease, and the resulting effects on humans. While it reflected some medical truths—West Africans and their descendants *do* have a greater degree of resistance to malaria and yellow fever—it also overstated the case. The argument emphasized inherited characteristics and ignored individual variation in order to assign low status to all members of a racial group and to exploit them. For blacks as well as whites, continued contact with a disease culture was needed to stimulate and maintain resistance, often at high rates of debility and mortality. In the case of slaves, continued contact with fevered environments came through the racial coercion of plantation slavery: this, as well as biolog-

---

45. Lining, "Description of Yellow Fever," *Essays and Observations*, II, 407 (on mulattos), 408–409 (quotations, my emphasis). On black susceptibility to fevers and whites' slow recognition of this fact, see Curtin, "Epidemiology and the Slave Trade," *Pol. Sci. Quar.*, LXXXIII (1968), 210–211; Kiple and Kiple, "Black Yellow Fever Immunities," *Soc. Sci. Hist.*, I (1977), 425–428.

46. Greene, *American Science*, 335–336, 452 n. 26. In *natural selection*, environmental conditions select among different characteristics; in *sexual selection*, animals or humans select mates according to different characteristics.

ical resistance, made them, as a population, more resistant to malaria and yellow fever than whites.[47] Whites' medical conjectures restated the paradox of the Lower South: free residents took up lines of inquiry common to the modern era but also used them, especially in the case of science, to defend their least modern institution. Although the emphasis on disease seemed to provide for whites a coherent answer, of sorts, why they used black slaves, it would create new problems once coastal planters confronted the demands of upcountry settlers for slaves to supply the labor needs of an unswampy environment.

For the moment, however, whites created a cultural interpretation of region, race, and work that justified their enslavement of blacks and defended them against accusations of sloth. As part of their ethos of activity (though not actual work), they defined for themselves a supervisory role over their slaves— one that emulated modern managerial functions. Nearly all planters accepted, as travelers noted, the Lower South's customs of task labor, employment of black drivers, and hiring out of skilled or superabundant laborers. But some planters paid closer attention to their workers and to the operation of their plantations, in the process providing additional checks on the Lower South's labor system. They watched overseers and drivers carefully, unwilling to allow deficiencies in plantation management to go undetected. Henry Laurens worried in 1765 that his overseer would select an improper driver for one of his estates and wrote him, "If you have not already made George a Driver I beg you will not do it, he is an eye Servant [whose work could not withstand close inspection], and a great Rogue, and therefore by no means fit to be an overseer of others." Laurens stressed, "You might as well set a Wolf to watch Your Sheep." In 1767, Richard Hutson wrote to his overseer after some of his slaves so resented the distribution of work on the plantation that they ran away. Hutson suspected that tasks were unequally divided and suggested that the overseer redistribute the labor to keep order on the plantation.[48]

Some planters wished to do away with the task system altogether and to

47. On the necessity of continued contact with a disease culture to maintain immunity to yellow fever and malaria, see Alfred W. Crosby, *Ecological Imperialism: The Biological Expansion of Europe, 900–1900* (Cambridge, 1986), 139; Burnet, *Infectious Disease*, 354.

48. Hamer *et al.*, eds., *Papers of Laurens*, IV, 602; Hutson to Mr. Croll, Aug. 22, 1767, Richard Hutson Letters, Charles Woodward Hutson Collection, SHC.

require slaves to labor in the fields for set intervals, obviating any disputes over or discrepancies in tasks. William Butler believed that a "gang" of slaves "will do their work more regular and uniform, and will be more under the Manager's Eye than if they were in different Tasks." Few planters accomplished this alteration, probably because slaves regarded tasking as a custom that, more often than not, worked to their advantage. Florida Governor James Grant discovered this when he tried to "assemble the Gang in the Field at a time" but that they "don't understand Roll calling." Grant seemed oblivious to the possibility that they understood but disapproved. Although most planters forged ahead with the task system, many had an interest in better regulating it. An exasperated James Habersham explained to William Knox that Knox's overseer had "taken the Negroes Account of their daily work without further examination," thereby deluding himself and Habersham as to the slaves' overall output. Rawlins Lowndes requested that his head driver, Ellick, "give a more full account of Charles' gang" by explaining "how it is organized—what it has done—how Charles plays the driver." Lowndes later wanted Ellick to inform him exactly how many corn hills "a hand can dig in a day." Georgian planter John Channing sent out a 105-foot chain (which marked out quarter-acre units of work) to his plantation, "for running out the Tasks" with "more exactness."[49]

Just as industrious whites watched their country slaves closely, so also they monitored their city slaves, who, if hired out to other whites, might elude supervision. Henry Laurens was unwilling to accept a percentage of a hired slave's wages without first determining whether the slave was earning as much as was possible. In July 1775, Laurens confronted his brother's hired-out slaves and was angry that Ishmael had not handed over money he had earned as a porter, that both Ishmael and George "were working jobbs about Town" without his knowledge, and that Cato was "passing his day in Play." Laurens made certain he "placed all that are able to work" where he could regulate their activities and earnings more easily. In 1794, Gabriel Manigault complained to

49. William Butler, "Observations on the Cultivation of Rice" (1786), 2, series 35-1786, SCHS; James Grant to Henry Laurens, n.d. (ca. 1765), Letterbook, MacPherson-Grant Papers, bundle 659, Ballindalloch; *Letters of Habersham* (GHS, *Colls.*, VI [1904]), 161; Rawlins Lowndes to Mrs. Lowndes, Oct. 23, Dec. 4, 1814, Rawlins Lowndes Papers, SHC; J. Channing to [Edward Telfair], Aug. 10, 1786, Edward Telfair Papers, box 3, folder 3, coll. 23-H, Duke.

his agent: "Carp[ente]r Quash has only paid £2.18, as wages. Be so good as to tell him that if he does not bring in wages as he ought to do, I have desired you to send him to Silkhope" plantation as punishment.[50]

Laurens's and Manigault's manipulative strategy—using threats and humiliation (like demotion to field hand) to influence their laborers—evidenced the recent shift in planters' treatment of slaves. Here again, white residents were taking up a modern theme, the idea of a universal humanity, and using it for a particular local need, that of ameliorating slavery, of smoothing its embarrassing rough edges. They had begun by conceding the essential humanity of their slaves, by seeing in slaves fellow persons with inherent human characteristics: ability to reason; tendency to become sentimentally attached to other people, especially kin; susceptibility to verbal threats and incentives. Whites used these discoveries toward two ends. They wanted to define a standard of behavior for themselves that dodged criticisms over the cruelty of the institution of slavery; and they sought to subject slaves to a manipulative form of discipline that, nevertheless, admitted of the necessity of negotiating with slaves over terms of work. The modern idea of humanity thus had negative and positive implications for slavery. It reassured whites that they were humane in their treatment of slaves while allowing them to exploit blacks' human characteristics for their own ends, but it also forced them to participate in a carefully defined process of give-and-take with their workers. By the Revolutionary era, whites who adhered to these new criteria set themselves apart from their seemingly less humane peers, just as industrious planters distinguished themselves from lazy ones. Thomas Boone warned his aunt in 1773 that, if she sold her estate, it "would carry away a parcel of old Family Negroes, who being past Labour, are supported by you, but would probably be required to work by a less indulgent owner." Henry Laurens declared in 1773 that he preferred an overseer who "makes less Rice with more hands but treats my Negroes with Humanity" over "one who should make twice as much Rice and exercise any degree of Cruelty towards those poor Creatures who look up to their Master as their Father, their Guardian, and Protector, and to whom their is a reciprocal obligation upon the Master."[51]

Reciprocity notwithstanding, once whites considered slaves' position within

50. Hamer *et al.*, eds., *Papers of Laurens*, X, 201; Gabriel Manigault to Mr. Owen, May 9, 1794, Manigault Letterbook, 1793–1805, SCL.

51. Thomas Boone to Margaret Colleton, Sept. 29, 1773, Margaret Colleton Papers, SCL; Hamer *et al.*, eds., *Papers of Laurens*, VIII, 618.

a common framework of human needs and obligations, they began to manipulate slaves' human sentiments in order to control them. Rather than resort to
a haphazard method of physical abuse, whites would assess the character of a
misbehaving slave, decide what emotional pressures might break the slave of
the particular behavior, then apply psychological stress to alter the individual's
behavior and that of the slaves who watched the punishment. Much as they did
with their children, whites now wanted to reform character and establish discipline. They shunned physical coercion, and, while their meliorism rendered
slavery less sanguinary, they brought a deeper, more invasive type of control
over slaves. Henry Laurens, for instance, decided in 1764 that his slave Abram
had to be sold, as an example to his fellows, for repeated bad behavior. Laurens
meticulously listed the five faults he felt the slave had (among other things,
Abram seemed overly "Fond of Women") against eight good qualities—including sobriety. Believing that Abram was essentially good, Laurens thought
he would mend his ways once he was away from the "pernicious connexions"
he had formed with some Charleston slaves.[52]

Other whites worried that slaves of whom they disapproved would seduce
their own servants away from virtue and duty. When M. Lazarus sent Mary
Ann, his Charleston housemaid, to Lewis Malone Ayer as punishment for her
stubbornness, he complained of "a mutual affection Existing between her and
a Very raskally fellow who I have often forbidden from coming near her." To
break the bond and "to make an Example" of her, Lazarus wanted Ayer to place
Mary Ann among the field workers on his plantation. Lazarus wished to
humble her by keeping her "at as hard lauber and coarse food as is on the
plantation" until she agreed with him that she had been wrong and would
behave better in the future—an admission that he evidently calculated as the
most humiliating part of her punishment. Following the same manipulative
strategy, South Carolinian Pierce Butler had in 1790 put Sawney, a house
servant, "in the field to punish Him for being insolent to his Mistress; but as I
suppose he is by this time pretty well humbled I can forgive him."[53]

Slaves' familial relations were an area whites picked out for particular
observation. Edward Rutledge discovered that his slaves were "more satisfied
when sold in Families and with their Connections." He considered selling

52. Hamer *et al.*, eds., *Papers of Laurens,* IV, 299.
53. Lazarus to Ayer, Oct. 2, 1809, folder 34, box 2, letter-sized documents, Lewis
Malone Ayer Papers, SCL; Pierce Butler to Roger Saunders, Sept. 6, 1790, Pierce Butler
Letterbook, SCL.

some of his slaves to a Mr. Parker, but if they did not want to go to him, Rutledge declared, "there will be no Bargain," remarking that Parker was "too humane, and too good to force them" to come to him. But the recognition that blacks cared deeply for their kin was also used against them, as whites discovered ways to twist affection into tractability. Georgia resident William Simpson did this when he calculatedly sold one man away from his wife until he submitted to Simpson's demands. Whites thought about other ways they could persuade their chattels to obey them. They concluded that slaves, as social and reasonable beings, could be motivated by verbal appeals rather than punishment. When John Channing left his Georgia estate in the hands of Edward Telfair while away in England, he impressed on Telfair that his first concern was management of his slaves. "I wish them to be treated as reasonable creatures," Channing emphasized, "that is, with humanity and kindness." Many slaveholders began to provide slaves with goods as incentives for their continued labor. Josiah Smith gave his workers clothing, beef, and liquor to keep them weeding rice fields during the summer of 1773; Peter Horry procured whiskey, rice, and a slaughtered bull for his slaves' 1812 Christmas feast.[54]

Because of these new manipulative strategies, master-slave relations became more interactive, more verbal, and more dependent on blacks' tentative trust that a white would keep his or her word in the bargain—however bleak the bargain. Slavery became a negotiated sphere between social unequals; the principle of humanity opened negotiations—the one, and terribly limited, progressive feature of humanitarianism as it was transplanted in the Lower South. Many slaveholders were thereafter more careful to listen to slaves' opinions and to tell them the truth. One Georgian who accepted his slaves' complaints in 1767, for example, did so because the conditions under which they worked, as he put it, were "unreasonable." Another Georgian refused to lie to any slaves, lest they "never take his word again." Peter Massie, James Hamilton's overseer, assured his employer that he had won the slaves' trust after promising to buy their corn. Massie had paid out about one hundred dollars for the corn in 1806 and reported that "the Negroes is very glaid that

54. Edward Rutledge to ——, Mar. 12, 1789, Edward Rutledge Papers, SCL; William Simpson to James Grant, June 15, 1767, bundle 243, MacPherson-Grant Papers, Ballindalloch; John Channing to [Edward Telfair], Aug. 10, 1786, folder 3, box 3, Edward Telfair Papers, Duke; Josiah Smith to George Austin, July 22, 1773, Josiah Smith Letterbook, SHC; Salley, ed., "Journal of Peter Horry," *SCHM*, XLIII (1942), 252.

they have got there money and those that was affried to trust me is coming and offering theirs."[55]

For the most part, however, whites motivated by the local work ethic assumed that slaves, like everyone else, needed to be prodded into a disciplined form of labor; productive activity maintained order among slaves, just as it reflected the moral rectitude of whites. In 1769, Ralph Izard complained to Peter Manigault about the unsatisfactory behavior of runaway slave Andrew and asserted that "the discipline of a rice Plantation is absolutely necessary for his Welfare." Jane Ball praised the benefits of work in 1803 when she wrote Isaac Ball about Hagar: "Keep her employ'd in the Garden as she is now use[d] to work and seems to be quite able [so] that it would be a pity to let her get ruined." William Johnson warned planters that it was necessary to train slave children to perform small tasks so that they would be properly prepared for a lifetime of labor. Delight over seeing white children hard at work in factories was locally expressed as determination to keep black children accustomed to labor in the fields. Thus was the work ethic pushed downward: Poor Richard, here in planter's garb, directed the labors of slaves using language adopted from European theory on the nature of humanity.[56]

The principle of humanity allowed whites to congratulate themselves on their efforts to improve their society. It provided a yardstick against which they measured their pre-Revolutionary and post-Revolutionary selves. In the early nineteenth century, William Moultrie wrote how he was "very much pleased to see the treatment of the slaves in the country . . . altered so much," inclining more to standards of "tenderness, and humanity."[57] Slaves doubtless felt little actual tenderness; cruelty toward them persisted, and they might well have wished for less interference from unctuous whites. In any case, the fundamental injustice of slavery was left in place. Humanitarian language allowed whites to substitute a gentler but no less effective form of slave discipline for a harsher

55. Hutson to "Mr. Croll," Aug. 22, 1767, Charles Woodward Hutson Papers, SHC; N. G. Bugg to Thomas Carr, July 12, 1793, folder 16, box 2, Carr Collection, UGA; Peter Massie to James Hamilton, May 11, 1806, folder for 1806, box 1, James Hamilton Papers, UGA.

56. Ralph Izard to Peter Manigault, Apr. 23, 1769, Ralph Izard Papers, box 1, folder 1, SCL; Jane to Isaac Ball, Jan. 21, 1803, Ball Family Papers, box 2, folder 19, SCL; Johnson, *Nugae Georgicae*, 36.

57. Fragment from early 1800s, folder 38, box 3, William Moultrie Papers, SCL.

one. This new method better suited the sentiments of men and women in this era, but it did not change their conviction that it was just for whites to hold blacks in perpetual bondage. Even more strikingly than in the case of scientific theory about disease, therefore, a modern ideology of human nature proved adaptable to strange demands. Planters' adoption of this ideology ran parallel to their admiration for the industrial order, revealing them to be not-so-distant relations of nonslaveholding upper and middle classes in the West. It is a truism that humanitarian behavior was often expressly designed to serve the interests of capitalism—this assertion has appeared in assessments of abolitionism ever since Eric Williams first attempted a thoroughgoing analysis of the connection between industrial capital and antislavery.[58] Humanity's similar influence on slaveholders and its usefulness to them reveal that this modern idea could teach members of a ruling elite to exploit others in a kindly fashion (one that deflected some external criticisms) even if they were not directly involved in industrial production.

℘ð Social Mobility

Though a local, albeit unusual, work ethic flourished in the Lower South, it was unevenly distributed through the population. Whites assumed, for example, that blacks had little interest in performing coerced labor and needed supervision to guarantee continued productivity. (Like travelers, nonetheless, they believed slaves, especially when hired out, were all too clever at earning money for themselves.) Whites conceded that they themselves needed to be inured to an active life. Courage in the face of disease, discipline throughout one's days, and a rhetoric that shamed slackers all facilitated this campaign, which recruited women and children as well as adult males. Those who most enthusiastically preached this ethic were members of the planter elite: the improvement-minded Pinckneys, Alexander Garden, Henry Laurens, David Ramsay, James Habersham, the South Carolina Balls, the Georgia Joneses. The

---

58. For an assessment of this debate, see the forum "Reflections on Abolitionism and Ideological Hegemony," in *AHR*, XCII (1987): David Brion Davis, "Reflections on Abolitionism and Ideological Hegemony," 797–812; John Ashworth, "The Relationship between Capitalism and Humanitarianism," 813–828; and Thomas L. Haskell, "Convention and Hegemonic Interest in the Debate over Antislavery: A Reply to Davis and Ashworth," 829–878.

local work ethic was, as in other parts of the modern world, cherished by members of the most-propertied class, who then prescribed it to everybody else.

In the Lower South, on the other hand, the ethic—articulated in racial terms—was also useful for those whites who wished to enter the ranks of propertyholders, either into the planter class or at a humbler level. Georgia settler Reuben King was typical. King arrived in Georgia in 1801 when he was twenty-two years old and obliged to apprentice himself to his brother, a tanner, to get a start in his new home. He was freed from servitude in 1802 and then went into partnership with his brother. When he was twenty-six, King set himself a life's plan of diligence, dividing his years into four parts, the first part (ages twenty-one to thirty-one) to be devoted to hard work, reading, and "agreeable conversation" in order to gain an "independent" economic condition, which he indeed achieved. Through constant work, by reading to improve himself, and by establishing good relations with his neighbors, King managed to acquire his own property and reputation. By 1860, his estate was worth forty thousand dollars. The penniless New Englander had become a rich antebellum planter.[59]

Members of the propertied elite recognized and applauded the labors of those below them; some even saw men like King as a catalyzing influence. Henry Laurens claimed in 1756 that poor farmers "by their persevercence have establish'd" indigo as "a Staple Comodity" and thereby "encouraged" richer planters "to re-Enter the Lists who before did not care to risque their money" on unknown crops. Penury necessitated industry. Proponents of self-disciplined labor could as easily, however, assume that lack of property meant lack of effort; whereas lazy planters appeared to squander their advantages (wealth, leisure, authority), the propertyless poor seemed to squander their own labor, their only means of getting ahead. Eliza Lucas concluded that, among South Carolinians, the "poorer sort are the most indolent people in the world or they could never be wretched in so plentiful a country as this."[60]

Such a line of analysis, like whites' reasonings about endemic fevers, was

59. Wood and Wood, eds., "Reuben King Journal," *GHQ*, L (1966), 199–200 (on his arrival in Georgia), 313 (apprenticeship), 319 (partnership), LI (1966), 83–84 (his itinerary). Signs of his labor and his constant habit of reading are apparent throughout the journal.

60. Hamer *et al.*, eds., *Papers of Laurens*, II, 343; Pinckney, ed., *Letterbook of Pinckney*, 39–40.

both inclusive and exclusive. The local work ethic gave whites from different backgrounds (newly arrived or native-born, planter or pioneer, male or female) common activities: individual discipline, an active life, and admiration for modern improvements. It welcomed even northerners, provided they could pass through the circle of fire drawn by local fevers. But this ethos also put down black marks against a list of persons unwilling or unable to submit to these efforts, including slaves, Indians, poor whites, and settlers who openly preferred quick economic return at the expense of societal benefit. These latter persons included those who made money they then used for leisure-class trumpery. This ethic was, nevertheless, clearly a product of a region where wealth (and its concomitant leisure) was a condition or goal of many. Though residents defined an ideal of responsible activity, it did not directly relate to real accomplishment; it defined a pattern of life, an improving life for those who already had wealth, rather than laid out avenues to success, and it smacked of self-fulfilling prophecy. To define particular goals of improvement, whites turned to more specific plans. But because of their specificity, these schemes made divisions over slavery and the region's economy erupt. The tension, for whites, over inclusion and exclusion became more explicit and more dangerous as some found themselves excluded from opportunity by others. Propertyholders in the region had long struggled to assert control over themselves and over their environment—the last thing they wanted was to be controlled by others.

Chapter 5

Projects and Power

The local work ethic proffered a potential welcome to struggling newcomers but also stigmatized those who did not defer to it. These terms of inclusion and exclusion, which tended also to divide those who already had wealth and power from those who did not, characterized the earliest innovatory schemes. The division over innovations—and more importantly the reasons for it—reveals the assumptions free residents had about the economy of the Lower South. Their disagreements with each other again show how whites drew upon earlier English debate over the state's role in economic affairs and reiterated contemporary Scottish ambivalence over how an older organic order had to be sacrificed to modern progress. Two issues were especially contentious: government-sponsored economic preferments and inequitable access to forms of property, especially slaves. Both possibilities threatened to curtail the rights of some citizens in favor of others.

At first, in the era before the Revolution, division over innovations was regional: coastal planters and upcountry farmers differed over plans to expand or to develop the Lower South. In this period, plans to alter agriculture took up the Age of Improvement's language of projecting and relied on scientific information; both of these features endeared projects to lowcountry planters but not to inland farmers. After the Revolution, division was more apparent between wealthy individuals and ordinary settlers regardless of where they lived. Elite projecting and scientific patronage were of less concern; worries over innovation in the early Republic instead acquired a political dimension and warned of corruption in the government's power over the economy.

Drawing upon the transatlantic scientific network and contemporary economic theory, lowcountry planters designed many of the earliest innovatory schemes, ones that reinforced the elitist orientation of much of the Lower

South's innovation. Yet despite their self-confident stance as patrons of projects, planters betrayed their inherent uncertainty over the region's optimal stage of development, especially the Lower South's reliance on slaves. Reluctant to increase the numbers of slaves and to spread this volatile population over more territory, planters searched for alternatives to rice cultivation along the coast, and they encouraged mixed agriculture and free labor in new settlements. Projectors regarded new areas, not as places in their own right, but as spaces where they—doubtful over a material success that depended on slavery—could construct models of economic variation for the benefit of the larger region. They wanted, accordingly, to freeze newer areas at a stage of development behind that of the coast, at a phase that avoided the lures of the market and of slavery. This vision contained a paradox: coastal planters had an admiration for science and an unease over human bondage that pointed up the modernity of their thought even as they clung to a nostalgic scheme for surrounding themselves with halcyon farming communities.

Achievement of their goal depended on the coastal elite's power. Learned-culture and patronage networks that stretched across the Atlantic Ocean, and even beyond, were key elements for members of this provincial, innovatory group. They used the network to seize control of an expensive, prestigious, and often exotic form of knowledge that could improve or alter agricultural forms. Access to information about agriculture in other parts of the world was therefore not a neutral gathering of wisdom, but both reflected and reasserted the power that coastal planters already had over the region. Progress was their stated aim, though within limits that demarcated authority rather than established opportunity. But in British America and, later, the United States—where whites were famous as bumptious defenders of their existing and anticipated rights—curtailment of opportunity was never acceptable. Settlers of new areas in the Lower South insisted that they wanted to follow the lowcountry's own successful trajectory: a route toward the market using the vehicle of slavery. Recent arrivals fought for a vigorous commercial network that would supply them wealth and political autonomy, they resisted manipulative financial innovations like land speculation, and they pressed for slaves. This last demand forced the region's explanation for slavery beyond its earlier and environmentally specific postulate.

Arguments that restricted any kind of economic opportunity to the lowcountry were precisely what newer settlers contested; they not only wanted slaves but also wished to turn new land (recently appropriated from Indians and, whites believed, aching to be tilled) into part of the region's commercial economy. They feared the ways in which external authorities might, through inept or corrupt schemes, prevent them from doing this. Even after settlers won concessions from planters, shifted away the debris of elite projects, acquired land, and accumulated capital, they still battled against agents of corruption. Apprehensions over how political power could impede progress toward wealth and aggrandize property in the hands of the few were of long standing. Such suspicions originated in England's financial revolution, especially argument between Walpole's innovating Whigs and Bolingbroke's Country opposition. Colonial carping over the folly or evil of projects drew upon the earlier English debate, and, after the Revolution, the problem of governmental influence over the economy played itself out in the controversy surrounding Alexander Hamilton's plans for economic development in the new Republic. The controversy divided Federalists and Republicans in each state, each of which had its own concerns and interested parties.

But discussion of economic development rarely followed a clear-cut divide between those who wanted government support of economic ventures and those who absolutely opposed it. Rather than a bipolar opposition, debate represented gradations of opinion over how to create a modern economy— never an outright rejection of this prospect. These gradations often depended on unlikely choices. Lowcountry planters, for instance, continued to live with a mixture of commercial agriculture and slavery, even as they recognized the contradictions of their economy and prevented new arrivals from replicating their own compromises. New settlers themselves expressed contradiction: they criticized colonial governments for supporting economic projects but, after the Revolution, welcomed state and federal control over ventures like land speculation. By this time, most Americans recognized that government would intervene in economic policy; they accepted it as a benefit of the modern age. Disagreement continued, however, over which policies the state ought to support and which citizens ought to influence policy-making. Public policy that supported the private interests of exclusive groups was rarely acceptable; government sponsorship of private ventures like land companies and franchises (and, later, banks) threatened *imperium in imperio:* involution of private power protected by the perverted authority of the state. Especially when policy favored established groups by denying poorer whites access to slaves and land, the power of the state—which prevented free newcomers from achieving status in the southern community—seemed corrupt.

In essence, new settlers, especially in their demands for slaves, were moving the region ever closer to a Herrenvolk interpretation of sociopolitical democracy. Such a democracy promoted political equality for one people only—whites—and rabidly defended them from inappropriate use of government power.[1] Controversy and compromise over plans for improving the Lower South established this trend. The Malcontent rebellion in Georgia (1740s) and the Regulation in South Carolina (1760s) were two well-known battles within the ceaseless struggle for white opportunity. Less familiar are two other important episodes: promotion of silk cultivation, which epitomized colonial projecting, and speculation over western lands in the Yazoo scandal, which capped post-Revolutionary protests over corruption of the state's power to stimulate economic growth and resulted in a Supreme Court decision on the relationship between law and property—not just within the Lower South but throughout the nation. Continual protest against and modification of innovation meant that new areas could not be frozen in time at a wishful point along the continuum of stages between savagery and commerce; the Lower South's distinctive mixture of commerce and slavery would instead keep moving west, and would keep revealing the problems and contradictions of the region.

&a Patrons of the Exotic

In the lowcountry, plantation agriculture was an acknowledged economic success. Irrigated rice was, here, what sugar was to the West Indies: a lucrative staple on the profits of which planters built a wealthy and leisured provincial culture. Existing levels of wealth and opportunities to gain more wealth were considerable, and successful planters achieved a high degree of cultural sophistication, partly a result of their ties to the mother country. They took up for themselves the role of projector as Daniel Defoe had defined it. Innovators regarded plants, mechanisms, and skilled workers as commodities they could exchange or purchase in order to diversify or strengthen their methods of agriculture; they saw the natural world, especially, as a storehouse of information about and supplies for agriculture.[2] In their search for perti-

1. On Herrenvolkism, see George M. Fredrickson, *White Supremacy: A Comparative Study in American and South African History* (New York, 1981), esp. 140–150.

2. A. Hunter Dupree, "The National Pattern of American Learned Societies, 1769–1863," in Alexander Oleson and Sanborn C. Brown, eds., *The Pursuit of Knowledge in the Early American Republic: American Scientific and Learned Societies from Colonial Times to the Civil War* (Baltimore, 1976), 21–32; Jack R. Kloppenburg, Jr., *First the Seed:*

nent information, coastal projectors contacted powerful organizations and individuals who could reinforce their own status, and they focused on semi-tropical crops and complicated machines as objects of research. Not all of these plants and devices were appropriate, but the point is not so much that specific schemes were successes or failures as that they all generally assisted planters in improving agriculture, providing a framework of innovation and economic flexibility within which the most promising schemes could flourish.

Imperial policy based on mercantilism provided the overarching framework within which transatlantic exchange of information took place. Since British America's beginnings in the late sixteenth century, colonizers had hoped that their settlements would yield commodities England could not produce and had to buy from other nations. Along with the well-known Navigation Acts of the late 1600s and early 1700s, other laws encouraged production of staples (including tobacco, dyes, lumber, fibers, and luxury foods like sugar, ginger, rice, and pimento) for markets in the mother country. Bounties stimulated approved patterns of production and trade, tariffs discouraged importation of foreign goods into Britain, and fines punished smuggling of the same. Britons particularly abhorred laying out money for products from the Catholic nations, France and Spain, with which they warred during the 1700s. In one patriotic statement, South Carolinian Charles Pinckney wrote a correspondent at the Royal Society of Arts that Americans ought to make indigo and silk in order to avoid enriching "these hated Rivals the french." Certain interest groups wanted production of selected commodities in the Lower South. A draper and dyer lobby in London, for instance, secured a bounty on Anglo-American indigo that lasted from 1748 to 1777, rewarding planters for devoting themselves to this new crop.[3]

Transfer of information and monetary awards both stimulated agricultural innovation in the Lower South. The form of these exchanges, through the

---

The Political Economy of Plant Biotechnology, 1492–2000 (Cambridge, 1988), 9–11, 14–15.

3. Lewis Cecil Gray, *A History of Agriculture in the Southern United States to 1860* (Washington, D.C., 1933), I, 292 (indigo lobby); David Leroy Coon, "The Development of Market Agriculture in South Carolina, 1670–1785" (Ph.D. diss., University of Illinois, Urbana/Champaign, 1972), 249–250; C. Pinckney to "Mr. Baker," Apr. 1, 1755, RSA, Guardbooks, reel 1 (quotation). For a discussion of mercantilism's effects on colonial economies, see John J. McCusker and Russell R. Menard, *The Economy of British America, 1607–1789* (Chapel Hill, N.C., 1985), 35–50.

hierarchy of patronage, reflected the very form of English-speaking society at the time. Hierarchical social relations were the rule in late-eighteenth- and early nineteenth-century society, both in the provinces and in the metropolis. Patronage, the protection and largess a person of high socioeconomic status gave to "friends" at the same or lower ranks, was both an adhesive for relations among people in different classes and a method for the upper class to control social mobility. Patrons and clients composed a large social network that extended from colonial governors to scullery maids—all of whom may have received their positions through the influence of friends. Like many scientific or improving activities, agricultural innovation took place within this system, depending more upon the encouragement of learned societies and educated or wealthy individuals than the efforts of ordinary farmers. Agricultural innovation thus expanded rather than challenged the existing structures of power, namely, European imperialism, merchant capitalism, and a hierarchical social system. The Lower South was comparable, for instance, to other provinces like colonial Brazil. There, agricultural improvement favored those in the upper strata of Portugal and Brazil, revealing how "not only the political but also the economic, social, and scientific ideas of the eighteenth century could serve the interests of some groups in society and work against those of others."[4]

The circle of power most useful to planters was scientific and European. Coastal planters participated in an exchange with the Old World that capitalized on their own natural world. They supplied botanical information about their region to men of science and to British officials interested in expanding the Americans' agricultural repertoire. In return, planters got information that improved their methods of cultivation; seeds and cuttings were entering wedges into a scientific circle. Sometimes these exchanges were explicitly negotiated. When Thomas Jefferson sent John Milledge, recently governor of Georgia, samples of seed rice from France's national garden, he asked

4. Harold Perkin, *The Origins of Modern English Society, 1780–1880* (London, 1971), 37–49; Perkin, "The Social Causes of the British Industrial Revolution," Royal Historical Society, *Transactions*, 5th Ser., XVIII (1968), 129–134; Margaret W. Rossiter, "The Organization of Agricultural Improvement in the United States, 1785 to 1865," in Oleson and Brown, eds., *Pursuit of Knowledge,* 279; Kloppenburg, *First the Seed,* 7–15, 53–54; Lucile H. Brockway, *Science and Colonial Expansion: The Role of the British Royal Botanic Gardens* (New York, 1979), 13–34; J. H. Galloway, "Agricultural Reform and the Enlightenment in Late Colonial Brazil," *AH,* LIII (1979), 763–779, quotation from 765.

for seeds from Georgia cotton (obtained "through your kind instrumentality") to send back. This maneuver would keep the wheels greased, should Americans require future information from the French. Such trading could acquire a personal dimension. Peter Manigault, when he asked his father to supply him with seeds for South Carolina laurel trees for a gentleman in Paris, admitted that he owed the man, perhaps a patron, a favor—one that could be paid off with a rather obscure commodity. Politics also regulated the flow of information. Before the Revolution, Benjamin Franklin (Georgia's colonial agent) sent a packet of rare East Indian seeds to Noble Wimberly Jones (speaker of the provincial assembly) for Jones to plant or distribute as he saw fit. Such contacts survived the Revolution. In 1783, Henry Laurens received ninety-nine packets of Indian seeds from Sir George Yonge, a prominent English civil servant.[5]

Before the Revolution, two British organizations assisted innovators. Britain's prestigious Royal Society was the focus for English science. Such was the Royal Society's importance to Americans that Alexander Garden believed a proposal for an experimental garden in South Carolina should originate from the organization because that would carry more "weight with the people" than if mere colonials made the same suggestion. But for practical rather than theoretical information, the Royal Society for the Encouragement of Arts, Manufactures, and Commerce (founded in London in 1754 and commonly called the Royal Society of Arts) provided patronage to Americans who would not describe themselves as learned scientists. Innovators reported to the Royal Society of Arts about prospects for new crops and about new methods of cultivating old staples. In return, the society endorsed selected schemes, offered premiums for new commodities, and gave awards to outstanding projectors.[6] By the 1750s, Garden had more contact with the Royal Society of Arts

5. Jefferson to Milledge, Oct. 10, 1809, John Milledge Papers, GHS; Peter to Gabriel Manigault, Aug. 21, 1753, Manigault Papers, series 11-275-11, SCHS; Noble Wimberly Jones to Benjamin Franklin, Jan. 13, 1778, Jones-Franklin Correspondence, UGA (from originals in the American Philosophical Society); Henry Laurens to Edward Bridgen, Sept. 16, 1783, Apr. 2, 13, 14, 1785, LP.

6. George F. Frick, in his "Royal Society in America" (Oleson and Brown, eds., *Pursuit of Knowledge*), has described how the society was a cultural center for scientifically minded provincials, but he has emphasized that ties between the society's fellows and Americans were more common than the society's official support of these

than anyone else in the Lower South because he was the region's outstanding scientist; the society regarded him as the proper agent to notify them of projects that might redound to their own and the nation's glory. One official wrote Garden that members of the society "must depend on you, who know the Genius of the People [in Carolina], that their Money may not be thrown away." In 1755, Garden described to the society cultivation of rice, indigo, and cochineal and solicited advice about rice milling. He criticized planters for their inefficient method of grinding rice in wooden mortars, using the manual labor of "*poor slaves*" who were often exhausted by this primitive task. Garden wanted the society to help develop mechanized milling, especially equipment run by draft animals instead of slaves.[7]

Other innovators also contacted the Royal Society of Arts for its support. In 1758, Charleston merchant Robert Pringle wrote the society about his attempts to raise logwood. In 1772, Samuel Bowen, resident of Georgia, sent a sample of his groundnut oil to the organization. In a 1766 letter to Samuel Moore of the society, Edmund Caiger warned that the poor farmers of South Carolina needed aid if their efforts to make silk were to continue. Supplicants like Caiger could win premiums and financial support from the Royal Society of Arts. Indeed, the largest amount of money the society gave to any of its clients was the £1,374 sent to Georgia between 1759 and 1767 to encourage silk reelers there. The society gave other premiums, such as the bounty they promised in 1768 for "fine Cotton." It also awarded gold medals for distinguished accomplishments. Members bestowed this award on Samuel Bowen in 1766 for making sago powder out of dried sweet potatoes and vermicelli noodles from soy beans grown in Georgia. (The first product thickened foodstuffs and starched textiles; the latter testified to a surprisingly sophisticated English palate.) Whites were well aware that the Royal Society of Arts' support might be the only way of promoting a given experiment. South Carolina's Governor William Bull requested in 1770 that the colony's agent lobby in the society's offices on behalf of Christopher Sherb, who was planting vines and making wine. Without assistance, Bull explained, "this poor adventurer" had little chance of winning a premium from the society and would then be forced to abandon his mer-

---

colonists (81). The quotation is from Alexander Garden to John Ellis, May 11, 1759, Linnaeus Correspondence, XVII, LSL.

7. ———— to Alexander Garden, June 30, 1756 (p. 243), Dr. Templeton's Transactions, and Garden to the Society, Apr. 20, 1755, Guardbooks, RSA, reel 1.

itorious scheme, which Bull recommended "as Agent, and as a Gentleman" of the province.[8]

The Royal Society of Arts conveyed, along with financial rewards, valuable information and materials to chosen clients who then picked out contacts of their own. When British silk expert Pickering Robinson, who resided in Georgia, wrote John Ellis that he had received seeds, cuttings, and literature from the society via Ellis, he explained how he would distribute lists of the premiums "among my Friends." In 1760, the society sent cuttings of currant and other vines to Alexander Garden, who decided to pass some along to Christopher Gadsden and Henry Middleton, men he deemed worthy of caring for them. One year later, the society responded to a Mr. English in South Carolina, who had asked them for information on tidally powered mills. The society's members doubted such mills could be useful in South Carolina (they guessed wrong) but promised to introduce English to experts who could answer his questions.[9]

Though British associations such as the Royal Society of Arts were important sources of patronage, innovators also contacted other European agencies. Scientists in the Lower South had always corresponded with continental Europeans, but these connections strengthened considerably during the era of imperial tension between the colonies and Great Britain. Under these circumstances, even the French seemed helpful. In a 1775 edition of the patriot newspaper *South-Carolina and American General Gazette,* for instance, the publisher offered to print by subscription a translation of Beauvais Rousseau's *Indigotier,* which could teach planters to raise indigo. (The editor pointed out that the Royal Academy at Paris had endorsed the work.) After the Revolution, citizens were interested in building up the economic strength of each state, assisted by the international world of science. It was at this time that John

8. All references are from the RSA: Robert Pringle to the Society, Aug. 7, 1758, Guardbooks, reel 1; entry on Samuel Bowen, Mar. 4, 1772, MS Transactions, 1771–72, reel 1; Edmund Caiger to Samuel Moore, Sept. 15, 1766, reel 2; Introduction, p. 3, reel 1 (on silk); Jan. 19, 1768, Minutes of Committee, 1767–68, reel 1 (on cotton); entry on Bowen, June 10, 1766, Minutes of Committee, p. 21, reel 1; Bull to Charles Garth, Jan. 20, 1770, Guardbooks, reel 1.

9. Pickering Robinson to John Ellis, Apr. 14, 1761, Ellis Manuscripts, II, LSL; Alexander Garden to Society, July 20, 1760, and entry on Mr. English, Feb. 17, 1761, Minutes of Committee, RSA, reel 1.

Milledge corresponded with Jefferson, well known for his contacts with European scientists, who responded by sending seeds of different kinds of rice from
France's National Garden. Milledge later emphasized to Jefferson that he had
distributed the seed to "Planters" he knew would cultivate it with care.[10]

After the Revolution as well, coastal residents formed their own agricultural
societies to work in tandem with European organizations or to replace the lost
protection of British learned societies. The most successful example was the
South Carolina Agricultural Society, established in 1785.[11] Among its founding
members were Thomas Heyward (the first president), who pioneered tidal rice
irrigation; Ralph Izard, who experimented with cotton and silk; and Thomas
and Charles Cotesworth Pinckney, who improved methods of rice cultivation
and milling. These men, like most of the society's members, were wealthy land-
and slaveholders who formed their state's political elite. Ralph Izard was one of
South Carolina's first two federal senators, and the Pinckney brothers filled
several state and national political positions. Their organization modeled itself
on the Royal Society of Arts by awarding gold medals and premiums, but it
gave itself a new, patriotic and national identity by establishing contacts with
learned men throughout the Republic—Jefferson was its first honorary member. Resident members of the South Carolina Agricultural Society were determined to keep abreast of European developments in agriculture. After Charles
Cotesworth Pinckney discovered a promising piece of English farm machinery
in 1792, he told his brother, "If it should answer, I will then propose to the
Agricultural Society to send for one." In the same year, the society resolved to
appropriate funds for buying olive trees in Marseilles. In 1793, Thomas Pinckney received Sir John Sinclair's assurance, as head of Britain's Board of Agriculture, that the board would correspond with the Agricultural Society on topics of mutual interest.[12] Thus did planters in the Lower South replace the

10. *South-Carolina and American General Gazette* (Charleston), July 14, 1775; Jefferson to Milledge, Oct. 10, 1809, and Milledge to Jefferson, Nov. 11, 1809, folder 7, John
Milledge Papers, GHS.

11. The Agricultural Society of Georgia (founded 1810), was short-lived. See James C.
Bonner, *A History of Georgia Agriculture, 1732–1860* (Athens, Ga., 1964), 110.

12. Brooke Hindle, *The Pursuit of Science in Revolutionary America, 1735–1789*
(Chapel Hill, N.C., 1956), 362–372; John C. Greene, *American Science in the Age of
Jefferson* (Ames, Iowa, 1984), 110–111; Coon, "Market Agriculture," 313–347; volume
with list of founding members, South Carolina Agricultural Society Records, series

lost beneficence of Britain's learned and royal societies with their own re-publicanized version.

Planters who contacted or organized learned societies did so to gain machinery from Europe and crops from warm regions. Cherishing how their own region, or at least an exotic vision of it, conferred climatological advantages, residents of the lowcountry looked for semitropical germ plasm in far-flung places like Asia. But they also wanted European machinery to process their crops; in this aim, they could indulge their admiration for industrial gadgetry by bringing pieces of it to their coastal plantations. This was a vision of improvement that lay somewhere between the exotic Eastern paddy and the efficient European factory—an unusual but often successful hybrid.

Residents were, to be sure, interested in some products of temperate zones. Joseph Clay and Company of Savannah made a small business of ordering seeds and implements from Philadelphia during the 1770s. Clay bought a plow "made very strong and fit for Ploughing in low Marsh Land" from Bright and Peckin in that city, and ordered seeds for oats, peas, onions, radish, cabbage, rye, lucerne (alfalfa), beets, lettuce, and spinach from the same establishment. Like contemporaries in South Africa and Australia, coastal planters wanted to introduce more and better varieties of sheep, especially fleecy merinos. Local knowledge of advances made in Europe was sometimes quite au courant. Henry Laurens, for example, experimented with the mangel-wurzel, or Huntington root, a tuber that enjoyed brief fame among philanthropists as a cheap foodstuff that, like the potato, would cure rural poverty. But Laurens was merely casting a wide net rather than stating any preference for European agriculture—he also experimented with breadfruit around the time he grew mangel-wurzel.[13]

34-162-1, SCHS; Chalmers S. Murray, *This Our Land: The Story of the Agricultural Society of South Carolina* (Charleston, S.C., 1949), 32, 49, 69; C. C. Pinckney to Thomas Pinckney, July 14, 1792, Pinckney Family Papers, series 1, box 4, LC; same to same, Nov. 13, 1792, Pinckney Family Papers, microfiche 38-7-7, SCHS; John Sinclair to Thomas Pinckney, Sept. 9, 1793, Thomas Pinckney Papers, SCL.

13. Letters of Aug. 4, 1773, Sept. 14, 1773, Letterbook, Dec. 14, 1772–Dec. 1773, Joseph Clay and Co., GHS. On sheep, see D. Humphreys to John Rutledge, Dec. 6, 1808, John Rutledge Papers, folder 22, SHC (Humphreys sent six merinos from New Haven); advertisement for New York merinos to be auctioned, *Georgia Journal* (Milledgeville), Jan. 1, 1812; Charles Cotesworth Pinckney to Harriott Horry, Mar. 2, 1816, Pinckney

Other planters were altogether dismissive of farming in colder climates and resented how Europeans (or northerners) imposed inappropriate notions of agricultural improvement on them. In 1761, Georgia settler Pickering Robinson rebuked the Royal Society for sending him a bushel of acorns: "We are anxious to clear—and not plant Forests in Georgia." Robinson then gave sharp instructions on how rare seeds and vine cuttings were to be packed and shipped to him. Bernard Romans stated that "*sain-foin, lucerne, clover,* and *timothy grass,*" darlings of improving farmers in Europe, "thrive not" in the lowcountry. Romans also took care to give a "detail of the agriculture practised, or practicable" along the coast while avoiding "the silly notions, whereby *England* is deceived in her ideas of *America.*" To some extent, disdain for northerly agriculture was justified; the Lower South made its fortune on vegetation transplanted from areas distant from the mother country. As David Ramsay emphasized, in 1809, all of South Carolina's crops (except maize, sweet potatoes, and Indian peas) were, not natives, but "exotics" brought from afar.[14]

Planters did look back across the Atlantic for European technology. They were most interested in two types of mechanisms: for controlling water and for cleaning grain. The first was a pressing need for the lowcountry, filled with swamps, surrounded by river and sea. Nicholas Langford, for instance, advertised in the *South-Carolina Gazette; And Country Journal* in 1768 that he had imported an English pump, "extremely useful to this province, particularly for the draining of swamps, and filling the indico vats" with water to make dye.

Family Papers, series 1, box 3, LC; Pinckney to George Washington, Feb. 27, 1811, Pinckney Family Papers, series 38-10-1, SCHS.

On Laurens, see Benjamin Vaughan to Sir Joseph Banks, July 12, 1788 (a discussion of Laurens's experiments with mangel-wurzel), and John Vaughan to Laurens, June 23, 1789 (on breadfruit), LP. Laurens's experiments with "the Huntington (or scarcity) root" were also described in the *American Museum,* IV (July 1788), 100. Mangel-wurzel has beetlike roots and is now fed to livestock, not humans.

For a discussion of the influence of European agricultural improvement, see Coon, "Market Agriculture," 1–37.

14. Pickering Robinson to John Ellis, Apr. 14, 1761, Ellis Manuscripts, II, LSL; Bernard Romans, *A Concise Natural History of East and West Florida* (1775; facs. ed., Gainesville, Fla., 1962), 130, 179; David Ramsay, *History of South-Carolina, from Its First Settlement in 1670 to the Year 1808* . . . (Charleston, S.C., 1809), II, 304. Cf. Julius Rubin, "The Limits of Agricultural Progress in the Nineteenth-Century South," *AH,* XLIX (1975), 362–373, who argues that the subtropical nature of the American South impeded its economic vitality.

While touring Europe, Georgian Robert Mackay bought a "Model of a Water Pump" with several other devices (including an orrery, camera obscura, and pedometer). Planters particularly valued Dutch expertise in using hydraulic power and in draining and flooding land. Hugh Williamson received information from the Society of Sciences at Haarlem to help him design the Cooper-Santee Canal in South Carolina. Thomas Pinckney collected drawings of Dutch agricultural machinery—including pumps and waterwheels—perhaps provided by William Vans Murray, United States minister at The Hague in the late 1790s.[15]

Pinckney's portfolio also contained diagrams of machines from other parts of Europe, including a Venetian underground cistern and a threshing machine, possibly one Pinckney saw during his diplomatic service either in England or in Spain. He and his brother, Charles Cotesworth, were searching for a threshing machine adaptable to rice, one that would save labor just as Alexander Garden had wished for rice milling several decades earlier. While posted at the Court of St. James's, Thomas Pinckney wrote agricultural expert Arthur Young in January 1793, asking about a threshing machine, "lately invented in Scotland," that Young had mentioned in his writings. Pinckney found another promising threshing machine near London and hired a "Mechanic" to make a model of it. In 1794 Pinckney discussed with Jefferson modifications for a Sicilian threshing machine, and in 1795 he searched for a device that Scottish statistician Sir John Sinclair described in his "View of the Agriculture of East Lothian." Working independently, Charles Cotesworth located "a Scotchman" who constructed threshing machines and planned to use the Scot's designs to erect twenty such mechanisms on his Snee Farm plantation.[16] Some

15. *South-Carolina Gazette; And Country Journal* (Charleston), Aug. 9, 1768 (see also advertisement of Henry Rugeley and Co., Dec. 10, 1771); Robert Mackay's Travel Diary, 1802–1804, Mackay-Stiles Papers, XXII, SHC; Harriott Horry Ravenel Collection, series 11-332A-22, 11-332A-20, SCHS. On Dutch techniques of irrigating and draining and their influence on English and South Carolina agriculture, see Coon, "Market Agriculture," 11–29. On Dutch influences in Georgia, see E. Merton Coulter, ed., *The Journal of William Stephens, 1743–1745* (Athens, Ga., 1959), II, 60. On Williamson, see Hindle, *Pursuit of Science*, 372. See also Charles Pinckney to Sylvanus Bourne, May 12, 1802, Charles Pinckney Papers, SCL (on Dutch loans and markets).

16. Harriott Horry Ravenel Collection, series 11-332A-22, SCHS; Thomas Pinckney to Arthur Young, Jan. 7, 1793, Pinckney Family Papers, series 37-56, microfiche card 3, Pinckney to Thomas Jefferson, Feb. 14, 1793, microfiche card 4; Pinckney to Thomas Jefferson, Jan. 29, 1794, series 37-57, microfiche card 1, Pinckney to Sir John Sinclair,

planters would also adopt sugar mills—examples of some of the most advanced forms of technology in the modern era, though these were developed in the New World rather than Europe and were more clearly suited to plantation agriculture.

Though their search for exotic plants sometimes led to crops that did quite well—witness cotton and indigo—it also misled innovators into pursuing unlikely things like citrus fruit, sugar cane, and silk. They focused on these foreign crops because they had a latitudinal understanding of climate. They realized their region was on a rough parallel with the Mediterranean, Asia, and the nearby West Indies and concluded that crops could easily be transferred between these parallel areas. This fallacious reasoning had had disastrous consequences in earlier phases of colonization when promoters assumed that any part of North America lying south of England was warm enough to sustain Mediterranean crops like vines and silk. Colonizers were not always wiser in the eighteenth century, and a myth of North American luxuriance continued. A Briton named Whitworth, who wished the Royal Society of Arts to introduce him to Alexander Garden, insisted that, because the colonies lay parallel to China, Italy, and Spain, their residents ought to be producing the commodities of these places.[17] A piece in the March 1767 *Gentleman's Magazine* declared that American farmers "between thirty and forty degrees of northern latitudes" (the varying zones stretching from St. Augustine to New York City) should be busy growing grapes, almonds, currants, and olives for themselves and British consumers. This would be more "patriotic" than paying the French, Spanish, Portuguese, and Italians for such products.

Though planters in the Lower South saw truth in statements like this, they also recognized that not all land in their region was suited to crops from southern latitudes. Soil science did not take form until the mid-1800s, but, before this time, those who worked the land had rough notions of which types supported which crops, using the physical appearance of the soil and its

---

Apr. 5, 1795, microfiche card 10; Pinckney Family Papers, series 37-57, SCHS. Charles Cotesworth to Thomas Pinckney, Oct. 28, 1793, Pinckney Family Papers, series 1, box 4, LC. Years later, Thomas wrote his sister that he had received "a chaff cutter" from a Briton named Vaughan; see Thomas Pinckney to Harriott Horry, Aug. 24, 1808, Pinckney Family Papers, series 1, box 8, folder 2, LC.

17. See Karen Ordahl Kupperman, "The Puzzle of the American Climate in the Early Colonial Period," *AHR*, LXXXVII (1982), 1265–1269, 1288–1289; C. Whitworth to Dr. Shipley, July 31, 1755, Guardbooks, reel 1, RSA.

natural products to make their judgments. In the Lower South, residents distinguished between three broad categories of land. John Drayton explained in his *View of South-Carolina* (1802) how that state was "divided into *Lower*, *Middle*, and *Upper* Country." Drayton elaborated on the idea that people as well as plants were products of physical places by explaining how, in Carolina, "the soil, the natural growth, and the political economy of its inhabitants" supported the logic of this threefold division. David Ramsay also detailed how South Carolina's "soil" was "naturally" divided into these classifications—coastal floodplain, upper coastal plain, piedmont—easily discriminated by farmers as well as tax collectors.[18]

Near the coast itself, four types of land (two dry and two wet) predominated: pine barrens, hardwood forest, cane savannah, and lowland swamp. Pine barren, everyone knew, was the worst land, shunned by all but the poorest settlers though capable of producing some foodstuffs and cotton. "Oak and hickory" land contained richer soil and, when cleared, was suited to grain and provision crops, cotton, indigo, and tobacco; of dry lands, it was the best type of soil. Cane savannah resembled hardwood areas in the types of crops it could sustain and had the added advantage that, unlike oak and hickory lands, it needed little clearing before cultivation. The richest and most-prized soil, however, was the swampland, or marsh, that lay along coastal estuaries. When some justices of the peace inspected marshland in Liberty and McIntosh counties, Georgia, in 1797, they concluded that these were soils unsurpassed in quality: they were "very level and consist cheifly of a fine blue clay with a mould [topsoil] of two or three inches." This heavy and wet earth (continually supplied with silt from estuarial flooding) gave the Lower South its most distinctive lands and its residents the idea—reasonable, if they meant to use this soil—that they could grow all manner of luxuriant crops found along the Yangtze or the Nile. Such land provided a perfect hothouse for experiments with exotic plants, and it insulated cultivators from the soil depletion that concerned farmers elsewhere.[19]

18. John Drayton, *A View of South-Carolina, as Respects Her Natural and Civil Concerns* (Charleston, S.C., 1802), 8–11; David Ramsay, *A Sketch of the Soil, Climate, Weather, and Diseases of South-Carolina* (Charleston, S.C., 1796), 4.

19. For descriptions of these four types of land, see Drayton, *View of S.-C.*, 8–10, 110–111; Harry J. Carman, ed., *American Husbandry* (1775) (New York, 1939), 270–275; [Thomas Christie], *A Description of Georgia . . .* (London, 1741), 4. The quotation is from a "Certificate of several Magistrats . . . ," Apr. 14, 1797, Liberty County Records,

Innovators in the Lower South were particularly fascinated with agriculture in the Near and Far East, because they themselves produced crops, like rice, that were ancient staples of Asia. They also knew that Asian rice (and later cotton) vied in European markets with their own products and wished to improve the quality and amount of their staples to maintain a competitive edge. John Drayton read accounts of China before he wrote his *View of South-Carolina;* a foldout table in his work compared methods of cultivating rice in South Carolina, China, Egypt, Sumatra, and Spain (see Plate 1). When Thomas Pinckney wrote a description of local rice cultivation in 1810, he assured his fellows in the South Carolina Agricultural Society that he had obtained "correct information concerning the production of this grain, in countries where, in consequence of its long establishment and extensive use, I was induced to believe that experience must have suggested the most advantageous mode of culture."[20]

Planters adopted other elements of the East. Georgia's trustees helpfully sent samples of bamboo to their settlers. When Andrew Turnbull brought Greek emigrants to New Smyrna in East Florida, he instructed them to build stone-lined canals for irrigating indigo and other crops. Turnbull had seen such canals in Egypt, and his adoption of Middle Eastern irrigation was a success— one of the few working features of this troubled settlement. James Simkins of South Carolina advertised in the *Columbian Centinel* in 1809 that he sold "Egyptian Grass Seed" because "few, if any, of the English grass Seeds [are] adapted to our Southern Climate."[21]

The most successful experiments with Asian agriculture, and astonishing examples of agricultural creativity, were the handiwork of Samuel Bowen.

GHS. See some spirited defenses of pine lands, dated May 1, 7, 1793, in the John Hall Papers, GHS. These documents were probably advertisements encouraging speculation in what would become the Pine Barrens scandal.

20. Drayton, *View of S.-C.,* 121n, cites two works on China; *Report of the Committee Appointed by the South Carolina Agricultural Society . . . to Which Is Added General Thomas Pinckney's Letter on the Water Culture of Rice* (Charleston, S.C., 1823), 16, Pinckney Family Papers, series 37-60, SCHS. (The letter was written on Dec. 12, 1810.) On the ever-present threat of competition, especially from Bengal, see Peter A. Coclanis, *The Shadow of a Dream: Economic Life and Death in the South Carolina Low Country, 1670–1920* (New York, 1989), 135.

21. Richard Beale Davis, *Intellectual Life in the Colonial South, 1585–1763* (Knoxville, Tenn., 1978), II, 957; E. P. Panagopoulos, *New Smyrna: An Eighteenth-Century Greek Odyssey* (Gainesville, Fla., 1966), 75–76; *Columbian Centinel* (Augusta), July 1, 1809.

Bowen, rather than the mistakenly credited Benjamin Franklin, introduced the soybean to North America. As a young man he sailed with the East India Company and claimed to have been a prisoner of war in China for four years; he viewed many parts of that country, observing Chinese methods of agriculture. After his release and return to England, Bowen arranged with James Flint, an officer of the East India Company, to emigrate to Georgia and experiment with Asian crops there. Flint, the first Englishman legally permitted by Chinese authorities to learn Chinese, well knew how jealously China guarded itself and its products; doubtless he and other colonial agents wanted an alternative source for Eastern crops. Bowen arrived in Georgia in 1764 and bought land along the coast, possibly using funds from Flint. He began in 1765 to grow soybeans—"Luk Taw" or "Chinese vetch"—from which he produced soy sauce and soy vermicelli noodles. As well as divining a London market for Asian foodstuffs, Bowen conjectured that soybean sprouts had antiscorbutic properties of value to the Royal Navy. He presented his results to the Royal Society of Arts and was doubtless a shoo-in for their gold medal of 1766. Bowen also received two hundred guineas from the king and patents for his methods of producing vermicelli, soy sauce, and sweet potato sago. Having in the meantime married into the Georgia elite, Bowen was an example of how individual skill, imperial connections, and a fertile southern climate could confer success and fortune.[22]

Records of Bowen's activities end before 1778 (he probably died then), though others took up similar experiments. Luigi Castiglioni reported in the 1780s that a man from the East Indies had set up a "sago" manufactory near Greenage, Georgia, "from which he made a huge profit." James Laurens wrote in 1773 that he grew small amounts of Chinese tallow and tea. His brother,

22. Bowen's own accounts of his Chinese adventures and his Georgia experiments are in the *Gentleman's Magazine*, XXXVII (1767) as well as in the *Georgia Gazette* (Savannah), Sept. 17, 1766. For scholarly work on Bowen, see T. Hymowitz and J. R. Harlan, "Introduction of Soybean to North America by Samuel Bowen in 1765," *Economic Botany*, XXXVII (1983), 371–379. See also Notebook 2, p. 48 (verso), Ellis Manuscripts, LSL, on "Mr. S. Bowen," "Mr. Flint," and their experiments with soybean sprouts and the antiscorbutic properties of water in which the sprouts had soaked; Dr. William Grant's notes on Samuel Bowen's experiments with Chinese vetch, Misc. Muniments, item 34, bundle 38, section 32, GD.1, SRO. On Flint's career in the East India Co., see Edward L. Farmer, "James Flint versus the Canton Interest, 1755–1760," Papers on China from Seminars at Harvard University, East Asian Research Center, Harvard University, XVII (December 1963), 38–66.

	SOUTH-CAROLINA.	SPAIN.	EGYPT.	SUMATRA.	CHINA.
How rice land is prepared.	Generally by turning up the land with an hoe; but sometimes it is done with a plough, and harrowed.	The land is turned up by a plough, and covered with water four inches deep.	The land is covered with water for a week. Afterwards men, women, and children, naked, up to the waist, walk and sink deep into the mud, and free the land from the old roots and stubble.	Buffaloes are turned into the land, which by wading and rolling over it, stir it up. After which a flat board, with weights on it, is drawn over the land to make it level.	The field is flowed with water, and ploughed with an ox plough, while the water is on. It is then harrowed in the same way.
How rice is planted.	It is sown in drills, from 16 to 18 inches asunder, at the rate of from 1 to 2 bushels the acre.	By transplantation; each plant, distant a foot from the other, and the ground covered four inches with water. Transplanted in June.	By transplantation in July.	By transplantation.	It is sown broad-cast, in loose mud; and is afterwards taken from thence and transplanted in loose mud, in quincunx order.
How rice is reaped.	By sickles, or reaping hooks.	By sickles, or reaping hooks. Sometimes by scythes.		By a particular kind of small knife.	By long knives, rather concaved at the edge. Also by sickles.
How gathered.	In sheaves, with a length of straw.	In sheaves.	In sheaves.	The ears of rice are cut short, one by one, and tied in a little sheaf, and thrown into a basket.	In very large sheaves; one man brings only two out of the field at a time.
How threshed.	By flails.	Trodden out, by driving horses & mules over it, on a stone, or stucco area.	The sheaves are spread on the floor, and a cart, with cutting wheels, drawn by oxen, passes over them, which separates the grain from the straw.	The sheaves are spread on mats in the barns; and the grain rubbed from the straw, by the feet of the labourers. This exercise sometimes draws the blood from	By flails.

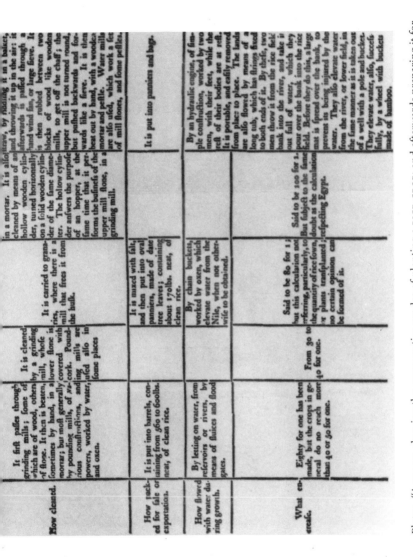

Plate 1. "A TABLE, shewing the comparative modes of planting a RICE-CROP; and afterwards preparing it for market, in the different countries of South-Carolina, Spain, Egypt, Sumatra and China." From John Drayton, A View of South-Carolina, as Respects Her Natural and Civil Concerns (Charleston, S.C., 1802), facing 125

Henry, experimented with "the Chinese Method of transplanting Rice" in the 1780s and found it saved labor yet made much more rice: 2,053 pounds compared with his usual yield of 1,500 pounds per acre. Encouraged by his Asiatic successes, Laurens appealed in 1787 to his London factors for a model of a Chinese rice mill, which they duly produced, evidently long accustomed to their client's requests for obscure devices and unusual advice.[23]

Coastal innovators looked to the Mediterranean as well as to Asia for promising agricultural strategies. One of the first Mediterranean crops they tried was citrus fruit. Citrus trees, thanks to Spanish settlers, had grown wild in the region since the 1500s but still needed some coddling to yield a sweeter and more salable product. In 1744, Robert Pringle told a correspondent that South Carolina had "been for some years past Improving in the Planting of Orange Trees" and that he had some ten thousand oranges in his orchard. He sent nine hundred oranges to his brother in London and also shipped quantities of fruit to merchants in New York and Boston to see how it would sell. It evidently sold well somewhere, because planters began planting large numbers of trees— Henry Yonge boasted to Charles Pinckney in 1747 that he had about two thousand orange trees on his aptly named Orange Island plantation. An unfortunate frost in the same year, however, killed many citrus trees in South Carolina. David Ramsay lamented in 1809 that severe frosts had recurred every seven to eight years, precluding large-scale cultivation of citrus, though a few hardy trees remained in gardens, especially in lower Georgia and eastern Florida. Experiments with citrus fruits showed how planters could overestimate their climate's ability to sustain semitropical crops on a commercial basis. Ramsay, again explaining how frosts prevented planters from "naturalizing tropical fruits," adjusted the old latitudinal reasoning: though South Carolina lay parallel to the Mediterranean, its climate more nearly resembled that of temperate Italy and France (and Asia, of course) than of the warmer Middle East.[24]

23. Hymowitz and Harlan, "Introduction of Soybean," *Econ. Botany,* XXXVII (1983), 371, 378; Luigi Castiglioni, *Viaggio: Travels in the United States of North America, 1785–87,* ed. and trans. Antonio Pace (Syracuse, N.Y., 1983), 128; Philip M. Hamer *et al.,* eds., *The Papers of Henry Laurens* (Columbia, S.C., 1968–), IX, 47–48; Henry Laurens to Edward Bridgen, Feb. 13, 1786 (quotation), and to Bridgen and Waller, Jan. 4, 9, 13, 1787, LP. George Jones procured "powdered Sago" in Georgia for export in 1790; see Jones to Edward Telfair, Aug. 6, 1790, Telfair Family Papers, folder 2, GHS.

24. Walter B. Edgar, ed., *The Letterbook of Robert Pringle* (Columbia, S.C., 1972), II, 732, 742; Henry Yonge to Charles Pinckney, July 8, 1747, Pinckney Family Papers, series

Connections with the European side of the Mediterranean did prove useful. Emigrant Du Mensil de St. Pierre made such a success of viticulture in South Carolina that in 1772 he won the Royal Society of Arts gold medal. In 1796, South Carolinian James Sanders Guignard paid ship's passage and wages to a Frenchman to make wine and brandy from Guignard plantation grapes. Stephen Cathalan, consul to the United States in Marseilles, supplied materials and information to Americans. In 1794, Thomas Pinckney ordered young olive trees from Cathalan. In 1806, Thomas Jefferson introduced Cathalan to John Couper of St. Simons, Georgia, who also wanted to cultivate olives. Other planters who went to Europe gathered their own information. When John Rutledge toured Italy in 1788, he made notes on local methods of growing rice, wheat, beans, and mulberry trees. At his diplomatic post in Spain in the 1790s, Thomas Pinckney observed whatever "might be beneficial" in the way of agriculture.[25]

The Caribbean was the third region that planters surveyed for likely crops. South Carolinians had had close ties with the West Indies since the 1670s. Emigrant West Indians formed an important component of Carolina's early settlement, and South Carolinians supplied sugar planters with naval stores,

---

4, box 15, folder of "Odds and Ends," LC; Ramsay, *History of S.-C.*, II, 52–53, quotation from 53. See Edgar, ed., *Letterbook of Pringle*, II, 732n, for a description of the 1747 frost. For later evidence of orange trees, see Thomas to Ann Couper, Aug. 31, 1810, Fraser-Couper Papers, folder 1, GHS; William Baldwin to Thomas Forman, May 20, 1814, Forman-Bryan-Screven Papers, folder 2, GHS.

Citrus fruits originated in Asia but spread (with Islam) to the Mediterranean, and from there Europeans carried them to the New World. See Alfred W. Crosby, *Ecological Imperialism: The Biological Expansion of Europe, 900–1900* (Cambridge, 1986), 156–157.

25. Introduction, p. 3, reel 1, RSA; oversized papers, Guignard Family Papers, box 1, folder 74, SCL; Stephen Cathalan to Thomas Pinckney, Mar. 25, 1794, Pinckney Family Papers, series 3, box 5, folder for March 1794, LC; Thomas Jefferson to Stephen Cathalan, Mar. 22, 1806, Mackay-Stiles Papers, microfilm, reel 4, XLIII, SHC; 1788 Journal, John Rutledge, Jr., Papers, cab. 24, Duke; Thomas Pinckney to ———, Mar. 16, 1796, Pinckney Family Papers, microfiche card 8, series 37-58, SCHS—Pinckney mentioned wheat cultivation in Virginia, so his addressee probably dwelt in that state and might have been Thomas Jefferson, to whom Pinckney had written in 1793 (series 37-56, card 8) and 1794 (series 37-57, card 1). Charles Cotesworth Pinckney's experiments with olives and capers might have resulted from his brother's information. See C. C. Pinckney to Eliza Lucas Pinckney, July 1, 1792, Pinckney Family Papers, series 1, box 4, LC.

lumber, meat, and other provisions from the early 1700s until the Revolution. Continuing trade and migration proved conducive to exchange of information.[26] Eliza Lucas, one of the Lower South's best-known innovators, drew extensively and fruitfully on the Carolina–West Indies connection during the 1740s. Her Antiguan family bought lowcountry property, and Lucas moved there with her mother and siblings, possibly to remove her ailing parent from the Caribbean's baleful climate. Lucas maintained contact with her father, who was governor of Antigua and remained behind. At her request that he send her some novelty to grow on his plantation in South Carolina, Governor Lucas supplied an assortment of seeds; his daughter reported in 1740 that indigo seemed most promising. The governor then searched about for a suitable West Indian to teach her how to make the plant into marketable dye. He tried to send a slave but settled instead on a white man, Nicholas Cromwell—a mistake, as it turned out, because Cromwell resented his hired status and removal to the Lower South. Lucas warned his new son-in-law, Charles Pinckney (who married Eliza in 1744), that Cromwell would not submit to the direction of an overseer but should be permitted to go his own way. Cromwell balked at teaching his skills to anyone, though this had been the whole point of his service. Eliza Lucas Pinckney thereupon discharged Cromwell and hired his brother Patrick, who proved no more tractable; he sabotaged the project by throwing too much lime in the indigo vats while the dye fermented. The Cromwell brothers were two early, unruly examples of imported talent uneasy, at best, with a dependent position within the hierarchy of patronage. The Pinckney-Lucas clan nevertheless gleaned enough understanding of indigo manufacture to pursue the experiment and publicize its results to others, and other innovators began to coax West Indians familiar with indigo to their plantations.[27]

26. On early West Indian settlement of Carolina, see M. Eugene Sirmans, *Colonial South Carolina: A Political History, 1663–1763* (Chapel Hill, N.C., 1966), chap. 2; Richard S. Dunn, "The English Sugar Islands and the Founding of South Carolina," *SCHM*, LXXII (1971), 81–93; Richard Waterhouse, "England, the Caribbean, and the Settlement of Carolina," *Journal of American Studies*, IX (1975), 259–281. For trade with the West Indies, see Clarence L. Ver Steeg, *Origins of a Southern Mosaic: Studies of Early Carolina and Georgia* (Athens, Ga., 1975), 114–117; and Peter H. Wood, *Black Majority: Negroes in Colonial South Carolina from 1670 through the Stono Rebellion* (New York, 1975), 13–34.

27. Elise Pinckney, ed., *The Letterbook of Eliza Lucas Pinckney* (Chapel Hill, N.C., 1972), 8; George Lucas to Charles Pinckney, July 12, 1745, Pinckney Family Papers, series

While indigo was becoming a commercial success, innovators planted other and less common West Indian plants. In the 1730s, Georgia's trustees hired botanists to tour the West Indies in search of plants for the experimental garden near Savannah—the trust's incubator for potential staple crops. Henry Laurens requested seeds for "guinea" and "Scotch" grasses and sugarcane joints from Peter Bachop of Jamaica in 1770. Laurens also revealed how he was already "growing Pine Apples" he had received from another source. In 1785, Laurens was growing grass and ginger from Jamaica; three years later he received information on the cultivation of West Indian guinea grass as forage for cattle.[28]

From this range of Caribbean exotics, planters picked cotton and sugar for special attention. They acquired cotton from islands that had produced it since the seventeenth century and had gradually improved strains derived from the Old and New Worlds. When Ralph Izard toured Europe and the Near East just before the Revolution, he wrote Henry Laurens: "I should have sent some Turkey cotton-seed, from Leghorn, but was informed there, that our own West India cotton was much better, and bore a higher price than that from the

---

38-1-5, SCHS; David L. Coon, "Eliza Lucas Pinckney and the Reintroduction of Indigo Culture in South Carolina," *Jour. So. Hist.*, XLII (1976), 61–76; Gray, *Agriculture in the Southern U.S.*, I, 290–291.

Gabriel Manigault hired a French West Indian to "learn the Planters to raise and make Indigo" in South Carolina. See John Farquharson to Gabriel Manigault (grandson of the Gabriel who raised indigo), June 24, 1789, Manigault Family Papers, box 2, folder 14, SCL. West Indians who came to the Lower South on their own initiative found they could market their skills there, as did a Frenchman from Santo Domingo, who offered in 1767 to teach planters how to make indigo (*South-Carolina Gazette; And Country Journal*, May 5, 1767). See also George Udney to William Middleton, Mar. 29, 1748, Middleton-Saumarez Papers, microfilm, section 2, SCL, on another indigo maker from the French West Indies.

28. Davis, *Intellectual Life in Colonial South*, II, 957; Bertha Sheppard Hart, "The First Garden of Georgia," *GHQ*, XIX (1935), 329–330; Joseph Krafka, Jr., "Medicine in Colonial Georgia," *GHQ*, XX (1936), 327–330; James W. Holland, "The Beginning of Public Agricultural Experimentation in America: The Trustees' Garden in Georgia," *AH*, XII (1938), 271–277; Hamer *et al.*, eds., *Papers of Laurens*, VII, 356–357; Henry Laurens to John McIntosh, Sept. 10, 1785, and "Mr. Irvine's directions for planting Guinea Grass," November 1788, folder of Miscellaneous Medical and Plantation Recipes from the Library of Congress, LP (this folder also contains an unsigned letter to Laurens about guinea grass).

Levant." Georgia planter Richard Leake sowed samples of West Indian cotton on his plantation in 1788 and referred to the second growth on his harvested cotton plants in 1792 and 1797 as "ratoon" cotton, using the West Indian term for subsequent growth on harvested sugar cane. In 1807, George Izard planted flax and hemp around his cotton fields to repel worms, as (he had learned) West Indians did.[29] West Indian cotton gins, as well, were prototypes for continental gins. The *Georgia Gazette* of December 4, 1788, offered for sale— five years before Eli Whitney patented his gin—a slave man from St. Croix who was "well acquainted with the Culture of Cotton" and "a compleat hand at ginning of it, and can construct a gin for that purpose." The British Caribbean was, literally, the seedbed of the later Cotton South.

Although West Indian sugarcane was not as successful as cotton, coastal innovators between Charleston and St. Augustine nevertheless produced a surprising amount of sugar. A small group of East Florida planters experimented with cane in the new British settlement during the 1770s; the next generation planted sugar in Georgia and Carolina during the financial slumps of the Napoleonic Wars.[30] Eliza Lucas Pinckney's children (Harriott Pinckney Horry and Thomas and Charles Cotesworth Pinckney) experimented with

29. Entries for Apr. 6, 1788, May 24, 1792, Aug. 15, 1797, Richard Leake Plantation Journal, GHS (see also Pierce Butler to Thomas Young, Oct. 28, 1793, Pierce Butler Letterbook, SCL, where Butler wrote about his "Ratoon Cotton"); George to Henry Izard, May 21, 1807, Ralph Izard Papers, box 2, folder 16, SCL; quotation from Anne Izard Deas, ed., *Correspondence of Mr. Ralph Izard . . .* (New York, 1844), 16–17.

On the probable origins of cottons familiar to North Americans, see Donald D. Brand, "The Origin and Early Distribution of New World Cultivated Plants," *AH*, XIII (1939), 114, which points to South America as the origin of sea island cotton (*Gossypium barbadense* L.), and southern Mexico as the origin of upland cotton (*Gossypium hirsutum* L.). S. G. Stephens, on the other hand, argues that the first cottons North American colonists grew were *G. hirsutum* varieties from the West Indies and that sea island cotton was probably a hybrid of *G. barbadense* (a long-staple cotton like sea island cotton) and *G. hirsutum* (short-fibered, but with sea island's fineness). See Stephens, "The Origin of Sea Island Cotton," *AH*, L (1976), 391–395.

30. A few settlers in British East Florida raised cane and made sugar and rum (in small amounts) during the 1770s. See William Turnbull to James Grant, May 27, 1771 (in which Turnbull claimed he had machinery to mill sugar), bundle 253, and F. G. Mulcaster to Grant, June 13, 1773 (on sugar planters in the colony), bundle 369, MacPherson-Grant Papers, Ballindalloch.

sugar during 1813–1814, gaining information about planting from Santo Domingo, among other places. Members of Georgia's McQueen and Mackay families also experimented with sugarcane at the same time. Both clans had friends in Jamaica; the information they gained and relayed about sugar cultivation perhaps came from these contacts. Other important cane growers included William Baldwin and John Couper. Baldwin was an amateur botanist who lived in the St. Mary area of south Georgia; he planted sugar there and at St. Simons during 1813 and 1814 and advised other planters on the suitability of their lands for the crop. John Couper grew both sugarcane and oranges at his St. Simons plantation in 1810. Couper even declared the area around St. Simons better suited to cane than the West Indies. He claimed that the region's mild frosts posed no problem to sugar cultivation, though here he was clearly indulging in boosterism—the Lower South could not compete with the Caribbean or, later, Louisiana in producing sugar.[31]

Thomas Spalding, the Lower South's most energetic sugar planter, did find a strategy that made the most of the region's warm but not quite tropical climate. Spalding began growing cane on Sapelo Island in 1806. He adapted to Georgia's shorter growing season by planting a new crop before his workers had harvested the old, rotating each planting among different fields. This strategy demanded quantities of labor and acreage far above the average even for most rice planters, making sugar the preserve not only of the most inventive but of the richest planters. Spalding's system worked, and in 1816 he published a definitive description of sugar planting in the United States. Cultivation had spread enough that, by this time, newspaper advertisements offered cane plants for sale or specified that available lands were suited to sugar.[32]

31. Thomas Pinckney's notes, Harriott Horry Ravenel Collection, series 11-332-25, and Thomas Spalding to Thomas Pinckney, Oct. 18, 1815, series 11-332-27, SCHS; Charles Cotesworth Pinckney to Harriott Horry, Nov. 16, 1814, Pinckney Family Papers, series 1, box 3, LC; Mary Ann Cowper (Jamaica) to Eliza McQueen (Georgia), box 1, folder 1, Mackay-Stiles Papers; M. C. McQueen to Eliza Mckay, Sept. 21, 1814, T. Butler to John McQueen, Aug. 20, 1815, box 2, folder 18, and diagram of sugar mill and transcript of notes on its use, XXVII, SHC; William Baldwin to General T. Forman, Feb. 27, 1813, May 20, 1814, and ca. 1814, Forman-Bryan-Screven Papers, folder 2, GHS; Thomas to Ann Couper, Aug. 31, 1810, Fraser-Couper Papers, folder 1, GHS.

32. E. Merton Coulter, *Thomas Spalding of Sapelo* (Baton Rouge, La., 1940), 111–119; Thomas Spalding, *Observations on the Method of Planting and Cultivating the Sugar-*

Considering their long-standing connection with Africa established by the slave trade, it is surprising that whites in the Lower South did not experiment more with African crops. Neglect of Africa paralleled their relative lack of interest in South America, probably because planters considered both places to have torrid climates too different from their own and because they were prejudiced against regions that lacked what they would recognize as civilized cultures. They experimented with truly tropical crops from unfamiliar areas only if such plants had already proved successful in the Europeanized West Indies: sugarcane, most obviously, but also things like Henry Laurens's guinea grass and pineapples, the latter natives of South America. Rather than importing African crops, planters more often discovered them in the gardens of their slaves. For these crops, blacks were the true experimenters and relied on a transatlantic network much different from that emanating from the Royal Society. Through the Atlantic slave trade, blacks had gradually transferred African plants (like sesame, guinea corn, okra) and American crops transplanted in Africa (peanuts and capsicum peppers) to lands where they were enslaved.[33]

Whites discovered uses for slaves' products only when they learned of external markets for them. This was clearly the case with peanuts. Blacks had often grown and marketed peanuts, but whites paid little heed until European chocolate manufacturers wanted the product for its bland oil. In 1807, George Izard relayed to Henry Izard the unexpected news that a British merchant offered "two Dollars" a bushel for an order of one thousand bushels of peanuts; in 1808, David Ramsay claimed that planters could make up to twenty pounds sterling per acre from peanuts. Much of this profit came indirectly through slaves' cash cropping: planters bought peanuts that slaves raised on their own time. George Izard persuaded his brother, for instance, that "the Negroes [might] be encouraged to raise a large Quantity of these for which they should receive a reasonable Price."[34] Sesame seed, which blacks called

Cane . . . (Charleston, S.C., 1816), in Coulter, ed., *Georgia's Disputed Ruins* (Chapel Hill, N.C., 1937). On cane plants and lands, see, for example, advertisements of David McCormick and George Street in the *Georgia Journal*, Dec. 17, 21, 1814.

33. Wood, *Black Majority*, 119–122.

34. Philip D. Morgan, "Work and Culture: The Task System and the World of Lowcountry Blacks, 1700 to 1880," *WMQ*, 3d Ser., XXXIX (1982), 572–574; Ramsay, *History of S.-C.*, II, 564–565; George to Henry Izard, June 26, 1807, Ralph Izard Papers,

benne or binny, was another African crop nearly invisible to whites until the market beckoned for it. James Crokatt, a South Carolina merchant who removed to London, sent back in 1747 a model of a mill to press out sesame oil (as well as samples of cochineal and Spanish indigo) for display at the treasurer's office in Charleston. Crokatt intended to lead planters' thoughts toward diversification, and residents did pay some attention to sesame during the depression of the 1740s. Production expanded again during the commercial vicissitudes of the War of 1812; at this time, local planters looked for sales yielding three dollars a bushel to cover the cost of growing the seed or (a more interesting possibility) the cost of buying it from their slaves plus a profit. Whether slaves had already calculated and charged a profit of their own is an intriguing question.[35]

Cultivation of things like peanuts and sesame helped reinforce a base of surprisingly autonomous slave labor in the lowcountry; it showed planters' reliance on slavery's flexibility as a form of production—which was especially the case with tasked slave labor. Slaves' relative autonomy would be significant for several phases of innovation in the Lower South. Their self-directed actions supported crucial years of cotton cultivation during the Revolution, when slaves acted nearly as independent producers of the fiber; their continuing desire for autonomy then shaped the expansion of tidal irrigation of rice after the war. But the independence cut two ways. Slaves were actively rebelling against white authority during the war, and their resistance continued after 1783; planters who granted new or extended old forms of autonomy at this time did so to ward off more overt forms of discontent. In this way, slaves'

box 2, folder 17, SCL. Other whites had already realized that there was a market for peanuts; the *South-Carolina Gazette; And Country Journal* for Sept. 3, 1771, listed 4,149 bushels of groundnuts among the annual exports.

35. Advertisement for Crokatt, *South-Carolina Gazette* (Charleston), Mar. 23, 1747 (see also advertisements for sesame, Oct. 27, Dec. 1, 1746). Georgia resident John McQueen learned that a Dr. Mease of Philadelphia wanted a bushel of the seed for some unstated purpose; see T. Butler to John McQueen, Nov. 3, 1815, Mackay-Stiles Papers, series A, box 2, folder 18, SHC. William Few of New York offered $2.00 a bushel for benne, and upped the price to $2.25 in an advertisement in the *Augusta Chronicle,* Apr. 15, 1809. A complaint about Few's low price is in the Henry Jackson journal, Sept. 1, 1811–Oct. 11, 1811, entry on p. 16 (verso), Jackson-Prince Papers, box 9, III, SHC. See also Henry Laurens's note to the American Philosophical Society, to accompany a keg of benne, Misc. Medical and Plantation Recipes, LP.

seeming cooperation with planters' innovations was also a reminder of the kind of assertion that had erupted into violence in the Stono Rebellion of 1739.

Lowcountry planters warily compromised with slaves' desire for independent activity to maintain or expand their own profits from commercial agriculture; slaves as well as scientists provided ideas—and made demands—that changed local practice. But whites' eagerness to use all of slaves' efforts to strengthen their economy did not make up for a growing uncertainty over slavery in general. Planters had been apprehensive over slavery as early as the 1730s. With each succeeding decade, and especially during the Revolution, they were ever more fearful that they had imported a resentful population and created an unstable institution that, whatever its economic payoff, threatened the security of the region. Their willingness to grant some autonomy to slaves summed up planters' uncertainty over what they should do: they retained slavery, yet were willing to modify it to keep the institution as a whole, even if this strategy meant minimizing day-to-day evidence of their own authority over slaves.

❦ The Case of Silk

Lowcountry planters' conflicting desires for change and continuity reappeared, in sharp relief, in their plans for the less-settled areas that surrounded the plantation belt. To prevent slavery from spreading ever further over the region, many planters in the parishes wanted a strategically underdeveloped band of settlement around them. They saw new settlements as laboratories for their projects, places for experiments with exotic products and free-white labor. Silk production was the most notable example of this expectation. Silk reeling reflected key elements of the coastal pattern of innovation, including supplying a rare commodity to the mother country, using elite patronage, and relying on foreign materials and labor. Promoters of silk had more interest in these elements than in achieving economic growth for the new regions supposed to produce silk; such places were to remain outposts removed from commercial ambition and from the slave labor that would realize such ambitions.

From the 1730s to 1800s, planters designed policies to accomplish their unwieldy collection of goals: to prevent slavery from moving west, to fulfill mercantilistic production of rare goods, and to provide military defense of

Britain's southern holdings against hostile Indians and Spaniards. The first scheme modeled on these lines was South Carolina Governor Robert Johnson's township plan, later copied by Georgia's trustees; both policies discouraged the black slavery and white amassment of land that would usher in plantation agriculture.[36] Subtler strategies lingered in calculated neglect of western areas in the decade before and two decades after the American Revolution. Though some coastal planters (notably Henry Laurens) encouraged westerners to buy slaves and set up commercial agriculture, others preferred not to have slavery move west.

Ambivalence over slavery was due, not to a moral position, but to a practical suspicion that slavery had dangers that would only worsen if the institution spread over more territory. Everyone conceded that slaves were a security risk; slaves rebelled, ran away, and jeopardized a settlement if it was attacked from outside. If new settlers had no slaves, the reasoning ran, they could better take immediate military action against Indians, against the Spanish, or against rebellious lowcountry slaves. Before the Revolution, Christopher Gadsden concluded that farmers in the interior were "the most intrinsically useful people we have" because all their produce was "clear gain"—that is, reinvested in land and improvements, not in slaves. Slaveless settlers also were, Gadsden believed, "always ready to assist" planters in regulating their own "very precarious property." This assumption ran parallel to coastal residents' belief that slavery, though unfortunately needed in fevered environments, was not a generally laudable institution. Timothy Ford claimed in 1794 that while "nature" forbade whites to work in the lowcountry's "fertile swamps," "she has not interdicted their labouring in the up lands" whose residents, free from fevers, ought themselves to wield ax and hoe.[37]

This climatic reasoning played into mercantilistic expectations for southern areas of British America. English merchants and manufacturers had a long list of exotic staples they wanted to have produced by British subjects instead of by potential enemies. Silk was a prime example. By the early modern era, Italy and France produced most of the silk worn by Europeans. Cultivating mulberry

36. See discussion of township plan in Chapter 2, above.

37. Gadsden cited in Robert M. Weir, ed., *The Letters of Freeman, etc.: Essays on the Nonimportation Movement in South Carolina, Collected by William Henry Drayton* (Columbia, S.C., 1977), 83–84; Timothy Ford [Americanus, pseud.], *The Constitutionalist . . .* (Charleston, S.C., 1794), 16.

trees for silkworm fodder, raising the worms, and reeling their cocoons into usable hanks of fiber flourished especially in the area around Lyon and in Italy's Piedmont. Continental warfare perennially disrupted the silk trade, though Britain made a strategic alliance with Savoyard ruler Victor Amadeus II during Queen Anne's War to curb Hapsburg expansion while speeding Italian goods to British consumers. British merchants preferred, however, to import raw silk that could be processed by workers in the Spitalfields district of London, rather than indirectly pay wages to Continental workers by importing finished cloth into Britain. Spitalfields spinners, for their part, complained about the underemployment and low wages that resulted from influxes of either Irish workers or foreign cloth; silk spinners rioted in 1737, in 1763, and most ominously in 1768, when they tied their protests to the Wilkes and Liberty movement. Britons and even colonists soon recognized silk and Spitalfields as bywords for clamor and popular radicalism.[38]

Given all these difficulties, making silk within some tractable English colony had long been a goal of mercantilistic planners. Promoters worked to shift some silk production from Europe just as it had earlier been shifted from Asia. In 1628, Virginia's Governor John Harvey received instructions to plant mulberry trees. After many setbacks (Virginians preferred tobacco to silk) mercantilist expectations for silk took shape a century later in the Lower South after a barrage of incentives aimed at settlers there. The South Carolina Assembly offered bounties on silk in 1736, 1738, and 1744. When Spain and Italy prohibited exports of raw silk from their countries in 1750, London merchants petitioned Parliament also to subsidize American silk production. In 1755, London manufacturers and traders endorsed Georgia's silk to the Royal Society of Arts to ensure that organization's support. The society thereafter sent rewards to silk reelers in South Carolina, kept in contact with silk expert Pickering Robinson in Georgia, and granted more than one thousand pounds

---

38. On Continental silk production, see Geoffrey Symcox, *Victor Amadeus II: Absolutism in the Savoyard State, 1675–1730* (New York, 1983), 43–46, 159–160, 187–188, 208–209. On London silk workers, see Bernard Bailyn, *Voyagers to the West: A Passage in the Peopling of America on the Eve of the Revolution* (New York, 1986), 279–283; Rosamond Bayne-Powell, *Eighteenth-Century London Life* (New York, 1938), 78–79; and George Rudé, *Paris and London in the Eighteenth Century: Studies in Popular Protest* (New York, 1971), 204–213, 253–257—Rudé discusses how London silk workers' riots of 1768 were connected to the Wilkes and Liberty protests.

sterling to this new colony. Land policies also encouraged silk reeling. South Carolina settlers destined to make silk received shares in townships, and Georgia settlers got headrights of five hundred acres from the trust so long as they agreed to plant their new estates with stands of mulberry trees.[39]

If economic incentives came from Britons, supplies and expertise came from foreigners via routes established by innovators who researched agriculture over the globe. Live silkworms ("Worm seed") came from Italy. These emigrant grubs disdained leaves from American black mulberry trees; Georgia's trustees thereupon sent for seeds of white mulberry trees from the Chelsea Physic Garden, nurturing the seedlings in their experimental garden before distributing the trees to settlers. Cultivators relied on Italian designs to construct sheds lined with shelves where the worms spun their cocoons. Savannah's silk filature, constructed in 1751, was also modeled on Italian buildings. In this and the filature at Purrysburg, South Carolina, small metal basins, each with its own fire beneath it, heated the cocoons in order to loosen the coil of thread so it could be untangled and reeled into a spinnable hank. For this painstaking task, Italians were the workers of choice. British merchants and manufacturers considered Italian reeled silk the most desirable product—the British East India Company even enticed Italians to Bengal to reel Asian silk! John Lewis Poyas, a silk spinner from Italy's Piedmont, and other Piedmontese settlers were brought to silk-producing Purrysburg. The Amatis and Camuse families, other Piedmontese, arrived in Georgia in 1732 to reel silk and to teach other settlers this delicate business. Joseph Ottolenghi (or Ottolenghe) then replaced the Camuses in 1753 under Georgia's new royal government. Ottolenghi, an Italian Jew from the wine- and silk-producing area of Lombardy, had moved to England and, after romantic and financial disappointments, converted to Anglicanism. He then went to Georgia as a missionary and artisan—to catechize African slaves and reel silk at the Savannah filature until it closed in 1771. All in all, silk reeling encouraged social as well as economic

39. Gray, *Agriculture in the Southern U.S.*, I, 52–54, 184–187; C. Robert Haywood, "Mercantilism and South Carolina Agriculture, 1700–1763," *SCHM*, LX (1959), 21–23; W. Calvin Smith, "Utopia's Last Chance? The Georgia Silk Boomlet of 1751," *GHQ*, LIX (1975), 26–27; petition, Mar. 29, 1755, RSA, Guardbooks, reel 1; transactions for Jan. 7, 1772, RSA, MS Transactions, reel 1; Pickering Robinson to John Ellis, Apr. 14, 1761, Ellis Manuscripts, II, LSL; introduction, p. 3, RSA, reel 1; Robert L. Meriwether, *The Expansion of South Carolina, 1729–1765* (Kingsport, Tenn., 1940), 19–20.

diversity in the Lower South, where French and Italian joined English as languages of business.[40]

But the Lower South's silk industry, despite its Italianate planning, enjoyed limited success. Between 1742 and 1755, South Carolina exported a meager 651 pounds of raw silk; the industry peaked in the year 1750 with a paltry, almost comical, 118 pounds. After a decade of faltering attempts, Georgians managed somewhat better. Exports quickened in the 1750s, and annual average exports from Savannah between 1755 to 1777 were 546 pounds. The high point came in 1766, when Georgia shipped out 1,084 pounds. Discouraged by the low output, British officials, during the 1760s, reduced the subsidized price from forty shillings per pound to one and six pence.[41] Measured by its individual cultivators, the silk project seemed even tinier. Indigo innovator Eliza Lucas Pinckney, for instance, who raised silkworms in the 1750s, presented to members of the royal family silk dresses of her own manufacture—lovely garments, perhaps, but no serious threat to the Italian silk industry.[42] On the whole, silk production seemed like a series of promotional gimmicks meant to stimulate the mother country's interest in a potential boom of production forever receding into the future.

Part of the problem was that silk culture was a tricky and labor-intensive business unsuited to new settlements. Raising mulberry leaves, feeding silkworms, and transporting cocoons needed a fair amount of investment, a high degree of care, and a great deal of centralized planning and control to erect costly filatures and inspect the final product. None of these qualities endeared silk to pioneers; the expense of production and inspectors' refusal to buy

40. Holland, "Trustees' Garden," *AH*, XII (1938), 283–284; Coulter, ed., *Journal of William Stephens*, I, 52, II, 87; P. J. Marshall, *East Indian Fortunes: The British in Bengal in the Eighteenth Century* (Oxford, 1976), 150–151; Meriwether, *Expansion of S.C.*, 35–37; Mary Thomas McKinstry, "Silk Culture in the Colony of Georgia," *GHQ*, XIV (1930), 225–229; B. H. Levy, "Joseph Solomon Ottolenghi: Kosher Butcher in Italy—Christian Missionary in Georgia," *GHQ*, LXVI (1982), 119–144; Harold E. Davis, *The Fledgling Province: Social and Cultural Life in Colonial Georgia, 1733–1776* (Chapel Hill, N.C., 1976), 142–143.

41. On export figures, see Gray, *Agriculture in the Southern U.S.*, I, 186, 187, and on prices see 188. See also Smith, "Utopia's Last Chance," *GHQ*, LIX (1975), 30–34.

42. Harriott Horry Ravenel, *Eliza Pinckney* (New York, 1896), 130–131; *Belfast News Letter*, Dec. 17, 1754. On later private experiments, see Ralph Izard to Alice Izard, Dec. 7, 1794, and order for white mulberry trees, Apr. 14, 1796, Ralph Izard Papers, box 1, folders 6, 8, SCL.

second-rate products frustrated settlers' desire for wealth. When Georgia's trustees graded payments to silk producers by the quality of their cocoons, residents protested that the profits sank too low. Silk reeling was tedious and costly: it took sixteen pounds of cocoons to produce one pound of reeled silk— yielding less if the reeler damaged some of the raw product. This kind of industry needed workers drawn from a large and impoverished population, like Spitalfields or rural Italy. Silk enthusiasts had here miscalculated. Areas that produced silk in the Lower South had the thinnest population and most expensive labor. At the end of the trusteeship (in the 1750s), Georgia numbered only about two thousand white residents; the few skilled workers there commanded wages of two shillings per day and shunned agricultural tasks. As South Carolina's Lieutenant Governor William Bull concluded, "If we turn our eyes to those countries where [silk] is made in abundance . . . there labour is very cheap; in our Province it is very dear."[43]

Only a subsidized price for silk made it a worthwhile enterprise. When British prices declined in the late 1760s, silk production fell markedly in the next decade. Economic historians have calculated that settlers in Trustee Georgia made about a 10 percent rate of annual return. This was respectable, but Georgians could have garnered profits of 25–43 percent had they planted rice using slave labor. In speculating how silk might do better in Georgia than in Italy, James Habersham instead unwittingly gave reasons why it came out the other way. Habersham realized that Italian reelers "work for Others," whereas "in Georgia every Family have a Property, and may enjoy themselves the Produce of their Labour." Habersham thought this meant Georgians would work harder at reeling, but he failed to follow his own logic. Incentive and independence gave Georgians the ability to do with their property what they, and not the trustees, wished.[44]

To gain more-obedient workers, promoters looked for poverty-stricken Britons and persecuted Protestants from Catholic areas of Europe. Provided havens in the British Empire, such grateful peoples would be likely to toil

43. Smith, "Utopia's Last Chance," *GHQ*, LIX (1975), 29–30. On workmen's wages, see Coulter, ed., *Journal of William Stephens*, I, 145; Sainsbury Transcripts of Records in the Public Record Office, XXXII (1768–70), 396–397, SCDAH.

44. On silk prices, see Gray, *Agriculture in the Southern U.S.*, I, 188; Ralph Gray and Betty Wood, "The Transition from Indentured to Involuntary Servitude in Colonial Georgia," *Explorations in Economic History*, XIII (1976), 360, 363; "Extract from a Journal of Mr. Habersham . . . ," p. 6, Habersham Family Papers, folder 1, Duke.

without any ambition to set themselves up as planters. Under this policy, Protestants from Switzerland, Germany, and Italy's Piedmont settled at Purrysburg. Swiss emigrants formed core groups in other Carolina townships as well as portions of Georgia; Scotch-Irish, Welsh, German, Moravian, and Scottish settlers also flocked to the Lower South. Some of these settlers were devoted to their patrons' vision of a diversified economy. Georgia's pietistic Salzburgers steadily reeled silk, building two filatures at their town of New Ebenezer and remaining doggedly loyal to the trust, as did the farming community of Highland Scots at Darien.[45]

Silk reeling was, therefore, one especially dubious portion of an overambitious, if well-meaning, design that encouraged societal harmony over commercial ambition. A resident of a township or of Trustee Georgia had to fulfill a bewildering series of roles: yeoman soldier, diligent subsistence farmer, participant in a diversified artisanal economy, opponent of black slavery, teetotaler, converter of Indians, tolerant observer of alien religious and cultural beliefs—especially those of Catholics from the Mediterranean. Each element of the overall plan to create a traditional economy was intended to support the others. Settlers whom Georgia trustees liberated from demon rum, for instance, worked better and lacked a substance that might open a destabilizing trade with Indians. But because this complicated list of goals did little to promote settlers' material interests, migrants showed little enthusiasm in the design. In South Carolina, as more whites moved inland and the threat of conflict with Indians diminished, the first layer of townships was absorbed into the expanding commercial economy.[46] What was a gradual process in South Carolina required an out-and-out struggle in Georgia, where the Malcontents wore down the trustees, then made the province into a plantation colony along the lines of its elder neighbor.

In their utopian design and ultimate failure, centers of sericulture resembled other late-colonizing schemes meant to expand settlement of the Lower South using white laborers and exotic crops. Several of these came to tragic conclu-

---

45. Meriwether, *Expansion of S.C.*, 35–36, 45, 79, 92–93; Kenneth Coleman, *Colonial Georgia: A History* (New York, 1976), 20–22, 40–50; William L. Withuhn, "Salzburgers and Slavery: A Problem of *Mentalité*," *GHQ*, LXVIII (1984), 173–192; Harvey H. Jackson, "The Darien Antislavery Petition of 1739 and the Georgia Plan," *WMQ*, 3d Ser., XXXIV (1977), 618–631; Betty Wood, *Slavery in Colonial Georgia, 1730–1775* (Athens, Ga., 1984), chap. 4.

46. Meriwether, *Expansion of S.C.*, 38–39, 85; Coon, "Market Agriculture," 339.

sions in British East Florida. To build up a population in Florida after Britain gained it in 1763, promoters offered large land grants to anyone who promised to settle a certain percentage of the acres with white workers. Rollestown (where Denys Rolle deposited London paupers) and New Smyrna (where Andrew Turnbull settled and tormented Mediterranean migrants) were planned as slaveless zones that produced luxuries for the mother country. But the former project barely took coherent form on paper, let alone in the Florida wilderness. The latter scheme was a brutal disaster, where 80 percent of the original migrants died in what a prominent historian has labeled a "florid concentration camp."[47] In the lowest portion of the Lower South, projecting was not only dubious, but deadly.

✌ The Upcountry Responds

Even in areas with thriving populations, settlers preferred schemes that paid them well, hopeful of buying slaves, on whose labor they could expand production. Outright prohibitions on slavery, even restrictions on sale of land and slaves meant to slow the spread of plantation agriculture, were galling. Settlers recognized that, for the most part, coastal residents' and imperial planners' reluctance to let slavery expand represented, not an ethical position, but a strategic decision to protect those who already held slaves and to strengthen the western empire by keeping its new residents poor and docile. Settlers, particularly in the upcountry, were therefore vigorous in defense of equal rights for whites to do things like hold blacks in slavery. To defend themselves from any meddling that eroded their independence, western whites fought for more influence in the region's politics. First the Malcontents, then the Regulators, and then opponents of land speculation attacked the entrenched sociopolitical privileges that settlers believed had impeded them since 1730 and the implementation of the township scheme.

Externally imposed schemes for developing the region usually urged the actual settlers to put aside their own ambitions. Not only was this self-denial more than coastal planters expected of themselves, but such a policy had been ineffective in building up population and wealth in new areas. Projects there-

47. Bailyn, *Voyagers to the West*, 430–474; the figure and the quotation are from 459, 460. On similar if less disastrous plans in Georgia under its royal government, see 547–566.

fore cost much and created little but discord. In response to planters' assertions that their schemes, however difficult and expensive, strengthened the empire and assured an economic development that averted degeneration, new settlers protested that these rationalizations served only lowcountry interests. They wanted property (including slaves) and the political rights British subjects or American citizens derived from property; gratitude from empire or lowcountry for dutiful services rendered was inadequate compensation.

Settlers also objected to planters' vision of an optimal, and static, stage of development. They protested that lack of commercial development left them in a near-savage state; they accepted the idea of progress from incivility to commerce and wanted to keep progressing. Patrick Tailfer, a leader of the 1740s Malcontent rebellion against the Georgia Plan, referred to this implicit developmental schema when he rebuked Georgia's trustees, who "afforded us the Opportunity of arriving at the Integrity of the *Primitive Times,* by intailing a more than *Primitive Poverty* on us." Dismissing the coastal pattern of innovation altogether, the South Carolina Regulators mocked how "the [Royal] Society of Arts" had, "in vain," "labour[e]d to set People here on making of Experiments" in dubious commodities like silk. The Regulators warned promoters to use incentives to harness the economic ambitions of farmers rather than wield policies that shackled them; "small Premiums to encourage Poor People" would save money and get results.[48]

Externally imposed political power, which failed to encourage economic development, could not even provide legal protection of new settlers and their property. The vigilante Regulators demanded the political and legal services that were guaranteed to all other British subjects but denied to them. If unable to gain these powers, the Regulators warned, the "Welfare, Security, and Prosperity and Trade of the Inhabitants" were chimeras. After some reluctance on the part of lowcountry officials, the colonial government passed the circuit court acts of 1768 and 1769, which promised rudimentary legal services to new areas of the colony. With that, the Regulation finally died down.[49]

---

48. Clarence L. Ver Steeg, ed., *A True and Historical Narrative of the Colony of Georgia by Pat. Tailfer and Others, with Comments by the Earl of Egmont* (Athens, Ga., 1960), 4; Richard J. Hooker, ed., *The Carolina Backcountry on the Eve of the Revolution: The Journal and Other Writings of Charles Woodmason, Anglican Itinerant* (Chapel Hill, N.C., 1953), 253, 254.

49. On the Regulation, see Richard Maxwell Brown, *The South Carolina Regulators* (Cambridge, Mass., 1963); Rachel N. Klein, "Ordering the Backcountry: The South

But many members of the plantation elite still could not bring themselves to see upcountry settlers as equals rather than as pawns. Even after the disappointments of silk, disappearance of South Carolina townships, and failure of the Georgia Plan, planters sought ways to control the fortunes of those in the interior. They were now jealous of the upcountry's emerging economic and political power. Unless they themselves had property in the West, parish-dwellers avoided establishing political and judicial services beyond their reach, let alone granting more legal representatives to the upcountry, lest the center of power shift westward. In 1795, Henry William DeSaussure argued instead for a subpolitical reciprocity between upcountry and lowcountry. So long as the newer section raised useful products for the coastal "market," DeSaussure vowed, lowcountry interests would support its "government" and "external protection." The upcountry, in other words, received limited political services in exchange for raw goods—it was a province in the lowcountry's empire. The lowcountry would be particularly grateful, DeSaussure went on to stress, "for the strength of the upper country to protect its weakness in times of danger," slave rebellion being the danger too dreadful for him even to name.[50]

Settlers were exasperated with this view, recognizing (as had the Regulators) how lack of political power precluded wealth and autonomy. The South Carolina upcountry began to achieve political parity only with the Compromise of 1808, which finally granted more legislative seats to the interior. This breakthrough was achieved only through strenuous lobbying and renewed debate. Robert Goodloe Harper (a coastal lawyer with upcountry interests) championed the interior's hardy husbandmen, rejecting the lowcountry assertion that representation ought to be based on taxable wealth rather than free population. Any state grounded on this policy, Harper argued, was, whether it knew it or not, creating an aristocracy; South Carolina needed instead to protect the rights of all its propertied citizens, not just of rice planters. He maintained that "instead of giving [the rich man] more votes, you should give him fewer, in order to ballance and check that tendency to inequality, which exists in every society, and is its most dangerous ingredient." Such a policy would hardly appeal even to moderate rice planters. Responding to Harper, arriviste and conservative Timothy Ford wrote the clearest statement of low-

---

Carolina Regulation," *WMQ*, 3d Ser., XXXVIII (1981). The quotation is from Hooker, ed., *Carolina Backcountry*, 258.

50. H. W. DeSaussure [Phocion, pseud.], *Letters on the Questions . . .* (Charleston, S.C., 1795), 15–16.

country disdain for upcountry newcomers when he claimed that "certain rights attach to the prior occupants of a country, which subsequent emigrants can claim no rights to divest." Coastal planters' arguments for their unique-ness—their environmental need for slaves, their physical assimilation to their distinctive region, their achievements in creating the wealthiest creole society on the continent—were all weapons against interlopers.[51]

Regional tension was not as dramatic in Georgia, where the Malcontents had already thrashed out many questions over property and political power. But much of Malcontent protest, like Patrick Tailfer's assertion that he and his fellows needed slaves to till fevered swamps, reinforced rather than challenged lowcountry beliefs. Boosters of the Georgia upcountry had still repeatedly to demand more representatives to balance their political strength with that of their elder, seaside cousins. The state seemed fairly unified; it gave strong support to the federal Constitution, and the strength of Federalism through-out Georgia blurred any intraregional divisions. But the West was obviously going to keep gaining new settlers, so established residents avoided granting representatives to an area that might gain the upper hand. Delegates at the Louisville convention that amended the state constitution in 1795 did little to alter representation, but ostentatiously proclaimed themselves friends of the people while passing some perfunctory amendments: shifting power from the senate to the lower house and moving the capital from Augusta to the frontier polis of Louisville (it then migrated to Milledgeville in 1804). As in South Carolina, the new state university was strategically placed in the upcountry, though this decision represented concern for the health of students as much as concession to western interests.[52]

Lowcountry neglect continued to hamper settlers in their efforts to achieve wealth and cultural maturity comparable to the coast's. New farmers felt trapped between the view of outsiders, that they were still endowed with the unlovely features of barbarity, and the opinion of their neighbors, that they were loveliest in a usefully underdeveloped state. Both visions assigned settlers

---

51. Robert Goodloe Harper [Appius, pseud.], *An Address to the People of South-Carolina, by the General Committee of the Representative Reform Association at Colum-bia* (Charleston, S.C., 1794), 199; Ford [Americanus, pseud.], *Constitutionalist*, 22, 25. See also Lacy K. Ford, Jr., *Origins of Southern Radicalism: The South Carolina Upcoun-try, 1800–1860* (New York, 1988), 106–108.

52. Lucien E. Roberts, "Sectional Problems in Georgia during the Formative Period, 1776–1798," *GHQ*, XVIII (1934), 207–227.

to a primitive condition they were eager to escape. Even when freed of the unwelcome ministrations of the Royal Society of Arts and its meddling protégés, settlers feared that privileged persons and cabals might erode their status as independent propertyholders who had a legal stake in their government. They now had republican suspicions of the potential corruption represented both by the enlarged powers of the state and by the rise of wealthy men able to bend politics to their will—the lurking aristocratic interest Robert Goodloe Harper had glimpsed in South Carolina.

These apprehensions took specific form within debate over the nature of property, a controversy sharpened when Americans, after the Revolution, were creating a new Republic of laws and a modern economy of commerce and credit. James Madison, for example, expansively defined property as "everything to which a man may attach a value and have a right," a statement that left a wide margin for discussion—and disagreement. Residents of the Lower South glossed the margin with two dilemmas: how the property rights of individuals should rank with the good of the public, and what the government's role should be in doing the ranking. In this region, disposition of public lands—how they should be distributed among white settlers—was the most pressing problem, because it determined who would reap the greatest rewards from the newly commercialized region. This local question tied into the national contention between Federalists and Republicans over the broad definitions that founders like Madison put forward.[53]

Settlers of new western regions tended toward the Republican opinion that public lands theoretically belonged to all white citizens and should not be snapped up by venturers who happened to have more money than ordinary farmers. Distribution or sale of small holdings to worthy farmers would instead, like "small premiums" from learned societies, offer incentive to the hardworking and make wealth for the polity; complicated, expensive, and preferential schemes cheated the people. Settlers were approaching the later Jacksonian position that simultaneously favored government support of the economy and criticized any economic preferments seemingly supported by

---

53. Madison is quoted in Marvin Meyers, ed., *The Mind of the Founder: Sources of the Political Thought of James Madison* (Hanover, N.H., 1981), 186. On discussions of the early Republic's difficulties in legally defining property, see Morton J. Horwitz, *The Transformation of American Law, 1780–1860* (Cambridge, Mass., 1977), esp. 31–53, 63–84, 109–139; Lawrence M. Friedman, *A History of American Law,* 2d ed. (New York, 1985), 177–201.

duplicity and corruption—baleful monsters that preceded Andrew Jackson's monster bank. These westerners were heading toward the "venturous conservatism" that later opposed the Whigs' American Plan, a position that combined a noisy celebration of prosperity with a vehement denunciation of the growth of powerful economic interests such as were already in place along the rice-planting coast. To an increasing degree, however, this was a question no longer clearly related to regional identity; as Harper's support of western interests indicated, Republican sentiments might be strong in long-established communities as well as among pioneers.[54]

At this point, debate divided entrepreneurs with money from poorer residents. Settlers were no longer newly arrived and powerless; they had removed the debilitating effects of planters' projects and could now acquire property and send products to market. But they were braced against land speculation. Speculation was the entering wedge of exclusive opportunity that fostered unfair accumulation of property among moneyed investors—who might hail from other states in the nation. Any monopolistic association or restrictive land policy was an instrument that could allow wealthy men to use money and influence to defraud the people. Republicans continued to pin the problem of speculation on Federalists; the radical Josiah Meigs went even further when he insulted the University of Georgia's Board of Visitors by calling them "a damned pack of . . . tories and speculators." Few actually favored land speculation—government policies were supposed to curtail it. The colonial governments of South Carolina and Georgia (and East Florida) had headright systems of land distribution: free inhabitants received land for themselves and for their dependents, paying quitrents or small fees. Headrights were expressly meant to thwart speculators, who would "bring in the stock jobbing temper, the Devill take the Hindmost."[55]

54. On the character of the venturous conservative, see Marvin Meyers, *The Jacksonian Persuasion: Politics and Belief* (Stanford, Calif., 1957), 33–56.

55. Meigs's statement is cited in Thomas G. Dyer, *The University of Georgia: A Bicentennial History, 1785–1985* (Athens, Ga., 1985), 22. The other quotation is from a statement James Oglethorpe made in 1742, "Letters from James Oglethorpe," GHS, *Collections,* III (Savannah, 1873), 121. On colonial land policies, see Sirmans, *Colonial S.C.,* 172–182, 217–222; Alan Gallay, *The Formation of a Planter Elite: Jonathan Bryan and the Southern Colonial Frontier* (Athens, Ga., 1989), 84–108; Charles Loch Mowat, *East Florida as a British Province, 1763–1784* (Gainesville, Fla., 1964), 54–56.

But officials also wanted to encourage investment in their territories and tried to facilitate this without allowing the rich to grind the faces of the poor. Incentives to invest, loopholes in standard land policy, beckoned to men on the make. In pre-Revolutionary Georgia, for example, Jonathan Bryan used capital and political connections to amass a principality of more than thirty thousand acres. Because opportunity still knocked for men like Bryan, social inequality among whites appeared early in the colonial backcountry; by the mid-1700s, probably one-third of southern frontiersmen held *no* land whatsoever. Land speculators were, meanwhile, reserving rather than using large tracts. Such investments could be sold once other settlers, through their toil, enhanced the commercial value of the region, thereby raising land prices.[56]

In South Carolina, speculation increased just after the Revolution when new territory, debtor legislation, and restored sources of credit all allowed investors to grab lands before ordinary settlers could—or to wrest land away from indebted settlers. Upcountry residents protested that this new phase of speculation seemed "to be of no other view but to make gain and distress the poor." After 1791, when South Carolina opened even more lands to sale, many speculators residing outside the region (notably, the soon-to-be-bankrupt Robert Morris) entered the frenzied market. A few celebrated cases of bankruptcy as well as continuing protest over how property was being wrenched from honest citizens made some investors stand aside from the stampede. One man who renounced speculation even claimed "it much worse than love" in the obsessive turbulence it created.[57]

Speculation peaked during the Yazoo land controversy in Georgia, though this final debate over distribution of territory also reached into South Carolina. Indeed, it drew attention throughout the nation. The Yazoo affair originated with postwar land speculation. Many Continental army veterans received bounty grants of confiscated loyalist lands in the Lower South. Altogether, veterans garnered a total of 750,000 acres, but not all men actually

---

56. On Bryan, see Gallay, *Formation of a Planter Elite*, 84–108, 127–152. On backcountry poverty, see Richard Hofstadter, *America at 1750: A Social Portrait* (New York, 1973), 175–177; and Jackson Turner Main, *The Social Structure of Revolutionary America* (Princeton, N.J., 1965), 49.

57. On the South Carolina spree of speculation, see Rachel N. Klein, *Unification of a Slave State: The Rise of the Planter Class in the South Carolina Backcountry, 1760–1808* (Chapel Hill, N.C., 1990), 178–190—the quotations are from 184, 190.

settled their grants. Some resold their holdings or passed title to others who then sold the acreage. Their actions set off a small spree of speculation that, as earlier in South Carolina, gnawed away at the principles of the old headright system. In the meantime, Georgia officials realized that selling some of the land recently and coercively obtained from the Creeks would remit revenue the state desperately needed after the war. In the 1780s and 1790s, several Georgia governors signed grants for land speculators, grants larger than the 1,000-acre ceiling allowed by law. Through the machinations of some speculators, the Pine Barrens scandal of the early 1790s duped individuals into buying nonexistent lots of land. These tracts, supposed to be lush oak and hickory holdings, were really acreage in poorer piney regions, impossible to claim because they lacked the landmarks bestowed on them in fictitious surveys. Fraud continued: by 1796, the amount of land granted away in Georgia exceeded that which was actually in its territory by three times—surprisingly, no one commented on the miraculous excess of acreage. Much of the best land that did exist ended up in the hands of speculators, who raised prices above the reach of ordinary settlers.[58]

Encouraged by this atmosphere of shady dealing, several land companies placed bids on vast stretches of public land, using funds pooled by wealthy investors. Such companies eyed the disputed chunk of Yazoo territory—wrested from native Americans and also claimed by the Spanish—in present-day Alabama, Mississippi, and Tennessee (see Map 3). A consortium of companies tried to buy 15.5 million acres in 1789 but failed to cover their bid with sufficient assets. A new group (formed by the Georgia, the Georgia-Mississippi, the Upper Mississippi, and the Tennessee companies) next presented itself. The new company, labeled the Yazoo, gained, by act of the Georgia Assembly, somewhere between 35 and 50 million acres of the barely explored tract for $500,000. The Yazoo Act passed in 1795 during the administration of Governor George Mathews, who had practiced his signature on earlier and no less dubious land grants. Several other legislators were implicated in the under-the-table transfer of territory, either because they held stock in the Yazoo

---

58. Kenneth Coleman, ed., *A History of Georgia* (Athens, Ga., 1977), 105–107; Alex M. Hitz, "Georgia Bounty Land Grants," *GHQ*, XXXVIII (1954), 337–348; George R. Lamplugh, "John Wereat and Yazoo, 1794–1799," *GHQ*, LXXII (1988), 503; Lamplugh, *Politics on the Periphery: Factions and Politics in Georgia, 1783–1806* (Newark, Del., 1986), 31–37; C. Peter Magrath, *Yazoo: Law and Politics in the New Republic, the Case of Fletcher v. Peck* (Providence, R.I., 1966), 1–4.

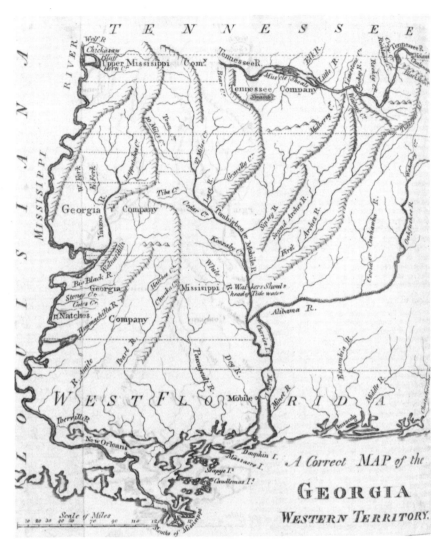

Map 3. The Yazoo Lands. *From Jedidiah Morse,* The American Gazetteer *(Boston, 1797)*

Company or because they had been so eager to render it assistance that they resembled men encouraged by bribery.[59]

Once the act was promulgated, it met with public outcry, much of it cast in antimonopolistic terms. Georgia politician James Jackson led the attack. Though himself a land speculator with roots in the lowcountry, Jackson resigned his seat in the United States Senate to run on an anti-Yazoo and prowestern platform for the Georgia legislature, seeing more political hay to be made there than in Washington. He attacked the Yazooists on several grounds. A veteran of the Revolution and of Indian wars, Jackson had long held that settling the Yazoo territory was "bad policy" because it could stir up trouble with the Creeks. Dangerous intriguers had nevertheless wrested sovereignty over public lands from the people, Jackson insisted, and they threatened the region's progress to greater wealth by illegally seizing public resources at the expense of the public. Summoning up several centuries worth of Anglo-American rhetoric against projects and corporations, Jackson called the Yazoo speculators creatures in a "combined Society" united by oaths of "Secrecy." The Rescinding Act that Jackson maneuvered through the legislature in 1796 denounced "monopolies in favor of a few, which tend to build up that destructive aristocracy in the new, which is tumbling in the old world." The repeal also claimed that "monopolies . . . will prevent or retard settlements, population, and agriculture" during the infancy of a growing region.[60]

Once the Rescinding Act declared the Yazoo Act null and void, anti-Yazooist Georgians burned the offending document, supposedly using a glass lens to make the sun's rays ignite the tainted paper with "fire drawn from heaven." The legislature purged its ranks and renounced its misdeeds. Had the story ended here, it would have remained merely another interesting variation on the republican theme of a strictly limited government role in the economy, one with certain opéra bouffe contrasts between cheerful avarice and public recantation. But the Georgia legislature declared invalid—a bit too hastily—all transactions resulting from the Yazoo Company. Their decision made a local

59. Coleman, ed., *Georgia*, 96–97; Lamplugh, *Politics on the Periphery*, 64–80, 104–119; Magrath, *Yazoo*, 5–7.

60. Lilla M. Hawes, ed., *The Papers of James Jackson, 1783–1798* (GHS, *Colls.*, XI [Savannah, 1955]), 77 (first quotation). On Jackson's political career, see Lamplugh, *Politics on the Periphery*, 81–103; and William Omer Foster, Sr., *James Jackson: Duelist and Militant Statesman, 1757–1806* (Athens, Ga., 1960). Remaining quotations in Magrath, *Yazoo*, 121, 129, 131.

story into a national dilemma and raised new questions about the power of the federal government in defining property rights through contract and credit.[61]

The action moved north, where, as the dust was settling in Georgia, shareholders in the Yazoo Company began to hear of the fracas. Most Yazoo shares had ended up in the hands of northerners, an indication of the extent to which many Americans (especially entrepreneurial New Englanders) were interested in the frontier South. These distant Yazooists were understandably dismayed when they learned that their holdings were worthless. The news got worse when they discovered that the Georgia legislature, by denying the legality of all transactions related to the original bargain, refused to repay anyone who had invested in any of the implicated land companies, whether they had stood directly to gain from the Yazoo Act or not. Investors found it hard to believe that Georgia's government had not erred at least once, either by courting the attentions of a corrupt monopoly and striking a bargain with it, or by breaking a contract that had drained finances from innocent parties. In either case, the state needed to take responsibility for citizens who lost money because of its mistake. When questioning about the behavior of Georgia legislators grew from murmurs of dismay to howls for an investigation, the United States Congress waded into the fray and debated whether the claimants ought to receive compensation. But Congress voted down this proposal, stymied by acrimonious debate among variously interested parties. Feeling still ran high against Georgia; men of Federalist persuasions, especially, believed that a business contract could not casually be broken, even by a sovereign power that claimed to be overseeing the larger, public benefits of its action.[62]

Congress having rendered an anti-Yazooist decision, supplicants next approached the courts. Nearly three-fifths of Yazoo claimants were from New England, and some formed themselves into a group called the New England Mississippi Land Company to pursue their claims. The Yazooist case *Fletcher* v. *Peck* (a collusive suit arranged between two claimants who had no real quarrel with each other) made its way from a Massachusetts circuit court into the Supreme Court in 1810. The case marked a number of firsts in the nation: the New England Mississippi Land Company was one of the first effective lobbies to pursue its goals in the federal arena and was the first lobby to use the Supreme Court as arbiter in a case of business law. *Fletcher* v. *Peck* raised

61. Coleman, ed., *Georgia*, 97; Lamplugh, *Politics on the Periphery*, 120–43; Magrath, *Yazoo*, 7–15; William Estill Heath, "The Yazoo Land Fraud," *GHQ*, XVI (1932), 274–291.

62. Magrath, *Yazoo*, 20–36.

questions not only about the nature of contracts but also about property as a dynamic force rather than static fact—as a shareholder's or creditor's note, for instance, rather than a tract of land. The complexity of the case increased with Georgia's after-the-fact dithering over whether it had the right to sell the Yazoo lands in the first place because title gained from the Indians was disputed. A possible, maximum definition of government intervention in economic and state affairs was hovering, a Federalist belief that national authorities could make policy regarding corporations, investment, state-level law, and Indian affairs. Rapidly charting his way through this terra incognita, Chief Justice John Marshall led a decision to declare the original Yazoo Act a lawful, however unwise, contract between the State of Georgia and the consortium of land speculators. The decision vindicated claims that a contract had to be respected even if corrupt, and even if it was one in which financial gain resulted from speculation rather than transaction in tangible property. Marshall excoriated Georgia for irresponsible trusteeship of its own economy, and, after some foot-dragging, the shamed state raised funds from sale of its public lands to repay claimants. Georgia had ceded much of the troublesome Yazoo tract to the United States government in 1802, and the final payments to claimants came from the Treasury.[63]

Refunds dragged on through 1814, by which time the scandal was eclipsed by the excitement (and controversy) over the Louisiana Purchase.[64] But the Yazoo incident had raised political questions not easily settled—indeed, ones reiterated over Louisiana. The feud helped coax out the nation's first third party, the Quids (from *tertium quid*, "third thing"), under the leadership of the erratic John Randolph of Roanoke. The Quids split from Jefferson's Republicans, protesting, among other things, their party's complicity in the Marshall decision, which invaded, Randolph declared, the rights of the sovereign state of Georgia. An extreme republican (more accurately, a follower of the Country ideology that had inspired opposition groups in Augustan parliaments), Randolph argued that Yazooism was an ominous, Federalist innovation in government. Randolph appealed to fellow Republicans, especially southerners, to resist further degeneration in the polity. He particularly emphasized how the federal government was pushing its way into questions of property and authority better reserved to the states, forming one of the first states' rights

---

63. *Ibid.*, 50–84; Jane Elsmere, "The Notorious Yazoo Land Fraud Case," *GHQ*, LI (1967), 425–442.

64. Magrath, *Yazoo*, 88–97.

arguments that hinted at a North-South division.[65] On a national level, also, the controversy revealed sectional division. Earlier congressional votes on the legality of Georgia's 1796 Rescinding Act (whipped up by Randolph's sardonic oratory) showed that Federalists from all states supported compensation of shareholders. Republicans divided over the question; southerners tended to support the Rescinding Act, and northerners favored the original contract.

But while the Quids' purist position provides a glimpse into the shattering debate over states' rights yet to come, it also shows the extent of contemporary agreement over economic policy. The issue of contracts seemed to yield the most agreement. Randolph had perceived correctly the meaning in Jefferson's disapproval of the Yazooists and support of Marshall's decision on the contract: most Republicans and Federalists were not so far apart and certainly did not divide on sectional lines. Southerners were themselves divided over the question whether slavery should move west, and northerners, like Yankee investors in Yazoo lands, were keen on profiting from an expanding plantation region. There was greater division over the question of government participation in economic activity; this was the most troublesome part of the Yazoo affair, and it revealed new settlers' own twist on the Lower South's paradoxical acceptance of modern economic trends. Western settlers had resented official policies—the township plan, Georgia's trusteeship, and the silk project—that restricted their initiative. But they nevertheless advocated that the federal government, no less, intervene in local affairs and take an anti-Yazoo stance, and they welcomed government limitations on speculation.[66]

65. Donald A. MacPhee, "The Yazoo Controversy: The Beginning of the 'Quid' Revolt," *GHQ*, XLIX (1965), 23–43; Magrath, *Yazoo*, 39–49.

66. Two examples reveal how sectional and ideological identities still presented alternatives that would not exist during the antebellum era. An early sectional dimension was clear in the 1791 statements of James O'Fallon, who invested in and acted as agent for a pre-Yazoo land company active in Georgia. O'Fallon, like Randolph, decried government policies that favored "*Yankee* Settlement" of the West over "the chartered rights of certain of the *Southern* States." In this case, however, and in contrast to Randolph, O'Fallon welcomed federal support of private companies and faulted neglectful "Federalists" for acting against the interests of his company. South Carolinian Robert Goodloe Harper nevertheless found that Yazooism pushed him toward Federalism. Though in an earlier, Republican incarnation Harper had held up the political rights of the upcountry yeomen, he switched to Federalism as a result of his pro-Yazooist position; finding it difficult to maintain a Federalist position in Carolina, Harper removed to Baltimore. Virginian Nathaniel Pendleton followed suit. After

Bluster over access to land formed, therefore, a controversy similar to the earlier one over access to slaves. Whites in the Lower South, however poor and recently arrived, emulated the long-settled residents who seemed walking advertisements of economic success. If the region had built itself on slavery and commercial agriculture and if it distributed political power to free persons who were the gainers from these economic structures, then the elite's attempts to prevent newcomers from becoming members of the club constituted self-interested duplicity. Had planters sought ways to eradicate slavery in the lowcountry, for instance, they would have been better qualified as critics of the institution. But machinations to curtail equality of opportunity among free whites smacked, in contemporary parlance, of aristocracy or monopoly—threats that Thomas Goodloe Harper and James Jackson had denounced. Settling the controversies raised by the Malcontents, Regulators, and anti-Yazooists forced planters to support what was becoming a Herrenvolk system of economic and political democracy, a democratic system, that is, only for whites, but which had to include all whites. A culture of potential white equality based on black slavery replaced earlier and more particular arguments for slavery in the lowcountry. The Indians, who reluctantly supplied the territory that caused all the fuss, saw that whites who argued among themselves also showed a racially united face, one carefully masked with political rhetoric. One Creek leader accordingly categorized Americans as "a sett of crafty, cunning, republicans."[67]

In the Lower South, an abundance of new land kept the problem of property rights and public interest before these citizens. Even after the Yazoo controversy, Georgians debated the disposition of their territory. The state needed revenue, and land sales would have raised it. A careful system of pricing and upper limits on amounts that could be sold would curb speculation, but sentiment still ran high against any method of sale that might benefit a privileged element. As Governor John Milledge put it, "The industrious poor"

---

settling in Savannah, where he practiced law, Pendleton was implicated in the Yazoo scandal. Fearing his legal career was damaged beyond repair, he fled to New York in 1795 and later served as Alexander Hamilton's second in the famous duel with Aaron Burr. See James O'Fallon Letter, 1791, GHS; Nathaniel Pendleton, "Short Account of the Sea Coast of Georgia in Respect to Agriculture, Ship-Building, Navigation, and the Timber Trade," ed. Theodore Thayer, *GHQ*, XLI (1957), 70–71. On Harper, see Magrath, *Yazoo*, 140.

67. John Walton Caughey, *McGillivray of the Creeks* (Norman, Okla., 1938), 184.

needed protection "from the grasping hand of the rich speculator." Weary and wary Georgians resorted to a method of distribution that was almost a theoretical opposite of a private land company: a public lottery. This was an unusual means of bestowing land on settlers, unique to Georgia and a fascinating instance of political waffling over the touchy question of how a government ought to divide public property among private owners. The lottery was probably the fastest retreat from finance to Fortuna in the early Republic—a rejection of the controversial modernity of corporation and contract law in favor of one of the most ancient methods of reaching a decision.[68]

The state lottery, established in 1803, took effect in 1805 and, almost incredibly, distributed nearly three-quarters of Georgia's lands. The laws regulating the lottery also constructed a revealing system by which settlers were rated according to their perceived value to the community. Indians—the land's original owners—and blacks were excluded because drawers had to be "white"; the stress on racial identity restated the trend toward Herrenvolkism. Political allegiance also mattered: only United States citizens were eligible. Out-of-state speculators could not participate, because ticket holders had to have resided in Georgia for at least a year. The drawings favored men; females could enter only if they were orphans in their minority or widows with legitimate children: feminine objects temporarily deprived of male protection. Those who supported families were also favored. Male or female heads of household got two draws; bachelors and orphans each got one. Drawers could be poor, but not destitute: tickets cost $.12½ each, a nominal fee, but winners were expected to pay $8.10 for lots of 202.5 acres and $19.60 for 490-acre grants to cover the costs of surveying and paperwork. Only legitimate children were eligible to draw as orphans; illegitimate minors could not be claimed even within a household composed of offspring from more than one relationship. This clause reflected racism as well as prudery: it eliminated most children of color, because few mulatto or mestizo children could qualify as legitimate offspring, and it reinforced the sense that family status was a method of determining community stability.[69]

Though an unusual method of settling territory, the Georgia Land Lottery nonetheless had precedents considered perfectly respectable. English lotteries raised funds in the early modern era when few individuals owned significant

---

68. Milledge is cited in Lamplugh, *Politics on the Periphery*, 186.

69. Virginia S. Wood and Ralph V. Wood, eds., *1805 Georgia Land Lottery* (Cambridge, Mass., 1964), ix–x; Coleman, ed., *Georgia*, 107.

amounts of capital and when the state's power to tax was strictly curtailed. The wheel of fortune rolled west. A lottery had collected money for the colonizing efforts of the Virginia Company. Colonial lotteries flourished thereafter, especially following the Seven Years' War when colonists needed to effect internal improvements, raise money for churches and schools, invest in business projects, and repair the physical and financial damages of the war. The impoverished Continental Congress authorized the first United States Lottery in 1777—South Carolinian John Lewis Gervais deemed it "the easiest way to levy a Tax or borrow Money." Lotteries continued under the Confederation, funding civic projects and organizing capital for economic ventures. These clustered in the North—two-thirds of Confederation lotteries were in New England, mostly in industrializing Rhode Island; only by the 1800s did lotteries in the poorer and newer Southwest predominate, though the Lower South had its own share of lotteries. Lotteries influenced the lives of some notable Americans. Slave Denmark Vesey (eponymous organizer of the 1822 slave conspiracy in South Carolina) bought his freedom using fifteen hundred dollars he received from a winning ticket in Charleston's East Bay Street Lottery, and a shrewd lad named P. T. Barnum got his start selling lottery tickets.[70]

Lotteries accumulated capital in amounts beyond the ability of individual entrepreneurs and allowed politicians to raise revenue without taxing prop-

70. John Samuel Ezell, *Fortune's Merry Wheel: The Lottery in America* (Cambridge, Mass., 1960), esp. 29–78, 111–112 (for Vesey); Hamer *et al.*, eds., *Papers of Laurens*, XI, 414–415 (Gervais); John M. Findlay, *People of Chance: Gambling in American Society from Jamestown to Las Vegas* (New York, 1986), 30–34, 39–43.

The short-lived Georgia Agricultural Society ran a lottery in the early 1800s, as did the more successful Agricultural Society in South Carolina. Upcountry lotteries raised money for a pier in Augusta (1796), for clearing the Ogechee and Canouchie rivers (1803), and for a woolen factory near Milledgeville (1815). See Records of the Agricultural Society, folder 46, Wayne-Stites-Anderson Papers, GHS; Murray, *Agr. Soc. S.C.*, 67—the society's first lottery of 1806 sold 3,000 tickets at $6.00 each. Advertisements for the other lotteries appear in *Carolina Weekly Messenger* (Charleston), Nov. 3, 1807; *Augusta Chronicle,* July 23, 1796; *Louisville Gazette* (Georgia), Apr. 20, 1803; *Georgia Argus* (Milledgeville), Mar. 1, 1815. Residents also kept track of lotteries in other states. Georgian Shaler Hillyer bought tickets from a New York lottery for the "Encouragement of Literature," and a South Carolina newspaper advertised a Delaware lottery supporting the College of New Jersey. See Hillyer to Messrs. Strong and Co., Nov. 27, 1806, Shaler Hillyer Letterbook, 1805–19, Hillyer Papers, UGA; *South-Carolina Gazette; And Country Journal,* Oct. 12, 1773.

ertyholders, but they had the considerable drawback of being associated with chicanery. Looking back on his youthful acquaintance with lottery agents, Barnum concluded that "such bipeds as 'humbugs' certainly existed before I attained my majority," before he himself embarked on a career of artful duplicity. As economic ventures, lotteries were *early* modern but not modern forms of finance: they did not contain the rational elements beloved of political economists; indeed, they revealed economic thinking at its least rational. Lotteries were, essentially, a form of gambling—here then was the gambling derided by travelers who described the Lower South! Aware of the dangers of gambling and lotteries, residents themselves tried to enact controls. A 1764 statute in Georgia, for instance, meant "to suppress lotteries, and prevent other excessive and deceitful gaming"; like laws prevailed in South Carolina before the Revolution. Upcountry settlers continued to worry over gambling after the war, perhaps seeing games of chance as especially dangerous to a region whose residents had yet to find solid economic footing. One "CITIZEN" editorialized in a Pendleton, South Carolina, newspaper that "excessive gambling . . . prevails in all the Back Country; and in every class of men." Another newspaper reprinted an essay from England ("But true every where") on how lotteries eroded "the morals" of the people.[71] Lotteries intoxicated the estimable citizenry, luring them from honest toil by hope of spectacular gain.

But this hazard had to be balanced against the competing dangers of taxation and financial speculation. In a lottery, at least, the only power at work was that of chance, the luck of the draw. To give away thousands of acres by this method showed the considerable fear Georgians had of the powers of the state and the wealthy, a fear that overshadowed even their need for revenue and their belief that western territory was in the public trust. Here the Georgia situation was exceptional. Though lotteries had elsewhere serviced other business functions, only in Georgia did a lottery distribute public land. Nowhere else was the territorial issue left to chance—one can imagine the uproar that would have greeted a proposal to distribute land gained in the Louisiana Pur-

71. Findlay, *People of Chance*, 40 (Barnum quotation); Allen D. Candler, comp., *The Colonial Records of the State of Georgia* (Atlanta, 1904–1916), XVIII, 608 (for other prohibitions of gambling, see XIX, 51–52); Thomas Cooper and David J. McCord, eds., *The Statutes at Large of South Carolina* (Columbia, S.C., 1836–1841), III, nos. 784, 807, IV, 911, 926, V, 1786 (in acts nos. 1595 and 1615, lotteries were authorized for charity and improvements); *Miller's Weekly Messenger* (Pendleton, S.C.), July 9, 1807; *Columbian Herald* (Charleston), Aug. 22, 1796.

chase by lots rather than by requiring payment into the national treasury. Englishman John Melish noted, for example, that if Georgians seriously thought new territory was public property, it then belonged "to every member of the community, and no alienation ought to take place without securing alike the rights of all; but this can never be done by a lottery, which is a game of chance,—and all cannot be gainers." John Milledge likewise regretted the decision to "gamble away all our inheritance" rather than invest it in worthy citizens through land sales.[72]

Georgia's troublesome territory helped define, again, the Lower South's uneasy position within a modern, commercial economy. The specific anxiety, at this point, was over the advantages individuals could gain by manipulating political power and capital, thereby preventing other free citizens from gaining any capital whatsoever. The local episode had even upped the ante. White propertyholders now faced the possibility that a central power like the Supreme Court would shape the fortunes of the nation and its states, a threat that made the earlier machinations of mercantilist projectors seem almost benign. Even as they welcomed political control over financial ventures like speculation, Georgians retreated from this tendency in federal power, taking up studiedly archaic tactics to make decisions about their economic growth. Their lottery presages the anticapitalist defiance of the antebellum South—a fierce resentment of a modern tendency to measure everyone and everything by money and a willingness even to gamble away an inherited asset rather than let it disturb family harmony.

The Lower South's expansion in many ways seemed to be shaping the region into the antebellum South. Insistence on whites' equal access to slaves and to land would become a cherished element of the South's racist political economy; access did not guarantee equality among whites, but it assured a comforting potential for white social mobility in the face of unwelcome realities like poverty, debt, and tenancy. In many ways too, the debate over expansion of slavery paralleled contemporary events in the Chesapeake and prefigured, within a part of the South itself, the later and cataclysmic North-South conflict over western territories and slavery. This latter point shows again how the

---

72. Entry for July 1807, Josiah Everett daybook, 1808–20, Curry Hill Plantation Records, microfilm 2-2200-C, GDAH; John Melish, *Travels through the United States of America, in the Years 1806 and 1807, and 1809, 1810, and 1811* . . . (London, 1818), 46–47; Milledge's words are quoted in Lamplugh, *Politics on the Periphery,* 190.

Lower South was—but was not—like its antebellum descendant: proslavery arguments were already present, but they still appeared alongside serious doubts over the utility and safety of slave labor. The Lower South was clearly already a distinctive region, yet it also continued to express a desire for reform and economic improvement that seemed more typical of the North than the South.

Several forms of apprehension over the regional economy's future were evident in coastal and upcountry expectations for change. Lowcountry planters, who had the most successful form of agriculture, nevertheless restlessly tinkered with new crops and machines and worried over slavery; they had the strongest connections to the modernizing, commercial world and therefore the strongest fears over their region's particular weaknesses. Upcountry settlers were still trying to attain what already prevailed along the coast. They were most removed from commercial networks, highly determined to enter them using the labor of slaves but also fearful that, once they were connected to the outside world, powerful forces could follow them home and make trouble.

The correlation is clear: the better established commercial agriculture was, the more its participants wanted to reform or diversify it—especially to prevent greater dependence on slavery. Conversely, the newer that settlers were, the less trust they had in complex projects and the more loudly they demanded slaves; they wanted a foothold in modern commerce—their *own* foothold that might lead to their own connections with scientific associations and botanic experts. There were exceptions to this pattern. English planners, themselves remote from the Lower South and not always clearly allied with the coastal elite, were strong supporters of experiments like townships, Trustee Georgia, and East Florida's settlements. Coastal planters were sometimes the most vocal critics of these utopian designs. Some newcomers, like the Georgia trust's faithful Salzburgers, did not hanker after plantations and slaves. By and large, however, controversy over extension of plantation agriculture revealed the Lower South's essential difficulties with the concept of a modern society. Profits from commercial agriculture carried wealthy whites (through books, travel, correspondence, or simple curiosity) close to a modernizing world; drawn into an improving ethos, they saw their region's flaws more clearly. Settlers not yet able to court learned societies and to buy books on Chinese agriculture wanted to enter a commercial economy, however flawed, and resented consignment to a developmental stage (like Georgia's primitive poverty) behind the rice-planting coast. They rushed headlong toward the dilemmas already established in the lowcountry.

Not until the early 1800s, when upcountry residents finally carved out a successful commercial region, did they and their coastal neighbors settle their differences and begin a final, mutual phase of diversification involving investment in manufactures during the War of 1812.[73] In the meantime, commercial agriculture remained the standard model of success, and only the details invited dispute: *where* slavery would be strongest, *who* would settle new territory, *what* activities were optimal. Fresh innovations often emerged as responses to these questions. Both coastal projects and western commercialization thus gave new features to an enlarging region. In many cases, whites did not even tamper with the model of commercial agriculture unless forced by some external crisis, an economic emergency that acted as a creative disruption and catalyst for schemes that might unite or divide the population. A tableau that gives meaning to whites' innovative behavior—their conflicted response to slavery, their fear of socioeconomic regression, their resentment of external criticism, their admiration for modern industrial economics, their apprehension over state-controlled economic preferments—is now in place.

73. It is arguable that lowcountry planters never fully accepted their neighbors as equals and never really acquired a taste for Herrenvolk politics. See William W. Freehling, *The Road to Disunion*, I, *Secessionists at Bay, 1776–1854* (New York, 1990), 216–223.

Part II

Realizing Modernity

"... we hope a new War will learn us

how to propagate some other usefull Articles."

—Henry Laurens, 1755

Chapter 6

Crisis and Response

Indigo and Cotton

Innovators were a minority of the lowcountry's population; most planters simply continued to grow rice. Only during commercial crises could projectors recruit fellow experimenters. In a crisis, the white population fell into two categories, innovative and responsive. The former group had always looked for ways to alter agriculture; the latter did so only if market conditions gave them little other choice. Whenever old patterns of transatlantic commerce disintegrated, innovators' contacts with the Royal Society, fascination with European gadgetry, and hopes of lessening the danger of slave resistance became useful in teaching others how to adapt crops, capital, and labor to meet the crisis. In a perverse way, lowcountry innovators even welcomed crises as opportunities to shake up their moribund cohort. As Henry Laurens said about one exigency, the War of Jenkins's Ear, "'Twas intirely owing to the last War that we became an Indigo [growing] Country and we hope a new War will learn us how to propagate some other usefull Articles which would not be attempted with any Spirit whilst the Planter can find his Account in continuing in the old Track."[1]

Though the Lower South had, by the mid-1700s, a maturing plantation

1. Philip M. Hamer *et al.*, eds., *The Papers of Henry Laurens* (Columbia, S.C., 1968–), I, 309. John J. McCusker and Russell R. Menard, *The Economy of Early America, 1607–1789* (Chapel Hill, N.C., 1985), 178; cf. Richard B. Sheridan, *Sugar and Slavery: An Economic History of the British West Indies, 1623–1775* (Baltimore, 1973), chap. 17, on the significance of wartime slumps and peacetime booms for the West Indian economy.

economy, it was entering an era of significant economic instability, most of it caused by war. Several episodes of conflict affected Atlantic trade: between Britain and the allied powers of Spain and France during the War of Jenkins's Ear (1739–1743); during the Seven Years' War (1754–1764); surrounding the worsening imperial relations between Britain and its colonies that culminated in the War of American Independence (1776–1781); and, later, resulting from the diplomatic tensions among Britain, France, and the United States that led into the War of 1812 (1812–1815). More than two decades were consumed with open hostilities, much of the rest of the time in assorted nonimportation resolutions, embargoes, and chilly international relations. All these troubles guaranteed projectors plenty of opportunity to persuade more cautious planters to seek inventive ways to turn a profit in the absence of stable markets. Profit was present even in disaster. War brought new prosperity to certain classes (often to merchants who serviced military forces) and had salutary effects on stagnant local economies because it fostered creative disruptions that established new patterns of economic behavior.

Examination of any war could turn up evidence of economic diversification or expansion, but the two episodes that finished out the colonial period merit particular attention. First, the War of Jenkins's Ear (named for the British tar purportedly mutilated by the crew of a Spanish *guarda costa*, or patrol vessel) temporarily severed commercial links between British colonies and territories held by Spain and France. Rice prices declined, and the Lower South's economy went into a period of recession that eroded the wealth of its free residents; the mean value of inventoried estates in South Carolina dropped from about £532 in the 1740s to £437 in the 1750s (see Table 2). To replace lost profits, a small group of South Carolina planters and farmers led the way in adopting new crops, especially indigo. Second, the movement for and then War of American Independence shut out British products from the 1760s to 1780s; clothing and blankets were most sorely missed. The lack of textiles for restive slaves became a pressing issue. To fulfill their need, whites and blacks produced cotton for domestic use in a process that eventually led to commercial production of cotton.

Though both indigo and cotton emerged from similar disruptions of warfare, each provides a different measure of the flexibility of the plantation economy. Indigo revealed the overall willingness of planters to adopt new commercial crops, but only as a way of maintaining the status quo. The dye was a product of the British Empire, a creation of imperial warfare and mercantilistic regulation that propped up established economic and political

TABLE 2. *Mean Value of Estates, 1740–1789*

	Pounds Sterling					
	1740s	1750s	1760s	1770s	1740s–1770s	1780s
South Carolina	532	437	589	1281		1,409
Georgia					364	452

Note: The extraordinary level of South Carolina wealth in the 1770s and 1780s is most likely due to underrepresentation of western-dwellers (who tended to be poor in this era) and overrepresentation of wealthy merchants and rice planters. Postwar inflation probably elevated prices for articles inventoried in the 1780s. Levels of wealth dropped after the Revolution, both in reality and because a more representative slice of the population made their way into official records.

Sources: Estate Inventories, SCDAH, GDAH.

interests; it made little qualitative change in the economy. Cotton resulted from a deeper crisis when an anti-imperial war completely disrupted plantation agriculture in the region. Rather than simply perpetuating the old pattern of production for a foreign market, cotton did something more interesting: it set up a domestic economy geared toward household and community consumption of basic goods. This alone was unusual for a plantation economy that had once bought most of its finished goods out of its commercial profits. As elsewhere in North America, textile production began to build a base for semi-industrial production. This low-grade manufacturing set up a capability for the Lower South to move both forward and back along a theoretical continuum between household and factory production. While indigo tested the adaptability of whites within commercial agriculture, cotton caused them briefly to range beyond it.

Another way of gauging the extent to which indigo and cotton variously altered the earlier socioeconomic system in the lowcountry is to examine what each crop did for people outside the plantation elite, especially poorer whites and black slaves. Not surprisingly, whites of all classes benefited more from the new crops than they would have from rice; both indigo and cotton created new opportunities for poorer whites, unlike the innovations in rice cultivation that would follow the Revolution. Slaves too acquired skills useful to production of indigo and cotton, expertise that expanded for them an earlier margin of independent activity. In the case of cotton, because this crop accompanied a more serious breakdown of the plantation economy, slaves used the staple to erode planters' power over them during the chaotic events of the war. But planters were able, even during this contested moment of the Revolutionary era, to use cotton to maintain their dominance. Both crops showed the flexibility of commercial agriculture yet also revealed planters' determination to preserve their control over the economy as a whole.

℘℘ An Imperial Blue

Henry Laurens had, if anything, underestimated the causal effect war had on indigo cultivation. At every point in the local history of the dye, war and its accompanying disruptions in commerce promoted indigo. The War of Jenkins's Ear prompted whites to adopt indigo, and the Seven Years' War further stimulated production of the crop for the British market. The Revolutionary War then upset these commercial networks, and prices for dye dropped. Indigo sales recovered after the Treaty of Paris in 1783 but declined again by 1796.[2] Indigo cultivation took place within an intensely imperial context; war for empire may have disrupted commercial agriculture, but Britain's imperial authority also protected indigo makers in the Lower South until the sun finally set on this portion of the British Empire.

The War of Jenkins's Ear began the cycle of crisis and response by removing markets for rice on the European continent. Unlike many plantation staples, the lowcountry's crop had gone, not to the mother country, but to other European consumers. When war broke out with Spain and France, markets in these countries and in Portugal were cut off entirely; the conflict that raged at sea also prevented merchants from easily reaching an even larger group of consumers in northern Europe. Rice prices concomitantly fell by 50 percent in the year after war broke out. Nor did they recover during peace. English financial ministers refused to take rice off the list of enumerated commodities in 1745, and rice planters failed to regain complete access to European markets. During the 1740s, therefore, some planters looked for new sources of income to buttress their standard of living. One statement of frustrated commercial ambition that appeared in 1744 was nonetheless peppered with exasperation

2. G. Terry Sharrer, "Indigo in Carolina, 1671–1796," *SCHM*, LXXII (1971), 95–97, 102.

over slowness in responding to the crisis: "Is it not then *full* Time . . . for the *Planter* to look about him and *try* whether he cannot *lay out* his *Time* and *Labour* or *part* of it, at least, to *greater* Advantages than he has done for the *Two* last Years?"[3]

The author of this statement recommended that planters turn to indigo, but this was only one of several crops under consideration. Innovators also experimented with articles produced in the Mediterranean (silk, wine, oil) but no longer available to British consumers; with commodities needed by the busy British navy, especially hemp; and with luxuries like ginger and cotton that subjects had once bought from Latin America. A South Carolina statute of 1744 placed bounties on all these items as well as on wheat, barley, and flax, which colonial officials hoped would provide incentive for migrants to move into and settle frontier areas that might face attack from France and Spain. These crops could more easily be grown without the labor of slaves than rice, an attractive prospect in the years following the Stono Rebellion. Coming as it did in 1739, the Rebellion coincided with the war (no real coincidence, as it turned out). Slaves knew that South Carolina was at war with the Spanish, who were eager to turn English chattels against their owners. Word was out that runaway English slaves were welcome in Spanish Florida, hence the attempt on the part of some slaves to fight their way to St. Augustine. For lowcountry whites, the foremost goals during these years of uncertainty were to diversify plantation agriculture and expand white settlement—the former lessened the empire's dependence on potential adversaries, and the latter built up imperial frontiers. No one crop seemed most likely; a mixture of commodities might serve best. Antigua's Governor George Lucas, for instance, who provided indigo seed to his daughter in South Carolina, also proposed sending "a Dutch family or Two" to introduce the manufacture of flax and hemp into the Lower South.[4]

3. David Leroy Coon, "The Development of Market Agriculture in South Carolina, 1670–1785" (Ph.D. diss., University of Illinois, Urbana/Champaign, 1972), 194; *South-Carolina Gazette* (Charleston), Oct. 8, 1744.

4. Thomas Cooper and David J. McCord, eds., *The Statutes at Large of South Carolina* (Columbia, 1836–1841), III, no. 708; George Lucas to Charles Pinckney, Dec. 23, 1745, Harriott Horry Ravenel Collection, series 11-332-4, SCHS. On Spanish Florida, the Stono Rebellion, and black resistance, see Peter H. Wood, *Black Majority: Negroes in Colonial South Carolina from 1670 through the Stono Rebellion* (New York, 1975); and Jane Landers, "Gracia Real de Santa Teresa de Mose: A Free Black Town in Spanish Colonial Florida," *AHR*, XCV (1990), 9–30.

Though items like hemp and wheat continued to have their promoters, indigo ended up as consort to the dominant crop of rice. Indigo overtook its competitors for two reasons. It had patrons both in the mother country and in the Lower South; it fitted well into the Lower South's plantation economy. The crop enjoyed the benefit of a London lobby. British merchants had long pleaded for legislation to encourage colonial production of dyes. They were in dire need of such laws because, though Britain was increasingly a manufacturer of cloth, it did not produce many materials needed for the textile industry within its own empire—indigo, for example, had never before been a staple in British America. The British West Indies produced some indigo (it had been a crop on some islands since the 1650s), but Caribbean planters' focus on sugar usually distracted them from secondary commodities. British drapers and dyers relied on imports of indigo from French or Spanish colonies in the Caribbean and Latin America, though this dependence gave the lie to mercantilistic assumptions of colonial trade. When war cut off supplies of French and Spanish indigo in 1739, imperial authorities could demonstrate how trust in foreign powers had, yet again, weakened the nation.

Some South Carolinians had already begun producing indigo. Members of the Lucas-Pinckney clan were key innovators, first experimenting with and then promoting the dye.[5] Eliza Lucas (later Pinckney) especially labored to introduce West Indian indigo cultivation, but she was only one of the most visible innovators (and the only female) within a wider network that included Carolinians, West Indians, and Britons. Lucas, for instance, collaborated with her Huguenot neighbor, Andrew Deveaux, who was praised by her father as "the greatest Indigo Planter in your Province." Once the first experiments were successful, people more gifted with words than plants took up the task of disseminating information about the dye, usually in provincial newspapers. Charles Pinckney, who married Eliza Lucas, observed her efforts and wrote a series of promotional articles in the *South-Carolina Gazette* under the pseudonym Agricola. Throughout October 1744 (when rice prices were again falling, this time to their lowest level in the century), the newspaper published further articles explaining how to get started with the crop. Another flurry of articles and pamphlets by Agricultor and Patricola appeared in 1747; Patricola beseeched planters to give up their "Darling Rice" for the "valuable Manufacture" of dye. James Crokatt, a South Carolina merchant based in London,

---

5. David L. Coon, "Eliza Lucas Pinckney and the Reintroduction of Indigo Culture in South Carolina," *Jour. So. Hist.*, XLII (1976), 62.

distributed more pamphlets and articles on indigo cultivation in the following years.[6] Following the tradition of didactic rural poetry (perfected by Hesiod—creolized by Ebenezer Cooke), one newspaper poet lauded the dye in mock-epic style:

> The Means and Arts that to Perfection bring,
> The richer Dye of INDICO, I sing.

And he set the method of growing indigo into surprisingly practical verse:

> Break off Delays, and thus prepare the Plain,
> Let Two Feet void 'twixt every Trench remain.[7]

British drapers, talented horticulturalists, pamphleteers and poets—all helped plant the Lower South's plain with indigo. But the rich dye, though it had friends on either side of the Atlantic, would not have succeeded had it not meshed with rice cultivation; most planters wanted a crop that temporarily replaced income, not one that required them seriously to rethink how they ran their estates. They learned, to their delight, both that indigo grew best on drier land where they could not grow rice and that it needed work at points in the season when rice did not make its greatest demands on labor. Most coastal plantations had high land for growing provisions (see Plate 2) that could be turned over to indigo. It was, as the South Carolina Assembly exulted, "an excellent colleague Commodity with Rice." Workers sowed indigo in spring, but the rows of bushes needed little care for several months, during which time rice could be planted. After the indigo had bloomed and was fully leaved (usually in July), workers gently—so as not to bruise the dye-impregnated leaves—pruned the upper branches of the shrub with sickles. Planters could expect new growth on the bushes after the first cutting and, if the season was good, another harvest in August and perhaps even a third in September. The

6. *Ibid.*, 61, 66–68, 75; George Lucas to Charles Pinckney, Dec. 23, 1747, Harriott Horry Ravenel Collection, series 11-332-4, SCHS. Patricola's article appeared on Mar. 2, 1747, and the advertisement for Crokatt on Mar. 23, 1747. On the general publicity blitz, see Coon, "Reintroduction of Indigo," 68–73. Rice prices fell from about four shillings and five pence per hundredweight in 1744 to two shillings and four pence in 1745. They would not recover until the end of the decade. See Peter A. Coclanis, *The Shadow of a Dream: Economic Life and Death in the South Carolina Low Country, 1670–1920* (New York, 1989), table 3-29, p. 106.

7. Hennig Cohen, ed., "A Colonial Poem on Indigo Culture," *AH*, XXX (1956), 41–44.

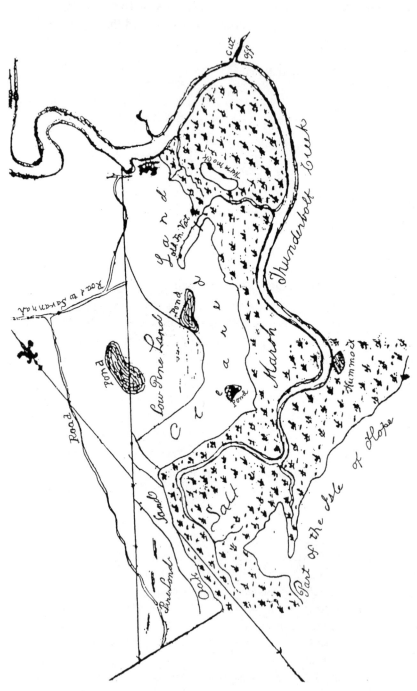

Plate 2. Indigo-producing Plantation. *Plantation of Elizabeth Box, Dec. 14, 1799, Chatham County, Deed Book 2A-270, Superior Court, drawer 233, microfilm box 6, GDAH.* This plat from Georgia shows how planters usually had several types of land on their estates. The oak land probably contained indigo fields, though the Old In. Vat was situated near a section of marsh that had been dammed to provide water for the indigo works.

second or first cutting was the richest, and the last simply the dregs of the season, so most of the crop would be cut and processed before the height of the rice harvest.[8]

Though it required little labor while in the ground, indigo needed much care in its manufacture, a difficulty for planters who regarded the plant as a temporary and part-time crop. Once cut, indigo needed quick processing before its leaves lost their luster. Workers placed the severed branches in the first of a series of three vats, each one smaller than the former, each one the recipient of a more concentrated product. These vats were serviced by one or more of the pumps that had fascinated innovators keen on importing European mechanisms (see Plate 3). The largest vat, called the steeper or the "hot" (its contents warmed as they fermented), contained the indigo on the bottom, held down by slats of wood and covered with water. The mixture steeped for anywhere from six to twenty hours, during which time the raw indican dissolved and fermented into indoxyl. The mass of fermented particles then drained off into the second vat, the battery or beater. Workers vigorously beat the thick liquid in order to oxidize it and thereby transform the indoxyl into indigo.[9]

Eighteenth-century planters did not, of course, understand the procedure in these chemical terms; they relied on visual and olfactory cues to regulate processing of the dye. The smell of the mixture got steadily stronger as fermentation progressed—it was almost overwhelming at the end when the indigo was truly putrefied. The color of what was in the vats changed, from a state in which the steeped vegetation was greenish yellow and exuded purple scum, to a final one in which the beaten mess turned dark green. At this stage, the person who supervised the fermentation and beating would begin to test droplets of the mixture on a clean and shiny surface (like a cup, plate, or mirror) looking for the "blue shimmer" and the separate granules that indicated that oxidation was complete. The supervisor then gave the order to stop

8. Harry J. Carman, ed., *American Husbandry* (1775) (New York, 1939), 272–275, 279; Coon, "Reintroduction of Indigo," *Jour. So. Hist.*, XLII (1976), 64 (quotation); Johann David Schoepf, *Travels in the Confederation, 1783–1784*, ed. and trans. Alfred J. Morrison (1911; rpt., New York, 1968), II, 157; *South-Carolina Gazette*, Oct. 29, 1744. On varying rates of production for different cuttings of indigo, see David Yeats to James Grant, Oct. 23, 1772, MacPherson-Grant Papers, bundle 250, Ballindalloch.

9. Coon, "Reintroduction of Indigo," *Jour. So. Hist.*, XLII (1976), 62–63; Schoepf, *Travels*, ed. Morrison, II, 158–159; *South-Carolina Gazette*, Oct. 19, 22, 1744.

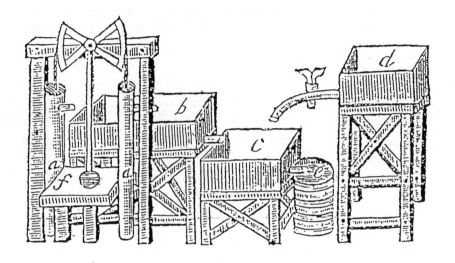

Plate 3. "Representation of the Machine Used in Making Indigo: *aa* Two pumps in a frame worked by a pendulum, to pump water into the steeper *b*; *c* the beater; *d* A vat of lime-water; *e* A tub set to receive the muddy water from the beater; *f* A stage whereon to work the pumps." *From* Gentleman's Magazine, *XXV (1755), 259*

beating and threw in a quantity of lime to fix the dye. "The hitting this Minute exactly," said one observer, "Shews the skill of him, who oversees the making of the INDIGO."[10]

Once the indigo was fixed, the sediment from the beater drained into the smallest vat, the "deviling," or settler. Most of the water seeped out of the settler, and workers removed the remaining paste, drained it further in cloth bags or wooden boxes, kneaded it on boards, formed it into cakes, and dried these thoroughly. At all times, from shrub to cake (see Plate 4), the nascent dye needed protection from light to prevent it from fading, from damp to prevent it from dissolving back into sludge, and from flies to prevent it from rotting. Successful indigo makers packed the dried cakes into casks or barrels for shipping. British clothworkers would then dissolve the imported cakes to make

10. Schoepf, *Travels,* ed. Morrison, II, 158–159; *South-Carolina Gazette,* Oct. 29, 1744. For two detailed descriptions of indigo cultivation that emphasized the visible cues of the process, see Archibald Johnston's and Alexander Frazer's accounts in bundle 549, MacPherson-Grant Papers, Ballindalloch.

Plate 4. Indigo Plant and Cake of Dye. *From John Gabriel Stedman,* Narrative of a Five Years Expedition against the Revolted Negroes of Surinam *(London, 1796). Permission of the John Carter Brown Library at Brown University, Providence, R.I.* A detail of the leaves is at the upper left; a cake of the final product is at the bottom.

dye. Variations in the composition of the final product, resulting from the quality of the plant and the technique of processing, created color variations that determined its value. The bluest, or "flora," indigo contained more indigotin and was highly prized; reddish and less valuable dye had more indirubin. Copper indigo, the cheapest variety, had stray minerals in it that created a coppery sheen in the cake. The finest dye was used to tint luxury cloth; the poorest, to color coarse woolens or ceramics.[11]

A difficult procedure, the proper preparation of indigo was somewhat like brewing beer or making sugar: the salability of the commodity depended on the wisdom of a person who divined the critical moment when the substance was ready, who understood what was called the "mystery" at the heart of a skilled, preindustrial task. Marveling at the process, Alexander Garden took a stab at explaining its scientific nature by saying it was "surprizing to see how exactly the various phaenomena of the Indigo beating, quadrate with, and confirm Sir Isaac's theory of the composition of the colorific particles of bodies." But while Garden knew his Newton, he, along with most whites in South Carolina, was unlikely to have known how to make indigo. Johann David Schoepf explained that it was instead skilled slaves who made the dye and that "a great value is set upon them." Slave experts were often worth two or three times more than field hands because they understood this mysterious process.[12]

The *South-Carolina Gazette* in 1777, accordingly, drew planters' attentions with an advertisement for thirty slaves, "among whom are, [an] Indicomaker." Slave carpenters who could set up indigo vats were also valuable and therefore tended to be hired out. Daniel Cain reported, for instance, that Robert Cahusac's estate gained income in the 1780s from "Pompy making Vats" for other planters.[13] Peter Gourdin's indigo supervisor gained unusual privileges

11. Schoepf, *Travels,* ed. Morrison, II, 159; *South-Carolina Gazette,* Oct. 29, 1744; [James Crokatt, ed.], *Further Observations Intended for Improving the Culture and Curing of Indigo, etc. in South-Carolina* (London, 1747), 2–3; G. Terry Sharrer, "The Indigo Bonanza in South Carolina, 1740–90," *Technology and Culture,* XII (1971), 450. On indigo used to dye stoneware, see Hamer *et al.,* eds., *Papers of Laurens,* II, 29.

12. Garden to Charles Whitworth, Apr. 27, 1757, Linnaeus Correspondence, XVII, LSL; Schoepf, *Travels,* ed. Morrison, II, 159.

13. *South-Carolina Gazette,* Apr. 14, 1777; March 1785–December 1788 accounts, estate of Robert Cahusac in account with Daniel Cain, Palmer Family Papers, box 1, folder 13, SCL. See also the statements of Jesse M. Cannico in his letter to John Ewing Colhoun,

because of his value. Gourdin specified in his will of 1775 that "Billy shall not be put to any field work, but be kept a jobbing on the plantation and in the proper seasons to tend the Indigo works about the Vatts as in my lifetime." Gourdin also stated that Billy "shall not be under the power or authority of any Overseer on the Plantation after my decease" and was to be freed upon the death of Gourdin's immediate heir. This last was a dubious piece of generosity—Billy would surely have few years left in which to enjoy freedom. More significant was his relative independence within the institution of slavery: Billy answered to the planter alone and, for part of the year, was recognized as the most important person on the plantation, more skilled than the planter himself.[14] Despite the 1739 scare over slavery, whites still opted to encourage skill and autonomy in some slaves.

As indigo spread and as expertise with the crop filtered through the population, more whites began to grow the dye. Many had begun to cultivate indigo for the market by the mid-1740s, regarding it as their only hope during recession. In 1745, James Michie wrote a Scottish associate of the "great hopes that Indigo will Answer extremely well here which raises the Spirits of most people." Real profits from indigo did not come, however, until King George's War commenced in 1748. From this point forward (except for a slump in the 1760s when soaring rice prices distracted planters from other crops), production expanded until the Revolution: between 1770 and 1775, indigo production increased 120 percent over 1750–1755. Indigo enjoyed such rapid and early success that in 1746 the South Carolina Assembly removed its bounty, stating that the crop was already profitable and that a tax to raise a bounty "would fall very heavy and unequal upon those persons who have no opportunity of making indigo."[15]

July 28, 1789, John Ewing Colhoun Papers, folder 1, SHC—Cannico mentions his reliance on the slave Pollidore and refers to the help with indigo "Flander" gave another planter.

14. Will of Peter Gourdin, Jan. 13, 1775, Gourdin Family Papers, series 34-15, SCHS.

15. James Michie to Sir Alexander Nisbett, Mar. 7, 1745, Tod Murray and Jamieson Collection, box 10, bundle 2, GD.237, SRO; Stuart O. Stumpf, "Implications of King George's War for the Charleston Mercantile Community," *SCHM*, LXXVII (1976), 173–174; Lewis Cecil Gray, *A History of Agriculture in the Southern United States to 1860* (Washington, D.C., 1933), I, 292; John J. Winberry, "Reputation of Carolina Indigo," *SCHM*, LXXX (1979), 244; Cooper and McCord, eds., *Statutes of S.C.*, III, no. 737.

Imperial bounties, on the other hand, continued to encourage colonists. The first bounty came in 1749 and offered (in addition to the market price) six pence per pound of British indigo to the merchant who imported the dye into the mother country. The merchant then passed part of the subsidy back to the colonial agent who sold him the indigo. Payment dropped to four pence a pound in 1764, but output had already increased so much that a high bounty was no longer essential to stimulate production. Under this policy, both the quantity and value of indigo increased, from 466,201 pounds (worth slightly more than two shillings per pound) in the years 1761–1770, to 795,074 pounds (worth almost three shillings per pound) in the period 1771–1774.[16]

A market for expert advice and specialized services emerged during these years. Henry Yonge sought out Charles Pinckney in 1747, for instance, as he struggled to grow indigo. Planters interested in getting better strains of plants to make better indigo or who needed varieties adapted to particular kinds of land could find seeds to suit them. Techniques of processing the dye also elaborated over time, and the scale of production enlarged on some plantations. Bernard Romans reported that some Florida planters used horses to operate beaters for large indigo vats. South Carolinian Plowden Weston claimed he owned a setup for indigo that included five steepers, an apparatus so large that two slaves had to pump for an hour to fill one vat full of water.[17] Possibly because of the larger scale of production, planters began to look for overseers who knew how to make indigo, as did a 1791 advertiser in the *Georgia Gazette* who wanted a man "acquainted with the new process of making indigo" to work for him. (The new process might have involved a different proportion of lime added to the fermented mixture.) Local artisans learned to

16. Winberry, "Carolina Indigo," *SCHM*, LXXX (1979), 242–244; Coon, "Market Agriculture," 255.

17. Henry Yonge to Charles Pinckney, July 8, 1747, Pinckney Family Papers, series 4, box 15, folder of "Odds and Ends," LC; Bernard Romans, *A Concise Natural History of East and West Florida* (1775; facs. ed., Gainesville, Fla., 1962), 136; Plowden Weston to Jonathan Lucas, Aug. 17, 1792, Lucas Family Papers, series 11-270, folder 66-5-13, SCHS. For specialized seed, see the April 13, 1774, *Georgia Gazette* (Savannah), advertisement for "HIGH LAND HAND-PICKED INDICO SEED" vended by someone who had cultivated the shrubs more for the seed than for the dye. The *South-Carolina Gazette; And Country Journal* (Charleston) of Mar. 22, 1774, advertised "sea-shore" and "wild" varieties of indigo seed for interested buyers.

make the complicated system of vats and pumps. For making twenty-six indigo-drying boxes, a set of vats, and a pump for Thomas Sacheverell in 1747, Robert Allen earned £34 12s.—almost the amount a skilled workman in colonial Charleston could expect to make in an entire month.[18]

Though indigo generated a respectable boomlet in the Lower South's economy and created some diversification within it as well, the product disappointed British merchants and dyers accustomed to a higher grade of dye from the Caribbean. Colonists themselves admitted that their product might be substandard. The *South-Carolina Gazette* of January 19, 1747, lamented, "Our Success, it must be owned, has not come up to our Expectations." The South Carolina Assembly passed a statute in 1749 designed to prevent frauds like mixing wet indigo paste with unwelcome substances like dirt, clay, ground slate, ashes, or foreign indigo—attempts to deceive merchants as to the local dye's weight or quality. Efforts to control quality proved ineffective, and Charleston indigo inspector Moses Lindo despairingly resigned in 1772, refusing to place the royal seal on an inferior product like Carolina indigo. South Carolinians (at least those who did not mix their dye with clay or slate) seemed at a loss to explain why their indigo was inferior to that of the West Indies. Governor James Glen believed that his people were not "conversant enough in this Commodity, either in the Culture of the Plant, or in the Method of managing or manufacturing it."[19]

The real problem was that most people cultivated indigo extensively rather than intensively and were careless in processing it. Increased quantity paid off (even when it resulted in inferior dye) because the market was protected by metropolitan policies that discouraged importation of higher-quality foreign indigo. With this advantage, colonists felt free to use too much lime in

18. Advertisement in *Georgia Gazette,* Dec. 15, 1791; account of work done by Robert Allen for Thomas Sacheverell, 1747, Elliott-Gonzales Papers, folder 2, SHC; see Governor James Glen's Report, 1751, in H. Roy Merrens, ed., *The Colonial South Carolina Scene: Contemporary Views, 1697–1774* (Columbia, S.C., 1977), for an estimate of a workman's annual wages (184). See also Andrew McLean's payments to Charles Simmons, June 25, 1784, Edward Telfair Papers, 23-H, box 3, folder 1, Duke.

19. Cooper and McCord, eds., *Statutes of S.C.,* III, no. 769; Winberry, "Carolina Indigo," *SCHM,* LXXX (1979), 246; [James Glen], *A Description of South Carolina* (London, 1761), 9, facs. rpt. in Chapman J. Milling, ed., *Colonial South Carolina: Two Contemporary Descriptions* (Columbia, S.C., 1951), 17.

processing the dye, to add impurities to it, to package and ship off indigo before it dried (the wet cakes rotted, but, concealed in a barrel, weighed more than dry dye), and to barrel their product ineptly. They received a government bounty for their crop unless it was outright unsellable, whereas foreign indigo cost, in addition to its often higher price, six pence per pound to import.[20] Indicative of planters' failure constantly to improve indigo production was their inability, between the 1740s and 1780s, consistently to maintain, let alone improve, the amount they made per worker. During the forty-year period of intensive indigo production, the amount ranged from 60 to 180 pounds per worker (see Table 3). The figure probably varied according to planters' interest in cultivation, their desire to make more or less dye at the expense of the product's quality, or their ignorance of how to grow or process the plant.

Such carelessness prejudiced British merchants against any Lower South indigo, even the small amount that actually was superior. By the 1760s, Henry Laurens despaired of ever getting a fair price for his dyes, which he felt were judged "upon caprice, the fashion, or the demand for it." He claimed London brokers believed that good Carolina indigo was really foreign dye smuggled from French or Spanish colonies; they routinely underpriced Laurens's indigo merely because it was from British North America. The low opinion officials had of the Lower South's product meant that, without imperial authorities to guarantee them a market, planters could not easily find buyers.[21]

Only East Floridians were skilled indigo makers, and their success indicates how the region's overall failure to produce quality dye resulted more from the desultory attentions of its cultivators than from its climate or soil. Floridians adopted the crop twenty years after South Carolina's first experiments yet quickly developed a knack for making excellent dye; many made it the sole staple of their plantations after other experiments failed. To be sure, they had little choice but to concentrate on the crop. East Florida lacked the extensive network of freshwater streams along its coast that would have allowed rice planting on the same scale as in South Carolina and Georgia, and sudden frosts stunted or killed the sugar that settlers tried to grow. Lumbering was an activity

20. Winberry, "Carolina Indigo," *SCHM*, LXXX (1979), 244–248; Sharrer, "Indigo in Carolina," *SCHM*, LXXII (1971), 97.

21. Hamer *et al.*, eds., *Papers of Laurens*, VI, 170, VIII, 228; Sharrer, "Indigo in Carolina," *SCHM*, LXXII (1971), 98–102.

TABLE 3. *Indigo Production per Worker*

			Weight in Pounds				
1749	1757	1767	1773	1775	1784(A)	1784(B)	1786
60–160	90–180	45	60	100	50	125	53

Sources: (1749) [James Glen], *A Description of South Carolina* (London, 1761), 9, in Chapman J. Milling, ed., *Colonial South Carolina: Two Contemporary Descriptions* (Columbia, S.C., 1951), 17; (1756–1757) Alexander Garden to Captain Rains, May 1, 1757, Guardbooks, reel 1, RSA (the same estimate appears in Garden to John Ellis, May 6, 1757, Linnaeus Correspondence, XVII, LSL); (1767) John Murray to Sir Robert Laurie, July 12, 1767, John Murray's Letterbook, bundle 290, Murray of Murraythwaite Muniments, GD.219, SRO; (1773) William Bartram, "Travels in Georgia and Florida, 1773–74; A Report to Dr. John Fothergill," American Philosophical Society, *Transactions*, N.S., XXXIII (1942–1944), 150; (1775) Harry J. Carman, ed., *American Husbandry* (1775) (New York, 1939), 286; (1784A) Porcher Family Account Book, pp. 69–70, College of Charleston (figured from George Wright's wages as overseer in 1784, with indigo at three shillings per pound); (1784B) Johann David Schoepf, *Travels in the Confederation, 1783–1784*, ed. and trans. Alfred J. Morrison (1911; rpt., New York, 1968), II, 157–159; (1786) Porcher Family Account Book, pp. 69–70.

limited to certain locations, and land speculation made money only for a powerful few.[22]

Other than quarreling with each other, therefore, indigo manufacture was the only pursuit common to Florida settlers. The disastrous history of this colony took on a melancholy blue tint. Indeed, the colony's intensive exploitation of its new settlers (black and white) may have been what made intensive production of indigo possible. In the most-troubled corner of the province, New Smyrna, indigo was the primary crop. The embattled community exported dye worth £13,500 in 1771 alone. Promoter Andrew Turnbull had already installed no fewer than 350 vats at New Smyrna and aimed for a total of 500—this was more factory than agricultural estate. New Smyrna's output expanded thereafter, totaling an astonishing 42,283 pounds between 1772 and

22. Leila Sellers, *Charleston Business on the Eve of the American Revolution* (Chapel Hill, N.C., 1934), 47; Romans, *Natural History of Florida*, 139.

1777. Governor Patrick Tonyn's twenty slaves made 1,200 pounds of dye in 1772, and the earl of Egmont's Amelia Island plantation produced 2,095 pounds in 1774. Quality did not seem to suffer from this prodigious output. William De Brahm claimed that Florida indigo was as good as that of Guatemala, and William Bartram viewed samples of what he considered "the best flora Indigo I had yet seen" in North America at Governor Tonyn's estate in 1773.[23]

Unlike planters to the north, who tended to rely on the expertise of their slaves, certain white Floridians themselves became adept at processing indigo. Andrew Turnbull plunged himself into experiments at New Smyrna in 1770, varying the time he steeped his dye and the amount of lime added to it. Other planters "followed his example" by steeping longer and adding more lime "and find it answer[s]" well. Turnbull also turned to other whites for advice on improving his indigo. His first crop of 1770 had a disappointingly purplish hue, and he approached a Mr. Skinner to find ways to "avoid that Episcopal Colour." Floridians also seemed to generate new wisdom about indigo instead of relying on information from outside. Turnbull declined an offer to bring in indigo makers from French New Orleans; another man criticized misleading advice perpetuated in a treatise endorsed by gentlemen scientists in Paris and warned planters not to get their skills from some "foolish Book." Some local empirics were so steeped in the dye that they became eccentric as well as expert. Turnbull claimed that John Ross "knows by the scent when the [indigo] Vatt is sufficiently beat." He also stated, "Jemmy Wallace is one of the best Indigo Crackers [poor whites] I have met with." The absentminded Wallace would evidently carry cured "Indigo in his Pocket, which he seems accidentally to think of, he takes it out, breaks it with his [finger]Nail, carrys his [stained] Hand to the Sunshine, then puts it under his Nose with an air of certain applause."[24]

23. E. P. Panagopoulos, *New Smyrna: An Eighteenth-Century Greek Odyssey* (Gainesville, Fla., 1966), 74–76; Turnbull to James Grant, Oct. 22, 1770, MacPherson-Grant Papers, bundle 253, Ballindalloch (number of vats); Louis De Vorsey, Jr., ed., *De Brahm's Report of the General Survey in the Southern District of North America* (Columbia, S.C., 1971), 214; William Bartram, "Travels in Georgia and Florida, 1773–74: A Report to Dr. John Fothergill," ed. Francis Harper, American Philosophical Society, *Transactions*, N.S., XXXIII, pt. 2 (1942–1944), 150; Daniel L. Schafer, "Plantation Development in British East Florida: A Case Study of the Earl of Egmont," *FHQ*, LXIII (1984), 179.

24. David Yeats to James Grant, Aug. 31, 1771, bundle 250 (first quotation), Andrew Turnbull to Grant, Nov. 18, 20 (last quotation), 1769, July 28, 1770 (second quotation),

While Florida's superior indigo partly resulted from a growing season slightly longer than that of South Carolina and Georgia, a more probable cause was the care taken with the product. Floridians made only nine pounds of dye per vat, a highly concentrated product that yielded an intense blue. South Carolinians, on the other hand, averaged twenty pounds per vat. Florida's first governor, James Grant, recommended that the British bounty allot more for Florida indigo than for Carolina: the former was worth about nine shillings per pound (much more if of the best quality), the latter a mere three shillings.[25] But East Florida's skilled planters were too few to impress British officials. Outside the aboriginal population, the new colony had only about three thousand souls—it was more sprawling town than province. In 1774, an agent working for the governor was able to sketch a brief inventory of how much indigo each individual produced, from New Smyrna's weighty yield to the humbler 600 pounds of Morris, "a Cracker." Floridians' neighboring and more careless indigo makers were too numerous to draw up into a single list. In 1771, St. Augustine exported 28,143 pounds of dye (a large increase over 1770's 6,189 pounds); New Smyrna exported 11,558 pounds; South Carolina churned out about 500,000 pounds, a glut of mediocrity that overshadowed any superior efforts made in smaller amounts.[26] Colonial indifference and imperial wariness thus ensured that indigo was granted an only temporary place within the British market.

The protected market vanished with the American Revolution. Imperial authorities found it easier to encourage new cultivators in more obedient provinces after the continental colonists took an independent path. During the

---

bundle 253; James Penman to Grant, Oct. 16, 1769, bundle 491 (third quotation), MacPherson-Grant Papers, Ballindalloch.

25. The estimates for indigo output are from Gray, *Agriculture in the Southern U.S.*, II, 294, but the same figures appear in Grant's letter to the earl of Hillsborough, Mar. 3, 1772, MacPherson-Grant Papers, bundle 242, Ballindalloch. In the 1790s, South Carolinians continued to get about 20 pounds per vat—see Jonathan C. Greninger to J. E. Colhoun, Sept. 3, 1791, John Ewing Colhoun Papers, folder 2, SHC.

26. Charles Loch Mowat, *East Florida as a British Province, 1763–1784* (Gainesville, Fla., 1964), 16, 77. On the indigo inventory, see Frederick W. Mulcaster to James Grant, Feb. 6, 1774, MacPherson-Grant Papers, bundle 369. Florida's total exports lagged behind those of both Georgia and South Carolina. In 1768, for example, St. Augustine exported 2,050 tons of goods; Savannah, 8,785; Charleston, 31,551 (Mowat, *East Florida*, table 5, p. 155).

war, loyalist East Florida made its patriotic contribution; by 1782, it provided 22 percent of the indigo imported into England. Britain was also, conveniently enough, increasing its hold over India. The East India Company sponsored individuals to set up indigo "factories" (large and expensive operations) around 1778 or 1779; a John Prinsep received a contract for thirty-five thousand pounds of dye at this time. The company set up eight to ten plantations in Bengal, and two more estates operated independently. Compared to Lower South planters, Indian producers had an easier time gaining cheap labor, training skills in workers, and investing in large and specialized factories. In post-Revolutionary America, production costs increased because planters had fewer slaves, more debts, and more damaged properties. New slaves were by then more expensive, and a series of natural disasters—floods, drought, pests, and frosts—savaged indigo crops in the Lower South.[27]

Meanwhile, East Indians used the same information network—between Old World learned societies and colonial settlers—that innovators in the Lower South had been employing to learn about new crops like indigo. William Roxburgh, for example, cultivator of the East India Company's garden at Calcutta, sought advice on indigo from Sir Joseph Banks of the Royal Society. Roxburgh wanted cuttings of both continental American and West Indian plants, claiming in 1793 that the dye "promises to become valuable" in India. A year later he assured Banks that "the manufacture of Indigo . . . [is] general here." Loyalists from America, among them a man named Gray, transferred American methods of indigo processing to Bengal, just as expatriate West Indians had once provided indigo experts and seeds to continental America.[28]

27. Mowat, *East Florida*, 78; P. J. Marshall, *East Indian Fortunes: The British in Bengal in the Eighteenth Century* (Oxford, 1976), 104–105, 153–154; Holden Furber, *John Company at Work: A Study of European Expansion in India in the Late Eighteenth Century* (Cambridge, Mass., 1961), 290–292; Blair B. Kling, *The Blue Mutiny: The Indigo Disturbances in Bengal, 1859–1862* (Philadelphia, 1966), 17–18, 20; Marjorie Stratford Mendenhall, "A History of Agriculture in South Carolina, 1790 to 1860: An Economic and Social Study" (Ph.D. diss., University of North Carolina–Chapel Hill, 1940), 47–51; Winberry, "Carolina Indigo," *SCHM*, LXXII (1971), 249; John Couturier to J. E. Colhoun, May 23, 1792, John Ewing Colhoun Papers, box 2, folder 14, SCL—they tried using chickens to catch grasshoppers in their indigo fields.

28. William Roxburgh to Sir Joseph Banks, Dec. 1, 1793, Add. 33,979.224, and Roxburgh to Banks, Dec. 30, 1794, Add. 33,979.292-93, Sir Joseph Banks Letters, BL. On Gray, see Mendenhall, "Agriculture in S.C.," 50; *Columbian Museum and Savannah Advertiser*, Oct. 15, 1799. A Floridian named Gray (perhaps the same man), who owned

Indigo eventually panned out in East India. There too it was propped up by the short-term interests of merchants and textile manufacturers, and the Asian product usually sold at a loss in London. Even after the Revolution, the United States supplied more than 50 percent of the indigo imported into Britain. United States exports declined in the early 1800s, however, as planters in indigo-growing areas discovered that cotton was a more lucrative crop. The Lower South's competition with Asia in producing semitropical luxuries ended in a draw: the region was losing the competitive edge with indigo but gaining a new one with cotton. Inability to maintain production of indigo was, nevertheless, not confined to North America. Neither Brazil nor Bengal, for example, continued production for more than a few decades, despite demand in Europe and despite the presence of government sponsorship in both places. Indigo too closely resembled silk. The dye was a small-scale luxury crop, unfamiliar to its new cultivators and requiring labor that was both skilled *and* cheap—a near impossibility in a colony.[29]

Indigo was, therefore, only a temporary solution to planters' need to diversify their sources of income, and, within the lowcountry, its effects on economy and society were temporary. Coastal slaveholdings, for example, did not change. From the 1740s through early 1760s, about half of the wealth in South Carolina estates was represented by slaves, this percentage increasing only slightly (from 48 to 51 percent). During the first phase of indigo cultivation in the 1740s, the Carolina lowcountry's wealth distribution hardly changed, in sharp contrast to the striking redistributions of wealth that took place during the Yamasee War depression of the 1720s and during the commercial boom that accompanied the Seven Years' War. Although smaller estates gained more capital in relation to large ones during the 1740s, this capital did not translate into more slaves or more wealth of any kind.[30] In part, the reason probably was that only a fraction of the agricultural population devoted itself to indigo

---

10 slaves, produced 800 pounds of indigo in 1774—see Frederick Mulcaster to James Grant, Feb. 6, 1774, MacPherson-Grant Papers, bundle 369, Ballindalloch.

29. "India Trade. Nawab's Debts," fols. 18–19, MS 1064, Melville Papers, NLS; Furber, *John Company*, 292; on the decline of indigo and cotton in Bengal, see Kling, *Blue Mutiny*, 20–21, 219–220; on Brazil, see Dauril Alden, "The Growth and Decline of Indigo Production in Colonial Brazil: A Study in Comparative Economic History," *Jour. Econ. Hist.*, XXV (1965), 35–60.

30. William George Bentley, "Wealth Distribution in Colonial South Carolina" (Ph.D. diss., Georgia State Univ., 1977), 111, 113.

cultivation for more than a few years. The scarcity of machinery to process the crop indicated this tendency. In colonial Georgia, only 3.7 percent of households had such equipment (vats, pumps, and drying boxes) to manufacture indigo, and in lowcountry South Carolina, only 4.8 percent of households had equipment (see Table 4). Indigo delivered what its proponents had wanted: stasis, a temporary recovery of the commercial increment lost in rice without any bothersome reshuffling of the economy.

The crop brought significant economic change only to areas outside the well-developed plantation belt on the coastline. In newer areas of the Lower South—upcountry Carolina, fledgling Georgia, fleeting East Florida—indigo did allow some settlers to earn enough money to invest in slaves and more land, because entry costs for the crop were fairly low. During the 1760s, Henry Laurens estimated that it had cost him seventy-five hundred pounds to set up a new rice plantation in Georgia but that an upcountry settler needed only one thousand pounds to establish a farm for indigo and provisions. Settlers who arrived at the right time found that indigo paid respectable profits as well. In 1772, after taking into account rising prices for land and slaves, William De Brahm claimed that a Georgia indigo farm could earn more than the 29 percent annual profit that a new rice plantation paid back to an investor. By growing indigo, men whom planters derided as "crackers" could become substantial farmers, if not planters themselves.[31]

❧ A Patriotic Fiber

In the lowcountry, indigo allowed most whites simply to rehearse for another crop. Cultivation of indigo was an instance of what one scholar has called "bonanza" farming, in which the specific crop was not as important as the general changes in agricultural strategies it engendered. Indigo's economic boom taught planters that flexible strategies could be profitable as well as risky. Whites were more willing to invest capital, land, and labor in new crops even after indigo bottomed out. Cotton was the next crop to which they looked, though only after another crisis—more properly, a revolution—convinced them that a new commodity could have its uses. Profit, a goal for indigo's

31. Rachel N. Klein, "Ordering the Backcountry: The South Carolina Regulation," *WMQ*, 3d Ser., XXXVIII (1981), 663; Hamer *et al.*, eds., *Papers of Laurens*, IV, 337, V, 668; De Vorsey, ed., *De Brahm's Report*, 162–163.

TABLE 4. *Estates with Indigo Machinery, 1740–1799*

	1740s	1750s	1760s	1770s	1740s–1770s	1780s	1790s
Georgia					3.7%	0.0%	0.0%
South Carolina	3.1%	5.3%	4.4%	5.6%		4.5	0.0

Note: Items counted include any vats, pumps, beaters, drying boxes that were specified as used for indigo.

Sources: Estate Inventories, SCDAH, GDAH.

producers, was almost beside the point during the War of Independence. Instead of filling a gap in income, cotton patched over societal tensions within the fully commercialized lowcountry as the plantation elite sought to maintain its dominance during the disruptions of the Revolution. During the nonimportation movement and the war, planters moved away from commercial agriculture to a domestic economy based on production of food and textiles. Household production then expanded into the market. Cotton producers invigorated internal lines of exchange for raw fiber and finished cloth, thereby stimulating both household and artisanal production. Whites perceived the manufacture of goods as a temporary substitute for agriculture and household crafts but not as a permanently useful activity, a pattern common to other portions of the continent, where the war's effect "was to *accelerate* American economic development and to *delay* the emergence of a more capitalistic society."[32]

Nearly all the North American and West Indian provinces had earlier produced small amounts of cotton. Various schemes to diversify the plantation economies of South Carolina and Georgia had encouraged its production. In the seventeenth century the Carolina proprietors had tried to force their colony's peripatetic residents, who preferred trading with the Indians for deerskins, to settle down and grow something useful like cotton. Colonial admin-

32. Sharrer, "Indigo Bonanza," *Tech. and Culture,* XII (1971), 447; James A. Henretta, "The War for Independence and American Economic Development," in Ronald Hoffman *et al.,* eds., *The Economy of Early America: The Revolutionary Period, 1763–1790* (Charlottesville, Va., 1988), 87 (quotation).

istrators who promoted townships in South Carolina directed township-dwellers to grow crops like cotton, hemp, flax, and foodstuffs rather than commercial staples. The South Carolina Assembly in 1744 passed legislation authorizing bounties on several commodities, including cotton, and in 1768 Britain's Royal Society of Arts offered premiums on the staple.[33] Georgia's trustees had promoted cotton cultivation at the colony's experimental garden and on individual estates in the 1730s; and in his celebrated orphanage at Bethesda in Georgia, evangelical George Whitefield intended that the inmates raise, spin, and weave cotton. None of these strategies proved successful for more than brief intervals. Though Georgians exported a bit of cotton on the eve of Revolution, most cotton shipped out of colonial Charleston and Savannah was actually West Indian cotton routed through the continent. Planters and would-be planters preferred growing more lucrative crops like rice. As Alexander Garden put it, rice was still "the slow but sure way of getting rich."[34]

Most cotton grown in the colonial era was meant for domestic use rather than for sale, and many of those involved in this phase of limited production were slaves. The lowcountry task system encouraged their semiautonomous efforts at growing things like cotton. When finished with their tasks, slaves raised crops for personal or household use—food, tobacco, fiber for making textiles. The lowcountry contained, therefore, two varieties of economic ac-

33. On townships, see Gray, *Agriculture in the Southern U.S.*, I, 52–59, 378–379; Converse D. Clowse, *Economic Beginnings in Colonial South Carolina: 1670–1730* (Columbia, S.C., 1971), chaps. 3, 4; Robert L. Meriwether, *The Expansion of South Carolina, 1729–1765* (Kingsport, Tenn., 1940), esp. 17–30; Coon, "Agriculture in S.C.," chap. 7. On bounties and premiums, see Cooper and McCord, eds., *Statutes of S.C.*, III, no. 708; Minutes for Jan. 19, 1768, Minutes of Committee, RSA, 1767–68, reel 1.

34. On cotton: Victor S. Clark, *History of Manufactures in the United States*, I, 1607–1860 (New York, 1929), 83–85; Kenneth Coleman, ed., *History of Georgia* (Athens, 1977), 52–53; Works Progress Administration, "Plantation Development in Chatham County," *GHQ*, XXII (1938), 317, 320; see the advertisement for imported West Indian cotton in the *Georgia Gazette*, Oct. 20, 1763, and the advertisements for exported Georgia cotton, May 28, 1766, Jan. 17, 1770; Kenneth Coleman, *Colonial Georgia: A History* (New York, 1976), chap. 7; James M. Holland, "The Beginning of Public Agricultural Experimentation in America: The Trustees' Garden in Georgia," *AH*, XII (1938), 271–288; Erwin C. Surrency, "Whitefield, Habersham, and the Bethesda Orphanage," *GHQ*, XXXIV (1950), 91–96. On rice: Alexander Garden to Society, Apr. 20, 1755, Guardbooks, Correspondence, RSA, reel 1.

tivity: one dominated by the commercial ambition of white planters and one shaped by the personal or communal needs of black slaves. Planters considered these latter activities of secondary importance to the plantation economy; indeed, they scorned any diversification of plantation activities that did not result from their own leisure-class experimentation, as was the case with sesame and peanuts. Referring to cotton cultivation, one South Carolinian wrote, with more disdain than grammar, "The Planter plants no more than just what serves their Plantations in some few trifling Articles to employ some old Superannuated Negroe Wenches."[35] Cultivation of fiber was significant to planters in other ways. Their insistence on their womenfolk's duty to turn European cloth into clothing for slaves, for example, worked another variation on their vision of a near-domestic harmony existing between master and slave.

Though cotton was not yet a commercial staple, its significance as a domestic article should not be underestimated. It was grown throughout the southern colonies, and most black and white women who lived in rural areas would have had some idea of how to clean, card, spin, and weave it. Tools for processing fiber—linen hackles, cards, reels, spinning wheels, and looms—were common items in Lower South households. In colonial Georgia, 14.6 percent of households had such items; in South Carolina, nearly a quarter had them (see Table 5). Prevalence of these devices contrasts sharply with the relative scarcity of equipment for indigo and indicates a surprisingly high level of domestic production in this plantation region. Widespread familiarity with textile production would speed expansion of cotton across the Lower South in times of commercial crisis. In the meantime, of course, innovators had been gathering information about different varieties of cotton from around the

35. Garden to Society, Apr. 20, 1755, Guardbooks, Correspondence, RSA, reel 1 (quotation); Philip D. Morgan, "Work and Culture: The Task System and the World of Lowcountry Blacks, 1700 to 1800," *WMQ*, 3d Ser., 563–599. Slaves' independent activities took on truly domestic connotations as their network of kin expanded during the second half of the 18th century. John Channing explained in 1770 that though he offered ready-made clothing to his male slaves, they "cho[o]se to have the Cloth given them and their Wives or Sisters to cut it out and make them up for them." Channing may have missed the point; many men might have made their clothes themselves to suit their own style and taste. But the planter did realize that slaves' desire to service their own needs might have been a way to express their autonomy as a community with its own internal relations. See Channing to William Gibbons, June 26, 1770, William Gibbons Papers, folder 4, 12-A, Duke.

TABLE 5. *Estates with Clothmaking Tools, 1740–1799*

	1740s	1750s	1760s	1770s	1740s–1770s	1780s	1790s
Georgia					14.6%	7.1%	5.3%
South Carolina	22.4%	23.0%	21.7%	29.7%		15.5	8.4

Note: Items counted include carding devices, reels, spindles, spinning wheels, looms.
Sources: Estate Inventories, GDAH, SCDAH.

globe, obtaining a data bank on which they could later draw.[36] Two spheres of activity were in place, planter-dominated and slave-controlled; both would undergird the later expansion of cotton.

During the imperial crisis that culminated in the American War of Independence, residents of the Lower South significantly increased cultivation of cotton for the first time. Americans who complied with the nonimportation resolutions of the early 1770s were cut off from British sources for all types of cloth and began to manufacture their own textiles. Growing cotton and flax became patriotic activities, and slaughtering sheep for mutton, rather than keeping them alive for shearing, was outlawed in some colonies. Using the republican language that urged the return of a traditional economy, orators and newspaper editors praised American husbandmen and housewives for making their own cloth rather than relying on the tainted products of an imperial oppressor. An editorial in 1773 in the *South-Carolina Gazette; And Country Journal,* for instance, gave some "New Thoughts upon LUXURY," warning of the national evils of degeneration, idleness, indebtedness, and vanity. The cure for these sins was in "oeconomy" and "labour"—both of which showed "honour" and "love for our country." Women, traditionally

36. Gray, *Agriculture in the Southern U.S.,* I, 182–184. On information about varieties of cotton, see, for example, Hamer *et al.,* eds., *Papers of Laurens,* V, 473, 549, VI, 219, 426; Alice Izard Deas, ed., *Correspondence of Mr. Ralph Izard* . . . (New York, 1844), 16–17; Andrew Turnbull to James Grant, July 28, 1767, MacPherson-Grant Papers, bundle 253, Ballindalloch; advertisement for a slave from St. Croix "well acquainted with the Culture of Cotton," *Georgia Gazette,* Dec. 4, 1788.

associated with spinning wheels and looms, were now celebrated as cloth-making patriots. The republican matron became a stock figure in political discourse and her studied frugality a point of Revolutionary pride.[37] Politicized arguments for rejection of commercial luxury reinforced doubts coastal residents might have had about their progress toward a more complex stage of economic development. Planters—the most commercially oriented agriculturalists on the continent—could temporarily revel in the role of virtuously precommercial republican.

Spurred on by political exhortation, those Georgians and South Carolinians who, like their northern neighbors, adhered to nonimportation, cultivated cotton and flax, and raised sheep for wool. This strategy was, for some whites, merely a continuation or an intensification of earlier activities that had met personal or domestic needs. But some individuals were more ambitious, and planters were, at least initially, the leaven in the lump. Their need for cloth was greater than that of small farmers for the simple reason that planters headed larger households. Slaves on large lowcountry estates had been furnished with coarse fabrics from British sources, and planters faced the formidable task of finding new sources. In 1774 absentee Ralph Izard wrote to Henry Laurens, who was managing Izard's affairs: "It will be very necessary for us to think of the means of clothing our negroes, if our disputes with England continue, which, I am inclined to think, they will. Pray, at all events, let there be a considerable quantity of cotton planted for me." Izard reiterated the next year that he wanted Laurens to order cotton planted on his estate, emphasizing to him, "There is no part of your last letter . . . that affects me so much, as the want of clothing for the negroes."[38] A language of human sentiments was thus sprinkled over the louder republican demands for economic independence.

37. Clark, *History of Manufactures,* 223–226; McCusker and Menard, *Economy of British America,* 363–364; Henretta, "The War for Independence and American Economic Development," in Hoffman *et al.,* eds., *Economy of Early America,* 45–87; *South-Carolina Gazette; And Country Journal,* Nov. 2, 1773; Mary Beth Norton, *Liberty's Daughters: The Revolutionary Experience of American Women, 1750–1800* (Boston, 1980), 15–20, 155, 163–170; Linda K. Kerber, *Women of the Republic: Intellect and Ideology in Revolutionary America* (Chapel Hill, N.C., 1980), 37–39, 42, 44–45, 48. On the patriotic rhetoric that stimulated wartime manufactures, see Drew R. McCoy, *The Elusive Republic: Political Economy in Jeffersonian America* (Chapel Hill, N.C., 1980), 64–66.

38. Deas, ed., *Correspondence of Izard,* 15–16, 174.

But Izard and Laurens were probably worrying more over slaves' discontent than their level of comfort—they feared rebellion more than they empathized with suffering, and hastened to grow cotton.

Here again, the planter elite acted as catalyst for the crop by sharing the fruits of their agricultural experimentation with others. Laurens himself helped distribute cottonseed in a circuit described through the Lower South and Caribbean. He obtained seed from Florida in 1767 and reported the same year that he "never saw anything grow more luxuriantly than Cotton does upon Broughton Island" in Georgia. He sent for more seed from Grenada in 1768 and posted samples of West Indian seeds to Governor James Grant of East Florida in 1769.[39] Planters who raised cotton also had to process it. During the struggle for Independence their main concern was to find appropriate technologies to card, spin, and weave. They were less worried about ginning the seeds out of raw cotton—curious, given how difficult the task was later said to be in the 1790s. But most varieties of cotton grown during the war were probably long-staple fibers with smooth and easily removed black seeds. Southern planters, like colonists throughout the New World, simply adopted East Indian *churka* gins for such cotton, often using prototypes improved in the British West Indies. Even so, obtaining equipment to turn cotton fiber into cotton cloth was difficult during the trade dislocations accompanying the Revolution. Though he had plenty of raw material in 1776, for example, Nathaniel Heyward's efforts to produce cloth faltered because he lacked the proper tools.[40]

Everyone interested in processing cotton was scrambling for equipment. In

---

39. Hamer *et al.*, eds., *Papers of Laurens*, V, 473, 549, VI, 219, 426. By the 1770s, Bernard Romans reported that he saw Floridians growing cotton. See his *Natural History of Florida*, 139.

40. Ernest McPherson Lander, Jr., *The Textile Industry in Antebellum South Carolina* (Baton Rouge, La., 1969), 3. Indian churka gins, with grooved rollers that took the smooth seeds out of long-staple cotton, had proved adequate when the East India Company had first begun manufacturing and exporting cottons to England in the mid-17th century. (India was the world's largest producer of cotton and cotton cloth until the 1790s. At that point British textile manufacturers, using short-staple cotton grown in the American South, undermined East Indian textile interest.) See Daniel H. Thomas, "Pre-Whitney Cotton Gins in French Louisiana," *Jour. So. Hist.*, XXXI (1965), 136, 139–140; and Chapman, *Cotton Industry*, 16, 43–52. John Earle of Skidaway Island, Georgia, planted black-seed cotton on his plantation in 1767 to provide clothing for his workers. See the *Columbian Museum and Savannah Advertiser*, Oct. 15, 1799.

1777 Georgia merchant Joseph Clay wrote to a commercial associate that "Cotten and Wool and Cards" to process these fibers "will bring particularly the latter a good price . . . indeed they are so necessary an Article that they will bring almost any price" in Savannah. Looms were even more difficult to find. One advertiser in the *South-Carolina and American General Gazette* entered what seemed a seller's market in 1777 when he published his wish "to purchase, a LOOM . . . for weaving of coarse Cloth for the cloathing of Negroes." In the same year and newspaper, Henry Calwell announced one inventive way around shortages of equipment and expertise: he wove homespun using yarn spun by workers who lacked looms.[41] Calwell's strategy indicated an early specialization among artisans or, more probably, between market-oriented artisans and individual workers in households, a gradual expansion of the domestic sphere into the larger economy. The lowcountry's economy had become both simpler and more complex; cut off from Atlantic trade, residents turned to each other, elaborating household but also community production. By the 1770s, for example, nearly 30 percent of South Carolina households had tools for processing fiber. A wartime adaptation, the distribution of such tools declined after the Revolution (see, again, Table 5).

Production of textiles increased during the early years of the war, as more patriots managed to buy, borrow, or hire equipment. In 1777, for instance, South Carolinians Nathaniel Heyward and John Lewis Gervais made enough cloth for their slaves—Gervais had at least 365 yards by November of that year. Georgia minister Henry Muhlenberg reported that his slaves grew and spun cotton for their clothing in 1777. At this point, the skills of women and slaves as clothmakers acquired new importance. In 1777 an advertisement for an overseer in a South Carolina newspaper specified a preference for a "married man, whose wife understands spinning." In the same year, Charlestonian Michael Hubert's slave boys wove "Negroe Cloth, Linnen, Sheeting and Towelling." A year later, an advertiser who wanted to sell a slave woman noted her ability to "card and spin Wool or Cotton extremely well." Notices for other slaves in one 1779 issue of the *Charlestown Gazette* included "carders and spinners" and a woman described as "a good spinner."[42]

41. *Letters of Joseph Clay* (GHS, *Colls.*, VIII [Savannah, 1913]), 25; *South Carolina and American General Gazette*, Sept. 11, Apr. 3, 1777.

42. Deas, ed., *Correspondence of Izard*, 296; Hamer *et al.*, eds., *Papers of Laurens*, XII, 88; Andrew W. Lewis, ed., "Henry Muhlenberg's Georgia Correspondence," *GHQ*, XLIX (1965), 431; *Gazette of the State of South-Carolina* (Charleston), Oct. 28, 1777;

Production of cotton not only provided planters in the Lower South with textiles but also gave them alternative uses for land and labor while European markets for rice and indigo were inaccessible. On the large estates that shifted to cultivation of cotton and other articles for domestic consumption, slaves were performing greatly changed tasks. Instead of growing a crop not primarily intended for their own consumption, as was the case with rice or indigo, slaves now grew and manufactured a product expressly meant for their own use. Slaves continued to produce goods for themselves, as they had done before the war, but were unlikely to parallel these activities with labor performed for whites.

Planters had little choice but to accept this development, because slaves had early realized that wartime instability could work to their advantage. In the embattled lowcountry, slaves seized the margin of autonomy allowed them by the task system and widened it until it became the prevailing condition on coastal estates. They also wanted a more lasting state of freedom. Large numbers of slaves (David Ramsay placed the figure at twenty-five thousand in South Carolina alone) ran away during the war, many to British troops who promised them liberty.[43] Slaves who did not abscond refused to submit to whites' authority and redefined property and productive activities to reflect their temporary sense of release. James Edward Colleton's 1780 crops, for example, were neglected because of "the Desertion of the Negroes . . . and their being under little or no Subjection to the Overseers." Thomas Pinckney stated in 1779 that, when British troops went through his plantation, they took most of the male slaves with them; those who remained "are now perfectly free and live upon the best produce of the Plantation." Pinckney hoped that the

---

South-Carolina and American General Gazette (Charleston), Apr. 24, 1777, Aug. 6, 1778; *Charlestown Gazette*, Jan. 26, 1779.

43. Philip D. Morgan, "Black Society in the Lowcountry, 1760–1810," in Ira Berlin and Ronald Hoffman, eds., *Slavery and Freedom in the Age of the American Revolution* (Charlottesville, Va., 1983), 109–112; Robert A. Olwell, " 'Domestick Enemies': Slavery and Political Independence in South Carolina, May 1775–March 1776," *Jour. So. Hist.*, LV (1989), 21–48; David Ramsay, *The History of the Revolution of South-Carolina* (Trenton, N.J., 1785), estimate of escaped slaves on 384. Lachlan McIntosh, Jr., separated slave men from the women and children at night after Independence was declared, probably to make it more difficult for them to plan to run away. See McIntosh to his father, Lachlan, Sr., July 22, 1776, in Lilla M. Hawes, ed., "The Papers of Lachlan McIntosh, 1774–1799," *GHQ*, XXXIX (1955), 54.

overseer, who had hightailed it to the swamp to hide from the British, would "be able to keep the remaining property in some Order, tho' the Negroes pay no Attention to his Orders," having once seen how the man cowered before other whites.[44]

Planters realized that discontented, footloose slaves would not produce the usual complement of staple crops. Markets for rice and indigo were not available, and many whites simply allowed blacks to raise products for their own subsistence, hoping to keep them stationary. Cotton was, therefore, not only a political adhesive within the ranks of Revolutionary whites but also a delicate point of conciliation between whites and blacks. South Carolinian Peter Horry described, at the end of the war in 1782, how slaves on a neighbor's plantation near Georgetown grew only sweet potatoes and cotton, food and clothing for themselves. These slaves nevertheless ran away, at which point Horry asked the owner's permission to cultivate and harvest the abandoned crops for the use of his own slaves, to give them food and clothing.[45]

As Horry's anecdote revealed, whites could not keep determined slaves from absconding if British troops or sympathetic tories were near enough to provide assistance. Slaveowners' practice of allowing slaves to do as little as was necessary for their own subsistence demonstrated how, amid the chaos of war, slaves could force their owners to reduce the work load by threatening rebellion or noncooperation. Georgian Ann Rabenhorst confessed in 1777 that she had been "a little afraid on account" of her slaves after tories passed through her neighborhood. The workers remained "orderly" because, Rabenhorst emphasized, they were busy growing food and "a great deal of cotton for Negro clothing." She further noted that the slaves, in addition to cultivating cotton, spun "to make their own clothing."[46]

While a subsistence economy took shape, whites chafed under their inability to act as commercial agents. In the absence of an external market, they

---

44. William Ancrum to James Edward Colleton, July 14, 1780, Margaret Colleton Papers, SCL; Thomas to Eliza Lucas Pinckney, May 17, 1779, Pinckney Family Papers, series 38-3-5, SCHS. See also the statement in Eliza Lucas Pinckney to ———, Sept. 25, 1780, Pinckney Family Papers, series 1, box 5, LC.

45. Peter Horry to "Colonel Grimké," June 10, 1782, Peter Horry Papers, SCL.

46. Lewis, ed., "Muhlenberg's Ga. Correspondence," *GHQ*, XLIX (1965), 431. Many of the slaves who fled were wearing the homespun of the region's changed economy. See the advertisements for wartime runaways in the *Georgia Gazette*, Oct. 12, 1780, Mar. 8, 1781, and in the *Gazette of the State of South-Carolina*, Aug. 4, 1779.

developed an internal one, especially for food and other necessities. Very early in the war, surplus cotton fiber appeared in local markets. John Lloyd assured Ralph Izard in 1777 that "cotton is produced in such plenty" in South Carolina "*that considerable quantities may be bought.*" In the same year, John Lewis Gervais's slaves wove a surplus of cloth to save for future use or to sell. A market for the commodity quickly expanded. By the late 1770s, newspapers advertised raw cotton, spun yarn, and homespun cloth for sale, accommodating the varied needs of those who lacked spinning or weaving equipment. Certain regions specialized in cotton production; thus inland cotton farmers produced fiber to sell to lowcountry merchants and planters. Gervais indicated as much when he assured Henry Laurens that he could easily get two to three hundred pounds of cotton from the "back Country" for Laurens's slaves to spin and weave.[47]

Once a surplus of raw fiber existed and whites had enough cloth to satisfy their immediate needs, they began to produce more elaborate textiles. Endowed with a large surplus, inland settlers produced a variety of goods. One colonel of a Georgia regiment claimed that he made all articles of his uniform using local supplies in the upcountry. Blankets for slaves were a specialized product of interest to coastal planters. Ralph Izard had wanted to make blankets as soon as trade with Britain ended in 1774. Izard seemed to regard the lack of British blankets as an interesting challenge to South Carolinians' ingenuity, cheering a more doubtful Edward Rutledge by promising that wartime hardship would "sharpen the invention" of their fellows.[48]

In addition to testing the inventiveness of Revolutionary patriots, cotton solved several problems all at once. It was, foremost, an example of import substitution, meeting domestic and local demand for scarce goods before and during the war. It also provided planters with a new crop that would utilize labor and land that would otherwise be idle and fallow during the war. It enabled blacks temporarily to subvert slavery's expectation that the fruits of their labor belonged to their owners and allowed a standoff between whites and blacks during wartime breakdown of social order and commercial activities. This was a new twist on an ancient theme: some people went off to wage war, and others stayed behind to maintain hearth and home; the clacking

47. Deas, ed., *Correspondence of Izard*, 296; Hamer *et al.*, eds., *Papers of Laurens*, XII, 88.

48. Clark, *Manufactures in the U.S.*, I, 224; Deas, ed., *Correspondence of Izard*, 31.

of looms accompanied the clamor of battle. But in the case of the Lower South, a racial division asserted itself—whites supported the war, and blacks fostered a subsistence economy.

A terrible irony lies at the heart of this phase of crisis and response. The crop that would characterize the bondage of their children and grandchildren briefly characterized slaves' wartime liberation from planters' full authority. This paradox reveals how, though import substitution served the needs of many, it was particularly significant as a way for planters to hold together their region during the extraordinary stresses of a colonial War of Independence. The crop measured the political allegiance of whites to the cause of Independence, and it softened blacks' threat, more radical than that of revolt against imperialism, of noncooperation with and resistance against slaveholders during the war.

But blacks' ability to make any rebellious statement was all too quickly absorbed into whites' assumption that they had reached a mutual compromise under trying circumstances. Planters gave a self-congratulatory assessment of a difficult fact: though many slaves had run away or resisted, many others had not. Slaves had to make a series of painful choices about whether they would depart by assessing many variables. They had to decide whether to leave behind kin or expose them to danger, whether to trust tories or British soldiers, whether an uncertain future was better than a known though enslaved existence. Planters were mostly oblivious to these complicated choices and usually concluded that slaves who did not desert were actually loyal to them. Not all planters could have believed this (those who lost considerable numbers of slaves knew better), but others refused to believe that a seeming fidelity might have complex sources. Such self-reassurance had informed Ann Rabenhorst's statement that *she* had managed to keep her slaves "orderly" by arranging for them to grow cotton and food. After the war, in a similar vein, Henry Laurens ordered blue cloth, metal buttons, shoes, stockings, and buckles to reward those of his slaves who had been "faithful." Even bolder had been Laurens's 1776 prediction that they *would* be faithful because they were "all to a Man . . . strongly attached to me." These statements about attachment, faithfulness, and order reveal, again, whites' stubborn conviction that slavery fitted into a humanly created social network constructed on the sentiments of all parties rather than on the coercion of the enslaved by the powerful. Cultivation of cotton during the war itself embodied this massive difference in perspective. Slaves used the crop to demonstrate their temporary freedom from the exploitiveness of plantation labor; planters used it to keep their region from falling apart entirely.[49] Again planters' perception of slaves' ability to defy their bondage was tellingly partial. Slaves could acquire expertise, feed and clothe themselves, and otherwise meet every crisis that befell the region, yet still whites refused to see them as other than faithful retainers. Indeed, the more autonomy slaves had (short of violent resistance), the more they may have seemed to their owners voluntarily "attached" to their condition.

The adoption of cotton also revealed an interesting pattern of shifts between commercial and domestic spheres. As was the case in the other new states, wartime economic experiments did not permanently alter the economy. Though residents of the Lower South took up forms of production not typical of plantation economies, they did not continue to diversify by encouraging more artisans or wage-earning laborers to work in tandem with commercial agriculture. Only during the next significant crisis, the War of 1812, would domestic manufacturing begin to firm up into a base for industrial production of cotton textiles. The Revolutionary retreat from commercial agriculture to a domestic economy ended when the war itself ended. Planters then added cotton to rice as part of the plantation complement, completing the cycle from market, to home, then back to market.[50]

✌ The Luxury Staple

Unlike the cotton grown in the lowcountry during the war, that grown after the Revolution was a purely commercial product—more so even than rice, a portion of which always wound up in local cooking pots. The coastal crop, sea island cotton, became the most specialized and most profitable cotton grown in the South. It was a silky, long-staple hybrid derived from South American and Caribbean varieties. Because its fibers were longer than those of green-seed cotton and were spiral-shaped, spun sea island cotton formed a finer and stronger thread suited to laces and luxury cloth, or to the woof of cloth woven with a warp of cheaper thread made from short-staple cotton. Textile manufacturers valued sea island cotton so highly that Edisto

49. See John Owen to Henry Laurens, Feb. 23, 1784, Laurens to John Owen and John Lewis Gervais, June 16, 1784, LP; Hamer *et al.*, eds., *Papers of Laurens*, XI, 223.

50. Henretta, "American Economic Development," in Hoffman *et al.*, eds., *Economy of Early America*, 87.

Island planters in South Carolina could annually make \$170–\$260 from each full field hand. The crop quickly proved a success; because it had easily removed seeds, sea island cotton did not languish while awaiting the development of a better gin (as did short-staple cotton), but moved into the textile market as soon as European manufacturing expanded at the end of the eighteenth century.[51]

Cotton, like indigo, nonetheless underwent a period of experimentation before it was suitable for British buyers. At first, the region produced many varieties requiring varied cultivation techniques. By about 1800, planters ended up with three main categories: a long-staple variety that had smooth black seeds and flourished along the coast, a smooth-seed cotton grown on a small scale in the interior, and a short-staple type that had bristly, green seeds and became the upcountry's (and the Cotton South's) darling commodity. Because innovators gained their seed from different portions of the continent and the West Indies, these three types were probably hybrids of any number of original samples, and neighboring planters might have been growing quite different strains of the same crop.[52] Even after they standardized the kinds of cotton grown for sale, cultivators still had a crop that offered a dizzying array of varieties, resembling indigo (though not rice) in its range of types and qualities. Lewis Du Pre explained in 1799 that, although black- and green-seed cottons were "the extremes," myriad strains between these poles "run into each other, by almost imperceptible gradations." Whitemarsh Seabrook claimed in 1846 that there were still ten to fifteen identifiable subvarieties of sea island cotton alone that were the result of decades of breeding. To make matters more

51. Donald D. Brand, "The Origin and Early Distribution of New World Cultivated Plants," *AH*, XIII (1939), 109–117; Stephens, "Origin of Sea Island Cotton," *AH*, L (1976), 391–399; Whitemarsh B. Seabrook, *A Memoir on the Origin, Cultivation, and Uses of Cotton* . . . (Geological and Agricultural Survey of South Carolina, *Pamphlets* [Charleston, S.C., 1844]), 40; Seabrook, "Memoir on Sea Island Cotton," *Proceedings of the Agricultural Convention and of the State Agricultural Society of South Carolina* (Columbia, 1847), supplement for 1846, 3, 5; Mendenhall, "Agriculture in S.C.," 137, 140–145, 148.

52. Gray, *Agriculture in the Southern U.S.*, II, 681, 689; Brand, "Origin of New World Plants," *AH*, XIII (1939), 114; Stephens, "The Origin of Sea Island Cotton," *AH*, L (1976), 391–395. North Americans developed hybrids of Mexican cotton in Mississippi during the 1810s and 1820s, but these varieties had no significant impact in the Lower South before 1815. See John Hebron Moore, "Cotton Breeding in the Old South," *AH*, XXX (1956), 96–97.

confusing, planters had not even settled upon sea island cotton as the low-country's favored fiber. Peter Gaillard, for example, planted considerable quantities of both long- and short-staple cotton on his midlands estate in 1806, and Ralph Izard produced "short staple cotton" on his Berkeley County rice plantation in 1812.[53]

It took some time, as well, for methods of processing the crop to sort themselves out. At first, planters indiscriminately packed all their cottons in bags, until they began to press short-staple cotton into bales in the early 1800s, reserving bags for long-staple cotton whose more delicate fibers would have splintered under the pressure of a bale press. Market value depended on the quality of the fiber and the way it was ginned. Long-staple cotton was in general worth more than short-staple, unless planters mistakenly ginned it on a saw gin meant for short-staple cotton, which tore the longer fibers as it yanked the seeds out of them.[54] The *Carolina Weekly Messenger* of October 24, 1809, stated that sea island cotton could be classified (in ascending order) as ordinary, stained, fine, middling, or very fine, with different prices on each.

A planter usually chose to specialize in a certain kind of cotton or, after some experiments, threw the crop over entirely. Some gave cotton up because it posed several problems that neither rice nor indigo had. Caterpillars were a persistent hazard from the 1790s onward, and many types of soil would not yield satisfactory cotton crops.[55] Faced with such obstacles, rice planter James

53. Lewis Du Pre, *Observations on the Culture of Cotton* (Georgetown, S.C., 1799); Seabrook, "Sea Island Cotton," *Procs. of the . . . State Agricultural Soc. of S.C.* (1847), 3, 6; entries for Mar. 27, Apr. 7, 1806, Peter Gaillard's planting book, Gaillard Family Papers, series 11-149, SCHS; Ralph Izard, Jr., to Alice Izard, Jan. 24, 1812, Ralph Izard Papers, box 2, folder 13, SCL.

54. Ezekiel to William Noble, May 30, 1796, Noble Family Papers, box 1, folder 11, SCL. The letter mentions that upcountry cotton was packed in bags. Sometimes long-staple cotton was baled—see John Palmer's account with the Frasers, Dec. 26, 1811, Palmer Family Papers, box 5, folder 87, SCL, in which Palmer made payment with "2 Bales Long Cotton." On saw-ginning long-staple cotton, see Gray, *Agriculture in the Southern U.S.*, II, 677.

55. W.P.A., "Plantation Development in Chatham County," *GHQ*, XXII (1938), 321–324. Seabrook claimed that caterpillars first appeared in Georgia around 1793, then spread into South Carolina (*Memoir on Cotton*, 42). See also Pierce Butler to Thomas Young, Oct. 28, 1793, Pierce Butler Letterbook, SCL; description of caterpillars on sea island cotton in July 1804, memorandum book, Lachlan Bain McIntosh Papers, folder

Hamilton wrote in 1805 that he was "very much disgusted with the hazardous manner of the Sea Coast Cotton planting." "To lose a Crop and afterwards to buy Provisions," complained Hamilton, "is worse than losing a stake at Dice when at leisure." If they adopted sea island cotton as a commercial crop despite its hazards, planters often bade a final farewell to indigo. Explaining this decision, Pierce Butler complained that, because grasshoppers preyed on indigo and caterpillars on cotton, he found it easiest to wrangle with only one pest at a time. Butler also noted that, unlike rice, cotton required labor at the same seasons as indigo yet needed different techniques for cultivation. It was easier for laborers to learn methods of tending one crop and then stick to it. Cotton also competed with indigo for the same kind of land; many planters could not have grown cotton, and indigo, *and* provisions on the same estate.[56]

Individuals often had preferences for particular kinds of cotton that emerged from the tangled cousinry of earlier years. Some were actively involved in crossbreeding to obtain optimal varieties. Richard Leake experimented with West Indian fibers, Chinese nankeen, and local varieties of cotton. He also mixed seeds in the same soil, then sorted out the seeds from the most promising plants for future experiments. Other planters knew of Leake's experiments—Alexander McIver asked Leake to sell him a bushel of his "Famous Cotton Seed" in 1793 along with directions for growing it. James Alger advertised in the February 19, 1795, *Georgia Gazette* that he was selling cotton seed from "the low black bush" that was "highly esteemed" by planters. Other experimenters tried to find optimal methods of cultivation. A methodical member of the Ball family planted twenty acres of cotton scattered over different types of soil on his three plantations in 1799. He intended to discover which crop would do best, "so that if Cotton keeps up the price I will go more fully on it next year" on whichever soil should prove most suitable.[57]

2, GHS; Henry William DeSaussure to Ezekiel Pickens, Sept. 10, 1805, Henry William DeSaussure Papers, SCL.

56. James Hamilton to Seaborn Jones, Feb. 16, 1805, James Hamilton Papers, SCL; Pierce Butler to Thomas Young, Oct. 28, 1793, Pierce Butler Letterbook, SCL.

57. On Leake's experiments, see entries for Apr. 11, Apr. 20, 1788, Apr. 2, 1792, May 24, July 25, 1793, Richard Leake journal, 1786–1801, GHS, and Alexander McIver to Richard Leake, Mar. 2, 1793, Richard Leake Papers, folder 2, misc., Keith Read Collection, box 15, UGA. May 1799 fragment, Ball Family Papers, series 516–11, SCHS. Charles William Janson also mentioned that planters experimented with nankeen; see Janson, *The Stranger in America* . . . (London, 1807), 367.

Experimenters soon found that their crop required painstaking work. Although slaves were spared (until about 1825) the onerous task of hauling salt grass and marsh mud to manure the fields, sea island cotton took more trouble to grow than short-staple cotton. It was harder to pick because its bolls were narrower. Once harvested, it had to be spread out to dry, usually in an enclosed shed filled with tables. Here, slaves removed stained or broken fibers and sorted the crop into different grades before ginning it. A discolored product with too many torn or tangled fibers guaranteed lower prices and the displeasure of British brokers, and fine cotton was worth the effort of careful processing.[58]

One sign of how cotton spread along the coast is in the distribution of equipment to clean it. By the early 1800s, between 9 and 10 percent of inventoried coastal estates had gins, roughly twice the earlier distribution of machinery for indigo. Most of these mechanisms were probably small gins that an individual could operate by hand cranks or foot treadles, but some planters wanted larger mechanisms with greater capacity. Just after the Revolution, William Mein used draft animals to operate a large cotton gin on his Savannah River estate. An advertisement for "TIDE SWAMP PLANTATIONS" in the May 24, 1798, *Carolina Gazette* described a gin adapted to waterpower, in this case from a stream. At this point, entrepreneurs began to erect the toll gins that would extract fees from poorer whites in the antebellum period, and from sharecroppers and tenants after the Civil War. Joseph Clay's Georgia plantation contained toll gins for both long- and short-staple cottons by the surprisingly early year of 1794.[59]

Ginning for commercial profit indicated a fairly high level of investment in the production of sea island cotton. Cultivation became the preserve of wealthy planters, mostly because the land that yielded the best crops was narrowly limited and, by the late 1700s, already in the hands of members of the planter elite. For optimal cultivation of sea island cotton, planters needed to be near the sea (within thirty miles of the coast) but on rich high ground away

58. John Drayton, *A View of South-Carolina, as Respects Her Natural and Civil Concerns* (Charleston, S.C., 1802), 130–131; *Carolina Gazette*, Sept. 12, 1799; Du Pre, *Observations on Cotton*, 12–14. On manuring of sea island cotton, see Seabrook, *Memoir on Cotton*, 25–26. On the size of cotton bolls, see Ulrich Bonnell Phillips, *Life and Labor in the Old South* (Boston, 1941), 154.

59. Gins from sample of estate inventories, GDAH, SCDAH (9.3% in Georgia, 9.8% in South Carolina); W.P.A., "The Plantation of the Royal Vale," *GHQ*, XXVII (1943), 98.

from salty water. Quality varied inversely with distance from the coast. A few men owned most of the suitable land and gradually monopolized the long-staple cotton trade with Britain, edging out cultivators with less suitable soils.[60]

By and large, coastal planters ended up where they had started—on top—though they traveled an interesting route along the way. Experiments with indigo and cotton revealed planters' remarkable adaptability: these were not commercial agents who sat on their hands whenever financial adversity struck. Nor were they stubbornly devoted to commercial agriculture, as their willingness to expand domestic production of cloth during the American Revolution revealed. They were even somewhat willing to cede economic opportunities to relatively unempowered groups. Poorer whites earned wealth from indigo, female patriots won recognition for the homespun they made for republican soldiers, slaves eased the pressures of plantation agriculture by processing indigo and raising cotton. But planters were determined to return to staple cultivation once secondary crops had served their purposes during periods of instability. Restoration of their hegemony indicated one incontrovertible fact: they had won all the wars that had presented them with economic crisis. After the battles ended, lowcountry planters were determined to make the most of whatever they had preserved during the conflict. The exclusive character of sea island cotton planting indicated this trend. This final secondary crop, which survived, like rice, until the Civil War, reflected a socioeconomic structure that, if anything, was more closed than it had been in 1739.

In the period from the War of Jenkins's Ear through the Treaty of Paris, planters chose both to strengthen and to depart from existing economic patterns in a process that falteringly led to the South's commercial service to the British textile industry. From the time Eliza Lucas sowed indigo to the time sea island cotton planters marketed their product as a luxury commodity, Britain's industrial enterprise was expanding. Both indigo and cotton were twisting paths in the South's march toward the British textile mill. The first commodity, a textile dye, was encumbered by mercantilist policies that proved too bulky for long-term use. The latter staple, though the South's most famous link with the British market, got its start in an era of anti-British sentiment. The detours these crops mapped took unpredictable directions. Cotton, given its multiple uses as both domestic article and salable commodity, provided an

60. Seabrook, "Sea Island Cotton," *Procs. of the . . . State Agricultural Soc. of S.C.* (1847), 3, 6; Mendenhall, "Agriculture in S.C.," 140–145.

especially good measure of residents' ability to move out of or back into commercial agriculture. But efforts at domestic manufacture were swallows that did not make up a spring of economic development. At most, the changes that emerged between 1739 and 1787 presaged the extensive growth characterized by the post-Revolutionary spread of short-staple cotton.

Not that the dislocations of the Revolution lacked a legacy. When the War of 1812 again disrupted transatlantic commerce, planters would not shy away from household and, this time, factory production of textiles, albeit in very small amounts of manufactures. Both varieties of economic activity—conservative and innovative—emphasized again the paradoxical nature of the Lower South, where taking a risk on a new crop often preserved static societal forms rather than forged new entrepreneurial options. After the Revolution, when planters shifted their attention back to their favored crop of rice, they revealed even less willingness to consider social change and generated more conflict over scarce resources as class lines acquired rigidity. Indigo and cotton were merely dainties that started the feast, crumbs of which planters let fall to others. Once the main course was carried in, they set about carving it up among themselves, though, here, the extent to which they had to pass some cuts back to slaves, however grudgingly, is clearer than ever.

Chapter 7

Crisis and Response

Tidal Rice Cultivation

Rice remained the coastline's distinctive crop, outlasting the crises that led whites to experiment with cotton and indigo and surviving even the Civil War and Reconstruction.[1] The continued cultivation of rice gave the lowcountry a superficial appearance of continuity even through the Revolution, one paralleled by coastal planters' determination to maintain the institution of slavery despite the ideological challenges of the Revolutionary era. But when lowcountry residents continued to grow their old crop, they expanded tidal irrigation, a new method of cultivating rice that required some deeper alterations in the region. Post-Revolutionary innovations in tidal rice irrigation restated the Lower South's tension between innovation and adherence to older economic patterns. Tidal planters had to transform the physical landscape of their region in ways that marked out important social changes, but they were entrenching slavery deeper into the lowcountry as they directed their slaves to dig new irrigation ditches and dams.

Tidal cultivation was peculiar to the lowcountry and gave the area distinctive features that continued to characterize it through the antebellum era. The coastline would be, after the war, an isolated area controlled by a minority of white planters but inhabited mostly by black slaves, two subpopulations who thereafter strategically minimized contact with each other. Post-Revolutionary rice cultivation also demonstrated the diminishment of economic opportunity

1. David O. Whitten, "American Rice Cultivation: 1680–1980: A Tercentenary Critique," *Southern Studies*, XXI (1982), 17–19.

along the coast (foreshadowed by the exclusive character of sea island cotton planting) and the final consolidation of a rice-planting elite. This development contrasted with earlier innovations, like growing indigo or cultivating cotton for domestic use, which had allowed participation of poorer whites in an era of greater social mobility. Though this socioeconomic consolidation, in part, reflected long-term trends in the lowcountry, tidal plantations also underwent alterations that belie this seeming lack of change. First, these estates bore the marks of struggles that had taken place between slaves and masters during the war years, and evidenced slaves' ability to gain more independence from planters. Second, the new method of cultivation set off a vigorous competition for natural resources between whites of varying social ranks, with rich planters emerging victorious. Last, tidal plantations required artificial reconstruction of the natural terrain. This alteration of nature forced coastal whites slowly to realize how they had dug themselves, their slaves, and their descendants into a permanently altered region. Planters began to wonder whether they were injuring nature and human nature (the latter in the persons of their slaves) as they used slave labor to impose an artificial landscape on the natural environment. One traveler would call tidal cultivation an "unusual manner of natural irrigation."[2] Residents began to worry that it was more unusual than natural, as pre-Revolutionary, Enlightenment optimism began to give way to a romantic questioning of societal progress.

Rivers

In the early eighteenth century, South Carolinians had cultivated rice on dry upland soil, using rainfall to water their crop. They next discovered that irrigated rice cultivation on inland swamps yielded larger crops, and by midcentury they had shifted most rice production to marshy areas along the coast. Inland swamp rice planters depended on ponds or reservoirs of fresh water drawn off from swamps or rivers to irrigate their crops (see Plate 5). They drained the swampland, divided it into squares separated by ditches, and surrounded it with banks to prevent reinundation. Slaves who had experience growing rice in West Africa were probably instrumental in the successful creation of early rice plantations. The efforts of blacks and whites, over the

2. Luigi Castiglioni, *Viaggio: Travels in the United States of North America, 1785–87,* ed. and trans. Antonio Pace (Syracuse, N.Y., 1983), 121.

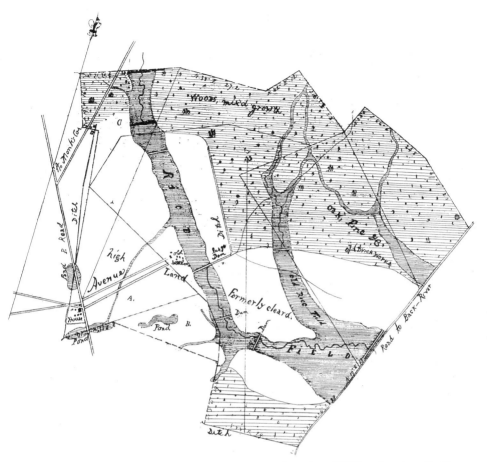

Plate 5. Old and New Methods of Rice Cultivation. *Plantation of William Loughton Smith, March 1805, series 32-46-7, SCHS.* In this estate plan for a plantation near Charleston, the Old Rice Fields (in the shaded portion at the top) follow the natural swamp along the waterways, the first kind of marsh to be used for rice planting. The new irrigation system is taking shape to the bottom. This larger shaded section has a ditch running alongside to the top; a parallel ditch is farther away on the bottom. Dams also run through the newer field at right angles to the ditches.

course of the eighteenth century, began to alter the natural world, turning it into one in which humans controlled water to make the land more productive. This pattern gradually extended to Georgia. But while reservoir cultivation worked most of the time, planters suffered considerable losses in their crops when sudden rains swelled surrounding water supplies and flooded the fields or when drought dried up reservoirs. They especially dreaded flooding. Peter

Manigault reported in 1766 that South Carolina had had "such incipient Rains that all the Rice Lands are under Water and numbers of people will not be able to plant this year." David Ramsay claimed that freshet floods in the 1780s caused financial ruin throughout one unlucky South Carolina district.[3]

Inland swamp cultivation also posed problems for planters because of its high demands for labor (about thirty working slaves per plantation)—the famously high demand that had created a black majority in the coastline's population and had fostered planters' tendency to cede some direct control over workers. Rice needed much weeding. The irrigation water that nourished the grain also encouraged growth of weeds; by late spring, all manner of opportunistic plants had sprouted in the thick mud of the fields. Rather than face the grinding months of toil with a hoe, ankle- or even knee-deep in muck, slaves tended to abscond, persistently eroding whites' authority over their labor. Josiah Smith feared his slaves would run away when the weeds were thickest in the spring of 1774 and hoped his overseer's moderate treatment of them, plus supplemental rations of beef and rum, would keep them at their tasks. The author of *American Husbandry* pointed out that South Carolinians had a revealing local expression for bad plantation managers: they were always

3. On the early development of rice cultivation: Lewis Cecil Gray, *A History of Agriculture in the Southern United States to 1860* (Washington, D.C., 1933), I, 279; Ulrich Bonnell Phillips, *Life and Labor in the Old South* (Boston, 1929), 116; Converse D. Clowse, *Economic Beginnings in Colonial South Carolina: 1670–1730* (Columbia, S.C., 1971), 122, 123, 126–127; Sam B. Hilliard, "Antebellum Tidewater Rice Culture in South Carolina and Georgia," in James R. Gibson, ed., *European Settlement and Development in North America: Essays on Geographical Change in Honour and Memory of Andrew Hill Clark* (Toronto, 1978), 97–98; David Leroy Coon, "The Development of Market Agriculture in South Carolina, 1670–1785" (Ph.D. diss., University of Illinois, Urbana/Champaign, 1972), 178–185; Peter H. Wood, *Black Majority: Negroes in Colonial South Carolina from 1670 through the Stono Rebellion* (New York, 1975), chap. 2; Daniel C. Littlefield, *Rice and Slaves: Ethnicity and the Slave Trade in Colonial South Carolina* (Baton Rouge, La., 1981); David Doar, *Rice and Rice Planting in the South Carolina Low Country,* Contributions to the Charleston Museum, no. 8 (Charleston, S.C., 1936), 7–41. On freshets: Peter Manigault to Thomas Gadsden, May 14, 1766, Peter Manigault Letterbook, series 11-493, SCHS; David Ramsay, *History of South-Carolina, from Its First Settlement in 1670 to the Year 1808 . . .* (Charleston, S.C., 1809), II, 7. See also how freshes "totally rotted the Rice" on several estates after freshet flooding: Charles Cotesworth Pinckney to Thomas Pinckney, Sept. 13, 1794, Pinckney Family Papers, series 1, box 4, LC.

"*in the grass*," not having enough labor (or enough willing labor) to keep their fields clean of weeds. Struggle over specific terms of work, therefore, characterized rice planting and reflected whites' newly acquired realization that they had to negotiate with slaves as they might with any other humans. Planters, because they used the task system, had already conceded some direct authority over labor. Slaves had greater control over their work (when they would perform their tasks, what they did on their own time) than their counterparts had in plantation economies that relied on gang labor. But slaves continued to dispute the fairness and uniformity of taskable units, and planters recognized slaves' power in redefining terms of labor. This was why Josiah Smith offered his workers incentives and why Richard Hutson, in 1767, admitted that his slaves had just cause to protest "unreasonable" working conditions and unequally divided tasks.[4]

Inland swamp irrigation, though it increased rice planters' profits, did so neither predictably nor invariably. Per capita output followed fluctuations in price and population more than anything else, and rice growing was as much a source of frustration over mobilizing labor as of increased income.[5] Some prescient innovators realized that the system would eventually yield diminishing returns and looked for an alternative way to irrigate their crops. The diurnal rising and falling of coastal rivers, caused by the flow and ebb of ocean tides, seemed a likely source of irrigation water. Coastal estuaries' changes in water level were quite striking. They rose six to eight inches at neap tides and eight to ten inches during the strongest spring tides, and the currents created by tides could ascend rivers for a distance of thirty to thirty-five miles.[6]

4. Josiah Smith to George Austin, Apr. 22, 1774, Josiah Smith Letterbook, SHC; Harry J. Carman, ed., *American Husbandry* (1775) (New York, 1939), 276 (quotation); Philip D. Morgan, "Work and Culture: The Task System and the World of Lowcountry Blacks, 1700 to 1880," *WMQ*, 3d Ser., XXXIX (1982), 569–570; Richard Hutson to "Mr. Croll," Aug. 22, 1767, Charles Woodward Hutson Papers, SHC.

5. In South Carolina, the per capita amount reached about 563 pounds between 1728 and 1732, but this would fall during the 1740s and 1750s and would not recover until just before the Revolution, probably because the price of rice had recovered and because more land was being taken up for commercial cultivation. See Peter A. Coclanis, *The Shadow of a Dream: Economic Life and Death in the South Carolina Low Country, 1670–1920* (New York, 1989), table 3-13, p. 82.

6. John Drayton, *A View of South-Carolina, as Respects Her Natural and Civil Concerns* (Charleston, S.C., 1802), 36; Ramsay, *History of S.-C.*, II, 297.

Boatmen could float part way up the Savannah River to Augusta using a strong tide yet had a hard time poling downward against the flow of the tide.

As early as the 1730s, planters noted tidal flow in rivers and, gingerly, began to flow estuarial water over their fields. During the next few decades, increasing numbers of cultivators would turn to tidal flooding for irrigation. In the January 22, 1741, *South-Carolina Gazette,* for instance, Joshua Sanders offered for sale fourteen hundred acres of land on the Combahee River that he described as "in a good Tide's way." James Habersham described to Henry Laurens in 1771 the welcome prospect of Georgia rice land "fully in the Tides way, and free from any Damage by Freshes." Bernard Romans said that, on the few rice plantations in Florida, the tidal rice swamp was the most valuable type of land, because it could be irrigated at will (regardless of the amount of rainfall) and cultivated "with much less labour and expence": the frequent inundation of the fields killed weeds that slaves would otherwise need to attack with a hoe. At this time, innovators were busily collecting information on irrigated rice cultivation in Asia and on hydraulic engineering in Europe. They knew that flooded fields produced the best rice crops but also realized that much effort and technical expertise would be needed to control estuarial flooding.[7]

Tidal irrigation of rice fields was not widespread before the Revolution, therefore, because it required significantly greater labor and capital than did inland swamp. George Milligen-Johnston observed that "the great Expence of damming out the Salt-water" prevented many South Carolinians from cultivating salt marsh on the banks of estuaries. Tremendous structures were needed to control tidal flooding (see Plate 6). A planter whose estate was on an estuary had first to build a permanent embankment about five feet high, three feet thick at the top, and twelve to fifteen feet thick at the bottom, its sides carefully sloped to prevent erosion. Workers reinforced weak points in the main bank by building wooden bridges over them and filling in these frames

7. Coon, "Market Agriculture," 178–181; James M. Clifton, "The Rice Industry in Colonial America," *AH,* LV (1981), 275; *The Letters of Hon. James Habersham, 1756–1775* (GHS, *Collections,* VI [Savannah, 1904]), 133; Bernard Romans, *A Concise Natural History of East and West Florida* (1775; facs. ed., Gainesville, Fla., 1962), 24. Planters also realized that a good, quick flood of water could kill pests and that a large water supply could guarantee the ability to flood at will. See Josiah Smith to George Austin, July 30, 1772, Josiah Smith Letterbook, SHC. On influences that shaped tidal cultivation, see Coon, "Market Agriculture," 181–182; and Chapter 5, above.

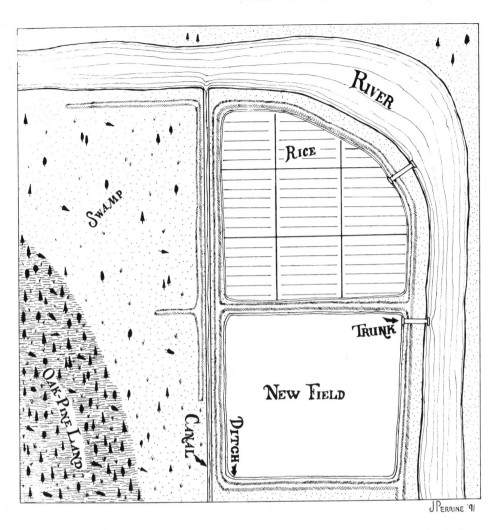

Plate 6. Hypothetical Development of Tidal Rice Fields. *Drawn by John Perrine.* A finished section of the field (labeled Rice) is in the bend of the river; below is an area newly cleared. Both sections have trunks to bring in water, and the canal to the left could be used to transport goods and workers or to bring in water should the planter wish to create more fields away from the river.

with more earth. A ditch ran all along the inner wall of this bank. The outer wall was pierced by trunks, or gates, that let water flow into the ditch, and the inner wall had drains that prevented the water from creeping too high. Smaller banks divided each section of the field from the next, and a system of internal ditches carried irrigation water to all sections.[8]

Each square of the rice plantation had to be enclosed by banks and each half-acre subdivided into 100–125 trenches for sowing. This complicated, expensive arrangement required care and time, for both its initial creation and subsequent maintenance. Allard Belin's men spent thirty-three days in the spring of 1792 reinforcing dams and banks and leveling rice fields, slightly more than the twenty-nine days that the women and men spent actually planting the crop. Any expansion required more infusions of labor. John Ewing Colhoun recorded in 1794 that, wanting to increase his ability to irrigate his fields, he planned to sink thirty new trunks along his "Spring Ditch."[9] Especially in the financially straitened decades before the 1760s (when they were using other crops like indigo to support their income), planters were wary of expanding rice production at such expense. They would soon be distracted, in any case, by the Revolution.

During the war, rice plantations were scenes of chaos. Most white men were drawn into the conflict, and blacks took the opportunity to flee or rebel against planters' authority. Authority was sometimes entirely lacking: Ralph Izard, engaged in the Revolutionary cause, bade farewell to five of his overseers who enlisted in the Continental army in the first year of the war alone. The situation worsened as the war ground on and as British invasion increased opportunities for slaves to defy planters and overseers. Eliza Lucas Pinckney complained in 1780 that her rice crop would be small as a result of "the desertion of the

8. [George Milligen (-Johnston)], *A Short Description of the Province of South-Carolina . . .* (London, 1770), 9, facs. rpt. in Chapman J. Milling, ed., *Colonial South Carolina: Two Contemporary Descriptions* (Columbia, S.C., 1951), 119; Hilliard, "Tidewater Rice Culture," in Gibson, ed., *Settlement in North America*, 105–109.

9. Drayton, *View of S.-C.*, 116–117; entries for spring, plantation journal for 1792, Allard Belin Journals, series 34-178-1, SCHS; memoranda for 1794, John Ewing Colhoun Papers, folder 3, SHC—these list several other tasks (carpentry, ditching, raising dams) necessary for renovation. On the division of labor among men and women, see entries for Apr. 28, June 1–7, 1792, Allard Belin Journals, series 34-178-1, SCHS; entries for Mar. 1, 1775 (spades given only to men) and for Mar. 20, 1784 (only one woman received a spade, no women received axes), Fairfield Plantation book, Pinckney Family Papers, series 37-60, SCHS.

negroes in planting and hoeing time." Planters also lost workers because slaves served, albeit unwillingly, in the war effort. Black men were commandeered as laborers or "artificers," working with army engineers to build fortifications; some slaves stayed away for several years before returning to their masters' plantations.[10]

Even more devastating than the loss of crops as a consequence of loss of laborers was the property damage that resulted from lack of willing workers to effect repairs. Wartime property damage was more extensive in the Lower South than any other region of the nation, owing partly to the virulence of battle there and partly to the nature of its landed property. When a rice dam broke or a ditch became clogged, it needed mending at once, so that water did not overflow and damage the rest of the irrigation system. With slaves, enemies, refugees, *and* water streaming through plantations in a chaotic fashion, damage remained and spread. In 1779, Thomas Pinckney worried that his overseer would be unable to "keep the remaining Property in some Order" on his estate. Georgian Josiah Smith described a desperate scene at his plantation in 1780. His rice dams had broken and would probably remain broken; some of Smith's slaves had vanished, others had been taken away by the tory overseer, and the rest could do little to put the property to rights, since most of them had smallpox.[11] The incentives Smith offered to slaves in peace could have little effect during war.

The end of the war and the restoration of civilian government brought only a small measure of order to the lowcountry. Loss of or damage to property was extensive; when the British took Charleston in 1780, losses of property in and around the city were already estimated at four thousand pounds sterling. After the final peace in 1783, many planters had to wait to accumulate new laborers and funds before piecing together their deteriorated properties. Henry Laurens was willing to let an expatriate East Floridian settle on one of his Georgia

---

10. Philip M. Hamer *et al.*, eds., *The Papers of Henry Laurens* (Columbia, S.C., 1968–), XI, 191; Eliza Lucas Pinckney to ———, Sept. 25, 1780, Pinckney Family Papers, series 1, box 5, LC. On acts regulating impressment of slaves, see William Edwin Hemphill *et al.*, eds., *Journals of the General Assembly and House of Representatives, 1779–1780*, The State Records of South Carolina (Columbia, S.C., 1970), 114, 197, 254. Men served as laborers, drivers, and artificers; women, as nurses. This was true in the British forces as well. See *Royal Gazette* (Charleston), Mar. 10, 1781.

11. Thomas to Eliza Lucas Pinckney, May 17, 1779, Pinckney Family Papers, series 38-3-5, SCHS; Smith to George Appleby, Dec. 2, 1780, Josiah Smith Letterbook, SHC.

plantations, paying only a token rent. Short-term profit was not his motive: Laurens only wished the property maintained so it did not continue steadily to lose its value. "Keeping up the foundation of Banks etc. which I had laid," Laurens explained, "will be a sufficient compensation to me." John Habersham recommended this strategy to Nathanael Greene, because it would be so difficult to plant again on a "neglected" estate. Georgia authorities even appointed overseers to some abandoned estates until ownership could be proven or restored, so that a distant claimant would not stand to inherit a property eroded and pillaged beyond redemption. Yet still these estates held great potential value. A summary image of the lowcountry's post-Revolutionary promise and disaster appeared in a 1784 poem in Savannah's *Georgia Gazette*. Restating the firm belief in the locality's luxuriance, the poet claimed of the Altamaha delta that it was "Another Nile, remote in Southern climes," but its "fertile soil" was, alas, "reserv'd for better times."[12]

Only after the Revolution would planters be able again to develop better methods of using their fertile soil. It nevertheless seems odd that tidal cultivation would expand, as it did, during this time of troubles. Tidal cultivation would eventually save labor by yielding more grain per worker, but to establish the new method required incredible amounts of labor, and maintenance took more time and more skill. The challenge could have daunted whites already discouraged from the war. Here again, however, war had acted as a creative disruption in the lowcountry. Wartime devastation meant that planters' estates *already* needed to be rebuilt. As long as they had to start from the ground up, they were more willing to consider ways to improve their properties. Georgian George Baillie made this clear when he stated, just after the newly minted peace in 1783, "The resettling of plantations that are so intirely gone to ruin, must be attended with nearly as much expence and difficulty, as the first settling of them." The 1780s formed, therefore, a watershed in the development of tidal planting. Innovators had earlier built up a crucial reserve of knowledge about techniques for exploiting tidal lands; a larger group of planters now had incentive to use these techniques. In Europe, increasing demand for foodstuffs and for cheap grain for distilling (as an industrial-era boom in population

12. Henry Laurens to Joseph Clay, Aug. 16, 1783, LP; John Habersham to Nathanael Greene, Nov. 1, 1782, Nathanael Greene Papers, Duke; *Georgia Gazette* (Savannah), June 3, 1784. For estimates of property damage in Charleston and on the use of overseers in Georgia, see Gray, *Agriculture in the Southern U.S.*, II, 595–596.

began) provided constant incentive as well for planters to produce and sell more grain. That tidal planting took off at this time is evidenced by how individuals began to claim they had "invented" specific techniques for planting tidelands. Most of these assertions were dubious—methods of using tidal flow had been known for decades and were not of a patentable nature—but revealed how there was a rush to utilize tidal fields that had not antedated the Revolution.[13]

Property damage was not the only obstacle to postwar innovation. This was also a time of financial hardship, debate over debtor legislation, and struggle to obtain loans from elusive European creditors. Planters were involved in these difficulties, but they did have, compared to poorer farmers, larger assets with which to start over. Especially in South Carolina, planters gained time for spreading out their financial obligations and recovering lost sources of income, mostly because they could borrow funds against the slaves who remained with them after the war. Costs were nevertheless high. By the early nineteenth century, for example, Georgia planter Thomas Spalding owed an astounding $100,000 for rebuilding and expanding his Sapelo Island estate. Clearly, creditors thought Spalding a good risk. Poorer agriculturalists had fewer assets against which to borrow and less time in which to pay.[14]

During this era, therefore, more wealth became concentrated in the top level of society. Amounts of both land and slaves increased in the upper ranks. In the meantime, falling levels of wealth in the population as a whole indicated that the coastline no longer offered economic opportunities to as many of its free inhabitants as it had before the war. This was a steady pattern in South Carolina, where the mean estate value (excluding real estate) for decedents dropped from $6,254 in the 1780s to $2,753 in the 1810s. In Georgia, settlers continued to acquire property, so levels of wealth continued to climb until the

13. Hilliard, "Tidewater Rice Culture," in Gibson, ed., *Settlement in North America,* 105, 109; George Baillie to John McIntosh, Sept. 7, 1783, John McIntosh, Jr., Papers, GHS. On markets for rice, see Coclanis, *Shadow of a Dream,* 133–134. Gideon F. Dupont would claim to have invented "Water Culture" and reported its methods to the South Carolina legislature in 1783. He petitioned for remuneration: Petitions to General Assembly, 1810, no. 119, SCDAH.

14. Jerome Nadelhaft, "Ending South Carolina's War: Two 1782 Agreements Favoring the Planters," *SCHM,* LXXX (1979), 50–64; E. Merton Coulter, *Thomas Spalding of Sapelo* (Baton Rouge, La., 1940), 41.

TABLE 6. *Value of Coastal Estates, 1780–1815*

	Mean Value in Dollars			
	1780s	1790s	1800s	1810s
South Carolina	6,254	4,370	4,723	2,753
Georgia	2,005	2,906	4,819	3,269

Sources: Estate Inventories, SCDAH, GDAH.

early 1800s but dropped thereafter as the newer region came to resemble its elder neighbor (see Table 6).[15]

Because of the increased socioeconomic stratification in the lowcountry, tidal cultivation was a class-based innovation: only those already in the planter class (or the rare well-heeled immigrant) could afford to expand production. Adoption of the new agricultural technique paralleled the final consolidation of a South Carolina planter elite and might possibly have accelerated the formation of such an elite in Georgia; although not a primary cause of this trend (which was set into motion at the start of the eighteenth century), tidal cultivation, because of its high entry costs, surely played into it. In 1796, Nathaniel Pendleton estimated that a new tidal rice plantation on Georgia's coast—with two hundred cultivated acres, four hundred acres of timber, and

15. Mark D. Kaplanoff, "Making the South Solid: Politics and the Structure of Society in South Carolina, 1790–1815" (Ph.D. diss., University of Cambridge, 1979), 16–18 (figures from 16). For other discussions of growing inequality, see Lee Soltow, "Socio-economic Classes in South Carolina and Massachusetts in the 1790s and the Observations of John Drayton," *SCHM*, LXXXI (1980), 283–305; Coclanis, *Shadow of a Dream*, 69–70. (Coclanis's statistics indicate that in 1763, 39% of landholders owned 500 or more acres, and 35% 1,000 or more. But in 1793, while an increased proportion [49%] had made it into the latter category, few had replaced them in the lower rank, which declined to 23%.) In the oldest plantation areas of South Carolina, this trend had begun before the Revolution. See George D. Terry, " 'Champaign Country': A Social History of an Eighteenth-Century Lowcountry Parish in South Carolina, St. Johns Berkeley County" (Ph.D. diss., University of South Carolina–Columbia, 1981), 281–289.

On continued social mobility in Georgia, see also Lee Soltow and Aubrey C. Land, "Housing and Social Standing in Georgia, 1798," *GHQ*, LXIV (1980), 448–458.

fifty slaves (forty of whom worked in the fields)—would cost $10,570, well beyond the reach of the ordinary investor.[16] Between tidal plantations and sea island cotton estates, lesser landholders were squeezed out.

Expenses were not the only problem. Would-be tidal planters also struggled with the tricky nature of their water supply. Tidal irrigation demanded a balancing act between the threat of salinity and the necessity for an adequate flow of water. Pendleton explained that tide swamp appropriate for rice cultivation ran the length of a river "from the place where the salt water ceases to flow, to the place where the tide itself ceases"; the best rice lands lay at a subtle point just next to where the saltwater ceased and the tide was strongest—"the proper pitch of the Tide." Even before the Revolution, some innovative planters studied Dutch and English methods of draining, diking, and irrigating land to learn how to turn natural resources into an artificial system of water control. After the Revolution, they resumed the research on hydraulic technology. The August 14, 1788, *Columbian Herald*, for instance, advertised the sale of "Belidor's Hydraulic Architecture, or the art of conducting, elevating and managing water" to planters who might wish to study this art. Planters could also hire experts; one man who said he understood "the reclaiming of land [from water] in every of its branches, both in Europe and America," offered his services to planters in 1806.[17]

Planters struggled, especially, to discover methods and mechanisms to irrigate their land without giving it a dose of saltwater. A not inconsiderable problem, this task confounded some planters. Francis Robertson gave up in 1798 and offered to sell his marshland to someone who was willing to drain the saltwater from it. Planters needed to drain brackish water off their fields, then bring in fresh water while keeping the saltwater at bay. Imported pumps like Charles Cotesworth Pinckney's English "Machine for throwing Water out of the Ditches" performed the first task. Local artisans also developed pumps, staving off costly and unpatriotic dependence on English technology. The South Carolina legislature granted a patent in 1786 on Peter Belin's "Water

16. Nathaniel Pendleton, "Short Account of the Sea Coast of Georgia in Respect to Agriculture, Ship-Building, Navigation, and the Timber Trade," ed. Theodore Thayer, *GHQ,* XLI (1957), 80.

17. *Ibid.,* 76; second quotation from John Wereat's letter to William Bingham, Sept. 22, 1782, Felix Hargrett Collection, box 3, UGA (though the phrase is found throughout tidal planters' writings); *Southern Patriot and Commercial Advertiser* (Savannah), Jan. 28, 1806.

Machines," which drained and desalinized salt marshes. To get fresh water back onto their fields, planters turned to resident artisans who developed floodgates suited to local conditions. Plowden Weston specified in 1792 that "a Trunk, or Floodgate" had "to keep out the salt W[ater and] vent the Fresh Water." Lowcountry workers rose to the challenge with an ingenious design. Their floodgates were large structures. One planter specified that each of his gates watered twenty acres. A floodgate was usually about four feet tall and had to run fifteen or twenty feet (sometimes more) through the width of a bank (see Plate 7). Each trunk had an outer and an inner gate; the outer swung open into the estuary, the inner toward the fields. When workers pulled the outer gate open, tidal water pushed open the inner gate and poured into the ditches. When the tide ebbed, the inner gate shut, retaining water. If a planter wanted the fields drained at low tide, the inner gate would be opened, and water would flow out the unlatched outer gate. On unpredictably salty rivers, gates were not automatic, but had to be raised and lowered like watery guillotines.[18]

Through growing experience, lowcountry residents learned to judge when to open or shut the gates. When the tide was high and the water fresh, planters seized the opportunity to irrigate their crop. John Ewing Colhoun's overseer thus explained in 1792 that because "the River has been perfectly fresh For sometime . . . I have given it plenty of Water always Changing it once a week." In 1802, Nathaniel Heyward recommended that both doors of the trunks should be slightly propped open when the river was sweet to allow constant freshening of the water in the ditches. This was the safest strategy during a storm of hurricane force, as the damage resulting from temporary flooding of

18. Robertson's advertisement in *Carolina Gazette* (Charleston), Oct. 4, 1798; Charles Cotesworth to Thomas Pinckney, May 1792, Pinckney Family Papers, series 1, box 4, LC; Thomas Cooper and David J. McCord, eds., *The Statutes at Large of South Carolina* (Columbia, 1836–1841), IV, no. 1337; Plowden Weston to Jonathan Lucas, Aug. 17, 1792, Lucas Family Papers, series 11-270, folder 66-5-13, SCHS. The dimensions are from Plantation Book, 1814–47, Mackay-Stiles Papers, XXVII, SHC (this trunk was 40 feet long—probably above the average). On other planters' construction of trunks, see Eliza Brewton Pinckney's letter to her father, Thomas Pinckney, Apr. 17, 1789, Harriott Horry Ravenel Collection, series 11-332-20, SCHS (her trunks were also about four feet tall); Albert Virgil House, *Planter Management and Capitalism in Ante-Bellum Georgia: The Journal of Hugh Fraser Grant, Ricegrower* (New York, 1954), 26. See also Hilliard, "Tidewater Rice Culture," in Gibson, ed., *Settlement in North America*, 108; and Phillips, *Life and Labor*, 117.

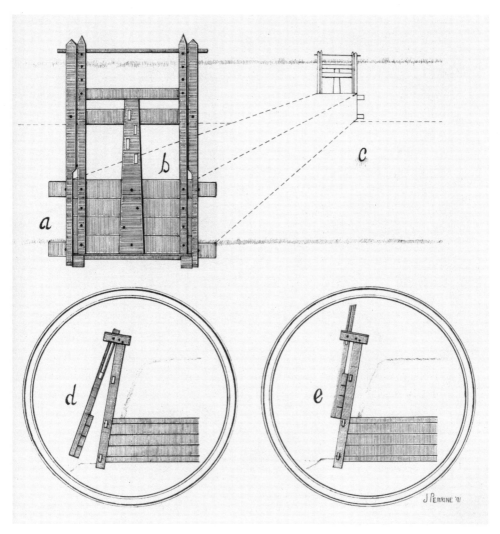

Plate 7. Cross-section of an Irrigation Trunk and Detail of Floodgates. *Drawn by John Perrine.* The trunk (oblong labeled *b*) runs through the earthen bank *c* (transparent in this image, its height is indicated by a grassy fringe at top and bottom) and has gates at either end. Gate *a* is locked closed. A worker could unlatch it (as in *d*) for automatic operation. Another design (*e*) could be lifted and locked.

the crop was less than that which could be done to the irrigation system if the closed floodgates burst under pressure.[19]

While learning to dodge hurricanes, planters made a series of discoveries about which estuaries were suitable to rice irrigation. One kind of lowcountry estuary contains brackish water, a vertically homogeneous mix of salt and fresh water. A second type—better for irrigation—has a sheet of fresh water overlying a moving wedge of saltwater. The saltwater pushes upstream with the tide and propels the freshwater layer above it up toward the river banks. This kind of river once included the Santee, Ashley and Cooper, Edisto and Ashepoo, Combahee, Savannah, Ogeechee, Altamaha, and the rivers around Winyah Bay. These estuaries themselves varied in value for rice cultivation. The Ashley-Cooper region around Charleston lost ground in rice production to areas around Georgetown, Savannah, and Altamaha. The Altamaha was especially rich: half of the total Georgia acreage suited to tidal cultivation (fifteen thousand acres) lay tangled in its delta.[20]

Observers began to note the variation among estuaries. Johann Martin Bolzius believed that there was "only salt water in the rivers" near Beaufort, and John Lambert noted that most Savannah River rice plantations were on the right side of the river (as an observer faced upriver), probably because the other side contained brackish water owing to some variation in tidal flow. Only after making some mistakes in planting were landholders able to determine the value of various estuarial swamplands. Ralph Izard believed that, if a swamp did not produce at least a barrel and a half of rice per acre, it was not worth the trouble of improving. Luigi Castiglioni related how the unlucky John Drayton surrounded his plantation on the Ashley River with banks to protect it from the salinity of the river and then irrigated his crops from a reservoir; Drayton was surrounded by water, but the wrong kind![21] Many

19. Archibald McK[?] to Colhoun, Aug. 16, 1792, John Ewing Colhoun Papers, folder 2, SHC; Nathaniel Heyward manuscript, 1802, SHC; House, *Planter Management*, 25–26.

20. Hilliard, "Tidewater Rice Culture," in Gibson, ed., *Settlement in North America*, 100–104; House, *Planter Management*, 22–23. On the Altamaha, see Coulter, *Thomas Spalding*, 76.

21. George Fenwick Jones, ed. and trans., "John Martin Boltzius' Trip to Charleston, October 1742," *SCHM*, LXXXII (1981), 95; John Lambert, *Travels through Lower Canada and the United States of North America, in the Years 1806, 1807, and 1808* (London, 1810),

other planters continued to use reservoirs either as their only source of water or along with tidal irrigation. One man advertised his Ponpon River estate of "prime tide land" in the June 18, 1787, *Columbian Herald* but added that the plantation also had forty-six acres watered by a reservoir. On other estates, planters called their inland swamp "old fields" and could get smaller yields from them, though developments in tidal irrigation probably helped improve methods of reservoir irrigation as well. Tidal irrigation did not, therefore, entirely replace other forms of rice cultivation. In parts of the lowcountry, it either spread quite slowly—in a process not fully completed even by the Civil War—or remained overshadowed by inland swamp planting. But in other areas the shift was dramatic: Saint Paul Parish, South Carolina, had an estimated 128 settled inland swamp plantations at the time of the Revolution, but only 8 in the antebellum period once tidal estates proliferated.[22]

Early tidal cultivation represented a struggle, therefore, not only to develop methods of using estuarial flow but to discover which estuaries were worth using in the first place. Appropriate tidal swamp was worth at least twice as much as inland swamp—up to four times as much if improved. Men blessed with such holdings were determined to get the most out of them. Their determination often translated into conflict among planters, particularly during the early years of tidal cultivation when they were not always sure whether they had suitable swamp or how best to irrigate it. The ill effects of their uncertainty were exacerbated by their use of rivers; rather than relying on private reservoirs, planters competed with each other for fresh water along public waterways.

Legislators had long recognized the potential for competition and had prohibited such unneighborly strategies like venting excess water onto or diverting water away from another planter's fields. Georgia's legislators enacted a law in 1763 to protect properties from "Damages which may Arise from Dams or Banks for reserving or stoping of Water" on nearby plantations, and a law of 1773 specified that erring planters would have to pay damages to neighbors;

III, 53; Ralph Izard to James Mills, Aug. 10, 1794, Ralph Izard Papers, legal-sized documents, folder 5, SCL; Castiglioni, *Viaggio,* ed. Pace, 122.

22. William B. Lees, "The Historical Development of Limerick Plantation, a Tidewater Rice Plantation in Berkeley County, South Carolina, 1683–1945," *SCHM,* LXXXII (1981), 51–53. On St. Paul Parish, see David Duncan Wallace, *The History of South Carolina* (New York, 1934), II, 379.

South Carolina had similar laws.[23] Tidal irrigation worsened this problem. Planters became more dependent on a predictable supply of water and needed to protect their irrigation systems (which represented considerable time and labor) from destructive flooding. Also, the way an individual planter directed the flow of an estuary might permanently alter the waterway, with resulting damage to the interests of other landholders. Conflicts erupted between competing rice planters and, more revealingly, between planters and poorer whites who tried to protect their lands from the errors and encroachments of unskilled or unscrupulous rice growers.

In response to the new demands of tidal irrigation, laws regulating dams became stricter and more detailed. A South Carolina statute of 1786 stated that rice field dams had to be opened by March 10 each year in order to prevent dangerous buildup of water. The statute levied a one-hundred-pound penalty on anyone who had not opened his gates by this date; Georgia passed a similar law in 1787. Such measures singled out planters with large and elaborate irrigation systems, as a South Carolina petition of 1799 (with sixty-seven names) illustrates. The signers complained that planters who shut their floodgates after the harvest made water back up in the river and flood over the properties of those who had inland swamps not protected by high banks. Such flooding made it impossible for the latter "to improve and put in order their Lands . . . and that at the only time of the year which is best suited to improving them." For similar reasons, when several large planters in St. James Parish, Goose Creek, petitioned the South Carolina Assembly for permission to create a canal that would help them cultivate crops and ship them down to Charleston, they met with protest. Two other residents sent a counterpetition arguing that the canal would ruin six hundred acres of their pasture and asking that their interests not be sacrificed to those who planted rice. Petition again met counterpetition in 1795 when landowners on Santee River wanted the waterway widened, but others nearer the mouth of the river feared that this measure would flood their lands with saltwater.[24]

---

23. See, for instance, a law of 1744 in Cooper and McCord, eds., *Statutes of S.C.*, III, no. 704; Allen D. Candler, comp., *The Colonial Records of the State of Georgia* (Atlanta, 1904–1916), XVIII, Act of Apr. 7, 1763, XIX, pt. 1, Act of Sept. 29, 1773.

24. Cooper and McCord, eds., *Statutes of S.C.*, IV, no. 1306; Robert Watkins and George Watkins, eds., *A Digest of the Laws of the State of Georgia* (Philadelphia, 1800), 348–350; Petitions to General Assembly, 1786, nos. 36, 37, 1795, no. 115, 1799, no. 62, SCDAH.

Squabbles also occurred between planters who lived next to each other. Just after the war, political enemies Henry Laurens and Christopher Gadsden were forced to cooperate in repairing a rice dam. (The former was a Revolutionary moderate; the latter, his radical critic.) Gadsden acidly suggested that Laurens hurry with his share of the labor, as the inner dam is *"all mine and done totally at my Expense"* yet sheltered Laurens's property "as a *common* boundary to us both." In 1789, South Carolinian Robert Clark complained that Elias Ball's irrigation system flooded his land whenever the river was high; Clark claimed that this happened because Ball refused to open his floodgates to relieve pressure along the waterway. Isaac Parker pleaded with John Coming Ball to *close* his gates when they released water that then surged toward his property, and Parker implied that Ball was using his overseer as a scapegoat in this tactic while professing innocence of its occurrence. In 1808, Conrad Augley and Isham Carr gave depositions that Alexander R. Chisolm had tried to prevent millowner William Loper "from having a sufficient resevoir of water to work his said mill" by draining off all the water to irrigate Chisolm's rice fields.[25]

Rice planters also quarreled over the borders of their land. Boundary disputes and a flurry of resurveying accompanied the shift to tidal irrigation, as new methods of cultivation raised questions about old landholdings. Planters were exploiting, sometimes for the first time, river swamp they had once assumed was of little use, and they wanted to determine the extent of these holdings. Moreover, their new irrigation systems could alter the flow of water and erode land, so that the boundaries of their property would change and could be challenged by a neighbor. This difficulty struck at the very foundation of an agricultural society based on individual ownership and development of land. Local law specified that in cases of disputed property, a committee of surveyors made a decision after studying old plats and traipsing out to see how the land lay. Isaac Parker and John Coming Ball resorted to this strategy after a year of wrangling with each other. Ball wanted it done in a hurry—"for I hear Mr. I. Parker is a Making all the interist he can against me" in the neighborhood. Arnoldus Vander Horst II and John Shoolbred, disputing over a piece of riverbank, had two court-appointed surveyors sent out to investigate and keep peace among the neighbors. In the meantime, the two men continued quarrel-

25. Richard Walsh, ed., *The Writings of Christopher Gadsden, 1746–1805* (Columbia, S.C., 1966), 199; Robert Clark's complaint, July 18, 1789, Ball Family Papers, folder 6, unnumbered box, SCL, and Parker to Ball, July 25, 1789, folder 5, box 1; June 16, 1808, depositions, Lewis Malone Ayer Papers, legal-sized documents, folder 11, SCL.

ing and made those around them (like it or not) share in their rivalry. When Vander Horst's slaves were discovered oystering on the disputed piece of ground in July 1810, for example, an angry Shoolbred stormed down to the river and cast loose their boats, leaving the scapegoat slaves stranded.[26]

The worst hazard of tidal irrigation—a possibility that made planters take a hard look at what their neighbors were up to—was salinization of waters and lands, which could thus be rendered useless. A 1796 petition from South Carolinian Charles Brown drew attention to this problem. He claimed he owned ten thousand acres that were flooded by saltwater and asked the state assembly for permission to block off the creek that brought in "the Salts with the Freshes." Before Brown could do so, a commission investigated whether his dam would shunt the saltwater toward some unsuspecting planter elsewhere along the creek. Another group of planters had unwisely constructed a canal to connect Back River with Cooper River before they had the plans properly investigated. To their regret, the canal introduced saltwater into the rivers, rice yields dropped, and the price of certain lands decreased to only a tenth of their original value.[27]

In their quarrels over prime swampland, competitors' statements reveal how socioeconomic status influenced the early history of tidal planting. Opponents—convinced they were gentlemen worthy of respect—insisted on being treated in accordance with their rank. They were incensed whenever they believed they were relegated to the status of hired overseers, mere actors in, rather than lords of, the tidal landscape. Isaac Parker, when he complained that John Ball's "overseer (contrary to our positive agreement,) refuses to let the flood gate be shut and threatens to resist any person who will attempt to do it," delicately reminded Ball of their shared rank by requesting him "as a gentle-

---

26. Cooper and McCord, eds., *Statutes of S.C.*, VII, 171, 177. The quotation is from Ball to Jonathan Pringle, Feb. 22, 1790, folder 6, legal-sized documents, Ball Family Papers, SCL. This last folder contains a subpoena (Jan. 4, 1791), for witnesses in the case of *Parker* v. *Ball*. See also Thomas Parker to Ball, Jan. 8, 1790, and Ball to Parker, Jan. 17, 1790, folder 6, letter-sized documents, box 1, SCL. For the dispute between Vander Horst and Shoolbred, see Arnoldus Vander Horst to Joseph Purcell, Dec. 21, 1801, John Hardwick to Vander Horst, Jan. 11, 1802, Vander Horst to Purcell, Mar. 9, 1802, Vander Horst Papers, series 12-194, and Vander Horst to ———, July 10, 1801, series 12-197, SCHS.

27. Petitions to General Assembly, 1796, no. 83, SCDAH; Charles Hateley to John Coming Ball, Aug. 6, 1792, Ball Family Papers, box 1, folder 10, SCL.

man and Man of your word, (of which I have not the least doubt,) to give him such directions." A neighbor of one of the Georgia Habershams complained of a similar breach in class etiquette. The man had neglected to cut open his dam but claimed that he "never mean'd to prejudice you or any other Neighbour with Water" and resented how Habersham had sent his overseer to issue a curt order to the neighbor's overseer rather than paid a courteous call himself: "I am not to be threatened by Overseers of any person else," the man objected; "I was the proper person to have been appli'd to, and not the Overseer."[28]

These heated interchanges suggest that tidal irrigation made only more apparent the existing economic inequality among whites. More conclusive evidence that it reshaped class relations lay in the system's material results. Tidal irrigation, supported by careful seed selection that had begun earlier in the eighteenth century, made productivity soar and enriched those who successfully adopted it. In 1793, James Heyward (who, with his brother Nathaniel, made early experiments with tidelands) boasted to Thomas Pinckney that the brothers' innovative "use of water" more than doubled their output and that they had the last laugh on those who had once seen fit to "laugh at our Dams." The Heywards' laughter was full of money. Inland swamps had produced between 600 and 1,000 pounds of rice an acre, but by the 1790s, tidal swamp planters could raise 1,200–1,500 pounds per acre. A slave could make five or six times as much rice on a postwar tidal estate as on a pre-Revolutionary inland swamp plantation, averaging between 3,000 and 3,600 pounds per worker. Coastal land values also rose. Inland swamp was worth only $20–$50 per acre while improved tide swamp sold for $70–$90 per acre—another indication that rice planting was no longer a possibility for men with modest resources.[29]

28. On Ball, see Robert Clark's complaint, July 18, 1789, Ball Family Papers, SCL (quotation from Isaac Parker to John "Cummin" Ball, July 25, 1789, folder 5). See also B. Mazyck to John Coming Ball, June 20, 1791, in folder 7, unnumbered box, of the same collection. On Habersham, see ——— to "Mr. Habersham," ca. 1800, Habersham Family Papers, folder 1, Duke.

29. On seeds: By the end of the 18th century, planters preferred what they called gold rice, a superior variety of white rice. See the advertisements in the *Georgia Gazette,* Jan. 20, 1791, for golden rice and in the *Southern Patriot,* Feb. 19, 1807, for seed rice "entirely free from red grains," a pesky volunteer rice that planters were eager to avoid.

On the Heyward brothers: James Heyward to Thomas Pinckney, Apr. 22, 1793, Pinckney Family Papers, series 3, box 4, LC. Heyward claimed that his brother's five plantations produced 3 barrels per acre and nearly 15 barrels per slave. These figures

Productivity further improved as the evolving method of irrigation passed through two early phases. Tidal planters first used a method called "flow culture." They drained and sowed their fields toward the end of March, then reflowed them to germinate the seed rice embedded in the trenches. During the late spring and summer they made successive flows to drown weeds and pests while nourishing the young plants; all told, they might use four to five major flows, or even more when weeds, insects, or lack of rain required them. Between flows, they drained the fields so slaves could loosen the soil around the growing plants, reinforce banks, repair floodgates, and remove the most stubborn weeds.[30] The methodical cycle of draining and flowing kept the crop nourished and killed most weeds, so slaves were freed from the endless hoeing that had dogged them on inland swamp plantations, though they still had constantly to adjust the irrigation system and to make even heavier repairs at the start of the growing season or after a hurricane.

Planters next refined flow culture into "water culture," what Nathaniel Heyward had recommended when he told planters to keep their floodgates always open to allow continual recirculation of water. Fields cultivated by this method were kept flooded. Workers simply raised the level of the water to keep pace with the rice as it grew taller until the crop had shoots with three leaves (about twenty days after planting). The fields were then drained for about three weeks while slaves hoed the crop and inspected the irrigation system. Slaves reflooded the fields and drained them again only at harvest. William

---

were a touch exaggerated—Heyward was claiming an average of 8,200 pounds of rice per slave, an indication that he was only figuring in full hands rather than all workers. The average was probably half the amount he claimed. On pre-Revolutionary rice yields, see Carman, ed., *American Husbandry*, 278.

On swamp productivity: Henry C. Dethloff, "The Colonial Rice Trade," *AH*, LVI (1982), 238–239. Lachlan McIntosh calculated (note ca. 1806, McIntosh Papers, folder 5, Keith Read Collection, box 17, UGA) that a tidal swamp would produce 1,650 pounds per acre—this would make more than 7,000 pounds per slave (35 slaves to 150 acres), which is a bit too high. Charles Cotesworth Pinckney estimated between 600 and 1,200 pounds per acre. For other estimates of production per slave and acre, see Coclanis, *Shadow of a Dream*, 97.

On slave productivity: Whitten, "American Rice Cultivation," *Southern Studies*, XXI (1982), 15.

On swamp prices: Lambert, *Travels*, III, 446.

30. For descriptions of flow culture, see Nathaniel Heyward MS, SHC; and Drayton, *View of S.-C.*, 119–120.

Butler, who pioneered water culture on Santee River in 1786, claimed that it was superior to "the slovenly method of flowing fields, and hoeing or chopping [weeds] thro' the water." John Drayton also praised water culture because, as it demanded only one hoeing between planting and harvest, each worker could manage more acres. Thomas Pinckney believed that "to pursue this system" of water culture "much less intelligence will be required in the cultivators," who would not have to worry about when to drain or reflow their fields. Pinckney further reported that in experiments he performed in 1810, he made 1,069 bushels of rice on twenty-two acres using water culture but only 990 bushels on the same amount of land using flow culture. He also stated that, because fresh water would constantly pass over rice fields, the swamps would not become the stagnant breeders of disease that flow-culture rice swamps (or inland reservoirs) became whenever the water in them was not changed for a long period of time.[31]

Final product of lowcountry planters' research on far-flung types of agriculture, water culture was the most Asiatic form of rice cultivation. The fields resembled Asian paddies, constantly covered, as they were, with a silvery sheet of water out of which the green shoots of rice appeared, leaved, and ripened. Water-culture planters also imitated painstaking Asian methods of hand transplanting and cultivation. Low spots where the seedling rice had drowned needed to be transplanted by hand, and, at the midpoint of the season when the fields were drained for hoeing, slaves had to pass through the fields and gently raise fallen stalks, "running their fingers under them in the manner of combing." Charles Cotesworth Pinckney used transplanting for large sections of his crop. So did Henry Laurens, who modeled his method of transplanting on that of China and estimated it increased his yield from 1,500 pounds per acre to 2,000. Water culture was, therefore, the last effort to perfect rice cultivation on tide swamp, though it had limited impact. Compared to the leap in productivity that resulted from the first adoption of tidal cultivation, water culture only slightly raised yields. Planters could undertake water cultivation

31. William Butler, "Observations on the Culture of Rice," first section, series 36-1786, SCHS; Drayton, *View of S.-C.,* 120. See also Nathaniel Heyward MS; House, *Planter Management,* 31. Pinckney in *Report of the Committee Appointed by the South Carolina Agricultural Society . . . to Which Is Added General Thomas Pinckney's Letter on the Water Culture of Rice* (Charleston, S.C., 1823), 18–20 (experiment), 21–22 (quotation), 23 (health). A bushel of rough or unmilled rice weighed approximately 65 lbs. (Carman, ed., *American Husbandry,* 278).

only if they had very level fields and if the nearby estuary was never subject to saltwater tides that could seep onto the fields and stunt or kill the rice.[32]

Struggles with earth and water—not to mention neighbors—would pay off for the gentlemen planters who emerged triumphant from the lists. Compared with inland swamp estates, their new plantations had larger rice crops, lower day-to-day demands for slave laborers, and a more certain harvest. Only a hurricane or severe flood of saltwater could damage their output.[33] Each tidal plantation made a permanent alteration in the landscape: symbol of wealth, distant landmark along a river, ambitious attempt to control natural phenomena. Nathaniel Pendleton concluded, "When a *tide swamp* plantation is properly banked and ditched, the crop will never, it cannot fail." John Drayton wrote, more modestly, that with tidal cultivation "the crop is more certain, and the work of the negroes less toilsome" during the growing season. Drayton also observed how tidal irrigation fertilized rice because the "inundations, and flowings of tides, bear to it, and precipitate thereon, the finest and most subtle particles of manure."[34] Rice planters thus had reason to compare their lands

32. The quotation is from the Heyward MS. For references to transplanting, see entry for June 13, 1790, Fairfield Plantation book, Pinckney Family Papers, series 37-60, SCHS; Henry Laurens to Edward Bridgen, Feb. 13, 1786, LP. Rice planters improved other aspects of their estates. Though the success of tidal irrigation deterred some innovations (planters stopped growing sugar, for instance), it stimulated other improvements. Planters brought in Bermuda grass to act as a binder for rice banks (to prevent erosion) and then experimented with the grass in their pastures (see Coulter, *Thomas Spalding*, 100). New forms of irrigation improved the yield of other crops, providing not only water but new topsoil. Rice planter Thomas Porcher, for example, irrigated his corn fields on Ophir Plantation in South Carolina (see entry for Apr. 10, 1799, plantation diary of Thomas Porcher, Stoney and Porcher Family Papers, SHC). This was one way around the problem of soil depletion that plagued southern planters in other regions.

33. On these unwelcome prospects, see the comments of Samuel DuBose, Jr., to William DuBose, Sept. 23, 1804, Samuel DuBose, Jr., Letters, SHC (hurricane); Jacob Read to Charles Ludlow, Nov. 6, 1804, Read Family Papers, box 1, folder 14, SCL (salt flooding). DuBose specified that it was "tide swamps" that suffered most from the 1804 hurricane.

34. [Pendleton], "Short Account," ed. Thayer, *GHQ*, XLI (1957), 76–77; Drayton, *View of S.-C.*, 8, 116. Because rice absorbs most of its nutrients through its stalk rather than its roots, the slow circulation and redepositing of silt from estuaries prevented

with those along the Nile: their waterways brought the floods of water and silt that had made lands in the Middle East bloom for centuries.

✌ Mills

Though tidal irrigation was a happy solution to Revolutionary-era crises in rice cultivation, it also created a crisis, this one in rice milling. To process their larger crops, planters had to replace preindustrial methods of milling with more efficient and mechanized mills. In this task, they could indulge the fascination with industrialization that had propelled them through many a factory. Quite willing to lay out capital and train labor in order to establish large-scale milling, planters gradually created a world around themselves that even more depended on physical reconstruction of the natural world for increased production of agricultural wealth. More than ever, these provincial planters were adept at entering a modern order—and at coming up with funds for buying into this order.

Nearly all rice mills in the Lower South were also, however, descendants of premodern West African technology. Before the American Revolution, slaves polished rice in upright wooden mortars using wooden pestles, devices clearly derived from African prototypes. This was a serviceable method that lasted for several decades—as late as the 1780s, Timothy Ford reported seeing South Carolina slaves pound rice in wooden mortars. But planters became discontented with the haphazard nature of hand-milling, because the process varied according to the skill, strength, and enthusiasm of the individual worker. Much rice ended up only partially hulled or it shattered in the mortar. Slaves had to sift out the marketable rice from the broken or rough bits, and the remaining product might still contain substandard grain. Henry Laurens complained of the generally poor quality of other people's rice and fretted that his own carefully processed grain would be mixed with or classed as an inferior product. Hand-milling made demands on slaves' energies that also concerned some planters. As Alexander Garden had emphasized to members of London's Royal Society of Arts, hand-milling could seriously weaken slaves. Georgian Josiah Smith complained to George Austin in 1774 that he needed better mills

---

long-term loss of nutrients. See D. H. Grist, *Rice,* 2d ed. (London, 1955), chap. 16; House, *Planter Management,* 24.

because, after the harvest, his slaves were fatigued and debilitated with the work of cleaning rice. Fearful of this outcome, Peter Manigault instructed an overseer in 1794: "If the Rice made at Goose-Creek is not yet beat out, I wd. wish to have it sold in the rough, to save Labour to the Negroes."[35] But Manigault would have preferred a laborsaving method of polishing rice, one that would raise its market value without taxing slaves' strength.

As early as the 1690s, whites had experimented with ways to mechanize milling. In South Carolina, an astonishingly active community of artisans (many of them Huguenot) and a colonial assembly eager to hand out patents had fostered several inventions. Mechanics were especially active during a 1730s economic boom facilitated by new land grants and high rice prices, but they also came up with inventions during the 1740s slump, when new devices promised to save labor for other tasks, like growing indigo. Most of these machines simply provided power to mortars, usually a row of them connected to a central mechanism. George Timmons of Colleton County, South Carolina, received a patent in 1743 for his (unspecified) "manner of lifting the pestles" in a rice machine. In 1744, John Tobler designed a treadmill propelled by two or three slaves. Adam Pedington and Samuel Knight received similar patents in 1756 and 1788, respectively, for their new designs for rice machines.[36]

Inventors also looked for ways to mill rice without using slave labor at all. Lowcountry planters had an abundance of draft animals (see Table 7), mostly horses or cattle, both of which could be used for milling. (Mules were not yet common. Planters were more likely to keep *bees* than mules—only 1.3 percent of Lower South estates had mules, but 7.6 percent had bees!) Some pre-Revolutionary planters had used livestock to power rice mills; advertisements for a horse-run mill and a cattle-turned machine within a barn appeared in 1768 editions of the *South-Carolina Gazette; And Country Journal.* Georgian

35. Joseph W. Barnwell, ed., "Diary of Timothy Ford, 1785–1786," *SCHM,* XIII (1912), 184; Hamer *et al.,* eds., *Papers of Laurens,* III, 394, IV, 137, 409; Josiah Smith to George Austin, Jan. 31, 1774, Josiah Smith Letterbook, SHC; Peter Manigault to John Owen, Feb. 20, 1794, Peter Manigault Letterbook, SCL. On African mortars, see Wood, *Black Majority,* 61–62.

36. See Cooper and McCord, eds., *Statutes of S.C.,* III, no. 698 for Timmons's patent, IV, no. 853 for Pedington's, V, no. 1400 for Knight's; Tobler's advertisement, *South-Carolina Gazette* (Charleston), Apr. 23, 1744. On the culture of inventions and patents in South Carolina, see Bruce W. Bugbee, *Genesis of American Patent and Copyright Law* (Washington, D.C., 1967), 75–82.

TABLE 7. *Coastal Estates with Horses and Cattle, 1740–1815*

	1740–1779		1780–1815	
	Horses	Cattle	Horses	Cattle
South Carolina	76.0%	63.0%	43.0%	37.4%
Georgia	53.7	50.0	42.9	41.0

Sources: Estate Inventories, SCDAH, GDAH.

James Wright used cattle and horses to run a mill that cleaned six barrels of grain each day. Elkanah Watson explained that at about the time of the Revolution South Carolina planters milled rice in mortars, "ten or twelve in a row, each containing about half a peck" and worked by pestles attached to a central mechanism run by horses. John Drayton claimed in the early 1800s that the most common device was this "pecker" mill run by livestock.[37]

On tidal plantations, however, rice output had increased by five or six times, and even mills run by livestock lagged behind the quickened pace of production. Plowden Weston complained in 1793 that his horse-powered mill was too slow: he could process only two or three batches each day. Their gluts of grain even made planters consider exporting rough rice to Britain and having it milled there. Jonathan Lucas, the Lower South's most talented millwright, planned to build a rice mill in London in about 1800. Aware of the ever-present threat of competition from Bengal, Lucas first persuaded Britain's Board of Trade to reduce the duty on American rough rice, as it had done for East Indian grain, with the expectation that milling would give employment to English workers. But in the meantime planters discovered how to handle rice using local hydraulic power and, for the moment, rejected the alternative of allowing the British working class to process their crop.[38]

37. See the July 22, 1768, and Nov. 8, 1768, editions for advertisements for Veitch's mill and for the barn and mill; *Letters of Habersham* (GHS, *Colls.*, VI [1904]), 216, 219; Elkanah Watson, *Men and Times of the Revolution . . .* , ed. Winslow C. Watson (New York, 1856), 52; Drayton, *View of S.-C.*, 121.

38. Plowden Weston to Jonathan Lucas, Mar. 22, 1793, Lucas Family Papers, series 11-270, folder 66-5-13, SCHS (Weston stated that it took more than four hours per

Planters first operated mills with modest sources of water. At about the time they abandoned reservoirs as sources for irrigation, they began to use these pools as sources of power. Georgian Lachlan McGillivray had an early water mill by 1764, but this type of machine did not spread over the Lower South until the 1770s and 1780s. Just before the Revolution, Bernard Romans reported that Florida water mills had proved cheaper than either slave mortaring or horse-operated milling. In 1783, Luigi Castiglioni admired William Allston's water mill near Georgetown; the machine activated "12 pistons for shelling rice, [and was] one of the first [so] constructed." By the 1780s, James Habersham's Georgia plantation, Silk Hope, had an artificial pond that operated a rice mill.[39]

Though millponds helped handle the postwar bounty of rice, planters soon discovered that these reservoirs had the same drawbacks as those for irrigation. Floods or drought could bring milling to an abrupt halt, and planters then had to scramble for alternative methods of milling until their reservoirs were at normal levels. William Frazer reported in 1792 that one of the Middletons' rice mills could not operate because heavy rains had sent water cascading over their milldams. Elizabeth Brewton Pinckney wrote her father, Thomas Pinckney, in 1798 that she had to put up a "fair weather machine" (probably a collapsible wooden mill run by livestock) until the rains came and replenished her water mill. Georgian John Bradley also complained in 1806, "We have had a Drought [so] that our Rice Machine has not been able to beat."[40]

As they slowly shifted their attention from reservoirs to rivers, planters

---

batch); Jonathan Lucas to Isaac Ball, ca. 1800, Ball Family Papers, box 2, folder 18, SCL. By 1850, most of the rice exported would be rough or paddy; see Gray, *Agriculture in the Southern U.S.*, II, 730.

39. W.P.A., "The Royal Vale," *GHQ*, XXVII (1945), 93; Romans, *Natural History of Florida*, 127; Castiglioni, *Viaggio*, ed. Pace, 121; *Letters of Habersham* (GHS, *Colls.*, VI [1904]), 128–129; R.F.W. Allston claimed that Jonathan Lucas built the first water mill in 1787 for a Mr. Bowman of Santee, but this date is clearly too late. See Allston, *Memoir of the Introduction and Planting of Rice in South-Carolina* (Geological and Agricultural Survey of South Carolina, *Pamphlets* [Charleston, 1843]), 17–18. Henry Laurens had a large mill constructed on one of his plantations in 1769. See March 1769 entry in Henry Laurens Journals, p. 221, College of Charleston.

40. William Frazer to Harriott Horry, Aug. 26, 1792, Pinckney Family Papers, series 3, box 3, LC; E. B. Pinckney to her father, Apr. 17, 1798, Harriott Horry Ravenel Collection, series 11-332-20, SCHS; John Bradley to William Scarborough, Apr. 23, 1806, Godfrey Barnsley Papers, box 1, folder 1, UGA.

realized that tidal estuaries were the best sources not only for irrigation but also for hydraulic power. Tidal estates already had systems of irrigation dams, ditches, and floodgates that could be modified to channel tidal power onto waterwheels as well as through irrigation ditches. These alterations were under way at the end of the colonial era. Henry Laurens recorded in 1777 his considerable payment of £450 currency to the appropriately named Andrew Miller "for building the Tide Machine" at Laurens's plantation in Georgia. John Drayton stated that such a mill conveniently ran on ebb tides controlled by rice field floodgates "which shut of themselves with the turn of the tide." Planters soon discovered that the problems tidal rivers posed to irrigation (such as influxes of saltwater or inordinately high flooding) could actually benefit mills. John Ball, Sr., remarked in 1802 that the river alongside his plantation was "brackish as high as the tide flows—but my Mill works away brisker than ever in consequence of getting in more tide water by the new flood gate."[41]

Heartened by their achievements, engineers and planters sought to mechanize as many steps in milling as possible using Oliver Evans's famous automated design for wheat flour developed in the mid-Atlantic region in 1785. A tidal mill that Jonathan Lucas constructed for Henry Laurens in 1794 contained a network of machinery, including an elevator to take grain up and down from the mill's entrance and an automatic packer to barrel the product. John Drayton boasted that mills modeled on Evans's design could take rice from the threshing floor to the market barrel all within the same mill and with little assistance from human hands (see Plate 8). Drayton reckoned that the automated pestles in rice mills struck thirty-two to forty-four times per minute and, under the supervision of only three workers, processed one hundred barrels of polished rice, at six hundred pounds each, per week. In 1811, Scotsman J. B. Dunlop described a Georgia rice mill that was also completely automated. He reinforced Drayton's boast that tidal rice mills contained the best mechanization available, stating that such mills would not "discredit

41. Hamer *et al.*, eds., *Papers of Laurens*, XI, 380; Drayton, *View of S.-C.*, 124, 124n; John Ball, Sr., to John, Jr., Jan. 12, 1802, Ball Family Papers, series 516-14, SCHS. Millwright Jonathan Lucas claimed he built the first tidal mill in South Carolina in 1791, but the assertion was probably only a way of advertising his services. See the list of mills Jonathan Lucas built, Lucas Family Papers, series 50-292 microfiche, SCHS. On the other mills, see Allston, *Memoir of Rice*, 18; Ramsay, *History of S.-C.*, II, 206–208, 206–207n.

Plate 8. "An Inside View of a Water Rice Machine as Used in South Carolina." *From John Drayton, A View of South-Carolina, as Respects Her Natural and Civil Concerns (Charleston, S.C., 1802), facing 122.* A. The Windlass for raising the Flood Gate. *B.* Holes for a Pin by which the Windlass & Flood Gate are secured. *C.* The main driving Cog Wheel, fixed on the Water wheel shaft. *D.* A large Wheel, revolving on the same Axle with the small Wheel *Y. E.* A Small Lanthorn Wheel impelled by the large Cog Wheel *D. F.* Mill Stones. *G.* Hopper. *H.* Funnel thro' which the rough Rice falls from the Loft. *I.* Funnel from the Mill Stones discharging into the Wind-fan Hopper. *L.* A Strap, worked by a

Crank for moving a riddle within the Fan. *M.* Hulls or Chaff passing thro' the Door.
N. The Hulled rice, discharging from the Wind-Fan into the Bin *O. P.* A Cog Wheel, Moving the Axle *S. Q.* The Pestles. *R.* The Mortars. *TT.* Two Moveable Beams, supporting the
Axle *S. U.* End of the Cross Beam, into which the Screw *K.* plays, and also supports the
long moveable Beam *VV.* on which the upper Mill Stone rests, raised at pleasure by Screw
K. W. A Band, which works the Pulley of the Wind-Fan. *X.* A long cross beam, connecting
the Beating & Grinding Parts.

England," world leader in industrial design. "Every thing necessary in the Cleaning of Rice is done in it by Machinery," Dunlop exclaimed. "The grain is removed from one appartment to another by artificial Elevators where it undergoes all its different processes." Dunlop noted how the final product was "packed by Mechanical power, and so much labour does it save that it is only necessary to deposit the Rough Rice in one appartment from whence it is carried off, by magic as it were, and produced in the appropriate part of the house fit for the market, and falling into the Cask in which they mean to convey it." This was the kind of mill a planter opened with a banquet or barbecue, the neighborhood gentry gathering to see the remarkable machinery set into motion like an enormous clock ticking off an accumulation of profit (though the mortar-and-pestle heart of the clock was still dependent on ancient African design, not European technology).[42]

Planters continued to modify tidal mills. Lewis Du Pre developed a screen moved by a pendulum for sifting polished rice from flour and broken grain; his design sifted better and more quickly yet used fewer screens, which were expensive to purchase or repair. Jonathan Lucas built at least one windmill for processing rice, though wind was not as widely used as tidal power.[43] Some planters endeavored to mechanize threshing and winnowing as well as milling. Slaves had used simple hand-operated wind fans to winnow rice since the mid-1700s (in the 1760s, Governor James Glen had claimed they were a new invention); these fans became standard equipment during the early nineteenth century. Most threshing remained comparatively labor-intensive. Slaves wielded hand flails against grain thrown on clayed barn floors. Threshing probably required less effort, time, and skill than had mortaring rice, so planters saw less

42. On Laurens's mill, see Allston, *Memoir of Rice*, 18; Drayton, *View of S.-C.*, 123–124. On Dunlop, see Raymond A. Mohl, ed., "A Scotsman [J. B. Dunlop] Visits Georgia in 1811," *GHQ*, LV (1971), 263.

43. Drayton, *View of S.-C.*, 122; Allston, *Memoir of Rice*, 18; list of mills Jonathan Lucas built, Lucas Family Papers, series 50-292, microfiche, SCHS. For further information on rolling screens (which seemed to be perfected in the 1780s and 1790s), see Nathan and D. Sellers of Philadelphia to Henry Laurens, July 23, 1802, Harriott Horry Ravenel Collection, series 11-332A-23, SCHS. On problems with screens that broke or needed to be replaced, see —— to William Johnston, Dec. 21, 1810, William Johnston Papers, box 1, folder 12, SCL; and Thomas Young to Thomas Chapman, July 14, 1801, McDowell-Davison Papers, SCL. For a windmill, see "A South View of Julianton Plantation in Georgia the Property of Francis Levett Esqr.," ca. 1800, Picture File for McIntosh County, Georgia, Duke.

need to improve the process. But some innovators could not help tinkering with mechanized threshing. The South Carolina Ball family had a threshing machine run by horses, and the indefatigable Pinckney brothers also looked for threshing machinery adaptable to rice.[44]

Planters could not resist experimenting, as well, with their era's new source of energy, steam. Most cultivators contented themselves with tidal mills, which utilized an indigenous source of power and neatly fitted into the existing system of irrigation. Indeed, tidal irrigation and tidal mills complemented each other because each made seasonally different demands on the dam and ditch complexes without hindering the other's operation. But in the early nineteenth century, as steam-driven machinery became a wonder of the modern age, some planters brought boilers to their estates. Steam mills worked where tidal mills could not—in towns, or at locations away from estuarial waterways—and when ordinary water mills failed to keep pace with crop production. The shift toward steam began in the late 1780s and quickened in the 1800s when coastal planters who had unsuccessfully experimented with sea island cotton and sugar turned back to rice, getting larger harvests that injected new profits into the region.[45]

Residents began adapting steam technology to local needs. In 1788, Isaac Briggs and William Longstreet advertised in the *Augusta Chronicle* of April 5 that they had a "new mode of applying *steam* to machinery" for mills or cotton gins. Innovators had to adapt boilers to withstand the region's brackish water without corroding. In 1813, William Lowndes heard, via Adam Seybert, of an

44. [James Glen], *A Description of South Carolina* (London, 1761), 7, facs. rpt. in Milling, ed., *Colonial S.C.*, 15; Drayton, *View of S.-C.*, 121. For threshing machines, see Hugh McCauley to Isaac Ball, Nov. 20, 1815, Ball Family Papers, unnumbered box, folder 13, SCL; and Chapter 5, above. See also William Lowndes to "Mrs. Lowndes," Nov. 16, 1811, William Lowndes Papers, folder 2, SHC (a discussion of a Virginia threshing machine and the application of steam to it), and Rawlins Lowndes to Mrs. Lowndes, June 27, 1813 (Lowndes wanted parts for a "wind fan and threshing mill"), Rawlins Lowndes Papers, SCL. But see too the plantation book entry for Nov. 5, 1810 (Ball Family Papers, microfilm R147, SCL), which describes how female slaves threshed rice by hand on Limerick Plantation in South Carolina.

45. Elias Ball (of Bristol) to Elias Ball (of Charleston), Sept. 11, 1787, Ball Family Papers, box 1, folder 4, SCL (Ball believed steam was better suited to sawmills than to rice mills); W.P.A., "Plantation Development in Chatham County," *GHQ*, XXII (1938), 323–324; House, *Planter Management*, 21; Benjamin Latrobe to John Vaughan, Nov. 14, 1802, Harriott Horry Ravenel Collection, series 11-332-21, SCHS.

English engine with salt pans that distilled the water before it passed into the boiler. The mechanism generated sixteen horsepower, Seybert claimed, but cost at least sixteen hundred dollars—a considerable outlay that only the wealthiest planters could afford. Inventor Benjamin Latrobe informed Lowndes that a copper boiler would best withstand muddy or saline water's corrosive effects. This device would be cheaper than distillation, but the boiler and pans still needed repair and periodic replacement.[46]

Because steam and tidal rice mills were expensive structures, they were scarcer than older kinds of equipment. Planters who had such mills often operated them as toll mills in order to make a profit on the large amounts of capital they had invested. The proportion of lowcountry estates that included milling equipment in their inventories declined. Between 5 and 13 percent of colonial estates had had such equipment (see Table 8), but this proportion dropped after 1800, reaching zero by the 1810s. Not entirely representative of the actual prevalence of milling equipment, these numbers suggest, instead, how mortars and pestles might have been relinquished to slaves and how large mills constituted real estate not identified in inventories. But the overall decline indicated that many estates probably had no backup if their mills failed; they, along with planters who had no way to mill their own crops at all, had to resort to commercial mills. These mills became the final goal for successful rice planters. Alice Izard therefore lamented how, though her son Henry had a rice mill and cotton gin that worked "by water," he was "too far from a Market to make a Merchant Mill profitable."[47]

Others were better situated. As early as 1798, the partnership of Gaillard and Mazyck ran a toll mill five miles above Strawberry Ferry in South Carolina. But most toll mills made their appearance later, reflecting the sharp increase in investment that mills demanded in the second decade of the nineteenth century. South Carolinian Jacob Read built his Paragon Toll Mill in 1811. The mill was situated on an impressive 200-foot dam, had a floorspace that measured 120 feet by 40 feet, and was 34 feet from floor to eaves, dimensions indicating the presence of a large machine within. Read bragged that it could polish three hundred tierces (about twelve hundred barrels) of rough rice each

46. Adam Seybert to William Lowndes, Aug. 23, 1813, Rawlins Lowndes Papers, SHC; Benjamin Latrobe to William Lowndes, June 11, 1813, Harriott Horry Ravenel Collection, series 11-332-26, SCHS.

47. Alice Izard to Mrs. [Mary Izard] Manigault, Oct. 26, 1815, folder 88, box 8, Manigault Family Papers, SCL.

TABLE 8. *Coastal Estates with Rice-milling Machinery, 1740–1809*

	1740s	1750s	1760s	1770s	1740s–1770s	1780s	1790s	1800s
South Carolina	7.7%	10.6%	13.0%	8.9%		5.5%	10.3%	0.9%
Georgia					5.6%	7.1	10.5	2.3

Note: The percentage drops to zero by the 1810s. Items counted include mortars and pestles, rice fans, and sieving and winnowing devices.

Sources: Estate Inventories, SCAH, GDAH.

week; he charged a 10-percent toll and collected half of the flour and broken rice sieved off from the finished product. He probably resold the products he received as payment in kind. In 1813, Read estimated that his yearly income from the mill alone would be about twenty-five thousand dollars.[48] Ralph Izard, Jr., set up a milling partnership with a Mr. Morris in 1812 to operate "a Mill on their place to which all the neighborhood are obliged to resort, and which according to these gentlemen will soon be made to bring in *ten thousand dollars* a year." Toll mills such as Izard and Morris owned capped the technological achievements in rice cultivation that took place after the Revolution and justified the large capital investments in rice mills.[49]

But if rice mills, especially when run with steam, brought a touch of industrial capitalism to the Lower South, this was a selective importation. Other aspects of rice production remained strikingly backward and reflected the region's continued reliance on enslaved human labor. Slaves, when transplanting rice by hand, harvesting it with sickles, or threshing it with flails, resembled peasants in Asia or slaves on an ancient Egyptian wall painting.

48. *Carolina Gazette*, Feb. 22, 1798; Jacob Read to "Sister Edgar," Oct. 5, 1811, folder 21, Read to Charles Ludlow, July 4, 1813, folder 23, Read Family Papers, box 1, SCL. A toll of 10% was standard. See Charles Cotesworth Pinckney to Thomas Pinckney, July 28, 1792 (discussing a miller named Bowman), Pinckney Family Papers, series 1, box 4, LC (10% was also a common toll for cotton ginning; see Chapter 8, below).

49. M. I. Manigault to Alice Izard, Feb. 18, 1812, folder 68, box 6, Manigault Family Papers, SCL.

Only when they stepped off the fields and onto the mill floor did slaves pass into the world of the factory. Tidal plantations and mills resembled (though in a subdued way) sugar plantations and mills in their complex blend of human bondage and near-industrial use of capital and machinery. Nor did the contradictions end here. Slaves continued to mortar seed rice by hand, but received cash from planters for doing so, a final demonstration of the extreme plasticity of modern slavery and the difficulty of clearly categorizing it (especially in places where agriculture was heavily capitalized and mechanized) as one static form of production.[50] Planters' ability to buy both machine parts and human beings reflected the considerable wealth and authority they had accumulated, though they would find it easier to control machines than slaves. Racial power, along the coast, was still contested.

Ⓓ‒ Power

The developments in rice cultivation that altered the lowcountry's natural environment capped three-quarters of a century of agricultural innovation along the coast. Income derived from indigo cultivation, stability gained from wartime cotton cultivation, and knowledge of hydraulic engineering and Asian agriculture combined into a success story, one in which planters assigned themselves roles as heroes and victors. Even though tidal irrigation did not completely replace inland swamp planting, it spread wide over the coast and gave the lowcountry a distinctive form that characterized it through the antebellum era. Most striking was the permanent alteration in the landscape. Rice growers had scraped flat their sections of the coastal plain, heaved up great earthen structures, forever altered waterways, and etched rectilinear structures onto their fields (see Plate 9). They changed a peculiar natural environment into one that now had artificial peculiarities, wonders and rarities to impress visitors. Even today, tourists visiting Middleton Plantation on

50. John Ball, for instance, paid 20 s. (currency) per bushel of Robin's and Sancho's seed rice (entry for April 1783, "John Ball's Planting Book," 1780–84, p. 16, John Ball, Sr., and John Ball, Jr., account books, Duke), and Henry Laurens bought rice from slaves in February 1765 (Henry Laurens Journals, p. 40, College of Charleston). Cf. Stuart B. Schwartz, *Sugar Plantations in the Formation of Brazilian Society: Bahia, 1550–1835* (Cambridge, 1985), chap. 5.

Plate 9. Tidal Rice Plantation. *Plantation of Daniel Huger, 1811, series 32-50-1, SCHS.* This tidal plantation near Charleston illustrates the system of dams and canals that controlled a natural waterway. The rice fields paralleled the river. Most of the straight lines around the fields are ditches and dams. The main canal runs along the left, fed by canals running away from the river. Two floodgates are indicated, one at bottom (Gate) and one toward the center of the canal (Flood Gate) near the Main Dam.

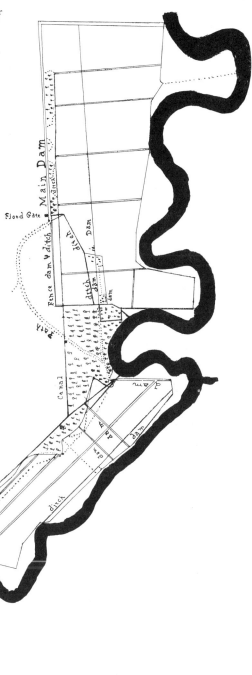

the Ashley River marvel at the artificially landscaped view between the river and the house: a series of terraces gently descends from the house to a pair of ornamental ponds. Beyond are the now-unused rice fields, which, when planted, integrated the entire vista—an agricultural landscape joined an aesthetic one to emphasize how humans had carved, mounded, and flooded the natural world for the wealth and glory of a very few of its residents. Whites recognized that this reordering of nature reflected their glory as members of a racial and economic elite. One man even expressed this power in terms of individual, masculine personality when he teased a lovesick friend about having "fallen upon a new plan of planting his Rice and instead of making Straight lines as here to for, he has whole Squares wrote in Poetry in praise of a favorite Lady."[51]

A system of internal navigation was the final stage in this creation of an irrigated landscape, and a step that most explicitly showed rice planters' power over their environment and within the political arena. Planters, especially in South Carolina, sought to improve their ability to get their increased crops to market and solicited government support of this goal. The Santee-Cooper Canal Company (the first successful canal-building venture) was incorporated by the state legislature to create such a public waterway. It used corvée workers, slaves drafted to supply labor as a tax on the planters who stood to benefit from the completed project. The network of canals that spread between the 1790s and 1810s gave the antebellum lowcountry its final, built form. One look at the Santee-Cooper Canal would show this. The canal, which widened and connected existing waterways to create an unbroken conduit, allowed planters upriver to speed their crops to Charleston. A public structure connected private estates to the market—all of them marked out in rectilinear form on a landscape that had once been covered with swamp and naturally flowing waterways. Nearly all landscapes show the influence of the human hand; this was a landscape where hands had been very busy shifting earth and water to create a system of permanent control over natural resources.[52]

51. J. Hill to Robert Mackay, Apr. 26, 1806, Mackay Papers, folder 374, Keith Read Collection, UGA.

52. On canal building in South Carolina, see Rachel N. Klein, *Unification of a Slave State: The Rise of the Planter Class in the South Carolina Backcountry, 1760–1808* (Chapel Hill, N.C., 1990), 244–246; Lacy K. Ford, Jr., *Origins of Southern Radicalism: The South Carolina Upcountry, 1800–1860* (Oxford, 1988), 16–17.

In this stage of its development, the lowcountry briefly resembled the classic "hy-

The wealthy and proud planter elite that now ruled the coastline would remain in place until 1861. Its accomplishments rendered the lowcountry a distinctive region: marked by an unusual crop and unique method of irrigation, it seemed set apart, culturally and geographically, from the rest of the slaveholding South, something that would be reiterated in political terms during the Nullification and Secession crises. The increased wealth of tidal plantations and their owners' touchiness and determination to dominate over resources had already been evident during the shift to tidal cultivation; the decades from the 1760s to 1790s constituted a crucial era in the formation of this insular class—nascent in the 1720s, infamous by the 1860s.[53]

But if tidal planting became the preserve of wealthy slaveholders, they were not willingly served in this enterprise by their slaves. Indeed, the very form of

---

draulic societies," supposedly shaped by "Oriental despotism," described by Karl Wittfogel in *Oriental Despotism: A Comparative Study of Total Power* (New Haven, Conn., 1957). Wittfogel drew a family resemblance among agricultural societies in which the state had totalitarian control of water and waterways; these states accumulated power to such an extent that they nearly erased individual ability to control labor, property, and wealth. Given the liberal tradition in North America, such a culture would have been impossible, but lowcountry planters did bash great dents in this tradition. South Carolina would be alone among the states, for instance, in not providing compensation to citizens whose property was taken for public projects like canals. See Morton J. Horwitz, *The Transformation of American Law, 1780–1860* (Cambridge, Mass., 1977), 64. Corvée was also a feature of hydraulic societies that the lowcountry adopted. Although these parallels are intriguing, true hydraulic societies can exist only in arid regions where control of water is a formidable power; the lowcountry was far from arid, and centralized control of its numerous waterways was impossible. The lowcountry more nearly resembled the subinfeudated Asian societies described by revisionists of the theory of oriental despotism. See E. R. Leach, "Hydraulic Society in Ceylon," *Past and Present*, no. 15 (April 1959), 2–26. Wittfogel's premise—that Asian societies tend toward despotism—is questionable in any case. Cf. Mart A. Stewart, "Rice, Water, and Power: Landscapes of Domination and Resistance in the Lowcountry, 1790–1880," *Environmental History Review*, XV (1991), 47–64. On the Santee-Cooper Canal, see the map in series 32-105-3, SCHS.

53. On how a "physical barrier" divided the lowcountry from the rest of the region, see Marjorie Stratford Mendenhall, "A History of Agriculture in South Carolina, 1790 to 1860: An Economic and Social Study" (Ph.D. diss., University of North Carolina–Chapel Hill, 1940), 133.

planters' newly reshaped estates revealed how slaves had, instead, managed to achieve a formal degree of independence from whites during the same years they helped create a new form of plantation agriculture. Collective slave rebellion had last appeared during the War of Jenkins's Ear, when English hostility with the nearby Spanish provided opportunity for slaves to take up arms against whites. Overt resistance to white authority again became apparent during the War of Independence, when a slave was more likely to be a runaway, a rebel, or a commandeered worker than a laborer for the owner. Because the war reversed the expectation that slaves worked for the profit of their individual owners, planters found it difficult to compel slaves (who had glimpsed some avenues of escape) to return to the old way of life. Even after the war, slaves staged small-scale rebellions that revealed the battered condition of lowcountry plantations and the weakened authority of planters. In 1768, Georgian Lachlan McIntosh recorded how "all my working Negroes left me last Night," possibly because of "the short prospect of provision." Continued threat of rebellious desertion reminded planters of their tentative control over slaves.[54]

In their struggle to avoid enslavement on the old terms, blacks could not only desert but proffer skills as a way of getting whites to make concessions. African slaves had earlier contributed knowledge of Old World rice cultivation to the lowcountry; their progeny's new skills reflected the creolization of the rural black population, whose members had gained knowledge of the land and water on which they were born and lived. Their wisdom helped reshape the environment. Native-born blacks, unlike absentee planters or transient overseers, were permanent residents of the coastal landscape and vital to its exploitation. Whites even recognized that slaves were sometimes more familiar with their property than they themselves were. When Elias Ball's father died, for instance, no one in his footloose family could determine how a certain piece of land was to be parceled out, because they simply did not know the land. One cousin who did know it was living abroad; he had no intention of returning, but he helpfully wrote that others could solve the problem: "Your Fellow Peter[,] Old Tom[,] Frank and many other of your Negroes knows the Spott" and could identify it to the family. Pierce Butler made clear how coastal slaves had a particular (though not always enviable) knowledge of rice cultiva-

54. Lilla M. Hawes, ed., "The Papers of Lachlan McIntosh, 1774–1799," *GHQ*, XL (1956), 157.

tion when he wanted to buy "a Gang of Negroes accustomed to Cultivate R[ice.] I want no cotton Negroes. I want People that can go in the Ditch."[55]

Slaves also had skills specific to the construction of tidal plantations. Planters probably received assistance in designing irrigation systems from slaves who had been taught by military engineers to construct fortifications during the war. Engineering was still a military science only occasionally adapted to civil problems (like defenses against water—a natural rather than human enemy in, for example, the Netherlands). Observers likened the ditches and dams of rice plantations to military fortifications; short of a tour of Holland and its famous dikes, as Ralph Izard noted, knowledge of military engineering was the best education that someone who built a tidal plantation could receive. Some male slaves continued to acquire such an education because they were drafted to construct canals, working with engineers for long stretches of time. Men belonging to the Ravenel family, for example, labored for three years on the Santee Canal during the 1790s.[56]

Blacks learned other skills as tidal irrigation proved successful. Large plantations often had trunk minders, men who regulated the trickiest part of the irrigation system. In 1784, the Middleton's Homeplace plantation included a slave man who "mends Trunks," and a man who "tends Trunks" lived at their Middle Settlement. The Ball family's Back River slave list for 1805 contained the name of a trunk minder, and their Pimlico plantation list for 1810 specified that one man was expert in mending trunks. Construction of floodgates was also a valued activity, and planters hired out their slave carpenters who had this skill. John Ewing Colhoun recorded that one of his slaves built the floodgates on his Bonneau's Ferry plantation in April 1794. William Moultrie evidently lacked slave artisans who could do this and noted among his May 1814 estate expenditures that he had to pay for "Carpenters work" in "building 2 flood gates for the Canal and putting one down" in the trunk.[57]

---

55. Elias Ball (of Bristol) to Elias Ball (of Charleston), Aug. 27, 1786, Ball Family Papers, series 516-8, SCHS; Pierce Butler to ———, Apr. 6, 1807, Pierce Butler Letterbook, SCL.

56. See Ralph Izard's statement about military engineering in Izard to Thomas Pinckney, Aug. 12, 1793, Pinckney Family Papers, series 3, box 4, LC; entry for Jan. 1, 1796, diary of René Ravenel and Henry Ravenel, Apr. 5, 1785–Sept. 10, 1851, Ford-Ravenel Papers, series 12-313/18, SCHS.

57. 1784 slave list for Homeplace Plantation, item 506, Thomas Middleton Manuscript Book, 1734–1815, SHC; 1805 list of Back River slaves, Ball Family Papers, series

While slaves' acquisition of some engineering skills was a poor substitute for that ability to flout white authority they had exerted during the war, they were able to use their limited strengths to create a formally recognized area of independence as a community with leaders drawn from within. The authority of the black driver was one important example of this post-Revolutionary trend. In the 1780s and 1790s, as tidal cultivation spread, so too did the tendency for lowcountry plantations to have drivers. In this era, they appeared more frequently in estate inventories than they had in colonial times, and whites were increasingly willing to commend their expertise with rice planting. One South Carolinian, accordingly, explained that his slave Jonathan was "without exception one of the best drivers in this state; and there are few White Men, who have a more general or better knowledge of planting." Another planter advertised for sale his "valuable Driver (many years experienced in the management of a tide swamp plantation)." Charles Cotesworth Pinckney remarked that, among Ralph Izard's plantations, the one "where you make most to the hand and really a good Crop, there is no overseer but only a Black Driver." (The phenomenon Pinckney acknowledged resulted partly because a driver was more honest than overseers, who were light-fingered with the salable rice left in their care.)[58]

Other planters also indicated that they trusted their drivers more than their overseers. When Henry Laurens's overseer refused to take advice from the driver Cuffy (as well as others on the estate), Laurens fired the white man. Another rice planter who advertised for a white overseer assured applicants that, rather incredibly, they would have time to carry on a trade if they had one, as the actual "business of the plantation is conducted by a black man." So much did Thomas Spalding rely on his slaves that, after his first few years of planting, he never again bothered to hire white overseers.[59]

11-515-11, SCHS; 1810 list of slaves at Pimlico, John Ball, Sr., and John Ball, Jr., Papers, folder 4, cabinet 24, Duke; memoranda for 1794, John Ewing Colhoun Papers, folder 3, SHC; May 1814 expenditures, William Moultrie Papers, box 3, folder 33, SCL.

58. Philip D. Morgan, "Black Society in the Lowcountry, 1760–1810," in Ira Berlin and Ronald Hoffman, eds., *Slavery and Freedom in the Age of the American Revolution* (Charlottesville, Va., 1983), 118; *Gazette of the State of South-Carolina* (Charleston), Dec. 20, 1784; *Columbian Herald* (Charleston), Jan. 13, 1794; Charles Cotesworth Pinckney to Ralph Izard, Dec. 26, 1794, Manigault Family Papers, series 11-276-80, SCHS.

59. Hamer *et al.*, eds., *Papers of Laurens*, VI, 444–446; *City Gazette and Daily Advertiser* (Charleston), Mar. 12, 1800; Coulter, *Thomas Spalding*, 85.

A second indication of how slaves increased a margin of independent activity lay in the lowcountry's task system, long a bone of contention between planters and slaves and sign of planters' new willingness to bargain with slaves. Around the turn of the century, rice field tasks took on firm and predictable characteristics, shedding the troublesome haphazardness of the colonial era. This was especially apparent on tidal plantations, because the irrigation system etched an orderly grid on the landscape. Small ditches in the fields that directed water from the main irrigation system also marked out quarter-acre units of work; each square contained trenches that could also be counted off into a task, seventy-eight at a time. There could be little confusion or debate over a slave's task, as all units could be measured by a 105-foot surveyor's chain: a square to be hoed, seventy-eight trenches to be dug, and so on. In addition, planters were careful never to make an individual slave complete an especially onerous task. If a square was slightly higher than the rest of the field, water there was shallower and weeds thicker; other workers were rotated in to help on such units, preventing one person from becoming too fatigued or discontented.[60]

The authority of the driver and the codified task both evidenced whites' relinquishment of direct control over planting. Each gridlike tidal plantation became a chessboard carved out from the natural landscape, a visible demonstration of how white and black players had faced off during the war, played a strategic game of defiance and concession, then agreed on rules for a continuing (though now implicit) contest. This result was, perhaps, the best characterization of how slaves in this portion of the New World managed to preserve their own and their community's integrity. As discussed earlier, they did not, like persistently rebellious Caribbean slaves or autonomous European or Asian peasants, emerge as clear victors from a certain number of matches. But unlike their counterparts in other parts of the American South, they would remain constantly active in what whites recognized as an unending contest between the races.

60. Morgan, "Work and Culture," *WMQ*, 3d Ser., XXXIX (1982), 569–570; Morgan, "Black Society," in Berlin and Hoffman, eds., *Slavery and Freedom*, 118. On problems over tasks in the prewar period, see Richard Hutson to "Mr. Croll," Aug. 22, 1767, Charles Woodward Hutson Papers, SHC. On measurement of tasks, see plantation book, 1814–47, Mackay-Stiles Papers, XXVII, SHC. The methodical Laurens had used a 105-foot measurement as early as 1772. See Hamer *et al.*, eds., *Papers of Laurens*, VIII, 291. For examples of the policy of rotating workers, see entries for June 6, 27, 1814, plantation book, 1814–47, Mackay-Stiles Papers, SHC; Heyward MS, SHC.

Drivers could sometimes be the decisive weight in the contested balance between black independence and white authority. They kept slaves working and minimally content with day-to-day conditions, and they were buffers between whites and the black labor force. Drivers rarely ran away and seemed to take seriously their privileged yet burdened role as the man between. Their complex role might also explain why, as Charles Cotesworth Pinckney had noted, drivers were more honest than overseers. If an overseer was caught pilfering rice, he and his family might suffer from a planter's wrath, but if a driver was thus detected, the entire work force (sometimes numbering in the hundreds) might be punished or be put under direct white authority for a time. But if drivers were important in keeping up production, planters recognized that black leadership could skew the delicate arrangement of racial power. In cases of rebellions or rumored rebellions, drivers (along with other skilled slaves) were automatically suspected as organizers. Robert Mackay and other Georgia planters detected one plan for a rebellion in 1806, around Christmas, when slaves had more free time than at any other season. Mackay claimed that the plot was led by "drivers and leading Negroes" who had made a successful appeal to "all the Sensible Drivers on the River." This problem probably motivated some planters to get drivers who were strangers to their work force. On Cannon's Point Plantation in Georgia, for instance, John Couper brought in a Fullah Muslim from the Niger Valley, Salih Bilali, he had bought in the Bahamas—someone he seemed to expect would be alien to the rest of his workers and slower to respond to appeals for collective resistance.[61] The drivers' role thus indicated whites' uneasy yet undeniable realization that their slaves formed a separate community with its own leaders.

Scholars of black slavery have recognized that slaves were able to carve out spaces for themselves within a society dominated by slaveowners. In the lowcountry, slaves not only carved out small places *within* rice plantations, they also carved out these plantations *as* places for themselves. John Boyle's South Carolina estate (Plate 10) indicates how slaves reshaped this new landscape for themselves. The strongest evidence for white dominance appears

61. On the scarcity of drivers among runaways, and their role as community leaders, see Morgan, "Black Society," in Berlin and Hoffman, eds., *Slavery and Freedom*, 119–120. Robert Mackay to Eliza Mackay, Dec. 29, 1806, Mackay-Stiles Papers, microfilm, SHC. On the Muslim driver, see John Solomon Otto, *Cannon's Point Plantation, 1794–1860: Living Conditions and Status Patterns in the Old South* (New York, 1984), 36. Couper might also have expected Bilali to be expert in African rice cultivation, or in Bahamian cotton cultivation, since Cannon's Point also produced cotton.

around the estate, especially with the repetition of the word "belonging" in reference to neighbors' landholdings. Inside, the plantation contained physical features (the spread of rice fields, the extensive irrigation system) asserting the racial and economic power of the planting elite but also revealing an internal, meaningful world for slaves. Slaves lived in two separate settlements—one in the upper left corner and the other toward the middle—each connected to the other by roads. Roads and canals also acted as conduits toward neighboring plantations. These features indicated a fairly large black community, yet one whose varied members had access to each other, on and off the plantation. Such a document nevertheless reflected pride of white ownership. It resembled (probably emulated) European maps of estates and family seats and, like Frederick George Mulcaster's fantasy of himself standing in a great "Hall," revealed planters' desire to resemble respectable landholders in the Old World.

There were also two cemeteries on this map, both to the left of the central settlement—one reserved, perhaps, for the white family. The inclusion of the cemeteries reveals how whites themselves were aware that the estates "belonging" to them might have communal meaning to their slaves, who had places of remembrance and honor for ancestors. To include settlements and cemeteries on such a map showed whites' recognition that slaves had stronger connections to certain portions of their land than they themselves did. The nonproductive landscape provided social meaning for its black residents, just as the productive landscape marked out negotiated terms of labor for them. This sense of place would survive even after slaves were emancipated. After the Civil War, when a freed slave named Morris learned that a new landlord was going to remove him from the Waccamaw River plantation where he lived, he confronted the white man, and his plea for permanency was recorded (albeit in a patronizing white version of black dialect). "I was born on dis place before Freedom," Morris objected. "My Mammy and Daddy worked de rice fields. Dey's buried here. De fust ting I remember are dose rice banks. I growed up in dem from dat high." Slaves' perception of attachment to a rice plantation— from the orderly form it placed on their work to the rootedness it gave them through the generations—reminded whites that the world they had made on the basis of slavery had also created a separate world for the slaves themselves.[62]

---

62. Quoted in Charles W. Joyner, *Down by the Riverside: A South Carolina Slave Community* (Urbana, Ill., 1984), 42–43. For the communal significance of slave burials, see Eugene D. Genovese, *Roll, Jordan, Roll: The World the Slaves Made* (New York, 1972), 194–202.

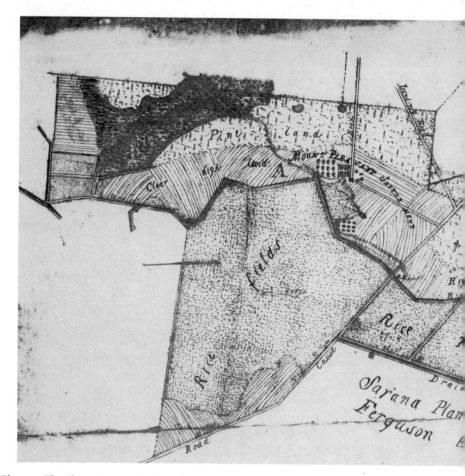

Plate 10. The Slave Community Revealed on a Plantation Map. *Plantation of John Boyle, Charleston District, April 1793, series 32-42-6, SCHS.* This plantation map gives a good sense of how slaves created an environment for themselves on rice plantations. There are two settlements, Mount Pleasant Settlement to the left and New Ground Settlement at the

The new, irrigated landscape along the coast thus revealed uneasy compromises between the blacks and whites who lived through the Revolutionary era. It also disclosed an emerging sense of doubt among planters about how their efforts to entrench plantation slavery by improving their estates were perhaps damaging the nature around them and the human nature of their slaves. Their unusual natural world had long been a point of pride because it had drawn the flattering attentions of an international scientific community—gentlemen

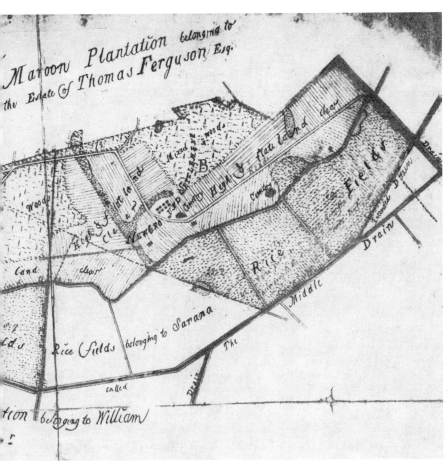

center. Two cemeteries are to the right of the new settlement. The roads and canals (double lines) were conduits for movement around and off the plantation. Above the old settlement is a Landing where boats could put off and dock.

planters had, often enough, swapped pieces of this natural world for information about agriculture in other regions. But when whites ordered slaves to dig up the land and redirect the flow of water, they changed an environment that had once supplied prize specimens to the likes of Linnaeus.

Tidal planters began to realize the consequences of their actions when they found themselves caught in a cycle of improvement and degeneration created by the less-than-predictable flow of water through their lands. Residents on the

Santee River, for instance, cultivated tidal lands for several years, then ruefully discovered that their efforts had exacerbated the dangers of flooding. They wanted to clear the now-more-turbulent river and cut more canals to drain off its increased water—transforming the river into a sort of canal itself, an artificially controlled waterway that needed continual tending.[63] As planters intensified their use of estuaries in this manner, expansion of traffic on these rivers had other unwelcome consequences. Whites, who thought slaves manned most of the craft on waterways, blamed slaves for damage without acknowledging that much river traffic served their own needs. A Charleston engineer warned one planter, who wanted to add a navigable canal to his plantation, that this alteration might irrevocably damage the natural order. He pointed to slaves who had widened the Ogeechee River in Georgia for easier navigation: they had cleared the river so well that saltwater rushed three miles farther upriver than before, spoiling rice fields well above the point of navigation. The engineer cautioned rice planters that their actions "may be attended with ruinous effects, which may not be foreseen" until it was too late. He warned: "Nature in the formation of her works has acted for the general welfare of man. It therefore behoves us to consider well the consequences before we deviate from, or counteract her ways." His was a skeptical realization of how humans could perform damaging actions, and this sentiment began to filter through the planter elite.[64]

David Ramsay, always the optimist, conjectured that damage due to human cultivation was undeniable but temporary. Ramsay conceded, for instance, that the expansion of rice planting had increased the prevalence of malaria but believed this would pass away. "These exciting causes of disease lie dormant in the native state of new countries, while they are undisturbed by cultivation," he postulated, "but when the ground is cleared and its surface broken they are put into immediate activity." Ramsay concluded that when "the original mephitic effluvia are exhausted and cultivation has improved the face of the earth, it again becomes healthy." He drew an intriguing parallel with Britain: fenridden when invaded by the Romans, perfectly dry by the modern age. This harked back to Enlightenment statements about how human cultivation benefited the environment (in this case, planters were analogous to the civilized

63. Petitions to General Assembly, 1795, no. 108, SCDAH.

64. Charles Hately to John Coming Ball, Aug. 6, 1792, Ball Family Papers, box 1, folder 10, SCL.

Romans, and Indians to the wild Celts), but the conceit was inadequate reassurance, because the analogy raised the possibility that several *centuries* could pass before damage and disease would subside.[65]

These warnings about rice planting and nature paralleled the statements whites began to make about slavery and human nature, culminating in John Laurens's conclusion that members of his class had "sunk" slaves "below the Standard of Humanity."[66] Few whites would go this far. But if their emerging uncertainty over the rectitude of slavery would never develop into anything as significant as actual reform of the institution, whites' doubts did show important changes in the lowcountry. The skeptical view of how humans could perform damaging actions on the world and each other was revealing, raising questions about the character of a society that depended on an artificial ordering of natural phenomena created by the labor of slaves. This attitude did not yet represent, however, a rejection of modern development or a belief that the local way of life was doomed. These were sentiments that appeared only in later generations. During the second decade of the nineteenth century, planters kept planting rice, but they also wondered about the nature of a society that depended on an artificial environment for its support—one that needed human hands as well as the hand of nature for its continuance. Eagerness to manipulate nature, yet belated realization of its consequences, makes this planting group most recognizably modern, situated as it was on a fault line between centuries of admonition about domination of nature and a new idea about the perils of human blundering. Planters dimly glimpsed, within their diked and trenched landscape, the wild beauty William Bartram had seen in Florida's untouched swamps with their brilliant contrasts between water and land, light and dark.

This emerging lament over the ill consequences of human endeavor, another variation on the tension between progress and stability, summarized a series of paradoxes that informed rice planters' endeavors. They had maintained slavery in their region, yet conceded more than ever to their slaves' dissenting vision of themselves as a semiautonomous people. They brought the steam and machines of industrial factories to their estates, yet slaves still used ancient implements—the hoe and the flail—for much of their work. They were inspired by a rationalist spirit of improvement to reshape their region, yet

65. Ramsay, *History of S.-C.*, II, 64, 69n.
66. Hamer *et al.*, eds., *Papers of Laurens*, XI, 277.

felt the early pangs of romantic melancholy over the loss of an untouched, natural order.[67] We leave them here, slipping into the studied regretfulness of their antebellum progeny, to examine their inland neighbors, who expressed ambivalence over the price of development in more forthright terms.

67. On romanticism, melancholy, and its connection to a sense of (ruined) place, see Michael O'Brien, *Rethinking the South: Essays in Intellectual History* (Baltimore, 1988), 50–51, 83.

Chapter 8

Creating a Cotton South

Rice planters' musings over their intensively used environment reflected the maturity of a region with a high level of social complexity. Within the interior of South Carolina and Georgia, society was newer and simpler. Differing from coastal areas in degree rather than in kind, the upcountry was passing through a stage the coast had experienced several decades earlier. Settlers of this area did not yet innovate within a system of commercial agriculture, but struggled to define one by staking out a geographic space within which cultivation for the market could flourish. One observer in upcountry Georgia used terms describing an actual creation when he concluded that its inhabitants were "setling again and beginning the World anew."[1] The world began with property; nature not defined by *meum et tuum* was, settlers believed, mere wasteland squandered by savages. Whites who moved into the upcountry first removed any residents who failed to turn western

1. *Letters of Joseph Clay . . .* (GHS, *Collections*, VIII [Savannah, 1913]), 191–192. On development of upcountry, see Robert D. Mitchell, "The Formation of Early American Cultural Regions: An Interpretation," in James R. Gibson, ed., *European Settlement and Development in North America: Essays on Geographical Change in Honour and Memory of Andrew Hill Clark* (Toronto, 1978), 66–90; Jack P. Greene and J. R. Pole, "Reconstructing British-American Colonial History: An Introduction," in Greene and Pole, eds., *Colonial British America: Essays in the New History of the Early Modern Era* (Baltimore, 1984), 14–15; Greene, "Independence, Improvement, and Authority: Toward a Framework for Understanding the Histories of the Southern Backcountry during the Era of the American Revolution," in Ronald Hoffman *et al.*, eds., *An Uncivil War: The Southern Backcountry during the American Revolution* (Charlottesville, Va., 1985), 15–20; Gregory H. Nobles, "Breaking into the Backcountry: New Approaches to the Early American Frontier," *WMQ*, 3d Ser., XLVI (1989), 641–670.

lands into tangible property, then used the land to make wealth for themselves through commercial agriculture.

To accomplish their goals, settlers carried black slavery inland, a decision that emphasizes yet again the region's yes-and-no response to the modern age—in this case, determination to enter a market economy but parallel conviction that enslaved labor was the optimal method of generating wealth. Both tendencies were conscious choices of the settlers, who were mostly small propertyholders from the mid-Atlantic region (garnished with a catalyzing minority of New Englanders) determined to achieve greater wealth in a region noted for its riches. Whites here did not innovate in response to crises; their creative adaptation of agricultural alternatives meant to avoid a crisis, one that would crack apart the recently laid and too thin commercial foundation and plunge settlers back into the primitive poverty with which the world had begun.

Migrants' overtly commercial ambitions—the self-awareness in their schemes for settling the upcountry—correct a misleading explanation of the origins of the Cotton South that overlooks settlers' own intentions. Scholars have argued that cotton itself built a bridge from a frontier West to a cotton-planting South and established a happy unity between rice and cotton planters. Ever since historian David Ramsay claimed in 1809 that "the culture of cotton" encouraged "personal industry" and replaced "poverty" and "idleness" in the upcountry, historians have concluded, as well, that through some mysterious transformation related to cotton, rustic and slaveless yeomen became planters. Some scholars have deduced that the mystery was the market itself, an external force that arrived in the upcountry in two forms of influence: the well-established pattern of commercial agriculture in the coastal Lower South, and the growing market for cotton in Britain that provided incentive for would-be commercial farmers once Eli Whitney's cotton gin removed the bottleneck in production. Other scholars have discovered that the antebellum upcountry contained populations that continued to shun commercial relations, seeing commercialization as a potential disruption to the independence and harmony of their communities. In this latter interpretation, the market was an object of aversion, though still a powerful external agent.[2]

---

2. David Ramsay, *History of South-Carolina, from Its First Settlement in 1670 to the Year 1808* . . . (Charleston, S.C., 1809), II, 448–449. On cotton as the key to a fully developed commercial economy, see William W. Freehling, *Prelude to Civil War: The Nullification Controversy in South Carolina, 1816–1836* (New York, 1965), 19–24; Freeh-

Both interpretations of market forces, though otherwise dissimilar, make the residents of the early Cotton South appear passive in their relations with the world beyond their region—either their socioeconomic role of cotton cultivator was created for them by others, or they retreated from the market whenever possible. The whites who settled the upcountry, however, were rarely interested in mimicking the lowcountry gentry, did not wait for industrial demand for cotton to create a place in the world for them, and did not flee the consequences of commercialization. Instead, they actively sought to enter a market that, they complained, lowcountry interests still withheld from them. One group of upcountry South Carolina petitioners gave voice to this grievance when it protested against being left "in a state of nature," restating the belief that without human cultivation the region was devoid of real value. The petitioners requested that the legislature fund improvements in internal navigation to help them get to the market, "thereby enriching many of your citizens."[3]

Many of the upcountry farmers who desired enrichment had cultivated staples for the market decades before the first cotton boom and used a model of commercial agriculture other than the one in the coastal Lower South. Indeed, the coastal model may have been relatively unfamiliar, known mostly because of some lowcountry planters' long-standing desire to keep newer areas from achieving anything like it. Whites who had migrated from the mid-Atlantic region (between the Delaware and the Roanoke rivers) did know about the well-established commercial cultivation of tobacco and grain. This

---

ling, *The Road to Disunion, I, Secessionists at Bay, 1776–1854* (New York, 1990), 220–223; Rachel N. Klein, *Unification of a Slave State: The Rise of the Planter Class in the South Carolina Backcountry, 1760–1808* (Chapel Hill, N.C., 1990), esp. 45–46, 248–268. Klein is careful to point out, however, that the rudiments of a commercial economy were in place before cotton cultivation was widespread—see 15–36. On the latter, anticommercialist interpretation, see, esp., Steven Hahn, *The Roots of Southern Populism: Yeoman Farmers and the Transformation of the Georgia Upcountry, 1850–1890* (New York, 1983).

3. On this pattern in the antebellum upcountry, see David F. Weiman, "Farmers and the Market in Antebellum America: A View from the Georgia Upcountry," *Jour. Econ. Hist.,* XLVII (1987), 627–647; Weiman, "The Economic Emancipation of the Non-Slaveholding Class: Upcountry Farmers in the Georgia Cotton Economy," *Jour. Econ. Hist.,* XLV (1985), 71–94; Lacy K. Ford, "Yeoman Farmers in the South Carolina Upcountry: Changing Production Patterns in the Late Antebellum Era," *AH,* LX, no. 4 (Fall 1986), 17–37. The quotation is from Petitions to General Assembly, undated, no. 1112, SCDAH.

mid-Atlantic model seemed to them better suited to the upcountry, and settlers who came from the older area adapted many aspects of its economy—from tobacco presses to the gang system of slave labor—to the new upcountry. The British market and the lowcountry plantation, like Whitney's cotton gin, reinforced, but did not create, tendencies toward commercialization and expansion of slavery. This is not to deny the later significance of these external factors, but to point out that human agency was at work as well: whites in the upcountry created the first cotton boom through a series of choices about economic development. Settlers leaped toward the market's siren call because they had taken great care not to lash themselves to the mast. By this point, upcountry demands for slavery won out over lowcountry stubbornness on this issue; settlers' determination to get slaves gives the lie to the belief that slavery was in any way declining before the widespread cultivation of cotton.[4]

Settlers struggled to define a coherent region—as opposed to a demarcational frontier or an ambiguous zone between areas of settlement controlled by different groups. To achieve this end, whites ripped out all the exasperatingly subcommercial features of the frontier (noxious weeds in their envisioned garden) and planted commercial crops and slavery in their stead. They next lobbied for government investment in a political and economic infrastructure that would, they promised, generate greater wealth for the region as a whole. The reluctance of lowcountry residents to assist upcountry settlers restated their continuing uneasiness about expanding black slavery. Settlers themselves worried over certain aspects of the commercial economy they were creating. Their ambivalence had two important manifestations: they realized that using slave workers to build the economy they desired might also destabilize a region they had so recently subdued; and they feared the consequences of an enlarged role for the government in ranking public and private benefits, an unease stated during the Yazoo affair but also during a parallel controversy over Whitney's cotton gin patent. Both fear of preferential economic policies and defense of a system of labor that was now under public debate emphasized the region's prevailing uncertainty over how its free residents might define themselves as participants in a modern economy and society.

4. Joyce E. Chaplin, "Creating a Cotton South in Georgia and South Carolina, 1760–1815," *Jour. So. Hist.*, LVII (1991), 171–200.

౭ಖ *The Geography of Opportunity*

Explanations of backcountry development have moved away from the pastoral belief (derived from Frederick Jackson Turner's thesis of a simple and egalitarian frontier shaping United States culture and politics) that near-subsistence frontier economies were significant features of the American experience, evidence of the virtuous fortitude of western settlers. Although this view has been reanimated in the contention that southern frontiersmen who leaned toward Jeffersonian republicanism were wary of economic development (which might upset the harmony within a dispersed and socially equal population), other studies have usually emphasized how frontier settlers welcomed select elements of commercialization. They hastened to set up market agriculture and even welcomed socioeconomic features, like white inequality and black slavery, characteristic of plantation societies. But one does not always see the consensual process—uniting dispersed and otherwise dissimilar whites through common ownership of slaves and cultivation of staples—that those scholars have described. Lack of shared vision about the upcountry's future also characterized settlement in the hinterland.[5]

The interior had for some time been removed from the spread of market agriculture that elsewhere characterized the Lower South. This is not to say that the frontier lacked population and activity; it contained *several* populations (Indian, white, black, mestizo) busy trading with each other for foodstuffs and raw materials like animal skins. The frontier was, therefore, a geographic space reserved for hunting and subsistence agriculture, primarily because the aboriginal population wished to keep it this way and would resort to war to ensure its continuance. (The Cherokees in South Carolina and Creeks in Georgia were especially powerful as opponents of white farmers.) White or mestizo Indian traders also wanted to preserve a place for their livelihood, and belligerent European powers were by this time adept at manipulating enmity between Indian nations to promote their imperial interests. The various nations, too, used Europeans against each other to gain wealth, weapons, or territory. Had whites remained a small and weak population, the shifting cycles of conflict along the frontier might have lasted a good deal

5. On this consensual interpretation, see Klein, *Unification of a Slave State;* Richard R. Beeman, *The Evolution of the Southern Backcountry; A Case Study of Lunenburg County, Virginia, 1746–1832* (Philadelphia, 1984), chaps. 7–9.

longer. But creole populations swelled as Indians themselves declined. By the middle of the eighteenth century, South Carolina whites had pushed the Cherokee, Creek, and Catawba nations out of the way of expanding settlement.[6]

Trade, war, parley, cultural interchange, migration were all parts of the frontier process. But whites on the lookout for land took a dim view of most frontier activities and vented much of their ire, unsurprisingly, on Indians. No matter that, by the eighteenth century, native Americans were probably the people in North America most altered by commerce, whites persisted in seeing Indians as members of primitive communities, because most of their trade resulted from hunting—that tell-tale sign of the earliest stage of human society. Because Indians did not turn the land around them into property, settlers disdained their claims to the territory: Indians' method of subsistence was savage and ignored the Christian god's dictum to subdue nature. The Georgia land lottery, inaugurated in 1805, exemplified this position. Georgia held a total of six land lotteries, the last from 1832 to 1833. Each time, the lands raffled away

6. On the frontier as an active zone of competition among many ethnic groups, see Francis Jennings, *The Invasion of America: Indians, Colonialism, and the Cant of Conquest* (Chapel Hill, N.C., 1976), esp. 15–31; James Axtell, *The Invasion Within: The Contest of Cultures in Colonial North America* (New York, 1985); Daniel H. Usner, Jr., "The Frontier Exchange Economy of the Lower Mississippi Valley in the Eighteenth Century," *WMQ*, 3d Ser., XLIV (1987), 165–192. Cf. Leonard Thompson and Howard Lamar, "Comparative Frontier History," in Thompson and Lamar, eds., *The Frontier in History: North America and Southern Africa Compared* (New Haven, Conn., 1982), 6–10. Nodes of settlement in the interior were usually linked to the Indian trade. This had been true of Camden in South Carolina, for example, and Augusta and Milledgeville in Georgia. See Joseph A. Ernst and H. Roy Merrens, " 'Camden's Turrets Pierce the Skies!': The Urban Process in the Southern Colonies during the Eighteenth Century," *WMQ*, 3d Ser., XXX (1973), 557–558; Kenneth E. Lewis, *Camden: A Frontier Town in Eighteenth-Century South Carolina* (Columbia, S.C., 1976), 18–21; Edward J. Cashin, ed., *Colonial Augusta: "Key of the Indian Country"* (Macon, Ga., 1986); James C. Bonner, *Milledgeville: Georgia's Antebellum Capital* (Athens, Ga., 1978), 1–10. On southwestern expansion more generally, see Verner W. Crane, *The Southern Frontier, 1670–1732* (Ann Arbor, Mich., 1956); J. Leitch Wright, Jr., *Creeks and Seminoles: The Destruction and Regeneration of the Muscogulge People* (Lincoln, Nebr., 1986), 41–127.

On the South Carolina advance, see M. Eugene Sirmans, *Colonial South Carolina: A Political History, 1663–1763* (Chapel Hill, N.C., 1966), 282–289, 296–301, 324–342; Wright, *Creeks and Seminoles,* 135–140.

were gained from Indian cession. The Creeks' last lands were distributed in 1827, and those of the Cherokees in the final lottery.[7] In the interior, the local work ethic took as its antithesis—not the sloth of an enervated elite, as in the lowcountry—but the hunting stage of human development.

Accordingly, and even though whites began to have a *racist* view of Indians (as a people innately and permanently different from whites), they relied on a *cultural* denunciation of preagrarian savagery that encompassed so-called white Indians as well. Whites who still participated in frontier activities had ingloriously, it seemed to farmers, fallen from civility to a savage method of subsistence. In the South, at least, the Leatherstocking did not personify any precommercial virtue. Settlers instead drew sharp contrasts between their virtuously productive lives and the profligate roving of frontiersmen and Indians, distinguishing between themselves and those who, according to travelers, resembled "nations in the first stages of Barbarity." South Carolina settlers, for instance, complained of the "Idle, worthless, vagrant People" who created an "unsettled Situation" in the upcountry. Especially when they were recovering from the Cherokee War (1760–1761), Carolina colonists saw a disturbing similarity between native Americans and the mobile white bandits who preyed on farmers. The bandits themselves played rather calculatedly on this parallel, as when the Haynes family was assaulted and robbed by white men disguised as Indians.[8] Long unwilling to go native—even in order to protest British policy before the Revolution, as patriots in the North had done—whites in the Lower South associated Indian costume with crimes against property.

What astonished settlers most was how whites might actually "*choose* to live by the wandering indolence of hunting," consciously rejecting civility for savagery, even becoming adopted members of Indian cultures. Alexander McGillivray (one-quarter Indian and a headman of the Creeks) had carefully

7. H. David Williams, "Gambling Away the Inheritance: The Cherokee Nation and Georgia's Gold and Land Lotteries of 1832–33," *GHQ*, LXXIII (1989), 519.

8. First quotation from Raymond A. Mohl, ed., "A Scotsman [J. B. Dunlop] Visits Georgia in 1811," *GHQ*, LV (1971), 264–265; second quotation from Richard J. Hooker, ed., *The Carolina Backcountry on the Eve of the Revolution: The Journal and Other Writings of Charles Woodmason, Anglican Itinerant* (Chapel Hill, N.C., 1953), 226, 227. For examination of the upcountry as frontier, see Richard Maxwell Brown, *South Carolina Regulators* (Cambridge, Mass., 1963), 36 (Brown draws the link between the Cherokee War and the Regulation on 1–12); Rachel N. Klein, "Ordering the Backcountry: The South Carolina Regulation," *WMQ*, 3d Ser., XXXVIII (1981), 661–680.

to introduce himself as "a Native of this [Creek] Nation and of rank in it"—whites would assume otherwise. Andrew Ellicott jeered at English adventurer and adopted Creek William Augustus Bowles for making similar claims: "He speaks in the style of a King, 'my Nation,' and 'my people' are his common expressions."[9] One South Carolina resident complained of whites "who depend wholly on hunting for a subsistence" without "attending to cultivation," and Georgia officials stated that mobile whites were not proper settlers for Indian territories because they too closely resembled Indians. James Habersham also denounced a "percel of stragling northward People," who had "no settled habitation, and live by hunting and plundering." Western properties were supposed to gain in value and contribute to royal coffers, Habersham maintained, and opening them to a new set of hunting people would "defeat the true Intention of the Indians ceeding [land] to the King."[10] Settlers concluded that they had to remove not only native Americans from the frontier but whites who had gone native as well.

As warfare, Indian cession, and white migration took their toll on the frontier, an upcountry region gradually took shape. After the end of the Cherokee War, South Carolinians expanded throughout the present-day boundaries of the state, excepting only the Cherokee-held northwestern tip and the Catawba nation, a semiautonomous Indian reserve. From the middle of the eighteenth century onward, the Carolina interior gained white settlers, but it was not until the 1770s that its population experienced significant growth, rising from twenty-two thousand to almost eighty-three thousand within the decade. By this time, upcountry whites constituted 50 percent of the colony's inhabitants and 79 percent of all South Carolina whites. The state ousted the remaining Cherokees after the Revolution, gaining even more land for the burgeoning

9. The first quotation is a 1769 statement of William Bull, cited in Klein, "Ordering the Backcountry," *WMQ*, 3d Ser., XXXVIII (1981), 668 (my emphasis). The next two quotations are from John Walton Caughey, ed., *McGillivray of the Creeks* (Norman, Okla., 1938), 74; and Benjamin W. Griffith, Jr., *McIntosh and Weatherford, Creek Indian Leaders* (Tuscaloosa, Ala., 1988), 53. On the white Creek leaders, see J. Leitch Wright, Jr., *William Augustus Bowles: Director General of the Creek Nation* (Athens, Ga., 1967); and more in Caughey, ed., *McGillivray of the Creeks*, 3–57. On other mestizos, see Griffith, *McIntosh and Weatherford*; Wright, *Creeks and Seminoles*, 60–62 (Wright discusses African-Indian "mustees" on 73–99).

10. Presentments from Edgefield County Grand Jury, 1786, Grand Jury Presentments, SCDAH; *The Letters of Hon. James Habersham, 1756–1775* (GHS, *Colls.*, VI [Savannah, 1904]), 199, 204.

population.[11] Georgia expanded westward several decades later. In 1815, only about half of the present-day state of Georgia was ceded by native Americans, and much of this was still sparsely settled. Starting in the 1780s, settlements spread westward from the Savannah River to the Oconee; by 1804, the Creeks ceded land between the Oconee and Ocmulgee. A large chunk running along the Georgia-Florida border would be ceded in 1814, and other cessions brought whites northward toward the Chattahoochee, but, overall, Georgia retained a distinctly frontier quality (see Map 4). South Carolina's upcountry may have been underdeveloped, but Georgia's was only coming into being, and even Georgia's coastal areas resembled the South Carolina upcountry more than that older state's lowcountry parishes.

This western space, forcibly cleared of all wandering, frontier activities, was ready for a new and sedentary population. Most upcountry settlers were, not Europeans (a few German and British immigrant enclaves were exceptions), but Americans from other colonies or (later) states. Colonial South Carolina was first in line for these internal migrants; in 1756 a Scotsman passing through South Carolina noted, "The Back Settlements of this Province are crowded with people from Pensilvania." Pennsylvanians and Virginians pioneered in pre-Revolutionary South Carolina, and, after the Georgia Indian Cession of 1763, Virginia tobacco planters began to move into Georgia to take up land. The pace of immigration quickened after the Revolution, especially to Georgia.

11. The Cherokee War, Seven Years' War, and Revolutionary war all continued the contest between Carolina settlers and their aboriginal neighbors. Even the imperial rearrangements that took place after the American Revolution did not decide the question of white expansion in the region. Spain replaced Britain as an interested European power, and the central authority of the new Republic replaced Whitehall as a curb on westward expansion. The firm of Panton, Leslie, and Company (sponsored by Spanish officials) sent agents to trade with the southeastern nations and was reluctant to see its trading grounds littered with farms, fences, and a Malthusian glut of English-speaking children. The Creeks (by this time allied with the Cherokees and Seminoles) had most to lose from white expansion and continued to court Spanish officials in order to gain weapons to repel would-be Jeffersonian farmers. Even the United States government entered the fray, with George Washington rebuking Georgians for grabbing the land (belonging to Chickasaw and Choctaw groups allied with the Creeks) that would make up the disputed Yazoo tract. See Sirmans, *Colonial S.C.*, 296–301, 324–342; Robert L. Meriwether, *The Expansion of South Carolina, 1729–1765* (Kingsport, Tenn., 1940), 160–261; J. Leitch Wright, Jr., *Anglo-Spanish Rivalry in North America* (Athens, Ga., 1971), 138–153; Wright, *Creeks and Seminoles*, 43–53, 103–127, 131–140.

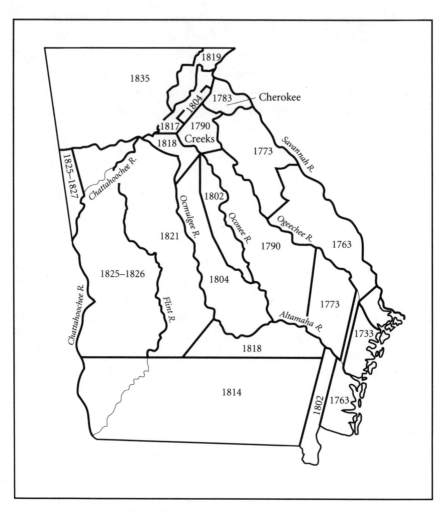

Map 4. Indian Cessions in Georgia. *After Ulrich Bonnell Phillips,* Georgia and State Rights . . . *(Washington, D.C., 1902)*

Creation of a new national perspective encouraged migrants to seek opportunity in other parts of the Republic. Veterans of the Continental army who had toured the South promoted the region by circulating information about its plenty. Georgian Joseph Clay explained this to Nathaniel Hall in 1783 when he wrote, "People are flocking into this Country to Settle beyond every Idea—the War has opened a knowledge of the Advantages that the So Countries afford hereafter not believed."[12]

Declining prices for tobacco and grain and lack of land in the Chesapeake and areas of Pennsylvania made settlement in the Lower South attractive to poorer whites and to settlers with assets that might yield more in a newer region with more land and opportunities.[13] (Table 9 provides a rough index to the availability of land in the Lower South compared to other parts of North America.) Only the newly opened areas of the Southwest and Northwest had lower population densities than the Lower South. Of regions that antedated the Revolution—New England, the Middle States, Upper South, and Lower South—the Lower South had the fewest people per square mile and, concomitantly, the most land for farmers. These facts were probably colored by the exaggerated idea of the region's wealth promulgated in travelers' narratives. Desire to go south, accordingly, reached obsessive proportions. One Virginian diagnosed this as "Georgia fever," whose sufferers "appear to be in a frenzy, and after turning around a few times, they stand still with their faces somewhat

12. Marjorie Stratford Mendenhall, "A History of Agriculture in South Carolina, 1790 to 1860: An Economic and Social Study" (Ph.D. diss., University of North Carolina–Chapel Hill, 1940), 35–36; John Murray to "Mr. Oswald," Jan. 31, 1756, John Murray's Letterbook, Murray of Murraythwaite Muniments, GD.219, bundle 290, SRO; G. Melvin Herndon, "Samuel Edward Butler of Virginia Goes to Georgia, 1784," *GHQ*, LII (1968), 115–116; *Letters of Joseph Clay . . .* (GHS, *Colls.*, VIII [Savannah, 1913], 186; Wilbur Zelinsky, "An Isochronic Map of Georgia Settlement, 1750–1850," *GHQ*, XXXV (1951), 194–195.

13. On growing inequality and land shortage in Pennsylvania, see James T. Lemon and Gary B. Nash, "The Distribution of Wealth in Eighteenth-Century America: A Century of Changes in Chester County, Pennsylvania, 1693–1802," *Jour. Soc. Hist.*, II (1968–1969), 1–24; Duane E. Ball, "Dynamics of Population and Wealth in Eighteenth-Century Chester County, Pennsylvania," *Journal of Interdisciplinary History*, VI (1976–1977), 621–644. On comparable trends in the Chesapeake, see Paul G. E. Clemens, *The Atlantic Economy and Colonial Maryland's Eastern Shore: From Tobacco to Grain* (Ithaca, N.Y., 1980), 97–105; Allan Kulikoff, *Tobacco and Slaves: The Development of Southern Cultures in the Chesapeake, 1680–1800* (Chapel Hill, N.C., 1986), 141–161.

TABLE 9. *United States Population Density, 1790–1810*

	Population per Square Mile		
Region	1790	1800	1810
Northwest		1.1	1.6
Southwest	1.3	2.8	4.8
Lower South	*4.4*	*6.4*	*9.0*
Upper South	17.2	19.3	21.6
Mid-Atlantic	17.9	21.7	27.0
New England	31.6	35.3	40.1

Source: U.S., Bureau of the Census, *Historical Statistics of the United States, Colonial Times to 1970* (Washington, D.C., 1975), I, 24–37. The regions include the states as follows: Northwest: Illinois, Indiana, Michigan, Ohio. Southwest: Kentucky, Louisiana, Mississippi, Tennessee. Lower South: Georgia, South Carolina. Upper South: Maryland, North Carolina, Virginia. Mid-Atlantic: Delaware, New Jersey, New York, Pennsylvania. New England: Connecticut, Maine, Massachusetts, New Hampshire, Rhode Island, Vermont.

towards the South, and then you will hear them utter with a loud voice: 'Georgia.'" The near-hallucinatory vision of plenty that Frederick Mulcaster had had of coastal Florida thus went west, along with the literal fevers introduced by the white population. Connecticut native Thomas Fitch gave a more-reasoned account of the lure of the South, estimating that "reputation" and "property" could be acquired in Georgia "about five times as fast [as] in any old state; for competition is inversely in that proportion." In 1792 William Murrell indicated the numbers and the states of origin of Revolutionary war veterans who made their way to the area around Camden, South Carolina. Murrell, who owned a store in Camden, noted in his business ledger the military wages due and the states of origin as part of the credit record of veterans who charged goods in the store. Of eighty-three outstanding accounts at his store, forty-eight were for individuals from South Carolina; but the next-largest group of veterans, thirty-three, more than one-third of the account holders, were from Virginia, Maryland, or Pennsylvania. In South Carolina, James Harrison used Virginia currency to figure expenses for building a house in the late 1780s, perhaps because an immigrant paid this way or perhaps because Harrison was a native Virginian quicker with his figures if done in a familiar medium. So much did post-Revolutionary Georgia remain an immigrant state that, when Levi Sheftall reported on a Savannah cricket match in 1801, the game was divided between teams of natives and of newcomers. (But the natives won, 57 to 25.)[14]

New Englanders, in addition, imparted a surprisingly Yankee quality to this southernmost region of the nation. Newly arrived in Georgia from Connecticut, Daniel Mulford estimated that half of Savannahians were from the North and that, under their influence, even the natives acquired "a strong tincture of Northern manners." Georgia governors Abraham Baldwin and Lyman Hall were both Yale men interested in establishing a southern institution based on their alma mater. They recruited Yale scientist and mathematician Josiah Meigs to head the new college in Athens and looked forward to the prospect of promulgating there the wisdom of the modern age. Under Meigs's tutelage, the school was to have an up-to-date academic structure that emphasized the sciences over the classics. Surveying the plenteous, albeit completely unimproved, acreage granted to the institution, Meigs ebulliently stated his goal "to kindle a scientific fire on this mount Pisgah."[15]

When they kindled new fires in the Lower South, migrants used material from what historical geographers have labeled "hearth" cultures. Each hearth

14. George R. Lamplugh, *Politics on the Periphery: Factions and Parties in Georgia, 1783–1806* (Newark, Del., 1986), 32 (quotation); Thomas Fitch to Daniel Mulford, May 11, 1808, Daniel Mulford Papers, I, GHS (quotation); entry for Oct. 15, 1792, Camden District ledgers, William Murrell Papers, SCL. The figures for accounts break down as follows: South Carolina 48, Virginia 23, Maryland 6, Pennsylvania 4, Georgia 1, New York/Connecticut 1, for a total of 83. James Harrison Account Book, p. 160, microfilm R406, SCL; note of Jan. 13, 1801, Sheftall Family Papers, Keith Read Coll., box 22, UGA. See also C. Anthony to James Clark, Sept. 3, 1782—on Virginians' migration to Georgia.

15. Daniel Mulford to Betsy Crane, Feb. 15, 1809, Daniel Mulford Papers, I, GHS. On the University of Georgia, see Roswell Powell Stephens, "Science in Georgia, 1800–1830," *GHQ*, IX (1925), 55–56; O. Burton Adams, "Yale Influence on the Formation of the University of Georgia," *GHQ*, LI (1967), 175–185; Thomas G. Dyer, *The University of Georgia: A Bicentennial History, 1785–1985* (Athens, Ga., 1985), 12–14 (quotation on 14); Robert Preston Brooks, *The University of Georgia under Sixteen Administrations, 1785–1955* (Athens, Ga., 1956), 9, 13–14; Louis W. McKeehan, *Yale Science: The First Hundred Years, 1701–1801* (New York, 1947), 53–58—these last two sources also emphasize Meigs's ardently republican politics. See also Josiah Meigs to Jedidiah Morse, Dec. 25, 1802, Josiah Meigs Papers, UGA–University Archives.

was a regional variation of colonial culture that moved with people as they went to new areas, providing the original spark for settlement patterns but also undergoing adaptation in new regions. The "backcountry hearth," derived from the mid-Atlantic region, provided most settlers with clear ideas about the possibility of creating an economy dependent on commercial agriculture, the likelihood of using black slaves to do so, and a focus on grain and tobacco as crops likely to fulfill these expectations. In this respect, the culture of the mid-Atlantic states overshadowed that of New England; though a Yankee enclave continued to be influential in Georgia, these northerners either conformed to the slaveholding expectations of the backcountry hearth or were self-selected to fulfill these expectations even before migration. A brief look at individual emigrants reveals their early use of slaves and their establishment of commercial agriculture. George Willis, who had been an overseer in King William County, Virginia, migrated south in the 1780s and by 1805 had acquired eleven hundred acres spread over three Georgia counties—he could then hire overseers of his own. Virginian Francis Cox brought seven slaves with him when he migrated to Georgia; he set them to work on shares when he acted as Joseph Clay's overseer in 1780, earning profits with their labor that he could later use to buy his own land and more slaves. Virginian Thomas Carr bought slaves in Savannah after he moved to Georgia in 1785 and was using them to grow tobacco by the end of 1790.[16]

Samuel Edward Butler best exemplified this southward transfer of people and a slaveholding culture. A small planter from Hanover County, Virginia, Butler migrated to Wilkes County, Georgia, in 1784. He was well aware that he belonged to a growing group of migrants. While passing through North Carolina, Butler "saw a Mr. Hughs from Macklenburg [Mecklenburg County, Virginia], moving to Georgia, 16 in family Black and White." On arrival in Georgia, Butler inspected available lands and selected four hundred acres, paying for the land with three adolescent slaves he had brought from Virginia and for the surveying fees with Virginia currency. He trekked back to the Chesapeake, sold his Virginia acreage and some slaves, then sent his remaining

16. Mitchell, "Early American Cultural Regions," in Gibson, ed., *Settlement in North America,* 66–90; George Willis journal, UGA; agreement between Clay and Cox, account book, Joseph Habersham Papers, GHS; Thomas Carr's receipt for slaves purchased from Thomas Glasock, May 24, 1785, folder 4, and W. Stith to Thomas Carr, Dec. 30, 1790, folder 10 (for tobacco), box 1, Carr Collection, UGA.

chattels and other personal property to Georgia. The move, while in some ways a risk, certainly improved Butler's lot—he had owned less than one thousand acres and only thirteen slaves in Virginia but acquired three thousand acres in Georgia as well as thirty-five slaves. On his death in 1809, his entire estate was worth a prosperous $12,728.[17]

This success was not overnight, however; it required clever selection of activities and determined exploitation of the upcountry's resources. Tobacco and grains, especially corn and wheat, established a base for the interior's prosperity. Starting in the colonial period, upcountry settlers produced tobacco and grain products, as Charleston merchant Alexander Gillon indicated when he advertised "Carolina TOBACCO in hogsheads, FLOUR, and ship BREAD" for sale in 1770.[18] Grain (especially corn, the early American staff of life) fed new settlers. John Drayton explained in the 1790s that wheat was grown "generally in the [South Carolina] upper country, where almost every one cultivates a little for domestic use." Grain cultivation probably increased in the upcountry after the Revolution; wheat production was expanding in the Chesapeake just as its population was moving south and reestablishing mid-Atlantic cultivation practices there.[19]

Cultivators in the Lower South soon began to produce grain for the market, first for provision-short planters, then for hungry Europeans. In the colonial

17. See Herndon, "Samuel Edward Butler," *GHQ*, LII (1968), 115–117, 120–125; and Herndon, ed., "The Diary of Samuel Edward Butler, 1784–1786 . . . ," *GHQ*, LII (1968), 205 (quotation), 207–208, 209.

18. *South-Carolina Gazette; And Country Journal* (Charleston), Mar. 6, 1770. The duc de La Rochefoucault also remarked how settlers from Pennsylvania, Maryland, and Virginia grew wheat and tobacco as they had done before migrating (François Alexandre Frédéric, duc de La Rochefoucault Liancourt, *Travels through the United States of North America . . . [1795–1797]* [London, 1799], I, 625).

19. John Drayton, *A View of South-Carolina, as Respects Her Natural and Civil Concerns* (Charleston, S.C., 1802), 139. See also Abner Davis to Samuel Jones, Jan. 9, 1789, Samuel and Thomas Jones Papers, GHS; François André Michaux, *Travels to the West of the Alleghany Mountains . . . in the Year 1802*, in Reuben Gold Thwaites, ed., *Early Western Travels*, III (Cleveland, Ohio, 1904), 292. On increased production, see Lewis Cecil Gray, *A History of Agriculture in the Southern United States to 1860* (Washington, D.C., 1933), II, 607–608, 818; Clemens, *Colonial Maryland's Eastern Shore*. Wheat easily fitted into cycles of tobacco production in the Chesapeake; farmers grew it in cornfields or on old tobacco land in rotation with corn and fallow intervals.

era, upcountry settlers had "furnished the Charles Town Market with their Flour." They managed to replace northern colonists as suppliers of breadstuffs to the lowcountry; in 1770, they made no less than 4,000 barrels of flour for coastal consumers, thereby fulfilling rice planters' expectation that inland farmers would service the lowcountry economy. Demand for breadstuffs was also rising in southern Europe, where markets began to set prices for American grain, including rice and wheat. In 1771, South Carolina legislators established inspection services for wheat flour and even granted a bounty on it, both indications that the product could be sold outside Charleston and needed encouragement and regulation. Settlers continued to produce grain after the Revolution. Jeremiah Kendall sent flour from his farm near Augusta to the Savannah market in 1782, and William Noble grew wheat along the Little River in South Carolina, sending flour to Charleston in 1796. Corn cultivation also expanded. In the year ending September 30, 1792, the region exported more than 100,000 bushels of corn. Some upcountry planters contracted to provision certain lowcountry planters, as John Chesnut did in the 1790s, boating 600 bushels of corn to the Middleton family in 1795.[20]

With grain, whites could make an easy move from domestic to commercial production. Their next step was to grow tobacco. Unlike grain, tobacco was cultivated almost completely for trade and represented greater devotion to the market. This was true even before the American Revolution—Georgia, for

20. Quotation from Louis De Vorsey, Jr., ed., *De Brahm's Report of the General Survey in the Southern District of North America* (Columbia, S.C., 1971), 70; see also Leila Sellers, *Charleston Business on the Eve of the American Revolution* (Chapel Hill, N.C., 1934), 31, 34. On inspection, see Thomas Cooper and David J. McCord, eds., *The Statutes at Large of South Carolina* (Columbia, 1836–1841), IV, no. 1066; Meriwether, *The Expansion of South Carolina*, 165–168; Hester Walton Newton, "The Agricultural Activities of the Salzburgers in Colonial Georgia," *GHQ*, XVIII (1934), 255–256; Klein, *Unification of a Slave State*, 18, 29. On European grain markets, see Clemens, *Colonial Maryland's Eastern Shore*, 177–180.

On post-Revolutionary production, see Jeremiah Kendall to Seth John Cuthbert, Jan. 4, 1782, Seth John Cuthbert Papers, GHS; Ezekiel to William Noble, May 30, 1796, Noble Family Papers, box 1, folder 11, SCL; receipt of Dec. 15, 1795, Chesnut-Miller-Manning Papers, series 12-33-39, SCHS—also see the other receipts in this series. On corn exports, see Gray, *Agriculture in the Southern U.S.*, II, 609; the figures break down into 99,985 bushels for South Carolina, 11,667 bushels for Georgia. Sellers of property began to specify that their holdings were suited to grain cultivation. See advertisements in the *Augusta Chronicle*, Mar. 10, 1787, Aug. 26, 1814, Feb. 13, 1796.

instance, exported 176,732 pounds of tobacco in 1772. Production increased in the 1790s; in 1792, Georgians exported more than 6,000,000 pounds, making their state the third-largest tobacco producer in the United States. South Carolinians exported only 643 hogsheads of tobacco in 1783, but their exports sharply rose to 9,646 hogsheads by 1799, an increase of fifteen times.[21] Thus, tobacco cultivation expanded after the Peace of Paris, and prices rose when nicotine-starved Europeans provided a larger market. (Prices would abruptly fall between 1810 and 1812, when Napoleonic ambition again disrupted trade.) South Carolina merchants Robert and Matthew Stewart wrote a business correspondent in 1786: "We cannot ship you the Tobacco agreeable to [earlier] directions, that article has got as high as 22/9 p[er] ct [hundredweight]. there is even a demand for it at that." So common was tobacco cultivation in upcountry South Carolina that records for a store in Camden District in 1798 included only seven accounts involving cotton on two pages of tobacco-dominated transactions.[22]

Although neither grain nor tobacco became a large-scale cash crop like cotton, both facilitated two needed components of a commercial economy: inspection and transportation. To gain these services, settlers raised insistent voices to their state governments, requesting a support of trade that was standard in older regions of America. Legislators in both South Carolina and Georgia responded by expanding facilities and regulations for inspecting flour. By 1801, Georgia had nine flour inspection stations in Savannah and Augusta and scattered through rural counties. Some of these were at mills, as with Jackson County's station at "Espy's Mill," and Scriven County's station at "Hudson's Mill."[23] Tobacco inspection was more complicated but, because

21. For Georgia, see Herndon, "Samuel Edward Butler," *GHQ*, LII (1968), 115–117. For South Carolina, see Gray, *Agriculture in the Southern U.S.*, II, 606; and Mendenhall, "Agriculture in S.C.," 40.

22. Robert and Matthew Stewart to Messrs. Stewart and Nesbett, June 22, 1786, Thomas Morris Papers, SCL; Camden Account Books, pp. 969–970, microfilm R474, SCL; Mendenhall, "Agriculture in S.C.," 40. Planters began to specify that estates they wished to sell or rent were suited to tobacco. See advertisements placed by Jacob Valk, Martha Young, and John Cobbison in *South-Carolina and American General Gazette* (Charleston), Dec. 3, 1779; *Georgia Gazette* (Savannah), Oct. 30, 1783; *Augusta Chronicle*, Jan. 21, 1792.

23. Augustin Smith Clayton, comp., *A Compilation of the Laws of the State of Georgia [1800–1810]* (Augusta, 1813), 27–28. On the trend toward government regulation, see

tobacco was a delicate product whose price depended more crucially on quality, even more necessary. One concerned Georgian wrote John Chesnut in 1785 about some poor-quality tobacco recently exported and feared the damage that could be done by lax inspectors "so lost to every Sense of Honor and regard for the infant State of this State as to pass and impose such trash" on merchants. Other upcountry petitioners also fretted that lowcountry-influenced legislators ignored their commercial interests. No fewer than 156 citizens from Union, Spartanburg, Greenville, Chester, and York counties in South Carolina put together a formidable petition in 1789 insisting on their need for a tobacco inspector at the Union County Courthouse. They complained of "their extreem remoteness from a Tobacco inspection" and stated that "the general interest of the back Country would be greatly advanced" by the legislature's concession to their request.[24]

Legislatures eventually proved responsive, much more so than in the case of flour. In South Carolina, tobacco inspection laws were passed in 1789, 1803, and as late as 1809; Georgia did the same in 1770 and 1785. By 1786, Georgia had six tobacco inspection stations in Augusta and Savannah and in outlying counties and along navigable rivers. More stations were added at two- or three-year intervals between 1787 and 1805.[25] Storage of tobacco was also a concern, because dampness or other damage lowered its value. Companies like James Barnes's in Augusta stored planters' tobacco while it awaited official inspection. Inspection laws, intended to encourage careful cultivation and packaging, resembled those in the Chesapeake—probably the model for Lower South legislation. Poor tobacco was declared "trash," for example, and then burned by the inspector. Additional rules controlled the actions of inspectors (who could, by uttering the syllable "trash," ruin a tobacco producer's finances for a

---

Mary McKinney Schweitzer, "Economic Regulation and the Colonial Economy: The Maryland Tobacco Inspection Act of 1747," *Jour. Econ. Hist.*, XL (1980), 551–569.

24. —— to John Chesnut, Aug. 4, 1785, Chesnut-Miller-Manning Papers, series 12-33-29, SCHS; last quotation from Petitions to the General Assembly, 1789, no. 103, SCDAH (see also 1783, no. 63, 1789, no. 84, 1791, no. 67, 1795, no. 126, 1797, no. 115).

25. On South Carolina, see Mendenhall, "Agriculture in S.C.," 55–56. For Georgia, see Allen D. Candler, comp., *The Colonial Records of the State of Georgia* (Atlanta, 1904–1916), XIX, 204–208, 380; Robert Watkins and George Watkins, eds., *A Digest of the Laws of the State of Georgia* (Philadelphia, 1800), 339–340, 361, 385–386, 530–531, 576; Clayton, comp., *Compilation of Laws of Georgia*, 121, 246.

year) to prevent them from favoring their own or friends' tobacco. In Georgia, heavy fines (five hundred pounds currency plus twenty pounds per contraband hogshead) deterred shipmasters from accepting uninspected tobacco that might bring Old World curses down on the heads of republican farmers.[26]

Efficient transportation was related to inspection—both preserved the market value of produce. Transport was a crucial public concern in South Carolina's upcountry because it was cut off from coastal ports, a factor that delayed development of this region in the eighteenth century. Riverboats glided over the few navigable waterways between the midlands and the lowcountry; they were how William Noble got his flour to Charleston in 1796. For landlocked areas, wagons were needed. Settlers began to lay out roads in the colonial period, and as many as three thousand wagons rumbled to and from Charleston each year.[27] Georgia was blessed with more navigable rivers than South Carolina and had less reason to improve roads unless to connect remote parts of the state with major waterways. The Savannah River was a lifeline between the frontier and Savannah's port. Augusta got its start as a station for the Indian trade, drawing in deerskins carried overland and boating them down the Savannah. The river became a crowded conduit once farmers wanted crops taken to the port. Further down in the state, both the Oconee (on which Georgians situated Milledgeville, the state's capital until 1868) and the Ocmulgee flowed into the Altamaha, which ended at Darien on the sea (Map 4). From Darien, seaworthy vessels carried goods to Savannah. Settler Daniel Mulford, for instance, took note of the traffic between the landing at Milledgeville and the port at Darien. Looking at Georgia's superior transportation, South Carolinians feared they would lose trade. A petition from Orangeburg and Ninety Six districts in Carolina pleaded for rivers to be cleared "for the easy carriage of Tobacco, Flour, Lumber and naval Stores to Charleston,"

26. James Barnes and Company's advertisement for their warehouse, *Augusta Chronicle*, Nov. 12, 1791; Clayton, comp., *Compilation of Laws of Georgia*, 240–241; Watkins and Watkins, eds., *Digest of Laws of Georgia*, 444–453; Lucius Q. C. Lamar, comp., *A Compilation of the Laws of the State of Georgia . . . [1810–1819]* (Augusta, 1821), 334–335.

27. Gray, *Agriculture in the Southern U.S.*, II, 684–685; Carl Bridenbaugh, *Myths and Realities: Societies of the Colonial South* (New York, 1963), 146–147; Sellers, *Charleston Business*, 34–35. See the references to transportation in Ezekiel to William Noble, May 30, 1796, Noble Family Papers, box 1, folder 11, SCL; Michaux, *Travels*, in Thwaites, ed., *Early Western Travels*, III, 300.

complaining that, unless this was done, "Georgia will by means of Savannah River draw most of their Produce to the Port of Savannah, much to the prejudice of the Trade of this State."[28]

To preserve its trade the South Carolina government funded several canal projects, but only when prodded by settlers who had petitioned for canals since the 1780s. Residents of Barnwell District, situated in "a Tract of fertile Land, thickly Inhabited, by Corn planters," complained that land carriage was "too great a draw Back." They wanted waterways cleared so they would no longer be "deprived [of] receiving the reward of their Labour." Some of these "canals," as this petition indicated, were simple and relatively inexpensive projects that widened or cleared obstacles from natural waterways. The Pine Tree Navigation Company, for example, petitioned for funds to open Pine Tree Creek near Camden and to establish an agricultural inspection station at the head of this canal. Efforts to dig artificial canals were less successful unless they were carefully regulated and well-funded projects that connected or extended existing waterways. The South Carolina legislature chartered four companies to clear rivers in the 1790s, but only the lowcountry's Santee-Cooper Canal Company managed to improve its designated stretch of waterway, one rather remote from inland settlers.[29]

Other transportation services better suited tobacco planters. Wagoners began to carry hogsheads overland to navigable rivers. This service flourished especially around Augusta; one farmer in Washington, for instance, sent tobacco and creditor's notes by wagon in 1792 to Augusta, where the goods and bills next took boat passage to Savannah. Two men who advertised boats for sale in the December 29, 1792, *Augusta Chronicle* specified the number of tobacco hogsheads each could hold—one man referred to his vehicle as a "tobacco flat." Another Georgian specified in 1799 that transporters were "engaged in preparing Boats for the exportation of Tobacco down the Oconee." In autumn of 1800, Le Roy Hammond offered to hire out a ninety-hogshead

28. Daniel Mulford to Levi Mulford, July 6, 1809, Daniel Mulford Papers, I, GHS; Petitions to General Assembly, 1786, no. 1, SCDAH. See also Nicholas Ware's comment that wagoners preferred carrying trade goods rather than agricultural staples because the former carried higher prices: Ware to Thomas Carr, May 18, 1807, Carr Collection, box 5, folder 35, UGA.

29. Quotation from Petitions to General Assembly, n.d., no. 1045, SCDAH; see also 1797, no. 115. On upcountry canals, see Klein, *Unification of a Slave State*, 244–246; Lacy K. Ford, Jr., *Origins of Southern Radicalism: The South Carolina Upcountry, 1800–1860* (New York, 1988), 16–19.

tobacco flat along with five or six boathands. Some agencies insured tobacco while in transit.[30]

The upcountry's commercial expansion—a product of individual efforts supported by state regulations—demonstrates how far the inland region had come since the Regulation. No longer neglected, settlers instead found legislators responsive to their requests. Their petitions for government expenditure show, better than any other source, how settlers had commercial expectations of the area upon their arrival there. But their insistence on public support of market agriculture did not obliterate an assumption that an active government was one that could do damage if corrupt and prone to venal favoritism. This fear would again assert itself once an economy based on cotton was in place and further government intervention seemed more invasive than helpful.

Upcountry farmers and planters eventually replaced tobacco and wheat with cotton as European markets for the first two commodities dwindled or proved less profitable. Tobacco began falling off in the 1790s, and cultivators shifted to commercial production of wheat to boost their profits, much as farmers were doing in the Chesapeake. Wheat prices then fell in early 1796, and production of grain declined. By 1808, millowners in Camden, South Carolina, stopped grinding because there was not enough wheat to justify commercial operation. At about the same time, David Ramsay claimed that upcountry settlers discovered they could earn more from cotton. In 1796, Ezekiel Noble in Georgia claimed that he could make much more producing cotton than he could wheat. This story is well known to historians: cotton production soared fantastically in the 1790s, encouraged by the development of more efficient cotton gins but even more by the expansion of the British textile industry. By 1800 the United States exported some forty million pounds of raw cotton, most of this from the Lower South; by 1815, cotton made up 33 percent of total United States exports.[31]

30. On wagons: L. Viul to John Gibbons, Aug. 6, 1792, John Gibbons Papers, box 2, folder 1, Duke. See also the tax receipt of Jem Williams, "a free Negroe Waggoner," July 10, 1800, in folder 5. On boats: M. Martin to Charles McDonald, Jan. 19, 1799, Isabel P. Lawrence Collection, folder 3, McDonald-Lawrence Papers, GHS (second quotation); Hammond advertisement, *Augusta Chronicle*, Nov. 29, 1800. Insurance agencies included, by 1792, the firms of Jackson and Nightingale of Augusta, and E. Jackson and Company of Savannah (see *Georgia Gazette*, May 3, 1792).

31. Gray, *Agriculture in the Southern U.S.*, II, 609; Klein, *Unification of a Slave State*, 248; Ramsay, *History of S.-C.*, II, 599; Michaux, *Travels*, in Thwaites, ed., *Early Western Travels*, III, 298; Ezekiel to William Noble, May 30, 1796, Noble Family Papers, box 1,

Though more whites were putting cotton into their tobacco and wheat fields, they continued to apply their knowledge of the two older crops to the new one. Techniques of cultivating green-seed cotton varied widely at first and were sometimes muddled with methods better suited to sea island cotton; cultivation practices took final form only around 1800. In the meantime, tobacco eased the transition to cotton because the two crops required remarkably similar techniques for their cultivation, mostly because both plants grew on freestanding stalks. During the eighteenth and early nineteenth centuries, both crops were either hoed up into hills of earth or plowed into ridges. Since the seventeenth century, tobacco had been topped and suckered—the top portion of each plant and superfluous side growths, or suckers, were trimmed off during the growing season to improve the quality of the remaining leaves. Cotton farmers adopted both these techniques, and topping and suckering plants became routine procedures in the nineteenth century.[32] The *Carolina Gazette,* for instance, explained in 1799 that cotton needed to be planted in ridges, then thinned and topped. Some planters even favored techniques derived from tobacco that were probably not appropriate for cotton. South Carolinian Lewis Du Pre recommended not only topping but "curing" cotton, a procedure of doubtful efficacy, but it indicates how farmers were shifting their attentions to cotton by referring to tobacco.[33]

Techniques of grain cultivation also influenced cotton culture. Planters advised that, to protect cotton from early frosts, cultivators should "turn down the stalk about the 20th of October, in the same manner as we turn down corn." On his land near the Ocmulgee River, Josiah Everett planted both corn

folder 11, SCL; Franklee Gilbert Whartenby, *Land and Labor Productivity in United States Cotton Production, 1800–1840* (New York, 1977), tables 3, 6.

32. Gray, *Agriculture in the Southern U.S.,* I, 184, II, 675, 689. Though techniques for tobacco and cotton may have been similar, there is no single causal connection between the former crop and the latter—West Indian techniques for planting cotton in rows and hills probably also were influential, as were European agricultural techniques. See Whitemarsh B. Seabrook, *A Memoir on the Origin, Cultivation, and Uses of Cotton . . .* (Geological and Agricultural Survey of South Carolina, *Pamphlets* [Charleston, S.C., 1844]), 22; entries for Apr. 6, 8, 1788, plantation journal, Richard Leake Papers, GHS; David Leroy Coon, "The Development of Market Agriculture in South Carolina, 1670–1785" (Ph.D. diss., University of Illinois, Urbana/Champaign), 3–4.

33. *Carolina Gazette* (Charleston), Sept. 12, 1799; Lewis Du Pre, *Observations on the Culture of Cotton* (Georgetown, S.C., 1799), 12. See also Gray, *Agriculture in the Southern U.S.,* II, 689; Drayton, *View of S.-C.,* 130–131.

and cotton in drills using plows. His procedure emphasized how similar methods were developed for both crops. Cultivators had originally grown corn in small hills (this was the pre-Columbian method) and grew cotton this way when they first turned to that crop. Georgian Richard Leake was still growing cotton in hills in 1788. By the end of the colonial period, however, other farmers grew corn in drills—rows of small holes in which workers placed seeds—and started using plows on both corn and small grains. Drills were still experimental; as late as 1812, one upcountry South Carolinian reported he sowed thirty-eight acres of his corn in drills and sixty-seven "the usual way." Following the newer method in the early 1800s, cotton growers sowed seed in drills, then adopted a technique of plowing the sprouted rows into ridges, strategies similar to those in contemporary grain cultivation.[34]

Use of plows spread quickly through the upcountry. Visitor John Lambert and coastal resident John Drayton both observed that, while lowcountry slaves employed hoes in rice fields, upcountry farmers depended on plows. Roughly half of upcountry estates had plows, in contrast to the relatively unplowed estates along the coast (see Table 10). With a plow, a worker could cultivate between three and six acres per day, an improvement on the single acre that could be handled with a hoe.[35] Plows might have features for different tasks: a straight-blade broke soil and made deep furrows, shovel plows raised ridges, moldboard plows turned clayey soil away from the cutting blade, and bull-tongue plows threw earth back on the roots of the plants. By 1797, John Ewing Colhoun had six plows of three different varieties on his estate in South Carolina. That year, Colhoun told his overseer to "dispatch all the Plowing" in

34. William Washington to Thomas Spalding, June 24, 1817, Spalding Family Papers, folder 1, GHS (first quotation); entry for Apr. 11, 1788, plantation journal, Richard Leake Papers, GHS; entry for June 1812, plantation book, Chesnut-Miller-Manning Papers, series 12-35-4, SCHS (second quotation); entries for spring of 1808, Josiah Everett daybook, 1808–20, Curry Hill Plantation Records, microfilm 2-2200-C, GDAH (use of drills); Whartenby, *Cotton*, 108; Gray, *Agriculture in the Southern U.S.*, II, 700–701, 813. See also Charles William Janson's description (in the early 1800s) of South Carolina green-seed cotton sown in drills and then plowed to form ridges, in *The Stranger in America* . . . (London, 1807), 368. Cf. Seabrook, who claimed that West Indian cotton planters and Jethro Tull influenced the development of ridge plowing in North America (*Memoir on Cotton*, 22).

35. John Lambert, *Travels through Lower Canada and the United States of North America, in the Years 1806, 1807, and 1808* (London, 1810), II, 454; Drayton, *View of S.-C.,* 140–142. On increased acreage, see Whartenby, *Cotton*, 112.

TABLE 10. *Estates with Plows, 1780–1815*

	1780s	1790s	1800s	1810s
South Carolina				
Lowcountry	7.3%	7.5%	3.6%	6.6%
Midlands	51.9	38.5	48.6	56.0
Upcountry	50.0	61.7	58.3	44.4
Georgia				
Lowcountry	7.1	5.3	18.6	23.5
Savannah River	—	38.5	58.2	58.6
Upcountry	—	62.2	57.9	64.4

Sources: Estate Inventories, SCDAH, GDAH.

February because "that is the greatest and principal Business" of planting. Other records, especially accounts kept with blacksmiths who made or repaired plows, further indicate how the business of plowing expanded and how planters had a preference for field workers who knew something about plowing.[36]

Development of a cotton baler, or press, also received a boost from the

36. On plowing: Whartenby, *Cotton*, 110–111; Gray, *Agriculture in the Southern U.S.*, II, 100–101; memorandum on Twelve Mile Plantation, 1797, and J. E. Colhoun to John Waddle, Feb. 4, 1797, John Ewing Colhoun Papers, folder 3, SHC. On blacksmith work: Thomas Carr's payments to Steele, Apr. 11, 1794, Carr Collection, box 3, folder 19, UGA; Josiah Everett daybook, 1808–20, Curry Hill Plantation Records, microfilm 2-2200-C, GDAH; blacksmith's receipts, Edward Oxford Papers, folder 1, GDAH; blacksmith's account, George Willis Journal, UGA. On plowmen: *Augusta Chronicle*, Nov. 8, 1794; *Farmer's Gazette* (Sparta), Dec. 13, 1806; Timothy Ford to Henry Izard, Jan. 31, 1806, Ford-Ravenel Papers, series 11-131-3, SCHS; records for Ford's production of short-staple cotton are in series 11-131-36.

Plows also connected cotton to another, earlier commercial crop: indigo. One advertiser, for instance, specified that slaves from a South Carolina indigo plantation included "some fine plough boys" (*State Gazette of South-Carolina* [Charleston], Feb. 18, 1790). See also George Washington to John Chesnut, June 26, 1791, Williams-Chesnut-Manning Papers, microfilm R962a-b, SCL. On indigo in colonial Carolina, see also Klein, *Unification of a Slave State*, 11, 16, 28–29; and Chapter 6, above.

know-how of tobacco and flour producers. Cotton pressed into bales appeared with regularity in historical records only in the early nineteenth century. Before that time farmers had packed cotton loosely into bags, and they continued to package sea island cotton in this manner throughout the antebellum period. But compacting short-staple cotton into bales would give it less volume and make transportation easier. As early as 1779, square bales of cotton made their debut along the Mississippi River in Louisiana, though not in the British colonies. (By way of contrast, in the Lower South's old competitor, the East Indies, balers were already common devices.)[37] British American tobacco planters, however, had been pressing their crop into hogsheads since the seventeenth century. When tobacco-growing migrants appeared in the Lower South, they packaged their product in hogsheads, indicating how they brought an expertise with agricultural presses with them. Othniel Beale, for example, had two "PACKING-SCREWS" on hand in his Charleston store in 1771. Also in Charleston, J. and T. Manson offered "An exceeding Good Tobacco Screw" for sale in 1788. Early in 1789 the city council of Charleston petitioned the state legislature to create regulations for tobacco presses so that hogsheads would uniformly weigh at least nine hundred pounds.[38]

At first, upcountry planters and farmers pressed their cotton into either square or round bales. Early on, they might simply have adapted tobacco presses—which packed tobacco into round hogsheads—to round bags of cotton without altering the general design of the devices. Round bales were probably a transition between bags and square bales in which planters used tobacco or flour presses to tamp cotton down into semicylindrical bags (see Plate 11). Eli Whitney's business partner Phineas Miller reported that he packed cotton in this manner, using an iron hoop around the mouth of the bag to facilitate even distribution of the cotton. In the first decade of the nineteenth

37. See the references to bagged cotton listed in exports in the *Georgia Gazette,* May 28, 1766, and in William Bryan's estate sale in the same newspaper, Jan. 15, 1795. In 1847 Whitemarsh Seabrook stated that sea island cotton planters did not use presses to package their crop. See Seabrook, "Memoir on Sea Island Cotton," *Proceedings of the Agricultural Convention and of the State Agricultural Society of South Carolina* [1839–1845] (Columbia, S.C., 1847), supplement for 1846, 20. Also see Gray, *Agriculture in the Southern U.S.,* II, 705. On East Indies, see U. Scott to Joseph Banks, Jan. 7, 1790, Joseph Banks Correspondence, Add. 33,979, III, fol. 13, BL; "India Trade. Nawab's Debts," fols. 109–119, MS 1064, Melville Papers, NLS.

38. *South-Carolina and American General Gazette,* Apr. 24, 1771; *Columbian Herald* (Charleston), Jan. 14, 1788; Petitions to General Assembly, 1789, no. 84, SCDAH.

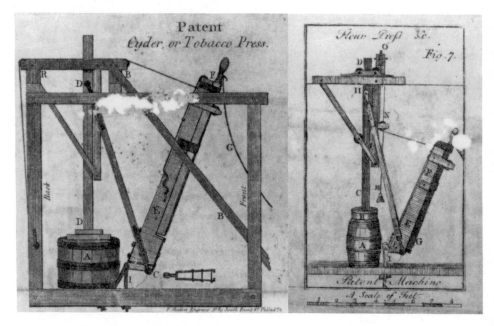

Plate 11. Patented Agricultural Presses. *Detail of patent certificate in Pinckney Family Papers, series 3, box 11, folder 1, LC.*

century, cotton planters used both round and square bales. John Chesnut's South Carolina cotton factors, for example, acknowledged their receipt of his seventy square and twenty round bales in 1803. In 1807 Augusta cotton factors McKinne and Company, Barrett and Sims, and Jones and Semmes offered to store cotton in bales, charging more for the square than the round, a sign that round bales were smaller or lighter than square ones. By the early 1800s, square bales were the rule, probably because they could be packed together without the wasted space that round bales (having no corners) had between them. Inspectors preferred square bales, because size and weight could be more easily correlated, hence controlled by law; planters preferred them because they used cheaper bagging than did round bales.[39]

39. Jeannette Mirsky and Allan Nevins, *The World of Eli Whitney* (New York, 1952), 99–100; MacBeth, Henry and Co. to John Chesnut, May 27, 1803, series 12-34-27, Chesnut-Miller-Manning Papers, SCHS; cotton factors' advertisements in the *Augusta Chronicle*, Oct. 3, 1807. On the issue of cloth bagging, see Osborn and Waring to Thomas Waties, Sept. 24, 1817, Thomas Waties Papers, box 1, SCL. On the uniformity of

From balers to flatboats, the commercial infrastructure already created for tobacco and grain gave cotton its biggest boost. The establishment of transportation and inspection facilities for grains and tobacco contrasted with the weakness of such infrastructure in earlier years. Indigo inspection, for example, had never moved beyond the coast during the colonial period, and a network of services that would have facilitated commercial expansion in the upcountry simply never developed until tobacco, especially, spread over the region. Once this network was in place, roads and freight boats could as easily carry cotton as tobacco, and transportation services gradually shifted from old crops to the new one after the cotton boom of the 1790s. Petitioners made clear their wish to convert facilities once meant for tobacco to service their new crop. A petition of 1796 from Camden, South Carolina, spelled out the need to "establish the Credit and Reputation of [cotton] in foreign Markets" and asked for a cotton inspection law "similar to that for the Inspection of Tobacco." Such a law would, the subscribers claimed, assist "Numbers of our poor fellow Citizens." Another petition, this from the South Carolina Cotton Company, stated that cotton merchants and planters needed inspection facilities in Charleston and requested permission to rent for that purpose buildings still used as tobacco warehouses. The company asserted that cotton had "in a great measure superseded Tobacco as an article of extensive cultivation" by the early nineteenth century. Inspection laws next elaborated on the special needs of cotton. They discouraged inventive but fraudulent practices (like mixing grades of cotton to get a better overall price or weighing down the bales with stones or a soaking-wet core of fiber) by requiring cultivators to mark their bales with their name and the district of origin. Careless or deceptive producers could then be tracked down. A clean bale of cotton would encourage, wrote some South Carolina petitioners in 1807, "that Harmony, Confidence, and Good-will which ought to exist . . . amongst Planters and Merchants."[40]

Individuals' innovatory efforts as well as prudent legislation improved the Lower South's cotton. Some cultivators imported seed of cottons grown in Louisiana and Mexico. A member of the Chesnut family who kept a plantation book in the 1810s recorded experiments with "Orleans" cotton that he planted

square bales, see the petition from Chatham County of November 1802, Wayne-Stites-Anderson Papers, folder 44, GHS.

40. John J. Winberry, "Reputation of Carolina Indigo," *SCHM*, LXXX (1979), 242–248; Petitions to General Assembly, 1796, no. 92, n.d., no. 1536, 1807, no. 79, SCDAH.

on "new Land" in 1811 and "on the river" in 1814, to see which soil suited it best. Thomas Carr planted Mexican cotton on his Georgia estate in 1812.[41] Like sea island planter Richard Leake, some planters conducted elaborate experiments. South Carolinian Peter Gaillard used his plantation, the Rocks, in Ninety Six District, as a large open-air laboratory during the 1800s. He grew different proportions of green- and black-seed cotton and tried to determine whether it was better to plant cotton between old beds in the fields or directly on them. He varied the time of first sowing, then compared the different amounts made per acre, the height of the plants, and the date of their first blossoming. He also varied the distance between rows of cotton (eighteen inches turned out to be optimal) and the distance between individual stalks in each row (from one-and-one-half to two-and-one-half inches), an early and successful experiment with thinning. Gaillard later tested Mexican cotton but, somewhat surprisingly, given the variety's later success in the South, declared it inferior to his own.[42] Cultivators early on improved soils to increase yield; manuring was not first intended, it seems, as a way of restoring fertility to worn land. John Palmer reported how he penned cattle on his cotton land in the early 1800s, claiming this tactic increased his crop fourfold. After ginning, Palmer saved cottonseed to manure his cornfields the next spring.[43]

Because of these experiments, cotton yields increased in the early 1800s before leveling off. Colonial production had set a fairly low baseline, one rather easy to improve on. In 1737, Georgia colonist Patrick Houston had raised 150 pounds of cotton per acre, which, when cleaned, amounted to about 40 pounds per acre. Yields increased by four or five times after the Revolution.

41. Entries for April 1811, April 1814, plantation book, series 12-35-4, Chesnut-Miller-Manning Papers, SCHS; entry for Apr. 4, 1812, Thomas Carr's diary, 1812–1813, Carr Collection, box 5, folder 45, UGA. On experiments with Mexican cottons around Natchez in the 1810s and 1820s, cf. John Hebron Moore, "Cotton Breeding in the Old South," *AH*, XXX (1956), 95–104.

42. For Gaillard's experiments: with green- and black-seed: see entries for Mar. 27, Apr. 7, 1807, April, June 1, 1808 (on the last date, Gaillard "patched over" areas of black-seed cotton with green-seed), Peter Gaillard's planting book (manuscript), Gaillard Family Papers, series 11-149, SCHS. On beds: Apr. 9, 1807. On time of sowing: Apr. 4, 1808, and records for 1799–1809 (pp. 35–36). On 1813 experiment with distance between rows: p. 52. On experiments with "thick and thin cotton": pp. 58, 74. On Mexican cotton: entry from 1817, p. 67.

43. John Palmer to David Ramsay, Dec. 3, 1808, David Ramsay Correspondence, series 51-132, SCHS (microfilm from collections in the Charleston Library Society).

David Ramsay estimated that a planter could get 150 pounds of clean sea island cotton per acre and 200 for green-seed cotton; John Lambert made similar estimates. In South Carolina, A. R. Lawton made about 573 pounds per acre (a combination of long- and short-staple cottons) in 1812, and 579 pounds in 1814; after ginning, these yields were about 150 pounds. James Guignard was making closer to 200 clean pounds per acre in the early 1800s, however, and Peter Gaillard made yields from 100 to 160 pounds per acre between 1799 and 1811.[44]

By the end of the first two decades of the nineteenth century, the median amount settled out to about 140 clean pounds per acre. At the same time, the average amount each slave made was slightly more than 600 pounds, a crop produced from about four acres. In productivity per slave, harvesting, rather than cultivation, seemed to be the determinant: a slave could plant twice as much cotton as he or she could pick. Some workers did slightly increase the amount of cotton they could pick, although the bottom level for output of picking per day did not appreciably improve. Daniel Turner pointed out that, whereas a slave picked 50–60 pounds a day in 1805, a slave could harvest 50–80 pounds in 1807. Nathaniel Marion claimed in 1811 that a worker could pick 60–90 pounds per day, but, in the same year, slaves at Curry Hill Plantation in Georgia picked an average of only 50 pounds per day. No techniques improved human unwillingness to speed up labor coerced from them. Whites had to rely on the enhanced output of only some of their laborers to increase their yield. Planters' problem of fixed yields would partly be solved in the 1820s, when they developed strains of cotton from breeding green-seed with Mexican and Louisiana cottons. These hybrids had larger bolls, which made it easier to pick out the fibers; they also had a longer staple and were more resistant to rot.[45] In the meantime, planters would, like lowcountry rice growers, have to rethink methods of managing and negotiating with slaves to increase productivity.

The expansion of cotton cultivation was nevertheless impressive even in the years before 1815. Creation of a commercial infrastructure, adaptation of older

---

44. P. Houston to ———, Nov. 12, 1737, Clerk of Penicuik Muniments, bundle 5360, item 4, GD.18, SRO; Ramsay, *History of S.-C.*, II, 215; Lambert, *Travels*, III, 69; crop lists for 1812, 1814, diary, A. R. Lawton Papers, SHC; Whartenby, *Cotton*, tables 13, 14.

45. Whartenby, *Cotton*, 102–105, tables 13, 14; Richard K. Murdoch, ed., "Letters and Papers of Dr. Daniel Turner: A Rhode Islander in South Georgia," *GHQ*, LIII (1969), 497, LIV (1970), 247; Nathaniel Marion to W. Johnston, Oct. 6, 1811, William Johnston Papers, box 1, folder 13, SCL; entry for Sept. 21, 1811, Josiah Everett daybook, 1808–20, Curry Hill Plantation Records, microfilm 2-2200-C, GDAH.

cultivation techniques, and improvement of agricultural yields all translated into good fortune for settlers. In one case, that of Virginian Samuel Edward Butler, individual rise in fortune perfectly mirrored the region's transfer of attention to cotton, its crucial shift from Upper South to Lower South forms of agriculture. In 1787, Butler produced about fifteen or sixteen hogsheads of tobacco on his new Georgia lands; at his death, his estate included two hundred pounds of cotton (as well as two looms and six spinning wheels to process some of this fiber), but not a trace of tobacco. Transplanted Virginian Wade Hampton I had what was probably the most dramatic success story—he cleared seventy-five thousand dollars on his first South Carolina cotton crop in 1799. Profits from cotton built wealth for its cultivators; their prosperity was a somewhat paler copy of the lowcountry's florid riches. During the first boom, from 1790 to 1815, levels of mean value for inventoried inland estates tripled in South Carolina and doubled in Georgia (see Table 11). More tellingly, on these estates the proportion of total mean value represented by slaves also increased, from 40 percent to 70 percent in South Carolina's midlands, from 58 to 61 percent along the Savannah River, and from 61 to 67 percent in Georgia's upcountry (see Table 12). Estate value composed of slaves declined only in South Carolina's upcountry, a reflection, possibly, of the difficulties with transport that hindered development of this westernmost area of the Lower South.[46] Elsewhere, the transition from frontier to Cotton South was over.

But not all white newcomers fared equally well within the region that replaced the frontier. Failure underscored the duality of prosperity and poverty within the upcountry; while a land of better opportunity for whites than older states, it was still possible to sink low there—and ill fortune might rankle more in an area reputed to be so full of promise. On one gloomy day in 1802, a Connecticut emigrant in Georgia, Reuben King, bitterly regretted his move to the newer state: "I am now all most Discouraged I am without Money without Credit and Nothing to Sell." King's position would improve, but many others never pulled themselves out of a slump.[47] Settlers who feared failure were on

46. Herndon, ed., "Samuel Edward Butler," *GHQ*, LII (1968), 209. On Hampton, see Ford, *Origins of Southern Radicalism*, 8. This decline of estate values might simply indicate that a larger (and poorer) proportion of the population was being inventoried, instead of a small number of wealthholders who had made the upcountry appear richer than it was.

47. Virginia Steele Wood and Ralph Van Wood, eds., "The Reuben King Journal, 1800–1806," *GHQ*, L (1966), 327.

TABLE 11. *Value of Inland Estates, 1780–1815*

	Mean Value (in Dollars)			
	1780s	1790s	1800s	1810s
South Carolina				
Midlands	4,875	1,009	1,548	3,621
Upcountry	3,463	786	1,234	2,296
Georgia				
Savannah River	—	1,041	2,481	2,839
Upcountry	—	1,076	2,047	2,087

Sources: Estate Inventories, SCDAH, GDAH.

guard against anything that gave a competitive advantage to any particular individual or group and might thereby upset the Herrenvolk promises of the recently created geography of opportunity.

✌ The Gin

In New Haven, there is a tomb (modeled on that of one of the Scipios in Rome) bearing the unequivocal inscription: "ELI WHITNEY. The inventor of the Cotton Gin." This lapidary claim, though widely accepted by historians, was energetically debated by Whitney's contemporaries and even questioned, as the inventor himself admitted, by his own friends.[48] Whitney's patented gin

48. Denison Olmsted, *Memoir of Eli Whitney, Esq.* (New Haven, Conn., 1846), 75–76. The model for the tomb was actually the sarcophagus of Lucius Cornelius Scipio Barbatus (consul 298 B.C.E.) discovered in Rome in 1780 and widely copied—sometimes in miniature as an ornament to grace the mantelpieces of consumers with republican sentiments. See Frances Haskell and Nicholas Penny, *Taste and the Antique: The Lure of Classical Sculpture, 1500–1900* (New Haven, Conn., 1981), 48. On the similarity of Whitney's tomb to Scipio's, compare the illustration in Olmsted, *Whitney Memoir,* 76, with Guntram Koch and Hellmut Sichtermann, *Römische Sarkophage* (Munich, 1982), plate 2.

TABLE 12. *Estate Value Held in Slaves, 1780–1815*

	Mean Value in Slaves			
	1780s	1790s	1800s	1810s
South Carolina				
Midlands	70.5%	40.4%	64.6%	70.3%
Upcountry	72.3	46.2	54.8	24.5
Georgia				
Savannah River	—	57.7	63.5	61.0
Upcountry	—	61.4	65.2	67.1

Sources: Estate Inventories, SCDAH, GDAH.

represented a curb on settlers' commercial ambition. They responded by claiming to see within his patent the old threat of monopoly: government preference, that is, for the few rather than for the public good. Quarrels over the gin questioned the state intervention in economic affairs that had characterized earlier efforts to generate services like tobacco inspection, restating the upcountry's contradictory position over the relation between politics and the economy. While welcoming mechanical invention and supporting monetary compensation of inventors, whites in the upcountry wanted to make sure that every useful development was fully available to them—not locked behind bars of monopoly and politicized preference. Whitney's gin reanimated the kind of struggle seen over land speculation, this time expressed in mechanical as well as financial terms.

The Lower South's concern over invention and over establishing legal right to new devices followed mainstream developments in the nation. Citizens of the early Republic realized that they lived in an age of mechanical invention and usually thought this a beneficial trend. They would state that, in Enlightenment terms, America's glory was emerging in an era of pervasive secular progress. Mechanics like John Fitch, Benjamin Latrobe, and Oliver Evans were heirs of Benjamin Franklin, lauded for contributing to an *American* culture of technology. But unlike Franklin, who grandly relinquished rights to his inventions and refused monetary compensation (endowing posterity with lightning rods and freestanding stoves), later inventors wanted to profit from their designs. This ambition meant that their efforts thrived in a lively, reckless atmosphere of dubious entrepreneurship and multiple claims to similar objects. The word "artifice," accordingly, came to indicate both useful invention and a mixture of greed and guile, just as "project" had conveyed negative and positive implications. As both Britain and America struggled to establish competing factories, development of technology operated in the world of international espionage. All in all, the machine's promises to the Republic were balanced by threats.[49]

To complicate matters, Americans were busy redefining the nature of property; this gray area would pose a central problem for assigning rights to new devices. Though the Constitution (Article I, Section 8) protected intellectual property in both mechanical and literary forms, property in ideas was still a vague concept. Republican legislators found it easier to define objects and even people as property than they did concepts, even if ideas were objectified in blueprints, manuscripts, or models. Uncertainty over the character of invention, and over the material rewards it might bring, preoccupied public officials. Citizens themselves, healthy skeptics of promoters who made exaggerated claims for potions and gadgets, were also suspicious of efforts to patent devices (or texts) that simply modified the work of others. Thomas Jefferson, casting his eye over a purportedly new threshing machine, insisted that an "invention" should differ from "a bringing together two things in full use before." Jefferson likewise grumbled over having to pay engineer Oliver Evans for his "rights" to an automated flour mill that seemed only to coordinate elements developed by others. Even in cases of machines truly invented or significantly modified, mechanics risked lawsuits if they claimed a patentable right. Invasive litigants harassed Oliver Evans too many times. Tired of defending his steam engine and milling machinery against rivals, Evans decided against further legal risk. He burned all his papers for new or disputed designs in 1809, thereafter manufacturing his existing designs rather than inventing new ones.[50]

49. See Brooke Hindle, *Emulation and Invention* (New York, 1981); Constance McL. Green, *Eli Whitney and the Birth of American Technology* (Boston, 1956), 13–14; John F. Kasson, *Civilizing the Machine: Technology and Republican Values in America, 1776–1900* (New York, 1976); Leo Marx, *The Machine in the Garden: Technology and the Pastoral Ideal in America* (New York, 1964), esp. 116–144, 145–156.

50. On the disputed nature of patents and copyrights, see Bruce W. Bugbee, *Genesis of American Patent and Copyright Law* (Washington, D.C., 1967), 1, 84–85, 128–129; Morton J. Horwitz, *The Transformation of American Law, 1780–1860* (Cambridge,

The Lower South was not, as yet, removed from this technological pell-mell. Colonial South Carolina was more vigorous in patenting mechanisms than any of the other colonies, partly because it needed to develop better rice mills. After the Revolution, the state established a law protecting intellectual property before any other state or even the national government did so. Lower South planters who strolled through factories admired them and wanted to bring their benefits home. Continuing interest in milling, threshing, and sugar processing also restated the Lower South's fascination with machinery and steam power. The culture of mechanical invention in the region was best characterized by William Longstreet, artisan, entrepreneur, and father of southwestern humorist Augustus Baldwin Longstreet. Longstreet tried building anything and everything, including a double-acting steam engine that used cold water to condense the steam and cool the pistons, steam-powered cotton gins and gristmills, and, in 1807, a steamboat that made a celebrated (if rather slow) run up the Savannah, clocking five miles per hour.[51]

Despite regional achievements in mechanical problems, upcountry planters were still wringing their hands over the problem of getting the seeds out of their cotton. Short-staple cotton, better suited to inland regions than sea island cotton, was much more difficult to clean. Cultivators tried to breed a smooth-seeded cotton that could grow inland. They ended up with some short-staple varieties that had smooth seeds, but even these strains languished in the upcountry. Cultivators were stuck with their sticky-seeded crop. They knew of two devices that could clean cotton, though both had their drawbacks. Ameri-

---

Mass., 1977), 122–124; Thomas Jefferson to Edward Rutledge, Dec. 27, 1790, Mrs. Francis D. Stewart Collection, SHC. For a discussion of Jefferson's antipathy to patents (including Evans's), see Hugo A. Meier, "Thomas Jefferson and a Democratic Technology," in Carroll W. Pursell, Jr., ed., *Technology in America: A History of Individuals and Ideas* (Cambridge, Mass., 1981), 28–30. On Evans himself, see Pursell, *Early Stationary Steam Engines in America: A Study in the Migration of a Technology* (Washington, D.C., 1969), 44–48.

51. Bugbee, *American Patent and Copyright Law*, 75, 92–94; Pursell, *Early Steam Engines*, 23; John Donald Wade, *Augustus Baldwin Longstreet: A Study of the Development of Culture in the South* (Athens, Ga., 1969), 9–11. See the advertisements for Briggs and Longstreet in the *Augusta Chronicle*, Apr. 5, 1788, and in the *City Gazette* (Charleston), Feb. 28, 1788. Longstreet would later advertise a model of a steam engine meant for saw- or gristmills—see *Augusta Chronicle*, Sept. 22, 1792.

cans had cotton gins adapted from East Indian *churkas,* ancient mechanisms that Europeans took with them to the New World. These machines worked by a crank, or treadle, that revolved two parallel cylinders in opposite directions, taking seeds out of cotton fiber fed between them. The cylinders on these roller gins had horizontal grooves that helped remove the seeds, though many seeds were crushed between the rollers and workers had to "mote," or pick out, the particles from the product. Colonists also used the even more primitive East Indian method of bowing cotton. A worker took a wooden bow, plucked the string, then held a hank of cotton near it. The vibrating string caught the fibers and twisted them away from the seeds; the worker stripped the clean cotton off the string and repeated the process. This procedure cleaned cotton more thoroughly than a roller gin but was, for any planter eager to get a crop to market, nerve-rackingly slow.[52]

Local mechanics modified roller gins, both to increase the machines' capacity for long-staple varieties and to adapt them to short-staple cotton. In 1788 Carolinian John Hart applied for a patent on his "Machine for the ginning of Cotton," not a new design, probably, but a modified churka. William Longstreet worked to improve gins throughout the 1790s and developed a steam-powered roller gin in 1792. Somehow, his gins kept catching fire (one machine perilously ignited in a shop filled with flammable cotton bales), and a singed and discouraged Longstreet eventually turned his talents to applying steam to other machines. His roller gin nonetheless remained widely used among sea island planters.[53] Joseph Eve, an inventor who lived both in North America and in the West Indies, developed a wind-operated gin in Nassau in the 1790s that cleaned cotton faster—up to 360 pounds a day. Eager to gain a more powerful machine, sea island and other cotton planters rushed to sponsor Eve's design. Thomas Spalding of Sapelo Island won the coveted role of Eve's patron, but others, including Pierce Butler, had also encouraged "the famous

52. On crossbreeding, see Green, *Eli Whitney,* 17. On bowing, see U. Scott (Bombay) to Joseph Banks, Jan. 7, 1790, fol. 2, Add. 33,979, III, Joseph Banks Correspondence, BL; Abraham Rees, *The Cyclopedia; or, Universal Dictionary of Arts, Sciences, and Literature,* 1st Am. ed., rev. (Philadelphia, [1810–24]), s.v. "Cotton" (referring to bowing in Georgia). On churkas in the New World, see Daniel H. Thomas, "Pre-Whitney Cotton Gins in French Louisiana," *Jour. So. Hist.,* XXXI (1965), 136.

53. Petitions to the General Assembly, 1788, no. 22, SCDAH; Pursell, *Early Steam Engines,* 23. On the fire in Longstreet's shop, see *Augusta Chronicle,* Dec. 26, 1801.

Ginn Maker" to come to the United States. Butler also heard, however, of a "young Man at Mrs. Greene's in Georgia, who has made a Cotton Ginn," one that would make nearly as much trouble as it did money.[54]

The young man in question, Eli Whitney, followed the post-Revolutionary stream of northerners who headed south looking for fortune. Indeed, his biography is useful in reiterating key characteristics of the north-south migration—especially Yankee fascination with the Lower South's plantation wealth and willingness to participate in a slave-driven economy. The twin themes of mechanical ingenuity and threat of penury drove Whitney throughout his life; when he precociously constructed a playable fiddle at the age of twelve, his father, a struggling farmer, could only gloomily respond, "I fear Eli will have to take his portion in fiddles." After graduating from Yale, Whitney went south as a tutor (New England was already chockablock with would-be tutors) and ended up at Mulberry Grove plantation in Georgia in 1792. New Englander Major General Nathanael Greene had been awarded Mulberry Grove—a confiscated loyalist estate named for earlier experiments with silk—in 1785 for his services within the Continental army and in defense of Georgia. Greene had died in spring of 1786, leaving his widow, Catherine, with a partially working rice plantation and the debts incurred to start repairs on it. Catherine Greene was assisted by Phineas Miller, native of Connecticut and yet another Yale graduate who had earlier acted as the Greene children's tutor. Greene was evidently the hub of a newly arrived community of New Englanders; Miller and Whitney were only two of several Yankees she guided there.[55]

Like many a new arrival to the Lower South, Whitney had a rough welcome. When he entered Mulberry Grove, he put the estate into quarantine because he had just been inoculated against smallpox. Catherine Greene sealed off the

54. Drayton, *View of S.-C.*, 133; Michael Craton, *A History of the Bahamas* (London, 1962), 191; Gail Saunders, *Bahamian Loyalists and Their Slaves* (London, 1983), 39; E. Merton Coulter, *Thomas Spalding of Sapelo* (Baton Rouge, La., 1940), 64. The quotation is in Pierce Butler to Nathaniel Hall, Sept. 16, 1793 (see also Pierce Butler to Eve, Mar. 31, 1794), Pierce Butler Letterbook, SCL.

55. On Whitney's youth, see Mirsky and Nevins, *World of Eli Whitney*, 32–45; Green, *Eli Whitney*, 20–39; quotation from Olmsted, *Memoir of Whitney*, 7. On his fortunes in the South, see Works Projects Administration, "Mulberry Grove from the Revolution to the Present Time," *GHQ*, XXIII (1939), 315–317, 321; Green, *Eli Whitney*, 40–43; Mirsky and Nevins, *World of Eli Whitney*, 53. Catherine Greene befriended, for example, Rhode Islander Daniel Turner. See Murdoch, ed., "Dr. Daniel Turner," *GHQ*, LIII (1969), 491.

plantation to prevent contagion from spreading and used the opportunity to inoculate her slaves. No sooner did Whitney recover from inoculation than he caught malaria; he continued to suffer relapses even years later in New England. (As residents warned, strangers had to be hardy to settle among them.) Thus the young inventor acclimated to the region, both to its physical hazards and peculiar customs. Describing his initial disorientation and discomfiture, Whitney wrote, "I find my self in a new natural world and as for the moral world I believe it does not extend so far South—Most of the productions of nature here are entirely new to me."[56]

All the more remarkable, therefore, that within a short period Whitney developed an improved gin for the new, to him, production of cotton. He ended planters' dilemma by adding three features to a roller gin: wire teeth on one roller to tear the seeds out of the fiber, a revolving brush on the other roller to sweep the cotton out of the teeth, and a slotted guard along the length of the rollers to sift out the loosened seeds. An ingenious design, it immediately solved the problem at hand. Scholars have found no ready source of inspiration. Whitney was evasive in his explanation of how he had come up with this solution. He breezily declared to his father that he had "involuntarily happened to be thinking on the subject and struck out a plan of a Machine" all at once. But truth is often duller than recollection. The row of wire teeth in Whitney's original model hinted at his probable prototype: carding tools, which used wire teeth embedded in cards to pull hanks of raw fiber into smooth tufts ready for spinning. Cards were domestic items used by women; Whitney worked with many such items. He used a hearth brush as well as some birdcage wire one of the Greene children had left to "hang in the parlour" in his original gin and had already designed a needlework frame for Catherine Greene.[57] Like so much of the adaptation that helped expand upcountry agriculture, Whitney's gin drew on existing devices and expertise.

Cobbling together his model from various materials, Whitney had an operable gin in early 1793. Phineas Miller, now married to Catherine Greene,

56. Olmsted, *Memoir of Whitney*, 12; Mirsky and Nevins, *World of Eli Whitney*, 47. Quotation from Whitney to Josiah Stebbins, Nov. 1, 1792, folder 1, Whitney Papers, Yale.

57. M. B. Hammond, ed., "Correspondence of Eli Whitney relative to the Invention of the Cotton Gin," *AHR*, III (1897–1898), 91–92 (on the design), 99 (first quotation), 123 (second quotation); Thomas, "Pre-Whitney Cotton Gins," *Jour. So. Hist.*, XXI (1965), 136; Green, *Eli Whitney*, 45, 47–48 (design and domestic materials).

agreed to bankroll a ginning company for Whitney, splitting the profits evenly as partners; he grandly summed up the arrangement to Whitney as a fusion of "your genius and my patronage." Whitney had already applied for a federal patent, one granted in March 1794. Armed with what they believed was legal protection for their device, the partners began making and operating toll gins. They offered to process short-staple cotton by toll, returning one pound of clean fibers for every five pounds of seed cotton. By 1796, Miller and Whitney had five gins at Mulberry Grove, ten in Augusta, ten at three other Georgia sites, and two in South Carolina. Some of these machines were large enough to be powered by water or livestock.[58] Theirs was an ambitious scheme, combining invention, manufacture, and large-scale operation of an important device under the control of one corporation.

Had Whitney merely held a franchise for manufacturing gins that could have been used by others (like Oliver Evans's concessionary scheme), he might have made a good deal of money, but his company's exclusive operation of all gins and its high rates elicited resentment. Miller and Whitney received the value of forty cents of every dollar's worth of ginned cotton; other toll machines, like mills, charged only about ten cents. Resentful planters had to pay for a Whitney gin or resort to slower methods of cleaning cotton. Some took a third route: appropriating the newly patented design. Whitney claimed his first model was stolen from a shed, and pirated versions began to pop up in the countryside. The inventor decided to fight the plagiarists in court.[59]

The resulting legal controversy hinged on the distinction between true innovation and mere improvement. Speaking of laborsaving devices in general, South Carolinian Thomas Lowndes argued, like Jefferson, that there was a difference between "an invention in its nature entire and compleat, and one which only went to improve a principle already known," which Whitney's gin seemed to have done. The two partners issued "A CAUTION" in the *Georgia Gazette* in early 1795, insisting that their patent depended on the feature of metal teeth, a design "perfectly different from any method heretofore practised for ginning cotton." Renegade gin makers countered that the design simply improved on the old roller gin; many further argued that their own machines

---

58. Green, *Eli Whitney,* 52, 78 (quotation); W.P.A., "Mulberry Grove," *GHQ,* XXIII (1939), 323; *Georgia Gazette,* advertisement of Mar. 6, 1794; *Augusta Chronicle,* advertisement for Mar. 15, 1794. Whitney described a horse-run gin in Whitney to Thomas Jefferson, Nov. 24, 1793, Whitney Papers, Yale.

59. Green, *Eli Whitney,* 66–67, 73, 74–76.

were comparable adaptations of this same prototype. Most pirated models used serrated metal plates or saws instead of wire teeth. Makers of these gins claimed that the design was significantly different from Whitney's wire-teeth model and did not constitute a patent infringement. Whitney denounced this line of reasoning, claiming intellectual property in the idea of fixing any kind of metal point to a gin and stating that a saw was only "a more expeditious mode of attaching the tooth to the cylinder." He had himself begun to make gins with metal saws, conceding that, though finer wire teeth cleaned cotton better, they tended to break or bend. His adoption of saws nevertheless meant he was using a development not specified in his patent.[60]

Continual poaching eroded Whitney's claim even as the legal battle went on. As early as 1795, artisans brazenly advertised in newspapers that they were handy with "cotton and other machinery," an open invitation for planters to employ them to make or modify cotton gins.[61] By 1797, Miller and Whitney came to the awful realization that most of these new gins were superior to their own. Miller admitted that "the common country made Gin" would "clean cotton much faster than ours": five hundred pounds versus two hundred pounds. Two years later, Miller wrote Whitney that "the people of the back country almost uniformly prefer making their own gins to using ours." He was able to list known trespassers by their names and counties of residence. Even more disheartening, Miller reported, "it seems to be a general opinion among our best friends that the machines which are made by the Country blacksmiths clean the cotton at least as well, and clean it in much larger quantity than ours." Miller concluded that because of these "surreptitious Gins" the partnership could not profit from commercial ginning.[62]

Rumors next spread that the Whitney gin snapped the staple of raw cotton, making it difficult to spin and of little worth to textile manufacturers. This

---

60. Thomas Lowndes to "General Read," June 19, 1809, Thomas and William Lowndes Papers, Duke; Green, *Eli Whitney*, 73; *Georgia Gazette*, May 7, 1795; Gray, *Agriculture in the Southern U.S.*, II, 681. On Whitney's best-known competitors, see Mirsky and Nevins, *World of Eli Whitney*, 113; Hammond, ed., "Correspondence of Eli Whitney," *AHR*, III (1897–1898), 92–98. On Whitney's legal case and his switch from wire to saws, see Olmsted, *Memoir of Whitney*, 41–43 (quotation on 41).

61. Advertisement of Francis Mercier, *Augusta Chronicle*, Sept. 12, 1795. On the spread of saw gins, see Gray, *Agriculture in the Southern U.S.*, II, 681.

62. Miller to Whitney, Jan. 19, Apr. 29, 1799, Whitney Papers, Yale; Miller to Seaborn Jones, Sr., Aug. 15, 1799, Seaborn Jones, Sr., Papers, GHS.

belief arose because planters were only beginning to distinguish among their several varieties of long- and short-staple cottons; they might have tried ginning long-staple cotton on saw- or wire-gins, tearing it into smaller and less salable pieces. Encouraged by these temporary difficulties, gin makers advertised roller gins that would, as entrepreneur Robert Watkins claimed in 1796, clean cotton "without injuring the staple."[63] Joseph Eve and William Longstreet also capitalized on the confusion between long- and short-staple cottons. Two prominent planters endorsed Eve's gin with the rather confusing statement that it was a roller gin capable of cleaning green-seed cotton. They also emphasized that Eve had created his gin in the Bahamas before Whitney had arrived in Georgia and in innocence of any mechanical developments on the continent. William Longstreet, who had already operated a successful business for roller gins, similarly dismissed accusations of patent infringement. Longstreet expressed weariness over the whole dispute when, in 1797, he advertised more of his gins and promised that this was "the last time that I will pester the good people of Georgia upon the old subject of Cotton Ginning."[64] To remove the stigma from their gin, Miller and Whitney arranged in 1795 for three New England factory owners to give affidavits that their gin, properly used, would cause no damage to the staple of cotton, and Whitney wanted to go to England to demonstrate his gin to skeptical manufacturers there.[65]

But trouble was closing in on all sides. Miller and Whitney began to bicker over who was doing most (or least) for the partnership. The company's capital was even unsteadier than its partners' relations. Miller warned Whitney, who was courting some wary backers, to "use great care to avoid giving an idea that we are in a *desperate situation,* to induce us to borrow money," even though the situation *was* desperate. Miller and Whitney maintained that everyone else reaped the benefits of the gins while "we get but a song for it in comparison with the worth of the thing." Determined to make some sort of profit, the partners agreed in 1799 to sell the franchise for manufacturing the gin and to

63. Green, *Eli Whitney,* 73–74. See advertisements for Watkins, *Augusta Chronicle,* July 16, 1796. See also the similar claims made by John Currie, *Augusta Chronicle,* Dec. 24, 1796, and Obadiah Crawford, *Columbian Centinel* (Augusta), Jan. 7, 1809.

64. Notices of Spalding and Waldburger, *Georgia Gazette,* Apr. 28, 1796; Longstreet's advertisement in the *Augusta Chronicle,* July 29, 1797 (supplement). See also the article on "black seed cotton" and roller gins, *Carolina Gazette,* Sept. 12, 1799.

65. Green, *Eli Whitney,* 77–78; Olmsted, *Memoir of Whitney,* 22–24. See the affidavits, *Georgia Gazette,* Nov. 26, 1795.

lease out existing gins.[66] This was, nevertheless, too belated a concession to upcountry residents who were already content to make their own gins.

The situation was never truly resolved. Phineas Miller died in 1803 before any state court granted legal patent on the gin. (Such were the Millers' financial straits that in 1801 they sold Mulberry Grove for much less than its actual value.) The first undisputed title to Whitney's gin came from South Carolina in 1802, but the state legislature immediately revoked the patent and would not regrant it until 1804. Georgia legislators finally supported Whitney's claim in 1806, but the federal patent expired the next year and was not renewed. While a good many native and transplanted southerners made fortunes on the new crop of short-staple cotton, Miller and Whitney were among the unfortunates who lost money on it—they could not even cover their court fees. Whitney bitterly recalled standing on the steps of a Georgia courthouse, where he "distinctly" heard "the rattling of the wheels" of several pirate gins in a building "within fifty yards," but was unable to convince the court that such gins violated the United States patent he held.[67] After Miller died, Whitney transferred his mechanical expertise to a more successful scheme: mass-produced firearms with interchangeable parts. He made a final, fruitless appeal to Congress for a renewal of the patent on his gin in 1812 and never got over his disappointment at the lack of recognition for his machine. Hence his defiant tomb.[68]

66. Hammond, ed., "Correspondence of Eli Whitney," *AHR*, III (1897–1898), 110–112; Green, *Eli Whitney*, 70–71 (first quotation), 82; Whitney to Josiah Stebbins, Dec. 20, 1801, Whitney Papers, Yale (second quotation).

67. W.P.A., "Mulberry Grove," *GHQ*, XXIII (1939), 324; Green, *Eli Whitney*, 79–93 (84–91 on the case in South Carolina and Georgia); Gray, *Agriculture in the Southern U.S.*, II, 681; Whitney to Robert Fulton, Mar. 31, 1811, Whitney Papers, Yale (quotation). There may have been other lawsuits surrounding the disputes over the patent. William Forbes Taylor petitioned for a refund from the state of South Carolina in 1802, testifying that he had paid Miller and Whitney for a "general licence" to use their machine—as approved by the state—then the state taxed the machine, and Taylor held South Carolina liable for his earlier payments for the gin. See Petitions to the General Assembly, 1802, no. 120, SCDAH.

68. See Green, *Eli Whitney*, chaps. 5–8, on Whitney's later career. Whitney evidently learned a trick or two from his canny rivals in the Lower South. To get a federal contract for his firearms, he made a celebrated demonstration (before President John Adams and President-elect Thomas Jefferson) of how his weapons were constructed of interchangeable parts. It seems that the performance was staged: the pieces he used

Though the controversy over the cotton gin had partly to do with an honest disagreement over the design itself, it was imbued, as well, with the old fear of government-sponsored economic advantage. Whitney was well aware that the ambivalent political economy of the region (and of the age) helped cast doubt on his claims. Observing the suspicion with which many contemporaries regarded financial speculation, Whitney asserted that, nevertheless, "He who speculates upon the markets, and takes advantage of the necessities of others . . . is called 'a man of enterprise.' " In contrast, "the pursuit of wealth by means of new inventions, is a very precarious and uncertain one;—a lottery where there are many thousand blanks to one prize."[69]

This was the case because the authorities were reluctant to defend monopolies that seemed to benefit individuals more than the citizenry at large, even if a person like an inventor did seem to have a prior claim on a certain property. Those who held these views offered eclectic arguments based on both traditional and modern economies. In classical republican terms, the public good outweighed the individual, and the power of the state should never support the latter over the former. For people interested in modern economic development, monopolies seemed to restrict the possible gains of open access to improvements: economic incentive was not a proper or sufficient reward for inventions that had larger economic benefits. Both views were apparent when Georgia resident James Jones concluded "that exclusive rights to any discovery in husbandry or any of the implements attending it, are injurious," and he indicated a submerged political dimension by claiming that "most of the Republicans whom I have had the opportunity of conversing with" agreed with this antimonopolistic contention. A committee in the South Carolina legislature similarly urged revocation of the state's patent on Whitney's gin, reasoning that "monopolies are at all times odious, particularly in free governments." Confirming suspicions that Miller and Whitney represented all that was insidious in government support of private ventures, their company's finances became entangled with those of the Yazoo Company. Miller and one of Whitney's brothers-in-law both invested in Georgia land; Miller's name was

---

were carefully filed to fit each other because they were not interchangeable at the point of manufacture. Robert S. Woodbury, "The Legend of Eli Whitney and Interchangeable Parts," *Technology and Culture,* I (1960), 235–253.

69. Cited in Olmsted, *Memoir of Whitney,* 56, 57.

listed among the culprits believed to have struck the tainted bargain with Georgia legislators.[70]

To be sure, the language of corruption was probably, in part, a screen for other, self-interested ambitions. Farmers who needed an easier way to clean cotton could use thundering rhetoric to get what they wanted. But placing the whole controversy in these terms still shows the power of this language to express anxiety over the way a commercial economy took shape in the up-country. Settlers had first worried that the new western lands were wasted when in the hands of Indians and Indian traders; they later insisted that the West would prosper more if its assets were not accumulated in too few hands.

&a Slavery

Controversy over the cotton gin evidenced reluctance on the part of upcountry settlers to accept all consequences of a modern economic system, including preferential distribution of economic or financial tools like intellectual property. They had parallel apprehensions over their slaves. Settlers feared that slaves, like Indians and frontiersmen before them, might erode the stable market structures recently transplanted to the upcountry. These were far from the newfound doubts over the morality of human bondage uttered by low-country planters. Unlike their lowcountry counterparts, upcountry blacks were still the minority, and whites were disinclined to view them with any sympathy, even the self-serving variety found among rice planters. Again it is clear how the upcountry was passing through phases pioneered by coastal South Carolinians in the early 1700s. The younger region was moving from a frontier economy where workers were loosely supervised to a settled economy in which nervous would-be planters kept tight control over new and hostile slaves. Whites were thus less willing to negotiate with and give humane treatment to their slaves, regarding them instead as potential rebels who could not be appeased by the kind of concessions tidal planters made after the Revolution.

Not that apprehension over the stability of slavery deterred white settlers

70. James Jones to Edward Telfair, Oct. 29, 179[?], Edward Telfair Papers, box 4, folder 3, Duke; Olmsted, *Memoir of Whitney*, 32 (second quotation); Green, *Eli Whitney*, 70–71 (Yazoo).

from installing the institution in the first place. The Lower South was the last section of the original colonies to absorb direct imports from Africa and last, at an awkwardly late historical moment, to make sustained arguments for the economic benefits of the transatlantic traffic in humans. Even more than the Malcontents' earlier and better-known insistence on owning slaves, the upcountry's demand for slaves was a bald statement of the greater region's increasing reliance on human bondage and its decreasing desire to restrict the institution to particular environments. Lowcountry claims that only a semi-tropical climate and labor-intensive crop made slavery necessary could not explain why slaves became more and more common in the upcountry. Instead, an argument for slavery based on how it enriched all whites (actually or potentially) was developed. All whites had to be granted access to workers who could be bought and sold, who were regarded as distinct and inferior members of a westward-moving nation.

But access to African slaves remained, for a time, a sore point in relations between upcountry and lowcountry. Coastal planters asserted, yet again, their reluctance to extend slavery inland. This fear appeared in David Ramsay's praise for cotton's purported ability to turn idleness to industry. Ramsay exulted that cotton gave the "poor" in the upcountry the "means of acquiring property without the degradation of working with slaves." Here was a contrasting set of assumptions: lowcountry residents assumed, even as late as the transition to cotton, that the new area would not need widespread slavery; upcountry settlers wanted slaves even before they grew cotton. Under guidance of the former sentiments (and also because of lowcountry planters' postwar indebtedness), the foreign slave trade into South Carolina was outlawed in 1787 and reopened only from 1803 until 1808, when the Constitution declared the trade closed. Charles Cotesworth Pinckney's threat to defy the proposed constitutional stricture was more an example of lowcountry arrogance than a promise to guarantee Africans to inland settlers. Indeed, lowcountry merchants and planters had supported local legislation to close the state's trade—against the interests of upcountry settlers who still lacked workers.[71] Inland petitioners protested this policy, arguing that they were trying to develop a new region within the Lower South and hinting that their state would gain strength

71. Ramsay, *History of S.-C.*, II, 248. On imports of slaves in and around the era of prohibition, see Candler, comp., *Records of Georgia*, XIX, pt. 2, 204–208, 380. On the controversy over the slave trade, see Patrick S. Brady, "The Slave Trade and Sectionalism in South Carolina, 1787–1808," *Jour. So. Hist.*, XXXVIII (1972), 601–628.

from their efforts. A petition in 1802 from South Carolina's Abbeville District, for instance, requested that the state reopen the slave trade, complaining that the act prohibiting importations was "a direct Bar to the Increase of the Wealth and population of the Upper and Middle Districts." Individuals petitioned to bring in slaves for their own use, swearing that they did not intend to use them for "speculation" but would use them "expressly for the purpose of the cultivation of cotton."[72]

Most slaves taken to the upcountry were Africans; only after the Atlantic trade closed in 1808 would new slaves principally come from the northern states. In the 1790s and early 1800s, South Carolina received an estimated four thousand slaves from the Chesapeake and fifteen thousand from Africa. Georgia imported the same number from the Chesapeake and forty-eight thousand from Africa. After the slave trade ended, Georgians bought an estimated thirteen thousand slaves from the Chesapeake between 1810 and 1820. Again, most of these new slaves went inland. Henry William DeSaussure wrote that Charlestonians believed most African slaves "are sold to the upper Country people," perhaps an overstatement that deflected national criticism of slavery and the slave trade away from the coast. Some upcountry planters did go on hasty buying sprees just before the Atlantic trade closed. In summer 1807, for instance, Richard Singleton bought twenty-three African slaves in Charleston, bringing them up to his plantation by wagon. Because of this rapid phase of importation, distribution of slaves in the interior dramatically increased in a short space of time. In upcountry Georgia, from 1794 to roughly 1810 or 1811, the proportion of slaves who lived on units containing at least twenty slaves increased from 11 to 24 percent.[73]

Like lowcountry critics before them, white settlers realized how slaves were a threat to societal stability. Two possibilities alarmed them: the especial hostility of new slaves, and the difficulty of maintaining slavery in a new region where

---

72. Petitions to General Assembly, 1802, nos. 129, 153, SCDAH. See also 1801, no. 113, in which Thomas Satur Jerman swore to take slaves from Georgia to South Carolina to grow cotton, not to sell.

73. On the estimates of slaves imported and on concentrations of slaves in the upcountry, see Allan Kulikoff, "Uprooted Peoples: Black Migrants in the Age of the American Revolution, 1790–1820," in Ira Berlin and Ronald Hoffman, eds., *Slavery and Freedom in the Age of the American Revolution* (Charlottesville, Va., 1983), 147–152; Henry William DeSaussure to Ezekiel Pickens, Sept. 10, 1805, Henry William DeSaussure Papers, SCL; Isaac Motte Dart to Richard Singleton, June 20, 1807, Singleton Family Papers, box 1, folder 4, SHC.

few other institutional supports yet existed. Daniel Turner, a Rhode Island physician who settled near St. Marys River, Georgia, expressed the first fear when he treated slaves belonging to local cotton planters. He confessed that he found "the business with negroes, particularly the new ones extreemly unpleasant." These Africans were only beginning to make the painful adjustment to a new place and to being owned by aliens—no wonder Turner found unsettling the business of witnessing their fear and anger. Though spared the horrors of the middle passage, even creole slaves had undergone the forcible removal and separation from families which Africans had endured. Thus, Virginian Samuel Edward Butler, for example, who had (as mentioned earlier) cold-bloodedly divided his slaves into three groups when he moved to Georgia: he sold three adolescents to a Georgian to pay for his new land, he sold others to neighbors before he left Virginia, and he took the remainder to his new farm. If the three young men sold on Butler's first trip were lucky, other members of their families were in this final group and not among the lot who remained in the Chesapeake, never to be seen again. Whites only cautiously admitted that transplanted creoles, like native Africans, harbored grief and resentment. Obadiah Jones, who transferred his lowcountry slaves into the interior of Georgia in 1804, described them as "well and quite cheerful," but, as he confessed, "very awkward" with their work. He did not openly consider that his slaves' demeanor (which he interpreted as cheer) might mask a discontent that manifested itself in poorly performed work.[74]

During periods of societal unrest, whites had to admit that their slaves' discontent was a threat. Whenever they heard rumors of slave conspiracy, whites blamed new slaves, especially acculturated creoles from the Chesapeake or West Indies who were familiar enough with white society to spot its weaknesses.[75] Slaves were also a precarious property because they were easily transported booty. During the Regulation, South Carolinians complained that bandits stole their slaves; during sporadic warfare with the Creeks, Georgians accused the Indians and their allies of taking their slaves; during the Revolution, slaveholders resented British regulars and tory partisans who beckoned to slaves beyond American lines. Whites were furious over how slaves *welcomed*

---

74. Murdoch, ed., "Dr. Daniel Turner," *GHQ,* LIII (1969), 485; Herndon, "Samuel Edward Butler," *GHQ,* LII (1968), 117; Obadiah Jones to Joseph Bryan, Jan. 20, 1804, Arnold-Screven Papers, series A, folder 2, SHC.

75. See Philip D. Morgan, "Black Society in the Lowcountry, 1760–1810," in Berlin and Hoffman, eds., *Slavery and Freedom,* 138–140.

being objects of theft, unwillingly recognizing how blacks could find freedom among the renegade groups in and around the hated frontier that moved west and south but did not disappear. Enclaves of banditti in South Carolina had black members who acted as if they were free, Seminole communities in upper Florida incorporated blacks and mustees, and runaway slaves who did not escape with the British during the Revolution still evaded capture after 1783. Determined communities of maroons held onto freedom in pockets along the Savannah River until crushed by state troops in the late 1780s.[76]

Black desertion and the existence of maroon communities raised the possibility that the upcountry could, at any moment, fray along its tentative edges and reenter a frontier existence. A maroon was, planters knew, a menacing antithesis of a slave: he or she was mobile, physically threatening to whites, and cunningly able to extract goods from the fragile commercial economy. Maroons along the Savannah River, for instance, routinely "committed robberies on the neighboring Planters" until it "was found necessary to attempt to dislodge them." In 1787, James Jackson complained of a band of maroons that first camped on Bear Creek, then fled to Harleston Swamp in South Carolina after being besieged by Georgia and South Carolina militias as well as hired Catawba warriors. Claiming that they were still fighting the Americans in the king's name, these maroons also raided neighboring plantations. Jackson, though hardly a sympathetic observer, nevertheless recognized the challenge maroons posed to slavery as a whole. He realized that it was the "freebooty they reap" as well as their "independants" that gave "strong charms of allurement" to other blacks weary of serving whites' commercial ambitions. One of Jackson's correspondents also revealed that white militias were mostly composed of poor men because the nonattendance fine levied on shirking citizens was a "trifle" for rich planters. This, too, was a reason for recruiting Catawbas.[77]

---

76. On South Carolina bandits, see Brown, *South Carolina Regulators*, 18, 31–32; on the Seminoles, see Wright, *Creeks and Seminoles*, 73–100; on maroons, see Jane Landers, "Gracia Real de Santa Teresa de Mose: A Free Black Town in Spanish Colonial Florida," *AHR*, XCV (1990), 9–30; Jerome J. Nadelhaft, *The Disorders of War: The Revolution in South Carolina* (Orono, Maine, 1981), 129; and Morgan, "Black Society," in Berlin and Hoffman, eds., *Slavery and Freedom*, pp. 138–139, n. 90.

77. The first quotation is from the *Charleston Morning Post*, Oct. 26, 1788; the next quotation is from James Jackson to South Carolina Gov. Thomas Pinckney, 1787, and the last is from James Gunn to James Jackson, May 6, 1787, Joseph Vallence Bevan Collection, folder 10, GHS.

Jackson, passionate defender of white property rights during the Yazoo affair, here sketched out an integrated vision of the upcountry: land controlled for settled cultivation, Indians and poor whites useful if subservient to this policy, and slavery a tightly controlled institution that increased the productivity of commercial agriculture. The problem was that the vision was not fully realized, and settlers feared their handiwork could simply erode before final consolidation of the new area.

Within these tense circumstances, whites justified harsh treatment of blacks in the name of stability. Carolinian Samuel Mathis kept a diary that described several violent encounters with rebellious slave women in 1781. This was the last year of the War of Independence, and the slaves around Mathis seemed desperate to escape—or they simply wanted to hide out until the damaging civil war in the upcountry was over and order restored. Mathis was equally determined to keep slaves immobile and working. He scuffled not only with his own slaves but with any who were around him, evidencing how racial conflict openly raged between whites and blacks irrespective of actual ownership. In this free-for-all atmosphere, for example, Mathis recorded that "S. Boykin and me chases E. K's Bett but she gives us the slip." He recovered a runaway ("wiked Jin") and whipped her. He had "a Divil of a Scuffle" with Jane, who "gives me the slip." He then "had a smart scuffle with Pegg [and] was forced to tie her," and some days later he "had a quarrell with Pegg and whip'd her." Esther escaped Mathis's physical wrath, but he "threatned her, and sett her to work" after she went to Camden without his permission. (Esther ran away two days later, and Mathis did not record recapturing her.) Mathis later joined Francis Marion's partisan forces to fight the British; as a veteran of a war of all against all, he probably made a good guerrilla.[78]

Between turbulent episodes like these, upcountry whites struggled to create a stable system of labor. As was the case with their agricultural forms, settlers disdained coastal precedent. They instead relied on methods from the Chesapeake: the gang system of work and the patrols that kept slaves from evading

78. Entries for Mar. 1, 17, 19, 26, 30, Apr. 4 (the scuffles with slaves) and for July 15, 1781 (Mathis's career with Marion), Samuel Mathis's 1781 diary, SCL. Sexual abuse is also a possibility here—especially in the case of the two men chasing Bett. On the chaos that accompanied the war in the upcountry, see Klein, *Unification of a Slave State*, 78–108. On white-black relations in the upcountry, see Mark D. Kaplanoff, "Making the South Solid: Politics and the Structure of Society in South Carolina, 1790–1815" (Ph.D. diss., University of Cambridge, 1979), 69–71.

whites' control. This implemented a much more invasive system of control than that in the lowcountry (with its task system and less energetic policing of slaves) but one better suited to the open hostilities between blacks and whites in the interior. Slaveholders from the Chesapeake put their laborers in gangs that functioned for set periods of time. When whites migrated from the Chesapeake to the Lower South, they brought this arrangement with them; by the antebellum era, most upcountry slaves worked in gangs. Settlers also wanted to police blacks. A 1786 petition of Augusta citizens, for example, requested patrols to prevent slaves from assembling at night or on Sundays.[79]

Settlers' attempts to discourage slaves from working for themselves was the greatest difference between upcountry and coast; an expanding commercial economy was not supposed to create an independent work ethic among slaves. Whereas lowcountry planters wanted slaves to work for themselves, whites in the interior saw therein a lessening of their control over blacks. A petition from citizens in Orangeburg asked that slaves be prevented from raising hogs and keeping horses (which gave them mobility), from growing produce "for home consumption and for market," and from having every other Saturday to work for themselves. This was a drastic curtailment of slaves' independent activity—especially the surprising prohibitions on their producing goods for their own consumption. The petitioners nevertheless warned that the state needed a universal ban on black enterprise, for "negroes that make cotton for themselves may act as factors for those [who] do not" and who, instead, would pilfer the crop from their masters; the petition sweepingly declared that "to authorise a slave to make cotton for himself is incouraging him to be a thief." Like Indians and frontiersmen, slaves were bound to transgress against the property laws that knitted together a market society. Reflecting this suspicion, one Georgian advertised in the *Augusta Chronicle* his "resolution, that if any of my Boat-Hands purchase corn, cotton, or any other produce of this nature, without my permission or a permission from my Patroon [head boatman] they shall be punished severely." He expressed his hope "that all owners of Boats will join me in this resolution, so that my negroes may not think hard of this usage"—an indication that slaves would regard this, in 1806, as a new and unwelcome policy.[80]

79. Gray, *Agriculture in the Southern U.S.*, II, 551–554; Augusta petition of Aug. 28, 1786, Cuyler Collection, box 1, UGA.

80. Petitions to General Assembly, 1816, no. 96, SCDAH; advertisement of F. Phinizy, *Augusta Chronicle*, Mar. 8, 1806.

This was, nevertheless, the emerging policy in newer areas. Georgia passed a law in 1803 fining whites thirty dollars if they bought any produce from slaves, and fining slaveholders thirty dollars per *week* if they let slaves work anywhere except on "their own premises." Only slaves who worked in Savannah, Augusta, and Sunbury were excepted; rural slaves could work only for themselves and exchange, presumably, only with each other. A law of 1806 placed further restrictions on Georgia slaves by forbidding them to act as patroons of boats between Augusta and Savannah; they had to work as boathands under white patroons. Such laws allowed whites to react quickly if they believed their slaves were gaining too much liberty. Jacob Rice, who lived in the Lexington District of South Carolina, prepared to sue John H. Eiffert in 1815 for "trading with his negrow Peter without permission or without a pass [?] from him."[81]

Remnants of tasking and hiring-out resurfaced, however, beneath the hegemonic form whites tried to establish. As in the lowcountry during the mid-1700s, conditions settled down in the upcountry by the early 1800s when commercial agriculture seemed an embedded and reassuringly prosperous activity. By this time, as well, slaveholders were taking up an ideal of Christian stewardship over slaves, as revivals increasingly characterized religious life in the upcountry. Christian humanity might have softened whites' earlier, more intractable attitude toward slaves, though (as was the case with the more secular humanitarianism that was more prevalent along the coast) this stance might also have represented more invasion into slaves' personal affairs. Whites nevertheless began to relinquish some control over blacks to facilitate their own economic ambitions, a concession welcome to slaves themselves. Slaves who came from the lowcountry (like Obadiah Jones's "awkward" workers) could easily remember how they had once worked as hired or tasked laborers. They had little interest in allowing whites' coercive policy—one part efficiency and two parts paranoia—to take hold; looser arrangements were more to their liking. If slaves worked more as they pleased, whites began to realize, slaves might be more productive. Because of the potential bottleneck of cotton picking, for instance, planters may have avoided harsh treatment of pickers to maintain the peace on their plantations. Pierce Butler realized that careful cultivation and hard driving ("more exacted as to labour than I allow of on my Estate") could yield up to 250 clean pounds of cotton per acre but decided

81. Clayton, comp., *Compilation of Laws of Georgia*, 133, 332–333; 1815 deposition from Lexington District, John Eiffert Papers, SCL.

against such tactics, implying that a moral economy, of sorts, regulated some plantations.[82]

Slaves gained other controls over the emerging system of labor. In contrast to the rich flatlands of black belt Mississippi and Alabama, upcountry land in Georgia and South Carolina was hillier, and cultivable soils were more scattered. Supervision of a field gang was more difficult, and slaves constructed from this problem a modified task system. John Lambert observed that, on cotton plantations near Jacksonboro, planters regulated workers by tasks. When John Chesnut hired some field hands in 1816, he worked them past the time for which he had paid their master. Recognizing, as a lowcountry planter would have done, that the slaves had worked on their own time, Chesnut then paid them cash "over their Task."[83]

The need for reliable transportation of crops, more than anything else, revealed how upcountry whites compromised their desire to master all of slaves' activities and movements. Despite their misgivings over mobile slaves, whites relied on slave boatmen to keep goods moving and were willing to hire these men out and grant them some extralegal autonomy. One Georgian hired his boat hands to Savannah River patroons, claiming they were "long accustomed to the river." In Augusta, Thomas Carr's inquiry into the whereabouts of a hired-out boatman revealed that such a slave could move far beyond the reach of a master but still kept in contact with other slaves through word-of-mouth messages; boatmen formed a floating community beyond direct supervision of whites. An Augusta resident named Bugg informed Carr that Carr's boatman was still working, but outside Augusta, according to "one of Col.o Hammonds boat hands." Another white named Zimmerman admitted that he could "give out word that [Carr] had hired" the slave for another customer, and this indirect message, passing among the black boatmen, would make the missing worker "come in." Zimmerman refused to do so, however, because after this falsehood "the Negroes . . . will never take his word again," and his business would suffer from slaves' ill opinion of him.

---

82. On Christian stewardship of slaves, see Klein, *Unification of a Slave State*, 290–293. Pierce Butler to F. D. Petit de Villers, June 2, 1807, Keith Read Collection, box 3, folder 57, UGA.

83. On upcountry tasks, see Whartenby, *Cotton*, 125, 128–129, 150; Lambert, *Travels*, III, 65–66; entry for Jan. 7, 1816, John Chesnut's plantation book, Chesnut-Miller-Manning Papers, series 12-35-4, SCHS.

Though the upcountry was becoming a fixed, commercial region, its water-ways remained fluid reminders of its earlier status as a zone where not only whites controlled economic activities.[84]

In the upcountry, settlers' determination to embed and then expand a commercial economy underlay the creation of a Cotton South. Their creative actions alter the historical image of cotton as an active, an almost animate force—something that swept over an unsuspecting, bucolic people in the hinterland and transformed them into slaveholding commercial farmers, whether they liked it or not. Cotton was not, as historians from David Ramsay onward have claimed, an invading force: it was more like William of Orange than William the Conqueror, an *invited* invader that created a kingdom for cotton. By first displacing Indians and peripatetic whites, settlers created the West of the popular imagination: a blank space, a void to be filled with opportunities for Euro-Americans only—though this was an artificial geography rather than a natural condition. By next bringing in slaves, tobacco presses, and expectations of wealth, migrants made the upcountry over into an agricultural region somewhat wealthier than the prototypical mid-Atlantic region, somewhat poorer than the neighboring lowcountry. Cotton did not insert these people into a commercialized economy, they inserted cotton into a commercialized economy they had already constructed; they were the creators of the new region, not its creatures. Most evident is whites' determination to import and exploit slaves, an impulse that preceded commercial cultivation of cotton by several decades. Had they not found that cotton would feed their ambition, settlers might have found something else that could. Any claim that some *thing* like the cotton gin or the British market created the Cotton South ignores how the real consequence of commercial cultivation in the upcountry, western expansion of slavery, was the conscious handiwork of intelligent and articulate people—a much uglier reality.

Settlers' cleverness at adapting old forms of agriculture to the new region had been successful, as had their resolution to squelch any conflict that threatened to undo economic promise and societal harmony (among whites). This pattern of inventive adaptation would be even more strongly manifested in development of machinery and mills to process crops for market. These later actions showed a continuing desire to improve and diversify the econ-

84. John B. Barnes advertisement, *Columbian Centinel,* Jan. 17, 1807; N. G. Bugg to Thomas Carr, July 12, 1793, Carr Collection, box 2, folder 16, UGA.

omy, even to the point of investing in manufactures, and demonstrated how the economic paths of the upcountry and lowcountry were converging. Uneasiness over expansion of slavery would, in future, split along North-South lines rather than divide southerners from each other. Elitist conceptions probably remained in place in the lowcountry—Herrenvolkism was an uneasy public stance that only partly covered the cracks—but coastal estrangement from upcountry did decrease.[85] Determined to join the modern economy— but selectively, in their own ways—the discrete regions of the Lower South came more and more to resemble each other and to segregate themselves from the rest of the Republic.

85. Ford, *Origins of Southern Radicalism*, 281–307; Freehling, *Road to Disunion*, I, 220–223.

Chapter 9

Factories and Fields

Commercial agriculture, which would reach its peak in antebellum production of rice and cotton for an international market, was a culmination of the ways in which free residents had long exploited the region's resources. By the 1820s, certainly, they had the archetypal southern economy: it discouraged diversification in goods produced for sale and delayed investment in a more industrialized economy, both of which might have directed the antebellum South into another economic form. But earlier in the nineteenth century, propertyholders in the Lower South had moved both back toward economic ventures based more on diversification and self-sufficiency, and forward toward manufacturing. They shifted in both directions during the commercial upsets of the Napoleonic Wars—their final, seemingly paradoxical solution to another economic crisis.

Wartime adaptation nevertheless evidenced more logic than contradiction. Subsistence, commercial, and industrial economies often ran into each other in surprising convergences. As scholarship on the development of capitalism in early America has contended, these categories were not only successive stages but also cycles. Domestic economies that produced clothing, for example, might expand beyond the household only as far as the town market but could also provide a base for subsequent factory production of these commodities using, especially, the work of women skilled in domestic crafts. To counteract recession and create substitutes for imports, the Lower South's population shifted commercial and domestic activities according to individual, household, or community needs. Many levels of productive activity emerged: household production of foodstuffs and artisanal goods, interhousehold cooperation in making things like cloth, production of raw goods for the international market, local marketing of raw and finished products, and manufacture of articles, especially textiles, by artisans and wage-earning workers. This was a national pattern of adaptation from Boston through Savannah; well into the 1800s, southern household manufacturing was as significant as that in the North.[1] Drawing upon this expanded sphere for manufactures, however, northeastern entrepreneurs made industrial production a permanent feature while elsewhere manufacturing was, as during the Revolution, a temporary expedient. In the Lower South, domestic manufactures briefly blossomed into factory production, then withered away after peace in 1815 restored alluring markets for raw cotton and rice.

Factory production, on the other hand, represented some intensive and qualitative transformations that grew out of earlier efforts to diversify and reinvest in forms of agricultural production. The region's small and scattered "manufactories"—no serious threat to industry in New, let alone Old, England—culminated an important phase of capital investment in machinery like commercial mills and gins. This trend did not go unnoticed. Though most free residents welcomed investment in useful and, during the War of 1812, patriotic ventures, they also resented the socioeconomic power that capitalization represented for the elite. No one directly attacked investment in factories or wage labor, probably because these were phenomena too fleeting to excite comment. The white population's only sign of discomfiture appeared over milldams. Dams, source of controversy in other parts of North America as well, sparked quarrels between different social strata, some wanting to protect investments they had made in mills, others protesting that blocking streams eroded common or natural advantages given by public waterways. Like controversy over land speculation and intellectual property, this subdued skirmish between common right and private advantage took the Lower South into the mainstream of modern America, which was busy charting the new legal difficulties posed by expanding capitalism.

1. On early industrialization, see Thomas Dublin, *Women at Work: The Transformation of Work and Community in Lowell, Massachusetts, 1826–1860* (New York, 1979), 1–13, 23–57; and Jonathan Prude, *The Coming of Industrial Order: Town and Factory Life in Rural Massachusetts, 1810–1860* (Cambridge, 1983), 67–99. On domestic manufactures in the South, see Franklee Gilbert Whartenby, *Land and Labor Productivity in United States Cotton Production, 1800–1840* (New York, 1977), 14; and Marjorie Stratford Mendenhall, "A History of Agriculture in South Carolina, 1790 to 1860: An Economic and Social Study" (Ph.D. diss., University of North Carolina–Chapel Hill, 1940), chap. 2, esp. 72–81.

Whites' unease over private development of natural resources represented, however, only one extreme of their wide-ranging debate over and alteration of the economy. Nor did their discomfiture yet show a sustained desire to curtail newer economic activities. What is significant is that whites did enter, however briefly, the house that the Industrial Revolution built. Free residents in the Lower South picked up and used whatever economic method seemed promising, from humble household labor to expensive mechanical contrivance. But their hunting and gathering embodied a desire simply to manufacture goods when it suited them; they thereafter abandoned their hastily organized ventures. They seemed more aimless than purposeful, plucking whatever caught their eye with the whimsy of a flower arranger rather than the method of the naturalist. It might be more accurate, however, to see their appetite as omnivorous instead of desultory. Planters and farmers used *any* means to keep goods flowing (sooner or later) toward the market. Cultivators cut timber, let livestock graze among the stumps, planted the cleared land, built gins and mills, dammed rivers to get hydraulic power to run these machines, floated the final commodities down the rivers, bought slaves, had wives and daughters make household goods from unsold products, invested their profits in larger economic ventures, hired free workers to support these schemes. Within a single year—say, 1812—all of these activities might have been going on in a single county. If a Chicago butcher used every part of a pig but its squeal, a sturdy yeoman or wealthy rice grower in the Lower South found use for every part of the Lower South's landscape but its aboriginal inhabitants—and wanted to dominate over all. Both rural diversification and factory production represented logical extremes of the region's ability to adapt to any hazard, to exploit any resource.

♠ Domestic Diversification

Not even the post-Revolutionary rush to expand rice production and to create commercial cotton cultivation erased a diversified economy in the Lower South. Lowcountry planters had, after all, long exhibited a tendency to swing back toward diversification in times of crisis, as they had done when growing indigo during the 1740s and cotton during the War of Independence. Outside the rice-growing coast, needless to say, a diversified rural economy remained the rule rather than the exception. The upcountry's array of products restated a pattern the lowcountry had once used when it was relatively underdeveloped in the early 1700s and one it readily took up again during hard times. The following account of the upcountry's diverse activities not only elaborates this point but describes how lowcountry planters could easily acquire a similar complement of tools and livestock whenever they desired.

Economic diversity was, relative to Europe, the general pattern in most New World regions. Rural communities throughout early America produced a variety of raw goods—lumber, flax, cotton, livestock, grain, fruit—and turned them into barrels, cloth, bacon, butter, flour, brandy; many of these commodities were intended for household use and, at most, made their way to local markets. But compared to northern regions, southern areas produced greater amounts of agricultural goods (grain, tobacco, cotton) for an overseas market. Desire to enter both domestic and international economies was, accordingly, always present in plantation regions. François André Michaux commented on how Pennsylvania Germans who settled in Lincoln County, South Carolina, practiced an amalgam of activities. Using their own and slaves' labor, these migrants grew cotton, corn, wheat, and oats; they sawed lumber and tanned leather, ginned cotton, ground grain, and made brandy. William Bartram similarly described how settlers in Wrightsborough, Georgia, "Plant Wheat Barley Flax Hemp, Oates, corn, Cotton, Indigo [and] Breed Cattle Sheep, and Make Very good Butter and Cheese."[2]

South Carolinian John Chesnut typified this dedication to variety. Chesnut grew tobacco in the 1780s and acted as a middleman for other producers. In the early 1790s, he grew corn and indigo, the latter crop for the market. He kept accounts of the lumber he sawed and sold from 1793 to 1797 and recorded sales of flour and pork in 1794. Only in 1802 did Chesnut finally have a cotton account with his factors, MacBeth, Henry and Company of Charleston. He then expanded operations by buying two wagons and a cotton gin in 1813. He purchased forty more gins in 1815, perhaps smaller ones to supplement the

2. François André Michaux, *Travels to the West of the Alleghany Mountains . . . in the Year 1802*, in Reuben Gold Thwaites, ed., *Early Western Travels*, III (Cleveland, Ohio, 1904), 292; William Bartram, "Travels in Georgia and Florida, 1773–74: A Report to Dr. John Fothergill," ed. Francis Harper, American Philosophical Society, *Transactions*, N.S., XXXIII, pt. 2 (1942–1944), 139. See also how John Farquharson explained to Gabriel Manigault in 1789 that the South Carolina upcountry's climate would support northern crops like "grain and all kinds of fruit," in contrast to the lowcountry. John Farquharson to Gabriel Manigault, June 24, 1789, Manigault Family Papers, box 2, folder 14, SCL.

more expensive model he already had. Though he was growing more cotton, Chesnut still raised other crops. In his plantation book for 1815–1816, he recorded not only his cotton but also his yields of corn, hemp, cattle, and lumber.[3] Descriptions of farms also evidence the upcountry's diverse pursuits, as did residents' willingness to accept many products as payment for goods or services. *Miller's Weekly Messenger* of Pendleton, South Carolina, took subscriptions in corn, wheat, bacon, tallow, whiskey, or homespun cloth—the editor must have worked amid quite a clutter. In South Carolina, merchant James Harrison took payments of raw goods (tobacco, whiskey, butter, tallow, beeswax) and crafts (saddles, hats, shoes, thread, cloth, hogsheads, casks, and tubs).[4]

The ubiquity of livestock was a good indication of how a diversified rural economy persisted inland. Like many frontier people, upcountry settlers relied

---

3. —— to Chesnut, Aug. 4, 1785, series 12-33-29 (for tobacco), receipts in series 12-33-39 (corn crop), receipts in series 12-33-37 and 12-34-1 (1791 and 1792 indigo crops), account with Joseph Kershaw, series 12-33-34 (lumber), receipt, series 12-34-6 (flour and pork); account with MacBeth, Henry and Co., 1802, series 12-34-24, agreement with William Pennock, Sept. 16, 1813, series 12-34-39, receipt of James Boatwright, Oct. 12, 1815, series 12-35-3, plantation book, 1815–16, series 12-35-4, John Chesnut Papers, SCHS. Other whites were similarly diversified. Along with 800 pounds of cotton, James Edward sent 1,000 bushels of corn, 1,000 pounds of corn straw, 100 bushels of peas, 50 hogs, and some flax to market in 1786. In 1796, the first year that he began to raise cotton, William Noble had already prepared hemp, butter, tallow, pork, and wheat flour for sale. In 1808 and 1810, John Everett cultivated potatoes, wheat, peas, oats, corn, peaches, turnips, pumpkins—and cotton—on his Ocmulgee Plantation in Georgia. See receipt of Andrew Williamson to James Edward, July 20, 1786, John Ewing Colhoun Papers, folder 1, SHC; Ezekiel to William Noble, May 30, 1796, Noble Family Papers, box 1, folder 11, SCL; Josiah Everett daybook, 1808–20, Curry Hill Plantation Records, microfilm 2-2200-C, GDAH.

4. *Augusta Chronicle*, Apr. 23, 1796; *Monitor* (Washington, Ga.), July 14, 1810; *Miller's Weekly Messenger* (Pendleton, S.C.), Aug. 14, 1813; James Harrison account book, microfilm R406, SCL—for the commodities listed, see pp. 30, 52, 75, 93; for artisanal products, see pp. 29, 49, 55, 75, 104, 164. See the similar payments Joseph Galluchat made to Georgia storekeeper Vardry McBee, Oct. 26, 1805, McBee Family Papers, folder 1, SHC. On the diversity of activities in the South Carolina upcountry, see also Rachel N. Klein, *Unification of a Slave State: The Rise of the Planter Class in the South Carolina Backcountry, 1760–1808* (Chapel Hill, N.C., 1990), 15–32.

TABLE 13. *Estate Value Held in Livestock, 1780–1815*

	Mean Value in Livestock			
	1780s	1790s	1800s	1810s
South Carolina				
Lowcountry	6.2%	5.8%	4.2%	3.6%
Midlands	14.8	25.2	16.2	10.0
Upcountry	13.7	27.8	21.8	6.3
Georgia				
Lowcountry	5.0	4.5	3.0	1.6
Savannah River	—	16.8	13.1	9.7
Upcountry	—	21.7	15.4	15.5

Sources: Estate Inventories, SCDAH, GDAH.

on grazing for their first profits. The South Carolina Regulators, for instance, had complained how bandits stole or killed their cattle, their most substantial form of wealth. After the Revolution, newer areas still used herding to build up a local economy—this was true of the area around St. Marys River in southern Georgia. Even after moving from pastoralism to agriculture, upcountry farmers depended on animals more than coastal planters did. Lowcountry estates (see Table 13) from the 1780s to 1815 tended to have livestock worth only about 5 percent of the total value. In the upcountry and midlands, on the other hand, livestock contributed from 6 to 28 percent of the average estate's value. As late as the 1810s, livestock formed 15 percent of the mean estate value in western Georgia.

Some animals were more prevalent than others (see Table 14). More than 80 percent of inventoried estates had horses, and about 75 percent had cattle. Swine were the next most common creature; about 70 percent of estates had at least one pig. Sheep appeared in more than 30 percent of estates—South Carolina and Georgia were places where sheep *could* safely graze. Though breeding of mules was apparently under way, mules and jackasses were surprisingly rare; they had yet to replace oxen and horses as draft animals. Mules, jacks, and jennies appeared on only 1.2 percent of estates and, as in the

TABLE 14. *Types of Livestock on Inland Estates, 1780–1815*

	Percentage of Estates Owning				
	Horses	Cattle	Swine	Sheep	Poultry
South Carolina	81.4	76.7	69.9	38.1	36.0
Georgia	83.2	75.1	69.9	30.4	34.1

Note: All estates with at least one of each type of animal are included.

Sources: Estate Inventories, SCDAH, GDAH.

lowcountry, were rarer even than beehives (17.7 percent of inland estates got honey from their own hives). More than 30 percent of estates kept poultry, including chickens, ducks, geese, turkeys—and sometimes doves. This distribution of animals in probate records does not reflect actual size of herds; all other animals outnumbered horses. The prevalence of horses simply indicated how a rural population depended on them for transportation. Like automobiles in the contemporary United States, horses were both common and valuable; most people with any property had one or two specimens they guarded more carefully than any other form of livestock. One planter, South Carolinian John Ewing Colhoun, had a typical distribution of livestock in 1797: forty-eight head of cattle, nineteen sheep, forty-three hogs, and sixty-odd ducks, geese, chickens, and turkeys. Colhoun did not bother to list his horses, presumably because he did not consider them farm animals per se. But the whole complement of livestock—cattle, horses, swine, and sheep—was considered optimal for a farm.[5] Though this collection of animals was not reflected in lowcountry inventories, it is possible that comparable distributions of animals were present there but owned by coastal slaves. Slaves' property would not be inventoried when their owners died, so any evidence from probate records would likely underestimate lowcountry distribution of livestock. Slaves did hold significant amounts of livestock, even horses. This fact, combined with some coastal planters' continuing interest in animal husbandry (as for breed-

5. Memoranda on Twelve Mile Plantation, 1797, John Ewing Colhoun Papers, folder 3, SHC.

ing merino sheep), indicates how the plantation lowcountry probably retained some of the diversity more apparent in the upcountry.[6]

Like lowcountry slaves, most upcountry whites probably raised livestock for their own use, consuming their meat, dairy products, wool, feathers, or leather themselves. But local markets also distributed animal products. Drovers herded stock to towns for buyers to choose from for breeding or slaughter. Increasingly, husbandmen produced more compact products—meat and butter transported more easily than living animals, which might lose salable flesh while going to market. John Green, Jr., overseer for John Ewing Colhoun's Twelve Mile River plantation in South Carolina, sent bacon, beef, and butter to Charleston consumers in 1793. Amounts of products that changed hands could be quite large. Georgian John Hammond offered 200–300 pounds of wool and 100 sheep for sale in 1798; in 1806, one advertiser in the *Farmer's Gazette* of Sparta, Georgia, wanted to buy 600–700 pounds of pork.[7]

Upcountry herds of swine and cattle—bacon and butter on the hoof—were temporary elements of an economy changing from grazing to tilling of the soil. Settlers demonstrated a more lasting interest in a varied agricultural landscape in their desire to have fruit trees and grape vines, just as coastal planters liked to have orange trees and vines in their gardens. Orchards and vineyards needed considerable time and care to bear fruit; these were not crops for a moment, but for the generations, ones that reminded new settlers of old homes and farms. Virginian George Willis, for instance, put in peach and apple trees very soon after he acquired land in Georgia. In 1793, Barack Gibbons planted 150 young apple trees near Louisville, Georgia. Benjamin Waring had six or seven varieties of grapes as well as peach and apple trees on his plantation near Columbia, South Carolina, and wanted to add more grape varietals and apricot and nectarine trees. David Creswell, when he put his Georgia plantation up for sale in 1800, described it as having roughly five thousand peach trees. John Singleton brought a bundle of young fruit trees up from Charleston in 1808, and John Brown of Milledgeville offered apple grafts

6. On slaves' property, see Philip D. Morgan, "Work and Culture: The Task System and the World of Lowcountry Blacks, 1700 to 1880," *WMQ*, 3d Ser., XXXIX (1982), 563–599. On lowcountry planters' interest in livestock, see Chapter 5, above.

7. John Green, Jr., to J. E. Calhoun, Aug. 12, 1793, John C. Calhoun Papers, Family Division, folder 1, Duke; *Farmer's Gazette* (Sparta, Ga.), Dec. 6, 1806; *Augusta Chronicle*, June 30, 1798.

for sale in the *Georgia Journal* in 1810.[8] A Lower South farmer evidently saw himself as an ancient patriarch, done over in American terms, seated under his own vine and peach tree—or orange tree.

But self-styled patriarchs were also eager to put machines in their gardens. Mechanization was the new promise of the new age, even out in the American countryside. Indeed, many technological developments were most apparent outside cities and factories. (Because most American factories operated by waterpower anyway, they lacked the essential element of modern technology, steam, which was mostly reserved for developments outside factory walls.) As Brooke Hindle has explained, "Americans—particularly the farmers—lived daily with machines" like stills, milling machinery, cotton gins, agricultural presses, and clocks. After the Revolution, the Lower South increasingly gained machinery. Lowcountry planters with enlarged profits from tidal rice put mills along their new irrigation systems. Newer and poorer settlers who were trained mechanics, like Eli Whitney, imported knowledge of machinery with them. New Englander Reuben King, for instance, was a tanner who built his own tanmill when he went to Georgia. King later adapted his skills to local demand: in 1803 he repaired a livestock-driven cotton gin for neighbor Henry Harford.[9]

Not only mechanics but every citizen found machinery compelling. The American press first described a steam-driven mill in the *Columbian Magazine* of July 1788. This information then reappeared in local newspapers; the *Augusta Chronicle* gave another description of the "Columbian Steam-Engine" for its readers in 1813. Probably drawing upon sources like periodicals and almanacs, South Carolinian William Richardson copied out engineers' tables for designing pumps, milldams, and water wheels. This was an old story along

8. Memoranda for 1785 planting of peach stones, 1802 grafting of apple trees, August 1808 report on peach orchard, George Willis Journal, UGA; Barack to William Gibbons, Feb. 3, 1793, Telfair Family Papers, box 10, folder 138, GHS; Benjamin Waring to Timothy Green, July 1, 1800, Benjamin Waring Papers, SCL; *Augusta Chronicle*, July 12, 1800 (Cresswell Plantation); John Singleton to Samuel Maverick, Dec. 27, 1808, Singleton Family Papers, box 1, folder 4, SHC; *Georgia Journal* (Milledgeville), Jan. 9, 1810 (apple grafts). Peaches, introduced by the French or Spanish, had gone wild in Georgia and South Carolina by the 17th century—some observers assumed the fruit was native. See Alfred W. Crosby, *Ecological Imperialism: The Biological Expansion of Europe, 900–1900* (Cambridge, 1986), 156–157.

9. Brooke Hindle, *Emulation and Invention* (New York, 1981), 4; Virginia Steele Wood and Ralph Van Wood, eds., "The Reuben King Journal, 1800–1806," *GHQ*, L (1966), 298 and 304 for building a tanmill, 443 for repairing a cotton gin.

the coast, where interest in factories and mechanization culminated in construction of tidal mills for the elite. Although not all upcountry settlers would have had the skills to use specialized information necessary to build mills, many were handy with tools and other machines. Captain Michael Gaffney observed of upcountry South Carolinians in 1800 that "every farmer or planter is his own shoemaker, tanner, tailor, carpenter, brazier, and in fact, everything else." In other words, in the absence of a large and well-settled slave population, upcountry whites had to do the skilled tasks lowcountry slaves did. As might be expected, carpenters' tools and even blacksmiths' tools were more common in the upcountry than along the coast, where unskilled whites could hire slaves: about half the inventoried upcountry estates had carpenters' tools, and 4–13 percent had smiths' tools (see Tables 15 and 16). The desire to extract profit from natural resources along the frontier even promoted devices less familiar to settled areas. Sawmills, nonexistent in England, were common in forested North America, where settlers were eagerly deforesting the landscape. Surveyor and engineer Gerard De Brahm claimed that the "Introduction of sawing, Stamp and grinding Mills in Georgia, was almost as early as the settling of the Province." Walter Augustine ran an early sawmill on his headright grant in coastal Georgia during the 1730s. When white settlement expanded, sawmills rose as western timber fell. In 1787, for instance, Robert Watkins operated a three-saw mill near Augusta that serviced nearby settlers impatient to rid their tracts of trees.[10]

Once settlers had removed timber from their land and sowed grain (first for their bread, then for export), they wanted gristmills. Sawmills were then replaced by (or adapted to) mechanisms for grinding grain, and a more lasting reliance on machinery spread. Ninian Barrett, who put his Georgia estate up for sale in 1807, stated that it had both grist- and sawmills as well as two stills and blacksmiths' tools to keep all the machinery in repair. In 1798, the Aera and Aetna Iron Works of South Carolina made and sold "MACHINERY for SAW and GRIST MILLS, RICE MACHINES, etc. etc.," indicating wider demand for quick replacement of parts. In 1814, H. and R. Thomas of Augusta also sold mill saws and mill saw files, cards for cotton-carding machines, and copper to make or

10. *Augusta Chronicle*, May 28, 1813; William G. Richardson ledger, 1800–48, pp. 100–105, SCL; journal of Captain Michael Gaffney, ca. 1800, SCL; Louis De Vorsey, Jr., ed., *De Brahm's Report of the General Survey in the Southern District of North America* (Columbia, S.C., 1971), 165; Works Projects Administration, "Drakies Plantation," *GHQ*, XXIV (1940), 209–210; *Augusta Chronicle*, May 12, 1787.

TABLE 15. *Estates with Carpenter's Tools, 1780–1815*

	Percentage of Estates Owning			
	1780s	1790s	1800s	1810s
South Carolina				
Lowcountry	20.0	21.9	11.7	8.2
Midlands	48.2	38.5	45.7	52.0
Upcountry	58.3	46.8	46.0	55.6
Georgia				
Lowcountry	14.3	23.7	20.9	29.4
Savannah River	—	38.5	58.2	48.3
Upcountry	—	51.4	54.6	55.6

Sources: Estate Inventories, SCDAH, GDAH.

repair stills. By the 1800s, most large gristmills were commercial operations that offered a variety of services and functioned as centers of exchange. One millowner near Washington, Georgia, who had a water-powered device that he ran commercially, sold barrels and packed flour with an automated press as well as ground grain. Holt's Mills in Georgia marketed the wheat, flour, corn, rye, barley, and oats it received as payment.[11]

Stills were also common, more widespread in newer areas than mills. Distilling converted grain and fruit into vendible commodities that would keep longer and transport more easily. Liquor was ubiquitous—Henry Jackson estimated that a typical Georgia farmer made between 300 and 400 gallons of brandy a year. In the early 1810s, Edward Oxford distilled brandy and retailed it for about a dollar per gallon. Oxford made 137 gallons in one busy month during 1815, though the price had fallen to about a quarter a gallon, perhaps because many more cultivators were distilling to supplement income lost during the war. Stills were lucrative enough, however, to be taxed, and news-

11. *Miller's Weekly Messenger,* Nov. 26, 1807; *Carolina Gazette* (Charleston), Jan. 25, 1798; *Athens Gazette,* Apr. 28, 1814; *Augusta Chronicle,* May 27, 1814; *Monitor,* Sept. 18, 1813; *Georgia Journal,* Aug. 26, 1812.

TABLE 16. *Estates with Blacksmith's Tools, 1780–1815*

	Percentage of Estates Owning			
	1780s	1790s	1800s	1810s
South Carolina				
Lowcountry	0.0	0.9	1.8	1.6
Midlands	7.4	0.0	5.7	12.0
Upcountry	0.0	12.8	8.0	3.6
Georgia				
Lowcountry	0.0	5.3	2.3	5.9
Savannah River	—	7.7	14.6	6.9
Upcountry	—	5.4	6.6	8.9

Sources: Estate Inventories, SCDAH, GDAH.

paper notices continued to indicate a demand for stills or for estates with distilleries.[12]

Above all else, cotton gins represented the deepening dedication to the market and to machinery during the 1790s and early 1800s; gins were to the upcountry what rice mills were to the lowcountry. The variety of mechanisms broadened as cotton cultivation became more common and its marketing better established. Saw gins were preferred for green-seed cotton and for later hybrids derived from Mexican cotton and came in several sizes. Some planters wanted several small gins rather than one large machine that required a greater outlay of capital and could hold up operations if it broke down; if a planter had one machine that failed, he had to resort to a toll gin or delay sending his crop to market. In 1801, James Symonds of South Carolina built "SAW GINS to go by

12. Henry Jackson's journal, Sept. 1, 1811–Oct. 11, 1811, p. 3 (recto), Jackson-Prince Papers, box 9, III, SHC; records of liquor business, Edward Oxford Papers, folder 16, GDAH; tax receipt for still, June 1801, Carr receipts, box 1, Joseph Henry Lumpkin Collection, UGA. See advertisements placed by John Cumming and L. Genty in the *Augusta Chronicle*, June 13, 1795, Jan. 28, 1804; and notices for Samuel Isaacs and Daniel Sims in *Miller's Weekly Messenger* of June 11, 1807.

hand" for farmers who wanted to clean their own cotton. John Chesnut providently bought forty such gins for $120 in 1815, each mechanism fairly cheap and replaceable at $3.00 apiece. But some planters preferred investing in large mechanisms that could rapidly service their own needs and perhaps turn a commercial profit. By the first decade of the nineteenth century, John Lambert claimed, an upcountry gin had a row of at least twenty and perhaps as many as forty saws and cleaned six hundred to nine hundred pounds of cotton per day. Planters could choose among graduated sizes of gins. Josiah Lanham, a mechanic near Edgefield, South Carolina, made gins at the rate of $2.50 per saw in 1809. Investment in such machines (larger and more complicated than early gins) made planters keen to operate them correctly. South Carolinian Richard Singleton received written instructions to prevent his new saw gin from being "much injured for want of proper method in attending" it. James Overstreet likewise instructed Lewis Malone Ayer, who bought an Overstreet gin in 1805, to "be sure at all Events not to work her too fast."[13]

Machinery exemplified the convergence between coastline and interior; just as the wealthiest coastal plantations tended to have rice mills, so larger up-country estates that produced cotton began to include, as a matter of course, gins (as well as saw- or gristmills) large enough to be noted as portions of the real estate.[14] As capital investment in machinery increased, some entrepreneurs began to operate commercial gins, western cousins to toll mills for rice. Many toll gins began as early competitors with Eli Whitney; like Whitney, Augusta resident John Hammond offered to gin out cotton for every fifth pound in 1796. Later toll gins had greater capacity and more services. In South Carolina, William G. Richardson owned machinery operated by cattle that cleaned and packed both long- and short-staple cottons. Richardson could also "moat" cotton (that is, remove stray particles from it), perhaps on a gin

13. *Georgetown Gazette* (South Carolina), June 24, 1801; James Boatwright's receipt, Oct. 12, 1815. Chesnut-Miller-Manning Papers, series 12-35-3, SCHS; John Lambert, *Travels through Lower Canada and the United States of North America, in the Years 1806, 1807, and 1808* (London, 1810), III, 69–70; *Augusta Chronicle*, May 6, 1809; William McCreight to Singleton, n.d., Richard Singleton Papers, box 1, Duke; Overstreet to Ayer, Nov. 3, 1805, Lewis Malone Ayer Papers, letter-sized, box 1, folder 19, SCL.

14. See advertisements for a plantation on Silver Bluff, *Augusta Chronicle*, Jan. 1, 1803; for Brittain Huckaby's estate in Greene County, Georgia, *Columbian Centinel* (Augusta), Nov. 19, 1806; and for C. Delavigne's plantation called China Grove in Edgefield, South Carolina, *Augusta Chronicle*, Aug. 26, 1814.

with finer saws or wire teeth, for customers who preferred not to task their workers with this tedious chore. Moses Alexander had a sizable "two story gin-house, with a gin in complete order—all of which moves by water" that he wanted to sell in 1814. Some gins may have been simple devices adapted for commercial use, but others were expressly designed for the market—steam power was always a giveaway of this, because steam engines cost too much for individual use. William Longstreet pioneered steam-powered ginning; he had a steam engine and gin enclosed in a building in Augusta by the end of 1801. Although some ginners could expand or contract with market demand, com-mercial ginning was risky enough to include the possibility of bankruptcy. A ruined George Fee saw his gin with forty-six saws sold at the sheriff's auction in 1806.[15]

For more clever or better-capitalized entrepreneurs, commercial gins of-fered power over local exchange and credit, an indication of ginning's growing economic significance. In South Carolina, A. Boles arranged for persons who owed him debts to settle their accounts in cotton at certain gins. Prices for ginning, in the meantime, dropped as more commercial gins arose and com-peted with each other. In 1801, S. Bivens, of Washington County, Georgia, charged every eighth pound of cotton for ginning and bagging—less than what Miller and Whitney and their rivals had charged. In 1815, George Izard re-ported, a South Carolinian named Carton owned "a gin worked by Horses, and a screw-press—and gets 10 P[er] C[ent] for cleaning and pressing for his Neighbours," another incremental decline in toll, though this might have reflected, as well, the financial straits of the war. Many commercial ginners nevertheless continued to enjoy good business because of the relative scarcity of gins. Residents of the upcountry's cotton belt were more likely to have stills than gins: between 1780 and 1815, only 10 percent of Georgia's inventoried population had gins, and only 4.6 percent in South Carolina; the figures for stills were 15.6 percent and 6.3 percent, respectively.[16]

The proliferation of gins at the same time as commercial mills and small manufactories signaled a wider shift toward larger investments. The number

15. *Augusta Chronicle,* Jan. 16, 1796 (Hammond), Dec. 26, 1801 (Longstreet), Aug. 2, 1806 (Fee), Nov. 18, 1814 (Alexander); William G. Richardson ledger, 1800–48, SCL, p. 16 (list of cattle), p. 46 (list of services).

16. *Miller's Weekly Messenger,* Oct. 22, 1807; *Louisville Gazette* (Georgia), Sept. 19, 1801; Harold W. Ryan, ed., "Diary of a Journey by George Izard, 1815–1816," *SCHM,* LIII (1952), 158; estate inventories, GDAH, SCDAH.

and capacity of sawmills peaked, for instance, during the cotton boom of the 1790s. (Farmers probably wanted more land cleared for cotton.) Small millers sawed timber for neighbors, as T. Glasock did in the Augusta area and as John Chesnut did in South Carolina. Larger mills operated commercially. These included the Savannah firms of R. Wayen, and Joseph Clay and John Habersham, which contracted for timber or sawed large orders of lumber in the mid-1790s. At this time, millers began tinkering with steam-powered equipment. William Longstreet was, it almost goes without saying, at the forefront of this new activity; he advertised in 1792 a model of a steam engine for saw- and gristmills.[17] Distilling also became commercialized, spawning machinery meant to produce great streams of liquor. Edward M'Farlin had a "Still Manufactory" in Georgia in 1813 and boasted he could "make any sized Stills, at the shortest notice." In 1816, a Hancock County plantation up for sale contained a steam-powered still, one obviously not for household use but meant to produce liquor for sale. Other entrepreneurs commercially baled cotton, and artisans made larger presses for their use. James Oliver operated a gin and baler on River Street in Augusta in the late 1800s; he ginned and packed cotton for $1.50 per hundredweight, or, for planters who had their own gins, Oliver baled clean cotton for $1.00 per 350-pound bale. By the early 1800s, planters could buy their own presses. In 1807, E. Clemens of Augusta took orders from planters for presses; Richard Singleton paid James Young $116 for two pairs of cotton presses in 1810; Thomas Waties paid Joseph Mayes $40 for making a "Cotton Screw" in 1811. In 1815, an advertiser in the *Southern Patriot, and Commercial Advertiser* sold "Compressing Screws" reputed to make fifty bales a day.[18]

In this way, the upcountry retained diverse agricultural activities (like making peaches into brandy) but was shifting toward more specialized and expensive investments (like using steam distilleries). The diversification that

17. *Augusta Chronicle,* Jan. 19, 1793 (Glascock); receipt of Dec. 31, 1795, series 12-34-13, and receipt of Sept. 6, 1796, series 12-34-14, Chesnut-Miller-Manning Papers, SCHS; *Georgia Gazette,* June 26, Aug. 28, 1794. For Longstreet's advertisement, see *Georgia Gazette,* Sept. 22, 1792.

18. *Augusta Chronicle,* Dec. 5, 1807 (Clemens), Sept. 9, 1809 (Oliver), Jan. 1, 1813 (M'Farlin), Jan. 19, 1816 (Hancock County); Richard Singleton to James Young, Oct. 4, 1810, Singleton Family Papers, box 1, folder 5, SHC; payment to Joseph Mayes, Mar. 16, 1811, Thomas Waties Papers, box 1, SCL; *Southern Patriot and Commercial Advertiser* (Savannah), Mar. 31, 1815.

had reappeared in the lowcountry during the Revolution remained a steady pattern in newer areas. But in the interior, artisanal and mechanical pursuits along with agricultural profits evidenced a more stable economy, one beginning to resemble that of the lowcountry. Indeed, leaving aside the still obvious gaps in wealth and size of slaveholdings, upcountry and coastal estates seemed to follow similar, cyclic movements between specialization for the market, reinvestment in new and mechanized ventures, and retreat to a diversified rural economy during recessions.

ৡ৹ Final Crisis

During the Napoleonic Wars, military conflict and disruption in trade formed a final exigency that tested both lowcountry and upcountry. Commercial instability—old foe of rice planters—was a nasty surprise to new cotton planters who had only just become accustomed to a higher level of income that depended on the external market. Between the rapid expansion of cotton cultivation during the 1790s and the Anglo-American cold war (especially the embargos and nonintercourse resolutions of the Adams and Jefferson administrations) that led to the War of 1812, cotton producers first enjoyed a dizzying expansion of the market, then endured its frustrating contraction. In 1810, a poem in Milledgeville's *Georgia Argus* grimly assessed the furtive market. At the moment, the poet warned, "cotton is selling" and "waiting a year for the price to enhance, / Believe me my friends is a mighty bad chance!" An exasperated George Izard was somewhat less poetic. "Curse that Bonaparte," Izard exploded. "Damn him, why lower the Price of Cotton? and of all years in the century, this year that my Purse is as lean as his was twelve years ago."[19]

Lest their purses continue lean, husbandmen looked to other ventures. Wheat (which had European markets outside Britain) took up some of the slack in cotton exports during the War of 1812, as it had done for tobacco in the shaky 1790s. Around 1808, David Ramsay estimated that farmers could make twenty dollars per acre of corn, which closely competed with the thirty-two dollars per acre of cotton they might earn if they managed to get their bales to market. In the lowcountry, planters experimented with sugar and sheep and paid slaves to produce secondary crops like sesame or peanuts. Under pressure

19. *Georgia Argus* (Milledgeville), Feb. 6, 1810; George Izard to Henry Izard, Feb. 13, 1807, folder 15, box 2, Ralph Izard Papers, SCL.

to diversify, planters discovered unexpected uses for familiar devices. John Milledge wanted to expand production of sesame during the War of 1812, for example, and found he could press marketable oil out of it using his cotton baler. War's extremity "opened the eyes of our Countrymen," Milledge exulted. "The Mechanical genius is exerting itself throughout our extended nation."[20]

But genius and its hard-won dollars could not always buy imported manufactures, also cut off by embargo or war. As during the Revolution, import substitution was necessary. One Georgia planter lamented, on the eve of peace in early 1815, that although he had a cotton crop, he could not sell it, and he and his fellows would "be required to exert all our financial talents, to command ways and means for domestic affairs." Residents, especially in the upcountry, expanded household production of many things, from shoes to rope, but they needed cloth most. Those lowcountry planters or upcountry farmers who had continued to make cloth even after the Treaty of Paris were in a good position to face new deprivations of a new war. Those who had moved more rapidly back to commercial agriculture had to make more adjustments. If they produced staple crops, farmers could trade them for or process them into commodities meant for domestic consumption whenever these staples could not be sold abroad. Thomas Smith, a rice planter, sold part of his crop to buy locally made homespun in 1814. Other planters reduced the amount of salable crops they grew and directed their workers' attention more to domestic articles. Thomas Pinckney explained in 1815, when the war ended, that this was the first year he bought cloth: "Hitherto I had spun yarn and had cloth wove which diminished plant[atio]n Expences while the Crops were sold low."[21] Patriotic rhetoric resembling that of the Revolution played a part in encouraging domestic manufactures during the Napoleonic Wars. Editors and orators admonished women to "turn again the spinning-wheel," told them to weave cloth, and warned of the derision that would greet "The Lounging House Wife."[22]

20. Mendenhall, "Agriculture in S.C.," 40–41; Ramsay, *History of S.-C.,* II, 580; Milledge to Thomas Jefferson, July 12, 1811, John Milledge Papers, folder 7, GHS.

21. W. B. Bulloch to William Stephens, Jan. 19, 1815, Bulloch Family Papers, folder 2, SHC. The Izards continued to make cloth—see Alice Izard to Ralph Izard, Feb. 16, 1795, folder 8, box 1, Ralph Izard Papers, SCL. The two examples in the text are from Thomas Smith to Davison McDowell, Sept. 25, 1814, folder 3, McDowell-Davison Papers, SCL; entry after listing of 1815 crop, plantation book, item 1, series 2, Pinckney Family Papers, LC.

22. *Georgia Argus,* May 22, 1810. See also *Carolina Gazette,* Feb. 27, 1800.

Especially in the cotton belt, housewives and other workers had a good base for domestic manufacture because cotton producers possessed quantities of raw material for textiles. Local markets for supplies were now well established and more specialized. Cotton changed hands as raw product, spun thread, or finished cloth, each form of the fiber representing a stage on the continuum between domestic and commercial economies.[23] Most upcountry households (between 64 and 83 percent, though the distribution ranged down to 46 percent in South Carolina's midlands) had some tools for making cloth (see Table 17). Coastal planters, fewer of whom had retained those tools after the 1780s, were more likely to buy cloth from inland producers (a trend underway during the Revolution), though Georgia's coast remained more similar to the diversified upcountry. Women in individual households continued to operate spinning wheels and looms, and other family or household members assisted in making cloth. These cooperative connections stretched across households. Hiring out their services, weavers joined local networks for making and selling textiles. They processed thread for people who grew and spun cotton but did not manufacture it further, doubtless because looms were more expensive and more difficult to operate than spinning wheels. Weavers were, therefore, most likely to enter the wage-earning ranks of semi-industrial workers.[24]

23. Josiah Everett exchanged cotton with his neighbors in Georgia, both borrowing and lending raw and spun cotton, indicating how local exchange networks accommodated different products for those who did or did not have spinning wheels. See the Josiah Everett daybook of ca. 1808, Curry Hill Plantation Records, GDAH. In the 1790s, Camden storekeeper William Murrell kept an account with Ann Pattison, who wove cloth and sewed clothing for him to sell to customers (Records for 1791–93, Camden District ledger, William Murrell Papers, SCL). Milledgeville baker and storekeeper P. Menard offered to buy locally produced homespun in 1809 (*Georgia Journal,* Dec. 12, 1809). A year later, the Milledgeville firms of Devereux and Thouatt, and Thomas and Scurry offered to exchange store goods for homespun—Devereux and Thouatt wanted a total of 2,000 yards (*Georgia Argus,* June 13, 1810). In Pendleton, South Carolina, Edward D. Smith advertised that he would accept homespun for any debts due him in 1813 (*Miller's Weekly Messenger,* Aug. 7, 1813). Farish Carter of Milledgeville wanted to buy homespun to resell at a store in Fort Hawkins along the Indian frontier (*Georgia Journal,* Sept. 22, 1813).

24. Cooperation was the case in the Harden family in Georgia; Lucy Ann Randolph did weaving for her married daughter, Mary Ann Randolph Harden. Edward Harden relied not only on his mother-in-law to weave cloth but also maintained an account with weaver James Anderson during 1814 and 1815. Mathew Smith kept an account with

TABLE 17. *Estates with Clothmaking Tools, 1780–1815*

	Percentage of Estates Owning			
	1780s	1790s	1800s	1810s
South Carolina				
Midlands	51.9	46.2	68.6	64.0
Upcountry	83.3	83.0	74.0	64.3
Georgia				
Savannah River	—	76.9	78.2	69.0
Upcountry	—	73.0	71.9	80.0

Sources: Estate Inventories, SCDAH, GDAH.

Three factors nudged workers and investors to the brink of the industrial world. First, cotton planters were raising greater amounts of cotton than they had during the Revolution, when surpluses were much smaller. By 1800 the United States was producing some 40,000,000 pounds of cotton a year, about 570–640 pounds per worker, making it possible to produce cloth on a larger scale. Second, all planters recognized that, unlike during the Revolution, commercial instability was temporary. They knew that external markets— albeit temporarily defunct ones—existed for rice and cotton and figured they could rapidly shift back to commercial cultivation once hostilities ceased. Last, white entrepreneurs were not hampered by the kind of chaos that had resulted from British invasion in the 1770s and 1780s. They concluded that manufactur-

weaver Matthew Dickson in South Carolina, paying him for shirting, blankets, and tow cloth. Georgian Thomas Carr hired Susan Wright to do weaving for his household, and the Palmer family in South Carolina contracted with artisans to weave homespun and bought homespun from local weavers—probably depending on whether the Palmers had surplus yarn or not. See Lucy Ann Randolph to Mary Ann Harden, June 12, 1812, box 1, folder 1, and account book (MS Book M1632), Edward Harden Papers, Cabinet 38, Duke; account with Mat. Dickson, June 20, 1785, to April 1789, Dickson Family Papers, oversized documents, SCL; Thomas Carr's payment to Susan Wright, Jan. 17, 1812, Thomas Carr's diary, 1812–1813, Carr Collection, box 5, folder 45, UGA; Palmer Family ledger, 1777–1811, pp. 6, 8, SCL.

ing would profitably shift capital and raw materials toward alternative activities during hard times. This trend had begun, in a smaller way, with
tobacco. Like cotton, but unlike grain, raw tobacco had a limited local market.
Once processed, however, tobacco goods would sell to local smokers and
chewers. In 1807, Joseph Henderson set up a tobacco factory in Campbelltown,
Georgia, to produce chewing tobacco in partnership with a tobacco grower on
the Savannah River. A few months later, Henderson dissolved the partnership,
moved his "manufactory" to Harrisburg, and made cigars. When D. Polock
advertised slaves for sale in 1812, he specified that one was "a fellow that
understands the manufacturing of Tobacco into Segars." In Milledgeville,
Samuel M. Mordecai offered to buy leaf tobacco or exchange it for "Manufac-
tur'd Tobacco," indicating that he operated or acted as an agent for another
factory.[25]

Cotton factories also expanded during the war. The defiantly tatterdemalion
patriotism that had surrounded cotton's introduction during the Revolution
continued when the crop was a mainly commercial one. Nationalistic preference for economic independence was, therefore, doubly important during this
era because it encouraged the efforts of Columbian corporations as well as of
republican housewives and spinsters; virtue could be expressed both individu-
ally and collectively. A "Company for the encouragement of Domestic Manufactures," for example, formed in Charleston in July 1808. Its chairman
published an appeal to patriots to raise cotton and wool for manufacturing
"blankets, negro cloth, and other common goods," concluding that when
citizens saw "commerce restrained," import substitution was a duty "friendly
to our national independence." In 1810, Henry Harden editorialized in the
Washington, Georgia, *Monitor* about the need to make textiles and rope.
Harden reminded readers, "Manufactures will be productive of that complete
independence which the free people of this country should lose no time to
establish." He also emphasized that the region already had a basis for factories
in its gins and mills, whose machinery could be converted to new uses.[26] Such

25. Whartenby, *Cotton*, table 6; Ernest McPherson Lander, Jr., *The Textile Industry in
Antebellum South Carolina* (Baton Rouge, La., 1969), chap. 1. See Henderson's advertisements in *Augusta Chronicle*, Jan. 30, Oct. 17, 1807; Polock's advertisement in *American Patriot* (Savannah), May 22, 1812; Mordecai's advertisements in *Georgia Argus*,
Jan. 9, 1810, and *Georgia Journal*, Nov. 13, 1809.

26. *Carolina Weekly Messenger* (Charleston), July 26, Aug. 9, 1808; *Monitor*, Aug. 11,
1810.

statements demonstrate the strength of the belief—even in plantation regions—that the Republic needed a diversified economy to free it from dependence on other, potentially hostile nations. The Charleston factory founded in
1808 represented the Lower South's initial response to this national ideal. Much
of this era's manufacturing was inspired, therefore, by a traditional economy's
insistence on greater gain for the community, expressed here in republican
terms. Individual profit was doubtless also a goal, but not one that received
much public attention.

Encouraged by patriotic exhortation, expanded surpluses of cotton, and the
promise of some gain, whites who had capital began to invest in manufacturing. By the end of the war three textile mills were in place in South Carolina. In
Georgia, the Wilkes Manufacturing Company ventured forth in 1810 with ten
thousand dollars raised in shares of one hundred dollars each. (It had to
request stockholders to pay another twenty dollars per share later in the year.)
Although some investors did try to cluster textile workers under a single
factory roof, as would be typical in fully industrialized economies, they more
often supported schemes that indirectly introduced socioeconomic relations
based on wages, only gradually moving away from earlier methods of household manufacture. Individual weavers sometimes agreed to a "putting-out"
system, for example, in which they took yarn from a factory, then wove it into
cloth in their own homes, participating in a transitional form of production
between the household and the factory. Hague Lawton, superintendent of
Wilkes Factory, hired weavers to work in their homes in 1813, paying twelve-
and-a-half cents per yard of plain shirting cloth. Lawton provided yarn to
weavers, yarn he either bought from spinners or had made by other contracted
workers. Other manufacturing that serviced textile production also emerged.
The Augusta firm of H. and R. Thomas made cotton cards and rewired old
cards in their "manufactory." Similar enterprises sprang up in South Carolina,
led by the South Carolina Homespun Company and smaller ventures. Some
products served plantation needs. John Palmer reported, "Some [South Car-
olina] Planters Cloths their Negroes intirely in Homespun . . . and we now
begin to make our own Cotton baging."[27]

27. See Lander, *Textile Industry in South Carolina*, 6–12; Alfred Glaze Smith, Jr.,
Economic Readjustment of an Old Cotton State: South Carolina, 1820–1860 (Columbia,
S.C., 1958), 112–114; *Monitor*, Sept. 22, Dec. 1, 1810, July 3, 1813 (on Lawton's activities),
Aug. 28, 1813 (on the stockholders' meeting); *Athens Gazette*, Apr. 28, 1814 (cotton

Whatever method of production they chose—household, interhousehold, or small-scale industry—whites in the Lower South were able to manufacture goods made scarce by foreign hostilities. Like market mills and toll gins, factories revealed the hand of an entrepreneurial class with enough capital and access to credit to underwrite some ambitious schemes. The concomitant alteration in society was noticeable enough to elicit some protest, though of a subdued sort that never directly addressed the questions of industrialization and wage labor. As in disputes over tidal irrigation, the new tensions wound along waterways, dividing men who invested in mills from rural landholders who defended common rights that not even wealthier entrepreneurs were supposed to violate.

Confrontations usually involved fish. Dams—power sources for commercial mills and gins—prevented easy passage of fish up and down rivers and could block them from smaller streams. This disadvantaged rural people who depended on fish for a portion of their diet. Access to fish in waterways had been protected by English common law since the Middle Ages, and early American settlers had also assumed that they should have common access to this resource. Though English custom sometimes allowed irate subjects to break open or even level offending dams (a tradition especially strong in fenlands), milder laws specified that dams could remain in place so long as they had fish passages or sluices. Such provisos made for a certain amount of peace between millers and rural-dwellers.[28]

Americans replicated this compromise in the Lower South. Colonial statutes regulated the size and placement of dams. To prevent serious misuse of waterways, millers often had to ask permission to construct dams, as John Henderson did for his "excellent Millseat" on the Enoree River in Newberry District, South Carolina. Rural folk still fulminated against millers. A 1787 petition from South Carolina's Orangeburg District (supported by 107 signatures) asserted that Ferguson's Mills on the Edisto River was "a public Nuisance" that blocked transportation and impeded "Fishery," thus violating "the

---

cards); John Palmer to David Ramsay, Dec. 3, 1808, David Ramsay Correspondence, series 51-132, SCHS (microfilm from collections in the Charleston Library Society).

28. See Gary Kulik, "Dams, Fish, and Farmers: Defense of Public Rights in Eighteenth-Century Rhode Island," in Steven Hahn and Jonathan Prude, eds., *The Countryside in the Age of Capitalist Transformation: Essays in the Social History of Rural America* (Chapel Hill, N.C., 1985), 25–50.

common Rights of Mankind." In Georgia, a law of 1793 protected "the natural and equal privilege of taking the fish" out of the Little and Broad rivers by stipulating that milldams needed sluices one-tenth the width of the stream. A similar statute regulated the Oconee in Georgia. Another law of 1796 ordered owners of Georgia milldams to install gates or locks for boats, a regulation much stricter than for fish sluices. Millers had to put in gates within four months of building a dam and, after this grace period, would be fined a stiff five dollars each hour that a boat or raft was detained.[29]

Greater concern for boats than fish reflected the Lower South's preoccupation with getting things to and from market. The same commercially minded citizens who signed petitions about fishing probably also saw economic benefit in the dams and eventually backed down. As a market economy spread ever further over the Lower South, state governments increasingly protected the interests of millowners over those of rural inhabitants. Millowners had helped bring this about by constant assertion of their right to develop property. They were particularly anxious over access to suitable mill seats. A seat or natural break in the streambed created a rapid flow of water; this, even more than the size or construction of a waterwheel, was key to hydraulic power. Like the proper pitch of the tide on estuaries along rice plantations, a mill seat was a natural resource worth fighting for. One petition accordingly protested against a law regulating the Saluda River: dams there had to have a sixty-foot slope so fish could slip upstream when the water rose over the dam. No fewer than 137 signers complained that the strong current at a natural mill seat prevented most fish from passing over any sort of slope, yet still millers had to alter dams in a way that reduced the power of their mills. The legislation was amended. Instead of sloping, Saluda dams needed only to have thirty-foot sluices that were opened from March to June, so millers lost power for only a three-month interval when they were unlikely to have new crops to process.[30]

Even when they had to respect some common rights, millers could expect acquiescence from the people, many of whom probably conceded that water-

29. Petitions to General Assembly, undated, no. 1602, and 1787, no. 8, SCDAH; Robert Watkins and George Watkins, eds., *A Digest of the Laws of the State of Georgia* (Philadelphia, 1800), 606–608, 609, 676–677.

30. On early mills and the nature of waterpower, see Louis C. Hunter, "Waterpower in the Century of the Steam Engine," in Brooke Hindle, ed., *America's Wooden Age: Aspects of Its Early Technology* (Tarrytown, N.Y., 1975), 179; Petitions to General Assembly, 1800, no. 137, SCDAH.

run mills and gins were improvements to the countryside. Compromise was common. Shaler Hillyer, for example, who built a milldam across the Broad River in Wilkes County, Georgia, could keep the dam no more than four feet above water level and had to construct a twenty-foot sluice for shad. He also had to maintain a boat canal for traffic between Petersburg and Augusta. But regulations on anglers were even more stringent and in Hillyer's favor. A fisherman could use only a line (not an obstructing net), had to stay at least two hundred yards from the dam, and could fish only from the first of February to the first of May. The regulation laid penalties of fifty dollars per offending "person," of ten lashes for a slave plus a twenty-dollar fine for his owner, and of thirty-nine lashes for a free black. Protection of Georgia millers stepped up in 1816, when the legislature stipulated fines and prison terms for people who willfully broke dams or banks. Thus ended the common-law tradition of public rights that an outraged citizenry once legally defended with violence against private property. A new trend was under way, one expanding in nineteenth-century law. Legislators increasingly held that private development of natural resources could benefit the public even if it eroded the property rights of certain individuals. Government intervention in economic affairs—as with control over land speculation and inspection of tobacco—was increasingly welcome.[31]

The Lower South was, therefore, a region gathering up some characteristics of industrializing economies: mechanical invention, growth of capital and entrepreneurship, conflict between men with capital and the rural population, government protection of private enterprise. It also had a labor force, both slave and free, able to work in manufacturing and with machinery. Protests that slaves could not act as artisans or machine operators, products of antebellum proslavery arguments, were scarce in these earlier times. Slaves, by the 1800s, performed most mechanical occupations found in the Lower South. South Carolinian Thomas Waties, for instance, hired slaves to make a "Screw press for Cotton" in 1812. Waties later hired a blacksmith named Prince to service his plantation's needs at eighty dollars per year, more than the sixty-five dollars Waties had already spent on blacksmith tools. Smiths like Prince were often hired out, evidence that their skills were better adapted to the market than to individual estates. Near Sparta, Georgia, Robert Rivers offered to hire

31. Lucius Q. C. Lamar, comp., *A Compilation of the Laws of the State of Georgia . . . [1810–1819]* (Augusta, 1821), 494–495, 582; Morton J. Horwitz, *The Transformation of American Law, 1780–1860* (Cambridge, Mass., 1977), 34–53.

out his slave blacksmith in late 1806. In 1813, Micajah Anthony also wanted to hire out a blacksmith in Washington, Georgia. Slaves also operated machinery. In 1794, William Kennedy and Company of Augusta needed twenty slave boys "to attend" a "cotton machine" or gin for them. In 1795, Kennedy again advertised for slave boys or girls (from ten to twelve years old) to mind his gin.[32]

Smiths and slaves familiar with machinery, like other skilled members of the slave population, developed noticeable characteristics of self-reliance, if not defiance. They seemed to be better able to bargain with whites, to be more educated, and more likely to be runaways. A South Carolina advertisement summarized some of these tendencies by describing runaway Andrew, a blacksmith, as a slave who "writes and reads English tolerably well." Planters who needed slave mechanics sometimes chafed under their dependence on an assertive class of worker. Rice planter Allard Belin, who regularly hired a workman named Billey to repair his mill, made peevish entries about Billey in his plantation book. Belin betrayed exasperation over the slave's ability to set his own wages and determine his own schedule, often emphasizing what Billey "said" rather than what he, Belin, believed. Billey delayed work because he "said he was sick," or "to hoe his Rice he said," or when he "said he had strained his Back." For all Belin knew, Billey told nothing but the truth, but the planter clearly felt at the mercy of this skilled and outspoken man's statements. Billey's strength, vis-à-vis the planter, was especially apparent when he told Belin that "New Years day his Mistres allowed him as his day and I must pay him for that days work which I did." The only thing better than paid holidays was freedom, which Billey tried to gain in an abortive runaway attempt in March 1797.[33] Investment in machinery and diversification of the economy may have solved many problems for Lower South whites, but slaves' rebelliousness was a difficulty that defied mere economic reform, however innovative the reform.

32. Overseers' wages, 1812 payment to Hopkin Seale, Thomas Waties Plantation Book, and receipt to John Waties, Oct. 1, 1812, Thomas Waties Papers, box 1, SCL; *Farmer's Gazette*, Dec. 13, 1806; *Monitor*, Dec. 25, 1813; *Augusta Chronicle*, Mar. 8, 1794, Apr. 18, 1795.

33. Entries for May 16 (runaway attempt), June 12, 13, July 14, 1797, July 8, 1798, Allard Belin plantation journals, series 34-178-1, SCHS. On Andrew, see *Carolina Weekly Messenger*, Jan. 19, 1808.

By the end of the War of 1812, two trends were under way in the Lower South. First, an economic system dependent on commercial agriculture and, increasingly, slavery, was moving westward as fast as the white population could carry it. (This tendency was no longer impeded by any foot-dragging or debate on the part of lowcountry planters.) Second, despite this spread of prototypical elements of the Old South, the region still displayed an interest in the modern world beyond. Local entrepreneurs' flirtation with factories best exemplified this latter trend and reiterated planters' admiration of the new industrial order. As was the case with arguments against the use of slaves in skilled or mechanical occupations, for instance, professions of horror against white wage labor awaited a later era. In this transitional period, wage labor that serviced manufacturing was not always associated with degradation and poverty. Farmers' daughters who knew how to spin and weave, like their New England counterparts, were the persons most likely to be drawn into cottage industry, and they were neither destitute nor dependent on a separate socioeconomic class of capitalists—they were temporary workers who would return to the household. Female artisans were, like others who supported wartime manufactures, willing to serve new economic functions for a time. It would be a large step from these tremulous beginnings and patriotic hopes over manufacturing to full-blown industrialization. But had investors seen permanent promise in factories, rather than republican duty and provisional expedient, it might have been the next step.

Epilogue

Slavery, Progress, and the "Federo-national" Union

If the Lower South seemed on the verge of further economic development as it moved toward manufacturing, it was a temporary phenomenon.
Factories disappeared after peace in 1815 reopened markets for rice and raw
cotton; manufactures served as temporary outlet for capital and labor during
the war but did not permanently diversify the economy. Most propertyholders
plunged back into the land, preserving their tidal mills and cotton gins but
neglecting economic ventures not directly tied to commercial agriculture.
Though their willingness to explore the modern territory of wage relationships
and capital investment—as early as 1808—indicated that whites regarded these
activities as plausible alternatives to agriculture, they entered them only under
economic duress. The region had several preconditions of further development, but these were not sufficient unless free residents were willing to forsake
planting for manufacturing in good times as well as bad. They were only part-
time entrepreneurs, loath to relinquish the known payoff of commercial
agriculture for riskier investments.[1]

---

1. But see Laurence Shore, *Southern Capitalists: The Ideological Leadership of an Elite,
1832–1885* (Chapel Hill, N.C., 1986), chap. 1, on how some capitalist ideology continued; Robert William Fogel, *Without Consent or Contract: The Rise and Fall of*

It is of course a truism that free participants in plantation economies were undone by their own success at planting, which continued to pay profits that distracted them from real development or diversification; this study has suggested that whites persisted in the same old track, not just out of stubbornness, but also through inventiveness—through their strategic switching back and forth between economic activities. In this regard, whites again restated how they were poised between the familiar and the new. If their position for the most part resulted from genuine and informed choices about modern economics, white propertyholders also began to craft a political justification of their regional particularity; only gradually, however, did their new position begin to erode an earlier ability to explain themselves without undue defensiveness. It is fitting, in this coda, to examine how free residents of the region still thought of themselves as cautious denizens of the modern age up until 1815, and also illustrate how they came to be more critical of their earlier conciliatory opinions as they assessed their position within a new nation of competing states. The form of their assessment—within political terms— signifies that planters' intensifying sense of peculiarity and isolation resulted, not from any inevitable development of plantation economics, but from the difficulty of arraying regional powers against federal powers, a difficulty that would worsen from 1815 onwards, until it culminated in the Civil War.

A guardedly optimistic view of commercial and modern progress had underpinned nearly all of whites' assumptions about economic activities since 1729. The prospect of commercial wealth and civility motivated them to seek information from the Atlantic world of trade and science, to plan new settlements, to diversify the economy in times of war, to denounce native Americans for their subcommercial mode of subsistence, to lobby for facilities to expand market agriculture, and to impress wayward whites and rebellious blacks into behaviors intended to further commerce. Though eager to use commercial agriculture toward these ends, whites harbored suspicions of rapid development and were wary of trading societal harmony and vigor for attenuated social ties, political corruption, and physical degeneration.

Georgian Henry Jackson gave a meandering account of all these doubts in a notebook he kept in the 1790s while a medical student at the University

---

American Slavery (New York, 1989), chaps. 3, 4, on how capitalism continued to develop in the South.

of Pennsylvania. Jackson was clearly someone who sided with the ancients against the moderns. Under the entry "Commonplaces," he first reflected on "How much the nature of a climate depends upon population," observing that an increasing population gave rise to a warmer climate and more "fevers." Jackson then made some notes on ancient history, remarking that Carthage, despite its "commercial" success, declined into "Avarice" and "Luxury" under the "effeminating influence" of wealth and barbaric allies. Switching back to the modern era, he finished with analyses of Holland and America, hypothesizing that "commerce appears to be inconsistent with true republicanism."[2] None of these attitudes was unique to the Lower South; all reflected residents' study of contemporary debates within politics, economics, and medicine and showed paradoxical combinations of modern thought with some of the region's less-than-modern features. Some examples of this eclecticism appeared in coastal planters' defense of slavery within the terms of an Enlightenment calculus of sentiments, in inland farmers' mixture of Scripture and conjectural history in their denunciation of Indians, in early ideas about race derived from up-to-date medical theory, in most free residents' coexisting desires for traditional and commercial economies—their inability to relinquish the familiar past as they sought an improved future.

Whites' unwillingness to plunge more rapidly into modernity was reinforced as they began to see themselves, certainly by the 1780s, as part of a national economy. Nationalism protected local interests; other states, planters and farmers argued, could serve economic functions they themselves shunned. This attitude showed how whites interpreted the nation's economy in terms of comparative advantage. They assumed each region within the United States had its peculiar climate and material resources that could contribute to an integrated, continental economy. Celebration of regional particularism, which encouraged Lower South whites to devote themselves to commercial agriculture (except during wartime disruption), was not rejection of national opinion. It was an interpretation, after all, that built upon James Madison's vision of an expanding polity beneficially divided among varied passions and interests, each of which built up the overall strength of the union.[3]

2. Henry Jackson notebook, 1796–97, Jackson-Prince Papers, box 9, I, SHC.

3. Douglass Adair, " 'That Politics May Be Reduced to a Science': David Hume, James Madison, and the Tenth Federalist," in Trevor Colbourn, ed., *Fame and the Founding Fathers: Essays by Douglass Adair* (New York, 1974); Roy Branson, "James Madison and the Scottish Enlightenment," *Journal of the History of Ideas*, XL (1979), 235–250.

By the 1800s, citizens of the Lower South defined the interested parties that composed this diverse polity by dividing them into three groups: members of professions, merchants, and those of the "*landed interest*." While giving the lion's share of praise to the last group, they maintained that, among the three divisions, "the dependence of each on the other is mutual," an interdependence that harmonized differing claims on the Republic. This was the position South Carolinian Charles Pinckney took in the Constitutional Convention of 1787, one he reiterated in his state's own ratifying convention, where he stated that the three "classes" were "dependent upon each other."[4] The nation was divided not only into classes (each one of which encompassed segments of each state's population) but into regions. Varying physical environments fostered diverse economic activities. David Ramsay concluded that "different climates and soils produce a great variety of the useful commodities." This was the view of regional particularity that ran through travelers' accounts, but one now used to create a national identity for citizens in smaller, republican governments strung through the continent's varying latitudes. Charles Pinckney explained how a "distinguishing feature in our Union is its division into individual states, differing in extent of territory, manners, population, and products." This view of connected fortunes was useful, as well, in making the final peace between lowcountry and upcountry. Ralph Izard related this vision to Edward Rutledge in a discussion over canal building in South Carolina. Canals would bring "happiness" to the state, Izard claimed, because "the uneasiness which has subsisted between the lower, and back parts, has been occasioned by the inequality of their circumstances. Enable the latter to bring their produce to Market . . . and they will be enriched . . . and we shall become an united, and happy people."[5]

Conceptions of unified happiness brought musings on national identity full circle. Montesquieu had hypothesized that the environment was the basic element of a nation's collective spirit, and observers in the late eighteenth and

4. Charles Pinckney, cited in Max Farrand, ed., *The Records of the Federal Convention of 1787*, rev. ed. (New Haven, Conn., 1937), I, 402, 403; and in Jonathan Elliot, ed., *Debates in the Several State Conventions on the Adoption of the Federal Constitution . . .*, 2d ed. (Philadelphia, 1876), IV, 322.

5. David Ramsay, "An Oration on the Advantages of American Independence," ed. Robert L. Brunhouse, American Philosophical Society, *Transactions*, N.S., LV, pt. 4 (August 1965), 185; Elliot, ed., *Debates on the Federal Constitution*, IV, 323; Ralph Izard to Edward Rutledge, Nov. 9, 1791, Ralph Izard Papers, legal-sized documents, folder 1, SCL.

early nineteenth centuries used environment (particularly climate) to categorize different groups of people, sometimes in unflattering ways. Whites in the
Lower South identified themselves in relation to their environment, but in a
defiantly positive way and with the intention of creating an ethos based on
improvement. When they had to provide an identity for themselves within a
federal system of government (something Montesquieu had not foreseen),
whites argued that their region's climate and terrain offered specialized advantages that supported the nation's material fortunes. National variations were a
larger reflection of the region's own internal variations—swampy coast and
red-soil interior—that gave it various forms of prosperity.

In its most literal form, this national vision translated into offers to swap
services interregionally. In 1793, Pierce Butler inquired of Connecticut manufacturer Jeremiah Wadsworth about the "state of manufactures in" the North,
offering raw cotton (rather than cash or creditors' notes) for Wadsworth's
textiles. Butler played to the national pride that could—especially during a
war—underpin this notion of regional specialization by adding, "As I know
your patriotism I will not trouble you with an apology for addressing myself to
you on this subject." David Ramsay also expressed faith in the economic
connections among the states. "Agriculture, commerce, ship-building, and
manufactures, support, and are supported by each other.—They are separate
links of one great chain, which binds all [Americans] together," making them
independent of Europe. Those who dwelt within a climate conducive to
agriculture could, accordingly, relegate some risky and possibly corrupting
economic functions to other states, thereby quarantining the ills of modernity.
Once established as a productive and diversified nation, Ramsay claimed,
America's overall expansion would feed "the reciprocal wants and capacities of
different portions of our now widely extended empire," an empire moving
ever further west.[6]

Ramsay's metaphor of a chain that bound the union showed the prevailingly
political dimension within this economic thinking. Ramsay claimed that, as
well as establishing a reciprocity of materials and services, "an emulation"
among the states would take place, "each contending with the other, which

6. Pierce Butler to Jeremiah Wadsworth, Oct. 10, 1793, Pierce Butler Letterbook, SCL;
David Ramsay, *An Oration on the Cession of Louisiana to the United States* (Charleston,
S.C., 1804), 10–11. On Ramsay's nationalism, see Arthur H. Shaffer, *To Be an American:
David Ramsay and the Making of the American Consciousness* (Columbia, S.C., 1991),
chap. 6.

shall produce the most accomplished statesmen." This was an image of connection but one also of potential conflict and loss of political harmony.
Ramsay denied that states with the best or most persuasive leaders might lord
it over others. "Our federo-national system is an improvement on all the
governments that have gone before it," a challenge to any benighted "admirer
of antiquity" like Henry Jackson. Federalism promised parity: "Do the people
of Connecticut govern the people of South-Carolina . . . ? By no means. Each
state governs itself, in all matters of domestic concern."[7]

But federal government was a possible source of tension—if the states shared
a common fortune, they might discover reasons to take an intrusive interest in
each other's business. Regional difference was, in this context, a danger.
Charles Pinckney saw the possibility of political dissension. "Nature has drawn
as strong marks of distinction in the habits and manners of the people as she
has in her climates and productions," and "inconveniences," as he cautiously
phrased it, could result from such variation. The problem was worsened,
Pinckney maintained, "by the variety of their state governments," even though
each was only a modification of the laudable republican form. Interregional
politicking was not merely a potential danger, Rawlins Lowndes warned delegates during South Carolina's debates on ratifying the federal Constitution.
The northern states had already flexed their confederated muscles to put limits
on the international slave trade and might, Lowndes predicted, eventually
"divest us of any pretensions to the title of a republic." Edward Rutledge and
Pierce Butler tried to calm Lowndes down (Butler pointed out that northern
shippers had an interest in southern commerce that should prevent them from
seeking the ruin of the plantation states), but Lowndes maintained that there
was a trend toward federal intervention in southern affairs. The message sent
southward, Lowndes warned, was: "Go: you are totally incapable of managing
for yourselves. Go: mind your private affairs; trouble not yourselves with
public concerns."[8]

7. Ramsay, "Oration on American Independence," ed. Brunhouse, APS, *Trans.*, LV,
pt. 4 (August 1965), 185; and *Cession of Louisiana*, 19. William Henry Drayton had
already stated, when he was a delegate to the Continental Congress in 1778, that "from
the nature of the climate, soil and produce of the several southern states, a northern
and southern interest naturally and unavoidably arise." See William M. Dabney and
Marion Dargan, *William Henry Drayton and the American Revolution* (Albuquerque,
N.M., 1962), 206.

8. Elliot, ed., *Debates on the Federal Constitution*, IV, 272, 273, 274, 324.

The skeletons Lowndes saw lurking in federal closets took on flesh during the four decades after 1819. That year marked a severe financial crisis that ended the first boom era for cotton. From the 1820s onward, sectional hostility mounted, from the Nullification Controversy, through the emergence of abolitionism and proslavery in the 1830s, and on to the final crises of 1860–1861—a remarkably compressed series of events that quickly eroded an earlier, trusting vision of national linkages. The problem of maintaining a distinctively regional economy would be elaborated on in the 1830s by southern political economist Thomas R. Dew; John C. Calhoun would propose as a solution the idea of a concurrent majority. In retrospect, the Lower South's decision to pursue commercial agriculture using slaves rather than a diversified economy with financial and industrial entrepreneurship seems disastrously ingenuous. Yet ingenuous more in a political sense than an economic one. In pursuing agriculture, after all, white residents of the Lower South exploited their region's comparative advantage and might have continued to do so undisturbed in the absence of other sources of national conflict. Political events, perhaps more than economic factors, encouraged an image of an anachronistic South, the handiwork both of northerners and southerners who played into the stereotyped notions of northern and southern peoples established in the early modern era.[9]

In the Lower South, whites' skepticism over commercial development and federal unity prepared them for external criticism, political separation, war, and even defeat. Their long-standing suspicion of pell-mell economic expansion allowed them, for example, to parry free-labor critiques of their more slowly adapting economy, and their gloomy belief that federal compromise was too fragile a construct played into their later rejection of the Union. Moreover, they also felt less and less reason to apologize for slavery. Accepting modern views of humanity, joined with evangelical demands for conversion of and charity to slaves, whites assumed that their relations with slaves were improving and were a sign of how the races were tied together through

---

9. On how continuing tension over economic development played into the emerging sectional controversy, see J. Mills Thornton III, *Politics and Power in a Slave Society: Alabama, 1800–1860* (Baton Rouge, La., 1978). On the crafting of sectional stereotypes, see William R. Taylor, *Cavalier and Yankee: The Old South and American National Character* (New York, 1957). On Dew and Calhoun, see Allan Kaufman, *Capitalism, Slavery, and Republican Values: Antebellum Political Economists, 1819–1848* (Austin, Tex., 1982), 102.

sympathy and a complementary inequality. To their mind, this connection was not heedlessly to be broken. In upcountry South Carolina a newspaper extracted statements "From Burk's Maxims," emphasizing, "We have obligations to mankind at large, which are not in consequence of any special voluntary pact." Instead, social ties "arise from the relation of man to man, and the relation of man to God, which relations are not matters of choice."[10]

When slaveholders insisted that Africans benefited from exposure to a "civil" society, that whites and blacks shared social bonds, that they knew their slaves as individuals, and that they therefore knew what was best for their slaves, they gave a modern theory of sentiments a regional and chilling twist. Yet embedding slavery in the theory did follow unfortunately its logic. Compared to the continuing ejection of native Americans from the expanding commercial polity, for instance, which severed whatever faltering ties of humane sympathy might have existed between Indians and whites, slaveholders' attitudes toward their slaves *were* in line with modern thought about the involuntary, customary nature of social relations. John Moultrie was thus able to assure himself that because his slaves had "been so long in my family I have a respectful attachment for them as my fellow Creatures." Fragments of an Enlightenment sensibility appear in his words, but Moultrie's inability to perceive that his slaves had little or no respectful attachment to him denied how force, not sentiment, kept his slaves in place on his rice fields.[11]

Perhaps because they saw slavery as an institution of social cohesion too delicate and dangerous to break apart, whites began displaying a do-or-die attachment to the institution of slavery and began revealing a paranoid suspicion of critics of that institution. Even if slaves posed a risk to military security, any proposals to reduce the region's dependence on them, openly discussed by whites before the Revolution, were no longer acceptable. New settlers had long protested that slavery and market agriculture were not the exclusive province of lowcountry planters, and they saw any such schemes as attempts to subvert their independence as small, virtuous producers—the hearty supporters of free government. Too, lowcountry planters were more likely to assume that they could not easily undo or reject an institution established, as Henry Laurens had said, on deep custom and prejudice. Under the strain of war in 1814, Mary Elliott Pinckney resolved to sell her lowcountry property and move to the upcountry, an area she believed was less prone to invasion and better able to

10. *Miller's Weekly Messenger* (Pendleton, S.C.), Apr. 17, 1807.
11. John Moultrie to Isaac Ball, Aug. 17, 1815, Ball Family Papers, box 3, folder 31, SCL.

guarantee a simple, stable life. Her brother, the writer William Elliott, berated her not only for her un-American cowardice but also for her willingness to break rank among the slaveholding elite. He argued that there was "no money . . . to be made in the Upper Country" (the siblings' belief in a precommercial and halcyon upcountry reasserts lowcountry prejudices about the newer region) and she would have "to settle again in the low Country" once peace was declared. Elliott assailed his sister with metaphor as well as reason—he stated that her essential weakness was represented by her desire "to exchange a bad negro, for a good hour," to reject the region's whole economic system because of its sometime inconveniences.[12]

Elliott's aphorism revealed a willingness to sacrifice harmony for slavery, a belief that, however difficult their situation, slaveholders should never cave in. Their conviction that the bonds between them and their slaves were ones of shared human need rather than racially prejudiced inequality was the most flawed adaptation the Lower South made to the modern era. The region had a system of human bondage newly formulated within an antirationalist celebration of human passions. The latter could not reform the former, but, instead, disastrously reassured slaveholders that they could improve their society without drastic change. In the early 1800s, when William Moultrie recorded his thoughts after taking a walk through his rice fields in St. John Parish, he congratulated himself on the "very interesting and amusing" "progress" being made there. He singled out the better "Rice Machines" and the superior "use of water," good examples, admittedly, of Lower South ingenuity. But Moultrie was also pleased with the way "the treatment of the slaves in the country is altered so much" to include principles of "tenderness, and humanity" precious to those of modern sensibilities.[13]

Tenderness and humanity—reassuring prospects of social cohesion—seemed preferable to the violent transformation that was the only other way of modifying slavery and commercial agriculture. Realizing the conservative forces that instead favored stability, Henry Laurens comforted his son, John, over John's failed attempts to raise a Revolutionary black regiment who would be freed if they fought against the British and, thus, would open the way to further emancipation. Henry was confident that the "work will at a future day be efficaciously taken up and then it will be remembered who began it in South

12. William Elliott to Mrs. [Mary] Charles C. Pinckney, Oct. 15, 1814, Elliott-Gonzales Papers, box 2, folder 13, SHC.

13. Fragment, ca. 1800, William Moultrie Papers, box 3, folder 38, SCL.

Carolina." The work was never taken up, because whites in the Lower South could adapt critiques of the revolutionary impulses of their age to make sense of themselves and their region. Their ability to do so is a painful yet necessary reminder of the selectivity of modern social thought. Whites in the Lower South did not err by ignoring modernity, but by embracing only what too well suited the ends of slaveholders. What took place in the early Lower South between 1730 and 1815 is disturbing, not because whites distorted the modern era's distinctive patterns of thought, but because they did not have to distort them much to pursue their own ends.[14]

14. Henry to John Laurens, Sept. 21, 1779, LP.

Statistical Method

Most of the tables in this work, and some other statistics used throughout, are drawn from a random sampling of probate records in the South Carolina Department of Archives and History and the Georgia Department of Archives and History. The sample came from the body of estate inventories for South Carolina and Georgia between 1740 and 1815, decades for which there are records for both colonies and the later states (there is no comparable body of probate records for East Florida). Each place was divided by decade and by geographical sections: South Carolina into lowcountry (the coastal districts), midlands (up to the piedmont), and upcountry; Georgia into lowcountry, river counties (along the Savannah), and upcountry. A 10-percent random sample of all extant inventories for each decade and subregion was then drawn. In colonial Georgia, however, all extant records were used in order to have a more meaningful body of data. The result is a total sample of 1,490 cases, divided among the six subregions and over the eight decades.

These data were used to illuminate the material basis for agriculture in the early Lower South. Although records from the United States Census could have also given data on land- and slaveholdings, they would have explained only the national era (for 1790, 1800, and 1810) and would not have contained meaningful material on other items of property. Probate records, in contrast, continue through the colonial and national periods and list tools along with other items of property. The probate records in this study were examined in two ways: for value and for presence or absence of specific items. Value was represented by the overall worth of an estate as well as the proportion of the total value held in slaves or livestock. Presence or absence of items ranging from cattle, to plows, to indigo vats was also recorded. The results are presented as simple values or as percentages. For the colonial era, all values are presented in pounds sterling; for the national period, in dollars.

There are problems with this type of data. Probate records tend, for example, to make a population look wealthier than it actually was. The destitute are rarely inventoried, so the poorest element of a population is missing. So are slaves who, especially in the lowcountry, did have some property, but property that would not be included in a white person's inventory. Because colonial records tended to ignore most (that is, poor) frontiersmen, pre-Revolutionary inventories—which overrepresent rich rice planters and coastal merchants—make the colonial Lower South seem (especially on the eve of the Revolution) almost fantastically wealthy. Similarly, the wealthiest elements of society are overrepresented. People tend to die when they are in later years, which is also when they tend to have more property than the population average. On the other hand, mean age at death is still unknown for much of the Lower South and varied a great deal according to internal region and over time. This is a caution to the reader that the estimates of wealth and prevalence of materials were probably lower in the actual population than in the tables that present the data, though the degree of distortion is, of course, unknowable. It is, in any case, the comparative value of the data that is important.

Bibliography

MANUSCRIPTS

Ballindalloch Castle Estate Office, Banffshire, Scotland
　　MacPherson-Grant Papers
British Library, London
　　Sir Joseph Banks Letters
College of Charleston, Special Collections Library, South Carolina
　　Henry Laurens Journal
　　Porcher Family Account Book
Georgia Department of Archives and History, Atlanta
　　Curry Hill Plantation Records, accession no. 79-116
　　Estate Inventories, Probate Court Records (sample)
　　Edward Oxford Papers, accession no. 66-502
Georgia Historical Society, Savannah
　　Joseph Vallence Bevan Collection
　　Joseph Clay and Company Letters
　　Seth John Cuthbert Papers
　　Forman-Bryan-Screven Papers
　　Fraser-Couper Papers
　　Joseph Habersham Papers
　　John Hall Papers
　　Jones Family Papers
　　Samuel and Thomas Jones Papers
　　Seaborn Jones Papers
　　Richard Leake Plantation Journal and Account Book
　　Liberty County Records
　　McDonald-Lawrence Papers, Isabel P. Lawrence Collection
　　John McIntosh, Jr., Papers
　　Lachlan Bain McIntosh Papers
　　John Milledge Papers
　　Daniel Mulford Papers
　　James O'Fallon Letter
　　Isaac Shelby Papers

Spalding Family Papers
Telfair Family Papers
Wayne-Stites-Anderson Papers
Guildhall Library, London
The Worshipful Society of Apothecaries of London, Manuscripts
Hargrett Rare Book and Manuscript Library, University of Georgia, Athens
Godfrey Barnsley Papers
Carr Collection
Cuyler Collection
James Hamilton Papers
Felix Hargrett Collection
Hillyer Papers
Charles Colcock Jones, Jr., Collection
Noble Wimberly Jones and Benjamin Franklin Correspondence (from originals in
the American Philosophical Society)
Benjamin Lincoln Papers
Joseph Henry Lumpkin Collection
Josiah Meigs Papers (in University Archives)
Keith Read Collection
William Tatham, "Botanical Observations"
George Willis Journal
Library of Congress, Manuscripts Division, Washington, D.C.
Pinckney Family Papers
Linnean Society of London
Ellis Manuscripts
Linnaeus Correspondence
National Library of Scotland, Edinburgh
Melville Papers
William R. Perkins Library, Manuscripts Department, Duke University, Durham,
N.C.
John Ball, Sr., and John, Jr., Papers
John C. Calhoun Papers, Family Division
Samuel B. Clark Papers
John Gibbons Papers
William Gibbons Papers
Nathanael Greene Papers
Habersham Family Papers
Edward Harden Papers
James Jackson Papers
Sylvanus and Cary Keith Papers
Thomas Legare Papers
Thomas and William Lowndes Papers
McIntosh County, Picture File
Edward Rutledge Papers

John Rutledge, Jr., Papers
Richard Singleton Papers
Edward Telfair Papers
Royal Society of Arts, London
   American Correspondence (microfilm, 2 reels)
Scottish Record Office, Edinburgh
   Clerk of Penicuik Muniments
   Miscellaneous Muniments
   Murray of Murraythwaite Muniments
   Tod Murray and Jamieson Collection
   Steuart of Dalguise Muniments
South Carolina Department of Archives and History, Columbia
   Records of the Secretary of State, Recorded Instruments, Estate Inventories (sample)
   Petitions to the General Assembly
   Sainsbury Transcripts of Records in the Public Record Office
South Carolina Historical Society, Charleston
   Robert Francis Withers Allston Collection
   Ball Family Papers
   Allard Belin Journals
   William Butler, "Observations on the Culture of Rice," 1786
   John Chesnut Papers
   Chesnut-Miller-Manning Papers
   Langdon Cheves I Papers
   Ford-Ravenel Papers
   Gaillard Family Papers
   Gourdin Family Papers
   Hering-Middleton Papers
   Lucas Family Papers
   Manigault Papers
   Peter Manigault Letterbook
   Maps and Muniments
   Pinckney Family Papers
   David Ramsay Correspondence (microfiche from originals in the Charleston
     Library Society)
   Harriott Horry Ravenel Collection
   South Carolina Agricultural Society Records
   Vander Horst Papers
South Caroliniana Library, Manuscripts Division, University of South Carolina,
  Columbia
   Lewis Malone Ayer Papers
   Ball Family Papers
   Pierce Butler Letterbook
   Camden Account Book
   Margaret Colleton Papers

Henry William DeSaussure Papers
Dickson Family Papers
Joseph Dulles Journal
John Eiffert Papers
Michael Gaffney Journal
Guignard Family Papers
James Hamilton Papers
Hammond, Bryan, Cumming Papers
James Harrison Account Book
Peter Horry Papers
Ralph Izard Papers
William Johnston Papers
Alexander Keith's Commonplace Book
John Lloyd Letterbook
McDowell-Davison Papers
Hezekiah Maham Papers
Manigault Family Papers
Manigault Letterbook, 1793–1805
Samuel Mathis Papers
Middleton Place Manuscripts
Middleton-Saumarez Papers (microfilm)
Thomas Morris Papers
William Moultrie Papers
William Murrell Papers
Noble Family Papers
Palmer Family Papers
Pemberton Diary
Charles Pinckney Papers
Thomas Pinckney Papers
David Ramsay Papers
Read Family Papers
Nathaniel H. Rhodes, "Observations on the General Doctrine of Fevers," 1800
William G. Richardson Ledger
Edward Rutledge Papers
Benjamin Waring Papers
Thomas Waties Papers and Plantation Book
Williams-Chesnut-Manning Papers (microfilm)
Alexander Wilson Papers
Southern Historical Collection, University of North Carolina, Chapel Hill
Arnold-Screven Papers
Bevard Papers
Bulloch Family Papers
John Ewing Colhoun Papers
Edith M. Dabbs Letter

Samuel Du Bose, Jr., Letters
Elliott-Gonzales Papers
Thomas Griffiths Diary
Nathaniel Heyward 1802 Manuscript
Charles Woodward Hutson Collection
Jackson-Prince Papers
A. R. Lawton Papers
Rawlins Lowndes Papers
McBee Family Papers
Mackay-Stiles Papers
Thomas Middleton Manuscript Book
John Rutledge Papers
Singleton Family Papers
Josiah Smith Letterbook
Mrs. Francis D. Stewart Collection
Stoney and Porcher Family Papers
University of South Carolina, Department of History, Columbia
Laurens Papers Project (from originals in the South Carolina Historical Society)
Yale University, Special Collections, New Haven, Conn.
Whitney Papers

PRINTED PRIMARY SOURCES

Abbot, Abiel. "The Abiel Abbot Journals. . . ." Edited by John Hammond Moore. *SCHM,* LXVIII (1967), 51–73, 115–139, 232–254.
Agricultural Society of South Carolina. *Papers Published by Order of the Agricultural Society of South Carolina.* Columbia, S.C., 1818.
Allston, R. F. W. *Memoir of the Introduction and Planting of Rice in South-Carolina. . . .* Geological and Agricultural Survey of South Carolina, *Pamphlets.* Charleston, 1843.
The American Gazetteer. 3 vols. London, 1762.
Bartram, William. "Travels in Georgia and Florida, 1773–74: A Report to Dr. John Fothergill." Edited by Francis Harper. American Philosophical Society, *Transactions,* N.S., XXXIII, pt. 2 (1942–1944), 121–242.
———. *Travels through North and South Carolina, Georgia, East and West Florida. . . .* London, 1792; facs. ed., Charlottesville, Va., 1980.
Bolzius, Johann Martin. "Johann Martin Bolzius Answers a Questionnaire on Carolina and Georgia." Edited and translated by Klaus G. Loewald *et al. WMQ,* 3d Ser., XIV (1957), 218–261.
———. "John Martin Boltzius' Trip to Charleston, October 1742." Edited and translated by George Fenwick Jones. *SCHM,* LXXXII (1981), 87–110.
Burke, Edmund. *An Account of the European Settlements in America.* 2 vols. London, 1775.

———. *The Speech . . . on . . . Conciliation with the Colonies. . . .* London, 1775.

Butler, Samuel Edward. "The Diary of Samuel Edward Butler, 1784–1786. . . ." Edited by G. Melvin Herndon. *GHQ,* LII (1968), 203–220.

Candler, Allen D., comp. *The Colonial Records of the State of Georgia.* 26 vols. Atlanta, 1904–1916.

Carman, Harry J., ed. *American Husbandry* (1775). New York, 1939.

Castiglioni, Luigi. *Viaggio: Travels in the United States of North America, 1785–87.* Edited and translated by Antonio Pace. Syracuse, N.Y., 1983.

Catesby, Mark. *Catesby's Birds of Colonial America.* Edited by Alan Feduccia. Chapel Hill, N.C., 1985.

[Christie, Thomas]. *A Description of Georgia. . . .* London, 1741.

Clay, Joseph. *Letters of Joseph Clay. . . .* GHS, *Collections,* VIII. Savannah, 1913.

Clayton, Augustin Smith, comp. *A Compilation of the Laws of the State of Georgia . . . [1800–1810].* Augusta, 1813.

[Cluny, Alexander]. *The American Traveler. . . .* London, 1769.

Cohen, Hennig, ed. "A Colonial Poem on Indigo Culture." *AH,* XXX (1956), 41–44.

Cooper, Thomas, and David J. McCord, eds. *The Statutes at Large of South Carolina.* 10 vols. Columbia, 1836–1841.

[Crokatt, James, ed.]. *Further Observations Intended for Improving the Culture and Curing of Indico, etc. in South-Carolina.* London, 1747.

Darlington, William, ed. *Memorials of John Bartram and Humphry Marshall. . . .* Philadelphia, 1849.

Davis, John. *Travels of Four Years and a Half in the United States of America . . . [1798–1802].* London, 1803.

Dunlop, J. B. "A Scotsman Visits Georgia in 1811." Edited by Raymond A. Mohl. *GHQ,* LV (1971), 259–274.

De Brahm, William Gerard. *De Brahm's Report of the General Survey in the Southern District of North America.* Edited by Louis De Vorsey, Jr. Columbia, S.C., 1971.

DeSaussure, H. W. [Phocion, pseud.]. *Letters on the Questions. . . .* Charleston, S.C., 1795.

Drayton, John. *A View of South-Carolina, as Respects Her Natural and Civil Concerns.* Charleston, S.C., 1802.

Du Pre, Lewis. *Observations on the Culture of Cotton.* Georgetown, S.C., 1799.

Elliot, Jonathan, ed. *Debates in the Several State Conventions on the Adoption of the Federal Constitution. . . .* 2d ed. 5 vols. Philadelphia, 1876.

Farrand, Max, ed. *The Records of the Federal Convention of 1787.* Rev. ed. 4 vols. New Haven, Conn., 1937.

Fauche, Jonas. "The Frontiers of Georgia in the Late Eighteenth Century: Jonas Fauche to Joseph Vallance Bevan." Edited by Lilla Mills Hawes. *GHQ,* XLVII (1963), 84–95.

[Fayrweather, Samuel]. "A Description of Whitefield's Bethesda: Samuel Fayrweather to Thomas Prince and Thomas Foxcroft." Edited by Lilla Mills Hawes. *GHQ,* XLV (1961), 363–366.

Ferguson, Adam. *An Essay on the History of Civil Society.* Edinburgh, 1767.

Ford, Timothy. [Americanus, pseud.]. *The Constitutionalist.* . . . Charleston, S.C., 1794.

———. "Diary of Timothy Ford, 1785–1786." Edited by Joseph Barnwell. *SCHM*, XIII (1912), 132–147, 181–204.

Gadsden, Christopher. *The Writings of Christopher Gadsden, 1746–1805.* Edited by Richard Walsh. Columbia, S.C., 1966.

[Glen, James]. *A Description of South Carolina.* London, 1761. Facs. rpt. in Chapman J. Milling, ed., *Colonial South Carolina: Two Contemporary Descriptions* (Columbia, S.C., 1951), 2–104.

Habersham, James. *The Letters of Hon. James Habersham, 1756–1775.* GHS, *Collections,* VI. Savannah, 1904.

Harper, Robert Goodloe. [Appius, pseud.]. *An Address to the People of South-Carolina, by the General Committee of the Representative Reform Association at Columbia.* Charleston, S.C., 1794.

Hazard, Ebenezer. "A View of Coastal South Carolina in 1778: The Journal of Ebenezer Hazard." Edited by H. Roy Merrens. *SCHM,* LXXIII (1972), 177–193.

Hemphill, William Edwin, *et al.,* eds. *Journals of the General Assembly and House of Representatives, 1776–1780.* The State Records of South Carolina. Columbia, 1970.

[Hewatt, Alexander]. *An Historical Account of the Rise and Progress of the Colonies of South Carolina and Georgia.* 2 vols. London, 1779.

Horry, Peter. "Journal of General Peter Horry." Edited by A. S. Salley. *SCHM,* XXXVIII–XLVIII (1937–1947).

Hume, David. *Essays Moral, Political, and Literary.* Rev. ed. Edited by Eugene F. Miller. Indianapolis, Ind., 1987.

Izard, George. "Diary of a Journey by George Izard, 1815–1816." Edited by Harold W. Ryan. *SCHM,* LIII (1952), 67–76, 155–160.

Izard, Ralph. *Correspondence of Mr. Ralph Izard.* . . . Edited by Anne Izard Deas. New York, 1844.

Jackson, James. *The Papers of James Jackson, 1781–1798.* Edited by Lilla M. Hawes. GHS, *Collections,* XI. Savannah, 1955.

Janson, Charles William. *The Stranger in America.* . . . London, 1807.

Johnson, William. *Nugae Georgicae: An Essay, Delivered to the Literary and Philosophical Society of Charleston, South Carolina, October 14, 1815.* Charleston, 1815.

King, Reuben. "The Reuben King Journal, 1800–1806." Edited by Virginia Steele Wood and Ralph Van Wood. *GHQ,* L (1966), 177–206, 296–335, 421–458, LI (1967), 78–120.

Lamar, Lucius Q. C., comp. *A Compilation of the Laws of the State of Georgia* . . . *[1810–1819].* Augusta, 1821.

Lambert, John. *Travels through Lower Canada and the United States of North America, in the Years 1806, 1807, and 1808.* 3 vols. London, 1810.

La Rochefoucault Liancourt, François Alexandre Frédéric, duc de. *Travels through the United States of North America* . . . *[1795–1797].* 2 vols. London, 1799.

Laurens, Henry. "A Narrative of the Capture of Henry Laurens, of His Confinement in the Tower of London, etc., 1780, 1781, 1782." *South Carolina Historical Society, Collections*, I (1857), 18–30.

———. *The Papers of Henry Laurens*. Edited by Philip M. Hamer *et al.* 12 vols. to date. Columbia, S.C., 1968–.

Lawson, John. *A New Voyage to Carolina*. Edited by Hugh Talmage Lefler. Chapel Hill, N.C., 1967.

Lining, John. "A Description of the *American* Yellow Fever . . . ," Dec. 14, 1753. *Essays and Observations Physical and Literary*, II. Edinburgh, 1756.

Linnaeus, Carolus. *A Selection of the Correspondence of Linnaeus*. . . . 2 vols. Edited by Sir James Edward Smith. London, 1821.

McIntosh, Lachlan. "The Papers of Lachlan McIntosh, 1774–1799." Edited by Lilla M. Hawes. *GHQ*, XXXVIII (1954), 148–169, 253–267, 356–368, XXXIX (1955), 52–68, 172–186, 253–268, 356–375, XL (1956), 68–88, 152–174.

McQueen, Don Juan. *The Letters of Don Juan McQueen to His Family, Written from Spanish East Florida, 1797–1807*. Edited by Walter Charlton Hartridge. Columbia, S.C., 1943.

Manigault, Ann. "Extracts from the Journal of Mrs. Ann Manigault, 1754–1781." Edited by Mabel L. Webber. *SCHM*, XX (1919), 57–63.

Melish, John. *Travels through the United States of America, in the Years 1806 and 1807, and 1809, 1810, and 1811*. London, 1818.

Merrens, H. Roy, ed. *The Colonial South Carolina Scene: Contemporary Views, 1697–1774*. Columbia, 1977.

Meyers, Marvin, ed. *The Mind of the Founder: Sources of the Political Thought of James Madison*. Hanover, N.H., 1981.

Michaux, François André. *Travels to the West of the Alleghany Mountains . . . in the Year 1802*. In Reuben Gold Thwaites, ed., *Early Western Travels*, III. Cleveland, Ohio, 1904.

[Milligen (-Johnston), George]. *A Short Description of the Province of South-Carolina*. . . . London, 1770. Facs. rpt. in Chapman J. Milling, ed., *Colonial South Carolina: Two Contemporary Descriptions* (Columbia, S.C., 1951), 111–206.

Miranda, Francisco de. *The New Democracy in America: Travels of Francisco de Miranda in the United States, 1783–84*. Edited by John S. Ezell. Translated by Judson P. Wood. Norman, Okla., 1963.

Montesquieu, Charles Secondat, Baron de. *The Spirit of Laws*. Edited by David Wallace Carrithers. Berkeley, Calif., 1977.

Morse, Jedidiah. *The American Gazetteer*. 2 vols. Boston, 1797.

Muhlenberg, Henry. "Henry Muhlenberg's Georgia Correspondence." Edited by Andrew W. Lewis. *GHQ*, XLIX (1965), 424–454.

Oglethorpe, James. "Letters from James Oglethorpe." *GHS, Collections*, III (Savannah, 1873), 1–156.

Olmsted, Denison. *Memoir of Eli Whitney, Esq*. New Haven, Conn., 1846.

Pendleton, Nathaniel. "Short Account of the Sea Coast of Georgia in Respect to

Agriculture, Ship-Building, Navigation, and the Timber Trade." Edited by Theodore Thayer. *GHQ*, XLI (1957), 70–81.

Pilmore, Joseph. *The Journal of Joseph Pilmore, Methodist Itinerant: For the Years August 1, 1769, to January 2, 1774*. Edited by Frederick E. Maser and Howard T. Maag. Philadelphia, 1969.

Pinckney, Eliza Lucas. *The Letterbook of Eliza Lucas Pinckney*. Edited by Elise Pinckney. Chapel Hill, N.C., 1972.

Pinckney, Mary Stead. *The Letter-book of Mary Stead Pinckney, November 14th, 1796, to August 29th, 1797*. Edited by Charles F. McCombs. New York, 1946.

Pringle, Robert. *The Letterbook of Robert Pringle*. 2 vols. Edited by Walter B. Edgar. Columbia, S.C., 1972.

Quincy, Josiah, Jr. "Journal of Josiah Quincy, Junior, 1773." Edited by Mark Antony DeWolfe Howe. Massachusetts Historical Society, *Proceedings*, XLIX (1915–1916), 424–481.

Ramsay, David. *A Dissertation on the Means of Preserving Health in Charleston and the Adjacent Low Country*. Charleston, S.C., 1790.

———. *History of South-Carolina, from Its First Settlement in 1670 to the Year 1808. . . .* 2 vols. Charleston, S.C., 1809.

———. *The History of the Revolution of South-Carolina*. Trenton, N.J., 1785.

———. "An Oration on the Advantages of American Independence" (1778). Edited by Robert L. Brunhouse. American Philosophical Society, *Transactions*, N.S., LV, pt. 4 (August 1965), 183–190.

———. *An Oration on the Cession of Louisiana to the United States*. Charleston, S.C., 1804.

———. *A Review of the Improvements, Progress, and State of Medicine in the Eighteenth Century. . . .* Charleston, S.C., 1801.

———. *A Sketch of the Soil, Climate, Weather, and Diseases of South-Carolina*. Charleston, S.C., 1796.

Rees, Abraham. *The Cyclopedia; or, Universal Dictionary of Arts, Sciences, and Literature*. 1st Am. ed., rev. Philadelphia, [1810–1824].

Robertson, William. *The History of America*. 2 vols. London, 1777.

Romans, Bernard. *A Concise Natural History of East and West Florida*. 1775; facs. ed., Gainesville, Fla., 1962.

Schoepf, Johann David. *Travels in the Confederation, 1783–1784*. Edited and translated by Alfred J. Morrison. 2 vols. 1911; rpt., New York, 1968.

Seabrook, Whitemarsh B. "Memoir on Sea Island Cotton." *Proceedings of the Agricultural Convention and of the State Agricultural Society of South Carolina* [1839–1845], supplement for 1846. Columbia, S.C., 1847.

———. *Memoir on the Origin, Cultivation, and Uses of Cotton. . . .* Geological and Agricultural Survey of South Carolina, *Pamphlets*. Charleston, 1844.

Smith, Adam. *An Inquiry into the Nature and Causes of the Wealth of Nations*. Edited by R. H. Campbell and A. S. Skinner. 2 vols. Oxford, 1976.

——. *The Theory of Moral Sentiments.* Edited by D. D. Raphael and A. L. Macfie. Oxford, 1976.

Smyth, J. F. D. *A Tour in the United States of America.* . . . 2 vols. London, 1784.

Spalding, Thomas. *Observations on the Method of Planting and Cultivating the Sugar-Cane.* . . . Charleston, S.C., 1816. In E. Merton Coulter, ed., *Georgia's Disputed Ruins* (Chapel Hill, N.C., 1937), 227–263.

Stephens, William. *The Journal of William Stephens, 1743–1745.* 2 vols. Edited by E. Merton Coulter. Athens, Ga., 1958–1959.

Tocqueville, Alexis de. *Democracy in America.* Edited by Phillips Bradley. 2 vols. New York, 1945.

Turner, Daniel. "Letters and Papers of Dr. Daniel Turner: A Rhode Islander in South Georgia." Edited by Richard K. Murdoch. *GHQ,* LIII (1969), 341–393, 476–509, LIV (1970), 91–122, 244–282.

Ver Steeg, Clarence L., ed. *A True and Historical Narrative of the Colony of Georgia by Pat. Tailfer and Others, with Comments by the Earl of Egmont.* Athens, Ga., 1960.

Watkins, Robert, and George Watkins, eds. *A Digest of the Laws of the State of Georgia.* Philadelphia, 1800.

Watson, Elkanah. *Men and Times of the Revolution.* . . . Edited by Winslow C. Watson. New York, 1856.

Weir, Robert M., ed. *The Letters of Freeman, etc.: Essays on the Nonimportation Movement in South Carolina, Collected by William Henry Drayton.* Columbia, S.C., 1977.

White, J[oshua] E[lder]. "Topography of Savannah and Its Vicinity: A Report to the Georgia Medical Society, May 3, 1806." *GHQ,* I (1917), 236–242.

Whitefield, George. *George Whitefield's Journals (1737–1741).* . . . Edited by William V. Davis. Gainesville, Fla., 1969.

Whitney, Eli. "Correspondence of Eli Whitney relative to the Invention of the Cotton Gin." Edited by M. B. Hammond. *AHR,* III (1897–1898), 90–127.

Wood, Virginia Steele, and Ralph Van Wood, eds. *1805 Georgia Land Lottery.* Cambridge, Mass., 1964.

Woodmason, Charles. *The Carolina Backcountry on the Eve of the Revolution: The Journal and Other Writings of Charles Woodmason, Anglican Itinerant.* Edited by Richard J. Hooker. Chapel Hill, N.C., 1953.

Wright, James. "Letters from Sir James Wright." GHS, *Collections,* III (Savannah, 1873), 157–375.

NEWSPAPERS

American Patriot (Savannah)
Athens Gazette
Augusta Chronicle
Augusta Chronicle and Gazette of the State
Carolina Gazette (Charleston)

Carolina Weekly Messenger (Charleston)
Charleston Morning Post (later *City Gazette*)
Charlestown Gazette
Columbian Centinel (Augusta)
Columbian Herald (Charleston)
Columbian Museum and Savannah Advertiser
Farmer's Gazette (Sparta, Ga.)
Gazette of the State of South-Carolina (later *State Gazette of South-Carolina*)
    (Charleston)
Georgetown Gazette (South Carolina)
Georgia Argus (Milledgeville)
Georgia Gazette (Savannah)
Georgia Journal (Milledgeville)
Louisville Gazette (Georgia)
Miller's Weekly Messenger (Pendleton, S.C.)
Monitor (Washington, Ga.)
Royal Gazette (Charleston)
South-Carolina and American General Gazette (Charleston)
South-Carolina Gazette (Charleston)
South-Carolina Gazette; And Country Journal (Charleston)
Southern Patriot, and Commercial Advertiser (Charleston)

BOOKS

Adams, Percy G. *Travelers and Travel Liars, 1660–1800*. Berkeley, Calif., 1962.
———. *Travel Literature and the Evolution of the Novel*. Lexington, Ky., 1983.
Appleby, Joyce. *Capitalism and a New Social Order: The Republican Vision of the 1790s*.
    New York, 1984.
———. *Economic Thought and Ideology in Seventeenth Century England*. Princeton,
    N.J., 1978.
Axtell, James. *The Invasion Within: The Contest of Cultures in Colonial North America*.
    New York, 1985.
Bailyn, Bernard. *Voyagers to the West: A Passage in the Peopling of America on the Eve of
    the Revolution*. New York, 1986.
Bateman, Fred, and Thomas Weiss. *A Deplorable Scarcity: The Failure of
    Industrialization in the Slave Economy*. Chapel Hill, N.C., 1981.
Batten, Charles L., Jr. *Pleasurable Instruction: Form and Convention in Eighteenth-
    Century Travel Literature*. Berkeley, Calif., 1978.
Baum, John Alan. *Montesquieu and Social Theory*. Oxford, 1979.
Bayne-Powell, Rosamond. *Eighteenth-Century London Life*. New York, 1938.
Beeman, Richard R. *The Evolution of the Southern Backcountry: A Case Study of
    Lunenburg County, Virginia, 1746–1832*. Philadelphia, 1984.

Berkeley, Edmund, and Dorothy Smith Berkeley. *Dr. Alexander Garden of Charles Town.* Chapel Hill, N.C., 1969.

Bertelson, David. *The Lazy South.* New York, 1967.

Black, Jeremy. *The British and the Grand Tour.* London, 1985.

Bloom, Edward A., and Lillian D. Bloom. *Joseph Addison's Sociable Animal: In the Market Place, on the Hustings, in the Pulpit.* Providence, R.I., 1971.

Bonner, James C. *A History of Georgia Agriculture, 1732–1860.* Athens, Ga., 1964.

———. *Milledgeville: Georgia's Antebellum Capital.* Athens, Ga., 1978.

Brathwaite, Edward. *The Development of Creole Society in Jamaica, 1770–1820.* Oxford, 1971.

Bridenbaugh, Carl. *Myths and Realities: Societies of the Colonial South.* New York, 1963.

Brock, William R. *Scotus Americanus: A Study of the Sources for the Links between Scotland and America in the Eighteenth Century.* Edinburgh, 1982.

Brockway, Lucile H. *Science and Colonial Expansion: The Role of the British Royal Botanic Gardens.* New York, 1979.

Brooks, Robert Preston. *The University of Georgia under Sixteen Administrations, 1785–1955.* Athens, Ga., 1956.

Brown, Richard Maxwell. *The South Carolina Regulators.* Cambridge, Mass., 1963.

Bryson, Gladys. *Man and Society: The Scottish Inquiry of the Eighteenth Century.* New York, 1968.

Bugbee, Bruce W. *Genesis of American Patent and Copyright Law.* Washington, D.C., 1967.

Burnet, Macfarlane. *Natural History of Infectious Disease.* 3d ed. Cambridge, 1962.

Bury, J. B. *The Idea of Progress: An Inquiry into Its Origin and Growth.* London, 1920.

Campbell, Mary B. *The Witness and the Other World: Exotic European Travel Writing, 400–1600.* Ithaca, N.Y., 1988.

Cash, W. J. *The Mind of the South.* New York, 1941.

Cashin, Edward J., ed. *Colonial Augusta: "Key of the Indian Countrey."* Macon, Ga., 1986.

Caughey, John Walton. *McGillivray of the Creeks.* Norman, Okla., 1938.

Chapman, S. D. *The Cotton Industry in the Industrial Revolution.* London, 1972.

Chitnis, Anand C. *The Scottish Enlightenment: A Social History.* London, 1976.

Clark, Victor S. *History of Manufactures in the United States.* Vol. I, *1607–1860.* New York, 1929.

Clemens, Paul G. E. *The Atlantic Economy and Colonial Maryland's Eastern Shore: From Tobacco to Grain.* Ithaca, N.Y., 1980.

Clowse, Converse D. *Economic Beginnings in Colonial South Carolina: 1670–1730.* Columbia, S.C., 1971.

Coclanis, Peter A. *The Shadow of a Dream: Economic Life and Death in the South Carolina Low Country, 1670–1920.* New York, 1989.

Coetzee, J. M. *White Writing: On the Culture of Letters in South Africa.* New Haven, Conn., 1988.

Coleman, Kenneth. *Colonial Georgia: A History.* New York, 1976.

——, ed. *A History of Georgia*. Athens, 1977.

Conkin, Paul K. *Prophets of Prosperity: America's First Political Economists*. Bloomington, Ind., 1980.

Coulter, E. Merton. *Thomas Spalding of Sapelo*. Baton Rouge, La., 1940.

Crane, Verner W. *The Southern Frontier, 1670–1732*. 1929; rpt., Ann Arbor, Mich., 1956.

Craton, Michael. *A History of the Bahamas*. London, 1962.

——. *Testing the Chains: Resistance to Slavery in the British West Indies*. Ithaca, N.Y., 1982.

Crosby, Alfred W. *Ecological Imperialism: The Biological Expansion of Europe, 900–1900*. Cambridge, 1986.

Crowley, J. E. *This Sheba, Self: The Conceptualization of Economic Life in Eighteenth-Century America*. Baltimore, 1974.

Dabney, William M., and Marion Dargan. *William Henry Drayton and the American Revolution*. Albuquerque, N.M., 1962.

Dalzell, Robert F., Jr. *Enterprising Elite: The Boston Associates and the World They Made*. Cambridge, Mass., 1987.

Davis, David Brion. *The Problem of Slavery in the Age of Revolution, 1770–1823*. Ithaca, N.Y., 1975.

——. *Slavery and Human Progress*. Oxford, 1984.

Davis, Harold E. *The Fledgling Province: Social and Cultural Life in Colonial Georgia, 1733–1776*. Chapel Hill, N.C., 1976.

Davis, Richard Beale. *Intellectual Life in the Colonial South, 1585–1763*. 3 vols. Knoxville, Tenn., 1978.

Doar, David. *Rice and Rice Planting in the South Carolina Low Country*. Contributions to the Charleston Museum, no. 8. Charleston, S.C., 1936.

Doerflinger, Thomas M. *A Vigorous Spirit of Enterprise: Merchants and Economic Development in Revolutionary Philadelphia*. Chapel Hill, N.C., 1986.

Dublin, Thomas. *Women at Work: The Transformation of Work and Community in Lowell, Massachusetts, 1826–1860*. New York, 1979.

Duffy, John. *Epidemics in Colonial America*. Baton Rouge, La., 1953.

Dunn, Richard S. *Sugar and Slaves: The Rise of the Planter Class in the English West Indies, 1624–1713*. Chapel Hill, N.C., 1972.

Dyer, Thomas G. *The University of Georgia: A Bicentennial History, 1785–1985*. Athens, Ga., 1985.

Evans, Eli N. *Judah P. Benjamin: The Jewish Confederate*. New York, 1988.

Ezell, John Samuel. *Fortune's Merry Wheel: The Lottery in America*. Cambridge, Mass., 1960.

Findlay, John M. *People of Chance: Gambling in American Society from Jamestown to Las Vegas*. New York, 1986.

Fischer, David Hackett. *Albion's Seed: Four British Folkways in America*. New York, 1989.

Fogel, Robert William. *Without Consent or Contract: The Rise and Fall of American Slavery*. New York, 1989.

Foner, Eric. *Nothing but Freedom: Emancipation and Its Legacy.* Baton Rouge, La., 1983.

Ford, Lacy K., Jr. *Origins of Southern Radicalism: The South Carolina Upcountry, 1800–1860.* Oxford, 1988.

Foster, William Omer, Sr. *James Jackson: Duelist and Militant Statesman, 1757–1806.* Athens, Ga., 1960.

Fox-Genovese, Elizabeth, and Eugene D. Genovese. *Fruits of Merchant Capital: Slavery and Bourgeois Property in the Rise and Expansion of Capitalism.* New York, 1983.

Fredrickson, George M. *White Supremacy: A Comparative Study in American and South African History.* New York, 1981.

Freehling, William W. *Prelude to Civil War: The Nullification Controversy in South Carolina, 1816–1836.* New York, 1965.

———. *The Road to Disunion.* Vol. I, *Secessionists at Bay, 1776–1854.* New York, 1990.

Friedman, Lawrence M. *A History of American Law.* 2d ed. New York, 1985.

Furber, Holden. *John Company at Work: A Study of European Expansion in India in the Late Eighteenth Century.* Cambridge, Mass., 1961.

Gallay, Alan. *The Formation of a Planter Elite: Jonathan Bryan and the Southern Colonial Frontier.* Athens, Ga., 1989.

Gaspar, David Barry. *Bondmen and Rebels: A Study of Master-Slave Relations in Antigua, with Implications for Colonial British America.* Baltimore, 1985.

Gay, Peter. *The Enlightenment: An Interpretation.* 2 vols. New York, 1969.

Genovese, Eugene D. *The Political Economy of Slavery: Studies in the Economy and Society of the Slave South.* New York, 1967.

———. *Roll, Jordan, Roll: The World the Slaves Made.* New York, 1974.

———. *The World the Slaveholders Made: Two Essays in Interpretation.* New York, 1971.

Gerbi, Antonello. *The Dispute of the New World: The History of a Polemic, 1750–1900.* Translated by Jeremy Moyle. Pittsburgh, Pa., 1973.

Gillies, Alexander. *A Hebridean in Goethe's Weimar: The Reverend James Macdonald and the Cultural Relations between Scotland and Germany.* Oxford, 1969.

Gray, Lewis Cecil. *A History of Agriculture in the Southern United States to 1860.* 2 vols. Washington, D.C., 1933.

Green, Constance McL. *Eli Whitney and the Birth of American Technology.* Boston, 1956.

Greene, Jack P. *Pursuits of Happiness: The Social Development of Early Modern British Colonies and the Formation of American Culture.* Chapel Hill, N.C., 1988.

Greene, John C. *American Science in the Age of Jefferson.* Ames, Iowa, 1984.

Greven, Philip. *The Protestant Temperament: Patterns of Child-Rearing, Religious Experience, and the Self in Early America.* New York, 1977.

Griffith, Benjamin W., Jr. *McIntosh and Weatherford, Creek Indian Leaders.* Tuscaloosa, Ala., 1988.

Grist, D. H. *Rice.* 2d ed. London, 1955.

Hahn, Steven. *The Roots of Southern Populism: Yeoman Farmers and the Transformation of the Georgia Upcountry, 1850–1890.* New York, 1983.

Hamowy, Ronald. *The Scottish Enlightenment and the Theory of Spontaneous Order.* Carbondale, Ill., 1987.

Hindle, Brooke. *Emulation and Invention.* New York, 1981.

———. *The Pursuit of Science in Revolutionary America, 1735–1789.* Chapel Hill, N.C., 1956.

Hirschman, Albert O. *The Passions and the Interests: Political Arguments for Capitalism before Its Triumph.* Princeton, N.J., 1977.

Hofstadter, Richard. *America at 1750: A Social Portrait.* New York, 1973.

Hont, Istvan, and Michael Ignatieff, eds. *Wealth and Virtue: The Shaping of Political Economy in the Scottish Enlightenment.* Cambridge, 1983.

Hook, Andrew. *Scotland and America: A Study in Cultural Relations, 1750–1835.* Glasgow, 1975.

Horwitz, Morton J. *The Transformation of American Law, 1780–1860.* Cambridge, Mass., 1977.

House, Albert Virgil. *Planter Management and Capitalism in Ante-Bellum Georgia: The Journal of Hugh Fraser Grant, Ricegrower,* part 1. New York, 1954.

Howard, Donald R. *Writers and Pilgrims: Medieval Pilgrimage Narrations and Their Posterity.* Berkeley, Calif., 1980.

Isaac, Rhys. *The Transformation of Virginia, 1740–1790.* Chapel Hill, N.C., 1982.

Jennings, Francis. *The Invasion of America: Indians, Colonialism, and the Cant of Conquest.* Chapel Hill, N.C., 1976.

Johnson, Paul. *Birth of the Modern: World Society, 1815–1830.* New York, 1991.

Jones, Alice Hanson. *Wealth of a Nation to Be: The American Colonies on the Eve of the Revolution.* New York, 1980.

Jordan, Winthrop D. *White over Black: American Attitudes toward the Negro, 1550–1812.* Chapel Hill, N.C., 1969.

Joyner, Charles. *Down by the Riverside: A South Carolina Slave Community.* Urbana, Ill., 1984.

Kasson, John F. *Civilizing the Machine: Technology and Republican Values in America, 1776–1900.* New York, 1976.

Kastner, Joseph. *A Species of Eternity.* New York, 1978.

Kaufman, Allen. *Capitalism, Slavery, and Republican Values: Antebellum Political Economists, 1819–1848.* Austin, Tex., 1982.

Kerber, Linda K. *Women of the Republic: Intellect and Ideology in Revolutionary America.* Chapel Hill, N.C., 1980.

Klein, Rachel N. *Unification of a Slave State: The Rise of the Planter Class in the South Carolina Backcountry, 1760–1808.* Chapel Hill, N.C., 1990.

Kling, Blair B. *The Blue Mutiny: The Indigo Disturbances in Bengal, 1859–1862.* Philadelphia, 1966.

Kloppenburg, Jack R., Jr. *First the Seed: The Political Economy of Plant Biotechnology, 1492–2000.* Cambridge, 1988.

Kolchin, Peter. *Unfree Labor: American Slavery and Russian Serfdom.* Cambridge, Mass., 1987.

Kramnick, Isaac. *Bolingbroke and His Circle: The Politics of Nostalgia in the Age of Walpole.* Cambridge, Mass., 1968.

Kulikoff, Allan. *Tobacco and Slaves: The Development of Southern Cultures in the Chesapeake, 1680–1800.* Chapel Hill, N.C., 1986.

Lamplugh, George R. *Politics on the Periphery: Factions and Parties in Georgia, 1783–1806.* Newark, Del., 1986.

Lander, Ernest McPherson, Jr. *The Textile Industry in Antebellum South Carolina.* Baton Rouge, La., 1969.

Lewis, Kenneth E. *Camden: A Frontier Town in Eighteenth-Century South Carolina.* Columbia, S.C., 1976.

Lindstrom, Diane. *Economic Development in the Philadelphia Region, 1810–1850.* New York, 1978.

Littlefield, Daniel C. *Rice and Slaves: Ethnicity and the Slave Trade in Colonial South Carolina.* Baton Rouge, La., 1981.

Litwack, Leon F. *Been in the Storm So Long: The Aftermath of Slavery.* New York, 1979.

McCoy, Drew R. *The Elusive Republic: Political Economy in Jeffersonian America.* Chapel Hill, N.C., 1980.

McCusker, John J., and Russell R. Menard. *The Economy of British America, 1607–1789.* Chapel Hill, N.C., 1985.

MacIntyre, Alasdair. *After Virtue: A Study in Moral Theory.* Notre Dame, Ind., 1981.

McKeehan, Louis W. *Yale Science: The First Hundred Years, 1701–1801.* New York, 1947.

McKendrick, Neil, John Brewer, and J. H. Plumb. *The Birth of a Consumer Society: The Commercialization of Eighteenth-Century England.* Reading, 1973.

McNeill, William H. *Plagues and Peoples.* New York, 1976.

McWhiney, Grady. *Cracker Culture: Celtic Ways in the Old South.* Tuscaloosa, Ala., 1988.

Magrath, C. Peter. *Yazoo: Law and Politics in the New Republic, the Case of Fletcher v. Peck.* Providence, R.I., 1966.

Main, Jackson Turner. *The Social Structure of Revolutionary America.* Princeton, N.J., 1965.

Marshall, P. J. *East Indian Fortunes: The British in Bengal in the Eighteenth Century.* Oxford, 1976.

Marshall, P. J., and Glyndwr Williams. *The Great Map of Mankind: Perceptions of New Worlds in the Age of Enlightenment.* Cambridge, Mass., 1982.

Marx, Leo. *The Machine in the Garden: Technology and the Pastoral Ideal in America.* New York, 1964.

Matson, Cathy D., and Peter S. Onuf. *A Union of Interests: Political and Economic Thought in Revolutionary America.* Lawrence, Kans., 1990.

May, Henry F. *The Enlightenment in America.* New York, 1976.

Meek, Ronald L. *Economics and Ideology and Other Essays: Studies in the Development of Economic Thought.* London, 1967.

———. *Smith, Marx, and After: Ten Essays in the Development of Economic Thought.* London, 1977.

———. *Social Science and the Ignoble Savage.* Cambridge, 1976.

Mercer, Philip. *Sympathy and Ethics: A Study of the Relationship between Sympathy and Morality, with Special Reference to Hume's Treatise.* Oxford, 1972.

Merchant, Carolyn. *The Death of Nature: Women, Ecology, and the Scientific Revolution.* San Francisco, Calif., 1980.

———. *Ecological Revolutions: Nature, Gender, and Science in New England.* Chapel Hill, N.C., 1989.

Meriwether, Robert L. *The Expansion of South Carolina, 1729–1765.* Kingsport, Tenn., 1940.

Meyers, Marvin. *The Jacksonian Persuasion: Politics and Belief.* Stanford, Calif., 1957.

Mingay, G. E. *English Landed Society in the Eighteenth Century.* London, 1963.

———. *The Gentry: The Rise and Fall of a Ruling Class.* New York, 1976.

Mirsky, Jeannette, and Allan Nevins. *The World of Eli Whitney.* New York, 1952.

Morgan, Edmund S. *American Slavery, American Freedom: The Ordeal of Colonial Virginia.* New York, 1976.

Mowat, Charles Loch. *East Florida as a British Province, 1763–1784.* Gainesville, Fla., 1964.

Murray, Chalmers S. *This Our Land: The Story of the Agricultural Society of South Carolina.* Charleston, S.C., 1949.

Nadelhaft, Jerome J. *The Disorders of War: The Revolution in South Carolina.* Orono, Maine, 1981.

Norton, Mary Beth. *Liberty's Daughters: The Revolutionary Experience of American Women, 1750–1800.* Boston, 1980.

O'Brien, Michael. *Rethinking the South: Essays in Intellectual History.* Baltimore, 1988.

O'Brien, Michael, and David Moltke-Hansen, eds. *Intellectual Life in Antebellum Charleston.* Knoxville, Tenn., 1986.

Otto, John Solomon. *Cannon's Point Plantation, 1794–1860: Living Conditions and Status Patterns in the Old South.* New York, 1984.

Panagopoulos, E. P. *New Smyrna: An Eighteenth-Century Greek Odyssey.* Gainesville, Fla., 1966.

Pearce, Roy Harvey. *Savagism and Civilization: A Study of the Indian and the American Mind.* Baltimore, 1967.

Perkin, Harold. *The Origins of Modern English Society, 1780–1880.* London, 1971.

Phillips, Ulrich Bonnell. *Life and Labor in the Old South.* Boston, 1929.

Pocock, J. G. A. *The Machiavellian Moment: Florentine Political Thought and the Atlantic Republican Tradition.* Princeton, N.J., 1975.

———. *Virtue, Commerce, and History: Essays on Political Thought and History, Chiefly in the Eighteenth Century.* Cambridge, 1985.

Proctor, Robert. *Racial Hygiene: Medicine under the Nazis.* Cambridge, Mass., 1988.

Prude, Jonathan. *The Coming of Industrial Order: Town and Factory Life in Rural Massachusetts, 1810–1860.* Cambridge, 1983.

Pursell, Carroll W., Jr. *Early Stationary Steam Engines in America: A Study in the Migration of a Technology.* Washington, D.C., 1969.

Ravenel, Harriott Horry. *Eliza Pinckney.* New York, 1896.

Richter, Melvin. *The Political Theory of Montesquieu.* Cambridge, 1977.

Riley, James C. *The Eighteenth-Century Campaign to Avoid Disease.* New York, 1987.

Rudé, George. *Paris and London in the Eighteenth Century: Studies in Popular Protest.* New York, 1971.

Saunders, Gail. *Bahamian Loyalists and Their Slaves.* London, 1983.

Savitt, Todd L. *Medicine and Slavery: The Diseases and Health Care of Blacks in Antebellum Virginia.* Urbana, Ill., 1978.

Schwartz, Stuart B. *Sugar Plantations in the Formation of Brazilian Society: Bahia, 1550–1835.* Cambridge, 1985.

Scott, James C. *Weapons of the Weak: Everyday Forms of Peasant Resistance.* New Haven, Conn., 1985.

Sellers, Leila. *Charleston Business on the Eve of the American Revolution.* Chapel Hill, N.C., 1934.

Shaffer, Arthur H. *To Be an American: David Ramsay and the Making of the American Consciousness.* Columbia, S.C., 1991.

Sheridan, Richard B. *Doctors and Slaves: A Medical and Demographic History of Slavery in the British West Indies, 1680–1834.* Cambridge, 1985.

———. *Sugar and Slavery: An Economic History of the British West Indies, 1623–1775.* Baltimore, 1973.

Shore, Laurence. *Southern Capitalists: The Ideological Leadership of an Elite, 1832–1885.* Chapel Hill, N.C., 1986.

Sirmans, M. Eugene. *Colonial South Carolina: A Political History, 1663–1763.* Chapel Hill, N.C., 1966.

Sloan, Douglas. *The Scottish Enlightenment and the American College Ideal.* New York, 1971.

Sontag, Susan. *Illness as Metaphor.* New York, 1978.

Spadafora, David. *The Idea of Progress in Eighteenth-Century Britain.* New Haven, Conn., 1990.

Stearns, Raymond Phineas. *Science in the British Colonies of America.* Urbana, Ill., 1970.

Stewart, John B. *The Moral and Political Philosophy of David Hume.* New York, 1963.

Symcox, Geoffrey. *Victor Amadeus II: Absolutism in the Savoyard State, 1675–1730.* New York, 1983.

Taylor, William R. *Cavalier and Yankee: The Old South and American National Character.* New York, 1957.

Thompson, E. P. *The Making of the English Working Class.* London, 1963.

Thornton, J. Mills, III. *Politics and Power in a Slave Society: Alabama, 1800–1860.* Baton Rouge, La., 1978.

Ver Steeg, Clarence L. *Origins of a Southern Mosaic: Studies of Early Carolina and Georgia.* Athens, Ga., 1975.

Wade, John Donald. *Augustus Baldwin Longstreet: A Study of the Development of Culture in the South.* Athens, Ga., 1969.

Wallace, David Duncan. *The History of South Carolina.* 4 vols. New York, 1934.

Waring, Joseph Ioor. *A History of Medicine in South Carolina, 1670–1825.* [Columbia, S.C.], 1964.

Whartenby, Franklee Gilbert. *Land and Labor Productivity in United States Cotton Production, 1800–1840.* New York, 1977.

White, Hayden. *Metahistory: The Historical Imagination in Nineteenth-Century Europe.* Baltimore, 1973.

Williams, Eric. *Capitalism and Slavery.* Chapel Hill, N.C., 1944.

Wills, Garry. *Inventing America: Jefferson's Declaration of Independence.* New York, 1978.

Wittfogel, Karl A. *Oriental Despotism: A Comparative Study of Total Power.* New Haven, Conn., 1957.

Wood, Betty. *Slavery in Colonial Georgia, 1730–1775.* Athens, Ga., 1984.

Wood, Peter H. *Black Majority: Negroes in Colonial South Carolina from 1670 through the Stono Rebellion.* New York, 1975.

Woodward, C. Vann. *Tom Watson: Agrarian Rebel.* New York, 1963.

Wright, Gavin. *The Political Economy of the Cotton South: Households, Markets, and Wealth in the Nineteenth Century.* New York, 1978.

Wright, J. Leitch, Jr. *Anglo-Spanish Rivalry in North America.* Athens, Ga., 1971.

———. *Creeks and Seminoles: The Destruction and Regeneration of the Muscogulge People.* Lincoln, Nebr., 1986.

———. *William Augustus Bowles: Director General of the Creek Nation.* Athens, Ga., 1967.

Wyatt-Brown, Bertram. *Southern Honor: Ethics and Behavior in the Old South.* New York, 1982.

Zacher, Christian K. *Curiosity and Pilgrimage: The Literature of Discovery in Fourteenth-Century England.* Baltimore, 1976.

ARTICLES AND ESSAYS

Abrams, Philip. "The Sense of the Past and the Origins of Sociology." *Past and Present,* no. 55 (May 1972), 18–32.

Adair, Douglass. " 'That Politics May Be Reduced to a Science': David Hume, James Madison, and the Tenth Federalist." In Trevor Colbourn, ed., *Fame and the Founding Fathers: Essays by Douglass Adair,* 93–106. New York, 1974.

Adams, O. Burton. "Yale Influence on the Formation of the University of Georgia." *GHQ,* LI (1967), 175–185.

Alden, Dauril. "The Growth and Decline of Indigo Production in Colonial Brazil: A Study in Comparative Economic History." *Jour. Econ. Hist.,* XXV (1965), 35–60.

Appleby, Joyce. "Ideology and Theory: The Tension between Political and Economic Liberalism in Seventeenth-Century England." *AHR,* LXXXI (1976), 499–515.

Appleby, Joyce. "Value and Society." In Jack P. Greene and J. R. Pole, eds., *Colonial British America: Essays in the New History of the Early Modern Era,* 290–316. Baltimore, 1984.

Ashworth, John. "The Relationship between Capitalism and Humanitarianism." *AHR*, XCII (1987), 813–828.

Ball, Duane E. "Dynamics of Population and Wealth in Eighteenth-Century Chester County, Pennsylvania." *Journal of Interdisciplinary History*, VI (1976–1977), 621–644.

Batz, William G. "The Historical Anthropology of John Locke." *Journal of the History of Ideas*, XXXV (1974), 663–670.

Becker, Robert A. "Salus Populi Suprema Lex: Public Peace and South Carolina Debtor Relief Laws, 1783–1788." *SCHM*, LXXX (1979), 65–75.

Bellot, Leland J. "Evangelicals and the Defense of Slavery in Britain's Old Colonial Empire." *Jour. So. Hist.*, XXXVII (1971), 19–40.

Berlin, Ira. "Time, Space, and the Evolution of Afro-American Society on British Mainland North America." *AHR*, LXXXV (1980), 44–78.

Brady, Patrick S. "The Slave Trade and Sectionalism in South Carolina, 1787–1808." *Jour. So. Hist.*, XXXVIII (1972), 601–620.

Brand, Donald D. "The Origin and Early Distribution of New World Cultivated Plants." *AH*, XIII (1939), 109–117.

Branson, Roy. "James Madison and the Scottish Enlightenment." *Journal of the History of Ideas*, XL (1979), 235–250.

Breeden, James O. "Disease as a Factor in Southern Distinctiveness." In Todd L. Savitt and James Harvey Young, eds., *Disease and Distinctiveness in the American South*, 1–28. Knoxville, Tenn., 1988.

Breen, T. H. "Horses and Gentlemen: The Cultural Significance of Gambling among the Gentry of Virginia." *WMQ*, 3d Ser., XXXIV (1977), 239–257.

Brown, Richard D. "Modernization and the Modern Personality in Early America, 1600–1865: A Sketch of a Synthesis." *Journal of Interdisciplinary History*, II, no. 3 (Winter 1972), 201–228.

Carrigan, Jo Ann. "Privilege, Prejudice, and the Strangers' Disease in Nineteenth-Century New Orleans." *Jour. So. Hist.*, XXXVI (1970), 568–578.

——. "Yellow Fever: Scourge of the South." In Todd L. Savitt and James Harvey Young, eds., *Disease and Distinctiveness in the American South*, 55–78. Knoxville, Tenn., 1988.

Cassedy, James H. "Medical Men and the Ecology of the Old South." In Ronald L. Numbers and Todd L. Savitt, eds., *Science and Medicine in the Old South*, 166–178. Baton Rouge, La., 1989.

Cates, Gerald L. " 'The Seasoning': Disease and Death among the First Colonists of Georgia." *GHQ*, LXIV (1980), 146–158.

Chaplin, Joyce E. "Creating a Cotton South in Georgia and South Carolina, 1760–1815." *Jour. So. Hist.*, LVII (1991), 171–200.

——. "Slavery and the Principle of Humanity: A Modern Idea in the Early Lower South." *Jour. Soc. Hist.*, XXIV (1990–1991), 299–316.

Chesnutt, David R. "South Carolina's Penetration of Georgia in the 1760's: Henry Laurens as a Case Study." *SCHM*, LXXIII (1972), 194–208.

Chinard, Gilbert. "Eighteenth Century Theories on America as a Human Habitat." American Philosophical Society, *Proceedings*, XCI (1947), 27–57.

Clark, Peter. "Migration in England during the Late Seventeenth and Early Eighteenth Centuries." *Past and Present*, no. 83 (May 1979), 57–90.

Clifton, James M. "The Rice Industry in Colonial America." *AH*, LV (1981), 266–283.

Coclanis, Peter A. "Bitter Harvest: The South Carolina Low Country in Historical Perspective." *Jour. Econ. Hist.*, XLV (1985), 251–259.

Coleman, Kenneth. "The Southern Frontier: Georgia's Founding and the Expansion of South Carolina." *GHQ*, LVI (1972), 163–174.

Coon, David L. "Eliza Lucas Pinckney and the Reintroduction of Indigo Culture in South Carolina." *Jour. So. Hist.*, XLII (1976), 61–76.

Craton, Michael. "Hobbesian or Panglossian? The Two Extremes of Slave Conditions in the British Caribbean, 1783–1834." *WMQ*, 3d Ser., XXXV (1978), 324–356.

Curtin, Philip D. "Epidemiology and the Slave Trade." *Political Science Quarterly*, LXXXIII (1968), 190–216.

Davis, David Brion. "Reflections on Abolitionism and Ideological Hegemony." *AHR*, XCII (1987), 797–812.

Dethloff, Henry C. "The Colonial Rice Trade." *AH*, LVI (1982), 231–243.

Duffy, John. "Eighteenth-Century Carolina Health Conditions." *Jour. So. Hist.*, XVIII (1952), 289–302.

———. "The Impact of Malaria on the South." In Todd L. Savitt and James Harvey Young, eds., *Disease and Distinctiveness in the American South*, 29–54. Knoxville, Tenn., 1988.

Dunn, Richard S. "The English Sugar Islands and the Founding of South Carolina." *SCHM*, LXXII (1971), 81–93.

Dupree, A. Hunter. "The National Pattern of American Learned Societies, 1769–1863." In Alexandra Oleson and Sanborn C. Brown, eds., *The Pursuit of Knowledge in the Early American Republic: American Scientific and Learned Societies from Colonial Times to the Civil War*, 21–63. Baltimore, 1976.

Egnal, Marc. "The Economic Development of the Thirteen Colonies, 1720–1775." *WMQ*, 3d Ser., XXXII (1975), 191–222.

Eisinger, Chester E. "The Influence of Natural Rights and Physiocratic Doctrines on American Agrarian Thought during the Revolutionary Period." *AH*, XXI (1947), 13–23.

Elsmere, Jane. "The Notorious Yazoo Land Fraud Case." *GHQ*, LI (1967), 425–442.

Ernst, Joseph A., and H. Roy Merrens, " 'Camden's Turrets Pierce the Skies!': The Urban Process in the Southern Colonies during the Eighteenth Century." *WMQ*, 3d Ser., XXX (1973), 549–574.

Ewan, Joseph. "The Growth of Learned and Scientific Societies in the Southeastern United States to 1860." In Alexandra Oleson and Sanborn C. Brown, eds., *The Pursuit of Knowledge in the Early American Republic: American Scientific and Learned Societies from Colonial Times to the Civil War*, 208–218. Baltimore, 1976.

Faust, Drew Gilpin. "The Rhetoric and Ritual of Agriculture in Antebellum South Carolina." *Jour. So. Hist.*, XLV (1979), 541–568.

Ford, Lacy K., Jr. "Republican Ideology in a Slave Society: The Political Economy of John C. Calhoun." *Jour. So. Hist.*, LIV (1988), 405–424.

——. "Yeoman Farmers in the South Carolina Upcountry: Changing Production Patterns in the Late Antebellum Era." *AH*, LX, no. 4 (Fall 1986), 17–37.

Fox-Genovese, Elizabeth, and Eugene D. Genovese. "The Slave Economies in Political Perspective." *JAH*, LXVI (1979–1980), 7–23.

Frick, George F. "The Royal Society in America." In Alexandra Oleson and Sanborn C. Brown, eds., *The Pursuit of Knowledge in the Early American Republic: American Scientific and Learned Societies from Colonial Times to the Civil War*, 70–83. Baltimore, 1976.

Gallay, Alan. "The Origins of Slaveholders' Paternalism: George Whitefield, the Bryan Family, and the Great Awakening in the South." *Jour. So. Hist.*, LIII (1987), 369–394.

Galloway, J. H. "Agricultural Reform and the Enlightenment in Late Colonial Brazil." *AH*, LIII (1979), 763–779.

Geertz, Clifford. "Deep Play: Notes on the Balinese Cockfight." In Geertz, *The Interpretation of Cultures: Selected Essays*, 412–453. New York, 1973.

Gifford, G. Edmund, Jr. "The Charleston Physician-Naturalists." *Bulletin of the History of Medicine*, XLIX (1975), 556–574.

Gray, Ralph, and Betty Wood. "The Transition from Indentured to Involuntary Servitude in Colonial Georgia." *Explorations in Economic History*, XIII (1976), 353–370.

Greene, Jack P. "Independence, Improvement, and Authority: Toward a Framework for Understanding the Histories of the Southern Backcountry during the Era of the American Revolution." In Ronald Hoffman *et al.*, eds., *An Uncivil War: The Southern Backcountry during the American Revolution*, 3–36. Charlottesville, Va., 1985.

——. "Search for Identity: An Interpretation of the Meaning of Selected Patterns of Social Response in Eighteenth-Century America." *Jour. Soc. Hist.*, III (1969–1970), 189–220.

Greene, Jack P., and J. R. Pole. "Reconstructing British-American Colonial History: An Introduction." In Greene and Pole, eds., *Colonial British America: Essays in the New History of the Early Modern Era*, 1–17. Baltimore, 1984.

Hamowy, Ronald. "Progress and Commerce in Anglo-American Thought: The Social Philosophy of Adam Ferguson." *Interpretation: A Journal of Political Philosophy*, XIV (1986), 61–87.

Hart, Bertha Sheppard. "The First Garden of Georgia." *GHQ*, XIX (1935), 325–332.

Haskell, Thomas L. "Capitalism and the Origins of the Humanitarian Sensibility." *AHR*, XC (1985), 339–361, 547–566.

——. "Convention and Hegemonic Interest in the Debate over Antislavery: A Reply to Davis and Ashworth." *AHR*, XCII (1987), 829–878.

Hasse, Larry. "Watermills in the South: Rural Institutions Working against Modernism." *AH*, LVIII (1984), 280–295.

Haywood, C. Robert. "The Influence of Mercantilism on Social Attitudes in the South, 1700–1763." *Journal of the History of Ideas,* XX (1959), 577–586.

———. "Mercantilism and South Carolina Agriculture, 1700–1763." *SCHM,* LX (1959), 15–27.

Heath, William Estill. "The Yazoo Land Fraud." *GHQ,* XVI (1932), 274–291.

Henretta, James A. "The War for Independence and American Economic Development." In Ronald Hoffman *et al.,* eds. *The Economy of Early America: The Revolutionary Period, 1763–1790,* 45–87. Charlottesville, Va., 1988.

Herndon, G. Melvin. "Samuel Edward Butler of Virginia Goes to Georgia, 1784." *GHQ,* LII (1968), 115–131.

Hilliard, Sam B. "Antebellum Tidewater Rice Culture in South Carolina and Georgia." In James R. Gibson, ed., *European Settlement and Development in North America: Essays on Geographical Change in Honour and Memory of Andrew Hill Clark,* 91–115. Toronto, 1978.

Hitz, Alex M. "Georgia Bounty Land Grants." *GHQ,* XXXVIII (1954), 337–348.

Holland, James W. "The Beginning of Public Agricultural Experimentation in America: The Trustees' Garden in Georgia." *AH,* XII (1938), 271–298.

Hunter, Louis C. "Waterpower in the Century of the Steam Engine." In Brooke Hindle, ed., *America's Wooden Age: Aspects of Its Early Technology,* 160–192. Tarrytown, N.Y., 1975.

Hymowitz, T., and J. R. Harlan. "Introduction of Soybean to North America by Samuel Bowen in 1765." *Economic Botany,* XXXVII (1983), 371–379.

Inscoe, John C. "Carolina Slave Names: An Index to Acculturation." *Jour. So. Hist.,* XLIX (1983), 527–554.

Jackson, Harvey H. "The Darien Antislavery Petition of 1739 and the Georgia Plan." *WMQ,* 3d Ser., XXXIV (1977), 618–631.

Johnson, Elmer D. "Alexander Hewat: South Carolina's First Historian." *Jour. So. Hist.,* XX (1954), 50–62.

Johnson, Michael P. "Runaway Slaves and the Slave Communities in South Carolina, 1799 to 1830." *WMQ,* 3d Ser., XXXVIII (1981), 418–441.

Kiple, Kenneth F., and Virginia H. Kiple. "Black Yellow Fever Immunities, Innate and Acquired, as Revealed in the American South." *Social Science History,* I (1977), 419–436.

Klein, Rachel N. "Ordering the Backcountry: The South Carolina Regulation." *WMQ,* 3d Ser., XXXVIII (1981), 661–680.

Koeniger, A. Cash. "Climate and Southern Distinctiveness." *Jour. So. Hist.,* LIV (1988), 21–44.

Krafka, Joseph, Jr. "Medicine in Colonial Georgia." *GHQ,* XX (1936), 326–344.

Kulik, Gary. "Dams, Fish, and Farmers: Defense of Public Rights in Eighteenth-Century Rhode Island." In Steven Hahn and Jonathan Prude, eds., *The Countryside in the Age of Capitalist Transformation: Essays in the Social History of Rural America,* 25–50. Chapel Hill, N.C., 1985.

Kulikoff, Allan. "The Transition to Capitalism in Rural America." *WMQ,* 3d Ser., XLVI (1989), 120–144.

———. "Uprooted Peoples: Black Migrants in the Age of the American Revolution, 1790–1820." In Ira Berlin and Ronald Hoffman, eds., *Slavery and Freedom in the Age of the American Revolution,* 143–171. Charlottesville, Va., 1983.

Kupperman, Karen Ordahl. "Fear of Hot Climates in the Anglo-American Colonial Experience." *WMQ,* 3d Ser., XLI (1984), 213–240.

———. "The Puzzle of the American Climate in the Early Colonial Period." *AHR,* LXXXVII (1982), 1262–1289.

Lamb, Robert Boyden. "Adam Smith's System: Sympathy Not Self-Interest." *Journal of the History of Ideas,* XXXV (1974), 671–682.

Lamplugh, George R. "John Wereat and Yazoo, 1794–1799." *GHQ,* LXXII (1988), 502–517.

Landers, Jane. "Gracia Real de Santa Teresa de Mose: A Free Black Town in Spanish Colonial Florida." *AHR,* XCV (1990), 9–30.

Leach, E. R. "Hydraulic Society in Ceylon." *Past and Present,* no. 15 (April 1959), 2–26.

Lee, Jean Butenhoff. "The Problem of Slave Community in the Eighteenth-Century Chesapeake." *WMQ,* 3d Ser., XLIII (1986), 333–361.

Lees, William B. "The Historical Development of Limerick Plantation, a Tidewater Rice Plantation in Berkeley County, South Carolina, 1683–1945." *SCHM,* LXXXII (1981), 44–62.

Lemon, James T., and Gary B. Nash. "The Distribution of Wealth in Eighteenth-Century America: A Century of Change in Chester County, Pennsylvania, 1693–1802." *Jour. Soc. Hist.,* II (1968–1969), 1–24.

Levy, B. H. "Joseph Solomon Ottolenghi: Kosher Butcher in Italy—Christian Missionary in Georgia." *GHQ,* LXVI (1982), 119–144.

Littlefield, Daniel C. "Plantations, Paternalism, and Profitability: Factors Affecting African Demography in the Old British Empire." *Jour. So. Hist.,* XLVII (1981), 167–182.

McKinstry, Mary Thomas. "Silk Culture in the Colony of Georgia." *GHQ,* XIV (1930), 225–235.

MacLean, Kenneth. "Imagination and Sympathy: Sterne and Adam Smith." *Journal of the History of Ideas,* X (1949), 399–410.

MacPhee, Donald A. "The Yazoo Controversy: The Beginning of the 'Quid' Revolt." *GHQ,* XLIX (1965), 23–43.

Meaders, Daniel E. "South Carolina Fugitives as Viewed through Local Colonial Newspapers with Emphasis on Runaway Notices, 1732–1801." *Journal of Negro History,* LX (1975), 288–319.

Meier, Hugo A. "Thomas Jefferson and a Democratic Technology." In Carroll W. Pursell, Jr., ed., *Technology in America: A History of Individuals and Ideas,* 17–33. Cambridge, Mass., 1981.

Menard, Russell R. "Slavery, Economic Growth, and Revolutionary Ideology in the South Carolina Lowcountry." In Ronald Hoffman *et al.,* eds., *The Economy of Early America: The Revolutionary Period, 1763–1790,* 244–274. Charlottesville, Va., 1988.

Merrens, H. Roy, and George D. Terry. "Dying in Paradise: Malaria, Mortality, and the

Perceptual Environment in Colonial South Carolina." *Jour. So. Hist.*, L (1984), 533–550.

Mitchell, Robert D. "The Formation of Early American Cultural Regions: An Interpretation." In James R. Gibson, ed., *European Settlement and Development in North America: Essays on Geographical Change in Honour and Memory of Andrew Hill Clark*, 66–90. Toronto, 1978.

Moore, John Hebron. "Cotton Breeding in the Old South." *AH*, XXX (1956), 95–104.

Morgan, Philip D. "Black Society in the Lowcountry, 1760–1810." In Ira Berlin and Ronald Hoffman, eds., *Slavery and Freedom in the Age of the American Revolution*, 83–141. Charlottesville, Va., 1983.

———. "Work and Culture: The Task System and the World of Lowcountry Blacks, 1700 to 1880." *WMQ*, 3d Ser., XXXIX (1982), 563–599.

———, ed. "A Profile of a Mid-Eighteenth Century South Carolina Parish: The Tax Return of Saint James', Goose Creek." *SCHM*, LXXXI (1980), 51–65.

Murrin, John M. "The Great Inversion, or Court versus Country: A Comparison of the Revolution Settlements in England (1688–1721) and America (1776–1816)." In J. G. A. Pocock, ed., *Three British Revolutions: 1641, 1688, 1776*, 368–453. Princeton, N.J., 1980.

Nadelhaft, Jerome. "Ending South Carolina's War: Two 1782 Agreements Favoring the Planters." *SCHM*, LXXX (1979), 50–64.

Nash, Gary B. "The Image of the Indian in the Southern Colonial Mind." *WMQ*, 3d Ser., XXIX (1972), 197–230.

Newton, Hester Walton. "The Agricultural Activities of the Salzburgers in Colonial Georgia." *GHQ*, XVIII (1934), 248–263.

Nobles, Gregory H. "Breaking into the Backcountry: New Approaches to the Early American Frontier." *WMQ*, 3d Ser., XLVI (1989), 641–670.

Numbers, Ronald L., and Janet S. Numbers. "Science in the Old South: A Reappraisal." *Jour. So. Hist.*, XLVIII (1982), 163–184.

Olwell, Robert A. " 'Domestick Enemies': Slavery and Political Independence in South Carolina, May 1775–March 1776." *Jour. So. Hist.*, LV (1989), 21–48.

Pascal, Roy. "Herder and the Scottish Historical School." *English Goethe Society Publications*, XIV (1938–1939), 23–42.

Paulson, Ronald. "Life as Journey and as Theater: Two Eighteenth-Century Narrative Structures." *New Literary History*, VIII (1976–1977), 43–58.

Perkin, H. J. "The Social Causes of the British Industrial Revolution." Royal Historical Society, *Transactions*, 5th Ser., XVIII (1968), 123–143.

Pocock, J. G. A. "Gibbon and the Shepherds: The Stages of Society in the *Decline and Fall*." *History of European Ideas*, II (1981), 193–202.

———. "To Market, to Market: Economic Thought in Early Modern England." *Journal of Interdisciplinary History*, X (1979–1980), 303–309.

Potter, David M., Jr. "The Rise of the Plantation System in Georgia." *GHQ*, XVI (1932), 114–135.

Ready, Milton. "The Georgia Concept: An Eighteenth Century Experiment in Colonization." *GHQ*, LV (1971), 157–172.

———. "The Georgia Trustees and the Malcontents: The Politics of Philanthropy." *GHQ*, LX (1976), 264–281.

Roberts, Lucien E. "Sectional Problems in Georgia during the Formative Period, 1776–1798." *GHQ*, XVIII (1934), 207–227.

Rose, Willie Lee. "The Domestication of Domestic Slavery." In Rose, *Slavery and Freedom*, ed. William W. Freehling, 18–36. New York, 1982.

Rossiter, Margaret W. "The Organization of Agricultural Improvement in the United States, 1785 to 1865." In Alexandra Oleson and Sanborn C. Brown, eds., *The Pursuit of Knowledge in the Early American Republic: American Scientific and Learned Societies from Colonial Times to the Civil War*, 279–298. Baltimore, 1976.

Rubin, Julius. "The Limits of Agricultural Progress in the Nineteenth-Century South." *AH*, XLIX (1975), 362–373.

Rutman, Darrett B., and Anita H. Rutman. "Of Agues and Fevers: Malaria in the Early Chesapeake." *WMQ*, 3d Ser., XXXIII (1976), 31–60.

Savitt, Todd L. "Black Health on the Plantation: Masters, Slaves, and Physicians." In Ronald L. Numbers and Todd L. Savitt, eds., *Science and Medicine in the Old South*, 327–355. Baton Rouge, La., 1989.

Schafer, Daniel L. "Plantation Development in British East Florida: A Case Study of the Earl of Egmont." *FHQ*, LXIII (1984), 172–183.

Schweitzer, Mary McKinney. "Economic Regulation and the Colonial Economy: The Maryland Tobacco Inspection Act of 1747." *Jour. Econ. Hist.*, XL (1980), 551–569.

Shaffer, Arthur H. "Between Two Worlds: David Ramsay and the Politics of Slavery." *Jour. So. Hist.*, L (1984), 175–196.

Sharrer, G. Terry. "The Indigo Bonanza in South Carolina, 1740–90." *Technology and Culture*, XII (1971), 447–455.

———. "Indigo in Carolina, 1671–1796." *SCHM*, LXXII (1971), 94–103.

Shepherd, James F., and Gary M. Walton. "Trade, Distribution, and Economic Growth in Colonial America." *Jour. Econ. Hist.*, XXXII (1972), 128–145.

Sheridan, Richard B. "Samuel Martin, Innovating Sugar Planter of Antigua, 1750–1776." *AH*, XXXIV (1960), 126–139.

Skinner, Andrew. "A Scottish Contribution to Marxist Sociology?" In Ian Bradley and Michael Howard, eds., *Classical and Marxian Political Economy: Essays in Honor of Ronald L. Meek*, 79–114. New York, 1982.

Smith, W. Calvin. "Utopia's Last Chance? The Georgia Silk Boomlet of 1751." *GHQ*, LIX (1975), 25–37.

Soltow, Lee. "Socioeconomic Classes in South Carolina and Massachusetts in the 1790s and the Observations of John Drayton." *SCHM*, LXXXI (1980), 283–305.

Soltow, Lee, and Aubrey C. Land. "Housing and Social Standing in Georgia, 1798." *GHQ*, LXIV (1980), 448–458.

Stephens, Roswell Powell. "Science in Georgia, 1800–1830." *GHQ*, IX (1925), 55–66.

Stephens, S. G. "The Origin of Sea Island Cotton." *AH*, L (1976), 391–399.

Stetson, Sarah P. "The Traffic in Seeds and Plants from England's Colonies in North America." *AH*, XXIII (1949), 45–56.

Stewart, Mart A. "Rice, Water, and Power: Landscapes of Domination and Resistance in the Lowcountry, 1790–1880." *Environmental History Review*, XV (1991), 47–64.

Stumpf, Stuart O. "Implications of King George's War for the Charleston Mercantile Community." *SCHM*, LXXVII (1976), 161–188.

Surrency, Erwin C. "Whitefield, Habersham, and the Bethesda Orphanage." *GHQ*, XXXIV (1950), 87–105.

Thomas, Daniel H. "Pre-Whitney Cotton Gins in French Louisiana." *Jour. So. Hist.*, XXXI (1965), 135–148.

Thompson, Leonard, and Howard Lamar. "Comparative Frontier History." In Thompson and Lamar, eds., *The Frontier in History: North America and Southern Africa Compared*, 3–13. New Haven, Conn., 1982.

Usner, Daniel H., Jr. "The Frontier Exchange Economy of the Lower Mississippi Valley in the Eighteenth Century." *WMQ*, 3d Ser., XLIV (1987), 165–192.

Vickers, Daniel. "Competency and Competition: Economic Culture in Early America." *WMQ*, 3d Ser., XLVII (1990), 3–29.

Warner, John Harley. "The Idea of Southern Medical Distinctiveness: Medical Knowledge and Practice in the Old South." In Ronald L. Numbers and Todd L. Savitt, eds., *Science and Medicine in the Old South*, 179–205. Baton Rouge, La., 1989.

Waterhouse, Richard. "The Development of Elite Culture in the Colonial American South: A Study of Charles Town, 1670–1776." *Australian Journal of Politics and History*, XXVIII (1982), 391–404.

———. "England, the Caribbean, and the Settlement of Carolina." *Journal of American Studies*, IX (1975), 259–281.

———. "The Responsible Gentry of Colonial South Carolina: A Study in Local Government, 1670–1770." In Bruce C. Daniels, ed., *Town and County: Essays on the Structure of Local Government in the American Colonies*, 160–185. Middletown, Conn., 1978.

Weiman, David F. "The Economic Emancipation of the Non-Slaveholding Class: Upcountry Farmers in the Georgia Cotton Economy." *Jour. Econ. Hist.*, XLV (1985), 71–94.

———. "Farmers and the Market in Antebellum America: A View from the Georgia Upcountry." *Jour. Econ. Hist.*, XLVII (1987), 627–647.

Whitten, David O. "American Rice Cultivation: 1680–1980: A Tercentenary Critique." *Southern Studies*, XXI (1982), 5–26.

Williams, H. David. "Gambling Away the Inheritance: The Cherokee Nation and Georgia's Gold and Land Lotteries of 1832–33." *GHQ*, LXXIII (1989), 519–539.

Winberry, John J. "Reputation of Carolina Indigo." *SCHM*, LXXX (1979), 242–250.

Withuhn, William L. "Salzburgers and Slavery: A Problem of *Mentalité*." *GHQ*, LXVIII (1984), 173–192.

Wood, Betty. "Thomas Stephens and the Introduction of Black Slavery in Georgia." *GHQ*, LVIII (1974), 24–40.

Woodbury, Robert S. "The Legend of Eli Whitney and Interchangeable Parts." *Technology and Culture*, I (1960), 235–253.

Works Projects / Progress Administration. "Drakies Plantation." *GHQ*, XXIV (1940), 207–235.

———. "Mulberry Grove from the Revolution to the Present Time." *GHQ*, XXIII (1939), 315–336.

———. "Mulberry Grove in Colonial Times." *GHQ*, XXIII (1939), 236–252.

———. "Plantation Development in Chatham County." *GHQ*, XXII (1938), 305–330.

———. "The Plantation of the Royal Vale." *GHQ*, XXVII (1943), 88–110.

Zelinsky, Wilbur. "An Isochronic Map of Georgia Settlement, 1750–1850." *GHQ*, XXXV (1951), 191–195.

Zuckerman, Michael. "The Fabrication of Identity in Early America." *WMQ*, 3d Ser., XXXIV (1977), 183–214.

THESES, DISSERTATIONS, AND PAPERS

Bentley, William George. "Wealth Distribution in Colonial South Carolina." Ph.D. diss., Georgia State University, 1977.

Chesnutt, David Rogers. "South Carolina's Expansion into Colonial Georgia, 1720–1765." Ph.D. diss., University of Georgia, 1973.

Coon, David Leroy. "The Development of Market Agriculture in South Carolina, 1670–1785." Ph.D. diss., University of Illinois, Urbana/Champaign, 1972.

Farmer, Edward L. "James Flint versus the Canton Interest, 1755–1760." Papers on China from Seminars at Harvard University, East Asian Research Center, Harvard University, XVII (December 1963), 38–66.

Kaplanoff, Mark D. "Making the South Solid: Politics and the Structure of Society in South Carolina, 1790–1815." Ph.D. diss., University of Cambridge, 1979.

Mendenhall, Marjorie Stratford. "A History of Agriculture in South Carolina, 1790 to 1860: An Economic and Social Study." Ph.D. diss., University of North Carolina–Chapel Hill, 1940.

Moltke-Hansen, David. "The Empire of Scotsman Robert Wells, Loyalist South Carolina Printer-Publisher." Master's thesis, University of South Carolina–Columbia, 1984.

Sydenham, Diane Meredith. "Practitioner and Patient: The Practice of Medicine in Eighteenth-Century South Carolina." Ph.D. diss., Johns Hopkins University, 1979.

Terry, George D. " 'Champaign Country': A Social History of an Eighteenth-Century Lowcountry Parish in South Carolina, St. Johns Berkeley County." Ph.D. diss., University of South Carolina–Columbia, 1981.

Index